Theories in Contemporary Psychology

Theories in Contemporary Psychology

ARRANGED AND EDITED BY

Melvin H. Marx

PROFESSOR OF PSYCHOLOGY,
UNIVERSITY OF MISSOURI

THE MACMILLAN COMPANY, NEW YORK

COLLIER-MACMILLAN LIMITED, LONDON

Library of Congress catalog card number: 63–15264

THE MACMILLAN COMPANY, NEW YORK

COLLIER-MACMILLAN CANADA, LTD., TORONTO, ONTARIO

Printed in the United States of America

Preface

In the dozen years since the appearance of *Psychological Theory*, the predecessor to the present volume, a large number of most important changes in the area of psychological theory have occurred. These changes have necessitated a correspondingly large number of changes in the content of the present book, if that content is to reflect the major facets of contemporary work.

The primary changes may be summarized as follows. First, there has been a drastic decline in interest in highly formalized theory, particularly of the Hullian hypothetico-deductive variety. Hull's grand objectives for a psychological theoretical system are now generally recognized as premature and overambitious. Second, there has been a somewhat correlated increase in interest in strictly positivistic and empirical types of scientific work. This kind of science is, at worst, blatantly antitheoretical, and, at best, tolerantly atheoretical.

These two retreats from theory have been matched, on the positive side, by certain upsurges toward different types of theoretical development. Two particular movements deserve comment. Most spectacular has been the advance of the *model*, particularly of the mathematical-type model. Less spectacular, but perhaps more important in the long run, has been the renewed prominence of what I have called in Chapter I a *functional* type of theory. This is theory which is closely tied to empirical footings and is designed to be developed gradually, rather than precipitately on the basis of scanty data and much speculation.

In accordance with the new emphasis in theory construction, the present book has been divided into three parts. The first two parts deal with various aspects of theory construction and consist mainly of reprinted selections. Part Three, however, is completely new. It consists of papers written especially for this book by various contributors on the present state of theory methodology in some of the major areas of psychology. Unfortunately, all of the important areas could not be covered because of space limitations; also, of those planned, a small number could not be included because of the inability of the prospective contributors to complete the papers within the time available. Nevertheless, it is hoped that these papers will help to

v

provide useful, overlapping bird's-eye views of the state of the art. Although their primary emphasis is intended to be on methodological problems, varying amounts of substantive information are necessarily provided.

Of the original forty-seven selections, seven have been re-used (and one of these, the introductory chapter to this book, has been completely rewritten and expanded). The selections retained are ones whose contemporary significance appeared to be most relevant. Application of this criterion was most difficult in many cases, but the need to reflect contemporary trends severely limited the space available for older selections.

Even more difficult decisions involved which of the many new papers should be included within the first two parts. Here arbitrary decisions were necessary if the scope of the book was to be maintained. Many worthwhile articles simply had to be excluded. In addition, a small number of very short excerpts were included, when such selections were judged to make a salient point. However, most of the selections in the first two parts are reprinted in their entirety.

The primary objective of the book remains as stated in the preface to the earlier volume: "to encourage a more critical understanding and a sounder utilization of the principles of theory construction." Implicit in this work is my own strong conviction that with the marked changes in viewpoints towards theory occurring since the previous volume, it is now even more important that all well-trained graduate students in the various branches of psychology be familiarized with the major problems and techniques of theory construction. Sophistication in theory evaluation and criticism is desirable even for those students trained in the more positivistic manner. Also, while creativity in theory construction cannot be prescribed by means of any set of rules, formal or informal, nevertheless there are certain gross procedural techniques with which one should be familiar. The empirical components of research are most often emphasized in scientific courses, even more so perhaps in the apprenticeship system which is now characteristic of the more effective graduate training programs. But training students in experimentation needs to be supplemented by training in interpretation, and the present work is predicated on the premise that sloppy "theorizing" can best be counteracted by familiarizing students with some of the problems which beset the theorist.

I would like to acknowledge the kindness of the authors, editors, and publishers who have granted permission to reproduce, and the efforts of the original contributors to the volume. I also most gratefully acknowledge the assistance of many of my students during years of teaching these materials; of several colleagues who kindly gave advice on special points; of some of the contributors to the volume who made suggestions (in particular Robert Leeper, who provided an assiduous and provocative criticism of Selection I); and finally of Mrs. Charity Flack and her clerical and secretarial aids, without whose struggles with the technical problems of manuscript preparation the book could not have been completed.

MELVIN H. MARX

Columbia, Missouri
August, 1963

Contents

Part One: Theory Construction

CHAPTER I. INTRODUCTION   3

1. The General Nature of Theory Construction
   Melvin H. Marx   4

2. Operationism and Logical Positivism
   S. S. Stevens   47

CHAPTER II. THE ROLE OF MODELS   77

3. The Model in Theory Construction
   Roy Lachman   78

4. The Uses and Limitations of Models
   Herbert A. Simon and Allen Newell   89

5. Men, Machines, and Models
   Alphonse Chapanis   104

CHAPTER III. MATHEMATICAL AND STATISTICAL MODELS   131

6. Growth and Function of Mathematical Models for Learning
   William K. Estes   132

7. Measurement Scales and Statistical Models
   Cletus J. Burke   147

CHAPTER IV. THEORETICAL CONSTRUCTS   161

8. Types of Constructs in Psychology
   Kenneth W. Spence   162

9. Events and Constructs in Psychology
                                    J. R. Kantor   179
10. The Dimension of Operational Clarity
                                    Melvin H. Marx   187
11. Formal and Informal Meaning in Constructs
                                    Howard H. Kendler 203
12. The Role of Neurology
                                    David Krech   211
13. The Analysis of Gross Functions
                                    Melvin H. Marx   213

Part Two: Special Problems

CHAPTER V. LEVELS OF EXPLANATION   225

14. The Conceptual Focus of Systems
                                    Egon Brunswik   226
15. Molar to Molecular
                                    F. H. George   237
16. Behavior and Neurophysiology
                                    David Krech   240
17. The Problem of Reductionism in Psychology
                                    Richard Jessor   245

CHAPTER VI. THEORETICAL EMPHASES   257

18. The Emphasis on Molar Problems
                                    Gordon W. Allport 258
19. The Emphasis on Basic Functions
                                    Kenneth W. Spence 272
20. The Principle of Gradualness
                                    Robert S. Morison 286
21. The Social Indifference of Psychology
                                    Richard A. Littman 303
22. Confusion in Attitudes Toward Clinical Theory
                                    Melvin H. Marx   311
23. The Flight from the Laboratory
                                    B. F. Skinner   323

Part Three: Fields of Study

CHAPTER VII. DEVELOPMENTAL AND SOCIAL
              FUNCTIONS   341

  24. Metatheoretical Issues in Developmental Psychology
                                              Edward Zigler   341

  25. Social Psychological Theorizing
                                              Leonard Berkowitz   369

CHAPTER VIII. PERSONALITY AND PSYCHODYNAMICS   389

  26. Theoretical Methodology in the Psychology of Personality
                                              Robert W. Leeper   389

  27. Theory Construction and Validation in Psychoanalysis
                                              Leonard Horwitz   413

  28. Affect and Emotion
                                              Henry N. Peters   435

CHAPTER IX. COMPLEX PROCESSES   455

  29. Verbal Learning and Psycholinguistics
                              Philip B. Gough and James J. Jenkins   456

  30. Thinking
                                              Donald W. Taylor   475

CHAPTER X. LEARNING PROCESSES   495

  31. Classical Conditioning
                                              William W. Grings   495

  32. Theory Construction and Instrumental Learning
                                              John W. Cotton   526

  33. Mathematical Models in Research on Perception and
      Learning
                                              Richard C. Atkinson   551

CHAPTER XI. SENSORY AND PERCEPTUAL FUNCTIONS   565

  34. Some Trends in Perceptual Theory
                                              H. Leibowitz   565

  35. Theories in Sensory Psychology
                              Conrad Mueller and William McGill   575

  Index   615

PART ONE
Theory
Construction

CHAPTER I

Introduction

THE PURPOSE OF THIS *introductory chapter is to present, in Selection 1, a general picture of the nature of scientific theory construction, with special reference to certain of the methodological problems that particularly apply to psychology; and to provide, in Selection 2, certain background material, mainly of historical interest but nevertheless necessary to a thorough understanding of contemporary science.*

Most of the points treated in the first paper are more intensively treated in papers reprinted in the following chapters of the book. The glossary at the end of the first selection is intended to provide the various scientific meanings for words that are not adequately treated, from this point of view, in the ordinary dictionary. Further elaborations of many of these terms will be found in the text, since so much of the confusion and controversy in this area tends to be fundamentally semantic in nature.

The bias in the paper is definitely toward what is described as functional theory. Because of the recent trend toward reduced inferential commitment and more strictly inductive types of theory, the case for the use of inferential constructs is most strongly emphasized. However, it is also the position of the paper that the optimal growth of psychological theory will occur if all types of theory construction are encouraged, as long as certain key safeguards are maintained. All have contributions to make. Any effort by proponents of one or another of the various types to exclude the others is to be regretted.

Among the most significant general scientific developments of this century has been the increasingly critical attention paid, by both scientists and philosophers, to the nature of science and scientific method. In this development the two most important formative influences have been the movement called "operationism," directly instigated by P. W. Bridgman's The Logic of Modern Physics, *and the broader philosophical position most commonly called "logical positivism," primarily originating in the famed "Vienna Circle" of philosophers. Operationism represents an attempt by scientists to improve the rigor of scientific language by requiring that concepts be defined in terms of the operations that produce them. Logical positivism, or "scientific empiricism" as it is also often called, represents an attempt by philosophers to rid philosophy of its so-called "pseudo-problems"—those for which no empirical answers are available—and thus align it more closely with modern science. One of the first psychologists to recognize the psychological implications of these movements was S. S. Stevens. The second selection of this introductory chapter presents his comprehensive treatment of the relationship of both these influences to psychology.*

1 | *The General Nature of Theory Construction*

MELVIN H. MARX

I. Introduction

OBSERVATION AND THEORY   Direct observation is generally agreed to be a fundamental task of natural science. An impressive array of highly reliable and useful scientific knowledge has been accumulated in this way. Unfortunately, however, answering scientific questions *simply* by means of direct observation and measurement is not always feasible. Many phenomena appear to be too remotely and too tenuously related to the immediately observable variables to permit a strictly empirical approach. Further, some problems of underlying relationships cannot easily be attacked by empirical techniques alone. For these reasons all modern

Prepared for this volume.

natural sciences have developed a large number of inferentially derived propositions or theories which are ultimately based upon, but not entirely reducible to, concrete empirical data.

The present situation in psychology with regard to appreciation of the role of theory seems to be particularly in need of clarification. Recent trends have been clearly away from an emphasis on formal theory and towards a non-theoretical—even anti-theoretical—orientation. While there are certainly good grounds for the widespread disenchantment with the overly ambitious objectives of some recent theoretical enterprises, there is at the same time no justification for the kind of theoretical vacuum which seems to be encouraged by an increasing number of positivistically oriented psychologists. Actually, psychology is very much in need of a realistic and well-reasoned approach to theory construction, and a fresh theoretical look at a host of old and largely unsolved behavioral problems. This need is well stated by Estes (1957, p. 617):

In his own experience, the writer has found that the steepest obstacle to theory construction in psychology is not the complexity of behavior. It is the mountain of stereotypes deposited by centuries of prescientific attempts to comprehend behavior and capped by the pronouncements of the academicians who have always known in advance, apparently by divine inspiration, exactly what kind of theory is possible and proper for psychology. This barrier must be undermined by uncertainty before it can be toppled by experiment. Once it is down, our experimental subjects will be able to tell us, through the medium of their behavior, what kind of theory psychology is entitled to.

The intention of the present work is not to attempt to legislate any particular kind of theory construction for psychology, but, on the contrary, to encourage a variety of approaches to theory. Nevertheless, some guidelines need to be emphasized and major procedural pitfalls pointed out. To these ends the present chapter is dedicated. It has the primary objectives of exposing the common ground that all scientific theory construction shares and of pointing up some of the more difficult aspects of the relationship between empirical and theoretical endeavors within the field of psychology. Hopefully, clarification of these issues will especially facilitate an understanding of the way in which observation (fact) and theory (conceptualization) necessarily interact in research and thus stimulate a more widespread recognition of their mutual interdependence.

FUNCTIONS OF THEORY   Several distinct functions are subsumed by theory. Most of these may be summarized by the statement that all theory tends to be *both* a tool and a goal. This statement means that theory is seen to be useful as an aid, sometimes perhaps an essential aid, in directing empirical investigations (the *tool* function) and also to be something valued as an objective in its own right (the *goal* function). Different scientists emphasize these two major functions according to their own methodological tastes. It should be apparent that at least a gross positive correlation exists between preference for a more restricted use of theory and an emphasis on its tool, or heuristic, role, and a preference for the more logically coordinated type of deductive theory and an emphasis upon theory as a goal. But the correlation is far from perfect; even the most logically organized theory must make possible predictions of empirical results, and even the most provisional hypothesis may be highly prized as an achievement in its own right (especially perhaps in a field where scientific development is in preliminary stages).

More specific variants of these two general functions are often cited. For example, the tool function is evident in the generally accepted proposition that theories guide research by generating *new* predictions not otherwise likely to occur (e.g., prediction of the existence of the planet Neptune from extrapolation of prior data in advance of its actual sighting). Guthrie has put this argument most succinctly in his simple statement: "Systematic theory . . . guides observation and discovery. There are no raw facts" (1950, p. 99). And the point is nicely illustrated by Boring's comment (1953, p. 176):

I remember how a professor of genetics many years ago showed me published drawings of cell nuclei before and after the discovery and description of chromosomes. Chromosomes kept showing up in the later drawings, not in the earlier. In other words, microscopes do not reveal concepts until the concepts have been invented.

The goal function of theory is evident in the proposition that theories integrate and order existing empirical laws, independently of their own degree of logical sophistication. Also implied in the statement is the premise that theory is useful because it provides an economical and efficient means of abstracting, codifying, summarizing, integrating, and storing information. Such systematic treatment of data is an important goal of many scientists; relevant in this connection is one of the most commonly cited descriptions of science: that it consists of *ordered* knowledge. Representative of this view is Frank's statement: "Science begins only when we invent a system of symbols which can bring order into our experience" (1958, p. 62).

II. Some Basic Definitions

The multiplicity of meanings with which the important terms that we need to consider are endowed makes impossible a comprehensive listing. An outline of the more important of the major definitions in current usage, for certain of the most critical terms, is therefore presented. (See also the glossary at the end of this paper.) Issues which are essentially philosophical or logical in nature are largely ignored. These are excluded primarily on the ground that the interminable argumentation so often characteristic of such analysis is more likely to impede rather than enhance the understanding of fundamental issues by the developing student of science, for whom the present work is mainly intended. (Suggestions for selected readings in the philosophy of science are included in the list at the end of this paper.)

LAW A scientific law is most often defined as a statement of regular, predictable relationship among empirical variables. Sometimes, especially in older usages, the term law means a strongly established theoretical or abstract principle. However, it is increasingly being used to refer to the basic regularities observed in natural phenomena and thus typically to represent the descriptive and the empirical, rather than the abstracted and the inferred, properties of data. (The term data refers to the recorded results of observations, often but not necessarily in quantitative form; the term variable refers to a factor or condition involved in the investigation—to a class of objects or events, or to a class of properties of objects or events.)

HYPOTHESIS Loosely defined, an hypothesis is any conjecture or surmise that states a relationship among variables. This term is a veritable workhorse in the scientific vocabulary and is defined "loosely" almost by necessity, so many and varied are the ways in which it is used. However, the hard core of usage involves the notion of a provisional explanatory proposition which makes certain definite predictions concerning empirical data.

Scientific hypotheses vary along a number of dimensions, certain of the more important of which may be here specified. First, hypotheses vary in regard to the directness with which they may be tested. The experimental hypothesis, for example, is directly tested by means of observations, whereas certain abstract hypotheses, from which experimental hypotheses may be derived, can be tested only indirectly by determining the cumulative effect of many observations. A second, and closely related, dimension is that of specificity. In general, of course, the more specific the hypothesis, the more amenable it is to direct test; but this is not a perfect relationship, since some abstract hypotheses can be stated with a high degree of theoretical specificity, and conversely, some experimental hypotheses may be unfortunately vague and ambiguous. A most significant subclass of this dimension is the degree of logical tightness that the investigator is able to build between his experimental (data-oriented) and his abstract (theory-oriented) hypotheses.

A third important dimension, the importance of which is not often adequately recognized, is the public-private continuum. Here the range is from the vaguest of hunches, which one scarcely recognizes himself, much less formulates or announces, to the most highly formalized and publicized of logical propositions. The decision as to when to publicize a hypothetical proposition is a difficult one, one on which scientists with different temperaments or work habits quite clearly differ. Indeed, this difference of opinion seems to be the basis for much of the controversy between the typical positivist, who prefers to keep his hunches to himself while letting them direct his research, and the formal theorist, who prefers to state them openly and publicly, once they have acquired sufficient promise to satisfy him.

The term "postulate" is sometimes used as a kind of synonym for hypothesis, especially in a more or less logically formalized, systematic procedure (e.g., cf. Hull, 1943). Here the postulate is a proposition that is indirectly tested by means of its implications, or theorems.

THEORY   It is especially important to keep separate the various different meanings of "theory," since a large part of the confusion surrounding this topic is attributable to a failure to do so. Thus, critical or derogatory statements intended to apply to one kind of theory are often indiscriminately attributed to a different kind, or to "theory" in general. Conversely, a commendatory statement about one kind of theory may similarly be indiscriminately and inaccurately applied. The following sections indicate four of the major ways in which the term has been used within science.

1. Most generally, theory is used to refer in a very broad sense to any aspect of the formal, or conceptual, processes of science as contrasted with the strictly empirical, or observational, aspects. This usage, while not necessarily harmful in and of itself, is of limited value and does help to confuse the other, more specific usages. (A comparable usage is to refer loosely to any innovation as an "experiment.") Frequently, moreover, theory as thus popularly used has a distinctly negative connotation, in the sense that the practicability of the proposition is challenged (cf. "theory," def. 2, English and English, 1958). Nevertheless, in spite of these limitations, this usage is so well established as to require recognition. In the present chapter, therefore, the term, when not qualified, will be used in this general sense, but with particular reference to the conceptual and inferential processes which attempt to organize and order empirical data.

2. Theory is used to refer to any generalized explanatory principle. Ordinarily, this kind of theory consists of a statement of functional relationship among variables. If the variables are expressed in empirical terms, then the term law is more likely to be applied to such a principle. If, on the other hand, the variables tend to be more abstract and less directly empirical, the term theory is more often used.

Theories of this sort are obviously very closely related to *hypotheses*. For this reason the latter term will be used in the present paper to refer generally to provisional explanatory propositions. It should be noted, however, that the theory is often distinguished from hypothesis mainly on the basis of a somewhat greater amount of confirmation or scientific acceptability. In this usage, hypothesis refers to the least confirmed proposition, theory to a more confirmed one, and law to the one which has the greatest degree of confirmation, having usually survived the test of time as well as direct empirical investigation. This distinction (cf. "theory," def. 1, English and English, 1958) is increasingly being replaced by the usages described elsewhere in this paper.

3. Theory is used to refer to a group of logically organized (deductively related) laws. This usage is coming to be a preferred one (cf. Bergmann, 1957). It is clearly more pertinent to the better developed sciences, such as physics, from which it originated. Also, it has an obvious affinity to the concept of *system*, in the sense in which that term broadly refers within psychology to a cluster of theoretical propositions and methodological biases (e.g., behaviorism, psychoanalysis), and even more to the less ambitious *miniature system*. The decline in popularity of the classic systems within recent years may help to account for the increased utilization of this sense of the term, since it can serve as a kind of substitute concept for "system."

4. In its most restricted sense, theory refers merely to summary statements which give order, in an essentially descriptive manner, to the cluster of laws which have been empirically developed in some subject matter. Here the emphasis is upon a radical empiricism or positivism, with an absolute minimum of inference and postulation, and dependence upon generalization within an inductive procedure. Obviously, this use of "theory" has only a slight affinity to the other ones.

CONSTRUCT   A construct is a special kind of concept. These rather closely related terms are frequently used as synonyms. However, the distinction here made would seem to be a useful one, following the typical sense in which they are more precisely used within scientific work.

A concept is a class name which refers to certain abstracted properties of the class. It is a generalized term, because it is intended to apply to all cases showing the referent properties. It is a symbol, because it stands for or represents something else.

As class names, concepts are used in a wide variety of situations. Three major types are here differentiated.

1. Concepts refer to *things* (objects, organisms) and *properties* of things. Man, child, dog, rodent, table, school—along with large, small, black, white, round, and elementary—are thus all concepts, since they

apply as class names (in the main, as nouns and adjectives) to a number of individual examples of each class. As Pratt (1939) has clearly pointed out, all concepts contain both *more than* and *less than* the observations from which they are derived. Thus, the concept "dog"—"dog in general," that is—is at the same time more meaningful than the observation of any particular dog, since it summarizes in a single word or other symbol the essence of an infinite number of observations, and less meaningful, since it invariably loses in concreteness and individuality.

2. Concepts refer to *events* (things in action) and properties of events. This usage is more complex than the first, since the nature of the action (play, fight, eat, sing, roll, burn; quickly, awkwardly, gaily, etc.) needs to be abstracted. Direct description of behavior utilizes this kind of concept (grammatically, verbs and adverbs).

3. Concepts refer to *relationships among things and/or events, and their various properties*. Here, in this most complex case, the term *construct* is generally used. The "building" or "making" implication of the term is evident in that more inference is required in the process of abstracting the properties identified by the construct. Justice, school spirit, statesmanship, loyalty, and friendship are everyday examples of this kind of complex concept, or construct; gene, atom, habit, personality, and anxiety are scientific examples. Since so much meaning needs to be inferred, and the construct often is so broad as to include a great variety of different relationships, difficulties of communication are compounded, relative to the simple concepts of type (1) and (2). Much of the controversy concerning the role of theory in science, and particularly within psychology, stems more or less directly from this fact. Precise description of referent behaviors are frequently lacking; as a result, psychological constructs, which generally refer to the inferred properties of the organism, tend to be imprecisely and ambiguously used.

Although the kinds of concepts outlined above represent salient cases, it should not be assumed that the particular hierarchical organization suggested is anything more than one way of ordering the tremendous linguistic complexity involved in conceptualizations. As an initial step into this jungle of words and other symbols, the proposed distinction between simpler concepts and constructs should be helpful.

III. Basic Elements of Theory Construction: An Overview

Three basic elements of theory construction are shown in Figure 1. *Observation* is recognized as fundamental to all science. *Constructs* are seen as the major substantive units of which theories are composed. *Hypotheses* are considered to be the major conceptual tools by which theories are constructed.

The major purpose of Figure 1 is to provide a kind of overview of the way in which these three salient elements of theory construction vary with regard to their major dimensions. Each of the three continua from practical affairs to science will be considered briefly; more detailed attention is accorded certain aspects of these problems in later sections. The present treatment is in no sense exhaustive but is intended to highlight certain of the more critical problems of theory construction.

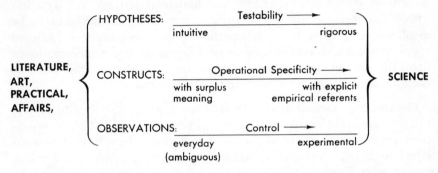

Figure 1.   The three basic elements of scientific theory construction.

OBSERVATIONS: CONTROL   Control of variables is held to be the essential characteristic of science, differentiating it from non-scientific procedures (see Marx and Hillix, 1963, Ch. 1, for a further discussion of this point; see also Boring, 1954, and Valentine and Wickens, 1949). It may be granted that everyday-life observations often constitute the groundwork for the origin of scientific problems and for preliminary conceptual and theoretical formulations (cf. Selection No. 10). However, notwithstanding the ability and ingenuity of some especially keen observers and reporters in literature, art, and related fields of endeavor, a certain degree of control of variables must be developed if science is to advance. Control in this sense refers to a reduction in the ambiguity with which variations in the data (dependent-variable measures) may be assigned to the major conditions whose influence is under investigation (independent variables). Elimination of extraneous conditions (controlled variables) is achieved in the main by experimental or statistical techniques.

It follows from the foregoing considerations that scientific progress is marked by a progressive shift from left to right in the diagram in Figure 1 for all three phases of theory construction. In each case there is a reduction in ambiguity of relations between the various components and an increasingly clear and often formal differentiation of their respective functions. The fact that scientific progress results in increasingly less natural and less lifelike concepts and theories obviously increases the difficulties of popularization and translation into practical action, but this is hardly avoidable (cf. Pratt, 1939, for an especially good discussion of this point). It is instructive to note, in this respect, how even Kurt Lewin, who may be considered to have been perhaps the most responsive of recent leading theorists to important human problems, translated such problems into the highly "artificial" terms and concepts of topological and vector psychology. Even in the case of popular vs. technically coined terminology, only an apparent advantage may accrue by using already familiar terms in new scientific and unnatural settings. As Thouless (1949) has observed, the use of popular, familiar terms may actually be disadvantageous in spite of its superficial appeal, because it is likely to result in a false and misleading sense of popular understanding, based upon the old but now inadequate meanings. This then simply increases the difficulties of popularization and re-translation.

CONSTRUCTS: OPERATIONAL SPECIFICITY   Operational specificity—the clearly stated relationship of the construct to its empirical basis in operations producing the data—is the most important characteristic of construct formation. Animistic concepts (e.g., "mind," "libido") and others having what Reichenbach (1938) has called "surplus meaning" may be tolerated in the early, pre-scientific development of a field, but their replacement by constructs more closely tied to the empirical operations must occur for effective scientific theory construction.

Although the physicist Bridgman (1927) is generally credited with the first emphasis on the importance of the operational principle in science, the need for clarity in definitions had long before been recognized, at least in practice, especially in the physical sciences. What was new in Bridgman's emphasis was the recognition that when different operations are involved, different concepts are generated, irrespective of any verbal similarities which may exist. Within psychology, both aspects of operationism are important: 1) the clarity of meaning in communication—the specification of empirical referents for concepts—and 2) the multiplicity of concepts, or meanings, which come from a corresponding multiplicity of operations, or empirical referents. Examples of this latter problem are discussed below, where the application of operationism to psychological constructs is considered in greater detail.

HYPOTHESIS: TESTABILITY   Testability is the absolutely essential characteristic of any scientifically useful hypothesis. A conjecture which cannot be tested in some way is of no immediate use to science, attractive as it may be for forensic and similar purposes. Moreover, the hypothesis must be so constructed as to be clearly *disconfirmable*—that is, it must be precise enough so that not all possible outcomes can be incorporated within its framework (a defect commonly ascribed to certain theoretical positions, such as the psychoanalytic).

The "intuitive-rigorous" continuum for testability of hypotheses refers to the extent to which adequate empirical (observational) tests can be performed. Adequacy here consists primarily of satisfactory logical relationships between hypothesis and data and reasonable control of variables in the observations. Since the latter point takes us back to the control dimension already discussed, the situation is obviously circular. But this is no accident. This is exactly the way in which science operates, with a continuous interplay of observation and hypothesis (or induction, if one prefers) medicated by constructs.

At this point it seems appropriate to emphasize a distinction between the so-called contexts of *discovery* and *confirmation*. The latter function, that of rigorously controlled tests of propositions, is the hallmark of science and has therefore been emphasized in this section; we have confidence in scientific propositions precisely because of their confirmation. *But*, we are also concerned with the significance or importance of scientific propositions, and in this regard confirmability has no direct relevance. That is, the significance of a proposition—its potential theoretical or implied importance—is independent of the empirical support it may subsequently receive. Problems of significance therefore belong to the context of discovery, and here science is similar to all other creative endeavors (which tend toward the left side of Figure 1). The only generally practical guideline that can be laid down for the encouragement of creativity is that the worker be thoroughly immersed in his work. The place for daring and imagination, the time for striking out boldly in new and previously uncharted directions—this is obviously the context of discovery, just as the place for caution and restraint and for the careful evaluation of hypothesis and data is in the context of confirmation.

We need to recognize most explicitly that *both* discovery *and* confirmation are necessary to effective scientific work. The most ingenious theories are limited scientific value until empirical tests are produced; the best confirmed proposition is of little value unless it deals with meaningful variables. Unfortunately, much controversy, even within science, has arisen from a failure to accept this dual necessity. This dichotomy enables us to understand and see in better perspective the overemphasis on either the discovery aspect (as is sometimes claimed to occur in psychoanalysis, for example) or the confirmation aspect (as is sometimes claimed to occur in scientific empiricism, for example). Finally, much useless argumentation seems to occur on strictly semantic issues, such as the question as to whether a particular person (say, Freud) is or is not a scientist; obviously, one's own definition of "scientist" determines the answer here. But however one defines a scientist, the necessity remains to recognize that both of these functions, whether or not they occur within a single individual, are essential to fruitful and productive science.

IV. Modes of Theory Construction

How best to develop sound theory is a problem that has generated as much heat as any in recent psychological writing. A variety of points of view may be found, with almost everyone admitting the desirability of "theory"—as defined by oneself, at least. Although the risk of oversimplifying a complex situation is a very real one in this case, the present treatment emphasizes four major positions along what is basically a continuum with regard to the amount of formal effort which should be exerted into the deliberate construction of theory.

These four varieties of "metatheory," or rules for theory, are schematically represented in Figure 2, arranged according to the *direction* of relationship between conceptual (theory-language) and empirical (data-language) levels. The student should understand that while these are salient types of theory-construction procedure, few, if any, actual theoretical endeavors would in practice conform exactly to these types. Careful examination of on-going theory-building would, however, probably reveal a number of close approximations to these modes, as well as many examples of intermediate conditions and some combinations of procedures. But theoretical efforts *can* be ordered in terms of the extent to which formalized inferences are explicitly used as guides, and this is essentially the kind of order depicted in Figure 2 and described in the following sections.

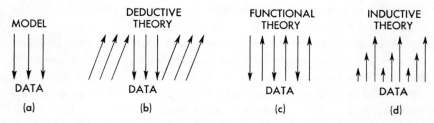

Figure 2.   Direction of interaction between theory and data in four types of theory construction.

MODEL   A model is any conceptual analogue, generally of a physical or mathematical nature, which is used to suggest empirical research. As indicated in panel (a) of Figure 2, the flow of influence in a model is entirely from the conceptual to the empirical level. That is to say, once a particular model has been selected, the researcher is not concerned at all about modifying the model itself on the basis of data obtained by means of it; this insensitivity to data is a major difference between the model and the other forms of theory.

Thus, a model is chosen solely on the basis of its heuristic, or tool, value. The consequent theoretical disinterest gives the investigator a considerably greater amount of freedom, since he is not required to be concerned with the substantive validity of his conceptualizations. Model thinking is strictly of the "as-if" variety, as Boring has nicely pointed out (1957), and this feature certainly accounts for some of the increasing popularity of this mode of theory construction.

The last point raises the question as to how an investigator proceeds, if he is really interested in developing theory, after he uses the model in the manner described. The answer to this question seems to be that he then proceeds to build theory in one of the other three major modes of construction, or some combination thereof. The main point is that as long as he continues to use only models, in the sense here discussed, he is not at all concerned with modification of the model itself; whether he uses the model as a framework or guide for the building of theory, as well as a guideline to data collection, will vary widely from one case to the next. One firm comment which can be made in this regard, however, is that if a conceptual model *is* used explicitly as the basis for theory construction, the procedure followed will be that of deductive theory. The papers of Chapters II and III (and Selection 33), all concerned with the various details involved in the use of models, provide a large number of examples of such use within psychology.

DEDUCTIVE THEORY This term is used to refer to any logically or deductively arranged cluster of laws where the emphasis is distinctly upon the conceptual structure and its substantive validity. Panel (b) of Figure 2 represents this kind of theory. The slanted arrows at the left suggest the more overt development of the theory from empirical data, and those at the right represent the explicit intention of the theorist to use data produced by his theory to modify it so as to produce new and better theory.

Perhaps most prominently represented in recent psychological history by Clark Hull (e.g., 1943), this classical position lays heavy emphasis upon the greatest amount of formal effort. It emphasizes the value of explicit formulations of explanatory propositions, logically interlaced, even when the empirical groundwork is admittedly inadequate. It stresses the research-directing function of such explicitly and formally organized theory, as well as the logical interrelationships which are seen to be the ultimate objective of science. It recognizes the ephemeral nature of the particular details of theory which are advanced, but trusts that errors of content will be taken care of by one's own empirical checks and by the "social corrections" produced by other people's criticisms and data.

A major kind of formal theory is that called *hypothetico-deductive* (or mathematico-deductive, if formal mathematical procedures are involved). Explicit statements of hypothetical propositions (postulates) with their corollaries are developed through deductive logic into empirical implications (theorems). Hull's system is of this type.

The great contribution such theory can make cannot be denied (particularly in the matter of stimulating empirical research, best exemplified by the tremendous influence that Hull had on the experimental literature in the first postwar decade). Nevertheless, a most marked reaction has taken place against this kind of highly formalized theory construction within the past decade. Mostly this has resulted from a growing discontent with the logical coordinations proposed; in the case of Hull's system especially, such inadequacies were more and more pointed out (e.g., Koch, 1954; Seward, 1954; Cotton, 1955).

Apart from the general inadvisability of attempting to construct an elaborate theoretical structure on minimal empirical grounds—and mistaking the finished product of the older mathematical and physical theories as indicative of their mode of development—other objections to this kind of theory construction have been raised. Such theoretical emphasis, according to the critics, tends to blind the investigator to alternative views, data, and methodologies (and so may come to fixate even a whole generation of researchers in a narrow, restrictive, and perhaps sterile path); gives the false appearance of too much certainty and knowledge (and so may mislead practice, as well as scientific investigation); emphasizes the personal, emotional elements in science rather than the substantive issues (and so may lead to experimental tests of particular theories and polemic publication directed more at personalities than at facts); and encourages speculation as to formal and logical relationships (and so may develop excessive concern with premature logical elegance at the expense of sound empirical investigation).

FUNCTIONAL THEORY   This term is here used to refer to the modest utilization of organized conceptualizations, with more explicit emphasis upon the provisional and tool character of theory. As panel (c) of Figure 2 indicates, the traffic is most definitely two-way; this kind of theory encourages the most intimate and continuing interaction of data and conceptualization. Both kinds of activity, empirical and conceptual, are emphasized, and they are given essentially equal status.

Choice of the term "functional" suggests the system called functionalism, and the similarity of name is not fortuitous. Functionalism flourished briefly in the United States during the first third of this century, mainly at the University of Chicago, and refuses to die out entirely, in the sense that functionalistically oriented psychologists continue to perform research chores with a characteristic deëmphasis on formalized theory but with a tireless quest for data and data-oriented explanatory principles.

In general, this position would attempt to salvage the positive values of a limited kind of theory construction, closely tied to empirical research, while eschewing the dangers associated with too premature and close an attachment to logico-deductive procedures. There is, of course, a wide spectrum of such compromise positions, so that specifications which cover all varieties are difficult to make.

The most persistent criticism of this position is that it lacks virility and enthusiasm and would accept a vapid eclecticism which seldom if ever makes positive contributions of its own (cf. Henle, 1957). As a compromise position, this procedure does lack some of the definitiveness of the extreme views. Nevertheless, to the extent that such positive contributions are forthcoming, this criticism will be stilled. Certainly nothing in the history of the functionalist researcher himself justifies a very great distrust of either his empirical devotedness or his ability to take a definite theoretical position for himself when he finds a secure empirical footing (cf. Hilgard, 1956, Ch. 10; Marx and Hillix, 1963, Ch. 6).

In his treatment of contemporary functionalism, Hilgard (1956, Ch. 6) selected the variable of distributed practice in learning as a specimen of functional research. This is a good illustration of functional theory for several reasons, but especially because of the close and continuing interplay of theory and experiment and the contribution of a variety of active researchers without firm prior commitment to fixed theoretical positions. In general, problems in the psychology of learning and memory have been favorite topics for functional researchers (e.g., Harvey Carr, John A. McGeoch, Arthur W. Melton, M. E. Bunch, Benton J. Underwood), although the use of the functional approach to theory is of course not restricted to any particular kind of problem. Thus, two recent and quite different examples of this type of theory construction are Harlow's (1959) error-set theory of discrimination learning and Festinger's (1957) cognitive-dissonance theory in social psychology. Additional illustrations are plentiful in any field of psychological endeavor. As a matter of fact, if any type of theory construction is to be considered representative of psychology, at least of American psychology, it would clearly be the functional mode.

INDUCTIVE THEORY   This term is used to refer to the kind of theory which consists essentially of summary statements of empirical relationships and so contains a minimum of inferential commitment and deductive logic. This positivistic view is represented in panel (d) of Figure 2, where the successively longer arrows are used to indicate the progressive nature of the development of theory, so defined. It is well exemplified by Egon Brunswik, B. F. Skinner (1938, 1950, 1956, and Selection 23 in this volume), and Murray Sidman (1960). Most of the arguments just cited against the classical, formalistic procedures have been made by the latter two men particularly.

On the positive side, this point of view holds that if we only develop our facts carefully enough, theories—as generalized, inductive principles summarizing empirical relationships—will take care of themselves. For the strict positivist, theories are nothing more than summary statements, and to try to produce them too far in advance of the acquisition of the facts themselves is therefore a serious mistake.

Critics of this extreme position have argued that the positivist *is* actually using some kind of informal theorizing, or logical deduction, in his choice of experimental problem and design; therefore, the process would be more effective if, rather than keeping it completely from public view, the investigator would explicate it, so that such conceptualizations (rationales underlying experiments, and the like) can receive the full benefit of the social-corrective operation which has proved to be so effective in scientific history. If social corrections are restricted to data-collection procedures alone, the progress of science in its effort toward more and more effective unifying theory—even in the positivistic meaning—will be seriously hampered.

A related argument concerns the claim that the strict positivist, in his fervent aversion to deduction, is less likely to be able to cope with certain intricacies of natural phenomena. In the more advanced sciences at least, deductive procedures have paid rich dividends in terms of elegant theoretical structures which order and unify large masses of data. The extent to which a strictly positivistic approach can successfully tackle such problems in the realm of behavior remains to be seen.

More extended criticisms of certain aspects of the strictly positivistic position, especially with regard to the use of inferential constructs, will be found in later sections of the present paper.

The behavioral positivist is also criticized on the grounds of certain procedural inefficiencies. Inferential terms, while certainly risky, are nevertheless seen as convenient intellectual tools; the data language by itself is cumbersome. Furthermore, the avoidance of systematic implications, as evidenced, for example, in Ferster and Skinner's otherwise most valuable *Schedules of Reinforcement* (1957), is distinctly inefficient. It is only fair to add, however, that not all positivistic efforts are *that* devoid of systematic implications; moreover, certain indications of changes in these matters, seen in some of the papers in the Skinnerian *Journal of the*

Experimental Analysis of Behavior, would move the general positivistic practice several steps closer to the functional, as described above.

One of the more salubrious by-products of the recent positivistic surge has been the reduction in the number of contrived "hypotheses" which investigators state their intention of testing. While this practice is most evident perhaps in regard to graduate student thesis research, it is by no means confined to this group. Certainly not all experiments need to be tests of formal hypotheses. On the other hand, some investigations may very legitimately be tests of hypotheses, and these should surely be regarded in a different light. Just as two decades ago an investigator was frowned upon, in certain circles, unless his study was a test of a formal hypothesis, so today one may be frowned upon, in certain other circles, unless the study merely "asks a question." Neither of these prejudicial tendencies is to be encouraged. The value of an investigation needs to be determined on grounds other than these.

V. Tests of Theory

EMPIRICAL VS. LOGICAL VERIFICATION   A number of interesting problems concern the manner in which hypotheses—and, more broadly, theories—are or are not verifiable in terms of their empirical consequences. Successful prediction of empirical data is commonly held to be the key requirement for the acceptance of the validity of an hypothesis. Here we must distinguish, however, between what may be called empirical and logical verification. The fundamental question is: Does confirmation of the implications of an hypothesis increase the probability of its being correct (its "truth value," in logical terminology)? From the standpoint of formal logic, empirical confirmation does not, since it involves the logical fallacy of "asserting the consequent" (e.g., Miller, 1939; Johnson, 1954; McGuigan, 1956; Turner, 1961). In essence, the reason for this apparent impasse is the impossibility, logically, of eliminating all possible alternative interpretations of the data. Only in purely deductive systems can implications of premises be logically verified.

Is this limitation a serious one for the scientist? Not really. Unless one is concerned with ultimate truthfulness—as a kind of philosophical or metaphysical Holy Grail—empirical verification should be sufficient. Consider the nature of the scientific enterprise. Change and modification are a most prominent characteristic of any developing, or well developed, science. No law or theory is to be accepted as final, or absolute. Even the best developed sciences have abandoned or at least modified certain of the most strongly established of principles; a recent example is the question raised concerning the basic symmetry in the nucleus of the atom. Relevant here also is the long-standing necessity within physics to retain two logically incompatible accounts of light—wave and quantum. From the point of view of the fundamental nature of science, therefore, absolute truth—or even increased probability in terms of formal logic—cannot be taken as a requirement for theory. All that can be asked is that our theory maintain its close relationship to observation. If empirical verification is all we can have, it seems to be a sufficient criterion for theory.

A certain logical restriction on the "truth value" of inductively obtained propositions must be noted, since these are sometimes advanced as intrinsically superior to the deductively oriented hypothesis. No induction, or generalizing from concrete specific observations, can ever be accepted as logically fully verified, for essentially the same reason which limits acceptance of deductive implications: logic cannot prove that exceptions to the generalization will not occur. More important, just as new theoretical positions may always be developed as alternatives to the older established theories, so new, more refined measuring or sensing devices (e.g., the electron microscope) may be developed as superior to the old inductive techniques and so render obsolete, or even incorrect, the older established generalizations. Thus, so-called "abstractive" hypotheses are in these respects little different from "imaginative" hypotheses, although this fact is sometimes apparently neglected by their most enthusiastic supporters (e.g., Turner, 1961).

In the same vein, little fundamental difference exists between the two procedures identified by the phrases "testing a hypothesis"—the orthodox scientific manner—and "asking a question"—the strictly positivistic style. A positive statement can easily be turned into a question, and vice versa, by grammatical means alone. No empirical differences need ensue from the two ways of framing the proposition. Some differences in interpretation of results (inductively by generalization, or deductively by theory) may occur, but the data themselves should be the same. And it is important to remember that "new data . . . are something in themselves which anyone is free to interpret theoretically in his own way or to accept as mere facts" (Barker, Dembo, and Lewin, 1943, p. 456).

PARSIMONY   One other point concerning the problem of testing theory merits attention. This is the role of the law of parsimony, sometimes called William of Occam's razor (in animal psychology, Lloyd Morgan's canon). Essentially, this says that the simplest of alternative explanatory propositions should be accepted. Much misunderstanding has accompanied the promulgation of this long-lived scientific principle, especially perhaps within psychology.

The principle of parsimony has often been criticized on the ground that it would eliminate complex propositions, or at least discourage their formulation, when in reality nature is not always parsimonious and the more complex view frequently turns out to be correct. Thus, the requirement tends to stall, rather than facilitate, scientific advance. This argument needs to be recognized as clearly defective. The doctrine of parsimony is relevant only to the *acceptance* of propositions—not to their testing or development. As a matter of fact, it should serve as a spur to scientific advance, since it puts the burden of proof on those who prefer the more complex alternative; let them find some evidence which *requires* it. Unfortunately, the spur is not always as effective as it might be, because so many of the objectors to the principle appear to be more interested in forensic activity than research. But that is hardly the fault of the principle.

The principle of parsimony helps to prevent the establishment of theories with insufficient empirical support. The longer such theories are permitted to remain in the scientific eye without challenge, the more difficult they are to dislodge and the more likely they are to clog up the avenues of scientific progress. This is particularly true if inadequate efforts to test them are made—perhaps because they are difficult or impossible to test as framed. And if they have become established largely through squatter's rights, even the advent of disconfirming empirical data may not be sufficient to move them. This established theory is what Conant (1947) referred to in his much-quoted statement to the effect that theories are not displaced by contradictory facts but only by superior—and often simpler—theories. The necessity of parsimony must be impressed particularly on all those who mourn the destruction of the "beautiful theory" by the "ugly fact."

Finally, the principle should be a most effective aid in the application of scientific research to practical affairs. Suppose that implementation of a particular theory is being considered in a school system, or a government agency, or a military organization. If some simpler alternative view will equally well handle the empirical data, a serious risk would be entailed in ignoring this important difference. Since most of our hypotheses turn out to be wrong, especially in the early phases of investigation, adding more hypothetical parts without sufficient data invites trouble. The principle of parsimony should thus be more widely recognized as a safeguard in the application of science as well as a stimulant in its pursuit.

VI. Problems in Construct Formation

OPERATIONISM   Put most succinctly, the operationism principle makes a very simple request: What are the empirical referents for your terms? As indicated above, this operational requirement is relatively difficult for the more complex intra-organismic constructs (tension, anxiety, ego strength, etc.) which abound in psychology, but it is a necessary one if clear communication channels are to be kept open.

The operational requirement can be considered as a kind of application, to semantics, of the principle of parsimony; that is, it demands the least in the way of symbol for the empirical referents which are specified. It does not legislate against richer, more complex symbols but simply requests that they be empirically supported—in this case, by explication of the manipulations or observations which identify the term. If such identification is not forthcoming, the term in question cannot receive the operational seal of approval. Of course, as is emphasized below, there is actually a continuum of various degrees of operational satisfaction; few terms are operationally perfect, and few are completely meaningless. The major function of operationism is to exert pressure on the operationally inadequate terms. Just as the principle of parsimony is designed to remove the excess fat and padding from the hypothesis or theory, so the operationism principle is designed to replace the fat of constructs with real muscle.

RESISTANCE TO OPERATIONISM   A great deal of misunderstanding and confusion has arisen with respect to the problem of operationism and its relation to intuitive functions. Some of this may be traced to certain kinds of pressures and motives which tend to restrict scientific work to the left side of the diagram in Figure 1. For example, in certain scientific as well as lay circles, the tendency is to ask large, highly general, practically important but experimentally meaningless questions, and to attempt to translate these too directly into theory construction and research programs. These problems come, of course, out of everyday-life situations, but they must be broken down into simpler and experimentally more meaningful questions before they can be effectively handled. The older schools or systems were most directly concerned with the large, philosophically-oriented type of problem; probably this helps to account for much of their failure to be scientifically more fruitful. The discouragement of such questions, except in preliminary formulations and long-range goals, and their replacement or at least supplementation by more specific and productive questions, seem to be necessary prerequisites for scientific advance in psychology. The large generalizations will then follow, as factual knowledge and empirically related theory are built up on a more solid basis.

The pressure for quick, useful solutions to urgent practical problems (cf. Chapter IV) and the alleged artistic and literary biases of some psychologists have also been regarded as detrimental influences, so far as scientific progress in theory construction and research is concerned. Whatever merit these charges may have, they are not meant—or at any rate should not be meant—to be depreciatory of practical applications or literary and artistic pursuits *per se*. The latter interests in particular, however, are regarded as being at the opposite end of the scale from scientific methods (cf. Figure 1) and are simply considered to be no more appropriate in a strictly scientific endeavor than the purely objective and experimental point of view is appropriate or desirable in the realm of art and literature. In this connection William James' well-known distinction between the "tough-minded" and the "tender-minded" is often cited, and Boring (1942) has presented an interesting elaboration of this notion, emphasizing the basic temperamental differences which account for differences in approaches.

A more serious misunderstanding of the demands of operationism has apparently resulted from an overly literal interpretation. Thus, Israel and Goldstein (1944, p. 186) ask, "How will the thoroughgoing operationist get started upon the investigation of a problem? . . . Unless he already knows the functional relationships, the operationist cannot formulate his problem in the form of a question concerning the functional connections of a certain set of events. . . ." The answer to this common type of objection is simply that problems and questions are originally formulated in relatively non-operational terms, but that, if scientific progress is to occur, they must ultimately be operationally refined. The difficulty seems to be that too many theorists fail to recognize the need for such refinement.

In answer to criticism of operational demands on the grounds that too much is demanded, let us emphasize that operationism is primarily a more or less formal attempt to *stimulate critical evaluation* of the relationship between logical constructs and their supporting empirical data. Not all concepts need to be defined literally in terms of the precise physical operations involved. But it is fair to ask that the observational basis of *any concept* be made as explicit as possible—that, at least, this particular problem be recognized as a problem and not simply ignored, as is very often the case. If this is not adequately done, the concept is certainly open to serious question, as are any conclusions based upon its use.

The need for careful operational analysis is of course greatest in just those areas of psychology where it is most difficult to apply. This situation has no doubt been responsible for a certain amount of the resistance to operationism which has appeared. Inner needs, phenomenological fields, personality structures, and the like become scientifically productive concepts only in so far as their observational bases can be directly evaluated in some way. Throwing the spotlight of critical inquiry upon many such concepts would certainly reveal an embarrassing lack of clarity—and probably very often evoke a strong emotional reaction in the theorist—

but, if science is to be a public and communicable enterprise, no other way of testing their validity seems to be available.

In summarizing this discussion, the fact should be stressed that all scientifically useful concepts in psychology are derived, ultimately, from observations. Failure to identify and localize the intuitive aspects of theory construction has been a major methodological defect in many of the higher-level types of theoretical work. Without some degree of willingness to subject all concepts to a critical, operational analysis, the vital self-correcting processes in science can hardly function effectively.

THE *IV-HC* CONTINUUM   Much of the controversy over psychological constructs in recent years has concerned the distinction between so-called intervening variable (*IV*s) and hypothetical construct (*HC*s). A portion of this book is devoted to this problem (see Chapter IV, especially Selection 10). The historical development will be only briefly outlined (see Meissner, 1960, for a recent review, stressing the more philosophical issues).

The use of the intervening variable was originally suggested by Tolman (1936), but its actual implementation was most seriously attempted by Hull (1943). In 1948, MacCorquodale and Meehl suggested that a distinction be made between two types of intervening constructs: 1) the *IV*, which they held to follow Tolman's original suggestion, since it is simply an abstractive construct; and 2) the *HC*, which on the contrary contains more meaning than is mediated by the specified stimulus and response referents. This important difference between the two types of construct is schematically shown in Figure 3, where the *S* and *R* represent stimulus and response referents respectively and the *?*s indicate the unspecified *S* and *R* factors in the case of the *HC*. Examples of these two types of constructs are considered in detail in the next section.

As constructs, then, *IV*s and *HC*s are held to differ mainly in two respects: 1) degree of *operational acceptability*, illustrated in Figure 3: *IV*s are pure summary or shorthand devices, whose total meaning is carried by the stimulus and response referents; *HC*s imply more ("surplus meaning") than is conveyed by their stimulus and response referents; 2) degree of *reality status: IV*s are not to be interpreted in terms of

Figure 3.   **Simplified schematic representation of two types of intervening constructs: the *IV* and the *HC* (see text for explanation).**

any physiological mechanisms—they are purely abstractive behavioral concepts; *HC*s imply some physiological mechanism—they "exist" therefore in the organism in a sense in which *IV*s do not.

The present thesis is that only the first of these continua is worth considering; the reality, or existential issue, is a hopelessly sterile one—for science if not for philosophy—and has contributed only to obfuscation of the more important operational dimension.

Let us therefore first quickly dispose of the reality issue, and turn then to the operational problem. Any behavior obviously must be mediated by some sort of physiological function; to ignore the fact is quite legitimate, but this does not deny that *some* process or mechanism *exists* for the *IV*. The important point is that none is *specified;* the present preference for handling this problem is to think of the *IV* in terms of "*whatever* process is needed to mediate the *S-R* relations" (see Selection 13). The surplus content of the *HC* can be physiological in nature, but this fact does not justify distinguishing between the two types of construct on the basis of reality status.

The thesis is sometimes advanced that "the whole controversy of intervening variables versus hypothetical constructs is a pseudoissue, the distinction itself a pseudodistinction" (Bergmann, 1953, p. 447). From the present point of view, this position is unacceptable only in so far as it applies to the operational distinction. Let us therefore review briefly Bergmann's rationale for rejection of this distinction.

Two major arguments are advanced. First, Bergmann has elsewhere stated: "If the right side *R* of a definition *D* contains itself a concept *C* claimed to be 'unobservable,' one *merely* has to expand *D* by substituting for *C* its definition. By repeating this elimination *as often as necessary*, one can *always* obtain an *R* that mentions only characters of the kind that we call immediately observable" (1951, p. 102; italics added). Plausible as this contention may be from a logical point of view, it is nevertheless a rather clear case of begging the question when considered from a scientific point of view. The ability to *specify* the definition, in terms of empirical referents, is exactly what is missing for the *C*s which carry the surplus meaning in *HC*s. Communication with authors to ascertain these definitions, even assuming that authors are able or willing to supply them, is hardly a feasible procedure. And how else can they be provided?

Second, Bergmann has argued on somewhat different grounds that *IV*s as well as *HC*s have surplus meaning, hence the pseudodistinction in this regard. He contends that *IV*s have "excess meaning" which "they acquire . . . automatically when they are put to use . . . in the formulation of fundamental laws" (1953, pp. 444–445). Again, this argument begs the question. A quite different kind of surplus meaning is involved. The difficulty of "putting to use" the *HC*s with *prior* surplus meaning is precisely what differentiates them from *IV*s. If *IV*s acquire a kind of "excess meaning" *only* when they are used in laws, they have already served their purpose, and incorporation into laws, as Bergmann himself points out, "is their one fundamental use" (1953, p. 445).

Thus the variation in operational clarity among constructs is held to be a most significant one, from the point of view of the practicing researcher. This statement holds regardless of whether the present usage differs, as Bergmann has noted (1953, p. 447) and was earlier pointed out (Selection 10), from the particular criteria for distinguishing *IV*s from *HC*s proposed first by MacCorquodale and Meehl.

CRITIQUE OF THE *IV*   Most of the other objections raised against the use of *IV*s fall into one of two major groups. On the one hand is the extreme positivistic protest (less strong than against the *HC* perhaps, but nonetheless clearly audible). Exception is taken, for example to "hidden mechanisms," to "mental fictions," or to "conjectures that postulate imagined properties" (Turner, 1961).

The rebuttal to these objections is simply to point to the widespread and quite successful use of such "imagined properties" in science. Psychological examples are less desirable, not only because of the scarcity of clearcut cases but also because of their more controversial status—to psychologists at least. For these reasons two examples will be mentioned from the field of biology: Charles Darwin's theory of organic evolution and Gregor Mendel's two-factor theory of inheritance. Since these are probably the two most important biological advances of the past century, they will surely qualify as adequate scientific illustrations.

Briefly, the case here may be put in the form of specimen questions: Was Darwin's construct, "survival of the fittest," a kind of "imagined property"? And how about the two factors ("genes") of Mendel? The fact that each of these constructs was closely tied to empirical data puts them on the *IV* side of the continuum but hardly eliminates their inferential status.

The second class of objection comes from the other side of the methodological fence, from those who prefer the *HC* to the *IV*. These arguments may be represented by two recurrent themes: 1) The *IV* is so narrow and situation-tied a construct that it cannot be easily generalized. A brief answer here should suffice. As has been pointed out elsewhere (Selection 13), the problem of generality is a persistent and pervasive one that bedevils all constructs. It is by no means peculiar to *IV*s, nor is it in any sense generated by the operational procedures, as is sometimes apparently assumed. On the contrary, the operational approach helps to delineate more clearly rather than obscure, the problem. It can be solved by processes of generalizing from *IV*s, the generalization processes themselves being operationally defined. 2) The *IV* is essentially a sterile kind of construct and does not permit the rich imaginative development which has been so characteristic of effective science (e.g., Benjamin, 1955). The answer here seems a simple one: The place for the imagination is in the form of hypotheses (or experimental questions), the effective number of which is limited only by the limits of experimental skill and patience in the investigator. Surely the fact that the constructs used are *IV*s and therefore clearly identifiable does not prevent the use of any kind of theory or model the researcher cares to devise.

One familiar example should be helpful in illustrating this problem more clearly. One frequently hears the derogation of the operational dictum, somewhat crudely put, that "intelligence is what the intelligence test measures." The fact that this kind of derogation can be so generally well received in psychological circles is very suggestive of a generally low level of understanding of this issue. Of course, "intelligence," as a gross or molar construct (or *HC*), is more than is shown by the intelligence tests, but this extra meaning is precisely what needs to be related to the test score or to some other operationally defined constructs.

Failure to recognize the role of the intelligence test score construct is probably attributable at least in part to an unfortunately widespread semantic fallacy: the apparent assumption that for each molar construct (frustration, motivation, anxiety, etc.) there exists some one definitive set of functions or processes, and that it is this which *is* frustration, etc. A more general appreciation of the fundamental lesson of operationism should facilitate understanding of the multiplicity of *different* empirical operations—and the consequent a priori multiplicity of meanings of the construct—even if a unitary process is ultimately uncovered.

This situation is shown in Figure 4. Any gross construct can be considered here as an example. Both "intelligence," just discussed, or "anxiety," to be considered next, afford good illustrations. The numbers in the figure represent the specific operational tests (such as particular ways of measuring intelligence or anxiety). The letters represent much wider, non-operational conceptualizations (*HC*s). The variety of such conceptualizations is indicated by the variation in the large circles; exactly what is not included in each is not clearly specified, but that different notions are to some extent involved is usually apparent. On the other hand, there is little question about the narrower meaning of the specific measures shown as numbers. In order to keep the illustration reasonably simple, it is assumed that all of the specific measures fall within the central hard core of meaning shared by the larger conceptualizations; even if this is unfortunately not always true, it is at least sometimes approximated.

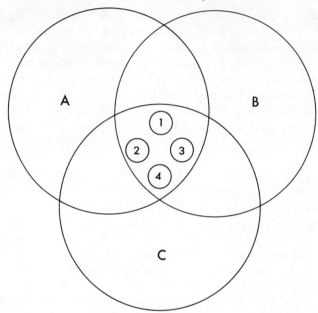

**Figure 4.   Two kinds of meaning in complex constructs
(see text for explanation).**

The heart of the problem, illustrated in Figure 4, is how to maintain
a reasonable degree of operational specificity, and thus clear communi-
cability, while at the same time extending the range of the particular
measures, thus approaching the scope and therefore the significance of
the constructs developed. One kind of solution to the present problem is
next described.

"Anxiety" affords an especially interesting and instructive illustration
of how a gross construct can be effectively analyzed by means of IVs.
Consider first an experimental paradigm widely used in rat and mouse
research. Typically, the subject is placed in a well-lighted but empty
"open field," such as a large tub, for a specified time interval. Measurement may be restricted to the amount of urination and defecation which
ensues during the interval. Now, anxiety can be defined simply and completely—for this particular standardized S-R situation—and the reader will
know exactly what meaning the writer intends to convey by the quantitative scores obtained. Further questions of the underlying physiological
basis of the construct, or its relationship to other constructs and variables,
will need to be answered on the basis of empirical investigations conducted as far as possible with similarly operationized terminology.

Consider next the kind of anxiety measured by the Manifest Anxiety
Scale (Taylor, 1953), where the term refers to a subject's score on an

inventory prepared from the widely used personality scale, the MMPI. Using human subjects, this inventory obviously plumbs a quite different kind of anxiety. It has proved quite useful in stimulating empirical investigations which relate it to other variables and constructs (see Spence, 1958).

Both the above illustrative *IV*s involve relatively standardized—specified—empirical situations and circumscribed response measurements. They therefore represent arbitrary decisions. These characteristics are important desiderata for *IV*s. Also note that because of their abstractive nature, *IV*s are more dependent upon the explicit development of hypotheses—as provisional relationships among variables—than are *HC*s with their built-in, and therefore relatively inaccessible, relationships.

Questions quickly arise concerning the relationship, if any, between these two "anxieties," and more particularly concerning their relationship, if any, to the variety of "anxieties" which can be found as *HC*s within the clinical and personality-theory literature. Note that these questions can *only* be answered in terms of empirical investigations which develop, with a carefully coordinated framework, the relationships among the various constructs (cf. Selections 13 and 15). Also important is that such analysis, as for example in the case of the so-called *E/C IV* described elsewhere (Selection 10), be recognized as an opening wedge or a starting point for research and not mistaken for any kind of terminal explanation. Such slow and laborious development, characteristic of scientific progress in all fields, is not appealing to those who want their questions answered here and now (cf. Chapter VI), or to those who are intolerant of the kind of ambiguity, or multiplicity of meanings, which is necessarily part of this process. Progressive narrowing of the various kinds of gross "anxiety" in terms of their empirical referents—and thus their operational meanings—will be accompanied by a progressive broadening of the scientifically acceptable conceptual and theoretical relationships among the constructs.

CRITIQUE OF THE *HC*   The basic objection to *HC*s is that, when used in theoretical propositions *which are accepted as explanations* of some phenomenon, they violate two major and highly respected canons of scientific procedure: 1) parsimony and 2) operationism. However, recognize that this violation involves only one of the two major functions of theory: its role as a goal. There is no reason at all why *HC*s should not be widely used to *guide* theoretical and experimental thinking (cf. the "context of discovery," discussed previously). Whether or not they are publicly expressed would then depend upon the taste of the investigator: the positivist or radical empiricist says no, keep them private (just *how* private is not clear—to oneself only? one's research assistant? one's colleagues?);

the theorist more partial to *HC*s is likely to want to advance them freely (as suggested previously, this procedure creates a serious risk, in that un-parsimonious hypotheses too freely advanced without empirical supports are hard to displace once well rooted in verbal argumentation).

Positivistic objections to *all* terms with surplus meaning, no matter how they are used, represent an unfortunate misapplication of the funda-mentally sound operational principle. They are reminiscent of the earlier behavioristic rejection in toto during the late 1920's and early 1930's of the concept of "instinct." The valid objection is to the use of "instinct" as an explanatory concept. But the term used in a strictly *descriptive* manner—to refer to a large number of important behavioral phenomena—is scientifically defensible. The fact that psychologists' attention needed to be recalled to these phenomena by the ethologists suggests a serious risk—the ignoring of significant phenomena—incurred in such wholesale rejection of terminology.

A comparable situation now exists with regard to such constructs as "motivation." Again, legitimate objections to this kind of gross construct used as an explanation, or without adequate empirical specification in theory, should not be confused with rejection of the term when used in an essentially descriptive sense to refer to important behavioral phe-nomena which require analysis (cf. Miller, Galanter, and Pribram, 1960). Such unrealistic standards not only discourage the kind of progressive theoretical-experimental attack which the phenomena involved need, but also blind too many students of behavior to the existence of the phe-nomena and so tend to stagnate research on them. Permitting words thus to become our masters rather than our tools can be prevented by a more realistic attitude towards their multiple roles in science.

Two kinds of surplus meaning may be distinguished in *HC*s. Since these have different implications for treatment, they should be identified. In the first case, the surplus meaning itself has a more or less clearly ex-plicated empirical basis—but the empirical referents for it are not pres-ently available. The solution to this operational gap is simple, at least in principle. It is to bring in the empirical supports and relate them to the empirical referents of the new construct. An example may help to clarify this situation. The construct "fear" is frequently used as a part of the ex-planation of avoidance conditioning. Bringing some empirical measure into the conditioning situation is not quite so simple in practice (cf. Solomon and Brush, 1956), but it is a necessary step if this surplus mean-ing is to be eliminated and explanatory progress achieved on this problem.

The second type of surplus meaning has no identifiable empirical referents. This, of course, constitutes a more difficult problem for the investigator, who must start more or less from scratch in producing empirical referents. Unfortunately this situation is probably more common than the first one.

As previously suggested (also see Selection 10), the *HC* can take two different lines of development: 1) it can be transformed, totally or partially, into strictly empirical hypotheses which can be directly tested; or 2) it can be transformed, more or less gradually perhaps, into a *IV*—by producing the appropriate empirical referents. In the first case, the construct disappears; it is no longer necessary in the presence of adequate, direct empirical measures. In the second case, the construct remains but is made more amenable to investigation by empirical referents. A good example of the first case is the discovery of capillaries, connecting the small arteries and veins, which was made possible by the invention of the microscope and eliminated the need for any construct of the sort previously advanced in the absence of a direct empirical look. Examples of the second case have already been thoroughly discussed (anxiety, intelligence).

If, however, *HC*s remain in their pristine state of operational infancy, the net effect seems to be that little scientific progress is made, no matter how hotly the theoretical issues may be debated.

VII. Types of Explanation

All scientific hypotheses, as attempted explanations, may be regarded as descriptions of functional relations between variables at a different level of discourse. Two major types of scientific explanation may be differentiated:

1. *Reductive*, by means of which particular phenomena are functionally related to other phenomena at a different and, in a hierarchical sense, more basic level of description.

2. *Constructive*, by means of which the phenomena are described in terms of more abstract, or higher-order, constructs and hypotheses on the same descriptive level.

The two types of explanation as they apply to psychology are shown diagrammatically in Figure 5. A single example may be given. Let us suppose that the behavior datum which we want to explain is a fairly simple one, a description of an animal *S* being presented with a certain type of food and eating. The chain of *reductive* explanation would then go approximately as follows: the eating behavior occurs because of certain stomach contractions and neurophysiological events, and these in turn occur because of certain biochemical conditions, etc. The *constructive* type of explanation would start with the same behavior and might proceed along the following line: the eating behavior occurs because of food deprivation (construct of hunger drive), which under similar con-

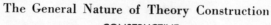
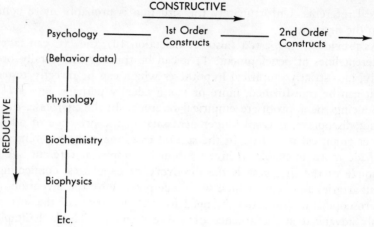

Figure 5.   Two types of scientific explanation.

ditions previously has been paired with the giving of food (construct of reinforcement) to produce a certain behavior tendency (higher-order construct of habit), etc.

Note that in each case explanation proceeds through an interlocking of the variables being described. When the variables which are used to explain are drawn from observations of a sort arbitrarily assigned to another level of description (for example, the physiological, if organ system functions are directly concerned), then the explanation may be considered to be of the reductive type. When the variables are drawn from observations made on the same level of description (the psychological, if behavior is involved), then the explanation may be considered to be of the constructive type. In either case the explanation proceeds to a more basic level of description—more basic in the sense that the original behavior data are found to vary systematically as functions of the changes in the other variables introduced.

A certain amount of controversial discussion has arisen over the relative merits, within psychology, of these two types of explanation. On the one hand, it can be argued that the constructive type is *methodologically* more fundamental than the reductive, in the sense that only after a certain degree of successful constructive explanation has been achieved can the various descriptive levels be readily related. On the other hand, the point is made that the *ultimate* objective of science is explanation of the reductive type. Without attempting to evaluate these claims, we shall simply state that whichever type of explanation seems to be most useful should be adopted (as a matter of fact, to separate the two types in actual practice often would be difficult). They are complementary, rather than mutually exclusive, and ought to be regarded as such.

VIII. Levels of Explanation

A somewhat related and equally sterile controversy has persisted in regard to the relative merits of the so-called *field-theoretical* and the *stimulus-response* types of theoretical and experimental approach. We should emphasize that these types of theoretical approaches are also to be regarded as supplementary, if not actually complementary, rather than mutually exclusive. Whether one prefers to stress theory at the most molar levels of description, or to work upwards, so to speak, from the relatively molecular and simplified levels of description, appears to be a function of a number of factors. Among these may be mentioned personal, temperamental influences, types of problems being investigated, etc. Obviously, many kinds of scientific attacks are possible upon different levels of complexity, or molarity, which however measured must always be regarded as upon a continuum (cf. Chapter V). It is therefore a most unfortunate fact that these two particular types of approaches—or any other two, for that matter—should be so often and so emotionally opposed to each other. Claims of *exclusive* excellence from either side and premature extrapolation of conclusions based upon the present meager and tenuous store of scientific knowledge in psychology may be seen as having little basis in fact. The only scientific test of any type of theoretical approach is its ability to generate fruitful experiments or other observations and to lead to more satisfactory and more comprehensive theories. While legitimate differences do exist between the field-theoretical and the stimulus-response points of view, and useful theoretical as well as empirical contributions have resulted from contrasting predictions thus made possible, no scientific development in the field of psychology today justifies the enthusiastic acceptance of any *single* type of theoretical-experimental orientation.

A glance at the situation in physiology is helpful in pointing up comparable problems in psychology. The physiologist may concentrate upon more and more detailed and refined analysis of highly technical problems within any one organ system—this has been the orthodox procedure, as a matter of fact—or he may concern himself with more molar interrelations of the various systems, as Cannon has done in his work on "homeostasis." There has been no wholesale or concentrated effort within physiology to dispense with either approach or even to treat them as in any way opposed to each other; they are recognized as complementary and necessary functions. Likewise, there is no essential reason why such calm acceptance of different purposes and approaches should not occur within psychology.

One particularly crucial problem within psychology involves the desirability of investigators' paying more theoretical and experimental attention to the way in which simple laws, particularly those involved in child development and personality organization, interact with each other. Such so-called "composition laws" (Bergmann, 1953, p. 445) require that the more elementary relationships first be at least roughed out. But failure to consider them as legitimate nomothetic (generalized law-making) endeavors has led in many instances to an over-emphasis upon the scientific value of idiographic efforts, which entail the intensive investigation and full descriptive account of the individual subject as a substitute for the general law. Certainly idiographic endeavors have their place, and a most important one, but their *scientific* value is strictly limited to the role they play in the establishment of nomothetic propositions. In contrast with practice, science is concerned *only* with generalizations which can be made upon the basis of a number of individual cases (Hunt, 1951; Falk, 1956). When more adequate attention is paid to the kind of law which combines simpler laws, perhaps a clearer understanding of the so-called nomothetic-idiographic issue will be achieved.

The problem of "reductionism" (cf. Selection 17), stimulated within recent years by the increasing popularity of the field-theoretical, or holistic, type of approach, has produced a great deal more heat and confusion than light and understanding. Scientifically, there is only one possible answer to the question whether so-called emergent behavioral functions can be successfully "reduced" to more primary and less complex ones within the same field. The answer must be a pragmatic one, dependent entirely upon the extent to which such reduction may eventually occur. Again, at the present time no reliable scientific basis exists upon which to make any very definite statement on this problem. Physical and biological analogies or emotionally biased beliefs in either direction have little support in scientific evidence and ought to be labeled more clearly for what they are—dubious analogies and emotionally grounded beliefs.

In this connection a certain amount of criticism has been directed within recent years against the various well-developed programs of theory construction based upon research with infra-human animals. Animal research has three major objectives: 1) to learn more about the nature of the various species per se; 2) to obtain comparative data, with special reference usually to implications that can be drawn for man; and 3) to investigate, with effective control of past experience and environmental conditions, certain problems for their own sake, rather than to concentrate upon one particular kind of subject, such as man. Frequently, more than one of these objectives are involved in a single type of investigation, and the investigators themselves may not bother to separate them. For our purposes, nevertheless, it is well to recognize them as separate and legitimate objectives.

The comparative objective is the one that is most often presumed, especially by those not themselves active in animal research, to be the major aim. Sometimes it is even seen as the only aim. Nevertheless, for many, if not most, of the basic researchers using animal subjects, the third objective is the primary, and perhaps the exclusive, one. Animals are used mainly for convenience in attacking particular problems—not for love of rat or monkey or pigeon or worm, nor for any compelling urge to apply the hoped-for results to human behavior. The problem of how far one can generalize from any given species to another, such as from the rat to man, is a strictly empirical one and can only be answered, for particular cases, by extensive experimentation. Certainly, theoretical generalizations need to be made carefully in this regard and should not be extrapolated from scanty data, as has occurred too often in the past.

Again, a glance at a well established and highly successful scientific field may be helpful in clarifying the situation. The research geneticist's primary—and many times practically exclusive—concern is with fundamental genetic functions, wherever they may occur. He has intensively studied the fruitfly *Drosophila* for the same reasons that the psychologist has so intensively studied the rat: convenience, ease of experimental control, large amount of previous work, etc. With the exception of certain recent work on human blood chemistry, it would be difficult, if not impossible, to point to a single fundamental genetic discovery based upon research on humans—or for that matter, upon other animal forms than *Drosophila*. There seems to be no reason why the behavioral scientist should not be allowed an equally unimpeded opportunity to employ infrahuman animals in the same general way and for the same general purpose—the investigation of basic behavioral functions, regardless of the degree to which the results may ultimately be related to human problems.

Finally, we should emphasize again that a diversity of interests and approaches is not only desirable but inevitable in as complex and heterogeneous a field as modern psychology. More, rather than less, experimental research and empirically-oriented theory is needed at all levels of explanations—the strictly molecular as well as the broadly molar. However, regardless of the level of complexity, or molarity, on which he works, the psychologist is obliged to follow the general principles of scientific theory construction, as outlined in the preceding sections. One of the most immediate needs in contemporary psychology is for a more realistic attitude towards these general methodological requirements. A major obstacle to more effective scientific progress seems to be a general disinclination to submit constructs and theories to a critical and rigorous operational analysis (whether or not that particular term is used) and a corresponding failure explicitly to recognize the invidious infiltration of emotional beliefs and extra-scientific values throughout all phases of theory construction. A more careful distinction between scientific and extra-scientific elements is necessary to keep both kinds of values in their proper place. The essential neutrality of scientific methodology cannot be sacrificed, no matter how urgent the immediate needs for knowledge and action may be, without a corresponding loss of the effectiveness of objective explanatory propositions of a high degree of empirically tested probability.

IX. Theory and Research Training

Before concluding this introductory chapter, we should correct one impression which might otherwise unfortunately be obtained from this volume as a whole, as well as from the present essay. This is the notion that the use of theory in actual scientific practice is an orderly process and that the best research is that which simply follows one or another of the procedures outlined.

The fact of the matter, as every experienced researcher knows, is that in practice effective research is most often unpredictable; that it evidences little uniformity; and that much of it apparently violates the customary prescriptions. Of all the popular stereotypes about science and scientists, those which overemphasize procedural uniformity and orderliness are perhaps the most clearly mistaken.

What implications does this situation have for the role of theory, especially in regard to training for research? How may this apparent contradiction between our textbook prescriptions and our laboratory behaviors be resolved?

In answering these questions a number of key points will be briefly summarized. The contradiction, while in some respects a real one, is much less serious than is often assumed. A careful look at some of its most important facets should help reduce some of the confusion surrounding it and so minimize its potentially harmful consequences.

First, and most generally, we should recognize that by far the greatest amount of diversity involves particular procedural problems rather than over-all objectives. Much as different sciences vary enormously in the particular techniques which they develop but nevertheless show considerable fundamental methodological commonality (e.g., use of controlled observation), so the various differing modes of theory construction share certain common features (e.g., their need to relate to data in a testable manner, to utilize operational constructs, to be parsimonious).

Second, we must be especially careful not to confuse the well-groomed theory which emerges as the ultimate product of the most advanced scientific research with the disorderly and frequently changing conceptualizations from which it developed. The common failure to make this distinction is often a major factor underlying the stereotype of science as a strictly neat and orderly intellectual enterprise. Actually, of course, to look upon the successful theory of textbook presentation as a prototype of theory *construction* is no more reasonable than to equate the finished poem with the early drafts or the final architectural blueprints with the preliminary sketches, to look for the printed book in the vats of ink and rolls of paper stock from which it is made, or to attempt to find the motor car in the various metals and other components processed in the automobile factory. The latter mistakes are of course seldom made, and perhaps with sufficient education we can reduce the frequency of analogous errors with regard to scientific matters.

Third, one must not confuse the common failures of particular individual scientists to conform to some expected norms with the question of the validity of those norms viewed over the scientific population as a whole. That is, the kind of general propositions advanced within this chapter as desiderata for the generation and evaluation of theory have a very considerable amount of general validity, even though only roughly approximated in the case of some investigators and perhaps grossly violated by certain others. A closely analogous situation exists with regard to the major attributes commonly, and accurately, attributed to the "scientific attitude": skepticism, empiricism, lack of bias, etc. Few scientists have all these characteristics in the degree to which they are ascribed to the ideal scientist; certain individual scientists, even some who have achieved high recognition for their theoretical or experimental contributions, are sadly lacking in many of these attributes. *But*, with regard to the scientific population as compared with other populations, little doubt exists that these attributes are more generally approximated and that, in the scientific group as a whole, they therefore not only are representative of the group but also in large measure help to account for the success of the scientific method as opposed to other means of acquiring knowledge. The same situation seems to hold for the exemplification within the scientific population and the influence of generalizations concerning theory construction and evaluation.

Fourth, the greatest inconsistencies exist in relation to the critical creative functions, or in what has been described above as the "context of confirmation." This is understandable in view of the little that is known of the effective variables underlying creativity of any kind, including the scientific. In the absence of sound knowledge, little agreement is to be expected—or sought.

Finally, as a direct consequence in part of the preceding point, variation in theory construction and manner and degree of influence is to be encouraged, rather than discouraged. Practice in theorizing, as an indis-

pensable component of research, is essential for effective research training. Formal coursework alone is entirely inadequate.

These are also the conclusions of the Estes Park seminar, which was
recently charged with the task of making recommendations for improvement of graduate training for research in psychology. The major theme of
the excellent report that was issued at that time is that there is very little
uniformity in successful research procedures—contrary to the various
stereotypes cherished even within educational circles—and that, as a result, standardization and formal training should be minimized and development of individual strengths maximized, preferably within the framework of the "apprentice system." In view of the strong stress in this report
on realism, rather than educational tradition, the views of the seminar
members on the role of theory in research training are of particular interest, and that section of the report is therefore here reproduced in full
(American Psychological Association Education and Training Board Ad
Hoc Committee, 1959, pp. 172–173):

How much and what kind of emphasis should be placed on theory in education for research? The good research worker generates good ideas. But what
constitutes an "idea?" And at what stage in the process of doing research does
the idea come? Most people will agree that worthwhile ideas do not come full
blown in all their glorious maturity out of an empty void. The process of getting and developing ideas is undoubtedly a confused mixture of observation,
thinking, asking why, cherishing little unformed notions, etc. Some people can
and do work very effectively with ideas that have an iceberg quality, that is,
most of the content is submerged in their own thinking and not made explicit
until a very late stage of the research. Other people are fond of making their
ideas more explicit earlier.

With the iceberg kind of thinking, it is obviously very difficult to communicate to someone else, such as a graduate student, what is a good idea, how to
have ideas, how to translate the ideas into experimental work, and the like. It
is obviously much easier to communicate such information when use is made
of a highly explicit and formalized theory from which rigorous derivations can
be made. As a consequence, it is easy in the training of research workers to
overemphasize highly formal rigorous theory where the rules of logic can
apply. It is equally easy to decry "theory" and to insist that one must stay only
on the empirical level.

We doubt whether either of these extreme positions, if adopted seriously, can
be anything but a hindrance to the research worker. The importance of the
vague notion, difficult as it is to explain, should be emphasized. The problem
really is how to communicate this usefully. But it should also be emphasized
that the notion cannot be allowed to remain forever vague; ideas must eventually achieve clarity and testability if they are to receive serious attention from
other researchers.

Testability is an important quality of good ideas and good theory. If theory
—in the sense of constructs which are invented and relations which are imagined
to exist among these constructs—is to be meaningful in the long run, it must
have direct implications concerning the empirical world. Confusion arises with
respect to the meaning of the word "implication." In doing research with the
iceberg type of thinking, the implication cannot be clearly spelled out and we

talk comfortably about intuitions, hunches, and the like. If the idea is at this level, it is probably bad to attempt formal statement.

But even when the ideas are more explicit, when terms are defined and a verbal theory takes shape, it is rare that the nature of the theory is such that derivation can be made rigorously using only the rules of logic and mathematics. This is particularly true during the earlier stages of the development of a body of knowledge. More often, implications from theory come about in a pseudo-logical manner with much "intuition" involved.

What is important in research is for the individual to be able to operate at whatever level his ideas are formulated. If he refuses to use ideas to guide him just because they are vague, or if he insists on trying to bring his ideas to a premature state of formalization, he will probably end up in triviality.

X. Summary and Conclusions

The preceding discussion may be summarized in the following major points:

1. An acute need exists within contemporary psychology for a wider recognition of the role that theory (broadly, conceptualization and inference) plays in relation to the empirical aspects of science. The interdependence of theory and observation must be emphasized in view of the recent disillusionment with highly formalized theories and the resultant trend toward a positivistic minimizing of theory in general.

2. The two great functions of theory are: 1) to serve as a *tool* whereby direct empirical investigation is facilitated and guided, and 2) to organize and *order* empirical knowledge so as to facilitate not only empirical predictions but also understanding of natural phenomena (by means of integrating conceptualization).

3. The three fundamental elements of all scientific theory construction, or conceptual ordering of empirical data, are: 1) *observations*—which must be under *controlled* conditions (that is, eliminate the role of extraneous variables so as to permit the relatively direct relating of dependent-variable effects to the independent variable, which is manipulated); 2) *constructs*—which must be *operational* (that is, have clearly specified and identifiable empirical referents); and 3) *hypotheses*—which must be *testable* (that is, clearly disconfirmable).

4. The four major modes of theory development are: 1) the use of a model, or conceptual structure, usually borrowed from some other field, whereby empirical investigation is provided firm guidelines, but strictly speaking, no effort is made to test the "truth value" of the model itself; 2) the *deductive* procedure, whereby postulate sets are logically arranged, as in a *hypothetico-deductive* framework, and empirical tests are indicated in terms of implications; 3) the *functional* procedure, whereby theory and data are developed interdependently, with neither straying too far ahead of the other but neither lingering too far behind; sometimes theory, some-

times data are emphasized as guides, with either clearly acceptable as such and scientific progress depending upon the degree of correspondence achieved between them; and 4) the *inductive* procedure, whereby inference is minimized and facts in the form of data are emphasized in their own right, with theory then following, rather than leading, data and serving only in a summary or covering function.

5. Whether scientific procedures emphasize induction, as in positivism, or deduction, as in classical theory, no guarantee of ultimate truthfulness can ever be achieved. Increased probability can be obtained not in any logical sense but only in terms of increased empirical predictability and fruitfulness of empirical investigation. But this necessary limitation should not be disturbing as long as scientific utility and not metaphysical certainty is our objective.

6. Operationally clear constructs (*IVs*) are most useful in theories per se. Constructs with surplus meaning (*HCs*) are useful mainly in the development of theory—and in the context of discovery rather than confirmation. The latter may be useful guides to planning of experimental design but are of dubious value in interpretations of data, because they violate the principle of parsimony as well as operationism. In attempting to eliminate *HCs* *completely*, the radical empiricist therefore runs the serious risk of throwing out many scientific babies in his operational bathing (although the suspicion may be nursed that the bathing is a public rather than a private ceremony); the arch-conservative intuitive espouser of *HCs* *only* obviously suffers from an overabundance of riches and is quite unable to achieve a satisfactory scientific digestion of data. Caught in the cross fire from these opposing and often highly emotional camps, the middle-of-the-roader needs to stand his ground and try to show how each of these types of construct has its place.

7. The two major kinds of explanation—*reductive* and *constructive*—are both needed in behavioral research and should be recognized as complementary.

8. A variety of *levels of explanation* is desirable within science, and the exclusive excellence of any particular level is to be rejected.

9. Theory has a most important contribution to make in research training, but one should not assume from this chapter or this volume that theory-making is an orderly process; quite the contrary, like research progress generally, theory construction is typically variable and unpredictable and cannot be properly taught merely by formal training.

In conclusion, the deliberate interlocking of theory and experiment ought to be viewed as the supreme challenge that science offers, rather than depreciated for the sake of theory (read: speculation) or experiment (read: data) alone. The devising of increasingly detailed means of tying empirical measures to conceptual inferences affords many scientists their deepest scientific satisfactions. Perhaps psychologists as behavioral scientists have lagged largely because they have failed to respond to this challenge. In this moderate but realistic view of theory, conceptual intuition and experimental ingenuity have a common meeting ground. It is sincerely hoped that the present work will aid at least a little in inducing the new generation of behavioral scientists, if not the old, to rally round this modest standard and labor in the interests of *both* fact and theory.

Glossary of Selected Terms

CONCEPT. A generalized class name which represents certain abstracted properties of the class.

CONSTRUCT. A concept that represents relationships among things and/or events and their properties (see intervening variable, hypothetical construct).

CONSTRUCTIVE EXPLANATION. Interpretation of phenomena in terms of constructs representing relationships of antecedent (stimulus) and consequent (response) conditions at the same level of analysis (in psychology, the behavioral).

CONTROL. 1) Of *variables:* the elimination of extraneous variation in an (experimental) situation so that measures of the dependent variable(s) may more accurately reflect the influence of the manipulation of the independent variable(s). 2) Of *events:* management of a situation made possible by scientific or otherwise ordered knowledge (as in the phrase that the objective of science is to describe, predict, and control).

CONTROLLED VARIABLE. A factor or condition whose influence on the dependent variable in a particular investigation is eliminated experimentally or otherwise.

COROLLARY. A proposition deductively related to a postulate and also empirically testable in terms of its logical implications.

DATA. Recorded results of observations, preferably of an experimental (controlled) nature.

DATA LANGUAGE. The terminology in which data are recorded, that is, the strictly empirical or observational language.

DEDUCTION. A formal logic in which specific conclusions are drawn from generalized premises.

DEDUCTIVE THEORY. See *Theory, types of.*

DEPENDENT VARIABLE. The factor or condition in an investigation which is directly measured; in psychology, generally some response or response measure.

EMPIRICAL. Observational; directly based upon sensory experience.

EMPIRICISM. A metatheoretical and scientific position that emphasizes observations and the data language rather than deductive logic and inference.

EXPLANATION. A principle or proposition in terms of which some other propositions or events can be understood; the process by which such clarification is produced.

FACT. A symbolic proposition, usually a verbal statement, that is generally agreed upon by some particular group of persons. (In science, facts range from scientific data, the recorded results of experiments, to abstract theoretical propositions, with a generally decreasing degree of acceptance, or "factualness," from the former to the latter.)

FUNCTIONAL THEORY. See *Theory, types of.*

HYPOTHESIS. A proposition, usually couched in the form of a conjecture or provisional explanation, that states a relationship among empirical or theoretical variables.

HYPOTHETICAL CONSTRUCT (*HC*). A construct representing a wide range of stimulus (antecedent) and response (consequent) conditions which are not specified; hence, an intervening (intra-organismic) construct with "surplus meaning" and a relatively low degree of operational specificity (usually distinguished from the intervening variable (*IV*), which is more strictly abstractive of the *S-R* relationship).

IDIOGRAPHIC. Referring to the intensive study of an individual subject; contrasted with nomothetic.

INDEPENDENT VARIABLE. A factor or condition that is experimentally or otherwise manipulated and whose influence on the dependent variable is under investigation.

INDUCTION. A logic in which specific propositions are accumulated to produce generalized conclusions.

INDUCTIVE THEORY. See *Theory, types of*.

INTERVENING VARIABLE (*IV*). A construct abstracted from the stimulus (antecedent) and response (consequent) conditions and having no meaning beyond this *S-R* relationship; hence, an intervening (intra-organismic) construct with a high degree of operational specificity and clarity (usually distinguished from the hypothetical construct (*HC*), which has "surplus" and unspecified meaning).

LAW. A statement of regular, predictable relationship among empirical variables.

METATHEORY. A set of general and super-ordinate rules concerning the construction of theory.

MINIATURE SYSTEM. A theoretical structure with definitely circumscribed objectives encompassing the data of some particular problem area.

MODEL. A conceptual analogue, generally brought in from some other field, whose function is to direct empirical research; differing from other types of theory in that its modification or improvement is not involved. (In psychology, models are most often of a physical or mathematical nature.)

NOMOTHETIC. Law-making in a generalized sense; contrasted with idiographic.

OBSERVATION. Noting and recording of events in scientific investigations.

OPERATIONISM. A movement in science which insists that adequate definitions of terms are those in which meanings are synonymous with the operations involved in measuring and that therefore, if a term has more than one set of identifying measurements, or empirical referents, it has more than one meaning.

PARSIMONY. The general principle that in science it is safer, in the long run, to accept the simpler of alternative explanatory propositions of a particular phenomenon.

POSITIVISM. A metatheoretical and scientific position that emphasizes parsimony and operationism in data language and eschews speculative theorizing.

POSTULATE. 1) A proposition concerning the relationship of variables that is indirectly tested by means of its theorems (implications); hence, a formalized type of hypothesis, usually occurring in a deductive theory. 2) A working assumption.

REDUCTIONISM. The general attempt to explain and interpret phenomena by means of analysis into simpler components and principles at a different level of analysis.

REDUCTIVE EXPLANATION. Interpretation of data in terms of other phenomena, or propositions incorporating such phenomena, which are at a different level of analysis; usually the relationship is a hierarchical one, as, for example, when behavior phenomena are interpreted in terms of biological ones, these in turn in terms of biochemical ones, etc.

SCIENCE. The enterprise by which a particular kind of ordered knowledge is obtained about natural phenomena by means of controlled observations and theoretical interpretations.

SYSTEM. An organization and interpretation of the data and theories of a subject matter with emphasis upon a particular methodology (metatheory) and working assumptions (postulates).

THEOREM. A specific implication of a more general explanatory proposition, a postulate, by means of deductive logic.

THEORY. 1) In a general sense, any more or less formalized conceptualization of the relationship of variables. 2) Any generalized explanatory principle. (See also *Theory, types of*, for kinds of theory resulting from different metatheoretical procedures.)

THEORY CONSTRUCTION. The process of producing abstract and generalized conceptualizations by various metatheoretical rules. (See *Theory, types of*, for major products of varying procedures.)

THEORY, TYPES OF. As here distinguished: 1) *Model* (q.v.). 2) *Deductive theory*, a logically organized (deductively related) cluster of laws. 3) *Functional theory*, more or less informal explanatory propositions which are closely related to data (empirical propositions) and without fixed logical form. 4) *Inductive theory*, descriptive statements summarizing clusters of empirical propositions with minimal inferential commitment.

VARIABLE. A class of objects or events, or properties thereof; a factor or condition that is conceptualized for scientific purposes. (See *Controlled variable, Dependent variable, Independent variable, Intervening variable*.)

Suggestions for Further Readings

The following annotated readings list contains selected books from which the student may obtain a more detailed and intensive account of various facets of theory and theory construction, both within and outside of psychology. Some of these are provocative and useful metatheoretical treatments with features which have not been incorporated into the present discussion.

In addition to the works specifically cited are a number of authoritative volumes, mainly collections of readings, in the philosophy of science [e.g., Feigl and Sellars' *Readings in Philosophical Analysis* (1949), Feigl and Brodbeck's *Readings in the Philosophy of Science* (1953), and Danto and Morgenbesser's *Philosophy of Science: A Reader* (1960)]. Of the strictly psychological journals, the *Psychological Review* is the major one primarily concerned with theory. The journal *Philosophy of Science* should also be mentioned in this connection, although most of its papers are at a level of philosophical and logical sophistication that may frighten the mere psychologist without special training in those fields. The series, *Minnesota Studies in the Philosophy of Science* (Vol. I, 1956; Vol. II, 1958; Vol. III, 1962), contains much of current interest in this area. Finally, the *Annual Review of Psychology* series contains from time to time, special articles on various aspects of theory, and many of its substantive reviews of special fields include a high proportion of theoretical emphasis.

Benjamin, A. C. *Operationism*. Springfield, Ill.: Thomas, 1955. This slim volume provides a good historical orientation to the general problem of operationism, including consideration of the applicability of the principle to psychology and sociology.

Bergmann, G. *Philosophy of Science*. Madison, Wisc.: Univ. of Wisconsin Press, 1957. Problems of theory construction—in particular, the deductive elements—are well presented in this book by an author thoroughly versed in the metatheory of physical science as well as psychology.

Braithwaite, R. B. *Scientific Explanations*. Cambridge, England: Cambridge Univ. Press, 1955. An intensive account of scientific explanation is presented from a logic-of-science point of view.

Estes, W. K., Koch, S., MacCorquodale, K., Meehl, P. E., Mueller, C. G., Jr., Schoenfeld, W. N., and Verplanck, W. S. *Modern Learning Theory*. New York: Appleton-Century-Crofts, 1954. A most detailed treatment of five of the classical learning theories (Hull, Skinner, Guthrie, Tolman, and Lewin). Although these critics judge primarily in terms of rather unrealistic—for the time—metatheoretical standards, the papers are nonetheless extremely valuable. Koch's long critique of Hull contains much of general interest in theory criticism.

Koch, S. (ed.) *Psychology: A Study of a Science*. Vol. I, Sensory, Perceptual, and Physiological Formulations; Vol. II, General Systematic Formulations, Learning, and Special Processes; Vol. III, Formulations of the Person and the Social Context. New York: McGraw-Hill, 1959. These volumes represent by far the most ambitious effort yet made to reveal the full scope of contemporary psychology. The papers vary enormously in style and scope and seldom contain very much which has not already appeared elsewhere in print, but they do provide an illuminating picture of the present status of theory and of metatheory in psychology. Although not all authors followed the editor's suggested outline, enough attempted to do so to provide a good amount of grist for the metatheoretical mill. B. F. Skinner in particular resisted the editorial suggestions and wrote instead his "Case History." Here the leader of the American positivistic movement in psychology recounts certain salient details of his own experimental background and reveals, in an absorbing account, some of the reasons for his methodological biases. Koch's introduction (Vol. I) and his Epilogue for Study I (Vol. III) are also especially interesting as generalized treatments; so, presumably, will be his final capstone to the study (projected as Vol. VII) when it appears.

Mandler, G., and Kessen, W. *The Language of Psychology*. New York: Wiley, 1959. This book offers a comprehensive account of metatheoretical problems and procedures, more or less from a classical point of view, as these apply to psychology.

Popper, K. *Logic of Scientific Discovery*. New York: Basic Books, 1959. The title is self-explanatory in the case of this work, which attacks a critical problem of scientific work.

Pratt, C. C. *The Logic of Modern Psychology*. New York: Macmillan, 1948. This classic work, although somewhat dated, remains an interesting introduction to the topic.

Sidman, M. *Tactics of Scientific Research*. New York: Basic Books, 1960. This provocative book is an excellent exposition and defense of the positivistic position and indicates its close ties to careful experimental research.

References

American Psychological Association. Education for research in psychology. *Amer. Psychol.*, 1959, *14*, 167–179.

Barker, R. G., Dembo, Tamara, and Lewin, K. Frustration and regression. In Barker, R. G., Kounin, J. S., and Wright, H. F. (eds.), *Child behavior and development*. New York: McGraw-Hill, 1943.

Benjamin, A. C. *Operationism*. Springfield, Ill.: Thomas, 1955.

Bergmann, G. The logic of psychological concepts. *Phil. Sci.*, 1951, *18*, 93–110.

Bergmann, G. *Philosophy of science*. Madison, Wis.: Univ. of Wisconsin Press, 1957.

Boring, E. G. Human nature vs. sensation: William James and the psychology of the present. *Amer. J. Psychol.*, 1942, *55*, 310–327.

———. The role of theory in experimental psychology. *Amer. J. Psychol.*, 1953, *66*, 169–184.

———. The nature and history of experimental control. *Amer. J. Psychol.*, 1954, *67*, 573–589.

———. When is human behavior predetermined? *Scientific Monthly*, 1957, *84*, 189–196.

Bridgman, P. W. *The logic of modern physics*. New York: Macmillan, 1927.

Conant, J. B. *On understanding science*. New Haven: Yale Univ. Press, 1947.

Cotton, J. W. On making predictions from Hull's theory. *Psychol. Rev.*, 1955, *62*, 303–314.

English, H. B., and English, Ava C. *A comprehensive dictionary of psychological and psychoanalytic terms*. New York: Longmans, Green, 1958.

Estes, W. K. Of models and men. *Amer. Psychol.*, 1957, *12*, 609–617.

Estes, W. K. The statistical approach to learning theory. In S. Koch (ed), *Psychology: a study of a science*. New York: McGraw-Hill, 1959.

Falk, J. L., Issues distinguishing idiographic from nomothetic approaches to personality theory. *Psychol. Rev.*, 1956, *63*, 53–62.

Ferster, C. B., and Skinner, B. F. *Schedules of reinforcement*. New York: Appleton-Century-Crofts, 1957.

Festinger, L. *A theory of cognitive dissonance*. Evanston, Ill.: Row, Peterson, 1957.

Frank, P. Contemporary science and the contemporary world view. In G. Holton (ed.), *Science and the modern mind: a symposium*. Boston: Beacon Press, 1958.

Guthrie, E. R. The status of systematic psychology. *Amer. Psychol.*, 1950, *5*, 97–101.

Harlow, H. F. Learning set and error factor theory. In S. Koch (ed.), *Psychology: a study of a science*, Vol. 2. New York: McGraw-Hill, 1959.

Henle, Mary. Some problems of eclecticism. *Psychol. Rev.*, 1957, *64*, 296–305.

Hilgard, E. R. *Theories of learning* (rev.). New York: Appleton-Century-Crofts, 1956.

Hull, C. L. *Principles of behavior*. New York: Appleton-Century, 1943.

Hunt, W. A. Clinical psychology—science or superstition. *Amer. Psychol.*, 1951, *6*, 683–687.

Israel, H. E., and Goldstein, B. Operationism in psychology. *Psychol. Rev.*, 1944, *51*, 177–188.

Johnson, H. M. On verifying hypotheses by verifying their implicates. *Amer. J. Psychol.*, 1954, *67*, 723–727.

Koch, S., and Hull, C. L. In W. K. Estes et al.,' *Modern learning theory*. New York: Appleton-Century-Crofts, 1954.

MacCorquodale, K., and Meehl, P. E. On a distinction between hypothetical constructs and intervening variables. *Psychol. Rev.*, 1948, *55*, 95–107. Reprinted in part in M. H. Marx (ed.), *Psychological theory: contemporary readings*. New York: Macmillan, 1951.

McGuigan, F. J. Confirmation of theories in psychology. *Psychol. Rev.*, 1956, *63*, 98–104.

Marx, M. H., and Hillix, W. A. *Systems and theories in psychology*. New York: McGraw-Hill, 1963.

Meissner, W. W. Intervening constructs—dimensions of controversy. *Psychol. Rev.*, 1960, *67*, 51–72.

Miller, G. A., Galanter, E., and Pribram, K. H. *Plans and the structure of behavior*. New York: Holt, 1960.

Miller, J. G. Symbolic technique in psychological theory. *Psychol. Rev.*, 1939, *46*, 464–479.

Pratt, C. C. *The logic of modern psychology*. New York: Macmillan, 1939.

Reichenbach, H. *Experience and prediction*. Chicago: Univ. of Chicago Press, 1938.

Seward, J. P. Hull's system of behavior: an evaluation. *Psychol. Rev.*, 1954, *61*, 145–159.

Sidman, M. *Tactics of scientific research: evaluating experimental data in psychology*. New York: Basic Books, 1960.

Skinner, B. F. *The behavior of organisms: an experimental analysis*. New York: Appleton-Century, 1938.

——. Are theories of learning necessary? *Psychol. Rev.*, 1950, *57*, 193–216.

——. A case history in scientific method. *Amer. Psychol.*, 1956, *11*, 221–233.

Solomon, R. L., and Brush, Elinor S. Experimentally derived conceptions of anxiety and aversion. In M. R. Jones (ed.), *Nebraska symposium on motivation, 1956*. Lincoln, Nebr.: Univ. of Nebraska Press, 1956.

Spence, K. W. A theory of emotionally based drive (D) and its relation to performance in simple learning situations. *Amer. Psychol.*, 1958, *13*, 131–141.

Taylor, Janet A. A personality scale of manifest anxiety. *J. Abnorm. Soc. Psychol.*, 1953, *48*, 285–290.

Tolman, E. C. Operational behaviorism and current trends in psychology. In *Proc. 25th Anniv. Celebr. Inaug. Grad. Stud.* Los Angeles: Univ. of South. Calif. Press, 1936. Reprinted in M. H. Marx (ed.), *Psychological theory*. New York: Macmillan, 1951.

Thouless, R. H. Some problems of terminology in psychological theory. *Brit. J. Psychol.*, 1949, *40*, Part I, 41–46.

Turner, W. S. A re-examination of the two kinds of scientific conjecture. *Psychol. Rev.*, 1961, *11*, 279–298.

Valentine, W. L., and Wickens, D. D. *Experimental foundations of general psychology* (3rd ed.). New York: Rinehart, 1949.

2 | *Operationism and Logical Positivism*

S. S. STEVENS

The scientist has always been proud of his hard head and his tough mind. When William James (1914) sat in judgment and divided the universe of temperaments into the tough- and tender-minded, the scientist knew where he belonged. He was happy to run with the goats, for he was an empiricist and he loved facts in all their crude variety. He was skeptical and cautious of word, and to "isms" of all kinds he was peculiarly unresponsive. The tender-minded were the rationalists. They had faith in intuition and were awed by the power of the mind. It was their opinion that by taking thought they could discover absolute principles of truth answering to the criteria of coherence and consistency and that, armed with these principles, they could legislate the bounds of science. They were the sheep whose wool shone white under the light of reason. They were most numerous in departments of philosophy.

Undoubtedly these two types are still with us, but it is the purpose of this review neither to shear the sheep nor tame the goats. Instead, its purpose is simply to invite attention to some recent developments in what we might call the Philosophy of Science.

The tough-minded scientist has always known that he could screen his integrity against the seductive pipings of the rationalist by ignoring philosophy. The tender-minded philosopher, gifted with his superior dialectic, has usually despaired at the stubborn naïveté of the scientist and has determined to leave the unrefined fellow to grovel alone, while he, the philosopher, calmly demonstrated the impossibility of proving anything by induction. Suddenly, however, we find, on the one hand, a coterie of philosophers plying us with what, if it is not science, is certainly not the brand of stuff we have ordinarily pigeonholed as philosophy; and, on the other hand, we are beset by a host of scientists of all disciplines campaign-

From S. S. Stevens, Psychology and the science of science, *Psychol. Bull.*, 1939, *36*, 221–263. Reprinted by permission of the author, the *Psychological Bulletin*, and the American Psychological Association.

ing for what, if it is not philosophy, is surely not the science we are used to.

The philosopher, Benjamin (1937ª), says of these scientists:

They begin with science, they talk about science, and they end with science, yet they do not conform at all to the tradition of scientific writing. . . . Their repeated reference to philosophical issues tempts one to classify them with this group, yet the writings approach these problems in a new spirit and with a new method, which seem quite foreign to traditional philosophy.

And concerning the widespread groups of philosophers participating in this movement, Reichenbach (1938) observes:

Though there is no philosophic system which unites these groups, there is a common property of ideas, principles, criticisms, and working methods. . . . It is the intention of uniting both the empiricist conception of modern science and the formalistic conception of logic . . . which marks the working program of this philosophic movement.

So numerous and insistent are the words of those who have been seized by the spirit of this movement that they swell the pages of several new journals—journals whose subject matter defies simple classification.[1] There are articles by philosophers, mathematicians, and scientists. But it is more than a mere scrambling of the sheep and the goats. A common spirit animates most of these writings. The common theme, despite its fundamental simplicity, despite differences of interpretation by newborn enthusiasts, and despite the disparagement of misunderstanding, is probably to be esteemed as a truly great advance in the Philosophy of Science, or the Science of Philosophy.

Numerous phrasings of this central theme have been cast by authors interested in various aspects of it, but they all assert essentially that *science seeks to generate confirmable propositions by fitting a formal system of symbols (language, mathematics, logic) to empirical observations, and that the propositions of science have empirical significance only when their truth can be demonstrated by a set of concrete operations.* There are thus two separate realms of discourse: the *formal* (or rational) and the *empirical*. It is the business of the philosopher to labor with the formal and discover and perfect the rules of the scientific language, and it is the business of the scientist to apply the formal symbolic model to the observable world in such a way that the concepts he generates will satisfy the rules of operational criticism.

---

[1] Some representative journals are: *Erkenntnis*, begun in 1930; *Philosophy of Science*, begun in 1934; and *International Encyclopedia of Unified Science*, begun in 1938. The advisory boards of these last two publications read like a who's who in science and philosophy. It would be a passionate optimist, however, who would expect such a band of hardy individualists to be entirely of one mind. Many of them have not yet spoken.

Elementary as these notions may appear, the development of their implications has commanded the interest of both tough- and tender-minded. The movement has proved disastrous for metaphysics, challenging for logic, and salutary for science. Philosophers and scientists in essential agreement are astonishing enough, but here we have them pleading for a common method. In this strange harmony we are witnessing the birth of a new discipline: the Science of Science. It is a triumph for self-consciousness. The science-makers are asking themselves how they make science and are turning on that problem the powerful empirical weapons of science itself; while at the same time a tough-minded outcropping among the philosophers is carefully combing the metaphysics out of logic in order to investigate more easily the common linguistic structure of science. In this quest the philosophers, like the scientists, resort to empirical methods. Witness the spirit of philosophy as exemplified by Nagel (1938):

It is difficult for me to take seriously the various attempts made historically by philosophers to legislate to the sciences just what they can and cannot investigate . . . on the basis of a deductive theory of mind and nature. . . . Furthermore, it seems to me an integral character of skilled workmanship to insist upon the fact that no statement or proposal has any meaning apart from the methods which are or may be employed to establish or execute them.

In succeeding pages we shall see how operationism, beginning at one end in the laboratories of scientists, evolved an enterprise co-ordinate with that of Logical Positivism, Physicalism, and Scientific Empiricism which, beginning at the other end in the armchairs of philosophers, settled on the problem of the proper scientific use of logic. And we shall see how the natural issue of this mating came to make up the unifying principles of the Science of Science. We shall see how this movement concords with "behavioristics," which is a behavioristic psychology tuned up to keep pace with a fast-moving logical criticism. And finally, we shall see what the impact of this movement means for some specific problems in psychology, and what is indicated as the future rôle of psychology in this scheme.

Operationism

Ten years ago Professor Bridgman, the expert on high-pressure phenomena, wrote a book[2] called *The Logic of Modern Physics* (1928). It has been judged an excellent book, animated by the single idea that "in general, we mean by any concept nothing more than a set of operations; *the concept is synonymous with the corresponding set of operations.*" This dictum stands forth in what many have found to be objectionable naked-

---

[2] For additional comments on some of the books and papers cited in this review, see the "Bibliography." [In the original publication.—Ed.]

ness, but, throughout more than 200 well-stocked pages, Bridgman demonstrates what he means by analyzing the operational meaning of the basic concepts of physics. There is nothing rationally a priori in his method (at least he honestly *tries* to exclude metaphysics). His introductory confession is: "The material of this essay is largely obtained by observation of the actual currents of opinion in physics." In this empirical spirit he observes the behavior of his colleagues and finds that what is considered an *explanation* "consists in reducing a situation to elements with which we are so familiar that we accept them as a matter of course, so that our curiosity rests." The reduction of the "situation" is made in terms of operations, but do we thereby arrive at exact and certain knowledge? No. "We never have perfectly clean-cut knowledge of anything, but all our experience is surrounded by a twilight zone, a penumbra of uncertainty, into which we have not yet penetrated," and consequently "no empirical science can ever make exact statements." The degree to which any of the laws of science wear the penumbrous halo can be told only by inspecting the operations which the laws are intended to generalize.

Bridgman's book is rich in example but poor in precept. That its author has occasionally been misunderstood has perhaps been due largely to this fact. The book gives numerous examples of operational method without prescribing explicitly what operational method is; it talks of "operations" without giving an explicit definition of the term; and it discourses on natural laws without pointing out how we get from particular operations to generalizations. In short, it is a thoroughly inductive enterprise, and the reader is often allowed to make the induction by himself. Nevertheless, the spirit of the book is unmistakable and its message is simple and powerful.

Philosophers rose to protest, or sometimes to defend, the notion of "operational meaning" because it assures the automatic elimination of even the choicest propositions of metaphysics: "If a specific question has meaning," says Bridgman, "it must be possible to find operations by which an answer may be given to it." No operations, no meaning! And so, as we have said, philosophers, and others, rose to protest. Finally, the pressure pushed Bridgman temporarily from his Harvard laboratory and on to the lecture platform at Princeton where he spoke what became another book: *The Nature of Physical Theory* (1936).

To say that this second book pleased all who were disciples of the first book is perhaps not quite true. The author had been able to say in his first book that fortunately he would "be able to get along with a more or less naïve attitude toward" psychology and epistemology, but in his second work he boldly lays hold on thought, language, and experience. Bridgman's discussion of these concepts was what the world had been waiting for, but once out of the well-charted sea of physics and adrift in epistemology, the author's bark, if we are to believe the critics, appears to have lost its rudder. One cannot avoid the impression that criticism of this second book has been of unmerited severity, but perhaps severe criticism is what must be expected by a man who challenges us with issues as vital as those proposed by Professor Bridgman. Objection has been made to such statements as: "In the last analysis science is only my private science." "What," asks editor Malisoff (1936), "can an operationist mean by a 'last analysis'?" Bridgman says his purpose in sailing the epistemological waters is "to map out the possibilities and limitations of the human mind in dealing with the problems presented to it." "Our complaint," criticizes A. F. Bentley (1938), "is not that he makes this inquiry, but that in it he employs all the bad devices he had ejected from physics." Some of his devices are assertions crutched on such terms as "essentially," "absolutely," and "intuitively." Nevertheless, Bridgman's critics agree that his discernment in physics remains as fine as ever—he is still simple and hardheaded. In physics he is an operationist, and it is in physics that we should judge him, if we are to presume to do so.

Just as Bridgman had set out to apply and make explicit the principles by which Einstein shattered the physicist's notion of the absolute, so did others seize upon the opportunity to try out these principles in other fields. Psychologists, long self-conscious of their own self-consciousness, were particularly alert to this budding self-inspection on the part of the modern masters of physics. If the physicists could examine the methods of their science-making and evolve helpful principles, perhaps psychologists could do likewise. Such, at least, was the attitude of those who were happy to confess blindness to any fundamental dichotomy between the methods of psychology and physics.

Operationism in Psychology

But psychology is more difficult than physics—at least psychologists often find it easier to get themselves into a mess in their field than physicists do in theirs. Of course, when the physicist strays into psychology, the result is apt to restore the psychologist's ego-level, but if the physicist fumbles it only serves to show that when doing open-field running among psychological concepts the critic must hold the ball more tightly. In view of the difficulty of keeping a grip on the operational principle, it is not surprising to find evidence of dissension among the psychological apologists [Professor Bills (1938) calls them "apostles"]. In spite of much scattered writing, the case for operationism in psychology has perhaps never been adequately briefed, but a few of its consequences have been made explicit, and some interesting applications have appeared.

We all remember Tolman's *Purposive Behavior in Animals and Men*

(1932). Whatever dismay we may have felt at the superabundance of his glossary, the fact remains that in coining the words of his new language he appealed most directly and explicitly to experimental operations. The book is a monument in the methodology of definition. In much the same spirit, Professor Tolman has more recently prepared for us "an operational analysis of 'demands' " (1936[a]). In his own field of expertness we find McGeoch making a critical inquiry into the possibility of "learning as an operationally defined concept" (1935). Boring treats of "temporal perception and operationism" (1936) in a short, poignant demonstration of how a classical problem turns out to be specious when its defining operations are made explicit. Seashore and Katz propose to bring order to the chaotic discipline of abnormal psychology by "an operational definition and classification of mental mechanisms" (1937). Lundberg, the sociologist, would do the same for the social sciences by replacing spineless intuitionism by "quantitative methods in social psychology" (1936), the foundation for which would be concepts operationally defined. And finally, Kantor examines "the operational principle in the physical and psychological sciences" (1938) and concludes that the principle, properly enlarged, can be employed to the psychologists' advantage. Now, these are not all of those who have taken notice of Bridgman's proposals. Nor do all these commentators see eye to eye with Bridgman or with each other regarding certain fundamentals. Furthermore, it is becoming alarmingly obvious that the phrases "operationally defined" and "operationally sound" are acquiring the sort of positive valence which leads to their being bandied about in indiscriminate fashion by writers who suppose that they can meet the operational test by announcing good intentions. Operationism is being threatened by its friends—largely, perhaps, because of the inherent difficulty of making a rigorous formulation of it.

What, then, are we to understand by operationism? All that any one man can do is to present his own version, and this I did in a series of articles in 1935 and 1936 (1935[a], 1935[b], 1936). There are some points there which invite revision, but, in general, the sins appear to be those of omission. The statement there needs expansion, but obviously this review is not the place for it. A résumé is more in order.

First, however, it must be emphasized again that the development of operational principles is properly an empirical undertaking. What do the science-makers do? What methodology has the maximum survival value? When do propositions have empirical validity? In short, operational principles are induced generalizations rather than a priori fiats. They are therefore subject to the usual hazards and uncertainty of inductive propositions. This empirical aspect of operational criticism has never been sufficiently stressed, and it is not surprising that operationists have sometimes been regarded as self-appointed legislators who try to prescribe rather than discover.

These, then, are some of the generalizations which I propose as verifiable:

1. Science, as we find it, is a set of empirical propositions agreed upon by members of society. This agreement may be always in a state of flux, but persistent disagreement leads eventually to rejection. Bridgman does not agree to this social criterion of knowledge and it was against this notion that he aimed a part of his Princeton lectures (1936). We must ask him, however, to produce the negative case. A physical law to which only Bridgman agreed would not be a part of physics—not, at least, until he won converts, and then there would be agreement.

2. Only those propositions based upon operations which are public and repeatable are admitted to the body of science. Not even psychology knows anything about private experience, because an operation for penetrating privacy is self-contradictory.

3. What becomes acceptable psychology accrues only when all observations, including those which a psychologist makes upon himself, are treated as though made upon "the other one." Thus, we make explicit the distinction between the experimenter and the thing observed. This distinction is obvious in physics; in psychology it is equally valid.

4. Although a particular experimenter may himself become the object of study by another experimenter, and he in turn by still another, at some stage of such a regress an independent experimenter *must be* (i.e., is always) assumed. The recognition of this "experimenter-regress" unravels many knots in psychology.

5. A term denotes something only when there are concrete criteria for its applicability; and a proposition has empirical meaning only when the criteria of its truth or falsity consists of concrete operations which can be performed upon demand.

6. When we attempt to reduce complex operations to simpler and simpler ones, we find in the end that discrimination, or differential response, is the fundamental operation. Discrimination is prerequisite even to the operation of denoting or "pointing to," because whenever two people reduce their complex operations for the purpose of reaching agreement or understanding, they find that unless they can each discriminate the same simple objects or read the same scales they still will not agree. Agreement is usually reached in practice before these most elementary operations are appealed to.

7. There are two types of propositions: *formal* and *empirical*. The formal propositions are arrays of symbols without empirical reference. They are language, mathematics, and logic *as such*. Empirical propositions are those in which these arrays of symbols have been identified with

observable events. Sometimes the two types of propositions intermingle and trouble results. For avoiding the obscurity of pseudo problems this distinction between the formal, syntactical model (symbols) and the operations for which it is made to stand is of prime importance. Hypotheses, for example, can be only formal statements—operationally empty—until they are demonstrated (see Appendix II*). Within the formal realm we speak sometimes of mathematical operations, but here we mean the manipulation of symbols carried out according to certain conventional rules. These are not the operations of operationism.

Although we shall have more to say later about the contrast between the formal and the empirical, at this point we might do well to see how history occasionally sets them off from one another and thereby emphasizes their distinctive natures. Historically, the algebra of complex numbers (numbers of the form $x + iy$, where x and y are real numbers and i is the square root of -1) was developed from the purest of purely mathematical motives. The rules for the manipulation of these numbers (their addition, multiplication, division, etc.) were worked out in conformity with the conventional laws of ordinary algebra and interesting relations were discovered. Gauss, for example, set a landmark in algebra by proving that every algebraic equation in one unknown has a root and that all roots of such equations are complex numbers (see Bell, 1937, p. 232). In Gauss's time these numbers were simply abstract symbols which could be combined according to the rules of the game we call algebra. They proved nothing about the empirical world or about science: they constituted, as they still do, a purely *formal* system. Then, with the advent of alternating electric currents, came also the need for a simple, effective "model" to represent electric circuits; and the electrical engineers discovered that if they let x stand for resistance, iy or inductive reactance, and $-iy$ for capacitative reactance, they could manipulate these symbols according to the rules of complex algebra and obtain new combinations of the symbols which they could then identify with some measurable aspect of an electric circuit. In other words, this formal system was found useful as a model, and out of its utility has grown the modern intricate theory of alternating currents. Therefore, when we can identify these complex numbers with various aspects of a circuit, we can say that the propositions containing these symbols are *empirical* propositions, testable by concrete operations.

These seven bald assertions about operationism are perhaps too brief to be convincing, but they may recommend the fuller development in the three papers already referred to. In the meantime we might profit

---

* In the original publication.—Ed.

by considering what operationism is not—still, of course, in only one man's opinion. Misunderstandings have been numerous and many of them could have been headed off had someone signaled what is non-operational. Let us, then, look at a few of operationism's contrasts.

What Operationism Is Not

1. It is obviously not a new school of psychology. Rosenzweig (1937) presented an admirable argument to show that the schools of psychology are really more complementary than antagonistic, but he was worried about operationism. He should stop worrying.

2. It is not a set of rules telling how to be a bright and original scientist. It does not even tell how experiments should be carried out. It has no precepts. At the risk of breeding disappointment we must say of operationism, as James (1914) said of pragmatism, that, "at the outset, at least, it stands for no particular results. It has no dogmas, and no doctrines save its method." Furthermore, its method is one which is applied *after* the scientific proposition has been made: it provides criteria for determining whether what *has been* said is empirically meaningful. In short, it tests inventions, but does not tell how to invent.

3. It is not opposed to hypotheses, theories, or speculation. It seeks merely to discover criteria by which these things may be detected and labeled. It is not opposed to poetry, art, or religion. It wants only to know the difference between these things and science. It wants to know under what conditions the consorting of science with metaphysics breeds pseudo problems. Scientists as people may be opposed to pseudo problems, but operationism's business, as a principle of criticism, is to discover them.

4. It is not a guarantee of agreement as to tastes or theories, but it points out how agreement as to facts is achieved by men capable of making the same fundamental discriminations. Operationism wants, most of all, to discover the bases of such agreement. What are the procedures which compel agreement among those engaged in open-minded pursuit of science? As to compelling agreement on tastes—that is probably a job in applied eugenics.

5. It is not positivism. The blemish on positivism was that in its reaction against rational metaphysics it pretended to base *everything* in science on experience. Operationism, however, acknowledges the rôle of the rational methods of mathematics and logic—formal disciplines which do not appeal to experience for verification, but only to conventions. Science uses these formal systems as models for representing its data. To deny them is to cure the disease by burying the patient.

When it is a matter of the significance of *empirical* rather than of *formal* propositions, needless to say, operationism adopts an uncompromising positivistic attitude.

6. It is not behaviorism. Like positivism, behaviorism erred in denying too much. Operationism does not deny images, for example, but asks: What is the operational definition of the term "image"? Of course there are different behaviorisms, and some of the renovated brands are truly operational. Tolman (1936[b]) has a variety which he dubs explicitly "operational behaviorism"—and perhaps it is. It is certain that the behavioristic emphasis has served capably in blasting a path through subjectivity, and without this path an objective Science of Science could not march.

7. It is not monism. It asks only whether any operational meaning can be given the proposition that there is but one irreducible substance or attribute. Can the truth or falsity of this proposition be put to experimental test? If not, we face a pseudo problem.

8. It is not dualism. Here again the problems raised are pseudo problems, because the propositions are not testable. As Bills (1938) so aptly says, "Parallelism would automatically reduce to a double-aspect formula, because where two sets of defining operations coincide perfectly they become identical operationally." Of course there can be no quarrel, except on the grounds of utility, with any arbitrary dividing or classifying of facts, but pseudo problems can be avoided only provided we remember that these classes are arbitrary.

The division of concepts into the categories of subjective and objective is justifiable—if at all—only on pragmatic grounds, and only *provided* both types of concept answer the operational test. Bills believes that "mentalistic" concepts like percept, image, and idea can be operationally defined. So do I. Kantor, however, is disturbed. He detects dualism. But Bills "cannot agree with Kantor that there is any necessary dualism implied in Stevens' position." Neither can Stevens. If we admit to our store of empirical science only those concepts which are operationally founded, can we not classify them according to our purposes?

Kantor (1938) would appear to supplant dualism with a kind of realism. Now, realism is a metaphysical doctrine, and perhaps Kantor did not intend a realism. Nevertheless, he appears to defend the proposition: Nature is not the same as our knowledge of nature. Operationism must here again pose its perhaps tiresome, but necessary, question: Can any operations be formulated which will either prove or disprove this proposition? If not, it is operationally meaningless, however much "emotional meaning" it may pack.

9. Finally, operationism is not pluralism. It should be apparent by now that operationism is not consonant with any "ism" which asserts something about the ultimate nature of reality.

The Problem of Generality

There is one more criticism we must take seriously before we continue. It has been urged that operationism reduces to a vicious particularism; that there is no provision for generalization; that instead of unification in science a strict servility to the operational principle nourishes an ever-expanding multiplicity of concepts. Here is what the critics say:

Margenau, in "Causality in Modern Physics" (1931), which he addressed to the philosophers, states that operationism "cannot be tolerated as a general directive. For, in the first place, it would, if carried to its consequences, dissolve the world into an unmanageable variety of discrete concepts without logical coherence."

Lindsay, in "A Critique of Operationalism in Physics" (1937), says: ". . . logically the operational method . . . implies that each concept is tied to a definite operation."

Lindsay and Margenau together, in their book, *Foundations of Physics* (1936)—a book which has brought them merited high praise—state: "On the basis of purely operational definitions, all concepts are strictly empirical and isolated" (p. 412).

Bills, in his excellent address on "Changing Views of Psychology as Science" (1938), says: "One of the ideals of scientific concept-makers is to reduce all concepts to a few fundamental ones. . . . Yet this is not, by any means, the likely outcome of operationally defined concepts. . . . For there is no universal set of operations."

Waters and Pennington, in their careful criticism of "Operationism in Psychology" (1938), assert: "The fact that the concept, for Bridgman, is *synonymous* with a corresponding set of operations cannot be over-emphasized. The slightest change in any aspect of a set of operations would mean, therefore, a new concept and would demand, likewise, a new symbol for its designation. A multiplicity of concepts could scarcely be avoided."

Since Bentley (the critic, not the psychologist), in his flashy tirade on "Physicists and Fairies" (1938), has a point to make here, we will let him speak first. He refers to Lindsay and Margenau when he says: "By distorting Bridgman grossly enough, either man can, of course, readily destroy what he has distorted. Both men distort alike; first by insisting 'operations' must be all hands and no mind; second by alleging that no operation in this world can have anything to do with any other operation, not even with its own repetitions of itself."

Whether there is distortion or not, the fact that so many have pounced on this supposed snare in operationism means that the rules and procedure for generalizing from operations must sometime be made explicit. These rules obviously can be stated, because science does generalize, and operationism seeks only to discover how scientists do what they do.

The process of generalization proceeds on the basis of the notion of classes. All objects or events satisfying certain criteria we call members of a class and to that class we assign a name or symbol. Common nouns originate in precisely this fashion, and it is apparent at once that no empirical proposition is ever without some element of generality. Classification can proceed only when we have criteria defining the conditions for class-inclusion, and these criteria are essentially operational tests. Thus the statement, "Dobbin is a horse," asserts that Dobbin is a member of a class. This proposition is empirically meaningful only provided its truth or falsity can be demonstrated by concrete procedures. Does Dobbin satisfy the criteria of the class, *horse?* If he is a certain size and shape, is covered with hair, feeds on oats and hay, etc., we are happy to acknowledge him as a full-fledged horse. But how do we know he meets our tests? Here we resort to that fundamental operation we have already called discrimination. If we can discriminate crucial differences between Dobbin and other animals we have named horses, we reject Dobbin as something not horse. In other words, we "correlate" our discriminations—those made on Dobbin with those made on other objects—and the "goodness" of the correlation determines where we shall classify the beast.

It may be objected that we can always tell Dobbin from other horses, i.e., discriminate differences, but we still would resent the suggestion that he is not a horse. The answer is that a certain latitude is always allowed—we seldom resort to j.n.d.'s in a case like this—and the amount of the latitude determines the precision of the concept. As Bridgman has insisted, no concept is without its halo of uncertainty, its penumbra. No empirical class is ever watertight; we can always plague the taxonomist with the borderline case.

On the basis of elementary discriminations, then, we make our first rudimentary classes and in doing so we have made the first step toward generalization. From there we advance to form classes of classes[3] and to discover the relations between classes—always, at the empirical level, in keeping with operational criteria. Occasionally we find that from a certain point of view two classes satisfy the same criteria, or are related by a simple law, so that we are enabled to combine them into a more inclusive class under a more generic tag. Nevertheless, in all of these classifications and combinations the same simple rule is followed: We combine

---

[3] This *empirical process* of forming classes of classes should not be confused with the *logic* of classes, in which the provision for an infinite hierarchy of classes led to the antinomies discovered by Russell. The empirical process has no *necessary* relation to a formal system of logic.

operations when they satisfy the criteria of a class; and the concept of that class is defined by the operations which determine inclusion within the class.

The matter can be illustrated by referring again to that example which appears to have been the jumping-off place for the critics: the concept of length. Bridgman's argument is that we measure the length of the table and the distance to a star by two different sets of operations and we have, therefore, two different concepts of length. True enough. And Bridgman proceeds thence to show that when dealing with very large distances or very minute ones, or with distances where velocities are involved, we do well to keep in mind the differences in our defining operations. However, in his concern for the perils of promiscuous class-matings he forgot to tell us when combining is legitimate. Length measured with a rod is different from length measured with a transit, but under certain statable conditions we can muster operations to determine the relation of these two sets of measurements, and, if they meet the proper criteria, we combine them to form a larger class defining length. Of course, if we had no operations for comparing the two lengths, we should have to veto their combination. In short, then, we can and do generalize the concept length, but we do it with operational sanction.

The Philosophical Movement

Just ten years ago, the year Bridgman published his *Logic of Modern Physics*, there appeared in Vienna a company of scholars bound together by mutual admiration and a common *Weltauffassung*—a scientific philosophy. Their discussions under the leadership of Professor Schlick accomplished a unitary enthusiasm which came to concrete form in the organization of *Der Wiener Kreis*.[4] The avowed intention of this "Circle" was to

---

[4] Some of the members of the Vienna Circle follow:

Moritz Schlick (1882–1936) fathered the group. Under his professorial paternalism the Circle met, discussed, and found its unity. (Schlick's unfortunate death, at the hand of a crazed student, occurred as he was climbing the steps of the lecture hall.)

Otto Neurath (b. 1882) contributed his own brand of enthusiastic originality. His spirited support of radical new theses provided important inspiration. Neurath coined the designations "Physicalism" and "Unity of Science."

Rudolph Carnap (b. 1891) labored with the problem of syntax—the logical rules of language. His energetic attack on the problem of the actual construction of a fundamental syntax for the "physical" language has created a whole new field of inquiry.

Philipp Frank (b. 1884), a theoretical physicist, applied the new theory of knowledge to the problems of physics.

Hans Hahn (1879–1934), a mathematician, investigated the foundations of mathematics and exact science in the light of the scientific *Weltauffassung* of the Circle.

replace philosophy by the systematic investigation of the logic of science which, for Carnap, is "nothing other than the logical syntax of the language of science." There are but two kinds of acceptable propositions: *formal* and *empirical*. Formal propositions concern syntax. They state the rules and procedure for combining words or symbols and have no empirical reference. Empirical propositions are assertions about the observable world and their truth or falsity can be tested by means of observational procedures. Since metaphysics consists of statements not susceptible to empirical test, it is either an array of syntactical (formal) sentences or else it is technical nonsense. Mostly it is nonsense. Philosophy must be purged of it; and, once purged, it becomes the business of philosophy, says the Circle, to investigate the rules of the language we use in formulating our scientific propositions. The goal of such philosophical research is to provide a secure foundation for the sciences.

This movement was not, of course, without its antecedents. Its most immediate point of departure was the famous *Tractatus Logico-philosophicus* (1922) by Russell's pupil, Ludwig Wittgenstein. The "Tractus" exhibited the close connection between philosophy and syntax; it made clear the *formal* nature of logic and showed that the rules and proofs of syntax should have no reference to the meaning (empirical designation) of symbols; and it showed that the sentences of metaphysics are pseudo propositions. But the roots of these notions can be traced even back beyond Wittgenstein. All who, like the positivists, struck out at metaphysics; all who, like Kant, sought to conciliate analytic (formal) methods with the synthetic (empirical); and all who, like the British empiricists, assaulted philosophy with logical weapons have something in common with the Vienna Circle. Hume, in particular, except when he was assuming the existence of a transempirical world, caught the spirit. He winds up his "Enquiries Concerning Human Understanding" (1902) with this counsel:

If we take in our hand any volume; of divinity or school metaphysics, for instance; let us ask, *Does it contain any abstract reasoning concerning quantity*

Friedrich Waismann distinguished himself with an investigation of the logical foundations of mathematical thinking.

In addition to these members of the Vienna Circle there were other groups whose scientific philosophy was so similar as to be scarcely distinguishable. In fact, one of the impressive aspects of this recent philosophical movement is the manner in which a common *Weltauffassung* appeared almost simultaneously among widely scattered groups of scientists, mathematicians, and philosophers. There was the Warsaw Circle, which boasted such able logicians as Tarski (b. 1901) and Lukasiewicz (b. 1878). At Berlin, prior to the recent cultural eclipse, there was another Circle whose outstanding advocate was Reichenbach (b. 1891). Logicians Russell (b. 1872) and Frege (1848–1925) fall into the same tradition, and in America C. W. Morris (b. 1901) is perhaps the best-known expositor of the common program. For a more complete listing of names, see Neurath's "Historische Anmerkungen" (1930).

or number [formal questions]? No. *Does it contain any experimental reasoning concerning matter of fact and existence* [empirical questions]? No. Commit it then to the flames: for it can contain nothing but sophistry and illusion.

A philosophy as distinctive as that of the Vienna Circle must inevitably become an "ism," and its disciples, Blumberg and Feigl (1931), lost no time in introducing the Circle's program to American scholars under the title of "Logical Positivism." A. F. Bentley (1936) promptly raised the question as to whether Logical Positivism is either logical or positive, but in spite of some obvious disadvantages, the name is not entirely unreasonable. Bentley, as his readers know, loves a *bon mot* and has a low threshold for alarm—he is aroused to criticism easily but not unpleasantly. The name Logical Positivism quite properly suggests the union of the formal and the empirical—a union which, in a well-ordered scientific household, is possible and legitimate.

Logical Positivism proposes to tell us how such a household should be run. A certain division of labor is required. The scientist, in his special field, continues to investigate the empirical relations among the variables he has at hand and these relations he represents by some form of symbolic language. The philosopher complements the scientist by probing the nature and the rules of this symbolic language. Statements about the empirical domain are called object-sentences; statements about language-forms are syntactical sentences. In any special science, such as psychology, both types of sentences frequently occur, because the psychologist must tell us not only about his facts, but also how he intends to use his words and symbols—he must provide his own definitions (see Appendix I*). The philosopher, on the other hand, can point out the logical implications of the psychologist's language and help him guard against the vicious combinations of the two types of sentences which lead to pseudo propositions.

Under this program it is not, however, the task of the philosopher to legislate for science. Science can use any logic it finds useful. Carnap (1937b), at this point, proposes a Principle of Tolerance to allay our fears: "It is not our business," he says, "to set up prohibitions, but to arrive at conventions." "*In logic*," he continues, "*there are no morals*. Everyone is at liberty to build up his own logic, i.e., his own form of language, as he wishes. All that is required of him is that, if he wishes to discuss it, he must state his methods clearly, and give syntactical rules instead of philosophical arguments." Consequently, he who sets out to scrutinize the logic of science must renounce the proud claim that his philosophy sits enthroned above the special sciences. He works in the same field as the specialist, only with a different emphasis. He ponders the logical, formal, syntactical connections. He studies rules which are basically nothing other than conven-

---

* In the original publication.—Ed.

tions and matters of free choice. Hence the labors of the philosopher in that which is his only legitimate domain, the logic of science, are bound to be barren unless they are pursued in close coöperation with the special sciences.

Logical Positivism, then, seeks 1) to clarify the language of science, and 2) to investigate the conditions under which empirical propositions are meaningful. The language of science (including syntax, logic, and mathematics) consists of arrays of words or symbols which we assemble according to certain rules. The analytic propositions of syntax and mathematics are absolutely necessary and certain, once the rules of the game have been laid down. These propositions neither tell us anything about the empirical world, nor can they be confuted by experience. They can no more be proved "true" than can the conventional rules of the game of chess (see below). They simply record our determination to use words and symbols in a certain fashion.

Mathematics, under this view, is a completely rational and deductive system and nothing is contained in one formula which is not implicit in all formulas. This, to many, is a fearful thought. Poincaré (1913) voiced his apprehension by asking: "If all the propositions it enunciates can be deduced one from the other by the rules of formal logic, why is not mathematics reduced to an immense tautology? . . . Shall we admit that the theorems which fill so many volumes are nothing but devious ways of saying that A is A?" The answer appears to be that regardless of how inventive mathematical discoveries may appear to be, they contain nothing not already implicit in the fundamental postulates of the system. The outcome of our symbol-juggling surprises and delights us and fills us with the illusion of discovery, simply because of the limitations of our minds. A man of sufficient intellect would disdain the use of logic and mathematics, for he would see at a glance all that his postulates and definitions implied. He would be aware of all possible discoveries under the rules. The rest of us, however, must continue to do our mathematics stepwise, proceeding from one tautological transformation to the next, and being surprised at the result.

The second aim of Logical Positivism—to discover the conditions of empirical meaning—leads to the notion that an object-sentence is one which is verifiable by means of some concrete procedure. At this point operationism and Logical Positivism are essentially indistinguishable and we shall say no more about them, except to note an error.

This is an error which the Logical Positivists themselves have acknowledged and corrected (cf. Carnap, 1937[a], p. 11), but since the slip was made in what is commonly regarded as psychological territory, we had best have a look at it. The Vienna Circle committed the all too common fallacy: It claimed to find a difference between *knowledge* and *immediate experience* (see Blumberg and Feigl, 1931). Knowledge is communicable, but the immediately given is private and noncommunicable. This from the mouth of a Logical Positivist! Indeed, by all the rules they have proposed, this sentence is not a testable proposition, for how shall we demonstrate the existence of the noncommunicable? But, as already indicated, the Logical Positivists have not been stubborn about insisting that it makes sense to talk of the private content of immediate experience as being different from the discriminable and reportable relations between experiences. Their past lapse in this regard is interesting only because it shows how easy it is for even the well-intentioned to talk nonsense when they invade this field of psychology. In "The Operational Definition of Psychological Concepts" (1935[b]) I have tried to demonstrate that an empirical (operational) definition of immediate experience is possible provided we note precisely what its advocates do when we ask them to indicate an example of it. Almost invariably they point to a situation involving an elementary discrimination such as: "I see red." Elementary discriminations, then are what is meant by the immediately given, and discriminatory reactions, of course, are public and communicable.

Physicalism

As thoroughgoing empiricists the Logical Positivists hold that all meaningful scientific propositions are derived from experience. More precisely, all such propositions are reducible to *protocol-sentences*—sentences relating to the simplest elements of experience. This notion, I take it, is equivalent to the operationist's view that complex propositions are shown to be meaningful when they can be reduced to simpler propositions for which there are operational tests. The simplest propositions of all would be those relating to elementary discriminations. Now, if all scientific propositions are reducible in this fashion, including propositions expressed in what is called *physical language*, it must follow that *all* propositions are translatable into the physical language—a language similar to that of contemporary physics. This is the thesis of Physicalism.[5]

---

[5] This is a somewhat oversimplified statement of Physicalism. Furthermore, Carnap (1937a) has recently introduced extensive qualifications and changes into the original views of the Vienna Circle regarding the relation of the various "languages" of science. His reasons for preferring the physical to the psychological language (pp. 9 ff.) do not appear to me to be binding, especially if the psychological language is made operational. If that is done, the choice becomes one based on convention or convenience. We could express all physics in psychological language, but that would be more traumatic to tradition than if we were to express all psychology in the physical language. The name Physicalism justifiably appeals to many as an unhappy designation, because it arouses prejudices by suggesting the primacy of a materialistic physics.

Physicalism was christened by Neurath (cf. 1931). Contrary to what the name suggests, it is not a metaphysical doctrine asserting that everything is physical, for such a proposition can have no testable meaning. It is, on the other hand, a thesis relating to language: The physical language is a universal language of science and the individual languages used in any subdomain of science can be equipollently translated into the physical language. Innocent as this assertion about language may appear, it is charged with far-reaching implications for psychology. In fact, the examples used to illustrate Physicalism make it appear that the doctrine was aimed directly against psychology—at least against the kind peddled by philosophers.

Physicalism makes it clear that the traditional but somewhat antiquated problem of psychophysical dualism is exclusively a problem of syntax. Using the common "material mode" of speech we might say: To every psychical state there is a corresponding physical state of the body and the two are lawfully connected. Couched in this form, such a sentence is a veritable gold mine for pseudo problems. Physicalism would throttle these problems by saying: All sentences purporting to deal with psychical states are translatable into sentences in the physical language. Two distinctly separate languages to describe physics and psychology are therefore not necessary. And in this assertion we have Physicalism's denial of metaphysical dualism. It is the Logical Positivist's way of saying that psychology must be operational and behavioristic.

The philosopher, Hempel (1935), calls this kind of psychology *logical behaviorism*. It differs from the primitive American stamp in that it does not prescribe that research shall be limited to stimulus-response connections. It is not, properly speaking, a theory *about psychology* at all, but only a logical theory about psychological sentences. The psychologist may study anything he pleases, but any verifiable psychological proposition he may utter is equivalent to some proposition in the physical language. An operationist would certainly agree to this notion. In fact, an operationist would point out that this view is correlative with his own dictum that any meaningful psychological proposition, even though it pertains to a toothache, is reducible to public, concrete operations.

The Unity of Science

How we get from Physicalism to the thesis of the *unity of science* is obvious indeed. If every sentence can be translated into the physical language, then this language is an all-inclusive language—a universal language of science. And if the esoteric jargons of all the separate sciences can, upon demand, be reduced to a single coherent language, then all science possesses a fundamental logical unity.

This idea of a unified basis for science, introduced into the Vienna Circle by the imaginative originality of Neurath, has launched a whole new movement in scientific philosophy. The newly-begun *International Encyclopedia of Unified Science* is tangible testimony to the vigor and seriousness of the enterprise.[6] Annual congresses provide a forum where the thesis is developed (Fifth Annual Congress . . . held at Harvard University, September 5–10, 1939); and out of this intellectual ferment there is emerging a substantial basis for an empirical and universal Science of Science. But before we inspect this newest of sciences—one which is obviously still warm in the womb of its philosophy-mother—let us look backward a few centuries.

How many men, since ancient Thales proposed that all is water, have dreamed the dream of a universal science is beyond a guess. The dream has taken many forms—mostly impracticable—for the history of science is a story of diversification and specialization proceeding almost geometrically with time. If there is unity in so much arborescence, where are we to find it? Certainly not in subject matter where differentiation is the rule. Perhaps, then, in method and logic.

In 1666 the twenty-year-old Leibnitz (Bell, 1937) dreamed his own dream about the unity of science and recorded it in *De Arte Combinatoria*. He himself called it a schoolboy's essay, but in it he proposed to create *"a general method in which all truths of reason would be reduced to a kind of calculation. At the same time this would be a sort of universal language or script, but infinitely different from those projected hitherto; for the symbols and even the words in it would direct the reason; and errors, except those of fact, would be mere mistakes in calculation."* How

---

[6] Neurath (1937) describes *unified science* as *encyclopedic integration*. The new "Encyclopedia" is to be constructed like an onion. The heart of the onion will be two introductory volumes consisting of twenty pamphlets, and in these volumes will be laid the foundations for a logical unity which will make possible future integration of scientific disciplines. The first layer of the onion enclosing the heart will be a series of volumes to deal with problems of systematization in special sciences, including logic, mathematics, the theory of signs, history of science, classification of the sciences, and the educational implications of the scientific attitude. Still outer layers will concern even more specialized problems. The encyclopedia will not be an alphabetical dictionary and its creators hope, quite piously, that it will not become a mausoleum but remain a living intellectual force.

At the present writing only three numbers (1, 2, and 5) of the "Encyclopedia" have appeared, but it is already clear that, although there is great community among the contributors, detailed unanimity is absent. As to the problem of unity in science, for example, Carnap finds as yet *no unity of laws* in science, but only *unity of language;* Lenzen finds a basis for unity in the fact that all science starts from experience; Neurath would get his unity by means of *encyclopedic integration;* Russell says the unity is essentially one of method; and Dewey hopes for unity by promulgating what he calls the scientific attitude.

long would it take to create this logistic? Leibnitz thought a few chosen men could turn the trick within five years. But chosen men were not at hand and two centuries passed before the creation of a universal symbolic logic was even begun. Almost another century of labor has been needed to lay a foundation in logic and syntax so tangible that many men together could vision the unity of science.

Leibnitz, though, if any single man, was father to the idea. He hoped for a universal logicalization of human thinking by means of a general calculus and a general terminology. He conceived a formal discipline to include a theory and art of forming signs to represent ideas and a general calculus giving a universal formal method of drawing consequences from the signs. Then, if two men were to find themselves in disagreement as to anything except matters of observation, they would settle their argument by calculating the right answer. Leibnitz' inspiration is perhaps not without its utopian aspect, but it cannot be denied that the modern logic of science has made progress towards Leibnitz' goal.

Perhaps our progress has not always been of the sort that would have delighted the boy of twenty, for metaphysics was no triviality in 1666. Today, however, it is clear that the unhappy symphonies of pseudo propositions that are metaphysics have all too frequently thwarted our efforts at clarification. Logical analysis has unmasked metaphysics; at least that is one of the boasted achievements of the recent philosophical movement. Opinion will probably never be unanimous on this issue, but disclosure of the empirically meaningless aspects of metaphysics is intimately bound to the other advances claimed by the Logical Positivists. By way of review at this point, these are some of the achievements of the modern movement:

1. It has been demonstrated that a unified language of science is possible. The syntax of this language is to be discovered by careful analysis of linguistic usage in science. And what unity there is in science is to be found in the unity of its logic and syntax.

2. Linguistic analysis has revealed the all-important distinction between the *formal* and the *empirical* aspects of science. Formal science consists of the analytic statements established by logic and mathematics; empirical science consists of the synthetic statements established in the different fields of factual knowledge.

3. The statements of logic and mathematics derive their validity from conventions, and, from the point of view of empiricism, they are materially empty and constitute a closed system of tautologies. Logic deals with language only—not with the objects of language. Likewise, mathematics deals with symbols—not with the objects which the symbols represent.

4. Empirical propositions have meaning when there exists a concrete

procedure (a set of operations) for determining their truth or falsity. Empirical significance attaches only to testable or confirmable sentences.

5. What we have called the "truth" of an empirical proposition is something which can never be absolute. Repeated tests of an object-sentence can add to its probability but never clinch its certainty. Induction, as Hume pointed out, is not a watertight method of proving anything empirical.

6. The notion that all scientific sentences are translatable into a common form—the physical language—requires of psychology a behavioristic approach. Psychology so conceived is called *behavioristics*.

These alleged achievements of the philosophers have been attained in the same spirit professed by the operationists: an empirical study of the actual doings of science-makers. Little wonder, then, that the two groups, although differing in emphasis, have arrived at substantially the same generalizations. Furthermore, these studies investigating the science-makers are the beginnings of a Science of Science. Like all other sciences, this one began before it was founded. Its founding and christening are of very recent date. They coincide with the harvesting of its first fruits.

The Science of Science

These first fruits of the Science of Science, it would appear, are the positive advances of operationism, of Logical Positivism, and of all who have looked seriously into the rules under which science is created. Except for these fruits, of which many are still green and some may even turn out to be wormy, the Science of Science comprises little more than an optimistic program. The fullest account of this program is supplied by C. W. Morris in his excellent essay on the "Foundations of the theory of signs" (1938[b]).

Morris is a philosopher at Chicago, and many will want to ask: What good is a science in the hands of philosophers? The obvious retort is that all our major sciences passed their childhood in the mansion of philosophy and only after they had grown tough and empirical were they bold enough to desert the tender-minded parent. It may be that once again a band of curious men have turned up in some unsuspected corner a new science with which they will charm away a few hardy scholars and leave the parental mansion tenanted by the tender-minded.

Let us turn now to an outline of the scientific study of science. Morris calls it "Metascience" or "Scientific Empiricism." Morris is enthusiastically full of new terms; in fact, a difficulty with his account is that he is overly generous in his willingness to enrich our vocabulary. Much of his coinage, however, is choice and merits more extensive circulation. Morris defends the thesis that *it is possible to include without remainder the study of*

*science under the study of the language of science, because the study of
that language involves not merely the study of its formal structure but its
relation to the objects it designates and to the persons who use it.* Language
is a system of signs or symbols and the general science of signs is to be
called *Semiotic.* Semiotic has a double relation to the other sciences: It is
both a science among the sciences and an instrument of the sciences. It is
not a "superscience" but rather a common science among the others.
Every scientist at some stage of his work must embody his results in linguistic signs, and consequently he must be as careful with his linguistic
tools as he is in designing his apparatus or in making his observations. In
his enterprise, the scientist unites empiricism with methodological rationalism, and Semiotic studies how this marriage is consecrated.

The study divides itself into three dimensions or levels, which we shall
discuss in turn:

1. Syntactics is the study of the relation of signs to signs.
2. Semantics is the study of the relation of signs to objects.
3. Pragmatics is the study of the relation of signs to scientists.

Syntactics refers to the formal disciplines commonly called logic,
mathematics, and syntax, where the relation of signs to one another is
abstracted from their relation to objects and to users or interpreters. At
present this is the best developed branch of Semiotic, but in the field of
the logical syntax of language there is still great labor to be done. The
investigation of language from the syntactical point of view is at once
both complex and fruitful. It has been possible accurately to characterize
primitive, analytic, contradictory, and synthetic sentences, and to show
that many sentences which are apparently object-sentences (and so concern things which are not signs) turn out under analysis to be pseudo
object-sentences which must be interpreted as syntactical statements about
language. An astonishing number of the scientist's sentences are syntactical
in this sense (see Appendix I*). They are propositions without material
content.

Ayer (1936, p. 63) gives us a "striking instance" of the way in which
propositions which are really linguistic are often expressed in such a way
that they appear to be factual. At first glance, the proposition, "A material
thing cannot be in two places at once," looks quite empirical, but critical
inspection shows that "it simply records the fact that, as a result of certain
verbal conventions, the proposition that two sense-contents occur in the
same visual or tactual sense-field is incompatible with the proposition that
they belong to the same material thing." The proposition, then, is a definition—it records our decision as to how we shall use the term "material

---

* In the original publication.—Ed.

thing." As this example suggests, the scientist frequently couches in the material idiom the propositions which he really intends as definitions, and thereby he tends unwittingly to generate pseudo problems out of his use— or misuse—of signs.

Of course, science is not the only activity in which we use signs. The artist, the musician, and the traffic cop are notable sign-users. What their various signs express or designate concerns semantics; what the effect of these signs is on society and the individual concerns pragmatics; but we can also inquire under what rules the signs are made, combined, and transformed, and that is syntactics.

Semantics refers to the rules determining under what condition a sign is applicable to an object or situation. Thus, the operational rule[7] laid down by Bridgman for determining the meaning of a term is, I take it, essentially a *semantical rule*. And the so-called "applicational definitions" used by the Logical Positivists to state when a term shall apply to an object come under this heading (cf. Blumberg and Feigl, 1931). Within the study of these rules belong all the problems relating to the correlation between the signs which comprise a scientific treatise and the discriminable aspects of the physical world to which the signs are meant to apply. The simplest semantical rule is that governing an *indexical* sign. Such a sign designates what is pointed at at any instant. The denotation of the sign is based upon the operation of pointing, which in turn, of course, involves an act of discrimination. We have already noted that discrimination is the simplest and most basic operation performable.

Many of the problems of semantics belong to psychology. Morris sees in the experimental approach made possible by behavioristics great promise for determining the actual conditions under which certain signs are employed. Unfortunately, rules for the use of sign-vehicles are not ordinarily formulated by the users of a language; they exist, rather, as habits of behavior, and semantics wants to know what these habits are and how they come to be established. Many pertinent experimental studies have already been made by psychologists seeking the conditions of concept formation and judgments of similarity, but more are in order. Tolman's discovery of sign-gestalts functioning in the life of the rat discloses

---

[7] In discussing operationism I have used the words *term* and *proposition*, *applicability* and *truth* (Stevens, 1935[b], 1936). In keeping with the spirit of Semiotic I ought perhaps to say that *terms* have *applicability* under semantical rules when the criteria governing their use are operational criteria. Then, sentences formed by combining these *semantically* significant terms into propositions are *empirically* significant (have truth-value) when their assertions are confirmable by means of operations. In other words, there is a justifiable distinction between the operational meaning of words and symbols (semantical significance) and the operational meaning of empirical propositions. I am not certain, however, that Morris would distinguish between empirical and semantical propositions in the same way.

semantics among the rodents, and Lashley's effort to discover what range of patterns are considered equivalent by the rat when he uses them as signs for food directs attention to the problem of functional substitutivity (to use Professor Boring's term) among symbolic forms.

The game of chess is frequently suggested (cf. Carnap, 1934, and Reichenbach, 1938) as an example of a system of conventional formal rules applicable to concrete objects and situations. Perhaps at this point we can better illuminate Semiotic by examining this ancient pastime. First let us consider a set of signs. We shall use three groups of symbols: 1) the letters *a, b, c, d, e, f, g,* and *h;* 2) the numbers 1, 2, 3, 4, 5, 6, 7, and 8; and 3) certain other signs such as Kt, B, Q, K, etc. Next we shall set up conventional rules for manipulating these symbols by allowing only combinations in which 1 sign from each of the three groups appears, such as, for example, Kt *c* 4. This combination shall be transformable into other combinations, depending upon the first symbol, Kt. Thus:

$$\text{Kt } c \text{ 4} \longrightarrow \text{Kt } e \text{ 5}.$$

But we shall not be allowed to write:

$$\text{Kt } c \text{ 4} \longrightarrow \text{Kt } d \text{ 5}.$$

Now, when we have stated all the rules governing these signs, what do we have? Quite plainly, what we have is a formal system—a set of signs governed by syntactical rules. We are engaged in the pursuit of syntactics.

Anyone who is a chess player will have guessed by now that these syntactical rules were *abstracted* from the game of chess. The point is that we can abstract them in this way and study them with no reference to anything beyond themselves. On the other hand, we can use them as a "model" to describe chess. In order to use them in this way we proceed to set up *semantical rules.* We say: Let the letters stand for the rows and the numbers for the columns of a chess board; let Kt stand for a particular small object (called a knight) which sits on a square of the board; then define Kt *c* 4 as equivalent to the statement that there is a knight on the square of co-ordinates *c* and 4; and define Kt *c* 4 $\longrightarrow$ Kt *e* 5 as equivalent to the statement that the knight is moved from *c* 4 to *e* 5. These semantical rules are statements about the use of language—they merely record our decisions as to how we shall use certain signs—and as semantical rules they are not empirical propositions. (This distinction between semantical and empirical statements was not made sufficiently explicit in operationism, but it needs to be stressed.)

We create an empirical statement as soon as we say that Kt *c* 4 is true, i.e., that there is, in fact, a knight on *c* 4, because this statement can be operationally verified. We can look to see whether our knight is there on *c* 4, or elsewhere. If the knight is on *c* 4 the statement is confirmed as true and if the knight is not on *c* 4 the statement is unconfirmed and is false. On the other hand, the statement "Kt *c a*" can never be considered an empirical proposition, because this combination of signs violates the rules of syntax and is meaningless—it cannot be tested operationally.[8]

From our game of chess we can abstract still another dimension or aspect. We can ask: What is the relation of these rules to chess players? Is the game hard or easy? What is its place in society, etc.? Here we are broaching pragmatical questions.

Pragmatics, as a part of Semiotic, studies the relation of signs to scientists. Here belong the problems as to how the scientist, as a behaving organism, reacts to signs; how science, as a social institution, interacts with other social institutions; and how scientific activity relates to other activities. This, indeed, is the aspect of Semiotic most challenging to the psychologist. It is the problem of the interpretation of signs. What is their effect on the man who sees or hears them? How do they determine behavior? How are they used and abused in shaping human destiny? A nebulous problem, one might complain, and overwhelmingly complex. "Yes, but none the less real and pressing," must be the answer.

The term "pragmatics" obviously suggests the philosophy known as pragmatism. The word was deliberately chosen to be thus suggestive. (In Semiotic we should say that the *pragmatical* aspect of the word is one of suggestiveness.) Pragmatism, more effectively than ever before, directed attention to the relation of signs to their users and assessed this relation as an aid in understanding intellectual activities. Pragmatics, as part of Semiotic, pays tribute to the achievements of Peirce, James, Dewey, and Mead, but it must not be thought identical with pragmatism as a philosophy.

Both pragmatism and pragmatics agree that the interpreter of a sign-vehicle is an organism whose "taking-account" of the sign consists in a *habit to respond* to the vehicle as it would to the thing designated by the sign. We thus find the problem of pragmatics cast in such a form that it can be handled by behavioristics—we deliberately avoid talking about the subjective effects of signs unless these effects are disclosed by public operations. Not only do we react to the signs appearing in sober scientific propositions, but our habits of response carry over to situations where signs obey neither semantical nor syntactical rules. We are often delighted by senseless jingles and moved to strong emotions by what analysis shows to be gibberish. In propaganda, where syntax is usually not violated, but

---

[8] Note the similarity between the statement "Kt *c a*" and Ayer's example discussed above. To say that a knight cannot be on *c* and *a* at the same time is very like saying that an object cannot be in two places at once. Both statements follow directly from the rules of our syntax and are therefore nonempirical sentences.

where semantical relations are sometimes distorted, the pragmatical effects (the induction of some form of behavior) may be profoundly disturbing. Clearly, psychology has a stake in the solution of all these problems arising in pragmatics.

One more facet of this many-sided problem deserves our interest. What Morris calls *descriptive pragmatics* occurs when a sign used by a person is employed as a means of gaining information about the person. The psychoanalyst studies dreams for the light they throw upon the dreamer, not to discover whether there are actually any situations which the dreams denote. Likewise, we may study the statements of newspapers and politicians, not as empirical propositions, but for their ability to disclose the faction whose interest is being served by this form of propaganda. And in much the same spirit, the psychiatrist inspects the signs used by his patient in order to diagnose an abnormality. The pragmatical aberrations found among the psychoses are extremely illuminating, for occasionally a patient lets his system of signs displace completely the objects they once stood for; the troublesome world of reality is pushed aside and the frustrated fellow gets his satisfaction in the domain of signs, oblivious to the restrictions of syntactical and semantical rules. The field of psychopathology thus holds great promise as a place to apply Semiotic and discover some of its laws.[9]

There can be no doubt that in the realm of human behavior the concept of sign holds a key place. And if, as the pragmatists contend, mental phenomena are to be equated to sign-responses, psychology bears an intimate relation to the science of signs. The theory of signs—being the co-ordinated disciplines of syntactics, semantics, and pragmatics—is the core of a unified science. "Indeed," exclaims Morris (1938[b]), "it does not seem fantastic to believe that the concept of sign may prove as fundamental to the sciences of man as the concept of atom has been for the physical sciences or the concept of cell for the biological sciences."

Epilogue

That then, in all too brief review, is the manner in which the Science of Science has been staked out. Whoever would probe the making of science

---

[9] Count Alfred Korzybski has written a bulky work called *Science and Sanity* (Lancaster: Science Press, 1933), in which he contends that in the miseducation of our youth we teach them semantical rules based upon static Aristotelian classifications which they must then use in dealing with a fluid dynamic universe. Such semantical habits are enough out of tune with reality to drive many people crazy. Korzybski would cure the resulting insanity by renovating the patient's semantics. Whatever our opinion about this etiology and cure, it is plain that much of Korzybski's concern is with what Morris would call pragmatics—the effect of signs upon the users of signs.

can learn all the answers by inspecting thoroughly the language of science. The investigator must remember, however, that *this language is an intersubjective (public) set of sign-vehicles whose usage is determined by syntactical, semantical, and pragmatical rules.* By making the Science of Science coextensive with the study of the language of science we have set spacious bounds to this field of inquiry—there is ample room for a variety of talents, and to bring all the diverse areas under cultivation will require co-operation among the specialties.

Three features of this lusty embryonic science stand out with particular prominence.

First, the rational and the empirical elements in science are disentangled and then reassembled according to a straightforward, workable plan. The formal, rational, analytic, a priori, deductive side of creative thinking, which has always been so dear in the hearts of James's "tender-minded," neither rules nor is ruled by the empirical, synthetic, a posteriori, inductive wing. Neither side can be called a usurper when both are understood, for they are not even in competition. Their union is achieved, not after the manner of Kant, who held out for a bastard hybrid which he called the "a priori synthetic judgment," but in conformity with the relation of sign to object.

Secondly, it is proposed that in our study of the science-maker we begin with the *products* of his activity—his finished propositions—rather than with his "experiences" or any other phase of his earlier behavior. This is a sensible place to begin. If we were to study the manufacture of any product, such as automobiles, we should probably find it useful first to ascertain what an automobile is and then to discover the conditions under which it comes into being. Science manufactures sentences, and we, as curious mortals, ask: What is a sentence and how is it made? The *complete* answer to this question is the Science of Science.

Thirdly, does it not appear that the Science of Science must go directly to psychology for an answer to many of its problems? Is it not also plain that a behavioristic psychology is the only one that can be of much help in this enterprise? A sign has semantical significance when an organism will react to it as it would to the object which the sign supplants. The psychologist works out the laws under which different stimuli evoke equivalent reactions. Signs, as stimuli, can be combined and utilized extensively in the control and direction of behavior, both individual and social. The entire activity of the scientist as a sign-using organism constitutes, therefore, a type of behavior for which behavioristics seeks the laws. If there is a sense in which psychology is the propaedeutic science (cf. Stevens, 1936), it is undoubtedly in its ability to study the behavior, *qua* behavior, of the science-makers.

Perhaps we are too close to this young Science of Science either to judge its value or see clearly how it came to be. We shall forego the value-judgment, since it would merely disclose the author's particular prejudice (already clear, no doubt), but an observation about the movement's immediate ancestry is not entirely out of order. It now appears, in retrospect, that the Science of Science emergéd as the reasonable outcome of revolutions in the three major fields: physics, psychology, and philosophy. These revolutions occurred almost independently, but a general community of spirit among them led directly to extensive cross-fertilization. Operationism as a revolution against absolute and undefinable concepts in physics, behaviorism as a revolution against dualistic mentalism in psychology, and Logical Positivism as a revolution against rational metaphysics in philosophy were the three forces whose convergence into a common effort is effected by the Science of Science.

Finally, the purpose of this review has been to call the attention of those of us who are psychologists to the critical principles involved in scientific method as evolved in recent scientific and philosophic movements. We have had little to say concretely about psychology or its facts, and undoubtedly many will be impatient with so much non-experimental discourse. "Who cares about philosophy?" they will say. "What matters is the product of the laboratory." While such robust empiricism is admirable, we must ask the indulgence of these tough minds. We must ask them to bear with us while we inspect our logical tools as carefully as we do our other apparatus. And we must ask them to weigh the implications for psychology of this statement by Quine, the logician (1936):

> The less a science has advanced the more its terminology tends to rest upon an uncritical assumption of mutual understanding. With increase of rigor this basis is replaced piecemeal by the introduction of definitions. The interrelationships recruited for these definitions gains the status of analytic principles; what was once regarded as a theory about the world becomes reconstrued as a convention of language. Thus it is that some flow from the theoretical to the conventional is an adjunct of progress in the logical foundations of any science.

References

Ayer, A. J. *Language, truth and logic.* London: Gollancz, 1936.
Bell, E. T. *Men of mathematics.* New York: Simon and Schuster, 1937.
Benjamin, A. C. *An introduction to the philosophy of science.* New York: Macmillan, 1937 (a).
———. The operational theory of meaning. *Phil. Rev., N.Y.,* 1937, *46,* 644–649 (b).
Bentley, A. F. The positive and the logical. *Phil. Sci.,* 1936, *3,* 472–485.
———. Physicists and fairies. *Phil. Sci.,* 1938, *5,* 132–165.
Bills, A. G. Changing views of psychology as science. *Psychol. Rev.,* 1938, *45,* 377–394.

Blumberg, A. E., and Feigl, H. Logical positivism. *J. Phil.*, 1931, *28*, 281–296.

Boas, G., and Blumberg, A. E. Some remarks in defense of the operational theory of meaning. *J. Phil.*, 1931, *28*, 544–550.

Boring, E. G. Temporal perception and operationism. *Amer. J. Psychol.*, 1936, *48*, 519–522.

Bridgman, P. W. *The logic of modern physics*. New York: Macmillan, 1928.

——. A physicist's second reaction to Mengenlehre. *Scripta math.*, 1934, 2, 3–29.

——. *The nature of physical theory*. Princeton, N.J.: Princeton Univ. Press, 1936.

——. Operational analysis. *Phil. Sci.*, 1938, *5*, 114–131.

Brunswik, E. Psychology as a science of objective relations. *Phil. Sci.*, 1937, *4*, 227–260.

Bures, C. E. The concept of probability. *Phil. Sci.*, 1938, *5*, 1–20.

Campbell, N. R. *Physics: the elements*. Cambridge: Univ. Press, 1920.

Carnap, R. On the character of philosophic problems. *Phil. Sci.*, 1934, *1*, 5–19.

——. *Philosophy and logical syntax*. London: Kegan Paul, 1935 (a).

——. Les concepts psychologiques et les concepts physiques sont-ils foncièrement différents? *Rev. Synthèse*, 1935, *10*, 43–53 (b).

——. Testability and meaning. *Phil. Sci.*, 1936, *3*, 419–471; 1937, *4*, 1–40 (a).

——. *Logical syntax of language*. London: Kegan Paul, 1937 (b).

Dingle, H. *Through science to philosophy*. Oxford: Clarendon Press, 1937.

Einstein, A. On the method of theoretical physics. *Phil. Sci.*, 1934, *1*, 163–169.

Feigl, H. The logical character of the principle of induction. *Phil. Sci.*, 1934, *1*, 20–29 (a).

——. Logical analysis of the psycho-physical problem. *Phil. Sci.*, 1934, *1*, 420–445 (b).

Hempel, C. G. Analyse logique de la psychologie. *Rev. Synthèse*, 1935, *10*, 27–42.

Hume, D. *Enquiries concerning the human understanding and concerning the principles of morals* (2nd ed.). Oxford: Clarendon Press, 1902.

James, W. *Pragmatism*. New York: Longmans, Green, 1914.

Kantor, J. R. The operational principle in the physical and psychological sciences. *Psychol. Rec.*, 1938, *2*, 3–32.

Lewin, K. The conceptual representation and the measurement of psychological forces. *Contr. Psychol. Theor.*, 1938, *1*, No. 4, 1–247.

Lindsay, R. B. A critique of operationalism in physics. *Phil. Sci.*, 1937, *4*, 456–470.

Lindsay, R. B., and Margenau, H. *Foundations of physics*. New York: Wiley, 1936.

Lundberg, G. A. Quantitative methods in social psychology. *Amer. Sociol. Rev.*, 1936, *1*, 38–54.

Malisoff, W. M. The universe of operations (a review). *Phil. Sci.*, 1936, *3*, 360–364.

Margenau, H. Causality in modern physics. *Monist*, 1931, *41*, 1–36.

——. Methodology of modern physics. *Phil. Sci.*, 1935, *2*, 48–72, 164–187.

McGeoch, J. A. Learning as an operationally defined concept. *Psychol. Bull.*, 1935, *32*, 688 (abstr.).

——. A critique of operational definition. *Psychol. Bull.*, 1937, *34*, 703–704 (abstr.).

McGregor, D. Scientific measurement and psychology. *Psychol. Rev.*, 1935, *42*, 246–266.

Menger, K. The new logic. *Phil. Sci.*, 1937, *4*, 299–336.

Morris, C. W. Scientific empiricism. *Int. Encycl. Unif. Sci.*, 1938, No. 1, 63–75 (a).

———. Foundations of the theory of signs. *Int. Encycl. Unif. Sci.*, 1938, No. 2, 1–59 (b).

Nagel, E. Some theses in the philosophy of logic. *Phil. Sci.*, 1938, *5*, 46–51.

Neurath, O. Historische Anmerkungen. *Erkenntnis*, 1930, *1*, 311–314.

———. Physicalism: the philosophy of the Viennese Circle. *Monist*, 1931, *41*, 618–623.

———. Unified science and its encyclopedia. *Phil. Sci.*, 1937, *4*, 265–277.

Poincaré, H. *The foundations of science*. New York: Science Press, 1913.

Quine, W. Truth by convention. In *Philosophical essays for Alfred North Whitehead*. New York: Longmans, Green, 1936, p. 90.

Rashevsky, N. Foundations of mathematical biophysics. *Phil. Sci.*, 1934, *1*, 176–196.

———. Physico-mathematical methods in biological and social sciences. *Erkenntnis*, 1936, *6*, 357–365.

Reichenbach, H. *Experience and prediction*. Chicago: Univ. of Chicago Press, 1938.

Rosenzweig, S. Schools of psychology: a complementary pattern. *Phil. Sci.*, 1937, *4*, 96–106.

Schlick, M. De la relation entre les notions psychologiques et les notions physiques. *Rev. Synthèse*, 1935, *10*, 5–26.

Seashore, R. H., and Katz, B. An operational definition and classification of mental mechanisms. *Psychol. Rec.*, 1937, *1*, 3–24.

Somerville, J. Logical empiricism and the problem of causality in social sciences. *Erkenntnis*, 1936, *6*, 405–411.

Stevens, S. S. The operational basis of psychology. *Amer. J. Psychol.*, 1935, *47*, 323–330 (a).

———. The operational definition of psychological concepts. *Psychol. Rev.*, 1935, *42*, 517–527 (b).

———. Psychology: the propaedeutic science. *Phil. Sci.*, 1936, *3*, 90–103.

Struik, D. J. On the foundations of the theory of probabilities. *Phil. Sci.*, 1934, *1*, 50–70.

Tolman, E. C. *Purposive behavior in animals and men*. New York: Appleton-Century, 1932.

Tolman, E. C. An operational analysis of 'demands.' *Erkenntnis*, 1936, *6*, 383–390 (a).

Tolman, E. C. Operational behaviorism and current trends in psychology. *Proc. 25th Anniv. Celebr. Inaug. Grad. Stud.* Los Angeles: Univ. of S. Calif. Press, 1936, 89–103 (b).

Waters, R. H., and Pennington, L. A. Operationism in psychology. *Psychol. Rev.*, 1938, *45*, 414–423.

Weinberg, J. R. *An examination of logical positivism*. London: Kegan Paul, Trench, Trubner, 1936.

Wittgenstein, L. *Tractatus logico-philosophicus*. New York: Harcourt, Brace, 1922.

Woodger, J. H. *The axiomatic method in biology*. Cambridge: Cambridge Univ. Press, 1937.

CHAPTER II
The Role of Models

THE PRESENT CHAPTER, CONSISTING entirely of selections new in this edition, attests to the growing prominence of models of varying sorts in theory construction. Roy Lachman's paper offers a useful review of the general role of models and should provide the student with a good introductory orientation. Herbert A. Simon and Allan Newell are among the pioneers in application of the electronic-computer model to problems of human thinking. Their paper outlines this work and covers, in addition, many more general issues involving models and their relationship to theories. The last paper, by Alphonse Chapanis, is of exceptionally broad scope and affords many illuminating insights into models and their utilities as well as their limitations.

3 | *The Model in Theory Construction*

ROY LACHMAN[1]

The scientific enterprise as here conceived consists of two related but discriminately different activities. One is the observation of objects and events, both experimentally and less formally. The other involves the use of mathematical and natural linguistic symbols, along with the rules for their manipulation, to represent these sensory experiences, to organize what is observed into some comprehensible order, and by proper symbolic manipulation to arrive at a representation of what has not yet been observed. The commentary that accompanies these latter theoretical undertakings frequently includes the term "model," the meaning of which can, at best, be imperfectly ascertained from the context. It has been claimed, not infrequently, that while some distinct referent can be delineated in physics, the term "model" has lost all semblance of meaning in psychology (e.g., Underwood, 1957, p. 257). Actually, the physical scientist has permitted himself wide latitude in the use of the term "model" and the psychologist has followed suit.

The plan of this paper is to analyze certain meanings and functions of the concept of a model; distinctions made will then be exemplified in some actual theories from contemporary psychology and classical physics. Implications of the properties of models for theory construction will then be examined in a systematic fashion. The consequences of this analysis for a sample of methodological problems currently at issue will be explored.

Two properties of the analysis to follow should be noted. First, although the profusion of ideas referred to by the term model is often

From R. Lachman, The model in theory construction, *Psychol. Rev.*, 1960, 67, 113–129. Pp. 113–117 and 126–129 reprinted by permission of the author, the *Psychological Review*, and the American Psychological Association.

[1] The author, now at Hilo Campus, University of Hawaii, is indebted to H. H. Kendler, M. Tatsuoka, M. K. Munitz, E. D. Neimark, Linda Weingarten, and H. Jagoda for reading the manuscript.

interrelated and compounded, it will be necessary for analytic purposes to separate the various meanings and functions into discrete categories. With this exception, the explication of the concept of the model will follow as closely as possible the actual scientific usage. Secondly, while the symbolic form of conveying the ideas of a model may take the form of a word, sentence, diagram, or mathematical calculus, the distinctions to be made concern the meanings of the concept of model and its functional properties within a theoretical system.

Since model has been used interchangeably with or in reference to various parts of a theory, it is necessary to distinguish such theoretical structures, if only crudely. For our present purpose, it will suffice to differentiate among the parts of certain theories: *a*) the principles, postulates, or hypothetical ideas, including the relations among them; *b*) the sentences, equations, or theorems, derived therefrom; *c*) the co-ordinating definitions relating theoretical terms to the observational sentences. The textual commentary accompanying the type of theory with which we are concerned may not explicitly designate all the parts of such a structure. It is part of the task of methodological analysis to isolate this structure. Finally, it will be useful to distinguish the formal theory from the *separate system* which is the model. This meaning of model may refer to, but need not necessarily refer to, what is frequently called the analogy. A model as an order structurally independent of the theory is the prominent notion. Equally important, more than one model generally functions for a theory. The model, consisting of a separate system, brings to bear an external organization of ideas, laws, or relationships upon the hypothetical propositions of a theory or the phenomena it encompasses. This external organization or model contributes to the construction, application, and interpretation of the theory. Precisely how this is accomplished can be clarified by analyzing the meanings and functions of the model concept.

Functions of Models

I. MODELS PROVIDING MODES OF REPRESENTATION   Empirical elements and relationships which constitute the phenomena to be organized by a theory are known to us by the symbolic system or language that designates these data. By introducing a model constituting a separately organized system, we are providing an additional system of representation for the phenomena and a suitable way of speaking about them. An essential characteristic of "modular"[2] representation constitutes the furnishing of *new* ways of regarding or thinking about the empirical objects and

---

2 Hereinafter the word "modular" is intended to pertain to a "model," not a mode.

events. Attributes and meanings of the model are transferred from their initial context of usage to the new setting. This application of unprecedented modes of representation can be executed on two levels. Objects and events formulated directly from observation are thought about in the new and unusual fashion prescribed by the model.

At another level, a model may provide novel modes for conceiving the hypothetical ideas and postulates of a theory. Consider the conditioning model: applied to perceptual phenomena, it illustrates the first or empirical level of application. If perception is *regarded* as though it were a conditioned response, to some *determinable* degree perceptual behavior should be capable of treatment in accordance with the laws of conditioning: frequency, stimulation interval, etc.; if so, the relationships and language of conditioning may be fruitfully applied. Howes and Solomon's (1951) findings may be so regarded. In this example, some such analogy with conditioning is said to provide an empirical or pretheoretical model (Koch, 1954). In contrast, the fractional anticipatory response mechanism—r_g theory—(Amsel, 1958; Kendler and Levine, 1951; Moltz, 1957; Spence, 1951,[a] 1951;[b] etc.) illustrates the second level of representative functioning for the conditioning model. Here, the postulated nonobservable fractional antedating response is conceived of as operating according to conditioning principles to *whatever* degree desirable. We assign any individual or combination of properties from the model to the theoretical construct guided by pragmatic considerations of predictive fertility and consistency of usage required for the integration of diverse areas. To reiterate this important point, a model may be applied to directly accessible (empirical) objects and events or to inaccessible and imaginary concepts of a theory. Though the levels of modular application considered are not discrete but represent extremes of a continuum, an important distinction should not be overlooked: while theoretical entities can be said to be anything we want them to be, this is not so for categories close to observation. The latter are spoken of only in an *as if* fashion. By invoking the conditioning model, perception, meaning, and verbal behavior are not said to be conditioned responses; it is only claimed that if represented and spoken of in such a fashion, important empirical consequences can be obtained. This point is well illustrated by Toulmin's analysis of the rectilinear propagation model of geometrical optics, "We do not *find* light atomized into individual rays: we *represent* it as consisting of such rays" (Toulmin, 1953, p. 29).

II. Models functioning as rules of inference   Given the assumptions of some theory along with the experimental arrangements, a train of reasoning leads to the prediction sentences. From what source do the rules for such inference arise?

In the language used to talk about a theory, the term model may refer directly to a mathematical calculus or to a system of relationships from some other source such as electronic computers, the classical laws of motion, the laws of conditioning, etc. Any one of these separate systems in conjunction with the initial conditions of a given experiment may permit the prediction of what is to be observed. Here, model signifies *the rules* by which the theoretical symbols (some, at least, having been empirically co-ordinated) are manipulated to arrive at new relations; the rules by which one sentence is inferred from another or the theorems are derived. The probability calculus utilized in statistical learning theory (Estes, 1959) exemplifies such a mathematical model, while some of the relations holding among electronic communication systems play a role in providing the inference rules or calculus for information theory (Grant, 1954). Another example is the laws of classical conditioning which, alone or supplemented, are the means by which inferences are drawn in application of r_g theory to a given experiment (Kendler and Levine, 1951; Moltz and Maddi, 1956).

Calculational rules of mathematical systems and the semantic principles of natural language are themselves rules of inference for the symbolism involved. In contrast to this mode of derivation, Munitz (1957,[a] p. 42) recognizes the necessity for distinguishing a more specific set of inference rules provided by certain equations and supplementary textual commentary which prescribe the precise manner in which the theoretical terms and symbols are to be connected; these occasionally are termed "implicit definitions." Although some models may imply how assumptions and implicit definitions are to be formulated, the terms "mathematical model" and "conditioning model" apparently refer to the general inference principles employed in the first sense rather than to the implicit definitions. This is illustrated in r_g theory by the relation or implicit definition $r_g \rightarrow s_g$, for there is nothing in the laws of classical conditioning that requires the hypothetical response to have a hypothetical response-produced cue. But it is precisely the laws of classical conditioning that function as the basis for the rules by which we arrive at the consequences of the several implicit definitions. An additional illustration is provided by statistical learning theory's operator or difference equations, the specific choice of which is in no way dictated by the rules of mathematics, although the operators may be suggested by some second model. While the operator equations determine the form of the learning function to be derived, it is only by the mathematical rules that the derivation itself is executed. It immediately follows that in the expressions mathematical model and conditioning model, the adjectives preceding the term model describe the *source* of the general inference principles. In both cases, this is a separate system external to the structure of the theory. The major source of statistical learning theory's inference rules are to be found in the texts on probability theory and the types of mathematics involved. The rules of inference for r_g can be found in the experimental literature on classical conditioning. For precision in derivation, it is obvious that the rules of mathematics are to be preferred. Furthermore, if it is not yet apparent, later analysis of specific theories will show that these modes of inference drawing do not follow the logic-book deduction of which some scientists and philosophers are so fond.

III. INTERPRETATIONAL FUNCTION OF MODELS   The inference rules or calculus of r_g theory is formulated by amending and adapting the rules contained in the conditioning model; the model serves the additional function of interpreting the calculus. This is not the case for theories with inference rules primarily adopted from a mathematical calculus; the mathematical model may be supplemented with one or more additional models which serve to interpret and make intelligible the inference rules employed. Estes' statistical learning theory (1959), for example, makes use of a stimulus-sampling model; this second model provides a mode of representation functioning as a coherent way of speaking about the theory. Moreover, it functions as one possible interpretation of the theoretical terms. Formulae and symbols are rendered intelligible by the modular interpretation which also shows how to apply the theory and suggests procedures for extending the use of individual parameters and the theory as a whole. Thus, the stimulus-sampling model would tend to suggest that in extending the scope of statistical learning theory to include motivational phenomena, deprivational states would be conceptualized as producing differential configurations of the stimulus set available for sampling; this is precisely what Estes (1958) has done.

Some applications of the conditioning model suggest, in addition to inference principles, the rules for their application to the phenomena involved, the interpretation of the inference principles. Here, the modular interpretation produces propositions such as: the strength of r_g increases to some asymptote as a function of the quantity, time, and magnitude of consummatory experience in the goal box. In psychology such symptom relations are generally termed "co-ordinating definitions" which designate the class of propositions tying together theoretical terms with their associated empirical sentences. The model as an interpretation of a theory guides the formulating of co-ordinating definitions. Hutten (1956, p. 87) adds saliently, "The model so becomes a *link* between theory and experiment. We explain and test the theory in terms of the model."

IV. MODELS PROVIDING PICTORIAL VISUALIZATION   Probably the most common meaning employed and service rendered by a model consists of the reproduction of the theoretical prototype in terms of mental pictures or images. Agents mediating this function range from a rigorously integrated separate system to a loose analogy with familiar sensory experience. The popularity of this modular activity follows from the ubiquitous desire for an intuitively satisfying account of any theory. Preoccupation of classical physicists with model building of this limited pictorial type initiated the counter-view that model construction was a disreputable enterprise. Duhem (1954), for one, considered model construction to be both superfluous and the refuge of weak minds. Residual forms of this position are in evidence today; Carnap (1955, p. 209), while recognizing esthetic, didactic, and heuristic value, finds models nonessential for successful application of theory. Although this may be true of some theoretical activity, as a generalization it is deficient on several grounds and it neglects certain essential aspects of the behavior of a good number of scientists. In modern physics, although visual representation is no longer a prerequisite for the acceptance of a theory, the pictorial model may serve decisively in the initial phase of theory construction. While contemporary quantum theory cannot provide coherent visualization, it did develop from "Bohr's atom" which was associated with a pictorial model. Moreover, some current theoretical efforts concerning the atomic nucleus utilize the shell and water drop models. Axiomatization of a theory, or the attempts to do so, does not compromise this argument. Construction of an axiomatic system, apparently, is not attempted until theory construction is well under way, usually with the aid of some model. It is necessary, therefore, to carefully distinguish simple pictorial functions from the less trivial enterprises described in the previous sections. A model providing satisfying intuitive pictures may also serve one or more of the functions enumerated above, with influence upon theory construction and application that cannot easily be overrated. Conversely, a model providing *only* visual representation serves, at best, didactically; even then, it probably does more to mislead the student than to teach him. Consider Lewin's (1951) topological and field-theoretical models. Following Braithwaite (1953, pp. 366n) we must agree that the essence of a calculus is not its symbolism but its inference rules, whereas Lewin's model functions as "a calculus that doesn't calculate." In contrast, the conditioning model, while possibly providing some S-R theorists with all the beautiful imagery associated with salivating dogs, also contributes the essential inference rules. The work of Staats and Staats (1957, 1958) provides an admirable illustration by their demonstrations that verbal meaning and attitudes may be treated as analogous to a conventional conditioned response whose laws furnish the calculus employed.

*   *   *

Criteria for Evaluating a Model

The modes of operation of several models within their respective theories have been demonstrated. It becomes necessary now to formulate criteria for evaluating a given model. Following Toulmin's (1953) analysis of science, which was influenced by Wittgenstein's (1922) views, several grounds for judging a model may be stated.

DEPLOYABILITY   The degree to which the terms in the model in their primary context of usage can successfully be brought to the new setting. In r_g theory, deployability means the extent to which the non-observable r_g can be assigned the properties of its observable counterpart, the conditioned response. As additional properties and laws of the separate system are assigned to r_g, the conditioning model is being deployed.

SCOPE   The range of phenomena to which the model is applicable. This means the number or extent of facts and data that may be derived by use of the model. According to this view, a theory does *not* contain formal limits; instead, the scope of applicability is empirically determined.

Delineation of the scope of a theory provides the guides and incentives for subsequent theorizing. This may take the form of changes in the initial theory or the construction of a more comprehensive system. In the latter case, the original theory frequently becomes a first approximation or a special instance of the general theory: the equations of the comprehensive theory reduce to the equations of the limited system for the special cases involved. The efforts of Estes and other mathematical model builders make it possible to envisage this future state of affairs in psychology.

While "scope" refers to the *empirical* derivatives of a theory which are generated with the aid of a model, "deployability" is an attribute of the set of relationships or meanings contained in the model that are employed in formulating the *logical* propositions of the theory. Generally, the more a model is deployed the greater will be the scope of the theory; the reverse, however, is not true.

PRECISION   For psychology, this in the present paper refers to the degree to which the consequences of a theory are unequivocally derived through application of the inference rules provided by the model. This feature is of special importance since the pre-quantitative character of most models in psychology often permits contradictory derivations.

Several implications of the viewpoint that generated these criteria merit specific consideration. A fundamental point concerns the criterion of truth. Although the terms true and false are applicable to empirical sentences, these adjectives are devoid of meaning when applied to a model or the theory the model serves. A model has lesser or greater deployability and scope and a certain degree of precision, but not truth or falsity.

An adjunct to the three judgmental criteria is the dichotomy between models providing calculi, co-ordinating definitions, and related functions and those yielding *only* pictorial imagery. The latter, in psychology, have taken the form of cognitive maps, *S-R* switchboards, behavioral fields, and a variety of peculiar things in the nervous system. When mistaken for more serious instruments, the *exclusively* pictorial model can generate a good deal of useless experimental labor, a point eloquently presented by Kendler (1952). Where the inferential or interpretative function is sacrificed for the best intuitive picture such as in a model reflecting, "the existential richness of human life . . ." (Allport, 1955, p. 11), the scientist usurps the poet's function.

One consequence of confusing modular terms with empirical sentences is the variety of cases continuously made against one or another model. For example, Harlow (1953) contends that simple behavior has explanatory value only for simpler phenomena and provides no information concerning complex behavior. This view loses all urgency when one seeks the basis for the distinction between simple and complex. Occasionally, the distinction is held to be self-evident. However, this cannot be seriously regarded, as that which is considered self-evident for one generation of science is frequently believed to be absurd by some other generation. More often, the distinction between simple and complex phenomena is predicated upon the more extensive knowledge accumulated concerning the former: what is relatively well understood is simple; that which is less well known is complex. Harlow (1953) and Asch (1952) have been most critical of the "simplicity" involved in the conditioning model. We may look forward to the day when the research being done by these scientists transforms "complex" incentive-motivational, exploratory and social behaviors into "simple" phenomena.

The Role of Analogy

There are no sufficient a priori grounds for determining how well some separate system will function as a theoretical model for another realm of phenomena. The successful theorist's imagination does, initially, grasp an analogy between the data of interest and the separate system. As the basis for selecting some model, recognition of a critical analogy has sometimes produced the most incredible accomplishments: de Broglie's wave mechanics and Einstein's relativity are two instances. Successful apprehension of analogy is not limited to the most illustrious examples, for as Munitz (1957[b]) has demonstrated, analogy has served a core function in man's interpretation of his environment from Babylonian mythology to modern science. Consequently, the logician has exerted some effort in the attempt to torture the notion of analogy into a neat classificatory scheme. With the exception of the recent heroic efforts of Braithwaite (1953), the basis for the analogical relationship between a model's separate system and the ideas of the theory it serves has not been explicated.

Modular Theories and Modular Constructs

One corollary of the methodological position outlined is the required distinction between constructs introduced by a model and those defined immediately in terms of observables. Stimulus elements and r_g are *theoretical or modular constructs*, whereas drive, defined in terms of the known laws concerning the energizing and facilitative effects of deprivation, might be termed an *empirical construct*. An essentially similar distinction has recently been made by Ginsberg (1954), so we need not pursue it further except for one additional consideration. Dichotomizing constructs along the lines suggested might provide one basis for categorizing scientific theories. Borrowing the classification of *empirical construct theory* and *axiomatic-model theory* from Spence (1957), we would suggest that whereas the former class of theory employs empirical constructs, the latter utilizes modular or theoretical constructs. Examples of axiomatic-model theories have been analyzed here; there are no examples of relatively pure empirical construct theory in psychology. Interestingly enough, Spence's (1956) theory might be considered a mixed type, as he employs empirical constructs such as drive and habit and theoretical constructs such as r_g and s_g.

In the course of the last century, theories of the axiomatic-model type were considered extremely objectionable to a number of scientists and philosophers such as Mach, Duhem, and Ostwald. Characteristic objections concerned the employment of concepts at another level of discourse, that is, the appeal to suprasensible occurrences. The great success of the axiomatic-model type of theory in classical physics eventually silenced the positivistic critics. In contemporary psychology, however, this viewpoint has sired the school of radical empiricism. Although the ingenuity and imagination of Skinner's experimentation are probably unequaled, his views on theory (Skinner, 1950) should be severely questioned.

The Model and Reality

On pragmatic grounds, most scientists find it necessary to acknowledge an external world independent of the observer. As a consequence, discourse is generated concerning the relationship between the models and constructs of science and the phenomena these represent. Since a successful model enables us to predict the future outcome of sets of events, the model is sometimes assumed to be a literal description of reality. For example, it might be argued that the kinetic theory predicts the behavior of gases and since a gas must be composed of something, why not the molecules pictured by the model? Such an assumption in no way interferes with the scientists' activity and may be disregarded. However, one consequence of that view is not so harmless. Occasionally it is argued that if there is a reality, then one and only one model can provide the best description of it. This last proposition and the assumption of reality correspondence upon which it is based are seriously discredited by the very content of physics and psychology. Numerous examples are available of several models serving the same class of events. Conversely, a single model can function in behalf of independent classes of phenomena. Whittaker (1942, p. 17) provides an admirable illustration of the latter state of affairs:

. . . it happens very often that different physical systems are represented by identical mathematical description. For example, the vibrations of a membrane which has the shape of an ellipse can be calculated by means of a differential equation known as Mathieu's equation: but this same equation is also arrived at when we study the dynamics of a circus performer, who holds an assistant balanced on a pole while he himself stands on a spherical ball rolling on the ground. If we now imagine an observer who discovers that the future course of a certain phenomenon can be predicted by Mathieu's equation, but who is unable for some reason to perceive the system which generates the phenomenon, then evidently he would be unable to tell whether the system in question is an elliptic membrane or a variety artiste.

Summary

The functions of models in theory construction were analytically categorized as a) representational, b) inferential, c) interpretational, and d) pictorial. Distinctions introduced were exemplified in the kinetic theory of gases, r_g theory, and statistical learning theory. Implications of the analysis for current methodological problems in psychology were examined.

References

Allport, G. W. *Becoming: basic considerations for a psychology of personality.* New Haven, Conn.: Yale Univ. Press, 1955.

Amsel, A. The role of frustrative non-reward in noncontinuous reward situations. *Psychol. Bull.*, 1958, 55, 102–119.

Asch, S. E. *Social psychology*. New York: Prentice-Hall, 1952.

Braithwaite, R. B. *Scientific explanation*. New York: Cambridge Univ. Press, 1953.

Campbell, N. R. *Physics: The elements*. New York: Cambridge Univ. Press, 1920.

Carnap, R. Foundations of logic and mathematics. In *Int. Encycl. Unif. Sci.*, Vol. 1. Chicago: Univ. of Chicago Press, 1955.

D'Abro, A. *The rise of the new physics*, Vol. 1. New York: Dover, 1951.

Duhem, P. *The aim and structure of physical theory*. Princeton, N.J.: Princeton Univ. Press, 1954.

———. Stimulus-response theory of drive. In M. R. Jones (ed.), *Nebraska symposium on motivation: 1958*. Lincoln, Nebr.: Univ. of Nebraska Press, 1958.

Estes, W. K. The statistical approach to learning theory. In S. Koch (ed.), *Psychology: a study of a science*, Vol. 2. New York: McGraw-Hill, 1959.

Estes, W. K., and Straughan, J. H. Analysis of a verbal conditioning situation in terms of statistical learning theory. *J. Exp. Psychol.*, 1954, 47, 225–234.

Ginsberg, A. Hypothetical constructs and intervening variables. *Psychol. Rev.*, 1954, 61, 119–131.

Grant, D. A. The discrimination of sequences in stimulus events and the transmission of information. *Amer. Psychologist*, 1954, 9, 62–68.

Harlow, H. F. Mice, monkeys, men, and motives. *Psychol. Rev.*, 1953, 60, 23–32.

Howes, D. H., and Solomon, R. L. Visual duration threshold as a function of word-probability. *J. Exp. Psychol.*, 1951, 41, 401–410.

Hutten, E. H. *The language of modern physics*. London: George Allen & Unwin, 1956.

Jeans, Sir James. *An introduction to the kinetic theory of gases*. Cambridge: Cambridge Univ. Press, 1940.

Kendler, H. H. "What is learned?"—a theoretical blind alley. *Psychol. Rev.*, 1952, 59, 269–277.

Kendler, H. H., and Levine, S. Studies on the effects of change of drive: I. From hunger to thirst in a T-maze. *J. Exp. Psychol.*, 1951, 41, 429–436.

Koch, S., Clark L. Hull. In Estes, W. K., et al., *Modern learning theory*. New York: Appleton-Century-Crofts, 1954.

Lewin, K. *Field theory in social science*. New York: Harper, 1951.

Moltz, H. Latent extinction and the fractional anticipatory response mechanism. *Psychol. Rev.*, 1957, 64, 229–241.

Moltz, H., and Maddi, S. R. Reduction of secondary reward value as a function of drive strength during latent extinction. *J. Exp. Psychol.*, 1956, 52, 71–76.

Munitz, M. K. *Space, time and creation*. Glencoe, Ill.: Free Press, 1957 (a).

———, (ed.). *Theories of the universe*. Glencoe, Ill.: Free Press, 1957(b).

Skinner, B. F. Are theories of learning necessary? *Psychol. Rev.*, 1950, 57, 193–216.

Spence, K. W. Theoretical interpretations of learning. In C. P. Stone (ed.), *Comparative psychology*. New York: Prentice-Hall, 1951 (a).

———. Theoretical interpretations of learning. In S. S. Stevens (ed.), *Handbook of experimental psychology*. New York: Wiley, 1951 (b).

———. *Behavior theory and conditioning*. New Haven, Conn.: Yale Univ. Press, 1956.

———. The empirical basis and theoretical structure of psychology. *Philos. Sci.*, 1957, *24*, 97–108.

Staats, A. W., and Staats, C. K. Attitudes established by classical conditioning. *J. Abnorm. Soc. Psychol.*, 1958, *57*, 37–40.

Staats, C. K., and Staats, A. W. Meaning established by classical conditioning. *J. Exp. Psychol.*, 1957, *54*, 74–80.

Toulmin, S. *The philosophy of science*. London: Hutchinson's Univ. Library, 1953.

Underwood, B. J. *Psychological research*. New York: Appleton-Century-Crofts, 1957.

Whittaker, E. T. *The beginning and end of the world*. London: Oxford Univ. Press, 1942.

Wittgenstein, L. *Tractatus logico-philosophicus*. New York: Harcourt, Brace, 1922.

4 | *The Uses and Limitations of Models*

HERBERT A. SIMON[1] AND ALLEN NEWELL

In contemporary usage the term "model" is, I think, simply a synonym for "theory." I am to speak, then, on "Theories: Their Uses and Limitations." This is a topic I can handle very briefly: the uses of theories are obvious, and their only limitations are that they are often bad theories.

However, the persons who arranged this meeting did *not* presumably intend that "model" should mean simply "theory." I suspect—but it is only a suspicion—that by "model" they meant "mathematical theory," and they intended to exhibit in this arena another instalment of the prolonged guerrilla warfare between mathematics and language.

With respect to these hostilities, I have two comments. First, I stand with J. Willard Gibbs: "Mathematics *is* a language"—and, to my ear, the most dulcet of languages. Second, I do not believe that the form in

Reprinted from L. D. White (ed.), *The state of the social sciences*, by permission of The University of Chicago Press. © 1956 by The University of Chicago. Published 1956. Composed and printed by The University of Chicago Press, Chicago, Illinois.

[1] Since most of the notions discussed here are by-products of my collaboration over the past several years with Allen Newell, I have asked him to permit me to present this paper as a joint product—which it is. For infelicities of form and manner, and for downright errors, I alone am responsible.

which we clothe our thoughts is a matter of indifference—or even of taste, as my last comment may seem to imply. It may be true that words without thoughts never to heaven go; but the converse is equally true: wordless thoughts, too, are earthbound. The matter has been put very well by Roget, the author of the *Thesaurus*. In the Introduction to his work he has this (as well as many other wise and even profound things) to say:

> The use of language is not confined to its being the medium through which we communicate our ideas to one another; it fulfills a no less important function as an *instrument of thought;* not being merely its vehicle, but giving it wings for flight. Metaphysicians are agreed that scarcely any of our intellectual operations could be carried on to any considerable extent, without the agency of words. None but those who are conversant with the philosophy of mental phenomena can be aware of the immense influence that is exercised by language in promoting the development of our ideas, in fixing them in the mind, and in detaining them for steady contemplation. Into every process of reasoning language enters as an essential element. Words are the instruments by which we form all our abstractions, by which we fashion and embody our ideas, and by which we are enabled to glide along a series of premises and conclusions with a rapidity so great as to leave in the memory no trace of the successive steps of the process; and we remain unconscious how much we owe to this potent auxiliary of the reasoning faculty.

If we interpret the term "word" literally, then Roget is probably wrong. But if he means that the form of our thought exercises a great control over the course of that thought, he is almost certainly correct.

To select a suitable language with which to wing our thoughts, we must understand what languages there are, and we must be able to compare them. In this paper I should like to discuss three main kinds of scientific languages or theories: the mathematical, the verbal, and the analogical. It will appear from our analysis that these three kinds of theory are really indistinguishable in their important *logical* characteristics; hence, that the choice among them must be based on certain *psychological* criteria. And since analogies, employed as theories, are somewhat less well understood than either verbal or mathematical theories, I shall devote the last part of the paper to two important current uses of analogies.

Before we can plunge into the comparison, however, we will need a clearer understanding of the nature of theory, and of these three types of theory in particular. The next two sections will be devoted to these preliminaries.

Models and the Modeled

It will be convenient for our purposes to define a theory simply as a set of statements or sentences. (They may, of course, be mathematical statements, or equations, instead of verbal statements.) It is important to observe that this definition refers to the form in which the propositions are clothed, that is, the actual explicit statements set forth. Thus, we distinguish the theory, so defined, from its *content*, to be defined next.

By the *content* (or logical content) of a theory I shall mean the totality of the empirical assertions that the theory makes, *explicitly or implicitly*, about the real world phenomena to which it refers. That is, the content of a theory is comprised of all the assertions about the world, whether true or not, that are explicitly stated by the theory or that can logically be inferred from the statements of the theory.

Consider now some body of phenomena, and imagine that there is a theory whose content tells the truth, the whole truth, and nothing but the truth about these phenomena. By this I mean that any statement that is true of the phenomena is stated in or derivable from the theory and that any factual statement contained in or derivable from the theory is true of the phenomena. Then we may define the *content of the body of phenomena* as identical with the total content of this particular theory.

The particular theory I have just mentioned is, of course, non-existent for any actual body of phenomena. The theories that actually occur do not have the same content as the phenomena to which they refer. They do not tell the truth—or at least they do not tell the whole truth and nothing but the truth.

The most conspicuous inadequacy of theories is that they do not tell the whole truth; they have a very much smaller content than the phenomena. Borrowing a term from statistics, we may call these errors of omission "Type I errors." But I think it can be shown that almost all theories also err in the other direction—they say things that are not so, as well as failing to say things that are so. Their errors of commission we may call "Type II errors." To the extent that theories commit errors of Type II—asserting some things besides the truth—they have, of course, a larger total content than the phenomena.[2]

The notion of content that I have introduced relates to the *logical* properties of a theory—to the facts that can be extracted from it by applying the laws of logic. Of at least equal importance to the scientist is its *psychological* or available content—the empirical propositions that the scientist is in fact able to derive from it. One theory can have exactly

---

[2] The ideas discussed in this section have been developed in a somewhat different manner by W. Ross Ashby in his book, *An Introduction to Cybernetics*, in which he discusses the relations among theories and between theories and phenomena by use of the concepts of isomorphism and homomorphism. We are indebted to Dr. Ashby for making his work available to us in preliminary mimeographed form. The printed edition of his book is to appear shortly.

the same logical content as another but be infinitely more valuable than the other if it is stated in such a way as to be easily manipulated, so that its logical content is actually (psychologically) available to the inquirer.

For example, one theory (a trivial one, but one that will illustrate the point) tells me that the number of years from the birth of Christ to the Hegira is DCXXII; and from the birth of Christ to the present, MCMLV. A second theory tells me that the former interval is 622 years; the latter interval, 1,955 years. From the second theory, I deduce readily that it is 1,333 years from the Hegira to the present; from the first theory I also deduce, but much less readily, that the interval from the Hegira to the present is MCCCXXXIII years.

The distinction between the logical and the psychological content of a theory helps us to understand Roget's assertion that language gives thought its wings. Man is not an omniscient logician; he is an information-processing system—and a very limited one, at that. The logical content of a theory is of use to him only to the extent that he can make that content explicit by manipulation of the theory as stated. All mathematics (and verbal logic, to the extent it is rigorous) is one grand tautology. The surprise that is occasioned by the Pythagorean theorem derives from the psychological properties of mathematics—from the new information obtained by processing the explicit statements of the mathematical theory—not from its logic.

Three Kinds of Theories

In the preceding section I have introduced the notion of the content of a theory and the important distinction between logical and psychological content (i.e., between what is inferrable "in principle" and what we can actually succeed in inferring). I have pointed out that theories can and do make errors of omission (Type I errors) and errors of commission (Type II errors). I should now like to characterize several types of theories in the light of these distinctions. I shall use as an example certain phenomena that are of central importance in economics: national income, investment, saving, consumption, and similar variables that occur in "macro-economics." I will distinguish three kinds of theories:

1. VERBAL THEORIES   An example of a statement in such a theory is: "Consumption increases linearly with income, but less than proportionately."

2. MATHEMATICAL THEORIES   The approximately corresponding statement in the mathematical theory is: "$C = a + bY; \ a > 0; \ 0 < b < 1$."

3. ANALOGIES   The idea that the flows of goods and money in an economy are somehow analogical to liquid flows is an old one. There now exists a hydraulic mechanism, the Moniac, designed in England and available in this country through Professor Abba Lerner of Roosevelt College, one part of which is so arranged that, when the level of the colored water in one tube is made to rise, the level in a second tube rises (*ceteris paribus*), but less than proportionately. I cannot "state" this theory here, since its statement is not in words but in water. All I can give is a verbal (or mathematical) theory of the Moniac, which is, in turn, a hydraulic theory of the economy.

The three types of theory I have just illustrated by an economic example could have been equally well illustrated by psychological or sociological examples. Corresponding to Guthrie's verbal learning theory we have Estes' mathematical counterpart, and a number of robots have been constructed by Shannon, Grey Walter, and others incorporating Pavlovian conditioning and associational learning.[3] Homans (*The Human Group*) has constructed a verbal theory of group behavior which I have mathematized. As far as I know, no electromechanical analogue has been constructed, but it would be extremely simple to make one if the task struck anyone's fancy.

Verbal, mathematical, and analogical theories represent, I think, the main kinds of theories there are, but it is of interest to consider a few special cases to see where these fit into the classification.

Geometrical theories appear at first glance to be mathematical theories. Thus, we can represent income and consumption as the abscissa and ordinate, respectively, of a graph, and represent the postulated relation by a straight line with a positive slope of less than 45 degrees cutting the ordinate above the origin. However, if we look at the matter a little more closely, we see that this geometrical theory is really a mechanical analogue of a mathematical theory, for we do not usually employ geometry in a rigorous axiomatic way but instead draw diagrams—which are, of course, actual physical objects in a space that we hope is approximately Euclidean. (For the benefit of non-economists, I should observe that most so-called "non-mathematical" economists are, in fact, mathematical economists who prefer arithmetical and geometrical analogues to algebra, calculus, and set theory. There are few verbal economists in the strict sense.)

Computing machines that have been programmed to represent a particular theory constitute a slightly more complicated case.[4] In a so-called

---

[3] See Robert R. Bush and Frederick Mosteller, *Stochastic Models for Learning* (New York: Wiley, 1955), and W. Grey Walter, *The Living Brain* (New York: Norton, 1953).

[4] To program a computing machine is to instruct it as to what it is to do in sufficient detail (and in an appropriate language) so that it can execute its tasks.

analogue computer there is generally a one-one correspondence between the circuits of the computer, on the one hand, and the equations of a mathematical theory of the phenomena, on the other. In the special case of a simulator there is a direct correspondence between the analogue and the phenomena. In addition to the Moniac, mentioned above, which can be considered a hydraulic simulator, Strotz and others have used electrical analogues to represent the theory of macro-economics.[5]

In the case of the digital computer—of which most modern general-purpose electronic computers are examples—there is no direct correspondence between the computer circuits and particular features of the phenomena. First, a mathematical theory of the phenomena is constructed, and then the computer is programmed to carry out the arithmetic computations called for in the mathematical theory. Thus, the computer is an analogue for the arithmetic process. *This is not, however, the only way of employing digital computing machines as theories*—an important point to which I shall return later.

Verbal and Mathematical Theories

We are now in a position to compare verbal and mathematical theories with respect both to their content and to the availability of that content to the theorist. At the very outset we are confronted with a paradox. It is usually argued that mathematics has certain logical advantages against which must be weighed its psychological disadvantages. A closer examination of the case shows that the truth is almost the exact opposite of this. In the arguments ordinarily used to compare the relative virtues of mathematics and words as languages, we find that the advantage claimed for mathematics is, in fact, largely psychological, while the advantage claimed for words is largely logical.

The mathematician is aware how difficult it is to squeeze more than an infinitesimal part of the logical content out of verbal theories, because of the awkwardness in their manipulation. On the other hand, the verbal theorist (assuming he knows enough mathematics to understand the issues) finds that the logical content of most mathematical theories is quite small compared with the logical content of verbal theories. I do not say that this is the only issue between the mathematician and the non-mathematician, but it is certainly one issue that is often stated explicitly.

Now, I am not a neutral in this particular dispute. I believe that the psychological advantage claimed by mathematics is real and vitally im-

---

[5] See Arnold Tustin, *The Mechanism of Economic Systems* (Cambridge, Mass.: Harvard Univ. Press, 1953).

portant and that the logical advantage claimed for words is often illusory. With respect to the psychological difference—the importance of ease of manipulation—my example of Roman and Arabic numerals will provide, perhaps, some food for thought.

The logical difference—the relative logical content of verbal and mathematical theories—requires additional comment. It can be verified, I think, by the examination of almost any verbal theorizing that makes claims of rigor that only a very small part of the logical content of the theory is or can be employed in the reasoning at anyone time. It is almost impossible to handle more than two or three simultaneous relations in verbal logic. Hence verbal reasoning (i.e., manipulation of theories stated in verbal terms) is replete either with logical gaps, or with *ceteris paribus* assumptions, or with both. For this reason the potential advantage derivable from the rich logical content of verbal theories is almost entirely lost by their intractability. The incompatibility of the theory with the information-processing skills of the scientist makes most of this logical content inaccessible to him.

Let me illustrate. Suppose we wish to theorize about the lynx and rabbit population in Canada. Lynxes eat rabbits; hence, if the lynx population is very large relative to the rabbit population, the latter will presumably decrease. On the other hand, if the rabbit population is too small, the lynxes will have a hard time finding a square meal and will also decrease in number. Now I should like a verbal theorist to predict for me the outcome of this competition. Will the lynx population become extinct, will the rabbit population become extinct, or both? Or will both species increase in number? And, if a large number of squirrels is introduced (which lynxes also like to eat), will the rabbit population increase or decrease?

There is a perfectly good mathematical theory, due principally to Volterra and Lotka (*Elements of Physical Biology*), that answers all these questions in a definite manner. (Roughly, the answer is that under reasonable assumptions there will be cyclical fluctuations in both lynx and rabbit populations; neither will become extinct; and under most assumptions the introduction of squirrels will decrease the rabbit population.) This theory has also been fitted to the data and has been found to hold reasonably well.

Now, of course, the illustration I have used is biological and has nothing to do with social phenomena. But Lewis F. Richardson has produced a mathematical theory of armaments races that is closely analogous to the lynx-rabbit theory. And he has been able to show the conditions under which an armaments race is consistent with peace and the conditions under which it leads to war. Moreover, the theory has been tested, to a certain extent, against data.

Other examples can be supplied;[6] but I do not wish to appear more partisan than I feel. The construction of good theory is such an ardous task at best that it is foolish to tie our hands behind our backs by limiting the range of tools that we utilize.

Of all three types of tools—words, mathematics, and analogies—analogies are perhaps the least frequently used and certainly the most poorly understood. Instead of continuing a discussion of the more familiar verbal and mathematical theories, I should like to turn my attention to the problems and possibilities of making fruitful use of analogy in social science theory.

Analogy as Theory

Analogies are the object of considerable distrust. An important reason for this distrust is that there have been some prominent examples in the not-too-distant past of their gross misuse—for example, Spencer's analogy between society and an organism and his uncritical social Darwinism.

I believe that the usual reason given for distrusting analogies (as contrasted with other theories) refers to logical content: analogies cannot be depended on to tell "nothing but the truth," while theories, it is alleged, can. That is to say, theories may be lacking in content, and hence be guilty of making Type I errors; analogies, on the other hand, have a great deal of content that has no correspondence with the phenomena—their serious errors are of Type II.

It is undoubtedly true—and Spencer's theory is only one of many examples that could be cited—that analogies are particularly susceptible to Type II errors. *But I believe it can be shown that verbal and mathematical theories are also susceptible to such errors.* The exaggerated use of the concept of instinct, for example, that characterized one period in the history of psychology can be traced simply to difficulties in handling the nature-nurture distinction in a verbal theory. The tendency of Freudian theory to proliferate mental entities—the id, the ego, the superego—probably has something to do with the preference of our language for nouns over verbs.

---

[6] I invite comparison of my mathematical "Homans model" ("A Formal Theory of Interaction in Social Groups," *American Sociological Review*, April, 1952) with the verbal theorizing by Henry W. Riecken and George C. Homans on the same subject in the *Handbook of Social Psychology*, ed. Gardner Lindzey, Vol. II, chap. xxii. A similar comparison may be made between the model that Harold Guetzkow and I have constructed of Festinger's theories of social influence ("A Model of Short- and Long-Run Mechanisms Involved in Pressures toward Uniformity in Groups," *Psychological Review*, January, 1955), and the verbal theory of Festinger himself ("Interpersonal Communication in Small Groups," *Journal of Abnormal and Social Psychology*, January, 1951).

Why should theories of all kinds make irrelevant statements—possess properties not shared by the situations they model? The reason is clearest in the case of electromechanical analogues. To operate at all, they have to obey electromechanical laws—they have to be made of something—and at a sufficiently microscopic level these laws will not mirror anything in the reality being pictured. If such analogies serve at all as theories of the phenomena, it is only at a sufficiently high level of aggregation.

A little reflection shows that the same is true of verbal and mathematical theories, but in a more subtle way. These theories must be fitted to a particular computing device—the human brain—and at a sufficiently microscopic level a theory will more closely mirror the neurological and psychological properties of that information-processing system than it will anything to be found in the outside world.

This was observed a long time ago by nominalistic philosophers, who noted that Aristotle's *Prior Analytics* bore a suspicious resemblance to Greek syntax. The same observation is the foundation of Kant's synthetic a priori and of modern phenomenology.

At this point you may wish to object. The theory, you will say, does not consist of the individual letters or words. It is the *meaning* of the statement or equation that contains the theory, not the mounds of ink or the neural circuits that are its physical embodiment.

Even if we were to change our definition of "theory" to agree, the same could then be said of the analogy. It would then not be the water and glass tubes of the Moniac that constituted the theory but rather the relations among variables that these exhibit. If propositions and equations live in the Platonic heaven of ideas, why cannot their earthly representatives be constructed of glass and water as well as of paper and ink?

The truth seems to be that we are accustomed to words and equations as analogies; consequently, we do not often mistake the paper and ink, or even the grammatical structure, for the meanings that are supposed to model the phenomena. Few of us are any longer convinced by the ontological argument—one of the classical Type II errors of verbal theory. Gradually over the centuries we have acquired the sophistication in handling words and equations that is essential to avoid errors of this kind.

We are not so accustomed to non-verbal analogies and particularly to electromechanical ones; hence, we do sometimes mistake the irrelevant properties of the analogy for parts of the theoretical model. But if analogies are intrinsically useful devices as vehicles of theory, this difficulty is certainly one we can learn to overcome.

In specific terms, the argument amounts to this: The content of the theory embodied in the Moniac is identical with the content of the theory embodied in the corresponding set of Keynesian equations or the corresponding set of verbal statements. All three are simplified aggregated theories of the economy, having virtually the same *logical* content. If we have a preference for one of these theories over the others, it must rest not on logical grounds but on information-processing considerations—the relative ease with which the theory can in fact be manipulated in order to extract from it the implicit logical content.

The relative power of words, equations, and computers to convey, psychologically, their logical content has to be determined case by case; and the answer, even in specific applications, may well depend on the time at which it is asked. For the ease with which a mathematical system or an electromechanical analogue can be manipulated will depend heavily upon the current state of the mathematical and computer arts, respectively. (For the last two thousand years no comparable progress has been made in the verbal art.)

I should like to devote the final portion of this paper to a discussion of the probably fruitfulness, as matters stand in the year 1955, of two analogical theories that have recently received considerable attention. These analogies present fresh and novel problems of methodology that should illuminate our general analysis. My first example will be the "natural" analogy—the organism analogy—that has been advanced by the proponents of general systems theory. My second example will be the digital computing machine as an analogy for human thought processes.

General Systems Theory: The Organism as Analogue

The premise that underlies the advocacy of "general systems theory" or "general behavioral systems theory" is that each of the classes of things designated a *system* is an analogy, in significant respects, of each of the other classes.[7] So an organism may be regarded as an analogue to a cell or to an organization, or vice versa. Our question is whether these analogies are likely to be useful, and whether some of the fallacies of earlier theorizing of this kind (e.g., Spencer) can be avoided.

First, let us specify the conditions of the problem. We suppose that there exists a theory, at some stage of development, for each of the classes of things we call "systems." There is a theory of cells, a theory of organisms, a theory of species (meaning by this term an organism and its descendants), a theory of groups, a theory of organizations, and a theory of societies. Each of these theories may include verbal, mathematical, and even electromechanical components. Each theory has a definable logical content.

A general systems theory is feasible to the extent that these several

---

[7] James G. Miller, "Toward a General Theory for the Behavioral Sciences," *American Psychologist*, September, 1955.

theories, as they develop, have common content. This is obvious enough. If there are no statements about cells that are not true also (with appropriate changes in correspondences) of organizations, then a general theory that embraces both classes of systems is simply not feasible. Miller, in his paper at this session, mentions a number of propositions that apply, or might apply, to all classes of systems. As he points out, whether they do in fact apply is a question that has to be answered by empirical research.

But if a general systems theory were feasible, would it be useful? I think this is simply a question of economy of learning, specifically, a question of transfer of training. The relevant questions are these: 1) How easy or difficult is it to set up a correspondence between the elements of, say, an organism and the elements of an organization? How does the effort required compare with the conjectured common content of the two systems? 2) Has one or more of these bodies of theory evolved so much beyond the others that it would prove a cheap mode of discovery to borrow from the former in order to add to the latter?

On the whole, I suppose I am rather skeptical with respect to the first question and a bit more sanguine with respect to the second. This reaction probably reflects little more than my own habits of thought and my desire to appear a man of Aristotelian moderation. However that may be, I remain unconvinced that the common content of the several systems theories is sufficiently great to justify the investment of much effort in the construction of an elaborate formal structure.

Beyond my general doubts, my skepticism has a very specific basis. One of the analogies that general systems theory proposes to encompass is the human organism. The human organism contains as one of its parts the central nervous system, which appears to be a completely general computer capable of constructing any finite proof—hence of imitating any other computing program; hence of serving as analogue for *any* conceivable theory. (Technically, such a general-purpose computer is known as a Turing machine.)

The same thing may be said in another way. Because of the flexibility of the central nervous system, the human organism can in principle be programmed to produce almost any physiologically possible output for almost any stimulus input. It seems unlikely that with this potential flexibility of behavior the analogy of this organism with a cell or even with an organism lacking such a central nervous system can have much content.

Having expressed these doubts as to how far the formal development of a general systems theory can be carried, I do not want to discourage the curiosity of the biologist who wishes to learn about social systems or the social scientist who wishes to study biology. It is probably useful for a scientist who wants to contribute to the theory of one of these systems to familiarize himself with the theories of the others. However incomplete, the analogy certainly has sufficient content to be of great heuristic value. I think I can cite a number of examples where this heuristic value has already been exploited in useful ways:

1. The lynx-rabbit cycle, already discussed, is a case in point. This biological theory was a major stimulus to Richardson's *Generalized Foreign Politics*, a theory of international competition; and it influenced also, directly or indirectly, Rashevsky's theories of social imitation and my own model of the Homans system.

2. W. Ross Ashby's theory of the central nervous system, set forth in his important book, *Design for a Brain*, might be regarded as a form of "neural Darwinism." Dr. Ashby has accomplished a transfer of the principle of natural selection from the theory of species to the theory of cerebral learning.

3. There is a broad class of frequency distributions, often encountered in biological and social data, that are highly skewed and may be regarded as the logarithmic counterparts of the normal, binomial, Poisson, and exponential distributions. The so-called Pareto income distribution in one instance; Fisher's log series distribution, which fits many biological "contagious" phenomena, is another; a third is the log-normal distribution; a fourth is a distribution, applicable for example to city sizes, that I have christened the "Yule distribution" in honor of the statistician who first provided it with a theory. The kinds of probability mechanisms that will generate distributions of these types and the reasons for their frequent occurrence in biology and sociology are beginning to be pretty well understood and will broaden the base of analogy among these phenomena.[8]

4. A final example is provided by information theory, first developed to handle certain problems of coding messages for electrical transmission, which has recently found exciting applications in genetics—specifically in contributing toward an understanding of how genes transmit the characteristics of the organism.

You will note that all the examples I have cited are at a relatively concrete level. They have not involved the construction of a common theory so much as an imaginative use of analogy to suggest special theories. It is perhaps also worth observing that what is transferred in these examples is largely the mathematical frameworks of the theories and only to a slight extent the more special content. I do not believe that there is between Miller and me any difference in principle on this point; there is, perhaps, a difference in strategy and tactics—a difference in the importance we attach to the construction of a formal general systems theory.

---

[8] See "On a Class of Skew Distribution Functions," *Biometrika*, December, 1955.

The Electronic Digital Computer as Analogue

As my final illustration of the relation of analogues to theories, I should like to talk about the fantastic modern toys that have been called "giant brains." Two supposedly fatal objections have been raised against regarding these systems as "brains." The first is that the anatomical structure of the central nervous system is demonstrably quite unlike the wiring diagram of a digital computer. The second is that the computers allegedly cannot do any "thinking" beyond simple arithmetic and that, like clerks and schoolboys, they must be instructed in detail what arithmetic to do.

The first objection is misdirected, and the second is not correct. The first objection rests on the common misconception about the nature of analogies that we have already discussed at length. Although the circuitry of a modern computer is clearly a very poor analogue to the anatomy of the brain, it does not follow at all that this disqualifies the functioning of a programmed computer from serving as an analogue to the processes of human thought.[9]

The usefulness, if there is one, in employing a digital computer as a theory of human thought processes rests not on any supposed similarities of gross anatomy but on the fact that the computer is a Turing machine. It is a general-purpose device that, subject to limits on its speed and memory, can be programmed to imitate the behavior of *any* other system—and, in particular, to imitate human thought. (Lest this statement depress my listeners, let me observe again that a human being is a Turing machine too. In fact, we can assert with considerable conviction that there is nothing a digital computer can do that a human being, given time, patience, and plenty of paper, cannot do also.)

Whether the computer will in fact prove a useful tool for the study of thought depends on whether it is powerful enough for the task within the limits established by time, memory size, and the complexities of programming it. The question, to put it briefly, is whether a computer can learn to play a reasonably good game of chess or to become a geometer at, say, the level of a high-school sophomore; and whether it can acquire and execute these skills using, at least qualitatively the same tricks and devices that humans use.[10]

---

[9] See John von Neumann, "The General and Logical Theory of Automata," in Lloyd A. Jeffress (ed.), *Cerebral Mechanisms in Behavior* (New York: Wiley, 1951).

[10] For an extensive discussion of the problem of programming a computer to learn chess, see Allen Newell, "The Chess Machine: An Example of Dealing with a Complex Task by Adaptation," *Proceedings of the 1955 Western Joint Computer*

The proposal to program a computer to play a game is not new. As a matter of fact, several reasonably powerful checkers-playing programs have already been constructed for digital computers. But in previous attempts of this kind the objective has been to get the machine to play a good game and not to simulate human problem-solving processes. Hence, the rational man of game theory and statistical decision theory (an entirely mythical being) has been taken as the model, instead of the problem-solving organism known to psychologists.[11]

I will not be tempted into a prediction as to how long it will be before we know how to teach these things to a computer. Nor do I wish to enter into the technical problems that are involved. This much I can say with confidence on the basis of some participation in such an undertaking. One cannot think seriously about the problem of programming a computer to learn and to solve problems without gaining very great insights into the ways in which humans learn and solve problems. Regardless of whether this analogy between machine and man can in fact be realized "in the metal," its heuristic value can hardly be exaggerated.

But apart from the heuristic value, what is the particular virtue of the computer analogy? Why not work directly toward a mathematical (or verbal) theory of human problem-solving processes without troubling about electronic computers? If we were sure that the construction of such a mathematical theory were within our powers, the question would have no answer. But it is at least possible, and perhaps even plausible, that we are dealing here with systems of such complexity that we have a greater chance of building a theory by way of the computer program than by a direct attempt at mathematical formulation. Let me indicate why I think this is so.

Remember, the proposal is not to program a computer to play chess but to program it to *learn* to play chess. It can be shown that to program something to learn means to program it to alter and modify its own program and to construct for itself new subprograms.[12] This means that, as the learning process progresses, the activity of the computer will be more and more self-programmed activity. The scientist will be no more aware

---

Conference, pp. 101–08. A remarkable analysis of the problems discussed in these concluding pages will be found in Edwin G. Boring, "Mind and Mechanism," *American Journal of Psychology*, April, 1946.

[11] The important differences between these two creatures are discussed in "A Behavioral Model of Rational Choice," *Quarterly Journal of Economics*, February, 1955; and "Rational Behavior and the Difficulty of the Environment," *Psychological Review*, January, 1956. For an example of a game theoretical approach to the chess machine, see C. E. Shannon, "Programming a Computer to Play Chess," *Philosophical Magazine*, March, 1950.

[12] Self-programming of digital computers has already been achieved at simple and elementary levels and is now a standard part of programming technology.

of the details of the program inside the computer than he is aware of the details of his own thought processes.

Suppose that we could achieve the goal of programming a computer to learn to play chess. How would we use the computer as a theory?[13] First, we would experiment with various modifications of the learning program to see how closely we could simulate in detail the observable phenomena of human problem-solving. The program that achieved this simulation would provide, at a suitable level of aggregation, a theory explaining these observable phenomena and would without doubt suggest a number of crucial experiments.

Second, human beings have great difficulty in introspecting—and particularly in introspecting reliably and comprehensively. The computer, however complex its over-all program, could be programmed to report, in accurate detail, a description of any part of its own computing processes in which we might be interested. Because of this, and because of our exact knowledge of the physical structure of the computer, we could find out directly a great deal more about what was going on in the computer than we are likely ever to find out directly, by introspective techniques at least, about what is going on in the human mind.

Third, it might prove easier to construct a mathematical theory of human problem-solving after we have constructed a mathematical theory of machine problem-solving. Ordinarily, we use a computer when we are confronted with a mathematical theory whose equations are too complicated to be solved explicitly. Then we program the computer as an analogue to the mathematical theory—which is, in turn, an analogue to the phenomena. The present proposal involves a quite different use of the digital computer in theory construction. If a computer were used to simulate human problem-solving activities, the analogy between computer program and the phenomena would be direct. Mathematical theory, as it first enters the picture, enters as a theory of the computer program and hence only indirectly as a theory of the phenomena.

Conclusion: Science as Analogy

The basic postulate underlying this discussion has been that, contrary to general belief, there is no fundamental, "in principle" difference between theories and analogies. All theories are analogies, and all analogies are theories. Two theories are not equivalent for the scientist simply because they have the same logical content. The choice between theories depends critically on the ease with which their logical content can be extracted

---

[13] For a penetrating discussion of the use of a computer as theory, see Walter Pitts, "Comments on Session on Learning Machines," *Proceedings of the 1955 Western Joint Computer Conference*, pp. 106–10.

by the manipulations of information-processing systems operating upon them and the ease with which errors of omission and commission can be detected and avoided. This is the real core of the debate about the relative virtues of mathematical symbols and words as materials of theory.

We must not suppose, simply because verbal and mathematical theories have been with us a long time, that methodology is a static matter—an unchanging substratum for the changing substance of science. Methodology requires a re-examination today, both because of the novel substantive problems that the behavioral sciences face and because of the novel devices that are now available to help us solve these problems.

A theory of man that takes account of his characteristics as an information-processing system is just beginning to emerge. Already, the theory suggests a system exhibiting a degree of complexity with which the sciences—and certainly the behavioral sciences—have not hitherto dealt. Modern electronic computers have been, and continue to be, the important influence, by way of analogy, on the emergence of this theory. If the argument advanced here is correct, these same computing devices may provide us with the materials for a methodology powerful enough to cope with the complexity of the theory as it emerges.

5 | *Men, Machines, and Models*[1]

ALPHONSE CHAPANIS

The history of psychology is a tortuous, winding road stretching back through thousands of years in time. If we look back along it we can make out many instructive features about the road itself, the signs along it, and the terrain and climate through which it has brought us to this present

From A. Chapanis, Men, machines, and models, *Amer. Psychologist*, 1961, *16*, 113–131. Selected portions reprinted by permission of the author, the *American Psychologist*, and the American Psychological Association.

[1] Based on the Presidential Address delivered to the Society of Engineering Psychologists at the sixty-eighth Annual Convention of the American Psychological Association, Chicago, Illinois, September 5, 1960. Preparation of this paper was supported by Contract Nonr-248(55) between the Office of Naval Research and Johns Hopkins University. This is Report No. 11 under that contract. Reproduction in whole or in part is permitted for any purpose of the United States Government.

moment. One thing which interests me greatly is that the highway which we call the history of psychology is littered with the wrecks of discarded models.

Aristotle, that venerable philosopher to whom we trace so much of our ancestry, made eloquent use of physical and mechanical analogies over two thousand years ago. See, for example, how he explains our ability to remember:

> Evidently we must regard this . . . as similar to a painting. For an active stimulus stamps on the soul a sort of imprint of the sensation, analogous to stamping with a seal-ring. For this reason, too, persons who are deeply moved by passion or by ardour of youth do not remember, just as if the effort and the seal were applied to running water. In other persons, because of their worn-out condition, like old buildings, or because of the hardness of their receptive principle, no impression is made (Hammond, 1902, p. 199).

Although it would not serve my purpose to review with you the history of mechanistic models which have been applied to the human organism, it is interesting to see how persistently and regularly they keep reappearing. For example, Descartes, inspired perhaps by the hydraulically operated, moving figures which were then in vogue in some of the public gardens, wrote in 1650:

> It is to be observed that the machine of our bodies is so constructed that all the changes which occur in the motion of the spirits may cause them to open certain pores of the brain rather than others, and, reciprocally, that when any one of these pores is opened in the least degree more or less than is usual by the action of the nerves which serve the senses, this changes somewhat the motion of the spirits, and causes them to be conducted into the muscles which serve to move the body in the way in which it is commonly moved on occasion of such action; so that all the movements which we make without our will contributing thereto . . . depend only on the conformation of our limbs and the course which the spirits, excited by the heat of the heart, naturally follow in the brain, in the nerves, and in the muscles, in the same way that the movement of a watch is produced the force solely of its mainspring and the form of its wheels . . . (Rand, 1912, pp. 172f.).

This was followed almost exactly a century later (1748) by LaMettrie's *L'Homme Machine*, a title which in turn was reincarnated exactly two centuries later in an edition of Carlson and Johnson's (1948) *The Machinery of the Body*.

There appears to be a certain pattern in all this activity. Like Descartes, modelists seem to be inspired by the latest physical theories and playthings of the times. Newton's mechanics brought forth models of man which treated him simply as a machine made up of levers and similar linkages. Watt's steam engine and the development of thermodynamics produced models of man which viewed him as nothing but a complicated heat engine. When servomechanisms mushroomed during World War II we heard that man is nothing but a servosystem. Somewhat more recently communication theory has been translated into models which purport to show that man is only an information-handling system.

THE CONTEMPORARY STATUS OF PSYCHOLOGICAL MODELS   By and large, the very old models of man have been tried, found wanting, and have long since been discarded. They are, to be sure, resurrected and discussed from time to time by the historians of psychology, but in the light of contemporary knowledge they usually appear quaint, naive, and amusing. Even some of the newer models of man have been under test long enough so that they are also beginning to lose some of their original aura and enchantment. The servomodel, for example, about which there was so much written only a decade or two ago, now appears to be headed toward its proper position as a greatly oversimplified, inadequate description of certain restricted aspects of man's behavior. When the model of man as an information-handling system first hit psychology everyone was measuring everything in bits. In today's scientific market, it is becoming apparent that the information model was greatly overvalued.

Despite this sobering history it seems to me that models are flourishing as never before in psychology. Everyone is constructing models of all sorts of things in experimental psychology. Indeed, it is almost as though there was a special form of magic attached to the word "model." Things which 10 years ago would have been identified with more ordinary words like hypothesis, theory, hunch, and empirical equation, are now very often called models simply because it is the thing to do.

Physical analogies are now even firmly implanted in our everyday speech. We say that a person may, at various times, be "all wound up," "tight as a drum," or "breathing fire." His "thread of life" is to some extent dependent on "the wheel of fortune." He works in a "pyramidal organization" and finds himself protected by the "checks and balances of the American Constitution." That such models carry over even into the arts is attested by the title of a recent Broadway hit, *I am a camera.*[2]

MODELS IN OPERATIONS RESEARCH   In this long, colorful, and rich history we can find justification enough for a systematic inquiry into the role of

---

[2] Parenthetically, models are not unidirectional since living organisms are often used as models for physical and mechanical systems. Note that cities "grow," due undoubtedly to the highways which serve as their "arteries." Aircraft, like birds, "fly," and automobiles, like horses, have always had "to be broken in." Satellites come equipped with "eyes," while missiles "seek" and destroy their targets. And, of course, nowadays we have machines which are electronic "brains," and so can "think" and "play" chess. Biological models are also used in the study of larger structures and organizations (see, for example, Haire, 1959). My interest here, however, is in models of biological structures and not in biological models.

models in the development and prosecution of our own specialty. But there is even more reason than this for us to look at models carefully. Engineering psychology, it seems to me, has much in common with operations research (OR), and operations researchers claim that model building is indispensable to the conduct of their work.

Operations researchers are almost as bad as psychologists when they feel impelled, or compelled, to define what it is they do. I use the following definition by Beer (1959, pp. 16f.) primarily because it agrees so closely with my own ideas of what OR is:

Operational research is the attack of modern science on problems of likelihood (accepting mischance) which arise in the management and control of men and machines, materials and money in their natural environment. Its special technique is to invent a strategy of control by measuring, comparing and predicting probable behaviour through a scientific model of a situation.

To examine more closely how engineering psychology and OR overlap would be too much of a diversion for me to undertake here, especially since I have recently had occasion to present my views on this topic in another place (Chapanis, 1961). Nonetheless, I think that most of us would agree that as engineering psychologists we are also concerned with "the management and control of men and machines . . . in their natural environment." To the extent that this is true I feel that the two disciplines have something in common. Moreover, I feel that this affinity will increase, rather than decrease, in the next few decades.

But notice the second sentence of Beer's definition. OR claims that its special technique involves the use of scientific models. If you have ever worked with operations researchers you have already discovered for yourself, I am sure, how much emphasis they put on the construction of models. Ackoff (1956), one of the leaders in the field, has formalized the steps involved in an OR attack on a problem in this way:

1. Formulating the problem
2. Constructing a mathematical model to represent the system under study
3. Deriving a solution from the model
4. Testing the model and the solution derived from it
5. Establishing controls over the solution
6. Putting the solution to work

In contrast to what we see in our sister field of operations research, engineering psychology is characterized by the paucity of its models and by its almost complete avoidance of model building as a method for the solution of its problems. Perhaps it is this state of affairs which led Conover to say recently that in his opinion one of the "most critical problems in human factors today" is the development of a "truly useful mathematical model of human behavior . . . that can be utilized in the analysis of man-machine systems" (Simon, 1959).

This divergence in methods of attacking man-machine problems is so striking that it constitutes another important reason for us to look closely at models in general. Are we overlooking an important technique? What are models anyway? Exactly what functions do they serve? What are some of the dangers involved in their use? These are some of the questions which have motivated me to write about "Men, Machines, and Models." When I have finished I hope that I may have helped you to formulate your own answers to these questions.

What Exactly Are Models?

As a point of departure, let us see if we can find a satisfactory definition of the word "model." Usually when you have the problem of arriving at a precise definition, you turn to a dictionary for help. In this case, unfortunately, that ordinarily reliable standard of English expression turns out to be of singularly little help. *Webster's* unabridged dictionary (Neilson, Knott, and Carhart, 1955), for example, gives fifteen definitions of the word model, none of which seems particularly consonant with the kind of model we mean when we speak of a "man-machine model." Among other things, Webster says that a model may be:

A person who poses
A copy, as "She is the *model* of her mother."
A woman who displays costumes to customers
The original pattern according to which other items are made
A tool used in molding cornices
The curvature in the back and belly of such musical instruments as the violin
An example to be imitated, as a *model wife*
A miniature representation of a thing

Of these possibilities, only the last one mentioned above seems to approximate the sense in which we have used the word model so far. Even in this case, however, it appears that the dictionary definition implies rather concrete *miniature* representations, such as model airplanes, model ships, and the like, rather than the symbolic representations to which the word model is often attached these days.

Another standard reference source, the 1959 *Encyclopaedia Britannica*, contributes little more of value to us. The article on "Models and Model-making" in that work discusses such things as burial models, toys, models in the motion picture industry, models for teaching and recognition training, models of airplanes for wind tunnel tests, and models of factories for testing layouts, lines of flow, and operating efficiency.

Perhaps the most important conclusion to be drawn from this brief excursion into documentation is that the scientific and engineering models with which we are concerned have a very special meaning, a meaning which has not yet found its way into the common English language.

If we turn to the model builders themselves for help in this definitional problem, we find ourselves no less confused. Models, we find from reading the literature, come in a bewildering variety. There are mechanical models, true models, adequate models, distorted models, dissimilar models, static models, dynamic models, structural models, iconic models, analog models, symbolic models, material models, formal models, mathematical models, and analytic models—just to name a few. Some authors avoid the problem. Underwood (1957), for example, starts his discussion of models by saying frankly: "I am not going to state a specific definition . . ." (p. 257). Other more philosophical writers have, frankly, left me floundering in a maelstrom of polysyllabic and largely incomprehensible words. For this reason I have abandoned all prior definitions of the word model in favor of one which makes sense to me. It is this:

Models are analogies.

Scientific or engineering models are representations, or likenesses, of certain aspects of complex events, structures, or systems, made by using symbols or objects which in some way resemble the thing being modeled.

It seems to me that this definition divests the word of much of the magic which seems to have become attached to it recently, and exposes at once the basic strengths and weaknesses of models. It suggests some of the reasons why models are useful in scientific and engineering work, but at the same time hints at some of the dangers and fallacies involved in their construction and use. But first, some amplifying remarks about kinds of models.

ON THE BASIC KINDS OF MODELS   One can find almost as many classifications of models as there are model builders. In an attempt to get at essentials again I would assert that there are only two basic kinds of models: replica models and symbolic models. Although the distinction between the two kinds of models is not always sharp, it is generally possible to classify models as one or the other.

The essential thing about replica models is that they look like the thing being modeled in some respect. I use the words "look like" here in a very loose sense to convey the general idea of a pictorial representation. A globe is a replica model of the earth because, in some respects, it looks like the earth. A model of an atomic submarine is a replica model because it looks like the real thing. Replica models are material models; they are, in short, tangible. Very often a replica model is made with a change in spatial or temporal scale. A replica model of the earth is smaller than the earth itself; a replica model of the atomic structure of uranium, on the other hand, is larger.

Symbolic models are intangible in the sense that they make use of ideas, concepts, and abstract symbols to represent the objects being modeled. The model of man in a closed-loop tracking system (Figure 1) is a

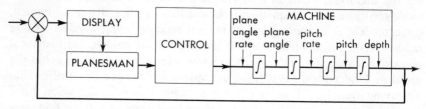

Figure 1.   A symbolic model of a closed-loop tracking system.

symbolic model. The model does not look at all like the real thing. Instead, lines and arrows are used to symbolize, by analogy, the flow of information from one element in the system to another. The major elements of the system are symbolized by blocks, and the movement of the vehicle itself (a submarine in this case) through a fluid medium is symbolized by mathematical symbols, integral signs. As should be apparent, mathematical models form a subclass of symbolic models.

Models may, of course, be mixed, that is, combine both replica and symbolic features. As a model of the earth, a globe is a replica model to the extent that it is spherical in shape and that the land and water masses are correctly scaled on the surface of the model. But a globe contains symbolic features because, for example, color codes are used to represent the depths of the oceans and the heights of land masses.

SOME THINGS THAT ARE AND ARE NOT MODELS   With these definitions before us, we can see that some things which are not called models in human engineering work could properly be so classified. Many types of displays, for example, clearly fall in this category. . . . The graphic panel in the control house, from which the operation of an entire modern oil refinery unit is monitored and controlled, . . . is a true *visual display* in the human engineering sense of the word, but it is also a *model* in our present sense of the word. The panel models or represents the major pieces of equipment in the refinery unit, the direction of flow of hydrocarbons in the interconnecting pipes, and state (temperature, pressure, and rate of flow) of the process at various points. Although the panel contains both replica and symbolic features, the latter predominate.

Some other things which we find commonly in human engineering work are mock-ups, simulators, mannikins, and training devices. All are properly models, according to my way of thinking. That these essential identities are recognized in some other places is shown by the following quotation which I have extracted from Paragraph 3.4.5 of Signal Corps Technical Requirement SCL–1787A, "Human Factors Engineering for Signal Corps Systems and Equipment" (13 April 1959): "Mock-ups shall be employed wherever essential to detail a human task or work-space lay-out. Mock-ups may vary from mathematical models to simple drawings of appropriate scale to three-dimensional simulators. . . ."

The fact that I consider certain visual displays, mock-ups, simulators, etc. to be true models does not mean that I am in favor of our calling them models. Too many things get called models these days and by and large engineering psychologists get along fine with their present system of names. When we consider the advantages and limitations of models later, however, we should keep in mind these models-which-are-not-called-models.

The word model, as I have already intimated, is overworked and I am much more concerned about things which are called models, but should be called other things. According to some of my OR friends, every mathe-matical equation, no matter how simple, and every curve fitted to an em-pirical set of data is a model (see, for example, Naddor, 1960). There is some logic in this position because, as Stevens (1951) points out so capably, the formal rules of mathematics are arbitrary conventions. They constitute a formal model, or rather a set of formal models (because there are different kinds of mathematics in existence) which often can be used to represent some aspect of the empirical world.

Nonetheless, I think it is possible to carry things too far. We have good words—"equations," "empirical equations," "rational equations," "fitted curves," and the like—to refer to many of our symbolic operations and I think there is much to be gained in precision of expression by using them. Recently, for example, I noted a title about a model of hypothesis behavior in discrimination learning (Levine, 1959). When I read the article, how-ever, I was disappointed to find that the author's "model" was primarily an empirical method for solving a set of simultaneous equations. If we were to follow his example we should start identifying as models the nor-mal equations we use for fitting curves by the method of least squares. Such loose and indiscriminate use of the word model is misleading and im-precise. We already have more exact ways of referring to these techniques. In this opinion, I realize that I am almost a lone voice speaking against the *Zeitgeist* of the times. Although I have no hope of reversing the trend, I can at least speak out in protest.

ON MODELS VERSUS THEORIES   There is also, it seems to me, much con-fusion between models and things which a short while ago were more often referred to as generalizations, hypotheses, and theories. In part this situation probably arises because the word theory has so many different connotations.[3] Still there is an essential difference between theory and model, and it is well to keep this distinction in mind.

A model is an analogy and no one expects an analogy to be completely accurate. When we use an electronic computer as a model for the brain, we obviously do not mean that our heads are full of transistors, wires, soldered connections, and magnetic cores. Nor do we believe for a moment that nerve impulses in the brain travel with the speed of electrical impulses in the computer. Neither do we grant that nerve spikes look like or have the manufactured precision of electrical potentials emanating from a power supply. With a model it is not even important that any of these conditions be true, for a model can tolerate a considerable amount of slop. It is only an analogy, a statement that in some ways the thing modeled behaves "like this." Modeling is playing a kind of child's game—a grown-up sophisticated version of a child's game to be sure, but a game nonetheless. The game is called "Make believe."

Theory, on the other hand, is a conceptual system which attempts to describe the real thing. The basic elements, or pieces, of a theory are actually supposed to be there in the thing about which you are theorizing and they are supposed to behave the way the theory says. Whereas a model can tolerate some facts which are clearly not in accord with it, facts which do not agree with theory are fatal to the theory.

This distinction is so important that I want to illustrate with a familiar example: the CIE system[4] of colorimetry. As you know, the CIE system is a valuable tool in engineering psychology for specifying colors, for calculating the transmittance of filters and the reflectance of colored surfaces, and for predicting how certain combinations of filters and lights will look. The xy chromaticity diagram (Figure 2) is a kind of chart or map of color space and is one of the end products of the system. The system is based on what is called a standard observer, a fictitious person whose visual characteristics are shown in Figure 3.

I think we would have to agree that the CIE system is a genuine model, a symbolic model, a mathematical model.[5] From the standpoint of our present discussion, however, perhaps the most important thing to say about the CIE system (or model) is that it is wrong. We have known this for years. It fails, for example, to predict adequately the luminances of highly saturated hues (see, for example, Chapanis and Halsey, 1955). In addition, the visual characteristics of the standard observer (Figure 3) are

---

[3] See, for example, the fine discussion by Boring (1953) on this question.

[4] Commonly referred to by its older designation of ICI system.

[5] Here again I am not proposing that we start calling the CIE system a model; its present title serves very well indeed.

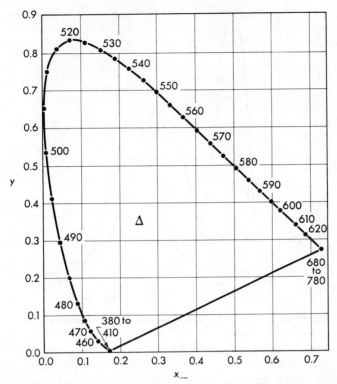

Figure 2.   The CIE *xy* chromaticity diagram.

mathematically derived functions which were arbitrarily contrived to make certain kinds of computations convenient and simple. No one for a moment believes that any real human eye has these characteristics. For these and other reasons, no one today would dignify the CIE system with the title of "a theory of color vision." There are just too many facts which are not in accord with the CIE model. Despite these inadequacies, take note also that there are no serious movements underway to scrap the CIE system. It is far too useful for that. Models, in a word, are judged by criteria of usefulness; theories, by criteria of truthfulness.

What Good Are Models?

Enough now of definition. What good are models? Models, I think, serve a number of useful functions.

MODELS DESCRIBE AND HELP US TO UNDERSTAND COMPLEX SYSTEMS OR EVENTS   First and foremost, models describe complex systems or events in simple terms so that we can more easily understand them. They do this

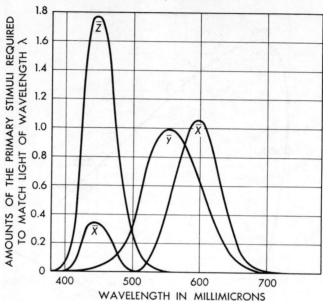

Figure 3.   **Standard CIE tristimulus values of unit energy.**

essentially by replacing intricate and complex systems with simpler and more familiar analogies. In this role models are indispensable teaching aids at every level of instruction from the nursery school through the university. In fact, this use of models is so commonplace and so well accepted that we can easily lose sight of it in any systematic treatment of the subject. Let us look quickly at a few examples.

The precise timing and sequence of events which transpire inside an internal combustion engine can be slowed down in a model so that its action becomes readily comprehensible. The movement of the planets in the skies can be speeded up in a model so that years or even centuries are compressed within reach of the human memory span. Models of the human body help the student to see the intricate organization and arrangement of our internal organs. Models of the earth help the student visualize and understand geodetic relationships with a clarity which mere words or symbols cannot hope to match.

We must not get the idea, however, that models are useful only in describing tangible structures and systems. They can also be used to describe theories, concepts, and ideas. A first-rate example of such an application is Broadbent's (1957) mechanical model for human attention.[6]

_____

[6] Broadbent actually described two models: one for human attention, the other for immediate memory, the latter being a somewhat more complex version of the former. Since both serve the same function, I shall discuss only one of them.

The model consists merely of a Y-shaped tube (Figure 4), mounted vertically, and a set of small balls. Each ball has a number so that it can be readily identified. The Y-tube has a narrow stem which will just take only one ball, though the branches are wider. At the junction of the stem and branches is a hinged flap which normally hangs straight downward, but which can be pivoted about its upper edge so as to close off either branch of the Y.

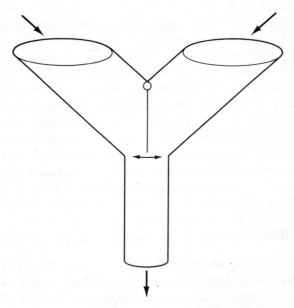

Figure 4.   Broadbent's model of human attention.
(After Broadbent, 1957.)

In this model the balls represent information from various stimuli. The branching arms represent different sensory channels. For example, one arm might be the eyes, the other the ears. Or, one might be one ear, the other the other ear. The bottom of the Y represents a response output, so that the process of dropping a ball into the arms and observing its emergence at the bottom is analogous to that of delivering a stimulus to some sense organ and observing a response.

The action of this model is, in some ways, analogous to the reception and processing of information from various sense channels. For example, if two balls are dropped simultaneously, one into each of the two branches of the Y, they will jam in the junction and neither will go through. This is similar to what sometimes happens when competing pieces of information arrive simultaneously over two different channels (Broadbent, 1952; Poulton, 1953). If, in the model, the hinged flap is used to close off one of the two arms before the balls are dropped, the ball entering the other branch will get through readily. This is roughly comparable to the effect of set introduced by prior instructions in experiments on multichannel listening. To continue, if the two balls are not dropped simultaneously, the first to arrive at the junction will usually push the flap over and emerge successfully. This is similar to what happens when messages do not arrive simultaneously in studies of multichannel listening (Spieth, Curtis, and Webster, 1954).

Some of the other experimental findings which can be simulated in this model are the reception and processing of stimuli of different intensities (Berlyne, 1950; Broadbent, 1954), the reception of information over previously quiet versus previously active channels (Hyman, 1953; Poulton, 1956), the effects of random versus systematic patterns of presentation (Webster and Thompson, 1953), and the effects of various speed and load stresses (Conrad, 1951; Mackworth and Mackworth, 1956).

Let us summarize now what this model does. First, because it is such a simple mechanical analog it helps us understand Broadbent's ·theoretical views on information processing.[7] Second, it is a convenient mnemonic device for recalling and integrating the results of a number of related experiments. It is, in short, a kind of crutch to help us understand and to lead us gently into a more formal, rigorous theory of human information processing. Broadbent himself claims no more for the model than this.

MODELS HELP US LEARN COMPLEX SKILLS   Closely allied to the above is the use of models, or training devices, for teaching specific skills. Models for this purpose range from extremely simple ones (aircraft silhouettes for recognition training) through enormously complex, full-scale models of submarines, control rooms, aircraft cockpits, or control consoles. . . . The brevity of this section should not be taken to mean that this use of models is relatively unimportant, but rather that it is too well-known to merit any extended discussion.

MODELS PROVIDE THE FRAMEWORK WITHIN WHICH EXPERIMENTS ARE DONE
The third role of models is particularly pertinent to engineering psychologists because so much of our research originates from, and is motivated by, real-world problems. What do we do when we do an experiment in

---

[7] In essence, Broadbent feels that the human perceptual system has such a limited capacity that a selective operation must be performed on all inputs to the system. The purpose of the selection operation is to make efficient use of the nervous system by selecting inputs which have much in common, that is, inputs which contribute little new information. The way in which selections are made depends in part on the organism and in part on the input (physical intensity, earliness in time, absence of recent inputs to the channel, rate and pattern of arrivals, and so on).

engineering psychology? We observe some aspect of man-machine inter-action in the real world which looks intriguing and for which we would like to have an empirical answer. We abstract from the real-world situation those variables, independent and dependent, which seem relevant and design an experiment accordingly (Rosenblueth and Wiener, 1945). Sometimes we may even say that we "simulate" the real world in the laboratory; at other times we may say that we use "simulators" in our laboratory experiment. Whatever we say, however, there can be no doubt about one thing: our experimental situation is a model of the real world. To a considerable extent the generality of our experimental findings depends on the fidelity of the model we have made of the real world.

Experiments as models differ from most other kinds of models in at least one important respect. The conclusions drawn from most ordinary models are arrived at by mathematical argument, by the application of formal rules of logic, or by somewhat less rigorous forms of reasoning. The conclusions are *deduced* from the basic concepts, assumptions, relationships, and principles built into the model. It is a tautological technique, because we can get out of the model only what we have already put into it. The conclusions follow inexorably from, and contain no more information than, what we have already put into the model. I like to think of it as something like asking a multiple-choice question. The answer you get is already contained in the question.

When we use experiments as models, however, we interrogate nature for her conclusions. We ask an open-ended question and the answers we can get are almost unlimited in variety.

MODELS HELP US TO SEE NEW RELATIONSHIPS Consider the impact of the information model on psychology (Figure 5). Why has this model had such an influence on contemporary psychology? Is it because we have

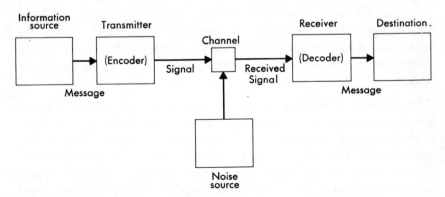

Figure 5.   A symbolic model of a communication system.

never had a model like this before? Not at all. Go back to some old text-books in psychology, before communication theory was born, and you will find diagrams like the one in Figure 5. To be sure you will have to cross out the words in Figure 5, and substitute words like stimulus, re-ceptor, nerve cell, effector, and response. But the diagram, the model, is an old one in psychology. Psychologists have been concerned about the way our sense cells encode information for thousands of years. Although they did not call it "encoding," they have always identified it as a central prob-lem in psychology. Similarly, psychologists have long been worried about the correlation between stimuli and responses, or, if you want to translate this into faddish terms, the information transmitted from input to output. No, I think we have to conclude that the novelty of the model is not what has made it so important.

The real reason for the impact of this model on psychology is that it made us see some old problems in new ways. When information theory was developed and applied to switching networks and to communication systems, it turned out that there was something called channel capacity which described the amount of error-free information that could be trans-mitted over a wire, the air waves, or along a carrier signal. This was some-thing which happened in machines. But since the human operator could be squeezed into the same pattern, an interesting question immediately popped into a lot of heads: "Maybe this channel capacity which we find in machines—maybe there's something like that in people too." And, as you know, this idea has generated a lot of informative research. The idea of the measure of information itself, the idea that information was some-how related to the number of possible alternatives, the concept of re-dundancy—all these came with the model when we borrowed it from the engineers and draped it around our own shoulders.

This role of models in jarring us from our conventional ways of thought (Deutsch, 1948–49) is an important one—especially if these new ways of looking at old problems generate research. The results of research—good data obtained from well-designed experiments—invariably outlive the models which stimulated the research in the first place. If some of us need models to motivate us to do good research, then by all means let us have models!

MODELS HELP US PREDICT WHEN EXPERIMENTS ARE IMPOSSIBLE   Another important use of models is to enable the engineer or investigator to make predictions about complex events when experimentation is either difficult or impossible. This may happen for any of a number of reasons. Some-times the events are so complicated that it would be prohibitively expen-sive to conduct an experiment. A good example would be attempts to test alternative methods of organizing a manufacturing plant. To use rigorous methods of controlled experimentation for such a problem might well exhaust the financial resources of the company.

*   *   *

MODELS ASSIST IN ENGINEERING DESIGN   Models are also extremely useful in many other types of practical design problems. In studying the layout of a factory and the flow of materials in a production process, or the efficient arrangement of men and machines in specialized work areas, models and mock-ups help the designer visualize how the final ensemble will look. Such three-dimensional models are much more powerful than drawings or symbolic representations. Many serious design errors are detected by three-dimensional models even after blueprints and plans have been thoroughly checked and approved.

MODELS AMUSE US   To evaluate properly the role of models in scientific and engineering work the final thing we must do is to recognize clearly that one of the reasons why scientists and engineers spend so much time with them is that they are fun. They are fun to design, fun to build, and fun to look at.[8]

More years ago than I like to remember, I attended my first Annual Meeting of the American Psychological Association while I was still an undergraduate student. The climax of those meetings was Hull's brilliant Presidential Address in which he first enunciated the formal behavior theory which was to have such a profound effect on psychology for the next several decades. In contrast to my memory of it the published version of Hull's address (1937) seems rather dull and dry because, among other things, it makes no mention of the model which he used to illustrate his talk. I can clearly remember the electric effect produced by that demonstration. The model was a suitably impressive collection of wires, lights, switches, and chemicals which, under its master's skillful hand, simulated simple stimulus substitution and forgetting, the effect of the order of stimulation on conditioning, experimental extinction, spontaneous recovery, secondary extinction, irradiation, summation, differentiation, external inhibition, and the redintegration of compound stimuli.

For all its ingenuity, Hull's model,[9] like so many others in psychology, has been long forgotten. Indeed, I have difficulty finding anyone who can

---

[8] Replica models are, I think, interesting and amusing to everyone, whether he be the inventor, an interested bystander, or a casual passer-by. In the case of most mathematical models, however, I am prepared to argue that it is only the inventor who has fun. The task of wading through many recent symbolic models is, in my opinion, tedious, difficult, and generally unrewarding.

[9] Although I speak of it in the singular, Hull's model actually went through some evolutionary changes—see, for example, Hull and Baernstein (1929), Baernstein and Hull (1931), and Kreuger and Hull (1931).

remember seeing it or hearing about it. Now that we have almost three decades' worth of perspective with which to look back on this model, what good was it? It yielded no deductive hunches for experimental test. It provided no new insights into the nature of the conditioned response. In fact, it did not even explain anything. I think the clue to the real function this model served is contained in one sentence which Baernstein and Hull (1931) used when they described it in the literature: "The strikingly mechanical appearance of its behavior [that is, the behavior of the conditioned reflex] offers a challenge to the construction of models which shall display similar characteristics." In short, it is my contention that Hull—an engineer turned psychologist—conceived and carried out the construction of this model primarily for the fun of it.

Let me illustrate my point with one other example, because I think it is important that we be really convinced about this matter. In a fairly recent article Jacobson (1958) describes in great detail the appearance, behavior, and construction of several models simulating a process which, for the moment, I shall not identify. One of these models consists of a large loop of "HO" gauge model railway track (see Figure 6). Inside the loop of track are four sidings. Two kinds of cars, A and B, move along the track. At the start of a demonstration eight cars, four A's and four B's, are placed on the outside loop in a random order. The demonstration starts when the demonstrator pushes a button which sets the eight cars into motion. An elaborate series of levers, switches, magnetic contacts, and

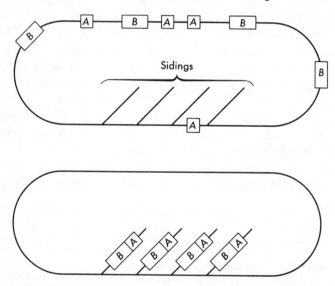

Figure 6.   The initial (above) and terminal (below) arrangement of items in one of Jacobson's (1958) models.

relays then sorts out the cars and distributes them on the four sidings so that at the conclusion of the demonstration each siding contains one A and one B car connected together (see Figure 6).

I have deliberately refrained from telling you what this model simulates, because I have found this a helpful procedure for evaluating models. Give someone a simple description of the model and then have him guess what the model simulates. What do you think?

Since Jacobson is a chemist, one reasonable interpretation might be that his model simulates the attraction of positive to negative ions. Unfortunately, that is not what the model is supposed to show. Another interpretation might be that it simulates the assortative redistribution of teenagers as they prepare to leave for home after a party. Here again, however, I must disappoint you, because this is not a model of social behavior, in the strict sense of that word. No, Jacobson's model is supposed to simulate the union of living cells in the process of reproduction!

Now that the secret is out, what function does this model serve? The analogies between the behavior of the model and that of real-life phenomena are so clearly strained that I do not think we need to take them seriously. Unlike Broadbent's model, Jacobson's contributes nothing to our understanding of reproduction. The author recognizes this himself and spends some time pointing up the deficiencies of his models. If you read the article carefully, however, I am sure that you will be left with the same impression as I was. Implicit in the detailed description of circuitry and mechanical details is the truth of the matter: this model was fun to build! Getting those little railway cars to shunt themselves onto the appropriate sidings was an interesting challenge. In addition, the sight of those toy cars moving around has, in the author's words, "spectator appeal."

I want now to clarify my position on this score. I am *not* against fun. In fact, I approve of it heartily. But in our quest for logical order and rational justification of our scientific behavior, we ought not to lose sight of the fact that much of what we do is motivated by the sheer fun of doing it. Scientists are people, too. Doing experiments, building theories, and constructing models are basically fun, in my opinion. Moreover, I am convinced that scientists often entertain models because their models entertain them. If we can once acknowledge this basic fact of life without feeling guilty, we will not then feel compelled to ascribe an important (and perhaps illusory) purpose to every model we see.

Some Dangers in the Use of Models

For all of their usefulness, models are subject to some extremely important sources of error. Indeed, we should even go further than this and say: *because* models are so useful in engineering and scientific work it is especially important that we recognize clearly what their limitations are. Only in this way can we avoid being trapped or misled into dangerous and fallacious conclusions. Models have so many limitations that it is difficult to know how to classify them. For purposes of exposition, however, I have assembled them under six major headings.

MODELS INVITE OVERGENERALIZATION In my opinion the worst error committed in the name of models is to forget that at best a model represents only a *part*—and usually only a small part—of the thing being modeled. There is an almost universal tendency to suppose that a model, once it is built or formulated, is more than it is. This shows up in many ways. In certain superficial ways the behavior of an electronic digital computer is something like that of the brain. Once we admit so much, the next step is easy. We forget that this is only an analogy and we lapse quickly into calling the computer a "brain." The next step is equally easy. Now we find ourselves saying, and, I am afraid, believing, that the computer *is* a brain. This is just so much rubbish! A computer is no more a brain than the Palomar telescope is an eye, or a bulldozer a muscle.

Models of the human operator can be convenient and useful. But we must remember that any replica or symbolic model of the human operator is at best a coarse and crude approximation of the real thing. The only reasonably accurate model of a human operator is another human operator. Even then everything we have learned as psychologists warns us that one person is not a good model for another unless the two are identical twins.

It is a difficult thing not to be wafted into a distorted world of illusion and hallucination by the heady and intoxicating fragrance of that magic word—model. My antidote is a simple one. Whenever anyone uses the word *model*, I replace it with the word *analogy*. The result is something like a breath of fresh air, or a cold shower, or some strong black coffee, in clearing the murky cobwebs from the discussion. Try it.

There are two other ways of looking at this same difficulty. One is to say that a model always fails to include certain variables and relationships which can be found in the thing modeled. Models are always incomplete. This is one reason why transfer of training is never complete when we go from practice on training devices to the real job. It is also part of the reason why the results of human engineering experiments are always subject to some error when we try to apply them to real situations. We must be sure that important variables in the real world were not overlooked in setting up that model of the real world which we call an experiment.

MODELS ENTICE US INTO COMMITTING A LOGICAL FALLACY Recall for a moment your freshman college course in logic. One of the classical fallacies which appears in almost every textbook of formal logic involves a simple conditional statement: if A then B. Let us assume for the moment that this statement is true. Now let us also assert that B is true. Does this mean that A is true, too?

In its simple symbolic form the fallacy is immediately apparent. But when it appears in the highly disguised form of a mathematical model, the fallacy is not so easily recognized. Let me put it this way. A mathematical model usually starts with a series of variables, constants, and assumed relationships. These are the A's of our conditional statement. From these is then deduced some consequence or some function of the model. This is the B of our conditional statement. If the deduced consequence or function is found to agree with some function in real life (this is asserting the truth of B) we sometimes find the model maker asserting that this proves the validity of the variables, constants, and assumed relationships which he started out with (the A's). Although everyone knows you can never *prove* a theory, it is easy to forget that this axiom is even more pertinent to models.

There are a number of instructive ways of illustrating this danger. Imagine, for example, that we have a box with two input leads and two output leads. We do not know what is inside the box, but we can vary the inputs and measure the outputs. Our eventual aim is to represent the box as an element in a mathematical model. Let me also tell you secretly that the output of the box, y, is linked with the input, x, in the following way:

$$\frac{dy}{dt} + ay = bx \qquad (1)$$

If the investigator guesses that the relationship inside the box is:

$$\frac{dy}{dt} + ay = \beta x \qquad (2)$$

he can test it by applying some selected input values to the box and measuring the resultant outputs. The outcome of such tests would undoubtedly show that Equation 2 fits the empirical points well.

But let us suppose the investigator had started out with the assumption that the equation linking the two is the following:

$$\frac{d^2y}{dt^2} = a\frac{dy}{dt} + \beta y = \gamma \frac{\cdot dx}{dt} + \epsilon x \qquad (3)$$

He would also likely find that there is good agreement between this equation and the performance of the box. Moreover, in the presence of noise and random elements d^2y/dt^2 and γ would not, in general, turn out to be zero. Here then are two different equations each of which might fit a selected set of empirical data quite well. If we now use Equation 3 in a mathematical model we might expose ourselves to serious error. For example, putting a feedback loop around Equation 3 could lead a system engineer to conclude that he is dealing with an unstable servosystem. However, if the true equation is not 3 but 1 the system might in fact be stable. The implications of such an error for engineering psychology I leave to you.

THE RELATIONSHIPS BETWEEN VARIABLES MAY BE INCORRECT   The third reason why models may be in error follows directly from what I have said above. It is that one or more of the functional relationships assumed to hold between critical variables in the model may be incorrect, that is, relationships in the model may not conform to those which actually exist in the object or event being modeled. This danger is one to which models of man are, I think, particularly prone. It is easy to be misled about the way variables are connected in human behavior, even when logic and common sense seem to be on your side (see, for example, Chapanis, 1959, pp. 5 f.).

Peters (1957) has a good illustration of this kind of error. His problem was to determine the effectiveness of a tripwired land-mine system under certain operational conditions. In typical OR fashion an analytic model was constructed to predict the effectiveness of the system as a function of several variables. One important variable was the probability that the tripwire would be seen. It seemed logical to assume that an enemy soldier would be able to see a long tripwire placed across his path much better than a short one. As the length of the tripwire is increased indefinitely, however, the probability of detection should level off at some reasonably high value. Figure 7 shows the relationship which was assumed to hold between length of tripwire and detection probability. The solution derived from the model was that the length of the tripwire should not exceed a certain value.

Since Peters was apparently properly sceptical about models, he ran a carefully controlled experiment to check the assumptions on which this critical relationship was based. A simulated minefield was constructed in a slightly wooded area of heterogeneous background. Tripwires were carefully laid out to simulate what might be expected under combat conditions. Each subject was instructed to search for and to try to find a series of concealed tripwires while following a marked path through the minefield. Five hundred and sixty trials were made with 35 subjects and 16 tripwires of 4 different lengths.

The results of these tests showed that the original formulation based upon logic and common sense was erroneous. The probability of detection did not vary with the length of the tripwire! On the contrary, detec-

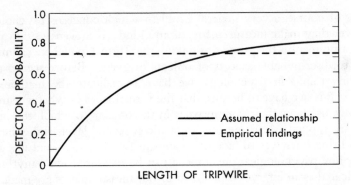

Figure 7. The solid curve shows a relationship between the length of a tripwire and the probability of its detection which was assumed for an OR model of a land-mine system. The dashed line shows the relationship discovered in an experiment on the same problem. (After Peters, 1957.)

tion probability was a constant over the critical range of lengths tested (see Figure 7). Revision of the model to take account of these empirical findings led to an entirely different solution, namely, that the over-all effectiveness of the system could be enhanced by increasing the length of the tripwire substantially.

The example I have quoted above is from a symbolic model, a mathematical model. Similar problems exist in replica models as well. Indeed, engineers know that in making replica models, there must always be some basic distortion of the basic variables (see, for example, Murphy, 1950). It is not sufficient simply to reduce the thing being modeled by some linear scale factor, because this radically alters the relationship between the length, area, and volume of the object. This is often referred to as the "square-cube" law which states that as a body is reduced in size, its area reduces with the square and the volume reduces with the cube of its linear dimension. This, of course, has serious effects on many properties of the model: the rate at which it cools or heats, its stresses and strains in acceleration, and its behavior when moving through liquids. The implications of these distortions for certain human engineering experiments in which scale models are used to represent the human operator are, I think, apparent.

An interesting, and perhaps not entirely trivial, illustration of the operation of this principle is the following: if you make an accurately scaled down model of an electric train, you will find that your model cannot stay on the tracks—the wheel flanges on your model (although accurately scaled) will be too small for the weight and mass of the model.

Underlying all of these considerations are some very basic questions about the validity of the very mathematics we use in our models of man.

This is, of course, a very general problem which concerns psychologists whenever they make measurements of any kind. As Stevens (1951) points out, measurement is the process of linking that formal model we call mathematics to discriminable aspects of objects or events. Before we go about measuring things in psychology we have to validate the mathematical model, that is, we have to be sure that the formal rules of whatever mathematics we use have their counterparts in the objects to which the mathematics are applied. Measurements are made at several levels and, whenever we can bring ourselves to face the issue squarely, we are painfully aware of how few psychological phenomena can be measured with anything as sophisticated as an interval scale. Most of our measurements are made with nothing better than an ordinal scale. This means, of course, that such elementary kinds of mathematical manipulations as addition, subtraction, division, multiplication, differentiation, and integration are not valid for these measurements. It is a humbling thought.

THE CONSTANTS ASSUMED IN THE MODEL MAY BE INCORRECT   The next reason why models may be in error is that the constants assumed for certain parameters in the model may be incorrect. Since these errors are made up in part of simple random errors of measurement, we can never hope to eliminate them completely. The best we can do is to reduce their magnitude to whatever precision is acceptable for the model. Whenever the model involves man and his characteristics, however, there are some other sources of error we must be concerned with. Several writers have already commented on the fact that psychologists have virtually no universal constants to describe human performance. Even when we can find so-called constants of human behavior we almost inevitably find on closer inspection that the constants have been determined for only one or two subjects, for a completely unrepresentative sample of subjects, or for unrealistic conditions. I have already written in detail elsewhere on some of these problems (Chapanis, 1949; 1959, pp. 253 f.). This scarcity of dependable, representative data about human performance will continue to be a source of error in all models involving humans for some time to come.

*   *   *

MODELS ARE TOO OFTEN NOT VALIDATED   Another very serious criticism which can be leveled against many models is that they are not validated, or, if attempts are made to validate them, the procedures used are scientifically valueless. This is not so much a criticism of the models themselves as it is a criticism of the model builders. I am sometimes frankly appalled by the faith which some model builders have in their own powers of analytical and synthetic reasoning when it comes to making models of human behavior. Those of us who have been in the business of human engineering for any length of time can point to any number of instances of poor human engineering design which originated in somebody's carefully reasoned, logical analysis of a work situation. I will state my bias on this score in no uncertain terms: I will gladly exchange 100 well-informed guesses at any time for the results of one carefully executed experiment.

Even when we find model builders attempting to make some validation of their models we sometimes find them using as scientific evidence the crudest form of observations collected under completely uncontrolled conditions. It is as though the Hawthorne experiments[10] had never occurred! Let us take one real example. Once upon a time the problem of traffic delays at toll booths was tackled by some OR people. They constructed a mathematical model, added it, multiplied it, integrated it, differentiated it, and came out with some conclusions about how the toll booths should be manned and operated. Then came the critical part. Is the model any good? Let us take the authors' own words: "The only way to find out was to try it. If it worked continuously for a week, it should be able to work indefinitely." They installed the new system at a toll collecting site and measured traffic flow and some other things for one week. Although the operation of the new system did not conform entirely to expectations there is no doubt that during that week, conditions were better than they had been previously. So say the authors: ". . . there is a good deal of satisfaction in seeing the validity of so much work actually established" (Churchman, Ackoff, and Arnoff, 1957). Please understand me. The authors may well have been correct. Their system may indeed have been better. But you will have to agree that this kind of test is *not* a model of scientific interference.

MODEL BUILDING DIVERTS USEFUL ENERGY INTO NON-PRODUCTIVE ACTIVITY
My final criticism of model building is that the modeler often becomes so intrigued with the formulation of his models that he constructs them for essentially trivial problems. Having at one's disposal a large electronic computing machine, for example, invites one to try out all kinds of things, because computers are such fun to play with. Considering the state of knowledge within psychology, however, the easiest problems to build models for are essentially unimportant problems. If it gives the modeler pleasure, I suppose we should not complain. But it does seem to me sometimes to be such a waste of talent.

So where do we stand now on the question of models? Should we as engineering psychologists model ourselves after our colleagues in operations research? I leave the answer for each of you to decide for himself. My mind is made up.

---

10 See Roethlisberger and Dickson (1939) and especially Chapanis (1959, pp. 73 f.).

References

Ackoff, R. L. The development of operations research as a science. *Operat. Res.*, 1956, *4*, 265–295.

Baernstein, H. D., and Hull, C. L. A mechanical model of the conditioned reflex. *J. Gen. Psychol.*, 1931, *5*, 99–106.

Beer, S. What has cybernetics to do with operational research? *Operat. Res. Quart.*, 1959, *10*, 1–21.

Berlyne, D. E. Stimulus intensity and attention in relation to learning theory. *Quart. J. Exp. Psychol.*, 1950, *2*, 71–75.

Boring, E. G. The rôle of theory in experimental psychology. *Amer. J. Psychol.*, 1953, *66*, 169–184.

Broadbent, D. E. Listening to one of two synchronous messages. *J. Exp. Psychol.*, 1952, *44*, 51–55.

———. Effects of noises of high and low pitch on behavior. *Med. Res. Council Appl. Psychol. Res. Unit Rep.*, 1954, No. APU222/54.

———. A mechanical model for human attention and immediate memory. *Psychol. Rev.*, 1957, *64*, 205–215.

Carlson, A. J., and Johnson, V. *The machinery of the body* (3rd ed.). Chicago: Univ. of Chicago Press, 1948.

Chapanis, A. How we see: a summary of basic principles. In panel on psychology and physiology, Committee on Undersea Warfare, *A survey report on human factors in undersea warfare*. Ch. 1. Washington: National Research Council, 1949.

———. *Research techniques in human engineering*. Baltimore: Johns Hopkins Press, 1959.

———. On some relations between human engineering, operations research and systems engineering. In D. P. Eckman (ed.), *Systems philosophy*. New York: Wiley, 1961.

Chapanis, A., and Halsey, R. A. Luminance of equally bright colors. *J. Opt. Soc. Amer.*, 1955, *45*, 1–6.

Churchman, C. W., Ackoff, R. L., and Arnoff, E. L. *Introduction to operations research*. New York: Wiley, 1957.

Conrad, R. Speed and load stress in a sensori-motor skill. *Brit. J. Industr. Med.*, 1951, *8*, 1–7.

Deutsch, K. W. Some notes on research on the role of models in the natural and social sciences. *Synthese*, 1948–49, 7, 506–533.

Haire, M. Biological models and empirical histories of the growth of organizations. In M. Haire (ed)., *Modern organization theory*. New York: Wiley, 1959, Ch. 10.

Hammond, W. A. *Aristotle's psychology*. New York: Macmillan, 1902.

Hull, C. L. Mind, mechanism, and adaptive behavior. *Psychol. Rev.*, 1937, *44*, 1–32.

Hull, C. L., and Baernstein, H. D. A mechanical parallel to the conditioned reflex. *Science*, 1929, *70*, 14–15.

Hyman, R. Stimulus information as a determinant of reaction time. *J. Exp. Pyschol.*, 1953, *45*, 188–196.

Jacobson, H. On models of reproduction. *Amer. Scient.*, 1958, *46*, 255–284.

Krueger, R. G., and Hull, C. L. An electro-chemical parallel to the conditioned reflex. *J. Gen. Psychol.*, 1931, *5*, 262–269.

Levine, M. A model of hypothesis behavior in discrimination learning set. *Psychol. Rev.*, 1959, *66*, 353–366.

Mackworth, J. F., and Mackworth, N. H. The overlapping of signals for decisions. *Amer. J. Psychol.*, 1956, *69*, 26–47.

Mosbaek, E. J. Economic analysis of repair versus discard alternatives: Polaris fire control system components. *Technical Military Planning Operation Rep.*, 1959. No. RM 59TMP–40. (General Electric Company, Santa Barbara, California)

Murphy, G. *Similitude in engineering*. New York: Ronald Press, 1950.

Naddor, E. Simplified models in operations research. In C. D. Flagle, W. H. Huggins, and R. H. Roy (eds.), *Operations research and systems engineering*. Baltimore: Johns Hopkins Press, 1960, Ch. 8.

Neilson, W. A., Knott, T. A., and Carhart, P. W. (eds.). *Webster's new international dictionary of the English language* (2nd ed., unabridged). Springfield, Mass.: Merriam, 1955.

Peters, G. A. Errors of estimate in operations analysis. *Operat. Res.*, 1957, *5*, 848–851.

Poulton, E. C. Two-channel listening. *J. Exp. Psychol.*, 1953, *46*, 91–96.

———. Listening to overlapping calls. *J. Exp. Psychol.*, 1956, *52*, 334–339.

Rand, B. *The classical psychologists*. New York: Houghton Mifflin, 1912.

Roethlisberger, F. J., and Dickson, W. J. *Management and the worker*. Cambridge, Mass.: Harvard Univ. Press, 1939.

Rosenblueth, A., and Wiener, N. The role of models in science. *Phil. Sci.*, 1945, *12*, 316–321.

Simon, C. W. Human factors research problems. *Hum. Factors Soc. Bull.*, 1959, *2*(12), 16–17.

Spieth, W., Curtis, J. F., and Webster, J. C. Responding to one of two simultaneous messages. *J. Acoust. Soc. Amer.*, 1954, *26*, 391–396.

Stevens, S. S. Mathematics, measurement, and psychophysics. In S. S. Stevens (ed.), *Handbook of experimental psychology*. New York: Wiley, 1951, Ch. 1.

Underwood, B. J. *Psychological research*. New York: Appleton-Century-Crofts, 1957.

Webster, J. C., and Thompson, P. O. Some audio considerations in air control towers. *J. Audio Engng. Soc.*, 1953, *1*, 171–175.

CHAPTER III

Mathematical and Statistical Models

PROBLEMS OF MATHEMATIZATION OF *theory and of measurement have received increasing attention within recent years as psychologists have sought more precise and powerful quantitative tools. The two selections in this chapter are concerned with the special role of models in mathematical and statistical applications.*

Mathematical models, particularly as applied to problems of learning theory, have enjoyed a remarkably rapid development in the past decade or so. William K. Estes has been perhaps the most active of all of the psychologists who have worked in this development. His sketch of the growth of such models is an unusually clear and cogent review of this field. The treatment of mathematical models in Chapter X by Richard Atkinson (Selection 33) should also be noted.

The second selection in this chapter is C. J. Burke's provocative defense of the proposition that measurement models, ordinarily assumed to be fundamental to statistical usages, are really irrelevant to such usages. This paper, in thus attacking certain of the orthodox assumptions which many psychologists have accepted concerning scales and statistics, should lay the groundwork for much discussion and help in the clarification of the issues.

6 | *Growth and Function of Mathematical Models for Learning*

W I L L I A M   K .   E S T E S

Attempts to formulate mathematical descriptions of learning and forgetting are as old as experimental psychology. But for a half-century dating; say, from the work of Ebbinghaus, little issued from these efforts that could be expected to excite wide interest or enthusiasm among students of learning. The status of this line of research at the time when I was a graduate student is epitomized by its treatment in McGeoch's *Psychology of Human Learning* (1942). For my generation of students, as for many to follow, this erudite text was the last word on the subject, without whose support no Ph.D. candidate would dare face preliminary examinations. One could not help noting, even upon the most casual inspection, that all of the material on learning curves and equations was carefully segregated in a special chapter—one which had nothing whatever to do with the rest of the book and was customarily assigned only because it provided such a gold mine of multiple choice questions. (I blush to admit that my own first undergraduate classes were required to master the esoteric terminology of positive and negatively accelerated curves, plateaus, and physiological limits—about as sterile an exercise as could well be devised.) The status of quantitative formulations of learning at that time was succinctly summarized by McGeoch in a footnote (1942, p. 65): ". . . equational statements of learning are of secondary importance to the subject at the present time, although it may confidently be expected that they will become more and more important as the quantification of our knowledge of learning increases."

It will be noted that McGeoch identifies mathematical formulations with equations for learning curves, reflecting accurately the prevailing

From *Current trends in psychological theory*. Pittsburgh: University of Pittsburgh Press, 1961, pp. 134–151. Reprinted by permission of the author and the University of Pittsburgh Press.

viewpoint among psychologists in the early 1940's. In order to illustrate for you the progress that has occurred over a fifty-year period in formulating equations for learning curves, I have assembled a longitudinal sample in Figure 1. The data points represent cumulative errors per trial in a standard paired-associates learning experiment run by B. L. Hopkins and myself (unpublished). The three empirical curves represent the same data

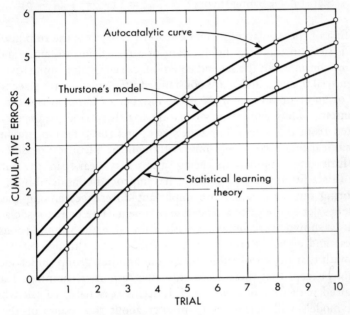

Figure 1. **Three learning functions fitted to the same empirical curve. The upper curves are displaced up the ordinate.**

and have simply been displaced up the ordinate to eliminate overlapping of the theoretical curves. The uppermost of the fitted curves has been computed from the "autocatalytic function" proposed by the chemist T. B. Robertson (1908); the middle curve represents the model advanced by Thurstone in 1930; and the lowermost curve is derived from contemporary statistical learning theory by a line of reasoning that I shall explain a bit later. It is interesting to note that however we measure progress in this area, it is not simply by the accuracy with which theoretical curves fit the data; although differences in goodness of fit among the three plots are difficult to distinguish by eye, the fact is that Robertson's equation provides the best fit of the three by a least squares criterion.

Some differences among the theoretical functions that do not show up in a graphic presentation will become apparent if we inspect the equations of the curves:

$$\text{Robertson:} \quad \log \frac{x}{A - x} = at - b$$

$$\text{Thurstone:} \quad e_n = \frac{n}{a + bn}$$

$$\text{Statistical learning theory:} \quad q_n = (1 - \frac{1}{N})\ (1 - c)^n$$

In the first of these, adapted from Chaisson (1930); x is the response measure;[1] t is time, in this case the duration of a trial being the unit; and A, a,
and b are constants. In the second equation, e_n represents cumulative errors
through trial n, and a and b are constants. In the third q_n represents probability of an error on trial n, N is the number of items in the list, and c
is a constant. Thus Robertson's equation has three free parameters to be
evaluated from the data, Thurstone's two, and the function drawn from
statistical learning theory only one. Although the adequacy of description
differs little among models appearing over a fifty-year span, the output in
terms of data fitted per free constant has improved considerably.

To bring out some still more important differences among the three
approaches, let us consider a related experiment. The paired-associate data
previously shown were obtained with a list of eight stimuli (consonant
syllables) and eight different responses (numbers 1 through 8). Concur-
rently with that group of subjects, we ran another group under identical
conditions except that there were only two responses (numbers 1 and 2)
each paired with four of the stimuli. It seems reasonable to ask what the
various models will permit us to predict about the results of the two-
response group, given the data for the eight-response group. For the first
model the answer is simple—nothing. Robertson's equation includes three
constants that must be evaluated by curve-fitting methods for each set of
data the equation is applied to; before it can be used to describe the two-
response data, the values of the constants must be re-evaluated for those
data; possibly some of them would turn out to have the same values, but
there is no underlying rationale to specify which, if any, should carry
over to the new condition and therefore no predictions can be made.

In Thurstone's model, an attempt has been made to provide the missing
psychological rationale. Thurstone conceived learning to be a process of
sampling from a population of acts, some correct and some incorrect for
any given task, with the successful acts being retained and the unsuccessful
ones having some fixed probability of elimination on each trial. In the

---

[1] To calculate the plotted curves, $(A - x)/A$ has been taken to represent probability of an incorrect response, and the function has been integrated over time with
this quantity as the dependent variable.

equation shown, the parameter b is assumed to vary inversely with the total number of available acts, and therefore with difficulty of the task. Thus one might hope that by making some simple adjustment in the value of the b constant, while holding the other constant fixed, one could generate a prediction for the two-response condition. However, according to my calculations, no such procedure yields a satisfactory prediction in the present case.

In the case of the statistical model, there is even more underlying theory, and consequently fewer degrees of freedom in carrying over the equation to a new situation. The principal assumption is that each stimulus and its correct response become associated on an all-or-none basis. The parameter c represents the probability that any one stimulus will become associated with its correct response on any given trial (if learning has not previously occurred). Therefore, the term $(1 - c)^n$ in the equation is simply the probability that any given item is still unlearned after n training trials. When the correct response to a particular stimulus has not yet been learned, the subject may still get a correct response by guessing, and the probability of doing so is $1/N$ (on the simplest assumptions). Therefore, the probability that a subject will fail to get any given item right on a test after n training trials is $\left(1 - \dfrac{1}{N} \right) (1 - c)^n$, and by summing this expression over trials we obtain the desired curve for cumulative errors. There is only one free constant, c, and once it has been evaluated for this experimental situation and population of subjects from the eight-response curve, we should be able to predict the curve for the two-response group simply by replacing ⅛ by ½ in the factor $\left(1 - \dfrac{1}{N} \right)$ representing the guessing allowance. The result of doing this is shown in Figure 2. The upper curve simply reproduces the one shown before for the eight-response condition. The lower curve shows how well we have been able to predict the results of the two-response condition by means of an equation which uses *none* of the two-response data for curve-fitting.

There is still another difference among the three developmental stages in quantitative theorizing that is worth mention. It concerns not the models per se but the purposes they serve. In the earliest period, the question at issue was simply that of whether equations, *any* equations, could be found that would describe the course of learning in standard experimental situations. By 1930, not only had this question been answered, but in fact an inconveniently large number of equations had been proposed, all with much the same ability to fit "typical" learning curves. In order to obtain any differential evaluations among them it was necessary to go deeper than the surface of the graph paper. The first substantial move in this

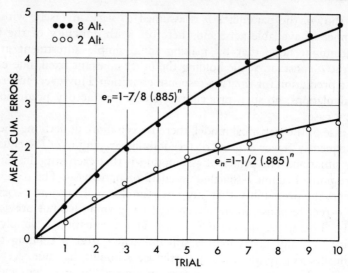

Figure 2. Equation derived from statistical learning theory fitted to data from paired-associate with eight stimuli and either eight responses (upper curve) or two responses (lower curve). The slope parameter was evaluated from the eight-response data only.

direction was taken by Thurstone, who set himself the task of finding plausible psychological assumptions from which one could deduce equations for learning curves. His apparently promising start did not come to immediate fruition, perhaps simply because Thurstone's theoretical work was not associated with an active experimental program; but progress during subsequent years has begun to show an encouraging tendency to follow the same autocatalytic function that the early quantifiers thought they saw mirrored in the performance of individual subjects. The "learning curve" for this line of endeavor shows no signs of approaching an asymptote, but it has reached a point at which we can afford to divide our attention between continuing efforts to improve our formulations and explorations of the utility that models already in hand may be prepared to offer in the service of other theoretical objectives.

One of the main functions of mathematical models, once they have attained some standing as descriptive devices, is to serve as tools to aid in testing substantive theories and hypotheses. The case of two-vs.-eight response alternatives in the paired-associate problem illustrates this point. The data shown in Figure 2 were not collected for purposes of testing the model. A number of previous studies had provided adequate evidence that the model yields a serviceable description of paired-associate learning under any one set of conditions. What we were concerned with was the role of number of alternatives as an independent variable. The few studies dealing with this variable had reported faster learning with fewer alternatives. However, we felt that none had fully controlled for the differential guessing allowances associated with differing numbers of responses and that consequently there had been no critical test of the hypothesis that learning is basically identical, and proceeds at the same rate, regardless of the number of alternatives. I do not mean to criticize the previous investigators; for the fact is that in the absence of a theory no suitable allowance for the guessing factor can be made. Guessing occurs only on unlearned items, and there is no way to tell by direct observation just how many items have been learned and how many have been guessed correctly on any given trial. With the aid of the model, we can make an exact estimate of the contribution of learning and guessing at every point of the performance curve, and thus evaluate the c parameter which represents rate of learning. Then if our assumptions are correct, the rate of learning will be the same when the number of alternatives is changed, and we can predict the result of this manipulation in advance by combining our estimate of learning rate with a new guessing allowance. As you have seen in the last figure, our data proved to support the hypothesis that rate of learning is independent of the number of alternatives. This is just one example of the type of case in which a model for learning serves the experimenter by helping him evaluate or partial out the effects of variables that cannot be separated by direct manipulation.

An important factor in making it possible for contemporary models to begin rendering these service functions is that, unlike earlier models which assumed a particular form for "the learning curve," the more recent ones typically express assumptions in the form of mathematical operators describing changes in response tendencies on single trials. Given the assumptions of a theory in the latter form, curves can be deduced for an infinite variety of experiments run with differing initial and boundary conditions. One main branch of research in mathematical learning theory (e.g., Bush and Mosteller, 1955; Burke and Estes, 1957; Bush and Estes, 1959, Part II) is concerned with deriving a body of theorems and formulas that follow from the assumption that learning on any one trial is described by a simple linear transformation of the response probabilities. These "linear models" are primarily descriptive, but they may also serve explanatory functions. Not explanation, as psychologists most often think of it, in terms of hypothetical neural mechanisms, but explanation of a sort familiar in physical science which accounts for the course of a process over a period of time by showing it to be a result of simple effects of variables operating on single trials. A contemporary illustration in psychology is afforded by an episode that may appropriately be termed "the case of the irrational rats."

The facts of the case are in essence that rats offered repeated trials in a T-maze with, e.g., .75–.25 probabilities of reward on the two sides, show remarkable ingenuity in avoiding the optimal strategy of always choosing the more frequently rewarded side. With a procedure that permits the animal to correct errors, several investigators (Brunswik, 1939; Estes and Lauer, cited in Estes, 1959; Parducci and Polt, 1958; Hickson, 1959) have found that probability of a given response tends to approach the probability of reward.

When animals are run under similar reward schedules except for a non-correction procedure, so that some trials go entirely unrewarded, the results are quite different. The majority of animals come to choose the more frequently rewarded side virtually 100 per cent of the time, while a few become equally fixated on the less favorable side. A typical result is that of Hickson and Carterette (1955); over the last 16 daily trials of a 56-day series run with a .75–.25 noncorrection schedule, they found that of a group of eleven rats, eight went 16 times and one 15 to the .75 side while the remaining two went 14 and 16 times to the .25 side. Clearly, what one would usually think of as a minor difference in procedure leads to a rather striking difference in results. And in neither the correction nor the noncorrection case does the outcome agree entirely with expectation based on traditional law of effect theory.

To analyze this two-choice situation in terms of the linear model, we consider the various types of trial outcomes that may arise; letting L and R designate responses and rewards on the left and right sides of the T-maze, p the probability of a left choice, and θ $(0 \leq \theta \leq 1)$ the learning rate parameter, these can be summarized as follows for the experiment with correction procedure:

Choice	Reward	New Probability of L Choice
L	L	
R	L	$p + \theta(1 - p)$
L	R	
R	R	$p - \theta_p$

The basis for the right-hand column is, of course, the usual assumption that reward on a given side increases the probability of that choice and decreases the probability of the other choice. The formulas given here for the new probabilities following rewards on either side are not the only ones that have been used in recent researches, but they are the simplest and will suffice for our purposes. Considering this schema, it is easy to see why, if the formulas are even approximately correct, the rats do not maximize their incomes by going always to the more frequently rewarded side when reward possibilities are intermediate between zero and unity.

If, say, probabilities of reward on the left and right are .75–.25, the probability of a left choice will be more often moved toward unity than toward zero, and thus, if it starts near .50, will initially start to drift toward unity. But even if p is brought near unity by an unusually long sequence of rewards on the left, eventually rewards will occur on the right and p will be driven back toward zero. Since on the average increments occur three times as often as decrements under this schedule, it seems intuitively reasonable that after a sufficient number of trials p will be found fluctuating around a mean value of .75, and this is what the model predicts.

Under a noncorrection procedure, the effects of rewarded trials must be assumed to be the same as under the correction procedure, but we now have also nonrewarded trials to contend with. There is considerable evidence from studies of partial reinforcement in the runway and T-maze to indicate that after a reasonably long partial series, a nonrewarded trial has very little effect on response probability (see, e.g., Weinstock, 1954). Thus we would expect that at least over the portion of an experiment for which asymptotic data are collected, the effects of reward and nonreward will be approximated by the following set of operators:

Choice	Reward	New Probability of L Choice
L	L	$p + \theta(1 - p)$
L	None ⎫	p
R	None ⎭	
R	R	$p - \theta_p$

The probability at the beginning of a trial, p, would be increased by a reward, decreased by reward on the opposite side, and left unchanged by nonreward. Now under a .75–.25 schedule, p will again tend on the average to drift toward unity; but here the similarity to the other case ends. If under this procedure p reaches unity,[2] no further rewards can occur on the right side to drive it away; similarly, if under a run of ill fortune (from the rat's point of view) p drops to zero, no further rewards on the left can occur and the animal will be expected to remain fixated on the right side even though this yields a much less than optimal return in terms of rewards per run. Predicting the exact proportion of animals that will be "absorbed" at unity rather than at zero, starting from any given initial probability, is a matter of considerable mathematical difficulty (see Bush and Estes, 1959, Part II), but it is safe to say that under the conditions of

---

[2] Strictly speaking, a linear model (Bush and Estes, 1959, Part II; Bush and Mosteller, 1955), as distinguished from a stimulus sampling model (Burke and Estes, 1957; Bush and Estes, 1959, Part I), does not permit p actually to reach unity; however, p may come so close to unity that the probability of its ever again decreasing is negligible.

initial probability and reward probability characterizing most studies that have been reported, a high percentage of animals should be predicted to end up choosing the more frequently rewarded side all of the time.

We recognize that the task of explanation is not complete for this class of experiments. We still would like to know, for example, precisely why the effect of nonreward changes during a partially reinforced series so that eventually nonreward is virtually neutral in its effects while at the same time the effect of reward remains essentially constant. But even while we continue looking for answers to these deeper questions, we may feel that our mathematical models have shed considerable light on a puzzling set of experimental results concerning matching and maximizing under partial reinforcement schedules.

Although we have not explicitly mentioned it so far, a noteworthy characteristic distinguishing the contemporary mathematical models we have considered both from earlier ones and from such theories as those of Hull (1943) and Hebb (1949), is the strategy of operating almost exclusively at the level of observable events. The probabilistic models for paired-associate learning and for maze learning have relied on careful analyses of observable stimulus and response variables in these situations and on assumptions formulated in terms of changes in probabilities of these variables as a function of reinforcing operations. It would be premature, however, to leap to the conclusion that the trend in the development of mathematical learning theory is toward complete elimination of any reference to unobservables, i.e., inferred or assumed events, or constructs. The fact seems to be that for any limited empirical area, taken by itself, hypothetical entities or mechanisms have trouble proving their worth and usually turn out to be clearly dispensable. Sometimes they play a useful role in suggesting the form of laws or models, but once the latter become operational, the hypothetical constructs can be discarded, much like the scaffolding after completion of a building. Only when we wish to bridge the gap between superficially distinct problem areas and to integrate hitherto unrelated findings do we find that interpretations in terms of hypothetical, "molecular" events turn out to be of critical importance. To illustrate this point, we turn to a final example of current mathematical theorizing, this time one beginning with the problem of retention and transfer but ending in an area customarily falling under quite a different chapter heading.

By reference to Figure 3 we can conveniently review the principal assumptions of a statistical model for stimulus fluctuation that have been applied to a number of studies of retention and transfer (e.g., Homme, 1956; Frankmann, 1957; McConnell, 1959) since its original publication a few years ago (Estes, 1955). The set-theoretical schema shown in this

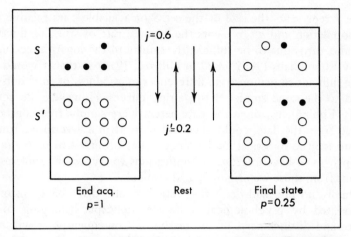

Figure 3. Theoretical schema from stimulus fluctuation model for retention loss following an acquisition period. Filled circles represent elements conditioned and open circles elements unconditioned to the reinforced response. Subsets S and S′, respectively, represent elements that are or are not available for sampling during a given period.

figure conceptualizes the idea that within any experimental situation there is constant, random fluctuation over any period of time in the particular stimulus components, or cues, that are available for sampling by the organism. If one of the rectangles shown in the figure is taken to represent the population of all stimuli, internal as well as external in origin, that may be available for sampling by the subject at any time during an experiment, then the portion, labeled S, above the horizontal dividing line corresponds to the cues that are available for sampling during a given short experimental period, and the portion below corresponds to the part of the stimulus population that is temporarily unavailable. The left-hand rectangle illustrates the state of affairs at the end of an acquisition period. The cues available during this period, represented by filled circles, are all conditioned, but those in the unavailable set, S′, represented by open circles, are not. Although the probability of the learned response has reached unity in this situation, it does not remain at this level, for during a subsequent rest interval, stimulus elements fluctuate back and forth between S and S′, eventually approaching an equilibrium condition in which the proportion of conditioned cues in the available set S is equal to the proportion in the whole population. From our statistical assumptions it is not difficult to derive an equation for the predicted curve of forgetting (Estes, 1955). This equation,

$$p_t = J + (1 - J)a^t,$$

Where J represents the size of the set S of available cues relative to the total population and a represents the average rate of stimulus fluctuation over time, turns out to be sufficiently similar to the logarithmic function used by Ebbinghaus (1885; cited in Hilgard, 1956) so that it would probably be difficult to demonstrate differences in goodness of fit if both were applied to the same empirical forgetting curves. However, the equation used by Ebbinghaus, since the parameters were simply free constants to be fitted from the data, could never fill more than a descriptive function. By contrast, the statistical model, once it has occurred to us to look for them, proves to have interesting implications for types of problems quite different from those we originally had in mind.

Certainly no one will deny that retention and drive have customarily been treated by psychological writers as concepts belonging to quite separate and distinct parts of the textbook. Consequently, it will not be particularly surprising that we had worked with the model in relation to distributional phenomena and the like for quite some time before the idea emerged of considering its implications for problems of motivation and drive. Once the possibility of a theoretical connection between these areas is suggested, however, it immediately seems quite appealing. One of the oldest, and in my view most underestimated, interpretations of the relation between motivation and learning is that of drive stimuli. But the most distinctive property of these stimuli is that the probabilities vary systematically with time during periods of deprivation. What is more natural, then, than that the stimulus fluctuation model should provide a conceptual tool for investigating the consequences of our assumptions about drive stimuli?

To see how such an investigation works out, we may turn to the theoretical schema shown in Figure 4. The assumptions underlying this analysis have been presented in more detail elsewhere (Estes, 1958) and I shall summarize them here in rather *simplified* form.

The rectangles in the figure may be taken to represent the set of drive stimuli associated with a given experimental situation: to be concrete, let us say they are all the cues whose sampling probabilities vary systematically with food deprivation. At t_1 the majority of these drive stimuli have been made unavailable as a result of a recent period of satiation. Over a subsequent period of time, stimulus fluctuation occurs; since the stimulus sources that produce satiation are not operative during the deprivation period, elements are more likely to enter than to leave the available set (S in Figure 3) and it increases in size, as we have illustrated in the change from t_1 to t_2. The diagram is intended to represent an experiment in which a series of learning trials is given with t_1 as the deprivation time, then, after a rest interval during which deprivation continues, additional trials are given at the higher deprivation, t_2. Within each series, the proportion of conditioned cues in the available set increases, as indicated by the increas-

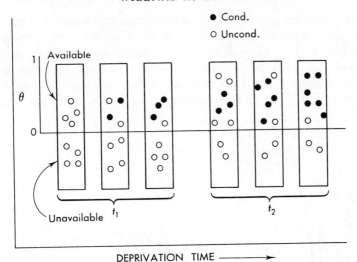

Figure 4. Theoretical schema for learning series under a low drive followed by shift to a higher drive. The parameter θ represents sampling probability for elements that are in the available set during a given period.

ing number of filled circles. Immediately after the shift in deprivation time, however, the proportion of conditioned cues available drops, leading in turn to a drop in expected response probability, before continuing to increase under the influence of additional reinforced trials. These notions lead to predictive equations for both pre- and postshift phases of an experiment in which deprivation time is abruptly changed either upward or downward, after the learning curve has reached an asymptote under the first condition.

Initial learning:

$$p_{n_1} = \frac{w[1 - (1 - \theta_1)^{n_1 - 1}]}{w_1 + w_e}$$

Postshift learning:

$$p_{n_1 + n_2} = \frac{f_{12}w_2(1 - f_{12})[1 - (1 - \theta_2)^{n_2 - 1}]}{w_2 + w_e}$$

In these equations, the subscripts 1 and 2 refer to the preshift and postshift phases, respectively. The parameters w_1 and w_2 represent the weights of the available sets of drive stimuli during the two phases, "weight" of a set being defined as the number of elements multiplied by the average sampling probability; w_e is the weight of any unconditioned extraneous or "background" cues present in the experimental situation; f_{12} is the proportion of elements that the two sets of drive stimuli have in common; and the factor $[1 - (1 - \theta_1)^{n_1-1}]$ is the probability that any available stimulus element will be conditioned to the reinforced response by the n_1th trial of phase 1. Some implications of these equations are illustrated in Figure 5. The first point of interest is the divergence of the learning

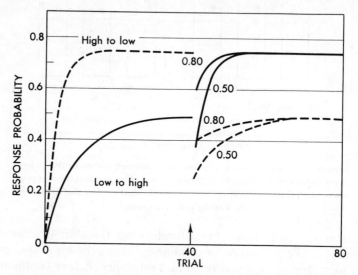

Figure 5. Illustrative curves showing predicted course of learning in groups shifted from high to low, or low to high, drives after reaching asymptote under the first condition. The parameter of the postshift curves is proportion of overlap between the high-drive and low-drive stimulus sets.

curves for low and high drive conditions during phase 1; this picture, which has been realized in numerous experimental studies (Estes, 1958; Spence, 1958), has been one of the chief lines of evidence taken to support the Hullian conception of drive (*D*) as an energizing factor. The results of our analysis show clearly, however, that the divergence of high- and low-drive curves cannot be considered to favor the *D* concept over the drive-stimulus concept. On the other hand, the two conceptions differ in their predictions about behavior following a shift in drive level. Hull's *D* factor, taken alone, would lead to the prediction that, under the conditions assumed in this example, response probability following a shift up or down should change instantaneously to the new level appropriate to the post-shift drive. According to the drive stimulus theory, a shift from high to low drive should be followed by an abrupt drop to a point *below* the low-drive asymptote, then a gradual increase with continued reinforcement until the low-drive asymptote is reached. Depending on the amount of overlap between the low-drive and high-drive stimulus sets, a shift from low to high drive may be followed by either a drop or a jump in response probability, in either case followed by a gradual increase to the high-drive asymptote. If, however, additional shifts are given after the subjects have again reached asymptote (so that all of the elements in both sets of drive stimuli have become conditioned to the reinforced response), response probability should change immediately and discontinuously to the appropriate postshift asymptote following each drive shift. Thus we see that, under certain conditions at least, all of the phenomena that have customarily served to support the concept of drive as an energizing factor are predictable from a theory of drive stimuli. Accurate quantitative determinations of response probability as a function of changes in drive level will be required in order to determine whether there are *any* phenomena that require the postulation of a *D* factor.

Here we must leave the story hanging in air, for to my knowledge the extensive literature on drive and learning includes no studies that are suitable for testing our predictions in all details. Perhaps this is not a bad denouement, for my purpose has been not to pass judgment on the *D* concept, but only to illustrate the way in which mathematical models are outgrowing the status of an isolated stepchild and are becoming inextricably bound up with other developments in learning theory. In the case of drive shifts, particularly, it would seem discrete to postpone evaluations until someone has gotten around to performing the indicated experiments. What does seem clear at this point is that the mathematical model has at least served the function of setting the stage for sharper differential testing of "drive as stimulus" vs. "drive as energizer." And, on the assumption that incompleted tasks are the best remembered, this may be a strategic point at which to close the present exposition.

References

Brunswik, E. Probability as a determiner of rat behavior. *J. Exp. Psychol.*, 1939, *25*, 175–197.

Burke, C. J., and Estes, W. K. A component model for stimulus variables in discriminating learning. *Psychometrika*, 1957, 22, 133–145.

Bush, R. R., and Estes, W. K. *Studies in mathematical learning theory*. Stanford, Calif.: Stanford Univ. Press, 1959.

Bush, R. R., and Mosteller, F. *Stochastic models for learning*. New York: Wiley, 1955.

Chaisson, A. F. An alternative approach to the mathematical study of learning curves. *J. Gen. Psychol.*, 1930, *4*, 352–359.

Ebbinghaus, H. (1885) *Memory*. Trans. by H. A. Ruger and C. E. Busenius. New York: Teachers College, 1913.

Estes, W. K. Statistical theory of spontaneous recovery and regression. *Psychol. Rev.*, 1955, *62*, 145–154.

——. Stimulus-response theory of drive. In *Nebraska Symposium on Motivation*. Lincoln, Nebr.: Univ. of Nebraska Press, 1958.

——. The statistical approach to learning theory. In S. Koch (ed.), *Psychology: a study of a science*, Vol. II. New York: McGraw-Hill, 1959.

Frankmann, J. P. Effect of amount of interpolated learning and time interval before test on retention in rats. *J. Exp. Psychol.*, 1957, *54*, 462–466.

Hebb, D. O. *Organization of behavior*. New York: Wiley, 1949.

Hickson, R. H. Response probability in a two-choice learning situation with varying probability of reinforcement. Unpublished doctoral dissertation, Univ. of Indiana, 1959.

Hickson, R. H., and Carterette, T. Asymptotic response probability under two conditions of random reinforcement, using a non-correction procedure. Paper given at MPA meetings, 1955.

Hilgard, E. R. *Theories of learning* (2nd ed.). New York: Appleton-Century-Crofts, 1956.

Homme, L. E. Spontaneous recovery and statistical learning theory. *J. Exp. Psychol.*, 1956, *51*, 205–212.

Hull, C. L. *Principles of behavior*. New York: Appleton-Century-Crofts, 1943.

McConnell, D. G. Spontaneous regression and recovery in a sequence of discrimination periods. *J. Exp. Psychol.*, 1959, *57*, 121–129.

McGeoch, J. A. *The psychology of human learning*. New York: Longmans, Green, 1942.

Parducci, A., and Polt, J. Correction vs. noncorrection with changing reinforcement schedules. *J. Comp. Physiol. Psychol.*, 1958, *51*, 492–499.

Ramond, C. K. Performance in selective learning as a function of hunger. *J. Exp. Psychol.*, 1954, *48*, 265–270.

Robertson, T. B. Sur la dynamique chimique de system nerveux central. *Arch. Int. de Physiol.*, 1908, *6*, 388–454.

Spence, K. W. Behavior theory and selective learning. In *Nebraska Symposium on Motivation*. Lincoln, Nebr.: Univ. of Nebraska Press, 1958.

Thurston, L. L. The learning function. *J. Gen. Psychol.*, 1930, *3*, 469–493.

Weinstock, S. W. Resistance to extinction of a running response following partial reinforcement under widely spaced trials. *J. Comp. Physiol. Psychol.*, 1954, *47*, 318–322.

7 | *Measurement Scales and Statistical Models*

CLETUS J. BURKE

During the past fifteen or twenty years, there have been several flurries of papers about issues related to statistics and measurement. A controversy has arisen over the interrelations of statistics and measurement; the two opposed viewpoints can be named the measurement-directed position and the measurement-independent position. Proponents of the measurement-directed position, who will be referred to in the sequel as "measurement-directeds," hold that statistical techniques are directed by measurement considerations. Proponents of the measurement-independent position, referred to in the sequel as "measurement-independents," hold that measurement and statistics are separate, independent domains and that therefore measurement considerations do not influence statistical techniques. We shall define the issue between these two positions and summarize their views on important questions, with special reference to practical applications of statistics. Finally, we shall try to re-examine the whole issue and propose a resolution.

The Measurement-Directed Position

Briefly, adherents of this position hold that measurement scales are frequently subject to certain laws of regularity which we shall call measurement models. Thus the measurement model for physical length or for physical weight is a system of ten or so axioms and the theorems which can be derived from them. The power and utility of a measurement scale derives, at least for certain problems, from the properties of the measurement model and its applicability to data. Statistical usage involves operations with numbers, such as the addition of numbers, which may be valid with some kinds of measurement scales and invalid with others. The validity of any statistical operation is to be decided on the basis of an underlying measurement model; for example, with any given measurement

---

Prepared for this volume.

147

scale, the statistical operation of taking the mean may or may not be valid. Since the operation of taking the mean involves the addition of numbers, it will be valid only when the measurement scale has an additive property.

The measurement-directed view has its roots in writings in physics and in the philosophy of physics but takes form in psychology essentially in the writings of Stevens. Stevens (1951) classifies scales of measurement into four classes, namely, nominal, ordinal, interval, and ratio scales. The nominal scale is simply a classification based on what Stevens calls a determination of equality (in other words, of common class membership), and the only permissible statistical measure of central tendency is the mode. The ordinal scale has order based on the empirical operation of the determination of greater or less, and the median is a permissible measure. The interval scale is based on the determination of the equality of intervals or of differences, and the arithmetic mean is a permissible measure. The ratio scale is based on the empirical operation of the determination of the equality of ratios, and the geometric mean or the harmonic mean are permissible measures of central tendency. We can readily see that this classification of scales is based on properties of a measurement model but that recommendations based on the classification are carried over into the domain of statistics.

The philosophical origins of the measurement-directed view seem to be Platonic. Until a few short years ago, much of psychology rested in Plato's special world. Psychological concepts and dimensions were conceived as existing independently of the body of psychological knowledge. Among the denizens of the Platonic world were entities such as intelligence, will, and feeling. The psychologist's task was to discover in the complex world of reality the laws governing the operation and interaction of such entities. We might remark parenthetically that physics, too, has spent much of its career in this world. In the past half century, a number of psychological workers from Watson through Kantor, Stevens, and Tolman to Skinner, Graham, and Spence have accomplished a revolution in psychological thought. As a result, the concepts of the psychologist are frankly recognized as scientific constructions made to organize the data of the behavioral domain. In contemporary literature such words as *construct*, *operation*, and *criterion* replace words such as *true* or *real*. Consequently, the Platonic world is now primarily of archaeological interest, but I suspect that living fossils lurk and defend themselves in the area of psychological measurement.

Much of the writing of the measurement-directed school can be understood on the basis of the following hypothesis, namely, there exists a Platonic world of real lengths and real temperatures, and in that world our present measurements of length and absolute temperature correspond to the truth, but our measurements of centigrade temperature do not. This Platonic world is composed of real intelligences which, as scientific measures, are every bit as good as the real lengths. In scientific practice, however, the intelligences are inferior to lengths, because we have not yet found the way to measure them which corresponds to the underlying truth. However, a Platonic world of real loudnesses also exists, and here in recent years we have found the proper way to measure. That this sort of hypothesis is found in the writings of Stevens is curious, for he is one of the psychologists who has promoted the revolution of the past thirty years away from such concepts in psychology.

The Measurement-Independent Position

Proponents of this position hold that the results of measurement operations are sets of numbers and, further, that statistical techniques are methods for drawing inferences about sets of numbers or making comparisons between sets of numbers. Hence, once the numbers are available, the statistician is free to proceed with his methods without bothering about any outside considerations. In particular, no properties of a measurement model can have any relevance for statistical operations.

On the philosophical side, the measurement-independent position rejects Platonism. So far as measurements are concerned, the scales may be more or less adequate for the scientific jobs they are expected to do. A completely adequate scale is a scale which exists within a comprehensive and successful scientific theory and which permits accurate and useful computations and predictions. According to this hypothesis, length has been a successful scale in physics because Euclidian geometry has been successfully applied, and temperature has been a successful scale because thermodynamics is a valid and enduring science.

Every empirical domain now covered by polished and viable theory whose history I have studied exhibits in its early development very crude measuring techniques. The workers in every field have reserved complete freedom in performing numerical and algebraic operations on the numbers resulting from the crude measurements. Such freedom of operation has often led to the discovery of important empirical laws which point the way to the final polished theory. Incidentally, empirical laws also point the way to the final adequate measurement scale, but one cannot reach even the first signpost on this way unless he has taken some crude measurement as a starting point and unless he has reserved for himself freedom for operating with the numbers resulting from that crude measurement. Such freedom, however, is categorically denied the scientific worker by the measurement-directed position.

The origins of the measurement-independent position are also partly in statistics. The view of statistics embodied in that position is, as has been previously asserted, that statistics is a set of methods which begins and ends with numbers, a set of methods which is concerned with inferences about sets of numbers, comparisons between sets of numbers, and ultimately statements about sets of numbers.

The Issues

There are a number of issues on which the two positions should be compared. They are in agreement with respect to 1) the definition of measurement and 2) the philosophical status of measurement properties. They are in disagreement with respect to 1) their view of statistics, 2) their view of the role of numbers in scientific work, 3) the resolution of certain difficulties in the application of statistical methods to monotonic transformations of simple measures, and 4) the criteria according to which selection is to be made from alternative non-parametric or distribution-free tests. These differences in the positions are, of course, all related to the fundamental difference on the question of the relevance or irrelevance for statistical procedures of measurement considerations. We shall proceed to compare the two positions with respect to the points of similarity and difference.

The points of agreement are easily disposed of.

1. Definition of measurement: proponents of the two positions have agreed, so far as one can tell, on a definition of measurement as the assignment, according to fixed rules, of numbers to objects.

2. Philosophical status of measurement properties: proponents of the two positions agree that the measurement properties of a scale refer to semantic relations between the numbers of the scale and certain phenomena outside the scale.

The points of difference require somewhat more discussion.

1. The view of statistics: the picture of statistics which characterizes the measurement-directed position makes statistics directly dependent upon measurement. Statistics is conceived as a group of techniques not for comparing sets of numbers but for comparing sets of objects. The comparison of the sets of objects must somehow involve more than the comparison of the sets of numbers which represent the objects. The "more" which is involved is a measurement model which sets out certain correspondences between properties of the objects and properties of the numbers. The position may be summarized in the following quotation from Stevens (1955[b]):

The kind of scale we work with depends, of course, upon the concrete empirical operations we are able to perform, and, as we might expect, the character of the operations determines the kind of statistics that are permissible.

This comes about because a scale erected by a given set of operations can be transformed in certain permissible ways without doing violence to the essential nature of the scale. As a matter of fact, the best way to specify the nature of the scale is in terms of its "group structure"—the group of mathematical transformations that leave the scale form invariant. And it follows quite naturally that the statistics applicable to a given scale are those that remain appropriately invariant under the transformation permitted by the scale.

The measurement-independents maintain that statistical techniques are techniques for the comparison of sets of numbers as numbers and, therefore, that measurement properties of a scale are irrelevant for statistical tests.

2. The role of numbers in science: adherents of both positions recognize the power of numbers in scientific work. The measurement-directeds ascribe this power entirely to the properties of numbers as they occur in measurement models. Whenever gains result from the use of numbers, attempts are made to derive the gains from properties of a measurement model. The measurement-independents hold that numbers have had great use and success in science simply because, after measurements have been made, difficult, clumsy, and sometimes impossible comparisons between objects can be replaced by easy, and often elegant, comparisons between numbers. Such comparisons will be statistical when statistical questions are involved. They may be comparisons of order or other properties when measurement models are involved. They may be, in addition, almost any sort of comparison which the ingenuity of a scientific theorist operating with a theory finds relevant.

3. Statistical methods and monotonic transformations: proponents of the measurement-independent position hold that, for statistical purposes, the important property of the measurement scale is order and, further, that in making statistical comparisons one deals with the numbers as numbers alone. The consequences of these two assumptions when applied to monotonic transformations undoubtedly influence the measurement-directed position.

One can obtain a set of measurements and run a test without finding statistical significance. One may then make a monotonic transformation of the numbers by looking up their logarithms, say, or taking their reciprocals. The monotonic transformation changes nothing about the order of the numbers, yet the same test on the transformed set may yield statistical significance. Stevens' writings, as well as those of Senders (1958) and Siegel (1956), make clear that their common viewpoint toward measurement and statistics is brought about at least in part by a desire for strictures to prohibit statistical turpitude. Without some sort of stricture, whether a person uses a set of numbers, or their logarithms, or some other monotonic transformation, is arbitrary. Thus the measurement-directeds seek to legislate statistical honesty by imposing measurement restrictions.

The measurement-independent position admits these difficulties. Of course, the investigator can reach one conclusion by applying a statistical test to a set of measures but another by applying the same test to a set of monotonic transforms. He can also reach different conclusions by applying different tests of the same hypothesis to the same set of measures. Either of these dilemmas is a statistical dilemma. For statistical purposes selection of the proper measurement with a given test or the proper test with a given measurement must be based on statistical grounds. A vast literature defines optimal statistical procedures and gives the conditions under which given procedures are optimal. The conditions are usually concerned with the form of the underlying population. Empirical information about the populations dealt with is necessary for making good choices of either a test or a transformation. Introducing irrelevancy to ignorance does not help solve the problems.

4. Selection of non-parametric or distribution-free tests: in distribution-free statistics a number of alternative tests for the same hypothesis frequently exist. To choose among them is difficult. The measurement-directed position invokes measurement properties for making the selection. The entire theoretical burden of Siegel's book on non-parametric statistics is concerned with the use of measurement properties for making such a choice.

The measurement-independents hold that the choice among alternative distribution-free tests involves difficult statistical problems. The tests are distribution-free only when the hypotheses being tested are true. Thus the probability of a type I error can be calculated without recourse to the distribution. But the power of a distribution-free test is scarcely non-parametric. In other words, when the hypothesis being tested is false, selection of a distribution-free test should be motivated by a consideration of the most likely alternative hypotheses. This observation points up a number of unsolved statistical problems. Since the problems are unsolved, the suggestion given here is of little practical value for a person wishing to make a selection at the present time. However, the proper problem is the determination of statistical criteria for the selection and is only hidden by the introduction of irrelevant measurement considerations. What must be carried forward is work on the type II error in testing various sorts of hypotheses by distribution-free methods.

There are several papers which deal with various aspects of the issues in general or philosophical terms. Bergmann and Spence (1944) have dealt excellently with the concomitants of the two viewpoints, giving special reference to the history of physics. The emphasis of the remainder of the present paper is on the statistical aspects of the issues.

Statistical Practice

As the positions of the measurement-directeds and the measurement-independents have been described, some differences certainly appear to exist. Whether the differences are of more than philosophical import depends upon whether they have any effects on statistical practice. We shall show concretely that the proponents of both positions approach their statistical problems in the same way but that the adherents of the measurement-independent position will work with greater statistical efficiency.

The operations of the measurement-independents in statistical inference are easily described. 1) They assess the sample data. Obviously, no statements of scientific interest can be made about populations without looking at the data at least in samples. 2) The relation of the sample to the population from which it arises is considered. Specifically, the sampling method is taken into account; usually a random sampling will have been made. 3) Statistical theorems are employed to make statements about the population on the basis of the sample data and the relation of the sample to the population. 4) A scientific interpretation of the results is made. For the interpretation the only important requirement is that the order of the numbers preserve some order in the underlying objects. A fundamental question is whether the measurement-directeds proceed in any different way. To see that they do not, the simplest procedure is to consider a few examples.

EXAMPLE 1. THE USE OF THE RESPONSES OF CHILDREN AS MEASURING IN-STRUMENTS   In Table 1 is given the simplest batch of data which could be collected to illustrate the point. There are two courses, A and B, and we are concerned with the lengths of the courses. We ask four children to walk the courses naturally, counting their steps. No child is told how many steps any other child takes. This is a physical measurement, to be sure, but a bad one. I suspect that the scale is not an interval scale, for

Table 1

Number of Paces Needed by Each Child to Measure Each Course

| | CHILD | | | |
Course	M	T	S	K
A	22	24	30	30
B	66	75	86	111
(B-A)	44	51	56	81

parenthood has taught me that even a fairly large child will take anywhere from four to ten times as many steps in walking two miles as in
walking one. Our problem is to find out whether one course is longer than
the other. We proceed by testing the hypothesis that they are of the same
length. For purposes of argument we shall agree that the scale is not interval; however, as we proceed, we shall see that this is of no great
importance.

The measurement-independent proceeds according to the following
steps: 1) He sets up the physical or geometrical hypothesis that the
courses are of the same length. 2) He assumes that the number of steps
taken by any child preserves the order of length but does not necessarily
have any stronger measurement properties. 3) From 1 and 2 he deduces
that any number assigned by any child is as likely to be assigned to
course A as to course B. 4) From 3 he deduces his statistical hypothesis,
namely, that the population mean of the difference between the numbers
assigned by the children to the two courses, A and B, is zero.

Note that the statistical hypothesis of step 4 has reference only to the
population mean of a set of numbers. Furthermore, this so-called null
hypothesis has been derived from considerations of order alone.

The measurement-independent will probably make an assumption of
normality and test the hypothesis by using the t-test, since the absence of
an interval scale does not, for him, prohibit the calculation of means and
variances. He will obtain a value of 3.6 for t on the given data, which is
significant with 3 df at beyond the five-per-cent level.

A measurement-directed will insist on a non-parametric test of the
hypothesis if he agrees that the scale is not interval. He goes through the
following steps: 1) He hypothesizes that the two courses have the same
length. 2) He assumes that order in the numbers reflects order in the
lengths. 3) From 1 and 2 he deduces that any number assigned by any
child is as likely to be assigned to course A as to course B. 4) From 3 he
concludes that for any child the number assigned to course A is as likely
to be larger as to be smaller than the number assigned to course B.

As with the proponents of the other position, the statistical hypothesis
of step 4 is a statement about, and only about, a population of numbers.
Again it has been derived solely from a physical hypothesis and considerations of order.

Proponents of the measurement-directed position would work up the
data by means of the sign test, obtaining a level of significance of $\frac{1}{8}$,
which is as strong a level as is possible for a double-ended sign test on
these data.

What should be clear is that: 1) The statement of the physical or geometrical hypothesis is the same in the two cases. 2) The assumption of the
preservation of order is common to the two cases. 3) The deduction of

the indifference of the assignment of numbers with respect to courses is the same in the two cases. 4) The relationship between the indifference of assignment of numbers and the statistical hypothesis is equivalent in the two cases, differing only as the hypotheses differ in detail of statement. Therefore, the only difference between the two positions in this example is the question of the statistical efficiency of the test selected.

The conclusion based on the statistical test can, of course, be wrong. The population may not be normal, in which case the method of the measurement-independent would be biased, but surely this merely statistical question is not among the points at issue. Or the sampling might not be random, in which case both methods would be biased, not necessarily equally. Finally, the experiment might be bad in that the order of step-numbers might not reflect order of length (for example, course A might be level but course B sharply inclined, or each child might be fatigued after walking course A, so that he would take more steps on course B), but such lack of preservation of order is equally damaging to both procedures.

Before passing to the next example, we remark that A and B can be any objects—physical, psychological, or whatnot. Our four children can provide the numbers of the slide as measures of any property of the objects A and B. The measures may be test scores, ratings of aggression, or anything. Whatever they represent, if we agree that their order is correct, aside from possible errors of measurement, then by the argument just concluded, the procedures characteristic of both positions are still defensible. The decision on procedure should be based on statistical criteria, entirely within the realm of numbers.

EXAMPLE 2. THE MEAN AND MEDIAN FROM A NORMAL POPULATION   This example is more abstract than the first, but it makes the same point. Suppose we have two random samples from populations known to be normal and of unit variance. We wish to test the hypothesis that the two populations have the same mean—or median, since the distribution is symmetrical —under the assumption that the scale is ordinal at best.

Measurement-independents will emphasize the normal form of the population and, seeking statistical stability, will use the t-test to compare the sample means. Measurement-directeds will emphasize the weakness of the measurement scale and will compare the sample medians.

The interpretive question on whether the measures reflect some desired extra-numerical property is not at issue, since adherents of the two positions test equivalent hypotheses by assessing information from identical samples of numbers. Hence, the measurement properties of the scale are simply irrelevant. But a great gain in statistical efficiency obtains for the measurement-independents. When the population is normal, the sample mean is more stable than the sample median. For every 100 subjects run by a measurement-independent, the measurement-directed must run 250 subjects to obtain the same experimental precision. His statistical luxury is again experimentally wanton.

EXAMPLE 3. LATENCIES IN HULLIAN THEORY   When a variable exists within the framework of a systematic theory, the structure of the theory tells us how to manipulate numbers representing the variable. To show the importance of theory for the present discussion, let us make the friendly assumption that the learning theory of Hull and Spence is comprehensive and successful and that all parameters have been evaluated. Then let us suppose that we have the problem of comparing two sets of response latencies.

Among the basic relations of the theory is one between response latency and momentary effective reaction potential. Response latency as a time measure has several well-understood and presumably desirable measurement properties but has a badly skewed and poorly-understood distribution; in fact, if the theory of Hull is accurate, the distribution of latencies is very bad—none of the moments exist. Momentary effective reaction potential, on the other hand, may be an abominable variable from the point of view of measurement models, but it has a simple, well-understood normal distribution. If a proponent of the measurement-directed position were faced with this problem in an experimental interpretation of the learning theory, I am convinced that he would use the t-test on the momentary effective reaction potential rather than mess with the difficult and unstable distribution of response latencies.

That the random variables on which statistical tests and estimates are based are themselves mathematical entities is simply a matter of fact. It follows therefore that statistical decisions cannot depend on measurement properties.

Re-examination and Re-evaluation

If the statistical practices of proponents of the two viewpoints are as we have described, the question arises as to why any disagreement exists at all. Why has not the position of the measurement-independents carried the day? A possible answer is that the issues have not yet been explored at sufficient depth and that adequate exploration will reveal weaknesses in the position. A second possibility is that misunderstandings have arisen through unclarity of language.

In connection with the second possibility, we might note that in the literature on measurement and statistics the term "measurement" is used with several meanings. We shall here distinguish four concepts, each of which is often called *measurement*, namely, *measurement model, measurement operation, measurement result,* and *measurement*. A *measurement model* is a theory based on a measurement scale. A *measurement operation* is a collection of empirical and numerical manipulations which leads to the assignment of a single number to a unique object. A *measurement result* is the single number assigned through a measurement operation. The fourth term, *measurement*, will be discussed at length below. We shall not review in detail the literature separating the four meanings of the term but will state a conviction that much misunderstanding can be avoided if the four meanings are kept clearly separated.

More serious misunderstandings may have arisen because of the first possibility, the possibility that the fundamental definition of measurement, although agreed upon by the two positions, has been given in insufficient depth. The definition given for measurement corresponds really to the definition we have just given for measurement operation. Yet, in interesting cases, whether in physics, psychology, or whatever science, a measurement operation clearly falls short of what we mean by measurement. If we examine practice instead of homily, we discover that scientific measurement is the attempt to assign a statistical population to a unique object.

Examples abound. The velocity of light is given as two numbers, an index of central tendency accompanied by an index of variability. Our first attempts to weigh a chemical object with great accuracy were guided by instructions to perform several weighings (*three* is the magic number of my own recollection) and to base the final weight on all. Nor is there any indication in finding or precept that repetition of precisely the same operations on presumably the same object will always lead to the same result. On the contrary, variability is expected as well as encountered whenever we try to make very accurate determinations of quantity.

This has been recognized before. But it has been described Platonically. The stick has been described as having a fixed but unknown number for its length and the scientist as making errors in trying to evaluate the number. Surely the length of the stick is more accurately described as a population of numbers whose properties depend upon the stick and the technique of measurement. In point of fact, one never assigns the population. At best, one performs finitely many measurement operations and thus draws a sample of finite size. Indeed, experience has shown that with certain scales and for certain purposes a sample of unit size suffices.

The stochastic view of measurement as the assignment of a population to an object is consistent with much of the language of measurement. When one speaks of making enough observations to get a stable result or describes the mean of several observations as better than any single observation, one is clearly in the realm of statistical estimation.

For many purposes—testing an additivity property of a measurement model, for example—it is necessary to represent each object by a single number. Such necessity does not contradict the stochastic view of measurement. The number to be used is simply an estimate of some parameter of the population, most often an index of central tendency. Historically, the population mean has almost invariably been estimated in measurement problems. There is no a priori reason, however, why one should not find an additive property characterizing a measurement scale which is based on population modes or medians.

In recognition of the needs set out in the previous paragraph, we distinguish between two classes of stochastic measurement. *Extended measurement* is the attempt to assign a statistical population to an object. *Restricted measurement* is the assignment of a single number to the object via extended measurement and statistical estimation. Restricted measurement can occur with respect to any parameter which can be estimated. Historically the concepts named here as *measurement operation* and *restricted measurement* have been inextricably confused.

The important point to be made is that, when scientific measurement is considered in proper depth, statistical models intervene between the measurement operations and the measurement models. The statistical models deal with the measurement results, which are already samples of numbers. Hence, measurement scales and models are based on statistical models.

Returning to the two basic positions on measurement and statistics, we see that they are both inadequate when viewed from the standpoint of stochastic measurement. The statistical practices advocated by the measurement-independents are the correct ones, but the independence of measurement and statistics postulated by adherents of this position is incorrect. The measurement-directed position is correct in asserting an interdependence of measurement and statistics, but the dependence which they postulate is in the wrong direction. Measurement scales are dependent upon statistical models which are themselves dependent upon measurement results. Each position has a partial, but only a partial, truth. However, the arguments of earlier sections of this paper showing the correctness of the measurement-independent view of statistical practice remain valid. Statistical problems should be solved with statistical theorems. Measurement models are irrelevant.

References

Bergmann, G., and Spence, K. W. Logic of psychophysical measurement. *Psychol. Rev.*, 1944, *51*, 1–24.

Boring, E. G. The logic of the normal law of error in mental measurement. *Amer. J. Psychol.*, 1920, *31*, 1–33.

Burke, C. J. Additive scales and statistics. *Psychol. Rev.*, 1953, *60*, 73–75.

———. The gazelle and the hippopotamus. *Worm Runner's Digest* (in press).

Campbell, N. R. *Physics, the elements*. London: Cambridge Univ. Press, 1920.

Comrey, A. L. An operational approach to some problems in psychological measurement. *Psychol. Rev.*, 1950, *57*, 217–228.

Davidson, D., Siegel, S., and Suppes, P., *Some experiments and related theory on the measurement of utility and subjective probability*. Rep. 4, Stanford Value Theory Project. 1955.

Gulliksen, H. Paired comparisons and the logic of measurement. *Psychol. Rev.*, 1946, *53*, 199–213.

Hull, Clark L. *Principles of behavior*. New York: D. Appleton-Century Co., 1943.

Senders, Virginia L. A comment on Burke's additive scales and statistics. *Psychol. Rev.*, 1953, *60*, 423–424.

———. *Measurement and statistics*. New York: Oxford, 1958. Chapter 2 provides a discussion of "Numbers, things, and measurement."

Siegel, S. *Nonparametric statistics for the behavioral sciences*. New York: McGraw-Hill, 1956.

Stevens, S. S. A scale for the measurement of a psychological magnitude: loudness. *Psychol. Rev.*, 1936, *43*, 405–416.

———. On the problem of scales for the measurement of psychological magnitudes. *J. Unif. Sci.*, 1939, *9*, 94–99.

———. On the theory of scales of measurement. *Science*, 1946, *103*, 677–680.

———. Mathematics, measurement, and psychophysics. In S. S. Stevens (ed.), *Handbook of experimental psychology*. New York: Wiley, 1951, pp. 1–49.

———. The measurement of loudness. *J. Acoust. Soc. Amer.*, 1955,[a] *27*, 815–829.

———. On the averaging of data. *Science*, 1955,[b] *121*, 113–116.

———. On the psychophysical law. *Psychol. Rev.*, 1957, *64*, 153–181.

Stevens, S. S., and Galanter, E. H. Ratio scales and category scales for a dozen perceptual continua. *J. Exp. Psychol.*, 1957, *54*, 377–411.

CHAPTER IV

Theoretical Constructs

THE PROBLEM OF THE kind of theoretical constructs to use in the development of useful scientific theories is obviously a key one. A variety of views have been expressed on this problem. In the first selection in this chapter the various types of theoretical constructs employed by psychologists are reviewed by Kenneth W. Spence, who, as a leading proponent of Hullian behavior theory, has been one of the most active and influential of the so-called "neo-behaviorists." J. R. Kantor, author of the second selection, has long been prominent for his "interbehavioral" psychology. This paper presents an up-to-date version of his views on constructs. The third selection, by Melvin H. Marx, analyzes the distinction between so-called "hypothetical constructs" and "intervening variables" originally made by MacCorquodale and Meehl, with an emphasis upon the dimension of operational clarity. An important distinction between formal and informal meanings in constructs is next provided in the excerpt from a paper by Howard H. Kendler. David Krech, in the excerpt following Kendler's, defends the role of physiological assumptions in constructs. Finally, in the last selection, an excerpt from a paper by Melvin H. Marx suggests a kind of progressive experimental and conceptual analysis as a means of breaking down originally complex constructs into more manageable pieces. A somewhat similar approach is represented in Selection 15, in Chapter V, from a paper by F. H. George.

161

8 | *Types of Constructs in Psychology*[1]

KENNETH W. SPENCE

I. Introduction

The task of the scientist has been described as that of attempting to discover ever more generalized laws by which the observable events within his field of study may be brought into interrelation with one another. To this end he develops and refines (mainly in the direction of quantitative representation) his concepts or variables, arranges highly controlled (experimental) conditions of observation and introduces theoretical constructions. While it is not the primary purpose of this paper to attempt a methodological analysis of these components of scientific method, it is necessary to begin our discussion by calling attention to two somewhat different roles or functions that one of them, construction of theory, plays in different fields of science or in the same field at different stages of development.

In some areas of knowledge, for example present-day physics, theories serve primarily to bring into functional connection with one another empirical laws which prior to their formulation had been isolated realms of knowledge. The physicist is able to isolate, experimentally, elementary situations, i.e., situations in which there are a limited number of variables, and thus finds it possible to infer or discover descriptive, low-order laws. Theory comes into play for the physicist when he attempts to formulate more abstract principles which will bring these low-order laws into relationship with one another. Examples of such comprehensive theories are Newton's principle of gravitation and the kinetic theory of gases. The former provided a theoretical integration of such laws as Kepler's con-

From K. W. Spence, The nature of theory constructions in contemporary psychology, *Psychol. Rev.*, 1944, *51*, 47–68. Reprinted by permission of the author, the *Psychological Review*, and the American Psychological Association.

[1] The writer is greatly indebted to Dr. Gustav Bergmann for reading the manuscript and making valuable suggestions.

cerning planetary motions, Galileo's law of falling bodies, laws of the tides and so on. The kinetic theory has served to integrate the various laws relating certain properties of gases to other experimental variables.

In the less highly developed areas of knowledge, such as the behavior and social sciences, theory plays a somewhat different role. In these more complex fields the simplest experimental situation that can be arranged usually involves such a large number of variables that it is extremely difficult, if not impossible, to discover directly the empirical laws relating them. Theories are brought into play in such circumstances as a device to aid in the formulation of the laws. They consist primarily in the introduction or postulation of hypothetical constructs which help to bridge gaps between the experimental variables. Examples of such theoretical constructs are legion in psychology, e.g., Tolman's "demand," Hull's "excitatory potential," Lewin's "tension system," and a host of other mentalistic and neurophysiologically-sounding concepts. It is the purpose of this paper to examine the attempts of psychologists to discover general laws of behavior, particularly the auxiliary theoretical devices they have employed in doing so.

II. Theoretical Constructs in Psychology

Like every other scientist, the psychologist is interested in establishing the interrelations within a set of experimental variables, i.e., in discovering empirical laws. At the present stage of development the variables (measurements) studied by the psychologist and between which he is attempting to find functional relations appear to fall into two main groups:

1. R-variables: measurements of the behavior of organisms; attributes of simple response patterns (actones), complex achievements (actions) and generalized response characteristics (traits, abilities, etc.). These are sometimes referred to as the dependent variables.

2. S-variables: measurements of physical and social environmental factors and conditions (present and past) under which the responses of organisms occur. These are sometimes referred to as the independent, manipulable variables.

While not all laws are quantitative, science typically strives to quantify its constructs and to state their interrelations in terms of numerical laws. The numerical laws the psychologist seeks may be represented as follows:

$$R = f(S)$$

The problem here is twofold: 1) to discover what the relevant S variables are, and 2) to ascertain the nature of the functional relations holding between the two groups of variables.

In general, two radically opposed positions have been taken by scientists, including psychologists, as to the best procedure to follow in solving this problem. On the one hand are those who propose the introduction of theoretical constructs as described above. On the other there are the more empirically minded persons who attempt to refrain from the use of such inferred constructs and try to confine themselves entirely to observable data. An excellent defense of this latter viewpoint, along with a constructive proposal as to how such an approach can hope to discover general quantitative laws in psychology, is contained in the recent presidential address of Woodrow to the American Psychological Association (1942). We shall leave consideration of the method proposed by Woodrow until later; certain criticisms he offers of the theoretical approach provide an excellent introduction to this method of discovering laws.

Beginning with the conception, more or less the same as that expressed at the start of this paper, that explanation in science consists in nothing more than a statement of established relationships of dependency (for psychology in terms of laws between measurements of environment and behavior), Woodrow goes on to protest that most psychologists seem to have been entirely too interested in postulating intermediate events occurring within the organism to explain the obtained measurements. The difficulty with such speculative constructs, he thinks, is that they cannot be measured because it is not possible to observe the interior of organisms. The result is that their specification must be left to the imagination. And as he says (p. 3):

. . . our imaginations have not failed us. The things we have stuck within the organism in the hope thereby of explaining behavior are almost without limit in number and variety. They include mental sets and cortical sets, traces, residues, synaptic resistances, inhibitory and excitatory substances, inhibitory and excitatory tendencies, determining tendencies, mental attitudes, sentiments, wishes, tensions, field forces, valences, urges, abilities, instincts, and so on and on. Very popular indeed is the animistic type of explanation.

While it must be admitted with Woodrow that many of the theoretical constructs employed by psychologists have never been too satisfactorily specified, one must protest the lumping together of all theoretical constructs in such a completely indiscriminate manner. As a matter of fact, Woodrow has included in his list certain conceptions which were never meant to be explanatory concepts. Thus such terms as set, attitude, sentiment, and in some instances drive, are what Carnap (1936–37) has termed *dispositional predicates or concepts*, because they refer to the disposition of an object to a certain behavior under certain conditions. They usually serve as names for events which do not appear in observable experience but instead are introduced into the scientist's language in terms of conditions and results which can be described in terms that refer directly to observable experiences. Such concepts are prevalent in all fields of science and serve a useful purpose.

Then, again, Woodrow has failed to distinguish in his list between what turn out upon analysis to be very different kinds of theoretical constructs. While some of them are little better than the animistic notions of primitive man, others have qualified as quite satisfactory in the sense that they have led to the formulation of behavioral laws. We turn now to the consideration of the different kinds of theories (theoretical constructs) that have been proposed in psychology.

III. Four Types of Theoretical Constructs

Theoretical constructs are introduced, as we have said, in the form of guesses as to what variables other than the ones under control of the experimenter are determining the response. The relation of such inferred constructs (I_a) to the experimental variables, measurements of S and R, is shown in the following figure. Here we have assumed an over-simplified situation for purposes of exposition.

S-variables   I-variables   R-variables
X_1 I_a R_1

Figure 1.   Intervening variables.

If under environmental conditions X_1 the response measure R_1 is always the same (within the error of measurement) then we have no need of theory. Knowing that condition X_1 existed we could always predict the response. Likewise if, with systematic variation of the X variable, we find a simple functional relation holding between the X values and the corresponding R values we again would have no problem, for we could precisely state the law relating them. But unfortunately things are not usually so simple as this, particularly in psychology. On a second occasion of the presentation of condition X_1, the subject is very likely to exhibit a different magnitude of response, or in the second example there may be no simple curve discernible between the two sets of experimental values. It is at this point that hypothetical constructs are introduced and the response variable is said to be determined, in part by X_1, and in part by some additional factor, or factors, $I_a, I_b \ldots$, i.e., $R = f(X_1, I_a, I_b \ldots)$. The manner in which these theoretical constructs have been defined by different psychologists permits a grouping of them into four categories: 1) animistic-like theories in which the relations of the construct to the empirical variables are left entirely unspecified, 2) neurophysiological theories, 3) theories involving constructs defined primarily in terms of the *R* variables and 4) theories involving constructs intervening between the *S* and *R* variables.

1. ANIMISTIC CONCEPTIONS   Little need be said about such instances of psychological speculation. They are included here merely for the purpose of completing the record. The invoking of such general concepts as the "soul," "mind," "élan vital," "entelechy," "idea," "libido," not to mention many more specific instances (e.g., insight, instinct[2]) in order to account for the apparent capriciousness of the behavior of organisms has been all too prevalent in psychology. When not safe from disproof by reason of the fact that their locus is usually specified to be in some region within the organism unaccessible to observation, these concepts are rendered invulnerable by failure to specify what relations they might have either to the *S* or *R* variables. While such vagueness renders them unverifiable, it does insure them a vigorous and long career among certain types of thinkers. Needless to say, such vague conceptions receive little attention today among scientific-minded psychologists.

2. NEUROPHYSIOLOGICAL THEORIES   The extent to which neurophysiological concepts, defined in terms of the operations and instruments of the neurophysiologist, are employed in psychological theorizing is not nearly so great as is sometimes thought. As a matter of fact, if we employ such variables to help us out in our formulation of behavior laws we are not, strictly speaking, theorizing for such concepts are not hypothetical, but are empirically defined. In such instances we have stated a law interrelating environmental, organic and behavioral variables. As yet we do not have very many such laws, except in the case of the simplest kinds of behavior (sensory responses, reflexes, etc.).

There are, of course, many theoretical constructs in psychology which are supposed to represent hypothetical neurophysiological processes, but whose properties are defined either in terms of the response variables (type 3 theory), in terms of environmental factors and the response variables (type 4 theory), or just assumed to be operating without making any specification of their relations to either the environmental or response variables (type 1 theory). Examples of these are Köhler's construct of brain field (1940) to explain perceptual and memory phenomena (type 3), Pavlov's constructs (1927) of excitatory and inhibitory states (type 4), and certain neural trace theories of learning (type 1).

It will be seen that this category really cuts across the other three. Further consideration of some of these theories will be given in our discussion of the final two classes of theory.

---

[2] Such terms, of course, when used as dispositional predicates serve the useful function of providing a name for the phenomenon.

3. RESPONSE-INFERRED THEORETICAL CONSTRUCTS   The fact that the behavior of organisms varies even though the objective environmental condition remains unchanged has led some psychologists to assert that the laws of such behavior cannot be formulated in terms of objective environmental variables even though additional hypothetical constructs are employed to bolster the effort. These writers have insisted that behavior must be accounted for in terms of the psychological situation. Thus Lewin in his book *Dynamic theory of personality* (1935) refers to what he describes as the complete failure of such German writers as Loeb, Bethe and other objectivists to develop an adequate theoretical interpretation of behavior in terms of the objective situation, i.e., the physical situation as described by the operations of measurement of the physicist and/or the objective social situation as described by the sociologist. It is always necessary, he insists, to describe the situation as the subject sees or perceives it, i.e., in terms of what it means to him. Typical quotations from Lewin's writings indicate the positive tone taken by such writers:

For the investigation of dynamic problems we are forced to start from the psychologically real environment of the child (1935, p. 74). Of course, in the description of the child's psychological environment one may not take as a basis the immediately objective social forces and relations as the sociologist or jurist, for example, would list them. One must rather describe the social facts as they affect the particular individual concerned (1935, p. 75).

One of the basic characteristics of field theory in psychology, as I see it, is the demand that the field which influences an individual should be described not in "objective physicalistic" terms, but in the way in which it exists for that person at that time. (1942, p. 217).

As Lewin implies in the last quoted excerpt it would seem that this type of "psychological" approach to the theoretical constructs of psychology is characteristic of the self-styled field theorists or Gestalt psychologists. Thus Koffka (1935) makes use of the construct of "behavioral environment" and the more inclusive construct of "psychophysical field" which includes the former and the physiological field, while Köhler (1929, 1940) refers to "phenomenal field" and to "brain field." Koffka and Köhler differ slightly from Lewin in that they introduce a physiological terminology in the description of the properties of some of their behavior-determining fields whereas Lewin does not. The methods of determining the structure and properties of these fields whether "brain field," "behavioral environment" or "life space" are, however, essentially the same, and as we shall see later, involve extensive use of the phenomenological type of introspection.

The nature of this type of theorizing may be made clearer by attempting to show how it fits into the schema we have already employed. Figure 2 makes use of the constructs of Lewin, who has been the most articulate

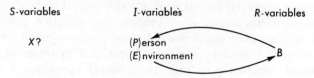

Figure 2.   Lewin's theoretical constructs.

of this group of writers so far as the exposition of the formal nature of his theorizing is concerned. Lewin employs the concept of life space to represent the totality of facts which determine the behavior (B) of an individual at a certain moment. The life space includes two groups of constructs, the person (P) *and the psychological environment* (E). Use is then made of certain concepts from geometry (topology and hodology) and dynamics to represent the existing relationships.[3] By means of what Lewin calls co-ordinating definitions these constructs are said to be related to empirical concepts.

Without going into detail, Figure 2 reveals an interesting fact. It is that little, if any, use is made of the S-variables in Lewin's theorizing.[4] The question immediately arises then as to what kinds of laws, if any, does Lewin arrive at. The functional relationship which frequently appears in his writings, $B = f(P, E)$, is obviously not a law of the type that psychologists were said to be interested in, i.e., $R = f(S)$. But if it is not this kind of a law, what kind is it? Some writers have implied that Lewin really does not attain any laws at all. They call attention to the fact that laws are statements of relations between *independently defined variables*

---

[3] There is considerable reason to doubt whether Lewin does much more than take over the terms of topology, making little if any use of the postulates (implicit definitions) of this formal system. Koch, after making a very thorough analysis of Lewin's formulations, states that Lewin "finds it expedient to abstract from the postulates (of topology) the properties with which they implicitly endow the constructs, instead of fully stating the postulates" (1941, p. 148). In this sense, then, it may be said that Lewin employs very fragmentary parts or sub-systems of topology. As for the formal system of dynamics it remains thus far closeted, to use Koch's happy description, in Lewin's mind. Like so many of these field theorists, Lewin sets up a most attractive program for theory. Taken in conjunction with his interesting experiments the illusion is nicely created that there is some connection between them.

[4] Lewin states that the objective physical and social surroundings "have a relation to the life space similar to that which 'boundary conditions' have to a dynamic system" (1942, p. 217). He believes that physicalistic behaviorism has made the mistake of treating such variables as if they were parts of the life space. Attention should be called here to the fact that Koffka concerned himself much more extensively with the objective environmental variables or the geographic environment as he called it. He discussed at some length the relations between the geographic and the behavioral environments—the traditional problem of perception (1935).

and they ask what are the two sets of independent variables in Lewin's formula.

The answer to this question is not easy, and the writer is of the opinion that it has not been met in all instances of field theory. However, an examination of the methods employed by Lewin and his students in determining the structure and properties of their fields reveals that they depend heavily upon the phenomenological introspections of their subjects or themselves. If we now think of these as a kind of verbal response or "perceptual" response, in which the subject tries to describe his own particular way of perceiving the objective situation, we see that Lewin's theory really does provide us with laws mediating between independent variables, i.e., between two different responses of the subject, or, as in some cases, between the experimenter's own perceptual responses and the subjects' subsequent response. Thus Lewin discovers what amount to laws of the following type: $R_1 = f(R_2)$.

Of course, such theorists do not always rely on such phenomenological introspections. Once certain laws of the above type have been formulated it is possible to formulate further laws between purely overt behavior items, neither of which are of this introspective, verbal type. There are also instances in which from the pattern of the observed response the theorist makes an inference as to the nature of the hypothetical field; and then by means of his postulates as to what happens in these fields he is able to make certain predictions as to subsequent behavior. An excellent example of the latter is Köhler's theoretical treatment (1940) of perceptual problems involving reversible figures and the effects of prolonged inspection in certain types of simple perceptual situations. Thus in the light of perceptual behavior to reversible figures, he formulated the hypothesis that percept processes are associated with fields of electric currents in the nervous system. Then by means of postulates based on knowledge about electrolytical conduction he was able to predict other perceptual behavior.

By and large, however, the field theorist depends heavily upon phenomenological introspection in introducing his theoretical constructs. In order to understand the field of the subject he asks him to describe how he perceives the situation, or he infers it on the basis of his own introspections. With engaging frankness Snygg has made an appeal for the recognition of the important role that phenomenological introspection plays in these theories.[5] Thus he writes in connection with the problem of prediction (1941, p. 413):

---

[5] Snygg also admits another obvious characteristic of such theoretical systems which some of its proponents have not always willingly acknowledged. Reference is made here to the fact that such systems are anthropomorphic.

By postulate B the determining locus of action is the behavior's p.f. [phenomenological field]. This is not open to direct observation by an outside observer. The process of prediction therefore involves two steps: 1) the securing of an understanding of the subject's field by inference or reconstruction, 2) the projection of the future field.

The first operation is of the common "Now why did he do that?" or "Under what circumstances would I have done that?" character. Much of the topological work of Lewin is of this type and essentially the same procedure was used by Shepard when from the behavior of his rats he inferred the existence of floor cues which he himself was unable to experience.

That this field approach to the problems of psychology has been fruitful and valuable is amply supported by the experimental contributions it has made, although in the writer's opinion, the theoretical superstructure has played a much less significant role than is sometimes credited to it. Furthermore, the phenomenological approach has its advantages, particularly in the complex field of social behavior of the human adult. It is obviously much easier to gain some notion as to the relevant variables determining such complex behavior by asking the individual to verbalize than it is to employ the procedure of trying to hypothesize them from knowledge of past history. Usually the latter is not available in sufficient completeness to make it even worthwhile to try to theorize as to the nature of such historical laws.[6]

A final point of no little importance is the failure of such field theories to provide us with laws which will enable us to control and manipulate the behavior-determining psychological field. Such laws are obviously a basic prerequisite to successful clinical therapy. While it may be true, as Snygg claims (1941), that psychiatrists and teachers find the phenomenological approach most valuable in diagnosing behavior disorders, it is difficult to understand how the response-response laws it provides can be of much use in guiding therapeutic treatment. The latter requires a knowledge of what to do to the individual, what changes in his physical and social environment to arrange, in order to bring about the desired behavior changes. The laws telling us how to proceed in such matters are historical laws and involve as an important component of them objective variables representative of past and present factors in the physical and social environments. Psychiatrists and clinical psychologists who employed a purely phenomenological approach might or might not be successful at diagnosis; it is difficult to see how they could ever prescribe satisfactory re-educative procedures.[7, 8]

---

[6] The situation in the case of animal behavior is somewhat different. Here one usually does have a pretty good record of the past history relevant to the present environmental situation.

[7] Bergmann has summed up this difficulty most succinctly in the form of the following questions:—"But even so, what is the predictive value of the suggestive meta-

4. Theoretical constructs as intervening variables between S and R variables   In sharp contrast to these response-inferred theories with their emphasis upon the phenomenological approach is the point of view that theoretical constructs in psychology are to be regarded as "intervening variables" which bring into relation with one another the dependent R variables on the one hand and the independent S variables on the other. As Bergmann and Spence (1941) have previously pointed out, two psychologists in particular, Hull and Tolman, have advocated, each in his own individual way, this type of psychological theory. In a little-known paper Tolman (1936) has presented an excellent account of such a theoretical program, while in his new book *Principles of Behavior* (1943ª) Hull has demonstrated in actual practice how such intervening variables provide us with a formulation of the basic principles or laws governing simple learning behavior. The following discussion makes no attempt to give a systematic account of this theoretical procedure. Instead we shall merely outline very sketchily its main features and then single out one or two aspects of it for more detailed examination.

According to Hull and Tolman, theoretical constructs, or intervening variables, have to be introduced into psychology either when we do not know all the important variables entering into a set of experimental events, or the precise nature of the interrelating function is not known. Consider, for example, the data obtained from conditioning experiments. These investigations have presented us with a wealth of data showing how the response variable changes or varies with the manipulation of certain other experimental variables. That is to say, various measurable aspects of response are studied as functions of the manipulable environmental variables and the data so obtained are plotted in the form of various curves.

The task of the psychologist here is to discover the precise nature of the interrelations holding within this set of variables. Instead of knowing merely that the response, R, is some function of the variables $X_1, X_2, X_3, \ldots X_n$, he desires to know the precise function. But in such

---

phor 'psychological environment'? Is it not the business of science to ascertain which objective factors in the past and present states of the organism and its environment account for the difference in response, so that we can actually predict it instead of attributing it, merely descriptively and after it has happened, to a difference in the psychological environment?" (1943).

8 Mention should perhaps be made here of the fact that the theoretical constructs (factors) that Spearman (1927), Thurstone (1935), and other factor analysts arrive at are response derived and hence fall into this class. These men do not, of course, use the phenomenological method, but beginning with response intercorrelations (empirical $R–R$ relations) they arrive at hypothetical factors by various methods of mathematical analysis. Like the phenomenologists their theoretical factors have no tie-up with the S variables.

a situation, involving as it does a large number of variables, the function relating the dependent and independent variables is so complicated that we are unable to conceive of it directly. It is necessary, say Hull and Tolman, to proceed by conceiving of it as broken down into successive sets of simpler component functions. These component functions begin by introducing new intervening constructs defined in terms of the independent variables. Further intervening variables are then introduced by stating them as functions of the first set of intervening constructs, until finally the dependent behavior variable is postulated to be a function of one or more of the intervening variables.

Thus Tolman, beginning with the empirical data that the response measure is some function (f_1) of two groups of independent variables (environmental variables and individual difference variables), writes (1938, p. 9):

In place of the original f_1 function, I have introduced a set of intervening variables, I_a, I_b, I_c, etc., few or many, according to the particular theory. And I have conceived a set of f functions to connect these intervening variables severally to the independent variables on the one hand, and an f_3 function to combine them together and connect them to the final dependent variable on the other.

It is characteristic of Tolman's theorizing, however, that it never gets beyond the programmatic stage. In his writings Tolman has merely shown how such a theoretical device as the "intervening variable" can provide for the definition and proper utilization within psychology of such mentalistic terms as "demands," "hypotheses," "traits," "discriminanda," etc., but he never actually reaches the point of formulating a specific theory. In the present context this would, of course, require the precise specification of the various functions relating the intervening variables to the independent and dependent experimental variables. Instead of risking guesses on such matters, however, Tolman seems to prefer to ascertain them empirically by a series of what he calls "standard experimental set-ups." He believes the data from these studies will mirror the functions obtaining between the experimental (empirical) and intervening (theoretical) variables.[9]

Quite in contrast to such an approach, Hull has ventured to make

---

[9] Tolman has been accused (and he has usually made no denial) of employing the phenomenological method in his psychology, and, because he has worked with animals, of being guilty of anthropomorphism. The present writer's interpretation is that it is Tolman, the experimentalist, who uses phenomenological introspection; Tolman, the theorist, introduces his intervening variables in terms of objectively defined variables. The difference between Lewin and Tolman on this point is interesting. Lewin, as we have seen, employs the phenomenological method primarily in his theoretical efforts, whereas Tolman uses it chiefly in the formulation of experimental problems.

guesses as to the precise nature of the functions introducing the intervening variables in his theoretical formulations. Thus he has attempted to formulate the basic laws of simple adaptive behavior (learning) by introducing a number of intervening variables.[10] Beginning with the experimental variables, he has introduced by means of specific mathematical functions such symbolic constructs as stimulus trace (s), habit strength ($_sH_R$), the limit of habit strength (M), excitatory potential ($_sE_R$), inhibitory potential (I_R), effective excitatory potential ($_s\overline{E}_R$), and so on. Ultimately the observable response variable, R, is stated to be some function of the final intervening variable (e.g., $R = f(_s\overline{E}_R)$). Despite the neurophysiological tone of some of the terms that Hull employs to designate these constructs, the mistake should not be made of interpreting them as physiological concepts. Their scientific meaning is given only by the equations introducing them, and in this respect they are strictly comparable to many similar, abstract, mathematical constructs employed by the physicist in his theorizing. The use of neurophysiological terms and such additional statements as Hull sometimes makes as to their possible locus in the nervous system merely serve the purpose of providing experimental hints to persons interested in such matters. It may or may not turn out that they represent actual neurophysiological states or conditions that will some day be measurable by independent neurophysiological procedures.

An example of the specific manner in which Hull introduces his theoretical constructs is shown by the equations which he employs to define the two constructs, habit strength ($_sH_R$) and the limit of habit strength (M). With all experimental variables except the number of reinforced trials (N) and the length of the delay of the goal reinforcement (L) constant, the two equations are:

$$_sH_R = M(1 - e^{-iN})$$
$$M = 100e^{-kL}$$

Grice (1942) has recently shown how such precisely defined theoretical constructs may be tested. He employed several mazes of different absolute lengths involving a shorter and longer path to the goal and ran different groups of rats on each maze. On the basis of the above two equations the following rational equation was then derived mathematically to describe the rate of learning the mazes:

$$\left[N = b \log \left(\frac{e^{-kL} - e^{-kHL}}{e^{-kL} - e^{-kHL} - a} \right) \right].$$

---

[10] Reference is made here to Hull's latest writings in which the "intervening variable" technique is made more explicit. As Bergmann and Spence (1941) have pointed out, Hull's earlier miniature systems (1937, 1940) really involved the definition of such mediating constructs.

Where N = number of pairs of trials on the two paths to learn the maze.

L = length of short path to goal.

H = ratio of long to short path length.

k, a, b = empirical constants.

This rational equation was then shown to fit the experimental data, whereas another equation

$$\left[N = b \log \left(\frac{\log H}{\log H - C} \right) \right]$$

derived from a logarithmic postulate[11] as to the relation of M to L was shown not to be in agreement with the experimental data.

Until constructs are introduced in some such precise fashion as Hull employs one really does not have a scientific theory, for it is only under such conditions that the possibility of verification or refutation exists. Unfortunately, much of what has passed for theory in psychology has been sadly lacking in this respect, a state of affairs which is largely responsible for many of the "theoretical" controversies, and for the low regard in which theory is held in some quarters in psychology. That theory construction has not always been intelligently pursued, however, is no reason for doing without theory. Without the generalizations which theories aim to provide we should never be in a position to predict behavior, for knowledge of particular events does not provide us with a basis for prediction when the situation differs in the least degree. The higher the level of abstraction that can be obtained the greater will be both the understanding and actual control achieved.

IV. The Ultra-Positivistic Approach

All the methods of ascertaining the laws of psychology we have discussed so far have agreed, in principle at least, that it is necessary to introduce some type of symbolic construct. It is also apparent that agreement ceases as regards the extent to which the proponents of these different views have insisted on rigorous and objective specification. We turn now to a quite different approach to the same problem—that of the ultra-positivist or empiricist, who tries to eschew all types of theoretical constructs. Usually the writings of such persons are limited to negativistic, critical attacks on all theory. Recently, however, Woodrow has come forward with a constructive proposal as to how general mathematical laws of psychology may be discovered by a method which he believes avoids the necessity of introducing theoretical constructs.

Woodrow's method consists in an attempt to obtain by mathematical

---

[11] $M = 100 - K \log L.$

curve fitting a general equation describing a wide variety of experimental facts. Thus, after plotting a series of experimental curves of such widely varying situations as learning to abstract, learning to associate numbers and letters, learning a maze, reaction time to different intensities of stimulation, the forgetting of monosyllabic words, brightness and pitch discrimination, the growth of intelligence, etc., Woodrow sought to fit these empirical curves by means of a single general equation. He found that such an equation could be found and that it took the following form:

$$Y = a + \sqrt{p^2 + k^2(1 - f^{x+d})^2}$$

This equation states a law between two experimental variables, a dependent response variable Y, e.g., errors, successes, latencies, etc., and an independent manipulable variable X, e.g., number of practice periods, intensity of the stimulus, preparatory interval, etc. But it will be noticed further that the law includes more than these two variables. It also involves certain constants or unknowns, termed parameters, the a, p, k, f, and d in the equation. We cannot stop to discuss these parameters in too great detail here. Suffice it to say that the specific shapes of the different empirical curves determine what parameters it is necessary to assume. Two of them, a and b, have no particular psychological significance, they merely express the fact that either one or both variables may have been measured by scales with an arbitrary zero. The parameter, k, is introduced because all his curves exhibit a limit to improvement, no matter how favorable the status given the environmental variable. Another parameter, f, is determined by the rate of approach of the curve to this limit and p, finally, is introduced to take care of the fact that the lower part of the curve sometimes shows positive acceleration.

As Woodrow himself points out, these parameters may be thought of, if one so wishes, as representing hypothetical states or factors within the organism.[12] Woodrow prefers not to do so, for, as he argues, it really makes little difference what the internal referents are since they cannot at present be independently measured anyway. From the point of view of finding a general equation or law that will fit the experimental data the important thing, Woodrow states, is to determine how many parameters are required and the mathematical function of each.

While in general sympathy with Woodrow's mathematical approach and his view that it is unnecessary to specify the factors or complexes of factors inside the organism which determine the values of the param-

[12] Woodrow writes (23, p. 4), "Now these parameters may refer to anything whatsoever, conscious, physiological, environmental, psychic, or purely imaginary. Here one is free to follow his predilections, whether for motives, excitatory and inhibitory substances, field forces, states of disequilibrium, inertia of the nervous system, abilities, or what not."

eters, the writer is, nevertheless, of the opinion that such an equation as Woodrow obtains by his analysis is, on the whole, rather barren and sterile. Its defect is not that the factors *within* the subject are not specified, but rather that it fails to give any indication whatever of the conditions or variables even *outside* the subject which determine these parameters. In this respect Woodrow's approach is similar to the field theorists'. We shall have occasion later to point out other resemblances between these two approaches.

This criticism can be made clearer, perhaps, by contrasting the end result of Woodrow's empirical procedure with Hull's rational approach to the same problem. Woodrow's law specifies but a single experimental variable determining the response:

$$Y = f(X_1).$$

Hull's theorozing culminates in a much more comprehensive law. Thus in the case of his theoretical formulation of simple adaptive behavior (learning) his derivation involves the following series of steps:

1. $\boxed{M} = f(T, G)$
2. $\boxed{H} = f(\boxed{M}, T', N)$
3. $\boxed{D} = f(T'')$
4. $\boxed{E} = f(\boxed{D}, \boxed{H})$
5. $\boxed{I} = f(N, W, F)$
6. $\boxed{\bar{E}} = f(\boxed{E}, \boxed{I})$
7. $R = f(\boxed{\bar{\bar{E}}}).$

Here the squared symbols are intervening variables or hypothetical constructs. The other symbols represent the dependent response measure (R) and the various manipulable, environmental variables $(T, G, T',$ etc.). By substituting in the successive equations, a single equation R as a function of seven environmental variables is obtained.[13]

$$R = f(T, G, T', N, T'', W, F)$$

The latter procedure thus comes much closer to achieving the goal of the scientist, that of discovering all of the experimental variables determining the response measure and the nature of the functional interrela-

---

[13] The reader may ask: Why have a series of equations that introduce intervening variables? Why not write the single equation from the beginning and avoid the hypothetical constructs? One obvious reason, of course, is that it is just not possible to conceive of such a complex function all at once. As Tolman says, one can arrive at it only by breaking it down into a series of simpler functions. The reader is referred to a recent article by Hull in which he gives other reasons for using intervening variables with multiple equations rather than a single equation (1943b).

tions holding between them. If this is achieved, the parameters become known functions of these experimental variables and thus become experimentally manipulable. Woodrow's formulation, on the other hand, provides us with very little more information than we had when we started.

It is also interesting to note that a strong case can be made out for the position that Woodrow's method is really not a great deal different from those theoretical approaches which infer their constructs from the characteristics of the response. In introducing his parameters Woodrow is, in effect, assuming or postulating some kind of hypothetical factor. Thus, on noticing that some of his curves show an initial period of positive acceleration, Woodrow assumes a factor, p, "whose influence is greatest when the magnitude of the environmental variable is small" (1942, p. 7). This factor is inferred, we see, from the characteristics of the response curve and is therefore in a certain sense akin to the hypothetical constructs of the field theorists which, as we have seen, are also inferred from the response characteristics. The important difference is that in arriving at these hypothetical factors Woodrow does not make use of the introspective report associated with a response but rather bases his constructs on the mathematical properties of a curve of successive response measures.

V. Conclusions

In summary, the present paper has stated the task of the psychologist to be that of discovering the general laws of behavior, and has attempted to present a brief and critical outline of five different methods of approaching this task. The conclusions that the writer believes may be drawn from this survey are:

1. That theory is still at a very primitive level in psychology, concerning itself primarily with the discovery of low-order laws rather than the integration of different realms of laws.

2. That there is a variety of different theoretical procedures possible in psychology.

3. That some psychologists, substitute, often quite unconsciously, phenomenological introspection and anthropomorphic thinking for theorizing. There is, of course, nothing wrong with such introspection; it has often served as a means of formulating interesting and valuable experiments. In such instances, however, the credit should not be given to a theory.

4. That many theories in psychology have provided us with response-response (R-R) laws rather than stimulus-response (S-R) laws.

5. That the most promising theoretical technique, especially from the point of view of discovering the historical stimulus-response laws, is the so-called "intervening variable" method proposed by Hull and Tolman.

References

Bergmann, G. Psychoanalysis and experimental psychology: A review from the standpoint of scientific empiricism. *Mind*, 1943, *52*, 122–140.

Bergmann, G., and Spence, K. W. Operationism and theory in psychology. *Psychol. Rev.*, 1941, *48*, 1–14.

Carnap, R. Testability and meaning. *Philos. Sci.*, 1936, *3*, 419–471; 1937, *4*, 1–40.

Grice, G. R. An experimental study of the gradient of reinforcement in maze learning. *J. Exp. Psychol.*, 1942, *30*, 475–489.

Hull, C. L. Mind, mechanism and adaptive behavior. *Psychol. Rev.*, 1937, *44*, 1–32.

———. *Principles of behavior*. New York: D. Appleton-Century, 1943(a).

———. The problem of intervening variables in molar behavior theory. *Psychol. Rev.*, 1943, *50*, 273–291(b).

Hull, C. L., Hovland, C. I., Ross, R. T., Hall, M., Perkins, D. T., and Fitch, F. B. *Mathematico-deductive theory of rote learning*. New Haven: Yale Univ. Press, 1940.

Koch, S. The logical character of the motivation concept. II. *Psychol. Rev.*, 1941, *48*, 127–154.

Koffka, K. *Principles of Gestalt psychology*. New York: Harcourt, Brace, 1935.

Köhler, W. *Gestalt psychology*. New York: Liveright, 1929.

———. *Dynamics in psychology*. New York: Liveright, 1940.

Lewin, K. *A dynamic theory of personality*. (Trans. by D. K. Adams and K. E. Zener) New York: McGraw-Hill, 1935.

———. *Principles of topological psychology*. (Trans. by Fritz and Grace Heider) New York: McGraw-Hill, 1936.

———. Field theory and learning. In *Forty-First Year Natl. Soc. Stud. Educ.* Part II. Bloomington, Ill.: Public School Publishing Co., 1942, 215–242.

Pavlov, I. P. *Conditioned reflexes*. (Trans. by F. C. Anrep.) London: Oxford Univ. Press, 1927.

Snygg, D. The need for a phenomenological system of psychology. *Psychol. Rev.*, 1941, *48*, 404–424.

Spearman, C. *The abilities of man*. New York: Macmillan, 1927.

Spence, K. W. Theoretical interpretations of learning. In F. A. Moss (ed.), *Comparative psychology* (rev. ed.) Englewood Cliffs, N.J.: Prentice-Hall, 1942, Chap. 11.

Thurstone, L. L. *The vectors of mind*. Chicago: Univ. of Chicago Press, 1935.

Tolman, E. C. Operational behaviorism and current trends in psychology. *Proc. 25th Anniv. Celebr. Inaug. Grad. Stud.* Los Angeles: Univ. of S. Calif. Press, 1936, 89–103.

———. The determiners of behavior at a choice point. *Psychol. Rev.*, 1938, *45*, 1–41.

Woodrow, H. The problem of general quantitative laws in psychology. *Psychol. Bull.*, 1942, *39*, 1–27.

9 | *Events and Constructs in Psychology*

J. R. KANTOR

Philosophy: Banished and Recalled

For several decades the double-barreled legend circulated in psychology that this discipline dates its coming of age as a science from the day that it separated from philosophy, and that it has accelerated its scientific advancement simply by confining itself exclusively to laboratory manipulations and leaving theories aside. Characteristic legend, setting forth the reverse of what was obviously happening even in the best established sciences, and notably in physics, which has always been regarded as the acme of science. It is probable that psychologists were not too much embarrassed by repeating the fable while acting contrary to it, because they took this to be just another instance of theory diverging from practice.

Happily the paradox was soon resolved. Psychologists began loudly to proclaim that philosophy was not only closely articulated with psychology but that by means of its help there was going to be produced in America "a behavioral discipline which will be a full-blown natural science."[1] In the paper from which this quotation is culled Hall asserts that the combination of two kinds of philosophy (Viennese Logical Positivism, American Pragmatism), two kinds of methodology (American Behaviorism, Operationism), all coupled with Pavlovian experimentation, will bring about a great science of psychology.

It must be admitted that psychologists assumed that the philosophy to be recalled would be a different kind from that which was banished. Certainly there were new names. What became acceptable was called philosophy of science and logic of science. Unfortunately, events negated

From *Interbehavioral psychology* (2nd rev. ed.). Bloomington, Ind.: Principia Press, 1959, pp. 257–265. First printed in the *Psychological Record*, 1957, 7, 55–60. Reprinted by permission of the author, Principia Press, and the *Psychological Record*.

[1] Hull, C. L. The problem of intervening variables in molar behavior theory, *Psychol. Rev.*, 1943, 50, 273–291.

this belief. As we shall see, the new philosophy, including all its analysis and structuring of language, remains still the same venerable epistemology and metaphysics. What had changed was a superstructural system. The metasystem or metalogic remained the same.[2]

Nevertheless, something was achieved for psychological thinking by this expulsion and recall of philosophy. There arose a growing appreciation by psychologists of the nature and significance of constructs and their relation to events. Certainly the intensified interest in the perennial problem of hypotheses in scientific work promised to have a useful outcome.

If only this appreciation did not exemplify the perversity that good principles do not always eventuate in good practice! What is a guarantee that the new interest in constructs or their role in science will prevent the assimilation of both events and constructs to traditional ways of thinking? If this could be prevented it would undoubtedly be of tremendous significance for psychological investigation. It is the goal of this paper to clarify somewhat the nature of events and constructs and thereby to indicate the proper envisagement of their relationships. We consider these important factors briefly.

Events and Constructs

Events may be simply described as anything that happens which may or may not become known or studied. Obviously if persons do not discover or become interested in certain objects, processes, or relations these will not be brought into the scientific domain. But unless our thinking is debauched by epistemological institutions we will not think that when scientists discovered electrical induction, radio waves, microscopic organisms, cosmic rays, the physiological changes in digestion, gestation or exhaustion, or the psychological processes of color discrimination, learning and unlearning they somehow created these events.

Of course no scientist would admit that he confuses events with his own creations, his own constructs. Nor does he in certain obvious situations. But we insist that much bad thinking in science is traceable to just this admixture of events and constructs.

What are the circumstances favoring this confusion? There are primarily two, the first being the necessity to deal with complex and elusive events, and the second that the scientist must work with many contrived events. As to the former, we know the difficulties that arise from the study of electrons, neutrons, and positrons when the investigator relies on cloud chambers, sensitive films, etc. As to the contrived events, great

---

[2] Cf. Kantor, *Psychology and logic*. Bloomington, Ill.: Principia Press, Vol. 1, 1945; Vol. 2, 1950.

alertness is required, for example, to keep distinct a) the work of trans-forming plutonium to americium and americium to its range of isotopes, from b) the starting material at the various stages, but such alertness means only following the simplest rule of scientific conduct. Such facts as we have mentioned enforce the need to observe the differences be-tween events and constructs instead of confusing them.

Constructs may be best described as products derived from inter-behaving with events. For example, the number set down as the result of applying a measuring rod to some object gives us a very definite con-struct. We go on from this to words of description, records of measure-ments or manipulations, mathematical or symbological equations, or formulae in all of their various forms. Once they are produced they may be used as tools in scientific investigation. The range of constructs is very wide, and often constructs are acts themselves. The acts of select-ing some specific type of events for study may be called operational constructs; taking an attitude toward events also may be a construct. In general, the term "construct" may be applied to acts as well as products of action. But constructs in any form or style are not to be confounded with the events or stimulus objects in connection with which they are engendered.

Keeping events and constructs separate and clear surely should fore-stall the old egoistic epistemological assimilation of events by constructs. There should be no problem as to whether or not things can exist inde-pendently of the knowledge of them. The creational view pictured in the standard mentalistic doctrine of perception is completely out of place in a naturalistic age. By the same token we achieve information about the potentialities and limitations of constructs when we employ them in connection with events in actual scientific situations.

"Variable," Variable, and *Variable*

Many of the problems concerning events and constructs are excel-lently pointed up by the way psychologists use the term "variable." It is employed for referring to an event as well as to a construct. Yet it is obvious how necessary it is to differentiate three things, namely, a) lin-guistic terms, b) event factors, and c) constructs.

a) As to the term "variable," it is worthy of note that mathematicians, who may claim priority for its use, frequently confuse it with the set of values with which they may be concerned at the moment. They also de-liberately confound constructs and terms when they describe a variable as a sign or symbol. If mathematicians may be allowed an excuse for thus confusing different things it lies in the fact that to a great extent mathe-maticians work with constructed events. Better it is, however, even for them to observe the differences between 1) constructs, and 2) the relations, the dependencies, and mutual connections, and constitute mathematical subject matter. Those who work with nonmathematical things must be even more careful.

b) Variables as events are easily pinned down. We have already pointed out that relations of various types are the events in the mathematical domain. In the more concrete sciences they are usually 1) phases, aspects, or units of objects, 2) actions, or 3) changes. In the psychological domain the immediate examples one thinks of are the response changes of organisms when stimulus objects change. Other examples are the various conditions of organisms (fatigue, satiation, toxications, etc.), of objects (complexly patterned, partially concealed or masked, etc.), or of the total situation which includes both organism and stimulus objects. Probably the terms "variant" and "factor" may be more advantageously used than the term "variable."

c) *Variables* as constructs are often similar to those mathematicians use. They are products of counting and measuring and take the form of numbers or relations. But they are not restricted to these forms. Sometimes the term "variable" is employed to refer to descriptive words for any variant or factor isolated from a complex event. And unfortunately, psychologists do not limit themselves to event factors but use the term "variable" for purely autistic constructs, that is, constructs that are not only not derived from events but do not correspond to any event at all. Psychologists will at once be reminded here of the notorious intervening variables.

The Case of Intervening Variables

The invention and propagation of the construct *intervening variable* affords an excellent study of the whole problem of constructs and their relation to events. If we trace the origin of the construct back to Tolman's 1936 article on operational behaviorism[3] we see that his purpose was to find a place for mental processes in his analysis of behavior. He says, "the sole 'cash value' of mental processes lies, I shall assert, in this their character as a set of intermediating functional processes which interconnect between the initiating causes of behavior, on the one hand, and the final resulting behavior itself, on the other." Again he says, "Mental processes are but intervening variables between the five independent variables of 1) *environmental stimuli*, 2) *physiological drive*, 3) *heredity*,

---

[3] Operational behaviorism and current trends in psychology, *Proc. 25th Anniv. Celeb. Inaug. Grad. Stud.*, Los Angeles: Univ. of South. Calif. Press, 1936; reprinted in Marx, *Psychological theory*, N.Y.: Macmillan, 1951.

4) *previous training*, and 5) *maturity*, on the one hand, and the final dependent variable, *behavior*, on the other."[4]

This straightforward mentalistic version was later modified so that the intervening constructs pointed to unobservable and unobserved events or phases of events. The scope of the construct was enlarged to include hidden neural processes in addition to purely psychic ones. Whether the intervening construct is limited to mental or neural processes or combinations of both, it does not correspond to psychological events.

In addition to imposing psychic qualities upon psychological events there is a complete transformation of such events. It is incontrovertible that psychological events consist of complex fields including reacting organisms and the objects with which they interact plus a number of setting factors. These are all acknowledged in some form in the various writings which feature intervening variables.

But note how the complex field has been distorted by imposing upon it unknown or unknowable variables. First the field is broken up into dependent and independent variables. Then the dependent variables is reduced to simple movements and the independent variables to "causal" conditions. No wonder the intervening constructionist believes he requires such free creations.

Why the notion of intervention altogether? As the numerous articles on the subject effectively indicate, variable intervention is simply a technique for loading the organism with internal principles and powers. As we have seen, one form of intervening elements merely consists of the old mentalistic constructs of *sensation idea, memory* and *thought* which guide and determine the movements of the organism. Has our whole recent objective and experimental tradition given us no more solid and dependable result than this? It is a sad reflection that all the help psychologists got from the logician, the operationist, and experimentation has resulted only in this reduction of events to arbitrary constructs.

But even if the intervening variables are presumed to be organic factors, for example, neural processes, there is no warrant for making a part of the action of the organism a determiner for the whole action, that is, the entire behavior segment or field. On the other hand, if the intervening determiners are completely imaginary neural processes, the whole notion of intervention goes by the board since the variables are only the words uttered to mention them.

A word must be said here about the argument that intervening vari-

---

[4] Not only the term "cash value" but the entire intervention idea is straight from James. In the *Principles of psychology*, Vol. I, p. 6, he says: "Can we state more distinctly still the manner in which the mental life seems to intervene between impressions made from without upon the body, and reactions of the body upon the outer world again?"

ables as created entities can be supported by some operational principle. We need only point out how often in the history of psychology some sign has been taken as proof of the existence of something asserted by the faithful. Small wonder then that the proponents of intervening variables have had to invent purely verbal anchorages for them. Even if we over-look the non-eventual ground of the intervening constructs, they are only necessary because what are really simultaneous factors in a field have illegitimately been transformed into antecedent and succeedent ele-ments. Granting that the notion of varying a stimulus in order to change a response has been derived from laboratory procedure, we still have here a confusion of constructs and events. This confusion stems from a misinterpretation of what is allowable in the constructional procedure. We turn, therefore, to a brief consideration of the problems involved in the process of scientific construction, including its role in the enter-prise, and the restrictions to be placed upon it.

Freedom of Construction in Science

How free is the constructional procedure? This question no doubt lies at the base of so much recent writing on the process of creating hypo-thetical entities and symbolic constructs. There can, however, be only one answer. Unless constructs are derived from events, they are likely to be autistic creations. Authentic psychological events afford no occa-sion for asserting the existence of hidden powers or entities. For example, anyone not influenced by the presupposition of traditional philosophy can easily see that what are called intervening variables are actually super-vening "variables." When intervening variables are identified with such factors as fatigue, previous training, or abnormality of the organisms they are extravening or setting factors.[5] If we persist in keeping before us the events with which we actually work, we will not confuse authen-tic hypotheses, namely, constructs regulated and controlled by the events that set the investigative problems, with the licentious products of autis-tic creation. It is an operational *non sequitur* to conclude, from the ob-vious fact that scientific work is primarily constructional, that hypotheti-cal entities may be arbitrarily created.

The Role of Construction in Science

No scientific rule is better established than the one that construction in science consists essentially of various operations with respect to events

---

[5] Cf. Kantor, *The principles of psychology*, Vol. I: *A survey of the science of psychology*, Chap. 2. New York: Knopf, 1924.

encountered. These operations consist of definite and palpable actions performed in order to ascertain the existence, nature, and relation of things and events.[6] These operations may be classified as a) observations and manipulations, b) descriptions, and c) explanations or interpretations. In each case the work of the scientist results in a product which may or may not be added to the scientific stock pile.

MANIPULATIVE CONSTRUCTION   Under this heading we place all the work of formulating a problem with respect to particular events and constructing some plan or hypothesis for attacking it and probably solving it. The activities here, including the work of constructing the needed apparatus, form a definite continuum. All of the activities constitute definite types of interbehavior, though some may be very subtle.

Of unique interest here is the point that only problems and hypotheses securely connected with events can be validated. Acceptable products can only be derived from such interbehavior with events. There can be no experimental validation of any autistic or conventional hypothesis. To take a classical illustration, no operation performed by Fechner could validate his hypothesis concerning the measurement of psychic states.

DESCRIPTIVE CONSTRUCTION   The primary aim of this work is to sum up the ascertained characteristics of an event. Among the actual products may be statements, diagrams, and numerical or topological formulae. The products may be laid out on a descending scale of validity and scientific usefulness, as 1) directly derivable from contacts with events, 2) analogically descriptive, 3) imposed by borrowing from some other field, and 4) completely invented.

EXPLANATORY CONSTRUCTION   While making such constructions the worker is largely motivated to make a system to interrelate events. Generally speaking, there is potentially more freedom here, provided by the possibility of ranging rather widely among data. Psychological events may be related, though not reduced to, events of physics, chemistry, various biological things and events, or social events. While any valid or useful explanation will not depart far from the original events, a greater latitude is present for originality in constructing maps, diagrams, propositions, formulae, and other sorts of products that will point to the characteristics and relations of things and events. The line is sharply drawn against constructs entirely unrelated to things and events or such as substitute for them, distort them, and misrepresent them. No creation of entities such as synaptic resistance, inhibitory potentials, cell assemblies, brain storage, or brain determination is permissible if the line between science and folklore is to be maintained. By way of summarizing

---

[6] Cf. Kantor, *The logic of modern science*. Bloomington, Ill.: Principia Press, 1953.

the problems of constructs in science, including psychology, we suggest that, whatever philosophy scientists require must be clearly different from both the kind banished and recalled. It must be a critical analysis of events, procedures, and constructions which must interlock with a naturalistic and non-traditional psychology. As a means of implementing this suggestion we conclude this paper with the following rules concerning scientific constructions.

Rules Regulating Scientific Constructions and Their Products

1. Term constructs and casual constructs must be carefully distinguished from descriptive and interpretive constructs and all of these from the original events.

2. Valid and useful constructs can only be derived from contacts with the events referred to, described, and explained.

3. To be avoided is the imposition of constructs borrowed from other domains even when they are derived from events.

4. Even more to be avoided as invalid and useless are constructional products derived from cultural and philosophical traditions.

5. Construction must be controlled to prevent the imposition of products, even though they may have been properly derived from investigative operations, upon the original events.

6. Obstructions to contact with events (lack of apparatus and techniques, and insufficiency of knowledge) warrant only the making of tentative constructs, but not autistic creations.

7. Since scientific work consists basically of operations upon events, there can be no valid constructs concerning unobservables.

8. No manipulation of sentences (reducing them one to another, substituting one for another, making one equivalent to another) can be substituted for operations upon events. In general, linguistic operations have only very limited functions.

9. Systems of constructs are no better than the individual product elements. No scientific value accrues to the heaping up of autistic elements into a grand system.

10. Valid constructional work in science can only be based upon the appreciation that the philosophy and logic of science must have reached as high a stage of development as current scientific research.

10 | *The Dimension of Operational Clarity*

MELVIN H. MARX

I

The improved scientific sophistication evidenced within recent years by psychological theorists has been largely characterized by an increased sensitivity to the need for operational validity in the formation and use of logical constructs. It has also become increasingly apparent, however, that operational validity, in and of itself, provides no guarantee of effective psychological theory construction. As constructs are made progressively more operational they must by definition be progressively divorced from the hypothetical content which seems to be regarded as a desirable if not essential component by a number of theorists. Within the past year both Tolman (1949) and Krech (1949), prominent theorists of so-called field-theoretical inclinations, have argued for the inclusion of a definite amount of hypothetical content in logical constructs. It is especially discouraging to find Tolman, whose introduction of the *intervening variable* (1936, 1938) contributed notably to the establishment of the recent operational trend, now apparently reversing his earlier position and stating that "to use Meehl and MacCorquodale's distinction, I would now abandon what they call pure 'intervening variables' for what they call 'hypothetical constructs,' and insist that hypothetical constructs be parts of a more general hypothesized model or substrate" (1949, p. 49).

One may certainly agree with Professor Tolman in his concern for the development of useful models. Nevertheless, it seems to be not only unnecessary but also distinctly dangerous to abandon the operationally defined intervening construct. It is the purpose of this paper, therefore, to attempt a clarification of the problem of the relationship between hypothesis and construct, as these are used in contemporary psychological theory construction. The hypothetical construct and the intervening

From M. H. Marx, Intervening variable or hypothetical construct? *Psychol. Rev.*, 1951, *58*, 235–247. Reprinted by permission of the author, the *Psychological Review*, and the American Psychological Association.

variable, to continue MacCorquodale and Meehl's (1948) terminology, are regarded as lying on a single continuum, each type of construct having a certain useful function in the development of theory but the fully operational type remaining the ultimate theoretical objective. If psychological theories are to be placed on a sound scientific basis, logical constructs of the more distinctly operational type must first supplement and *eventually* replace those of the hypothetical construct type. However, it should be noted that there has probably been a tendency to overlook the value of constructs of the hypothetical type on the part of the more objectively oriented stimulus-response theorists (e.g., Hull, 1943[a], 1943[b]; Spence, 1944, 1948), as well as an opposite tendency to minimize the value of the operational type on the part of the field-theorists. If the wholesale abandonment of operationally valid constructs is not required for the effective use of less operationally-defined constructs, neither is the wholesale abandonment of the latter type required for the effective use of the former.

In attempting a clarification of this problem the present paper has a twofold objective: first, to point out the *different* functions of each type of construct, and thereby justify their continued supplementary use; second, to describe a type of intervening variable which gives promise of offering an operationally sound alternative to the hypothetical construct but whose potential usefulness has not thus far been formally recognized.

II

Since the terminological distinction recently proposed by MacCorquodale and Meehl will be followed, a summary of their interpretation of the terms "intervening variable" and "hypothetical construct" will be useful. These authors distinguish between "constructs which merely abstract the empirical relationships (Tolman's original intervening variables) and those constructs which are 'hypothetical' (i.e., involve the supposition of entities or processes not among the observed)" (1948, pp. 106–107). They then summarize three characteristics whose presence is typically indicative of the purely abstractive kind of construct—the "intervening variable," as they propose to call it—and whose absence is indicative of the "hypothetical construct." These characteristics are:

First, the statement of such a concept does not contain any words which are not reducible to the empirical laws. Second, the validity of the empirical laws is both necessary and sufficient for the "correctness" of the statements about the concept. Third, the quantitative expression of the concept can be obtained without mediate inference by suitable groupings of terms in the quantitative empirical laws. (1948, p. 107).

In the present discussion a somewhat less detailed differentiation is required between the two terms, although the general tenor of Mac-Corquodale and Meehl's distinction is retained. By intervening variable is meant any intervening construct with a maximum amount of operational validity, or direct empirical reference, and by hypothetical construct is meant any construct with a relatively low degree of operational validity. These two terms, while specifically applicable to behavior problems, may thus be related to a wider methodological framework.

It is also necessary to recognize that a clear-cut distinction can not always be drawn, in actual practice, between these two "types" of constructs. Any such impression, based upon the treatment by MacCorquodale and Meehl or the following discussion, should be quickly discouraged. For the sake of convenience in exposition, however, their essential continuity will not generally be emphasized in the following sections.

III

We may begin our consideration of this problem with a brief examination of the origin and development of logical constructs. A series of stages in this development will be roughly classified and briefly described.

1. PRE-SCIENTIFIC ORIGINS   From an historical point of view, logical constructs, like scientific problems and hypotheses, originate in the common-sense reflections of men. At a somewhat more sophisticated stage of concept development various refinements may be made which tend to sharpen the dictionary definitions of concepts, and thus gain a certain degree of verbal appeal, but do little to tighten the relations between the concept and the relatively uncontrolled observations which produce it. Such refinements are typically made in philosophy, theology, politics and similar fields. Distinct and dogmatic biases in some of these fields often provide a certain consistency to conceptualizations but scarcely improve their operational validity. Little interest is shown in operational definitions.

2. PRELIMINARY SCIENTIFIC FORMULATIONS   As objective scientific interests arise in a special subject matter area two basically conflicting needs, which may be seen as fundamental to the subsequent conflict between hypothetical content and operational validity in constructs, become apparent. On the one hand, there is the immediate need for a scientific formulation of problems. Old questions have to be reworded in such a manner that relevant and controlled data can be collected. On the other hand, there is also the increasing pressure for continued operational refinement of the conceptual system that has been taken over, by and large, from the grossly non-operational systems of the earlier pre-

scientific periods. The result is that the pioneering scientist is typically forced to compromise—that is, to brush up his conceptualizations, at least making some gestures in the direction of more operational validity, but actually retaining a certain significant degree of hypothetical content.

a. *General role of hypothetical constructs.* Let us examine more closely the role of the hypothetical construct in the preliminary phases of a new scientific development, such as has been represented within the past few decades by psychology. Of the host of concomitant problems facing the scientist none is more important than the need to ask, as simply and objectively as possible, the kind of straightforward questions which can be given direct empirical answers. Now such questions, it should be apparent, are not easily discovered—not, that is, if they are to have that systematic usefulness that is required of any comprehensive scientific development. In all phases of science such empirical questions must be derived from some kind of prior hypotheses (cf. Cohen and Nagel, 1934, ch. 11). In the framing of these hypotheses the scientist must of course use whatever conceptual materials are at hand. In the absence of previous operational refinements he will be forced to rely, in a manner that ought to be explicitly recognized as a temporary expedient, upon such operationally inadequate conceptualizations as we are calling hypothetical constructs. How quickly such constructs can be replaced by more operational ones will, of course, depend upon a number of complex factors, among which may be mentioned the difficulty of the specific subject matter, the ingenuity and scientific skills of the investigators, etc. It is fairly obvious that large differences of this kind have thus far accounted for the appreciable variations in scientific development among the divisions of behavior study.

b. *Problems of semantic usage.* Effective scientific construct formation is complicated by certain unavoidable terminological difficulties. Although these operate at all stages of scientific development they are most apparent, and probably most serious, during the early phases.

It is important to recognize, at the outset, that this semantic problem is actually distinct from the problem of operational validity, although the two are easily and commonly confused in practice. That is, the question of operational validity concerns simply the problem of relating constructs, however they may be named, to the particular empirical data from which they were derived (cf. Pratt, 1939; Marx, 1963). We are now concerned with the independent problem of choosing names for constructs which, whatever degree of operational validity may be present, will most effectively express their observational basis as well as their theoretical implications to those other persons with whom the scientist wishes to communicate.

An immediate problem is posed, as new constructs are introduced or old ones modified, by the necessity of either 1) using old words, or other symbols, which ordinarily already have acquired a variety of vaguely overlapping meanings, or 2) coining new words or other symbols which may carry relatively unambiguous meaning but are seldom received with much enthusiasm by those outside the immediate systematic framework within which the new concept was developed.[1] In neither case, unfortunately, is there likely to be a long-lasting clarity of meaning achieved, since in spite of the best precautions each reader tends to read into the word, and to a lesser extent perhaps the other types of symbols, his own meanings and biases. This tendency then becomes more difficult to avoid as the term is circulated more widely, perhaps gaining in popularity and thus being increasingly related to other, less carefully defined conceptualizations. The use of isolated letters of mathematical symbols, exemplified by Hull's systematic behavior theory (1943[a], 1950), does appear to have the advantage of at least reducing the rate of such popular contamination.

From the standpoint of the subsequent user of the various symbols that represent scientific concepts, a suggestion by Maslow (1945) seems to merit serious consideration. He has proposed the formal use of what many of us probably tend to do more or less implicitly and informally —namely, the appending of a subscript, consisting of the original author's name or initial, to indicate the specific meaning that is intended by the use of the particular symbols.

This technique carries the disadvantage of being too awkward for common usage and, more important, of having to contend with the frequent variability that occurs within the usage of particular terms from time to time by the same author. Nevertheless, it has the very important advantage of recognizing not only the great variety of different meanings invariably acquired by common words but also the tendency, if not the privilege, which in actuality writers have of using words in ways that suit their own particular purposes. The common failure to appreciate this latter fact is a particularly unfortunate source of confusion. For example, the question, "What *is* perception?" (or "cognition," or "learning," etc.) is a type which is all too frequently found, either formally stated or implied.[2] Or, to use somewhat more sophisticated examples, the

---

[1] A modification of these two methods which seems to have certain advantages may also be mentioned. This consists of using familiar words in a new grouping. Examples would be Skinner's *reflex reserve* (1938), Hull's *fractional anticipatory goal reaction* (1930, 1931) and Hovland's *inhibition of reinforcement* (1936).

[2] It may be helpful to enumerate some of the more obvious answers to this kind of a question. The concept "perception," for example, may refer to 1) a field of study, 2) a set of more or less specific motor responses, 3) certain physiological processes, 4) a kind of subjective experience, 5) an intervening variable (or hypothetical con-

questions as to whether "fear" is distinct from "anxiety," "conflict" from "frustration," etc. tend to overlook the simple fact that authors may use these words in such a variety of ways as to make possible practically any answer they may wish. Explicit recognition of this fact and more careful attention, as a result, to the observational determinants of such shifty words would certainly save a considerable amount of the type of discussion and argumentation that helps to keep a large part of psychological theory on the "debating society" level of discourse.

3. ADVANCED SCIENTIFIC ANALYSIS   From the point of view of effective theory construction, scientific advance may be considered to be a function, in large part, of the extent to which hypothetical constructs can be transformed into operationally purified intervening variables. In attacking this problem we may first consider the three major outcomes of the use, in preliminary scientific formulations, of those hypothetical constructs with which the scientist undertakes his early theoretical endeavors.

a. *Continuation as hypothetical constructs.* Unfortunately, the most frequent outcome of the use of hypothetical constructs seems to be that they are simply retained as hypothetical constructs, often being modified through a process of more or less extensive verbal reorganization. Thus many of the psychoanalytic constructs have acquired, through a series of primarily verbal accretions, all sorts of alleged explanatory properties, with a progressive widening of the gap between them and specific empirical verifications. This process is well described by MacCorquodale and Meehl (1948, pp. 105 ff). It is this outcome which is responsible for so much of the dissatisfaction, on the part of many psychologists, with the use of hypothetical constructs. The distinctly negative reactions produced by the more flagrant bad examples of such theorizing tend also to transfer to theory and theory construction in general, as Spence (1950) has observed. This unfortunate situation, by no means peculiar to psychology but perhaps for many reasons more prominent there, is the price that must be paid if the more desirable fruits of such activity are to be enjoyed. Probably the only real solution is a continuing pressure on the users of constructs and the developers of theory to improve the operational validity of their formulations.

b. *Suggestion of empirical research.* The most obvious scientific values that derive from the use of hypothetical constructs are those that involve the suggestion of empirical, preferably experimental, research. As mentioned earlier, it is this particular function of the hypothetical construct which both Tolman (1949) and Krech (1949) have recently emphasized.

---

struct). Which of these is meant must of course be determined if possible from the context.

In this respect exception must be taken to the conclusion of MacCorquodale and Meehl that "hypothetical constructs, unlike intervening variables, are inadmissible because they require the existence of entities and the occurrence of processes which cannot be seriously believed because of other knowledge" (1948, p. 106). It is precisely this characteristic of enabling an investigator to go beyond present knowledge and not be tied down to currently orthodox formulations (which may of course later be viewed as wholly inadequate) that helps to justify the usefulness of such hypothetical constructs as guides to experimentation. Köhler's investigation of the figural after-effect and related perceptual phenomena (1940, 1944) is an excellent example of this point. The only valid basis on which such hypothetical constructs may be rejected involves their failure to lead to adequate empirical tests.

Although one must recognize the potential fruitfulness of the use of such models as may be generated by means of hypothetical constructs it is necessary to exercise considerable caution with regard to the conclusions which are drawn from empirical results obtained in this way. If the model is regarded only as a tool to be used in suggesting empirical investigation and then discarded, or modified and retained as a useful guide to experimentation, little danger of unjustified theoretical interpretation is likely to be present. More commonly, however, there is a tendency to regard the empirical results obtained as supporting, in some way, the *theoretical* validity of the original model and the particular hypothetical constructs which have been used. Such conclusions can not be legitimately drawn, and, as a matter of fact, should be quickly and vigorously labeled as inadmissible, *unless* in the process of investigation and theoretical reformulation the constructs have acquired a more adequate degree of operational validity (that is, have moved significantly in the direction of true intervening variables).

That some disagreement on this point exists is, I think, fairly obvious. For example, Krech writes as follows: "Because it is assumed that these hypothetical constructs exist, and because of the extrinsic properties that they are assumed to have, the correlations between experimental conditions and results are now seen as *necessary* correlations, as inevitable consequences of the functioning of these hypothetical constructs" (1949, p. 75). Now, it is essential to note that if such "postulated actually existing structure" is finally reduced to direct experimental measurement and purely empirical statements it can no longer be regarded, in any useful sense, as a *construct*. And if it continues to be defined indirectly through experimental measurement, and thus remains a construct, any *necessary* correlations of the kind Krech indicates can result only if operational refinement appreciably reduces the original ambiguity of the construct and it thus moves in the direction of the intervening variable.

In clarification óf this point it may be helpful to make a gross qualitative distinction between two types of hypothetical constructs: those which postulate the existence of some specific entity or process, the direct empirical identification of which is regarded as a major objection; and those which are deliberately designed to serve only as constructs and thus do not elicit attempts at direct empirical identification. Operational validation of both types is, of course, possible. As noted above, this leads in the case of the first type to purely empirical propositions, and in the case of the second type to the intervening variable kind of construct. It must be recognized, however, that in actual practice the scientific usefulness of the first type does not depend upon its "existence" in a specific empirical sense. An unfortunate amount of confusion seems to have been produced by the somewhat naive expectation that certain hypothetical constructs—for example, the gene—may some day be "seen," in a literal sense, through some sort of direct and specific identification of the entity or process "as it really is." Whether or not this is ever done (and parenthetically it may be observed that most such claims are to be regarded as highly tenuous, at best), it must be said that, from a more realistic point of view, all that need be expected in the way of direct empirical identification is the development of a series of progressively more refined empirical propositions. These typically bear only the slightest resemblance to the originally postulated construct.

The necessity for operational validity in scientific constructs is in no way reduced if the development of a system of formal models is regarded as the primary objective of science, rather than merely as a useful device to direct and unify empirical investigations. For example, Rosenbleuth and Wiener, who adopt the former position, nevertheless also state that "the successive addition of . . . variables leads to gradually more elaborate theoretical models: hence to a hierarchy in these models, from relatively simple, highly abstract ones, to more complex, *more concrete* theoretical structures" (1945, p. 319, italics added). It would certainly seem that the only way in which theoretical structures can be made "more concrete" is through co-ordinating empirical measurements of the kind that characterize operationally valid constructs.

It may be suggested that a large amount of the apparent confusion in psychology on the role of such theoretical structures has been due to the tendency to think in terms of the way in which they have been employed, with eminent success, in the physical sciences. The potential usefulness of theoretical structures of so high a degree of abstraction need not be denied. Nevertheless the most immediate need of psychology would rather plainly seem to be the careful development of a large number of low-level empirical laws, and low-order theories based upon the use of intervening constructs of the more operational type. Higher-order theoretical generalizations may then be built upon a sound empirical framework, in accordance with orthodox scientific procedure (cf. Feigl, 1945; Rosenbleuth and Wiener, 1945) rather than developed from above, as has too often been attempted in the past and is encouraged by the premature emulation of theoretical models based upon the highly abstract physical pattern.

Support for this point of view is readily adduced from consideration of previous attempts in psychology to construct elaborate theoretical models. With regard to Freudian psychoanalysis, for example, it is instructive to note the generally more favorable reception by academic psychologists of those constructs such as repression and other so-called "dynamisms" which involve relatively close functional relations to empirical operations than those high up in the theoretical superstructure, such as id, ego and super-ego, which bear only remote and tenuous relations to their observational bases. The extent to which any such theoretical superstructures have actually contributed to the development of psychology in a sound scientific direction may be seriously questioned. Their disadvantages are obvious. Broad systematic frameworks certainly serve some useful functions, but in the present state of psychology the most valuable formal models, like the most valuable experiments, seem to be those with definitely restricted objectives.

c. *Transformation into intervening variables.* As has been emphasized throughout the discussion, the ultimate objective of all theoretical construct formation is believed to be the operationally valid, intervening variable type of construct. Although no hard and fast rules can be easily prescribed for this important transformation and no completely black and white distinctions made, a few of the more obvious factors may be mentioned. In general, it is essential that the operationally inclined theorist think in terms of *experimental* procedures as well as theoretical structures. One of the most common characteristics of those theorists who are inclined to rest content with hypothetical constructs is their general tendency to be concerned with verbal distinctions and their general neglect of a critical analysis of the observational bases of their conceptual framework. A second factor which encourages the early transformation of hypothetical constructs into intervening variables is the tendency to set up definite, more or less formal hypotheses. Obviously, the more hypothetical content that can be placed into formal hypotheses the less need there will be for including it in the constructs that are used.[3] Thirdly, the operationally inclined theorist will make a

---

[3] In this respect it is interesting to note that Tolman's major point in favor of use of hypothetical constructs, rather than the intervening variables with "merely operational meaning," is that the latter "really can give us no help unless we can also imbed

deliberate effort to set up hypotheses which are susceptible to more or less direct *empirical test*, and to work out the implications of the hypotheses that can be so tested. This means that he is more likely to be concerned with specific as well as general problems. The operationally disinclined theorist, on the other hand, often tends to favor hypotheses which are either themselves relatively untestable, or the empirical consequences of which are not easily determined. A further characteristic of such hypotheses may be seen in the fact that it is frequently difficult if not impossible to refute them. Finally, the operationally inclined theorist is generally more interested in the problem of *quantification*, while the operationally disinclined type of theorist is more often content with purely qualitative distinctions.

Before leaving this general problem of modification of constructs it may be suggested that too rapid an attempted transformation into purely operational intervening variables seems to have certain disadvantages. The major risk of such over-expansion is that associated with the premature development of an overly rigid systematic position, especially if there is a concomitant attempt to stifle off continued exploratory efforts at other levels of explanation. The growth of such rigid positions into cult-like systems, with blind acceptance of certain key principles, serves to offset the genuinely sound scientific advances that can result from such concentrated research programs.

IV

Two particular types of intervening variables, each of which seems to have a distinct function in the development of sound scientific theory in psychology, will now be discussed.

a. *The orthodox type of intervening variable.* As ordinarily conceived, the intervening variable is a kind of shorthand expression for the performance of certain specific empirical operations. This type of construct often but not necessarily (cf. Skinner, 1938; Tolman, 1938) has been given a strong quantitative flavor and placed into a highly mathematical framework (cf. especially Hull, 1943[a], 1950). The advantages of such a conceptual tool have been well described in many other papers (e.g., Tolman, 1936; Hull, 1943[a], 1943[b]; Spence, 1944, 1948; MacCorquodale and Meehl, 1948; Marx, 1963) and need not be reviewed in detail here. Hull's systematic behavior theory may be considered a good example of

them in a model from whose attributed properties we can deduce new relationships to be looked for" (1949, p. 49). This, of course, is exactly what Hull's systematic behavior theory (1943[a], 1950) has attempted to do, largely without the use of hypothetical constructs—although Tolman would probably prefer to use a "model" other than the one Hull has fashioned.

the potential value of this use of intervening variables. As even certain of his critics have said (e.g., Hilgard, 1948), the development of this type of rigorous scientific system marks a definite objective toward which psychological theories should in the future point.

b. *The E/C type of intervening variable.* I should now like to call attention to a somewhat different use of the intervening variable technique which has been occasionally employed but apparently without formal recognition, and which I think offers considerable promise. Like the orthodox type of intervening variable, this type is a shorthand expression which represents the performance of certain specified empirical operations. Although sharing the generally desirable operational characteristics of the orthodox type it does in addition have the peculiar advantage of contributing to the semantic clarification of psychological language.

In essence, this usage simply provides a particular name—representing the postulated intervening variable—to account for whatever specified behavioral differences are empirically found to result from a specified set of stimulus operations. Since a construct of this kind must generally be a function of a comparison between experimental and control conditions, the term E/C is suggested to mark it off from the orthodox usage. It may best be illustrated by an example from the experimental literature.

In a recent study by Mowrer and Viek (1948) hungry rats were given the opportunity to eat moist mash from the end of a small stick offered them through the bars of a shock grid. An electric shock was delivered ten seconds after they had begun to eat, or following an additional ten-second interval if no eating occurred within the first ten seconds. The experimental animals were able to turn off the shock by leaping off the grid, an act which they quickly learned to perform. The control animals were unable to influence the shock directly, but each control animal was given exactly the same duration of shock on every trial as its matched experimental animal. Under these conditions experimental and control animals received identical amounts of electric shock, as objectively measured, but there was an important behavioral difference. The experimental animals ate significantly more frequently and more quickly than the controls. The "sense of helplessness," which is the verbal tag that Mowrer and Viek gave to the assumed psychological function more consistently present in the control than in the experimental animals, may be regarded as a true intervening variable type of construct since it can be tied down, on both the stimulus and the response sides, to empirical measurements.[4]

---

[4] It should be noted that this is true in spite of any doubts that may be entertained concerning the particular term chosen and the further theoretical implications sug-

The semantic advantages of this use of the intervening variable should be apparent. When we speak of any E/C intervening variable we mean— or *should* mean—nothing more than whatever intervening function needs to be assumed in order to account for the experimental-control differences empirically observed. However, in deciding which verbal label to give this intervening variable we may draw upon our own informal observations, or upon some particular theoretical framework. This use of the intervening variable technique thus makes it possible not only to give a purely operational meaning to the constructs used but also to relate them to some prior observations or theoretical system in a way that should help to move these in the direction of a more clear-cut operationism.

There is an obvious semantic danger in this process, however, which needs to be clearly faced. It is most apparent when the names chosen to represent the intervening variables have otherwise acquired a large number of vague and varied meanings. The danger is that such relationships will be emphasized and that subsequent investigation of the basic behavioral functions will be correspondingly diverted. Use of relatively neutral symbols, like letters of the alphabet, may be helpful in discouraging this kind of verbal regression, but these seem to be more readily applied in connection with the orthodox type of intervening variable.

The problem of the generality of intervening variables of the E/C type also needs to be considered. If concepts of a high degree of generality are essential objectives of scientific theory, how can they be obtained through the use of constructs postulated specifically to refer to a particular set of experimental operations?

Two answers to this question may be suggested. In the first place, any particular construct can be given strict, operational meaning through the E/C technique, and can subsequently be broadened to refer to an increasing number of different kinds of experimental situations. Such a broadening of meaning, or generalization, must of course be done with considerable caution. The great advantage of using successive E/C situations, however, is that if anyone cares to question such a generalized construct he may refer directly to the identifying experiments. The degree to which any given construct can be thus generalized will largely depend upon the extent to which the specific empirical situations upon which it is based may be related. In this respect it is useful to recall Stevens' solution for the basic problem of generality in operationism, which may be summarized in his statement that "we combine operations

---

gested. In the present case, for example, I have elsewhere (1952) questioned Mowrer and Viek's choice of the term "sense of helplessness" on the grounds that their theoretical interpretation of the experiment is not adequately supported.

when they satisfy the criteria of a class; and the concept of that class is defined by the operations which determine inclusion within the class" (1939, p. 234).

The controlled manipulation of experimental designs upon which successful development of such generalized concepts will depend must be recognized as a difficult but by no means impossible task. Moreover, it is one which psychologists must somehow effectively tackle if they intend to improve the scientific systematization of their theoretical frameworks. As a simple but concrete example of the manner in which related experimentation may in actual practice be performed, mention may be made of a modification of the Mowrer and Viek design, emphasizing a so-called "sense of control," which has recently been used by Marx and Van Spanckeren (1952) in a study demonstrating a certain amount of learned "control" of the audiogenic seizure by rats. This construct is definitely of the intervening variable type since it has been given a thoroughly operational meaning, in spite of its subjective sound, in terms of the E/C differences.

Consideration of the relationship between the E/C type of intervening variable and the orthodox type provides us with a clue to a second solution of the problem of generality. E/C intervening variables are considered to be most useful in the exploratory phases of scientific theory construction and experimentation, as a means of spotting new variables, probing for gross functions, etc. As experimental investigation progresses the E/C variables should ultimately be reducible to the more general orthodox type, and in fact should aid greatly in the discovery and delimitation of these in the later stages of systematic theory construction. Translation of such complex variables as "sense of control" into relatively more abstract and general constructs may then be expected to result from their continued experimental analysis. From this point of view the essential continuity of the E/C and the orthodox types of intervening variables is evident.

The other major advantages of the E/C usage of the intervening variable may now be briefly summarized. In the first place, and most importantly, it provides a technique which seems to combine the best features of both the hypothetical construct and the orthodox intervening variable. That is, it offers the experimenter an opportunity to draw upon the suggestions of a theoretical model and yet remain on a strictly operational level of discourse. It thus provides a high degree of freedom of experimental investigation without sacrifice of the methodological rigor that normally accompanies the use of the orthodox intervening variable. This is an especially important characteristic in the present stage of psychological science, with the concomitant needs for more exploratory work and the careful identification of the empirical bases of constructs.

Secondly, it permits the formal separation of the hypothetical from the conceptual components of theory construction, and requires that the investigator think more in experimental and less in purely verbal terms. Thirdly, by enabling the empirically-minded investigator to indulge, cautiously, in a small amount of construct formation, it encourages the development of a greater amount of theoretical orientation on the part of psychologists whose antipathy to theory and theory construction largely stems from their distrust of hypothetical constructs and accompanying speculation. An increased interest in theory construction by this kind of investigator is regarded as a highly desirable objective.

The successful use of the intervening variable of the E/C type involves several important requirements. It obviously depends, in common with all sound scientific work, upon the experimental validity of the empirical data. It also necessitates a certain amount of ingenuity in the design of the experiment, but once the proper theoretical-experimental attitude is acquired this may be less difficult than it at first appears. It demands that the investigator, once he has performed an experiment and defined his intervening constructs purely in terms of his experimental operations, now continue to apply those particular conceptualizations in an operationally sound manner, as he attempts to relate them to the wider theoretical framework from which they have been derived. This means that, as implied earlier, a clear line needs to be drawn between theoretical implications that are to be directly made upon the basis of the experimental results and those that are merely suggested by them. Finally, it requires that the investigator think in terms of narrow, experimentally manipulable problems—even if they are imbedded in a significantly wider theoretical framework. This is an especially desirable requirement, since it should result in an improved experimental sophistication on the part of those whose speculations too often tend to outstrip their empirical foundations.

In conclusion, it may be noted that there is in this discussion no intention to imply that the E/C usage represents anything more than a refinement and a formalization of currently accepted scientific procedure. However, it is hoped that this technique will encourage that active *experimental* search for new variables and new relationships between variables which is essential for the continued scientific advancement of psychology.

V

In summary, the following conclusions are offered:

1. The hypothetical construct, as defined by MacCorquodale and Meehl (1948) and recently justified by Tolman (1949) and Krech

(1949), is to be regarded as in general a temporary expedient in the development of sound psychological theory.

2. Hypothetical constructs are most useful in the early, preliminary phases of scientific work. Their use may have three major outcomes:

a. They may be continued, perhaps in modified form, on a grossly non-operational level of discourse. This practice cannot be scientifically defended.

b. They may lead to important empirical investigations, in which case they serve a useful function in suggesting research. However, the empirical results must not be regarded as constituting evidence in support of the theoretical validity of such conceptual models unless in the process they are given increased operation validity.

c. They may be transformed into operationally valid intervening variables, which are the only kinds of constructs ultimately admissible in sound scientific theory.

3. Two types of intervening variables are currently being used in psychology, each with an important function:

a. The orthodox type of intervening variable is simply a shorthand symbolic expression, often quantitative in character, of a specified set of experimental operations. It is necessary in the relatively advanced stages of theory construction.

b. The E/C type of intervening variable is likewise a verbal expression of a specified set of experimental operations, but is more directly related to the experimental-control differences in the experiment. It offers, through the method of successive approximation, an opportunity to clarify semantic usage in psychological theory construction. Its relatively greater flexibility as a methodological tool makes it especially useful in the exploratory stages of scientific investigation, when theoretical constructs need to be progressively released from their pre-scientific ambiguity. It is thus regarded as an operationally valid alternative to the hypothetical construct.

4. It is strongly recommended that psychological investigators pay more attention to the formal operational requirements of their theory construction, and in particular attempt more explicit use of both types of intervening variables.

References

Cohen, M. R., and Nagel, E. *Logic and scientific method.* New York: Harcourt, Brace, 1934.

Feigl, H. Operationism and scientific method: Rejoinders and second thoughts. *Psychol. Rev.,* 1945, *52,* 284–288.

Hilgard, E. R. *Theories of learning.* New York: Appleton-Century-Crofts, 1948.

Hovland, C. I. "Inhibition of reinforcement" and phenomena of experimental extinction. *Proc. Nat. Acad. Sci.,* Wash., 1936, *22,* 430–433.

Hull, C. L. Knowledge and purpose as habit mechanisms. *Psychol. Rev.,* 1930, *37,* 511–525.

———. Goal attraction and directing ideas conceived as habit phenomena. *Psychol. Rev.,* 1931, *38,* 487–506.

———. *Principles of behavior.* New York: D. Appleton-Century, 1943(a).

———. The problem of intervening variables in molar behavior theory. *Psychol. Rev.,* 1943, *50,* 273–291(b).

———. Behavior postulates and corollaries—1949. *Psychol. Rev.,* 1950, *57,* 173–180.

Köhler, W. *Dynamics in psychology.* New York: Liveright, 1940.

Köhler, W., and Wallach, H. Figural after-effects. *Proc. Amer. Phil. Soc.,* Phil., 1944, *88,* 269–357.

Krech, D. Notes toward a psychological theory. *J. Personal.,* 1949, *19,* 66–87.

MacCorquodale, K., and Meehl, P. E. On a distinction between hypothetical constructs and intervening variables. *Psychol. Rev.,* 1948, *55,* 95–107.

Marx, M. H. The general nature of theory construction. [Selection 1 in this volume.]

Marx, M. H., and Van Spanckeren, W. J. Control of the audiogenic seizure by the rat. *J. Comp. Physiol. Psychol.,* 1952, *45.*

Maslow, A. H. A suggested improvement in semantic usage. *Psychol. Rev.,* 1945, *52,* 239–240.

Mowrer, O. H., and Viek, P. An experimental analogue of fear from a sense of helplessness. *J. Abnorm. Soc. Psychol.,* 1948, *43,* 193–200.

Pratt, C. C. *The logic of modern psychology.* New York: Macmillan, 1939.

Rosenblueth, A., and Wiener, N. The role of models in science. *Phil. Sci.,* 1945, *12,* 316–321.

Skinner, B. F. *The behavior of organisms.* New York: D. Appleton-Century, 1938.

Spence, K. W. The nature of theory construction in contemporary psychology. *Psychol. Rev.,* 1944, *51,* 47–68.

———. The postulates and methods of "behaviorism." *Psychol. Rev.,* 1948, *55,* 67–78.

———. Cognitive versus stimulus-response theories of learning. *Psychol. Rev.,* 1950, *57,* 159–172.

Stevens, S. S. Psychology and the science of science. *Psychol. Bull.,* 1939, *36,* 221–263.

Tolman, E. C. Operational behaviorism and current trends in psychology. In *Proc. 25th Anniv. Celebr. Inaug. Grad. Stud.* Los Angeles: Univ. South. Calif. Press, 1936.

———. The determiners of behavior at a choice point. *Psychol. Rev.,* 1938, *45,* 1–41.

———. Discussion (from, Interrelationships between perception and personality: a symposium). *J. Personal.,* 1949, *18,* 48–50.

11 | *Formal and Informal Meaning in Constructs*

HOWARD H. KENDLER

* * *

Tolman has expounded the pragmatic use of the intervening variable to bridge the gap existing between the independent and dependent variables. Rather than treat separately the relationship each independent variable bears to the many dependent variables, Tolman proposed the grouping of certain independent variables; these groupings or component functions would then be connected logically to constructed intervening variables; these in turn would be connected to one another, and finally to the dependent variables. This *intellectual construction* has as its aims the economic description of the known empirical relationships, and the prediction of new phenomena. Tolman's blueprint for theory construction has been used by himself, Hull (1943) and others in their theorizing. The core of these theories has been the intervening variables, e.g., habit strength, cognitive map, etc. Basic to the entire question of what is learned is the specific interpretation given to these intervening variables (theoretical constructs). We shall see that secondary, and unnecessary, elaborations about the meaning of these intervening variables have led to what some have considered to be conflicting views as to what is learned.

There would be no confusion about the meaning of such terms if it were always remembered that these intervening variables serve as *economical devices* to order experimental variables in relation to the dependent variables. They are *"shorthand" descriptions*, and nothing more, of the influence on behavior of several independent variables. The *only meaning* possessed by these intervening variables is their relationship to both the independent and dependent variables. Because this point has been ignored or misunderstood, an immense amount of confusion concerning the "real meaning" of these intervening variables exists.

From H. H. Kendler, "What is learned?"—a theoretical blind alley, *Psychol. Rev.*, 1952, *59*, 269–277. Pp. 271–276 reprinted by permission of the author, the *Psychological Review*, and the American Psychological Association.

A somewhat similar situation existed in theoretical physics with regard to the gravitational action between distant bodies. For many physicists the idea of action at a distance was odious; it did not appear conceivable that a phenomenon could be "caused" by a relationship. In order, therefore, to make the phenomenon more "meaningful," different kinds of space-filling mediums capable of transmitting forces from one body to another were hypothesized. But there is no justification, as Bridgman (1927) points out, "for the attitude which refuses on purely *a priori* grounds to accept action at a distance as a possible axiom or ultimate of explanation."

Nagel uses a neat example to describe the above type of error which has been labelled the fallacy of reification or hypostatization. He writes:

Suppose, for example, that Smith invites to his home his foreign friend Forgeron, so that the latter may see for himself what family life is like in America. But suppose that after enjoying Smith's hospitality for some time Forgeron was to complain that though he met Smith's wife and children, had meals in common with them, took part in their recreations, and so on, he had never been introduced to Smith's Family Life. It is clear in this case just what is the nature of Forgeron's error: he mistakenly assumes that "Family Life" is the name of some supra-sensible "entity," distinct from the complex activities in which Smith and the members of his family are normally engaged (1951, p. 236).

In the very same sense the construct of learning, whether it be conceived in terms of modifications in cognitive maps or *S-R* connections, does not refer to an object, thing or entity as suggested by those who are concerned with the question of what is learned. These intervening variables possess no meaning over and above their stated relationships between the independent and the dependent variables. The basic error underlying the problem of what is learned is the assumption that these intervening variables are entities capable of being described and elaborated upon, independent of their operational meaning. The fallacy of reification yields the problem of what is learned. The realization that learning is not a "supra-sensible entity" disposes of it.

Intuitive Models vs. Operational Meaning

It would be interesting, and perhaps fruitful also, to go beyond our initial methodological analysis in order to understand the psychological factors underlying the confusion surrounding the question under consideration. After all, psychological theorizing is just another form of behavior. Why cannot we attempt as psychologists to understand why meaningless questions are asked and concepts are reified?

It appears to this writer that the confusion surrounding the meaning of theoretical constructs stems from the failure to distinguish sharply between personal thought processes leading to the invention of theoretical constructs and the *operational meaning of the term*. The first is a problem in the psychology of creative thinking (in this case the psychology of the psychologist), the second is a problem in epistemology. Why Hull (1943), for example, chose to define habit strength in the manner he did is a function of his intellectual abilities, his style of thinking, his personality, his interests, etc. In order to know what habit strength is, one need not know the intimate details of Hull's background or have a knowledge of his intellectual functioning; one need only know how this concept is tied down to "observable events," i.e., its operational definition. The thought processes of the psychological theorist may, as they usually do, involve the use of some sort of a model. It becomes necessary, when such models are used as *thinking aids*, that the model not be confused with the scientific concept stemming from it. Too often learning psychologists have been misled into believing that the intuitive models which they associate with their intervening variables possess existential properties above and beyond the operational definition of the intervening variable.

Although psychologists are very willing to admit the existence of individual differences in motor skills, aptitudes, and many other behavior characteristics, they appear markedly reluctant to admit that such differences may exist in creative thinking. Would it be valid to say one must think "phenomenologically" as does Tolman, or within a Darwinian framework, as Hull appears to do, or "algebraically" as does Spence, or in terms of psysical models as does Köhler? It is granted that only a valid and extensive knowledge of the psychology of thinking could answer this question. If we refuse to ascribe certain unique and mystical qualities to the process of creative thinking, i.e., if we consider it just as another form of behavior, then we may extrapolate from our knowledge of other behavior. We know that people learn mazes in different manners, runners sprint with different styles, and, if we are to believe Kinsey, people woo in different fashions. Certainly within our limited knowledge of the variables involved in productive thinking, it would appear questionable to assume that only one style of thinking would be fecund; and it would be hazardous, as well as somewhat presumptuous, for any theorist to insist that every other theorist think in his style.

The above point obviously does not imply that theorizing is purely a matter of personal taste. At some stage in the development of a theory, the theorist must meet the requirements of his scientific audience, i.e., the operational definitions of his theoretical (intellectual) constructs must be made clear to everyone who is sincerely interested in them. This does not mean that the theorist must reveal his private cerebration (for purposes of clarity, it may be best if he did not), but that he must state the relations which his theoretical constructs bear to the observable variables so that their "validity" may be tested.

In evaluating the "validity" of a learning theory it should be recognized that the most we can expect is that the theoretical estimates of the dependent variable be in agreement with the observed responses in an experimental situation. All learning theories must fulfill this function, i.e., generate valid estimates of the to-be-observed response. In this sense *all learning theories are response theories.*

The above analysis leads the writer to conclude that Tolman's recent division between place learning as contrasted with response learning is not sufficiently cogent; it suggests a qualitative distinction where none exists. Such a distinction arises only if one considers differences in intuitive models to be basic to theoretical differences—a position to which this paper would take exception. Using the same sort of logic, one would also be forced to conclude that Guthrie's conviction that movements are learned or Hull's belief that receptor-effector connections are required are as invalid as Tolman's feelings that cognitive maps are learned.[1]

Our initial point was that the pseudo-problem of what is learned emerged from the methodological error of considering learning an entity rather than a process. Our second point is that this methodological error is due to the contamination of the operational meaning of theoretical constructs by their intuitive properties. This contamination has led to spurious formulations of theoretical differences. Rather than persistently

---

[1] In actual practice there are two differences which appear to separate the cognitive theorists as a group from the S-R theorists. Firstly, the two appear to possess somewhat different thinking styles. Aside from certain scientific requirements, the selection of the specific terms in a theoretical structure seems to be determined by the personal needs of the theorist. Perceptual and cognitive terms appear to be intuitively satisfying to the cognitive theorist while they tend to evoke suspicion among S-R theorists. I suspect that if Hull had labeled what he now calls habit strength "dynamic cognitive field expectancies" without modifying its postulated relationships to the independent variables, much of the opposition to this concept would disappear and probably some new opposition would arise from certain quarters. The second difference is related to the problem as to what point in the "theoretical bridge" between the independent and dependent variables should the nature of the response be indicated. The S-R theorist usually specifies the nature of the response relatively early, while the cognitive theorist does not specify the nature of the response until rather late in his theorizing. In fact, they have been frequently criticized, with some justification, because they do not always translate the cognitive map of the organism into specific action; in other words, they do not always bridge the gap between the independent and dependent variables. The point on the "theoretical bridge" at which the initial response estimate is introduced may prove to be an important stratagem in theory construction. Since I have emphasized the operational meaning of concepts rather than their connotative meaning, and because so few contemporary theorists have come to grips with the problem of the location of the initial response estimate, it is felt that the above two differences are not *basic.*

pursue both the obvious and subtle connotative meanings of the words used in theorizing, it would be much more productive to attempt to relate the constructs systematically to the manipulable variables and behavior measures. Only then can the explanatory power, inherent in the concepts, be tested.

The "Cause" of the Confusion

Why have learning theorists indulged so much in unnecessary elaborations of their theoretical constructs at the expense of determining their relationships to the observable variables, i.e., the substitutions of models for operational definitions? It is the writer's belief that the answer to this question lies in different conceptions of the nature of scientific explanation.

Again, it may be appropriate to interject into our discussion certain speculations concerning the psychological basis of misconceptions of scientific explanation. Most, if not all, psychologists were confronted with the question "Why?" prior to their exposure to scientific training. It is safe to assume that intuitively satisfying "explanations" were achieved during this pre-scientific era of personal development. There is a strong suggestion that some of these pre-scientific explanatory techniques have lingered on and have been confused with scientific explanation.

Feigl (1945), in a brief perspicuous exposition, states that the demand for explanation "is answered by deductions either from empirical laws or from theories." He enlarges upon this dictum as follows:

Deduction from empirical laws may be styled 'low grade' explanation. It merely puts the fact to be explained into a class of facts characterized by the same empirical law. Thus the explanation for the fact, e.g., that there is a mirror image of a bridge in a river, is achieved by subsuming this fact under the law of reflection in geometrical optics. This law is simply the common denominator of all the various phenomena in which light-reflection is the essential feature. A 'higher-grade' explanation we find in the Maxwell-electromagnetic wave theory, which serves as a basis for deduction for a variety of optical phenomena; reflection as well as refraction, diffraction, interference, dispersion, polarization, etc., etc. (1945, p. 286).

Psychology has achieved only a few "low-grade explanations." For example, Hull was able to deduce from his initial goal gradient hypothesis the locomotion gradient of rats in a runway, blind alley elimination, the more rapid elimination of long blind alleys as compared to short blind alleys, the backward order of elimination of blind alleys, and similar phenomena. In a much less formal manner Freud has attempted to integrate such phenomena as slips of the tongue, dreams, hysterical symptoms, tics, etc., by assuming certain unconscious mental processes.

This requirement for a deductive component has too often been ignored in attempts at explanation. The reason for ignoring the requirement of a deductive component in scientific explanation stems from the failure of some writers to distinguish clearly the requirements of scientific explanation from those attributes of propositions which are capable of instigating in some a feeling of "understanding" (the "a-ha" phenomenon). The contention of this paper is that some of the arguments surrounding the question of what is learned have stemmed from such confusion, i.e., between scientific explanation and, for want of a better term, "psychological understanding." This sort of confusion has been particularly noticeable in many of the formulations involving physiological and/or phenomenological terms.

A common misconception among some psychologists concerned with discovering the physiological correlates of behavior is that their area of interest excuses them from the task of developing a theoretical system capable of generating valid deductions. Believing that they are dealing with the "real causes" of behavior,[2] they feel that the mere specification of the physiological factors or, more commonly, the mere speculation concerning the physiological processes is sufficiently explanatory. For example, Birch and Bitterman (1949), in a recent polemic against S-R reinforcement theory, conclude that it is *necessary* to postulate a physiological process of sensory integration to explain conditioning. This conclusion is reached in spite of their admission that ". . . we know very little about the conditions under which sensory integration occurs." Actually, they do not specify any physiological variables or behavior measures to which "sensory integration" is connected. The result is that their formulation is incapable of generating any deductive implications—and consequently is void of any explanatory ability. Adequate explanatory systems in physiological psychology, as well as in other areas of psychology, must have a deductive component.

The above should not be interpreted as an attempt to make an invidious comparison between behavioral and physiological theories. The development of psychology can and should be furthered by serious and rigorous attempts at formulations of both behavioral and physiological theories. This writer believes (on an intuitive basis) that, at the present time, the program of independent development at both levels would be the most strategic, followed, of course, by an attempt at co-ordination. Another procedure would be to develop behavioral and physiological formulations interdependently and simultaneously. There is no reason

---

[2] It has always been a mystery to me why, if one desires to be entrapped by the metaphysical problem of "real causality," one should be satisfied to stop at the physiological level without descending into the physico-chemical, or the atomic, or the sub-atomic level.

why such attempts could not be successful. The tendency, however, has been merely to use some physiological-sounding terms, extracted in all likelihood from the private thought processes of the theorist, without specifying their relations (hypothetical or established) to the experimental variables and behavior measures. Although such a procedure provides a ready "answer" to the question under consideration ("what is learned"), these answers contribute nothing to our understanding of the learning process.[3]

A similar problem is raised by some theories which use phenomenological terms as labels for their theoretical constructs. It appears that for many learning psychologists it is essential that their theoretical constructs be phenomenologically consistent, i.e., capture the quality of naive introspective experience. There is little doubt that the theoretical constructs used by psychological field theorists reflect "inner experience" in a more satisfying manner than do associationistic constructs. There is no basic methodological objection (or virtue) to the use of either set of terms *as long as they are related to observables, and as long as they are used in formulations with deductive capacities.* This rule, however, is not always followed. All too frequently, constructs by themselves (e.g., structuring,

---

[3] The problem of the physiological properties of intervening variables has been raised in a somewhat different form by MacCorquodale and Meehl (1948). They argue that it is important to distinguish between two types of theoretical constructs, hypothetical constructs and intervening variables. The former "involve the hypothesization of an *entity, process,* or *event* which is not itself observed . . ." while the latter ". . . do not involve such hypothesization." These writers demand ". . . of a theory of learning that those elements which are hypothetical . . . have some probability of being in correspondence with the actual events underlying the behavior phenomenon. . . ." Referring to some of Hull's early theoretical papers in this Journal, MacCorquodale and Meehl write:

"We suspect that Professor Hull himself was motivated to write these articles because he considered that the hypothetical events represented in his diagrams may have actually *occurred* and that the occurrence of these events represents the underlying truth about the learning phenomena he dealt with" (1948, p. 104–105).

Here again, the personal cogitations of the theorists are confused with the operational meaning of the concept. Although it may appear "clinically justified" to assume that Hull had some conceptions of physiological mechanisms co-ordinated to some of his theoretical constructs, the meaning of those constructs should be confined to their operational definition. Other theorists who work within the S-R reinforcement theoretical framework have no such intuitive physiological conceptions. Should we therefore have two (or possibly more) conceptions of these physiological sounding concepts, the constructs varying not in terms of their operational meanings but rather in terms of the individual's intuitive conception? For purposes of communication, it appears wise to separate all the private cogitations from the operational meaning of concepts. The important point is whether the behavioral theory can be divorced from the "physiologizing" without damage to the deductive capacity of the theory. In the case of Hull's theory it would certainly seem possible.

insight), which describe vividly phenomenological experience, are presented as scientific explanation.

I am convinced that the selection of any theoretical model, be it physiological or phenomenological, or for that matter, physical, mechanical or statistical, is in the last analysis a decision having *no truth character*. That is, in spite of the fact the choice of a model may, and usually does, influence both experimentation and theorizing, *the choice itself* cannot be evaluated as being right or wrong. It is a matter purely of personal taste. The most we can do is to attempt, in a sincere and conscientious manner, to understand the implications of such decisions, but we should not be led astray by believing we can experimentally test their validity.

What then should the learning theorist do? Instead of seeking an answer to the question of what is learned in a manner based upon inadequate conceptions of scientific meaning and scientific explanation, it would be better for learning theorists to come to grips with their undertaking in a positive forthright fashion, i.e., to anchor their theoretical concepts to observables and unhesitatingly test the explanatory capacities of their formulations.

By means of such a constructive approach, the time wasted in needless arguments of the sort which has centered around the sterile question of what is learned would be reduced and, perhaps, even be eliminated.

References

Birch, H. G., and Bitterman, M. E. Reinforcement and learning: the process of sensory integration. *Psychol. Rev.*, 1949, *56*, 292–308.

Bridgman, P. W. *The logic of modern physics*. New York: Macmillan, 1927.

Feigl, H. Rejoinders and second thoughts in symposium on operationism. *Psychol. Rev.*, 1945, *52*, 284–288.

Hull, C. L. *Principles of behavior*. New York: Appleton-Century-Crofts, 1943.

MacCorquodale, K., and Meehl, P. E. On a distinction between hypothetical constructs and intervening variables. *Psychol. Rev.*, 1948, *55*, 95–107.

Nagel, E. A philosophical critique of traditional psychology. *Nation*, 1951, *172*, 235–236.

12 | *The Role of Neurology*

DAVID KRECH

*   *   *

On Neurological Speculations

Perhaps the first guiding principle which one should set down for the psychologist intent on neurological speculations is that he should pay proper respect to present neurological knowledge and theory. With such an obvious statement I would agree, but only if I were permitted to specify the meaning of "proper respect." "Paying proper respect" is not the same as "being subservient to." That is to say, I would not interpret the above guiding principle to mean that the psychologist must not venture into territory which the neurologist has not yet explored, nor that he must be reluctant to disagree with what the neurologist has already determined. The reasons why I insist on this permissiveness are, I believe, crucial to an understanding of the proper relationship which must be worked out between neurology and psychology.

Essentially we are faced with the problem, when we try to combine psychology and neurology, of either *trimming down our psychology* to the possibilities inherent in present-day neurology, or else *expanding neurology* (even if only by piling speculation upon speculation) to encompass what we already know about psychology. It is the former which has been done in the past and it is that procedure which has resulted in an understandable impatience with "neurologizing" among psychologists. Thus MacLeod (1949) points out that previous attempts ". . . tended to restrict psychological investigations to just those processes for which simple physiological counterparts could be found, and by implication to brush aside as of secondary importance the very phenomena which originally inspired curiosity. . . . The psychologist in his desire to be ac-

From D. Krech, Dynamic systems as open neurological systems, *Psychol. Rev.*, 1950, 57, 345–361. Pp. 345–347 reprinted by permission of the author, the *Psychological Review*, and the American Psychological Association.

cepted in the fraternity of the natural scientists almost lost sight of his original objective. The ultimate problems of cognition were becoming gradually obscured by an ever thickening veil of sense-receptors and nerve-fibers." Such sterilization of psychology is inevitable, in my opinion, so long as we approach the problems of the neural bases of behavior as *neurologists* rather than as psychologists. We must be psychologists first and neurologists second. But, and this is my major contention, if we are psychologists first we will, by that very token, become *better neurologists*. To build up neurological hypothetical constructs for psychological theory must not involve, at any point, a denial of, or compromise with the data of behavior and experience. *It is the psychological data, in the last analysis, which must provide the tests of the adequacy of any theory of brain action.* And we will find, I believe, that if we go about our neurological speculations in this spirit, that the most cherished principles of present-day neurology will have to be reexamined and overhauled and the entire field of neurology redefined. There is another point to stress in this connection. The unity of science will not be achieved by *reducing* psychological principles to neurological ones, and neurological ones to physical ones. What we must seek is to make physical principles *congruent* with neurological ones, neurological ones with psychological ones, and at each point the most inclusive set of data must be the test of how well we achieve this congruence. Again, this means that we must test the adequacy of our physical principles by how well they can encompass neurological data, and neurological principles by how well they can encompass psychological data. As we go from the data of one scientific field to another in our search for unity, we should not seek to *reduce* the data, but we should seek to *redefine* the principles so that borderlines begin to disappear. I will, later in this paper, make this point with specific reference to the relationship between biological and physical principles, but the general position I am taking here is that *the more inclusive field must enlarge the concepts of the less inclusive if we are ever to achieve a genuine unity of science.* It is because of all of the above considerations that I insist on the psychologist's right to differ from present-day neurological theory.

But if all of the above tells us what I do not mean by "paying proper respect to present neurological knowledge and theory," what is it that I do mean? First I would assert that the speculating neurological psychologist is not absolved from the responsibility of knowing the neurologist's work and theory. Whenever we make neurological statements we must examine them in the light of current neurological thought. If our statements violate present theory we must show awareness of that fact, make the disagreements explicit, and justify our preference. Another thing I do mean by "paying proper respect" is that, everything else being equal,

I prefer those speculations which do the least violence to orthodox neurological theory. But the phrase "everything else being equal" must be
kept constantly in mind and refers to the usefulness of the speculations
for psychological theory, *i.e.*, for their ability to handle molar behavior
and conscious experience. Finally, I subscribe to the principle that, everything else being equal, I prefer those neurological hypotheses which are
most amenable to direct empirical verification, given our present research
techniques. The reason for this is that the attributes we give to our
neurological hypothetical constructs must be open to eventual direct
study—and the sooner, the better. So much, then, for our guiding principle that our neurological theorizing should pay proper respect to
present neurological knowledge and theory.

*   *   *

Reference

MacLeod, R. B. New psychologies of yesterday and today. *Canad. J. Psychol.*,
    1949, *3*, 199–212.

13 | *The Analysis of Gross Functions*

MELVIN H. MARX

*   *   *

1. OPERATIONAL CLARITY   A strict standard of operational clarity
should be maintained in applying the present intervening-variable technique to complex behavioral situations. Although the proposed usage in
broadened framework differs somewhat from the orthodox usage, the
intervening variable as I envision it must continue to be a true, operationally valid intervening variable. It is to be used in the original sense
intended by Tolman (1936) and MacCorquodale and Meehl (1948), who
pointed out that it must be simply and completely defined in terms of the
stimulus manipulations or observations, and the response measurements.

From M. H. Marx, Some suggestions for the conceptual and theoretical
analysis of complex intervening variables in problem-solving behavior, *J. Gen.
Psychol.*, 1958, *58*, 115–128. Pp. 119–126 and 127–128 reprinted by permission
of the author, the *Journal of General Psychology*, and the Journal Press.

It is thus a shorthand device for representing the relationships between the stimulus, or situational, factors, and the resulting responses.

2. INTERVENING VARIABLES IN EMPIRICAL RESEARCH   Underwood maintains that "the greatest need at present for understanding thinking is a set of empirically well-established laws between stimulus dimensions and response variables" (1952, p. 210). I agree essentially with what Underwood has said, but I believe that even such avowedly empirical research will be most effectively performed within a framework where careful attention is given to the problem of intervening constructs.

In the first place, we may as well be concerned explicitly with intervening constructs, because in actual practice we use them anyway. They can be handled more effectively if we bring them out into the open. Underwood himself gives extended consideration to response biases, which are clearly mediating variables. Systematic attention to problems of conceptualization and theorizing should help to stimulate experimentation through the direct suggestion of empirical attacks. This is most strikingly exemplified by the success of Hull's theorizing in this respect.

Moreover, early and continuing formal concern with intervening variables should help to avoid much semantic confusion. In dealing with a series of more or less related studies, investigators often confuse issues by using the same term to cover a wide variety of different empirical relationships. This confusion could be avoided by careful attention to semantic usage. Also, such attention to the problem should help to develop and maintain a high level of operational adequacy in constructs. Hypotheses of some kind are necessary for any research problem. These may be explicit, as in Underwood's proposed research, or merely implied in the experimental designs of the investigator. Concern for operational adequacy should help to keep the hypotheses separate from the intervening variables (1951).

3. SYSTEMATIC DELIMITATION OF THE INTERVENING VARIABLE: S AND R OBSERVABLES   Because of the complete dependence upon the stimulus and response observables, their specification in the abstraction of the intervening variable is a critical task which the theorist needs to perform. He will need to characterize with precision the kind of antecedent stimulus and resultant response conditions with which he is concerned.

Once the S-R referents for the intervening variable have been broadly specified, the theorist needs to specify in detail the important dimensions that may be manipulated and measured. In other words, he must carefully categorize the "structure" of the stimulus-response situation. Only then can the intervening variable be used in any refined way in experimentation or theory construction.

4. PROGRESSIVE DIFFERENTIATION OF INTERVENING VARIABLES   How should we proceed to differentiate the intervening variables involved in problem solving? Let us start with a single intervening variable (IV). Figure 1 shows this variable. An immediate problem arises in connection with the naming of this IV. Since the approach suggested here is deliberately kept free of prior theoretical commitments, it seems best for illustrative pur-

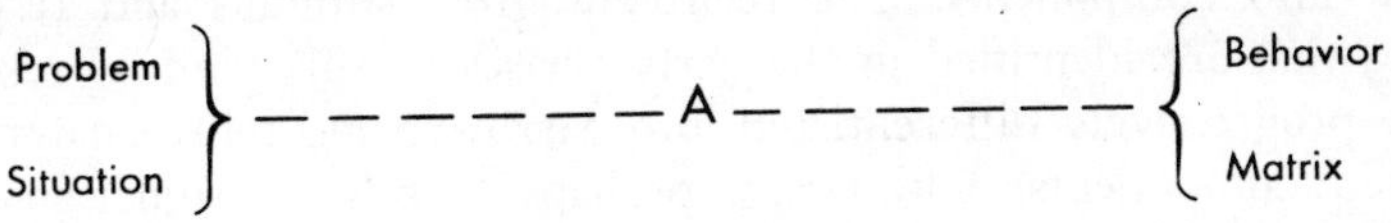

Problem \
Situation / — — — — — — A — — — — — — { Behavior
                                         Matrix

Figure 1

poses simply to letter this gross IV, and call it "A." This emphasizes the dependence of the construct on the stimulus and response measurements for its meaning. It also keeps it free of the surplus meaning which would be sure to be carried by any term we might choose. Some investigators might feel justified in giving the IV a label which derived from some other framework, thus relating it to the prior framework. For our present purposes, however, the suggested procedure should free us of arguments about what verbal tags should be applied until after empirical work has been done that might justify the tagging.

The gross IV, A, is in simple mediating relation to the stimulus and response sides of the formulation. I do not assume that we are dealing with an "empty organism," but this approach does not require the prior specification of the particular mediating functions that account for the relationship between stimulus and response. Instead, the IV as here used simply refers to *whatever mediating functions are necessary* to account for the occurrence of the problem-solving responses in the problem situation. Analysis of this grossly yet operationally conceived construct can then proceed through progressive experimental specification of component aspects. Such analysis can proceed in *either* of two major directions: *a*) towards the specification of physiological mechanisms, and *b*) towards the specification of more refined relationships between the S and R variables.

The first step in this differentiation is indicated in Figure 2. Here are introduced two IVs, A_1 and A_2, into which the IV A has now been differentiated. Each of these two new IVs is directly referable to certain

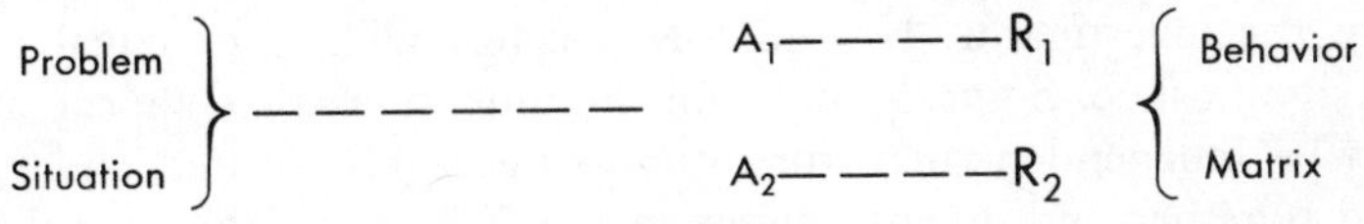

Problem \
Situation / — — — — — —
                          A_1 — — — — R_1 { Behavior
                          A_2 — — — — R_2 Matrix

Figure 2

specified stimulus and response variables. This fact is now indicated by breaking down the behavior matrix into component R's. For example, R_1 might be some measure of responses which do not lead to a solution of the problem; R_2 might be the class of responses which succeed in solving the problem.

Another step in this differentiation is breaking down the gross-stimulus situation into components. The relatively gross stimulus and response variables that are identified in the early phases of this kind of research must be progressively differentiated into narrower and more analytically conceived components. Ultimately, perhaps, a scheme something like that represented in Figure 3 may be achieved. Here a large number of

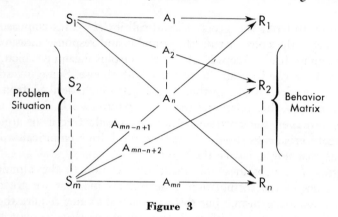

Figure 3

such stimulus dimensions are shown in their potential relationships to a large number of response dimensions, without regard for the various combinations, on both sides, which would in actual practice represent the previously analyzed factors.

Figure 3 indicates that there are m times n intervening variables in any given situation, where m is the number of possible significant response dimensions and n is the number of significant stimulus dimensions. Obviously, it would be a tremendous job to work out all these relationships empirically. If this point is raised as an objection, the only possible answer is that science is hard work, and there is no substitute for such work. Of course, the investigator must use his judgment in selecting the most promising relationships to study. Many stimulus dimensions will appear to be unimportant, and many response measurements will not be of interest to the investigator. Not all S-R pairings will be of equal experimental significance. Some S and some R dimensions that appear at first sight to be independent may turn out to be highly related and can be grouped together and given a common tag. These variables would then "converge" on what Koch (1954) calls systematic independent or dependent variables. So "*mn*" will probably be a much larger number than the investigator actually need deal with within particular experimental frameworks.

If the scheme presented in Figure 3 represents the analysis of a particular experimental situation, as I have intended it, then the problem of generality arises. The solution to this ubiquitous problem would seem to lie in relating different experimental situations through dimensional analyses of the sort described in a previous section of this paper. Demonstration of the essential continuity of different problem-solving situations would certainly be facilitated by the progressive delimitation of *S* and *R* variables, as here proposed. Further discussion of this problem is considered to be beyond the scope of the present paper, but it is obviously a critical one. Although the proponent of operational definitions is often accused of a failure in this regard, the problem of generality is not created by the use of operational procedures; rather, it is pointed up by them and brought out into the open where it can be more readily attacked. The facade of apparent generality that is achieved through easy verbalizations is certainly expendable.

The extent to which the proposed method differs from any extremely positivistic approach, such as that advocated by Skinner (e.g., 1950), depends upon the extent to which any particular investigator cares to use explicitly "theoretical" devices. My own feeling is that a considerable amount of deductive activity is inescapable, and that it therefore should be made explicit. Operational requirements should be satisfied at all times. This means that the specification of the investigated relationships among *IV*s will more or less follow the general hypothetico-deductive procedure described by Hull (1943). This does not mean that there need be recourse to any prior conceptual or theoretical framework, although such may of course influence the direction of research in an informal manner. Theory would develop primarily in a "grass-roots" manner, from the bottom up, as far as the formal structure of the conceptualization is concerned.

Whether old or new terms are eventually introduced in attempting the development of a more comprehensive, "theoretical" framework, will be a matter of individual choice. In any case, the program is intended to be basically descriptive in method and in its use of constructs. Theory is to be introduced by the conceptual manipulation of variables, in the manner previously suggested (Marx, 1951).

Some Basic Rules for Construction of *IV*s

Figure 3 has certain implications. First, we see that *each IV will be differentiated from all of the others in terms of specified stimulus and response observables*. Either the stimulus or the response dimension, or both, will be different from any pair of *IV*s.

The critic may object that *a*) some of the *IV*s will have identical stimulus conditions and behavioral representations, or *b*) some of the *IV*s will be represented, on the behavior side, only by assumed responses which are not directly observable. If the investigator uses the procedure suggested here, neither of these problems will arise. There can be no true *IV* unless the stimulus or response differs from those defining any other *IV*. And unless there is a behavioral representation, there can be no *IV*. Of course, the investigator may look for and find a new behavioral representation based on a new or more refined response measure. Then he *has* a new *IV*. Possible ways of getting such measures involve using *a*) direct questioning and acceptance of the resulting verbal responses, *b*) overt but indirect behavioral representation, such as that involved in projective techniques, and *c*) refined physiological techniques.

The above criticisms arise only because we frequently talk about things that are not *IV*s; they are assumptions, hypothetical constructs, hunches, intuitions, or whatever other names we wish to call them; or they may be terms introduced from other contexts which as yet have no defined meaning in the new context. If the investigator wishes to use them in the new context, he must produce stimulus manipulations and response measurements to demonstrate their meaning; these manipulations and measurements may be more refined than previous ones. For example, suppose a theorist is concerned about the *IV* "emotion," as defined in some other context, and is uncertain about its behavioral representations in the problem solving context. His task is then to manipulate the stimulus conditions in such a manner as to obtain related responses that can be assigned specifically to this *IV*, and to no other *IV* involved in this experimentation. He might introduce simple response measures like asking questions, or complex ones involving special apparatus (for example, *GSR*-measuring devices). If there are adequate specified relationships between the stimulus and response measures in the new and old contexts, he may be justified in using the old term "emotion" in the new context. He would *not* be justified in carrying over via such terms any of the *theorizing* about emotion that may have taken place in the old context.

Finally, progress toward anything approximating a complete integration of a number of complexly interacting *IV*s must be gradual, and in this process it will not be necessary continuously to identify each *IV* that has previously been defined. Once particular *R* measures have been related to *S* manipulations, it may be assumed that such *R* measures are demonstrable, as long as the essential *S* components are present. This is comparable to the manner in which animal experimenters assume that rats deprived of food for a certain period of time are motivated by "hunger." This assumption is made even in the absence of the kind of direct response evidence that would ordinarily be used in the complete operational definition of the term.

Relation of This Methodology to Orthodox Usage of *IV*s

It is instructive to make a more concrete over-all comparison of this methodology and the orthodox usage of *IV*s in the manner intended by Hull (1943, 1951). In this treatment I am not recommending the abandonment of the Hullian method, but rather its supplementation.

1. ANALYSIS OR SYNTHESIS   All effective scientific enterprise must involve both analytic and synthetic activities. The methodology proposed here is essentially analytic, whereas the Hullian methodology is essentially synthetic. Hull has attempted first to posit a number of presumably fundamental behavior constructs, and then on the basis of certain hypothesized relations among these has proceeded to build up to more complex problems.

Hull's system has already demonstrated its advantages by attracting adherents and stimulating research over the past decade. It suggests rigorously testable hypotheses with relative ease. However, there are also risks attendant upon Hull's methods. Research may be sidetracked onto easily testable problems whose theoretical implications are insignificant. Harlow (1953) expresses this criticism in his recent attack on the so-called "tissue-tension" theories. This particular risk is less serious in the analytic methodology proposed here. Moreover, the generalizability of constructs thus analytically fashioned should be considerably less open to question.

2. CHAINING OF VARIABLES   I would take a much more cautious approach than Hull to the problem of the chaining of *IV*s. Keeping closer to S and R referents allows us to make less tenuous assumptions. Fewer gaps need appear in the theoretical structure. Although Hull's system is seemingly tight and well-knit relative to its few competitors, it still suffers from a considerable amount of ambiguity. The surplus meaning in certain of his key constructs has been discussed by MacCorquodale and Meehl (1948), and recently more comprehensively by Koch (1954). The fact that there are difficulties in chaining *IV*s is illustrated by Hull's recent radical shift in the variables defining $_sH_R$ and $_sE_R$ (cf. 1943, 1951). Basic shifts of this nature would be less likely to occur if the R referents of all chained *IV*s were required to be directly testable.

3. FORMALIZATION AND MATHEMATIZATION   I am dubious about the fruitfulness of the exact mathematical formulations developed by Hull and his collaborators (Felsinger et al., 1947; Gladstone et al., 1947; Hull

et al., 1947; Yamaguchi et al., 1948; Yamaguchi, 1951^a, 1951^b) to represent behavioral relationships. Methodologically, as pioneers in an important but difficult area, they should be highly commended. But it seems to me that they have ignored the extreme specificity of the experimental conditions under which their data were obtained. Perhaps this is a necessary restriction under which any such efforts must labor. In any case, it seems to me that the task as they have undertaken it is bound to become a hopeless one when the variability imposed by simple variations in experimental parameters is compounded by that resulting from the introduction of new parameters. If this is a fair picture of mathematization at a simple level, similar efforts at more complex levels of behavior might be fruitless.

The above remarks need qualification. In the first place, they do not apply to the use of quantification for statistical purposes—that is, as involved in the evaluation of data. This kind of quantification is an essential requirement for any serious and thoroughgoing research effort in which we wish to generalize our results to populations. In the second place, they are not directed at the use of mathematics as a *tool* for better expressing the relationships among intervening constructs. They are directed at the premature development of mathematical formulations as *goals* in and of themselves.

Furthermore, I am not attempting to make a prediction about the *eventual* outcome of the efforts to develop mathematical formulations in behavior theory. I simply do not feel that psychology as a science is mature enough to justify widespread mathematization of this type. Our present ability to point to relevant variables, much less relate them in even a rudimentary fashion, is quite limited. Also, once we have personally invested in such mathematical treatments, we tend to become concerned with technical improvement of formulae rather than with the discovery of important relationships among variables. Our greatest present need is for more penetrating discoveries rather than for more refined mathematical formulations.

*   *   *

References

Felsinger, J. M., Gladstone, A. I., Yamaguchi, H. G., and Hull, C. L. Reactions latency ($_st_R$) as a function of the number of reinforcements (N). *J. Exp. Psychol.*, 1947, 37, 214–228.

Gladstone, A. I., Yamaguchi, H. G., Hull, C. L., and Felsinger, J. M. Some functional relationships of reaction potential ($_sE_R$) and related phenomena. *J. Exp. Psychol.*, 1947, 37, 510–526.

Harlow, H. F. Mice, monkeys, men, and motives. *Psychol. Rev.*, 1953, *60*, 23–32.

Hull, C. L. *Principles of behavior*. New York: D. Appleton-Century, 1943.

———. *Essentials of behavior*. New Haven, Conn: Yale Univ. Press, 1951.

Hull, C. L., Felsinger, J. M., Gladstone, A. I., and Yamaguchi, H. G. A proposed quantification of habit strength. *Psychol. Rev.*, 1947, *54*, 237–254.

Koch, S. Clark L. Hull. In W. K. Estes et al., *Modern learning theory*. New York: Appleton-Century-Crofts, 1954.

MacCorquodale, K., and Meehl, P. E. On a distinction between hypothetical constructs and intervening variables. *Psychol. Rev.*, 1948, *55*, 95–107.

Marx, M. H. Intervening variable or hypothetical construct? *Psychol. Rev.*, 1951, *58*, 235–247. [Selection 10 in this volume.]

Skinner, B. F. Are theories of learning necessary? *Psychol. Rev.*, 1950, *57*, 193–216.

Tolman, E. C. Operational behaviorism and current trends in psychology. In *Proc. 25th Anniv. Celebr. Inaug. Grad. Stud.* Los Angeles: Univ. of Southern California Press, 1936. [Reprinted in E. C. Tolman, *Collected papers in psychology*. Berkeley, Calif.: Univ. of California Press, 1951, pp. 115–129; also in M. H. Marx (ed.), *Psychological theory: contemporary readings*. New York: Macmillan, 1951, pp. 87–102.]

Underwood, B. J. An orientation for research on thinking. *Psychol. Rev.*, 1952, *59*, 209–220.

Yamaguchi, H. G. Superthreshold reaction potential ($_sE_R$) as a function of experimental extinction (N). *J. Exp. Psychol.*, 1951, *41*, 391–400.

———. Drive (D) as a function of hours of hunger (h). *J. exp. Psychol.*, 1951, *42*, 108–117.

Yamaguchi, H. G., Hull, C. L., Felsinger, J. M., and Gladstone, A. I. Characteristics of dispersions based on the pooled momentary reaction potentials ($_sE_R$) of a group. *Psychol. Rev.*, 1948, *55*, 216–238.

PART TWO
Special Problems

CHAPTER V

Levels of Explanation

A CERTAIN AMOUNT OF the systematic controversy gen-
erated within psychology has been said to be the result of a
failure to recognize the fact that different points of view will
naturally follow from the acceptance of different basic prem-
ises and the use of varying theoretical and experimental ap-
proaches. Differences in the level of explanation at which
various theoretical and systematic endeavors are designed to
operate seems to be one of the most important factors in the
production of such controversy. The selections in the present
chapter deal with this problem of varying levels of explana-
tion and are included in the expectation that a fuller apprecia-
tion of the role of such basic differences will result in a reduc-
tion of at least some of the more superficial disagreements.

In the first selection, Egon Brunswik provides a useful sys-
tematic framework that emphasizes the "conceptual focus" of
certain of the major systematic positions in psychology, with
special reference to their molar-molecular characteristics. The
second selection is an excerpt from an article by F. H. George.
It presents a succinct suggestion for the transformation of
molar to molecular units. In the third selection, David Krech
represents the neurophysiological point of view. Finally, a
comprehensive examination of the old problem of "reduction-
ism" is offered by Richard Jessor.

14 | *The Conceptual Focus of Systems*[1]

EGON BRUNSWIK

In the present paper the attempt is made to order systematically some of the conceptual tools which have been used in dealing with psychological topics. In the opinion of the author, a suitable starting point for such a consideration is furnished by a scheme of the following kind (Figure 1).

The drawing represents an organism within its surroundings as described by an observing physicist in terms of measurement and computation. This observer might be able to distinguish different layers within the whole causal texture with reference to the organism. Some of these which became most outstanding in psychological discriminations might be designated by the terms (c) remote past, (b) the realm of palpable bodies in the actual environment, (a) stimulus events located on the retina or on other stimulus surfaces of the organism, (0) intra-organismic events, (A) muscular reactions, or behavior in the narrower sense of the word, (B) effects of these reactions with regard to the relationship between organism and surroundings, as e.g., the reaching of a goal, and finally (C) the more remote consequences and final products of life activities including stabilized mechanical or conceptual tools for further use. For the purpose of further explanation, some of the customary terms not used in this list are included in the chart.

The layers indicated are not supposed to designate singular sequences in time, but rather to furnish a general scheme for cross-sectional classification and co-ordination of physical events, or features of the physical world, with reference to their causal relationship to an organism. The scheme possesses a certain symmetry, with layers designated by corresponding letters (a and A, b and B, c and C) conceptually related to each other.

From E. Brunswik, The conceptual focus of some psychological systems, *J. Unif. Sci.*, 1939, *8*, 36–49. Reprinted by permission of the author and publisher.

[1] Paper sent in for the fourth International Congress for the Unity of Science (Cambridge, England, 1938).

LAYERS:

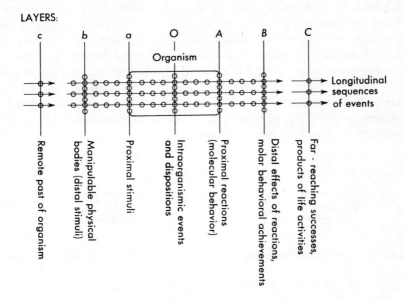

Figure 1.   Scheme of the organism in its surroundings.

Four main types of interest seem to be possible within this system: 1) emphasis upon events belonging to a certain cross-sectional layer and the internal relations of these events among each other, 2) emphasis upon a certain type of causal chains, that is, interest in longitudinal sequences, 3) emphasis upon the external relationships of distant cross-sectional layers among each other, 4) emphasis upon the interrelations of discrete longitudinal patterns among each other.

Concepts and laws referring to 1) and 2), that is, to single events or to cross-sectional or longitudinal internal relationships, are non-psychological. Roughly speaking, these internal relationships constitute the core of the problems treated in physics proper as far as the left part of the picture and particularly (b) is concerned. They constitute the core of the biological sciences in the narrower sense of the word as far as the middle of the picture is concerned, and the "letters" or "Geisteswissenschaften" as far as the right part is concerned. On this latter side those physical features of the world are represented which still reveal the fact that their causal ancestry is partially built up from causal patterns typical to life activities. For example, a mechanical tool made by man would be considered to belong to this group only by virtue of its particular form in connection with a limited number of certain "relevant" properties regardless of all the other traits.

We are now going to attempt to characterize some of the psychological disciplines, or systems, as they grew up historically, in terms of our scheme. In every instance, not the programmatically propounded general frame will be taken as the standard, but rather the conceptual texture of the work actually performed in a sufficiently detailed fashion. This has to be done, since in an arm-chair sense nearly any of the systems might justly consider itself all-inclusive and able to be considerate in face of every objection without doing violence to its own conceptual framework. In short, we are going to treat systems not in terms of what they could have included but what they did include.

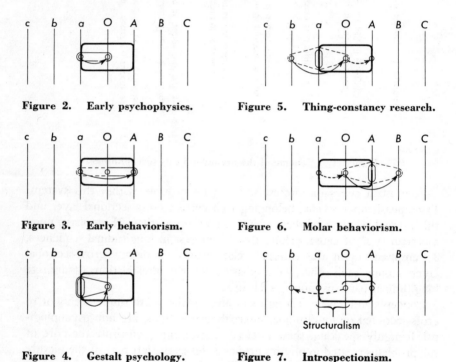

Figure 2.   Early psychophysics.

Figure 5.   Thing-constancy research.

Figure 3.   Early behaviorism.

Figure 6.   Molar behaviorism.

Figure 4.   Gestalt psychology.

Figure 7.   Introspectionism.

Early experimental psychology still was characterized by the ideology typical of the most paradigmatic nonpsychological sciences. In particular its interests were, as far as the very beginnings are concerned, chiefly longitudinal in the sense characterized above under 2). The first type of experimental research to win importance in psychology was classical psychophysics. Its interest centered around a rather limited fragment of a kind of longitudinal chain, per se. The initial link was defined in terms of what Koffka has named proximal stimulation, that is, stimulation in terms of the causal chains as they just enter the sense organ. The guiding ideal of the psychology of that time was expressed by the wish to know as much as possible about the functional mechanisms of the sense organ and of nervous conduction—in short, about "mediation problems"—and thus to be enabled to pursue the causal chains as closely as possible, in a step-by-step fashion, so to speak. There was, however, as we follow the development from the Johannes Müller to the Fechner era, a noticeable shift of emphasis toward the relationship, per se, of the two end terms of the longitudinal fragment concerned, namely, the relationship between "stimulus" and "sensation." At the same time the problems of the casual "mediations," as such, were losing ground. It is this becoming more and more interested in a by-and-large causal correlation between discrete layers regardless of the technicalities of their interconnection which brought psychology proper into existence as a discipline distinguishable from physiology.

Figure 2 gives a schematic picture of early psychophysics using the scheme of Figure 1 as a frame of reference. The focus of concept-formation is located at the layers of proximal stimulation and of internal response as well as at their gross interrelation as indicated by the arrow. The interest in mediation problems still vital is represented by the slope covering the entire ground leading from the one term to the other in longitudinal direction.

The categorical structure and the actual research interest of the early "conditioned reflex" behaviorism as represented by Pavlov or by Watson is similar, in principle, to that of early psychophysics. The chief conceptual emphasis appears to be shifted, however, from the implicit to the overt response in terms of bodily movements, as such. The interest in mediation problems is centered around the motor rather than the sensory processes, as indicated in Figure 3. In fact, of course, every psychophysics or introspective psychology had to utilize verbal, that is, a particular kind of motor, responses. These responses were supposed to be, however, true representatives of inner states. The aimed-at-focus of concept formation of these disciplines might therefore be considered to lie in the internal life of the individual.

The further development of psychology as an exact science can be characterized as a progressive extension of the range of consideration from the fragmentary or molecular viewpoint to larger units of a "molar" nature. This goes with an increasing emphasis upon gross by-and-large correlations between kinds of events schematically located at a distance from each other, on the one hand, and with a—on the whole—more and more subordinate interest in mediation, per se.

A first important step was Gestalt psychology. Considering the most characteristic core of problems actually treated by Gestalt psychology in the field of perception, the chief difference as compared with traditional psychophysics lies in an extension of the notion of the stimulus to that of a stimulus pattern. The response is treated as a response to the sensory configuration as a whole whereby the laws of dynamic interaction within each of the cross-sectional layers of the sensorium are made the central issue. Gestalt psychology, though totalitarian or molar, is, however, still fragmentary insofar as it is, in its most elaborate parts, a psychology "from the retina inward," so to speak. There is, as in psychophysics, a great deal of interest in mediation problems, as can be seen from the numerous attempts to explain physiologically the facts found. All this is represented schematically in Figure 4.

A further extension of the psychology of perception is given by including into the scope of consideration the manipulable solid bodies, located in the farther environment, and their recognition as the specific determiners of the reaction. The beginnings of this line of interest can be traced back to Helmholtz. This trend, however, did not become conscious of its own character until the last few decades and after the earlier stages of Gestalt psychology already had been completed. In this discipline, the stimulus is not any longer defined in proximal terms but in distal ones. The actual research centers around the question to what extent the perceptual system is able to liberate itself from the disturbing variability of the proximal representation of similar distal stimuli and thus to focus the response upon the latter and not upon the former as the determining event. In other words, the question is how far the organism has established mechanisms which are able to extrapolate, with a sufficiently large chance of success, the causal chains from the retina backward and thus, figuratively speaking, to reach out cognitively into the farther surroundings.

A fairly univocal attachment of a class of reactions to bodily properties, like extension or reflectively to color, despite changes in the mediating causal pattern is called "thing constancy." We might, then, as well describe these reactions by means of the other term of the external relation in question, or, in short, in terms of their "objects attained." The focus of concept formation is thus shifted away from the organism itself into its farther surroundings, or, more precisely, into a relationship of the organism with layer (b). In other words, the organism is characterized by its ability to achieve something with regard to its environment, not by the intrinsic character of its reactions or by the nature of certain physiological forms of mediation.

In the opinion of the author, there is scarcely another discipline which would reveal as clearly as does constancy research the extent to which the organism is able to render irrelevant the particularities of mediation. Let us take a frequently quoted example. Among the chief constituents of the system of cues which enable the organism to extrapolate the sizes of the surrounding bodies from the retinal stimulus pattern, are the so called "distance-cues," as, for instance, binocular disparity or the perspective distortion of right angles. There are numerous kinds of distance cues. Most of them differ radically from each other as long as we consider intrinsic properties or the physiological mechanisms operated by them. They have in common nothing but a higher or lesser probability of being caused by a certain environmental depth-pattern. And yet they are responded to by the central system of the organism in an identical manner, or, in short, they are "equipotential." It is this feature of organismic reaction and achievement which forces psychology, as it approaches its genuine molar and relational problems, more and more into a focusing upon the end terms of far-reaching relationships. The particular "how" of the mediation processes, on the other hand, necessarily will attract only subordinate interest.

In other words, we do not consider it a matter of choice, whether psychology does focus its concepts on one or on another layer or on a correlation of layers among each other. In looking without preconceptions at nature populated by organisms, gross correlations of higher or lesser degree between kinds of events rather remote from each other in space or time will strike the observer. The network of occurrences participating in such correlations might be conceptually picked out and its constituents labeled as the given foci of life patterns. Psychology has to focus its descriptions on what the organisms have become focused on, not on events systematically located at the interstices between these foci. *Ordo idearum sit idem ac ordo rerum.* There has to be a discipline to deal with these foci and their gross correlations, per se. Otherwise there would remain a white spot on the landmap of possible scientific knowledge. By all of its history, it is psychology which is predestined to fill this gap.

In short, molar psychology of achievement is a deliberate "lump" treatment. This feature seems to be the chief obstacle which stands in the way of its acceptance. Correlations between distant layers never hold to an ideal degree. There are always "exceptions" due to the lack of perfection of the cues and means establishing these correlations. In every instance, there is only a higher or lesser degree of probability for the reaching of the usual end. This feature becomes especially clear where we have to do with the so-called instincts. Dealing with instruments of this kind in terms of their achievement leads to an apparent lack of exactitude. It takes a certain courage, a neglect of some of the attitudes sacred to scientific tradition, to give up the safety of molecular correlations, cheap as they are, in favor of the equivocalities or "vaguenesses" of molar correlations. But we have to prefer vagueness focused upon essentials to security and strict univocality focused upon non-essentials. This holds especially as long as we are lucky enough to find everything prepared to become strictly physicalistic in our "vaguenesses," quantifying them by the means of correlation statistics and other related mathematical tools.

There always remains a certain self-restriction required in order not to become too curious about the mechanisms causing the "exceptions" and dispersions mentioned, before the task of a bird's-eye-view-inventory of gross correlations had been completed. Of course, there are various ramifications. Looking for exceptions and their causes might, besides being a mere side track, become a corrective measure which enables us to find still more superordinate correlations. These superordinate correlations, however, should be our ultimate aim. Furthermore, concepts and methods referring to mediation problems will have to come back to psychology proper as soon as the precise limitations of the complex achievements in question are subject to closer examination. These problems are out of the scope of psychological consideration only so far as that first phase of research is concerned in which far-reaching gross achievements become discovered and examined in first approximation. On the whole, however, psychology should develop "from above," not "from below." It might proceed to sub-foci of a more and more particular kind and ultimately converge towards and merge with its complementary sciences of a genuinely molecular type.

The schematic representation of constancy research (Figure 5) has to be drawn in the following way: an arrow from a certain type of events in (b) to a certain type of events in (0), representing the primary interest; a slope around the group of sub-foci which constitute the "family" of equipotential cue patterns and which circumscribe the extent of variability of the mediational pattern and thus the degree of safeguardedness of the achievement under varying conditions of mediation; and finally a slope around the whole unit of processes involved, including mediation processes. The latter slope has been dotted in order to indicate the subordinate nature of the mediation problems. A further dotted arrow is drawn to connect the event in (0) with an overt response. This is done to indicate that Psychology in Terms of Objects wishes to be, in principle, strictly behavioristic, i.e., refuses to extrapolate without particular controls from the measurable verbal utterances into the field of their internal "meanings."

A picture symmetrical to that of constancy research is yielded by a chief part of the research done within the conceptual frame of molar or purposive behaviorism, as represented by Tolman (Figure 6). The difference is merely a material one, constancy research being concerned with problems of reception and cognition, or the organismic achievement of a backward extrapolation of causal chains, whereas molar behaviorism deals with problems of overt action and its further environmental effects. In molar behaviorism, as contrasted to molecular behaviorism, results are expressed in terms of reaching a certain goal, not in terms of movements made. The comparative irrelevancy of ways and means, that is, their equipotentiality with regard to a certain end is systematically recognized and attempts are made to prove it experimentally. As it was done for the proximal stimulus cues in the extended psychophysics of perceptual thing constancy, molar behaviorism realizes that the essentials of behavior will become lost in a description focused on proximal determination. Thus both disciplines are essentially environmentalistic, not mediationalistic or physiologistic.

In both constancy research and molar behaviorism a certain interrelation of longitudinal causal chains is made one of the central issues, namely their equipotentiality within the larger instrument of well-established far-reaching causal couplings. Emphasis is withdrawn, to a certain extent, from a step-by-step determination of these mediating chains of events. Such a restriction is not essential, however, to a molar point of view, as is shown by the type of approach represented by Hull. His general frame of consideration coincides in its most essential features with that of the disciplines mentioned. A still stronger line of interest is focused, however, on the "family" of mediational patterns, per se. These patterns are analyzed in an essentially associationistic or conditioned reflex fashion, that is in a molecular longitudinal way. In the opinion of the author, the chief objection to such an attitude is a merely practical one, namely, distraction from the gross "first-approximation" treatment of cognitive or behavioral achievement.

The idea of a pure achievement analysis is accomplished, more thoroughly than in any of the other branches mentioned, in the psychology of "tests." At first glance this might seem to be a strictly cross-sectional affair within events in layer (B), these events being correlated among each other statistically. The correlational analysis implies, however, the reference to organisms performing various combinations of achievement. Mediation problems are usually kept entirely outside of consideration.

It might even be said that correlation statistics as a general scientific instrument received a decisive impetus from test psychology (Pearson, Spearman, Thurstone, and others). Starting from rather complex achievements relatively detached from straight sensory or muscular activities, test psychology had the chance to grow up without meeting a resistance comparable to that met by Gestalt psychology or the other molar disciplines mentioned above. The methods developed in test statistics are, therefore, most likely to become paradigmatic to all future molar psychology. As an illustration it might be mentioned that, according to a recent American survey, the term correlation is among the two or three most frequently quoted terms to be found in the textbooks used in this country.

In recent times statistical analysis led to a closer reference to a small number of hypothetical "factors" or basic abilities independent of each other underlying the countless variety of actual performances. This is one of the instances where the stage is set for a genuinely psychological physiological psychology, focused not on layer (0), as such, or on its interrelations with layers (*a*) or (*A*), but on the far-reaching interrelations between (0), on the one hand, and (*B*)—or (*b*)—on the other.

A few words only about disciplines like social psychology, genetic psychology, psychoanalysis. They all seem to be focused primarily on molar interrelations of the organism in its actuality with some complex features of the remote environment, present or past. They fulfill the requirements of a molar psychology as long as they concentrate upon an attempt to segregate abstractively the focal or relevant traits within the patterns they investigate from the actually irrelevant ones.

A certain type of genetic attitude possesses, however, a close resemblance to molecularism. Considering the systematic description of gross achievement or adjustment of the organism to the environment as the primary subject matter of psychology, inquiry about the history of such mechanisms in some cases might easily lose contact with the essential features of the achievemental pattern actually in question. In such instances, asking "why" becomes comparable to the "how" problems of the mediationalistic type. For example, to be concerned primarily as to whether a certain organismic instrument is due to heredity or to learning might occasionally become just another burden for the investigator of that instrument, co-ordinate with the claim of the physiologically minded criticist whose first concern is to know as much as possible about all the single steps involved in the mechanism in question. Like molecularism, geneticism for its own sake involves the danger of diverting psychology into knowing more and more for the price of knowing it about less and less, or about smaller and smaller fragments of the units which constitute the task of psychology.

In the common language of science, molecular as well as genetic descriptions have often been called "explanations." In contrast to that, molar achievemental analysis is "descriptive" in the most restricted sense of the word. As a deliberate "lump" treatment, it refuses to aim at explanation for its own sake. It is a psychology "in terms of . . . ," a terminological affair, a way of registering and conceptually looking at gross correlations in their straightforward actuality.

Up to this point of our considerations psychology has been treated as if it were built up by means of strictly scientific methods, that is, in principle, as physics was of a certain group of causal correlations. For a large part of psychology this holds true, in principle at least. The events involved are subject to measurement and the interrelations to quantitative treatment. Or, as Lewin would put it, "Aristotelian" concept formation in terms of absolute dichotomies between qualitatively different "principles," as, e.g., the traditional antithesis of "insight" versus "learning," has already been largely substituted by a "Galilean," that is, by more "diagrammatic" forms of thinking in terms of gradual discriminations.

We do not wish, however, to conclude this paper without glancing at some of the forms of psychology which do or do not fully subscribe to such a methodological ideal.

First of all, there is introspectionism. Common to all introspectionism is the tacit assumption of a strict one-to-one relationship between verbal utterances and "inner events." Only by virtue of such an attitude is it possible to consider, as is done by introspectionism, words or other events located in layer (A) as valid representatives or "symbols" for inner experiences (0). In all objective psychology verbal utterances are taken not as symbols, but merely as "symptoms" the meaning of which is supposed to be accessible only by means of special correlational investigations. In Figure 7, the substitution mentioned is represented by a parenthesis.

Another kind of substitution is, however, much more fundamental in introspectionism. As emphasized especially by the so-called act-psychologists, e.g., Brentano, the essence of consciousness is characterized by its pointing toward, or aiming at, an object. This relationship has been called intentionality. Though it was said that intentional objects should not be confused with the physical environment, it still can be made clear that introspectionism became infiltrated with a conceptual structure taken to a large extent from the layer of palpable bodies (b). Yet there was no chance of a quantitative treatment on a physicalistic basis, since the relation of (0) to (b)—or to something formally analogous to (b)—had been accepted as univocal without experimentation. Furthermore, this relationship was regarded as a qualitative entity of its own kind entirely incomparable with the causal relationship, to which it is also supposed to be opposite in direction. This relationship was admitted without further control, from a mere inspection of layer (0). This is indicated in Figure 7 by a dashed arrow $0 \rightarrow b$ which is also pointing in the opposite direction from the corresponding arrow $b \rightarrow 0$ in Figure 5. In philosophy, the problems of "dualism" have to a large extent arisen from confusion and uncritical mutual substitution of the two cross-sectional layers structurally similar to each other. This substitution is comparable to that committed by introspectionism. The fallacies of an uncontrolled substitution of layers by each other have recently been emphasized by Heider.

Introspectionism can be subdivided into two main branches. The one is represented by men like Wundt or Titchener, and also by Mach. It is sometimes called "Structuralism." Its chief feature is to look for basic elements out of which all the complex experiences may "consist" (without questioning whether the grammar of the word "consist" permits such an application). Structuralism coincides in time with the early molecular sensory psychology characterized by its emphasis upon mediational features like proximal stimulation and the structure of the sense receptors. It is obvious that in this general attitude—sometimes characterized as "glorification of the skin"—the mosaic-nature of the events at the sensory surface has been directly carried over to the hypothetical structure of inner events (cf. Figure 7). Thus these came to be understood after the pattern of the sense organ. In structuralism, therefore, not only layers (0) and (A) and layers (0) and (b), but also layers (0) and (a) appear in uncontrolled confusion.

The second branch of introspectionism might be called phenomenalism. It is somewhat related to act psychology, and sometimes the term phenomenology is applied, not quite unmistakably, to it. It is the kind of introspection represented by Gestalt psychology and the Würzburg school of psychology of thinking. There was sufficient sophistication within phenomenalism about the naïve entanglement of structuralism with sensory elementarism, with mediationalism and with functional "explanation." Unbiased "description" of the pre-analytically-given was aimed at. The structuralist's "consist of" was given up in favor of the phenomenalist's "resembles." Everyday language and even slang was used deliberately. Characteristic examples are the description of the phenomenon of the shadow by Hering as a tiny skin of darkness lying upon the surface of the object, the true color of which shines through the former, or the introduction of the term "Aha-Erlebnis" by Bühler in order to refer to the experience of sudden insight. In this way, phenomenalism grew into a kind of conceptualized and systematized poetry, bringing, in principle, all the various concepts and terms of the common qualitative language into one comprehensive system of resemblances. Since all "qualities" might be regarded as gross reactions of the organism to some features of the environment and thus be systematically located in layer (0), phenomenalism is the strictest expression in existence of an 0-internal system of psychological concept formation.

As a system of mutual resemblances, phenomenalism can be represented by means of a spatial order. The best example for such a quasi-spatial arrangement of qualities, though limited to a certain modality, is the three-dimensional Hering color pyramid. It is built up on an entirely phenomenalistic basis regardless of the physical relationships of colors among each other. Thus it deals with reactions only, not with stimuli. It was the first attempt to deal with psychological problems on a "topological" basis by assigning a certain place in a spatial order to each quality. These qualities could then be determined in terms of basic "dimensions" defined by certain outstanding qualities.

On a somewhat different basis, topological considerations have been recently introduced into psychology by Lewin. In his Topological Psychology, the actual "life space" is represented by a spatial scheme. As is true for phenomenalism, however, not the surroundings defined in terms of physics are taken as a frame of reference, but rather the environment as it is cognitively or functionally responded to by the organism in the particular instance. In a certain way topological psychology is similar to the "Unweltforschung" of Uexküll. It deals, deliberately, not with stimuli or stimulus relationships, but rather with a pattern of reactions to be schematically located in 0, and from 0 dynamically onward until a new equilibrium is reached. Its chief merit is that it furnished an adequate conceptual tool for a description of this organized pattern of "field" intervening between the stimulating surroundings (c, b, a) on the one hand, and the acted-upon surroundings (A, B, C), on the other. Though quasi-spatial and highly generalized, topological psychology is not quantitative and not physicalistic in the usual sense. It enters the picture at a systematic locus symmetrical, or complementary, to the psychology of perception. Psychology of perception deals with the relationship of the world as it "is" for the organism in question, and of the world as it "is" for the observing discursified human being. Only the former is represented in topological psychology.

In conclusion: psychological research today presents itself as a pattern of fragments. These fragments tend to crystallize around the program of a gross correlational analysis in terms of achievement, converging "from above" with the disciplines dealing with molecular problems. Environmentalism seems to take the lead before mediationalism and molecular geneticism (as e.g., some of the questions of "explanation").

15 | *Molar to Molecular*

F. H. GEORGE

*   *   *

A word on the interpretation given to the words "molar" and "molecular" lar" seems apposite as these words are indeed many meaninged.

Granted that we see all of science on a simple plan of assumptions,

From F. H. George, Formalization of language systems for behavior theory, *Psychol. Rev.*, 1953, *60*, 232–240. Pp. 238–240 reprinted by permission of the author, the *Psychological Review*, and the American Psychological Association.

consequences of assumptions, tests of consequences, etc.—going on indefinitely in a spiral, where we might equally well have written postulates,
theorems, experiments to test theorems, postulates, etc. Granted also that
we accept the need for precise propositions on some sort of a hierarchical
model as has been suggested, with the added flexibility allowed by glossary and contextual definitions, then we should also expect to find that
the molar-molecular apparent dichotomy really represents two points on
a continuum, at least in one sense. This distinction is important because
propositions which are vague, nontestable, etc. on molar levels may be
testable on molecular, and vice versa. This even applies to different molar
and different molecular levels. The problem can be simply illustrated
diagrammatically. Figure 1 is a representation of the essence of behavior

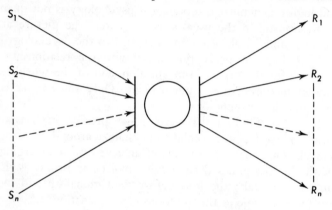

**Figure 1.   A schematic representation of a pictorial model
of behavior.**

where Ss stand for stimuli, Rs for responses and O for the organism—to
be regarded essentially, of course, as in an environment and in a space-
time manifold. The molar theorist now acts as shown in Figure 2. He
attempts to describe behavior in terms of varied and complex stimulus
and response conditions without carrying out tests, observations, etc. on
the internal state of the organism. Thus the vagaries that attend making
inferences about learning from performance are accounted for by logical
constructs (these are represented by the "tags" in Figure 2, strung together and involving any number). A consideration of latent learning,
delayed reward, etc. from molar theory itself is sufficient to show internal
variation cannot always be neglected, even if this was not obvious from
our knowledge of physiology, endocrinology, etc. Figure 3 illustrates the
molecular viewpoint in essence. Here the molar constructs are broken
down into molecular constructs where ⊞ represents diagrammatically
the subdivisions of □. The great advance is simply that ⊞ can be re-

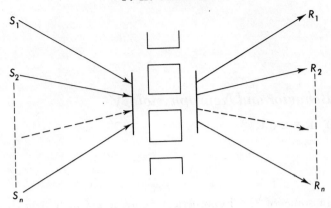

**Figure 2.   A schematic representation of a pictorial model
of molar theory.**

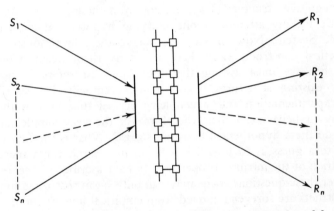

**Figure 3.   A schematic representation of a pictorial model
of molecular theory.**

garded as part of ☐ and part of a molar theory and testable as such, and at the same time is testable on the neurological, endocrinological level. The double purpose is served of making explicit our molar constructs and opening up a further testing ground for their validity.

This whole matter is complex but the term molecular should be regarded roughly in the light of tying our molar constructs to the organic data and thus hoping to reduce the work to be done by a single logical construct and thus to reduce the surplus meaning, and also the vagueness.

*   *   *

16 | *Behavior and Neurophysiology*

DAVID KRECH

*   *   *

What are some of the hypothetical constructs which have been suggested for psychological theory? To list them all would be a long and perhaps too depressing a task to undertake, but among some of the more current ones are such constructs as motives, needs, tensions, beliefs, attitudes, cognitive structures, expectations, hypotheses, etc.[1] Add to that pluralistic list my attempt at one unifying hypothetical construct, the Dynamic System. Now, if we are to take these as seriously-intended hypothetical constructs (and there are many theoreticians who so intend), then we must assume that the above list refers to postulated actually existing structures which might eventually be described by direct experimentation and which have crucial functions in the entire economy of behavior. I must therefore ask the very simple questions: Where do these hypothetical constructs exist? What is the first approximation to a guess as to how I can begin my search for a more direct examination of the intrinsic properties you have ascribed to them? Failure to answer these questions adequately can only mean that these hypothetical constructs are forever removed from empirical investigation.

What sort of answers have been given, or can be given, by those psychologists who can be labeled as "psychological psychologists" (as opposed to, for example, "physiological psychologists")? It seems to me that usually the answers have shown, or will show, the same confusion that I have displayed in my definition of Dynamic System. The basic

From D. Krech, Dynamic systems, psychological fields, and hypothetical constructs, *Psychol. Rev.*, 1950, 57, 283–290. Pp. 284–288 reprinted by permission of the author, the *Psychological Review*, and the American Psychological Association.

[1] I want to make it clear that I am discussing these concepts only when they are used as hypothetical constructs. What I have to say in the following discussion does not apply to these concepts when they are used as intervening variables in the MacCorquodale and Meehl sense, *i.e.*, as merely names for stimulus-response correlations. In other words, my present paper can have relevance and interest only to those psychologists who want to use hypothetical constructs in their system-building.

nature of this confusion derives from the fact that once we accept the position of a purely psychological psychology we are forced to place all would-be hypothetical constructs in a sort of never-never land—a domain which is forever inaccessible to scientific inquiry. I want now to indicate briefly my reasons for believing this, and to point to some variants of confusion which derive from this basic inadequacy. I should like to anticipate my argument a bit, however, by specifying that this confusion appears only when the question of using hypothetical constructs is involved.

Ask a purely psychological theoretician who proposes to use hypothetical constructs in his theory-making where his constructs—his tensions, expectations, cognitive structures or needs—are located, and ask him just what they are and how they can be studied more directly so that we can eventually check on his theorizing, and he will say something which boils down to the statement that these hypothetical constructs are in the psychological field, are psychological processes and can be studied by psychological analysis. Persist in your attempt to pin him down further and ask whether tensions or expectations or needs or cognitive structures are merely short-hand terms for certain behavior patterns and he will, of course, deny the implication and point out that he is using them as hypothetical constructs, i.e., these tensions, expectations, needs, etc., are *determinants* of behavior and not behavior itself. Ask him, then, whether these terms refer to conscious experiences, and again he will be forced to answer in the negative. Again he will insist that these terms refer to the processes which lie behind experience and are not to be identified with experience, and he will remind you further that not all needs or tensions or attitudes have conscious correlates. Ask him, finally, whether tensions or needs or cognitive structures are names for neurological activities, and again he will say no, if he is a purely psychological psychologist. (I will discuss the case of the not-so-pure psychologist in a moment.) What then are tensions and needs and cognitive structures? They are not behavior, they are not conscious experiences, they are not neural events. How can we ever study the intrinsic attributes of these non-behavioral, non-experiential, non-neural actually existing structures? The answer again is: They are psychological processes going on in a psychological field and are amenable to psychological analysis. But this answer, in my opinion, is double-talk when we are dealing with hypothetical constructs. I do not object to such an answer because this "psychological field" is now unavailable to more direct examination than through the study of stimulus-response correlations. That may be unavoidable and merely reflects the present preliminary stage of our science. But what I do object to is that such an answer does not even offer the slightest guess or hunch or even fantasy of how the scientist is *ever* to get beyond the study of correlations between the immediate data of psychology—stimulus and response. This situation, as I will attempt to show presently, is not a fatal one so long as we keep our theorizing on a descriptive level, or an *"operational"* level (in the narrow sense of the term), or on a correlational level. And there are many psychologists, of course, who intend to do just that. With them we have no quarrel at the present time. But this position of purely psychological psychology is an impossible one to tolerate when we attempt to use hypothetical constructs.

But not all purely psychological psychologists are consistent in their answers to the questions of Where and What. There are those who, in reaction to the difficulties of maintaining a purely psychological position simultaneously with an attempt at using hypothetical constructs, show a bewildering inconsistency in their use of terms. That is, they sometimes define tensions, needs, cognitive structures and the like as hypothetical constructs, and sometimes as conscious experience or as behavior. Thus, for example, they will make statements which can be summarized as follows: "The individual's behavior is determined by his psychological field. His psychological field is determined by his perceptions, needs, tensions, cognitive structures, etc. His perceptions, needs, tensions, cognitive structures, etc., are determined, in turn, by his psychological field." This amounts to saying that a) the "psychological field" as a hypothetical construct, is a cause of behavior, b) that "psychological field" is a resultant of other hypothetical constructs—perceptions, needs, etc., c) that perception, needs, etc., are caused by the psychological field. If it is argued that this is a misreading of the position, that all that is meant by the original set of statements is that attitudes and tensions and beliefs and needs are merely the units of the psychological field and that all of these units taken together compose the psychological field, then, I believe, we are still badly off. Either the term "psychological field" refers to the sum total of our conscious experiences at any given moment, or it refers to that *plus* other non-conscious psychological events, or it refers *only* to non-conscious psychological events. If the first interpretation is correct, then the psychological field is merely a name for a specific category of behavior (*i.e.*, "conscious experience") and as such it is not a hypothetical construct which is to be used to explain itself. If the second or third interpretations are taken, then we have, of course, the identical problem with which we confronted the psychological psychologists in the first place—Where and What are these non-conscious psychological events? However, it is my opinion that many of us have shifted from one interpretation to the other, and without realizing the consequences we have been playing a sort of innocent shell-game with the hypothetical construct here at one moment and gone another.

But, the objection may be raised, there are no such purely psychologi-

cal psychologists as I have been attacking. The point will be made that I
have been attacking a S_____ Man. I have two answers to that. In the
first place I would deny the allegation and assert that we have among us
quite a number of purely psychological psychologists. Some of my best
friends belong in that category. My second point would be that even the
impure psychological psychologists—those who are willing to grant the
possibility that neurological events may have something to do with
behavior—are caught in exactly the same difficulties of attempting to
localize hypothetical constructs in an unknown and an *unknowable*
land. The only difference between them and the purists among the psychologists is this: Where the purist attempts to place his hypothetical
constructs in a never-never land without further qualifications, the impure one does so but with an almost shamefaced yearning for an alliance
with the forbidden land of neurology. The theoreticians who fall into
this latter category make much use of such terms as "psychoneural (or
neuro-psychic) processes," "co-ordinated with neural events" and
"isomorphically related to a system of neural events." Just what is a need
or a tension or a cognitive structure when it is described as a *neuro-
psychic* event? Such a description, it seems to me, can only mean that a
need is a neurological event *in addition to* a purely psychological event.
Why are we not content with defining a need or a tension or a cognitive
structure as a neural event and letting it go at that? Obviously we have
been reluctant to do so because we have felt that needs or tensions are
something more than neural events. But what is this "something more"?
I suspect that the reasons behind our feeling that "something more" is involved are of two kinds. In the first place, as I have already indicated, we
sometimes think of a need as behaivor or conscious experience, and sometimes as a hypothetical construct. As behavior or conscious experience it
is obvious that a need is *not* a neural event and so we must add "something more." In the second place, when we do think of a need as a hypothetical construct which lies behind the experience or behavior, we operate on the implicit assumption that a hypothetical construct must itself
contain the flavor or attributes of the events it controls. And, of course,
the attributes of a purely neurological event do not include the attributes
which characterize the experience of need. Therefore, again, we feel that
we have to add "something more" than the purely neurological to our
would-be hypothetical construct.

The assumption that a hypothetical construct must have the qualities
of the events it determines is, however, a wholly unnecessary one and,
indeed, tends to diminish the scientific usefulness of hypothetical constructs. Just as the genes which determine the red eye color of the
fruitfly do not have any kind of "redness" about them, so is it not necessary that the hypothetical construct of "need" have any of the qualities

which we experience when we say we "feel a need" or when we say that that organism is behaving in a "needful fashion." We must always remember that hypothetical constructs have their intrinsic properties, and it is just because they have such properties that they can be so powerful in predicting *new* data. Otherwise they serve no useful purpose, for if we insist on limiting the description of the properties of the hypothetical constructs to those we can observe by direct description of the phenotypic data, then we have succeeded in merely cluttering up a perfectly useful and straightforward descriptive process. It is because the almost-neurological psychologist persists in being a purely psychological psychologist in his actual definitions, that he is no better off than the purist.

I must admit that upon rereading the above paragraphs I am left with an uneasy feeling that I have missed the point of most of the theoretical discussions and system-buildings of the last fifteen or twenty years. The theme of many of those discussions was that only a psychological analysis of behavior is a fruitful and theoretically mature analysis for psychologists. Perhaps I *have* missed the point, but I prefer to believe that the difficulty lies in the fact that we have never examined very carefully the implications of what is involved in a purely psychological approach to psychology. It now seems to me that a purely psychological approach to psychology has had, and still has, tremendous values—but only for one aspect of the study of psychology—the descriptive one. For system-building which uses hypothetical constructs it is completely inadequate. The purely psychological approach permitted us freedom of operation. It gave us autonomy from the restrictions of an inadequate behaviorism and an equally inadequate neurology. One of the effects of such freedom was a significant improvement in our descriptions of behavior and experience and a permissiveness in coining and using new descriptive terms for new observations. Such descriptions and such correlational analyses are still necessary and are still the proper concern of the psychologist. As long as we remain on that level and do not venture beyond the use of intervening variables in our systemization of our correlations, the purely psychological orientation may be helpful. But the moment we introduce hypothetical constructs into our theory building, then the purely psychological approach becomes untenable.[2] I have argued that it is untenable because it makes forever impossible any attempt to approach the study of our hypothetical constructs in any more direct manner than

---

[2] The apparent paradox appears that the purely psychological approach becomes most useful to the most "tough-minded" of the psychologists (those who would remain on the descriptive or correlational level) and least useful to those who would venture into the fantasies of hypothetical construct invention. The reasons for this are, I believe, obvious to the reader by now.

through the examinations of the original stimulus-response correlations. This is so, I must repeat, because the psychological position places hypothetical constructs in a domain which, *by definition*, is forever removed from any direct observation (for that domain, it will be remembered, is neither behavioral, experiential or neurological).

*   *   *

17 | *The Problem of Reductionism in Psychology*

RICHARD JESSOR[1]

The recent upsurge of interest in physiological determinants and physical models of behavior has raised or reopened certain fundamental questions about the logical status of psychology as an autonomous discipline among the sciences. Some of the discussions may fairly be summarized as implying that physiological or physical concepts are in some sense more basic than those of psychology and that, therefore, causal explanation of behavior will ultimately be expressed in those terms. The controversy over the nature of the hypothetical construct (*HC*) in psychological explanation is a current example. Krech (1950) has insisted that *HC*s must have neurophysiological reference or locus, and that psychologists should be content to define such things as needs, tensions, or cognitive structures as neural events. While this particular view has been criticized (Bergmann, 1953; Kessen and Kimble, 1952), and there is much agreement that neurophysiological content is irrelevant in *HC*s (Rozeboom, 1956), the more general orientation—that fundamental explanation will be reductive—continues to be influential.

Psychologists are not alone in being concerned about this problem. Anthropologists such as Kroeber and White have felt called upon to defend the autonomy of their discipline against those who have tried to explain

From R. Jessor, The problem of reductionism in psychology, *Psychol. Rev.*, 1958, *65*, 170–178. Reprinted by permission of the author, the *Psychological Review*, and the American Psychological Association.

[1] The author was a Social Science Research Council postdoctoral fellow at the University of California during the time in which this paper was prepared.

culture in terms of the concepts of psychology or even biology. (White caustically comments that some anthropologists "have sold their culturological birthright for a mess of psychiatric pottage" [1949, p. xix]). In turn, prominent biologists such as Needham, Haldane, Woodger, and Bertalanffy have argued that their own discipline cannot be considered simply an application of chemistry and physics.

Obviously, an inherent attraction of reductive explanation is its implications for possible ways of unifying the separate scientific disciplines. Since the unity of science is an ultimate aim of many scientific workers, the reductive point of view is not likely to be abandoned in the absence of reasonable alternative approaches to that goal. A commitment to reductionism, either because of its implications for the unity of science, or because of the belief that it represents more fundamental explanation, undoubtedly influences the strategy of work of many scientists.[2] For this reason alone it would seem worth while to assess the doctrine in some detail.

Some considerations of the reductionism problem have tended to dismiss it. One basis for dismissal is the assertion that the answer to the problem is entirely empirical in nature, depending on the course of future developments of science about which speculation is admittedly dangerous. This view seems unwarranted; while the ultimate relations among the sciences will be an empirical outcome, at any given point in time, the relations among the sciences are legitimate and important questions for logical analysis. Another basis for dismissal, especially where the disciplines involved are psychology and physiology, is the adoption of the reductionistic view as a logical or an in-principle certainty. The soundness of this view, also, is open to question, as will be shown. The purpose of this paper, then, is to examine the problem of reductionism and to try to make a small beginning in separating issues which are logical in character from those which are empirical. In the course of our analysis, it will be contended that there are certain *logical* barriers to any present-day physiological reductionism.

The Doctrine of Reductionism

The essence of reductionism would seem to include four related general propositions. *a*) The several disciplines or sciences may be considered as hierarchically ordered from, e.g., physics at the base through chemistry, biology, and psychology, to the social and historical disciplines at the

---

[2] Sound empirical work, of course, requires no defense, whether motivated by reductionistic aims or not. Nothing said in this paper should be interpreted as depreciating the value of empirical or theoretical efforts to bridge the gap between disciplines.

top.[3] *b*) The second essential aspect of reductionism is the proposition that the terms or concepts and the relations or laws of one discipline may fully and without loss of meaning be translated into or deduced from those of another discipline. *c*) Such deduction or derivability proceeds only in one direction, from lower to higher[4] levels in the hierarchical ordering, and hence the term "reductionism"; terms and laws of the higher discipline are "reduced" to those of a lower one. Thus, in our earlier example, the psychological term "cognitive structure" is considered translatable into—deducible from—terms belonging to neurophysiology. *d*) The final aspect is the implicit or explicit proposition that the lower the level of terms employed to explain a given phenomenon, the more causal or fundamental or basic the explanation. This is really only a corollary of the first point if certain assumptions about the nature of the hierarchical ordering are made. These four propositions together would seem to constitute the essential meaning of reductionism as a general doctrine. An adherent of that point of view may not, of course, subscribe to all of its aspects.

The primary focus of this paper is upon the issues attending the reduction of psychology to physiology, and our evaluation of the doctrine will for the most part be oriented toward that specific context. Within that context, the following comments are illustrative of the position which supports the doctrine. "Logically and in principle, physiological reduction is a certainty. Every bit of behavior and everything that can, like conscious contents, be defined in terms of behavior has its physiological correlate" (Bergmann, 1953, p. 442); "Relative to the 'molar' (or macro-)

---

[3] Finer discriminations can, of course, easily be made by including the well-known "border" disciplines such as biochemistry or social psychology. But the fact that there is no sharp break between the sciences, and that it is frequently difficult to tell where one leaves off and the other begins, need not, in itself, challenge the autonomous existence of the several disciplines. What may be implied by ordering them in a hierarchy from lower to higher will be discussed shortly; for the moment it is only important to consider that this is one of the notions essential to the doctrine of reductionism.

[4] Terms in this paper referring to "position" in the hierarchy of the sciences, e.g., higher-lower, upward-downward, top-bottom, are by no means to imply any valuative judgment. The *meaning* of position in the hierarchy has been variously specified, for example, as referring to levels of abstraction or levels of integration, or as referring to the order of historical evolution within the universe of the subject matter of the sciences, or even to the order of historical emergence of the sciences themselves (White, 1949). As pointed out later, the concept of levels of science is not an analytically clear one (cf. Kroeber, 1952). For present purposes it is sufficient to take note of the existence in scientific discourse of such a hierarchical concept, and to recognize the traditional general ordering which places the physical sciences at the base, the biological sciences in the middle, and the social sciences at the top of the hierarchy.

account given by behavioristic psychology, the neurophysiological account is a micro-description of the very same events and processes" (Feigl, 1953, p. 623); and finally, ". . . molar behavioristics is in theory completely reducible to underlying neurophysiological principles. . . . A completely deterministic neurophysiology must of necessity permit derivation of all molar behavioral laws" (Rozeboom, 1956 (pp. 261–262). An obvious corollary of these statements is the logical reducibility of physiological principles in turn to those of chemistry and ultimately of physics.

Any challenge to these kinds of statements and their implications can be seen to require both logical and empirical arguments. We shall try to show where each kind is appropriate.

To begin with, to speak of reducing one discipline to another requires that the terms or concepts of the one be distinguishable from those of the other. This is not an easy requirement. Woodger (1952) calls it an interesting methodological question to inquire how one knows what belongs to the language of neurology and what belongs to that of psychology. Similarly, in commenting on the new terms which will accrue as science develops, Hempel (1952) notes that it is by no means certain that each of these terms will be readily classifiable as physical or nonphysical. What seems to be a necessary preliminary for our examination of physiological reductionism is some general criterion for separating or identifying the terms of psychology and physiology. If this is accomplished by defining psychology in a certain way, it should make apparent some logical barriers to the possibility of a physiological reduction.

A Functional Definiton of Psychology

Admittedly, the definition of any scientific discipline is somewhat arbitrary; despite this, it is certainly possible to obtain adequate agreement on criteria for segregating one discipline from another or for grossly circumscribing the domain of a particular science. Among psychologists there is considerable agreement that the scope and subject matter of concern is the behavior of whole, human[5] organisms. The difficulty with such a general statement is that the term "behavior" is not without ambiguity; psychologists have been notoriously neglectful in providing a systematic definition of a response. This laxness has, it is felt, obscured the conceptual boundary between psychology and physiology. The present discussion of behavior as a psychological concept follows the implicit orientation of all functional behavior theories, and more specifi-

---

[5] The writer assumes that the study of animal behavior by psychologists is merely propaedeutic to a science of human behavior.

cally, the approaches of Kantor (1942), Brunswik (1939, 1952, 1955), and Tolman (1949).

The central point of these approaches is that behavior, *qua* psychological, refers to an organism-environment *interaction* or *relationship*. Tolman (1949) specifically states that the complete identification of any behavior-act requires reference to its relation to particular goal-objects and the intervening means-objects with which it has commerce. Kantor's interbehaviorism makes essentially the same point. In considering the question of where to establish the boundaries of a behavior, Bentley (1941) similarly concludes that behavior must be recognized as a transdermal process or event whose description must immediately and functionally include the environmental and situational settings. Within this framework, then, behavior viewed psychologically is interactional or relational in nature; its specification or identification at the referential level requires the specification of a particular context and a set of relationships thereto. Our definition of psychology, therefore, excludes the study of organisms or physical environments per se, and behavior may not be referred to either alone. The laws of behavior of a discipline so defined refer to the dynamics of organism-environment functional interaction. The terms or concepts of those laws describe what may be called an interaction or behavior space.

This definition of psychology was undertaken as a means of providing a criterion for deciding whether a behavior term, or a law involving such a term, properly belongs to psychology or physiology. Our criterion requires of psychological terms that they have immediate reference to a functionally defined environment or context. Before drawing the implications of these considerations for reductionism, a further comment on this kind of definition may be in order. Some objection may be raised to the relational or transdermal character of the definition in that there is provided no palpable locus for a psychologically defined behavior. Those who raise such a query seem to be operating within what Woodger (1956) picturesquely describes as a "finger and thumb" philosophy of metaphysics, i.e., the notion that a thing is real or exists only if it can in principle be picked up between the finger and thumb. Interactions or relations, though not simple physical objects, are nevertheless real and concrete and can be precisely specified by the conditions and course of their occurrence.

Incomplete Derivability of Terms

It may now be asserted that the reference of psychology, as defined, is profoundly different from that of physiology. The terms and laws of the latter refer to intra-organismic or intradermal processes, or, at most, relations between an organism or its parts and the space defined by physics. They refer, in short, to the functioning of anatomical structures or processes described by body parameters. To state one of the major contentions of this paper, the absence in contemporary physiology of any systematic terms for describing the functional environment or context of behavior would seem to preclude, *on logical grounds alone*, any complete reduction of psychology to physiology. These necessary and sufficient conditions for the terms of psychology cannot be described in physiological (or physical) terms alone. This "incompleteness" of the lower discipline's language, in being able to specify only the physiological correlates but not the environmental correlates of a behavior or response, constitutes the logical impediment. This point obviously requires elaboration and further support.

Let us take as an example an occurrence described in common-sense, non-systematic language—the wave of an arm as two persons pass each other—and compare the systematic descriptions of it by the two disciplines being discussed. The systematic language of the physiologist enables him to rely on only body parameters or physical terms. He may thus speak of arm-displacement, changes in muscle-tension, metabolic rate, blood-volume distribution, and neural reactivity. In none of these terms is it systematically possible to take cognizance of the social context. On the other hand, the psychologist may describe the event as waving a greeting to a friend, or even, since micromediation is generally of little interest to him, and equifinality generally taken for granted,[6] simply as greeting a friend. If psychological laws refer to interactions between organisms and functionally defined environments, only these latter descriptions of events can logically lead to the achievement of such laws. A discipline such as physiology, lacking such contextual terms, cannot therefore be considered *logically* equivalent; hence its adequacy cannot be guaranteed, even in principle, as a complete reduction base for psychology.

One of the strongest empirical sources of support for some of these considerations may be found in the research analyses of Campbell (1954, 1956) and Smedslund (1953, 1956) evoked by the recent controversy over "what is learned." As mentioned earlier, the term "response" has been conceptually neglected; this neglect seems, in turn, to be related to the inadequate attention given to the environment or context of behavior by many psychological theorists (cf. Jessor, 1956, in this connection). Brunswik (1939, 1952, 1955), however, is one of those who has called

---

[6] That is, the same psychological event may be served by (partly constituted of) an almost infinite variety of different physiological events.

attention to the problem in his emphasis upon *distal* achievement in the adjustment of an organism to its ecology. Beginning with this orientation, and appraising a variety of learning experiments, especially those dealing with transposition, both Campbell and Smedslund conclude that the learned response must be defined in environmental terms in order successfully to accommodate—predict—the actual research findings. Campbell states that ". . . the learned response is to be essentially defined in terms of a shift in the organism-environment relationship rather than a motor response defined in terms of organism or body parameters alone" (1956, p. 105).

Scrutiny of the literature on reductionism has showed only meager if any attention to the specific issue raised in this paper. Two writers may be cited whose remarks, made in other contexts, are pertinent to the logical soundness of our contention. In his Tarner lectures (1952), Woodger stresses the role of environment as a determinant at various biological levels from zygote to whole human organism. He rejects the body-mind dualism in favor of speaking about persons and developing a person-language. The notion of person requires, for its very definition, environmental specification, and the latter, he observes, requires words belonging to sociology. To treat persons otherwise, i.e., in terms of body parameters, loses sight of this fact: "But this is the only way in which we can treat them so long as we confine ourselves to the physical sciences, since these sciences do not provide a vocabulary for speaking about them in any other way" (1952, p. 261). Hempel has discussed the problem in relation to the possible derivability of all the laws of empirical science from those of physics (a logical corollary of physiological reductionism). Affirming that not all the terms of empirical science are definable by means of the vocabulary of physics, he asserts that ". . . a law containing, say, certain biological terms cannot, in general, be logically derived from a set of physical laws, which contain no biological terms at all . . ." (1957, pp. 320–321).[7] Both of these writers seem in support of our point of view that there are logical barriers to any thorough-going physiological reductionism. The barriers reside in the absence of terms in the "lower" discipline which would enable the logical derivability of descriptions of the functional context of behavior and, thereby, the derivation of the laws of psychology.

At least two kinds of questions can be raised about our analysis and are worth consideration at this point. The first of these is the possibility of overcoming the logical problem we have raised simply by incorporating

---

[7] To achieve such a derivation requires some law connecting the biological concepts with the physical concepts. "But those connecting laws are not purely physical in character" (Hempel, 1951, p. 321). And they have the character of *empirical* laws.

into physiology the category of terms we have suggested that it lacks. This is frequently what is implied by the phrase "in principle" in assertions about the possibility of reductionism. But as Sellars (1956) has pointed out in another connection, this makes the entire problem an empty truism in that it involves a "tacit redefinition" of physiological theory to encompass psychology. Such a redefinition is a statement about the *future* state of the sciences involved, and it therefore transfers the discussion from logical to empirical grounds. That is, the question of whether a future physiology will be able to encompass psychology depends entirely upon the nature and direction of on-going empirical development of *both* disciplines. It is to be noted here, too, that the meaning of reduction is always and only relative to a given state of the disciplines concerned. To suggest adding terms to physiology in order to make psychology deducible from it implies the "elevation" or "expansion" of physiology just as much as it implies reduction of psychology. (In connection with these issues, see the Meehl-Sellars discussion of the logic of emergentism, 1956.) Finally, it seems unlikely that scientific theory develops or advances by simple accretion of the terms of other theories. We will return to this point shortly, in considering reductionism and the unity of science.

The second kind of question which may be raised is implicit in the earlier quote from Bergmann. He bases his affirmation of the logical certainty of physiological reductionism on the proposition that ". . . everything that can be defined in terms of behavior has its physiological correlate" (1953, p. 442). The essential point of this position would be that the environmental reference of behavior upon which we based our definition must, if effective, be represented within the organism in its physiology or, especially, neurophysiology. This is, in a sense, a proximal approach to behavior rather than a distal one. Certain arguments may be brought to bear against this position, such as the absence of strict one-to-one proximal-distal correlation—e.g., in perception—and the theoretical significance of vicarious functioning or equifinality. The major reply which may be made, however, is that the "recovery" of actual behavioral phenomena from physiological correlates requires the conceptual co-ordination of these correlates to environmental contexts. Thus the issue raised originally reappears, the necessity for terms to represent or describe the context of behavior. That such co-ordination can or will be accomplished in the future is an empirical rather than a logical problem, and therefore not a logical certainty.

Our discussion of reductionism up to this point has concerned itself largely with the logical problems inherent in the second and third essential aspects of the doctrine as outlined at the start of this paper. Proper attention to the first and fourth aspects would extend the paper beyond practical space limitations. Instead, we shall simply sketch some of the issue requiring attention.

The first aspect has to do with the hierarchical ordering of the several scientific disciplines. Despite the widespread acceptance of the hierarchy notion—witness the frequent reference to "levels" of science, the employment of terms like "basic" to contrast disciplines, and the characterization of certain disciplines as "emergent" from others—it is not an analytically clear concept. Kroeber (1952) remarks on the absence of any adequate attempt to examine systematically what the levels constitute or mean in terms of a theory of knowledge. Most of the discussions of what is meant by levels resolve into two positions which are generally considered to exclude one another. One point of view conceives the levels of science to be a matter of methodology only, i.e., to refer to the kinds of procedures employed by the various sciences, the size of their units of analysis, etc. The other point of view considers the levels to refer to substantive differences in the events or phenomena dealt with by the various disciplines. Psychologists will be familiar with this contrast from the Littman-Rosen (1950) analysis of the molar-molecular problem. A third possibility is that these two positions are correlated rather than mutually exclusive, namely, that substantively different events require particularly appropriate methodological procedures for useful analysis.

Each of these three views has certain implications for the doctrine of reductionism. For example, the methodological position would seem to favor the doctrine, since it assumes the events or phenomena to be the same and only the descriptions of them to be different. If only the descriptions differ, e.g., in size of unit, it should be logically possible to reduce the larger units to their smaller constituents. On the other hand, to assert a substantive difference between levels would seem to be unfavorable to reductionism. The events or phenomena of higher levels are considered different from—not the same ones as—those of the lower levels, and therein lies the difficulty in reducing descriptions of one kind of event to those of another kind. No vitalistic or dualistic considerations need be involved in speaking of events as different; certainly organic events may in general be separated from inorganic ones, for example. Feigl's double-language theory (1953) of the mind-body problem espouses the methodological position in insisting that the factual reference of the mentalistic, behavioristic and neurophysiological languages or levels of description is identical, i.e., involves the very same events and processes. Others concerned with the problem seem to adopt the substantive position; thus White (1949) speaks of culture as a distinct class of events, a distinct order of phenomena. Woodger tentatively concludes that ". . . perhaps, in spite of superficial appearances, person-acts and behaviour [defined in physical or physiological terms] are not quite the same things . . ." (1952, p. 284). The position taken by the present writer in differentiating psychological from physiological terms may be seen as compatible with the substantive view. What may account for substantive differences, whether the substantive vs. methodological distinction itself is useful or defensible, the issues involved in emergentism, and any fuller analysis of the implications of the hierarchy of sciences for reductionism must be deferred for discussion elsewhere.

The final aspect of the reductionism doctrine has to do with the idea that causal explanation is advanced by the employment of terms of a lower-level discipline. In psychology, this notion identifies causal explanation with neurophysiological reference. The key reason for this approach would seem to be the belief in the higher levels as simply derivable from, or applications of, terms and laws of lower disciplines. Once this idea is abandoned, causal explanation could just as logically proceed upward to sociological and anthropological concepts. Knowledge of causality is probably best divorced from the hierarchy of sciences notion and considered instead to vary with the scope of the network in which any concept is embedded.

We have tried to examine some of the logical and empirical problems related to the doctrine of physiological reductionism. Some of the considerations have led us to doubt that psychology can be reduced to physiology, though certainly many of the questions are of an empirical sort. Nothing thus far asserted in any way denies the possibility or the desirability of the unification of the sciences, the synthesis of psychology and physiology. What is questioned is that such synthesis must proceed by reduction, by one discipline devouring or incorporating the other. All of the sciences are developing, and their influence upon each other does not only proceed upward from physics. Bertalanffy (1951, 1952), for example, sees certain biological developments, such as the notions of open systems, requiring extensions of the conceptual system of physics. Unity of science for him refers only to the structural isomorphy of laws in the different fields of science, the approach of General Systems Theory. Psychologists can also see the conceptual system of physiology as influenced by the data and concepts of psychology (Hebb, 1949). Thus, unification of the sciences may proceed from above as well as from below. The continued autonomous development of each of the sciences will at least serve to specify the properties required of any synthetic unifying scheme. This is probably part of what Brunswik had in mind when he wrote: "Insistence on reduction as a universal goal of science can only result in blighted spots on the landmap of scientific enterprise" (Brunswik, p. 237).

Summary

This paper has had as its aim the instigation of renewed attention to the doctrine of reductionism, especially in terms of its implications for the relationship of physiology and psychology. Despite the empirical character of the ultimate answer, it is asserted that the questions involved in the doctrine may properly be the concern of a logical analysis. After briefly sketching four propositions which constitute the essential notions of reductionism, the argument focused upon the logical possibility of a complete translatability or derivability of the concepts and laws of psychology from those of physiology. The central contention was that the latter, lacking terms to describe the behavioral environment, was logically inadequate as a base for a thoroughgoing reduction of the former. The remainder of the paper commented upon the relationship of the doctrine to the idea of a hierarchical ordering of the sciences and to the possibility of achieving a unification of science.

References

Bentley, A. F. The behavioral superfice. *Psychol. Rev.*, 1941, *48*, 39–59.

Bergmann, G. Theoretical psychology. In C. P. Stone (ed.), *Ann. Rev. Psychol.*, 1953, *4*, 435–458.

Bertalanffy, L. von. Problems of general systems theory. *Human Biol.*, 1951, *23*, 302–312.

———. *Problems of life.* New York: Wiley, 1952.

Brunswik, E. The conceptual focus of some psychological systems. *J. Unif. Sci.*, 1939, *8*, 36–49.

———. The conceptual framework of psychology. Chicago: Univ. of Chicago Press, 1952. (*Int. Encycl. Unif. Sci.*, Vol. 1, No. 10.)

———. In defense of probabilistic functionalism: A reply. *Psychol. Rev.*, 1955, *62*, 236–242.

Campbell, D. T. Operational delineation of "what is learned" via the transposition experiment. *Psychol. Rev.*, 1954, *61*, 167–174.

———. Adaptive behavior from random response. *Behavioral Sci.*, 1956, *1*, 105–110.

Feigl, H. The mind-body problem in the development of logical empiricism. In H. Feigl and May Brodbeck (eds.), *Readings in the philosophy of science.* New York: Appleton-Century-Crofts, 1953, pp. 612–626.

Hebb, D. O. *The organization of behavior.* New York: Wiley, 1949.

Hempel, C. G. General systems theory and the unity of science. *Human Biol.*, 1951, *23*, 313–322.

Jessor, R. Phenomenological personality theories and the data language of psychology. *Psychol. Rev.*, 1956, *63*, 173–180.

Kantor, J. R. Preface to interbehavioral psychology. *Psychol. Rec.*, 1942, *5*, 173–193.

Kessen, W., and Kimble, G. A. "Dynamic systems" and theory construction. *Psychol. Rev.*, 1952, *59*, 263–267.

Krech, D. Dynamic systems, psychological fields, and hypothetical constructs. *Psychol. Rev.*, 1950, *57*, 283–290.

Kroeber, A. L. *The nature of culture.* Chicago: Univ. of Chicago Press, 1952.

Littman, R. A., and Rosen, E. Molar and molecular. *Psychol. Rev.*, 1950, *57*, 58–65.

Meehl, P. E., and Sellars, W. The concept of emergence. In H. Feigl and M. Scriven (eds.), *Minnesota studies in the philosophy of science,* Vol. I. Minneapolis: Univ. of Minnesota Press, 1956, pp. 239–252.

Rozeboom, W. W. Mediation variables in scientific theory. *Psychol. Rev.*, 1956, *63*, 249–264.

Sellars, W. Empiricism and the philosophy of mind. In H. Feigl and M. Scriven (eds.), *Minnesota studies in the philosophy of science,* Vol. I. Minneapolis: Univ. of Minnesota Press, 1956, pp. 253–329.

Smedslund, J. The problem of "What is learned?" *Psychol. Rev.*, 1953, *60*, 157–158.

———. *Multiple-probability learning.* Oslo: Akademisk Forlag, 1956.

Tolman, E. C. *Purposive behavior in animals and men.* Berkeley, Calif.: Univ. of California Press, 1949.

White, L. A. *The science of culture.* New York: Farrar, Strauss, 1949.

Woodger, J. H. *Biology and language.* Cambridge: Cambridge Univ. Press, 1952.

———. *Physics, psychology and medicine.* Cambridge: Cambridge Univ. Press, 1956.

CHAPTER VI
Theoretical Emphases

THIS CHAPTER CONTINUES THE consideration of the general problem with which Chapter V was concerned. It offers, in the first two selections, a combination of two sharply contrasting views as to the nature of the theoretical and methodological emphasis which modern psychology should adopt. In the first selection, Gordon W. Allport presents in concise form the major arguments for his insistent demand that scientific orientation in psychology be maintained on a strictly molar and practical level. In direct contrast, Kenneth W. Spence has been equally insistent on the necessity for psychology to utilize rigorous orthodox scientific procedures and to work on as basic a level as possible. The second selection presents his arguments, as applied to modern "behaviorism."

In reading and evaluating these opposed points of view, it is necessary for the student to realize that, to a certain extent, Allport and Spence are talking about quite different problems. A clear recognition of this point should help to prevent confusion of the basic issues and allow full scientific recognition and freedom both to those who wish, with Allport, to work on problems of immediate importance, and to those who wish, with Spence, to carry on fundamental research of the more analytic type. However, it is also necessary to realize that in the former, no less than the latter, case such recognition will depend upon the degree to which sound scientific standards are successfully maintained. Since the two general points of view are each representative of a wide segment of current

257

psychological opinion, and reflect the so-called "fission" that has developed between professional and scientific psychologists, the issues merit a full discussion.

In the third selection, the biologist Robert S. Morison presents a most cogent argument for scientific procedures in psychology, thus more or less supporting the Spencian position. Richard A. Littman's paper points up the difficulties of attempting to combine scientific and practical affairs, and argues for their clear separation. The next paper, by Melvin H. Marx, considers some of the sources of various confusions found in the attitudes of psychologists toward theory in clinical problems. Finally, B. F. Skinner takes out after all sorts and manners of fellow workers, and espouses a strict laboratory type of psychology. This interesting and provocative paper should provide much discussion, regardless of how one feels about the validity of the attacks.

18 | *The Emphasis on Molar Problems*[1]

GORDON W. ALLPORT

Within the span of remarkably few years, the quantity and quality of investigations in the fields of personality and social psychology have established not only their scientific dignity but likewise their popularity and promise within the psychological profession. The official formation of this large Division within the American Psychological Association is a formal recognition of these facts.

At the same time the significance of this occasion extends beyond the boundaries of the profession. In forming this Division we are, wittingly or unwittingly, stating our readiness to assume a certain responsibility. We are announcing, in effect, that as a group of scientists we believe we

From G. W. Allport, Scientific models and human morals, *Psychol. Rev.*, 1947, *54*, 182–192. Reprinted by permission of the author, the *Psychological Review*, and the American Psychological Association.

[1] Address of the Divisional President before the first annual meeting of the Division of Personality and Social Psychology of the American Psychological Association, September 4, 1946.

have a contribution to make in interpreting and in remedying some of the serious social dislocations of today. For if we did not believe in the potentialities of our science would we thus formally establish it?

The test of our fitness to exist and to prosper, I submit, will be our ability to contribute substantially in the near future to the diagnosis and treatment of the outstanding malady of our time. The malady I refer to is not war, for modern warfare is but a symptom of an underlying morbid condition; it is not the threatening fission of one world into two, ominous as this threat may be; nor is it our apparent inability to control for our safety and profit the transformation of matter into atomic energy, though this crisis too is now upon us. I speak rather of the *underlying* ailment, of the fact that man's moral sense is not able to assimilate his technology.

While technological warfare, technological unemployment, and the atomic age—all by-products of physical science—have overtaken us, mental and moral science have made no corresponding gains in allaying the rivalries and anxieties induced by technology, in devising methods of social control, nor in enhancing human co-operation and solidarity. It is, I venture to point out, precisely our own young science, whose formal establishment we are now celebrating, that has failed to keep pace with the needs of the times.

In taking stock of the situation I observe how many of use seem so stupefied by admiration of physical science that we believe psychology in order to succeed need only imitate the models, postulates, methods and language of physical science. If someone points out the present inutility of mechanical models in predicting any but the most peripheral forms of human behavior, we are inclined to reply: Wait a thousand years if necessary and you will see that man is a robot, and that all his mental functions can be synthesized in kind as successfully as we now synthesize table salt, quinine, or a giant calculator. While we righteously scorn what one of us has called "the subjective, anthropomorphic hocus pocus of mentalism" (Boring, 1946), we would consider a colleague emotional and mystical should he dare speak of "the objective mechanomorphic hocus pocus of physicalism."

Let our progress be gradual, we say. By sticking to peripheral, visible operations we may some day be able to approach complex problems of motivation, and then come within hailing distance of the distresses of mankind. We hope that these distresses will keep a thousand years until we are ready to cope with them, and that in the meantime a free science will be permitted to linger along and take its time. But even if such improbable conditions were fulfilled, I question whether we should endorse this counsel of patience or the premises upon which it rests.

The machine model in psychology had its origin not in clinical or social experience, but rather in adulation of the technological success of the physical sciences. Since psychologists, like everyone else, are enmeshed in the prevailing ethos, they too, unless especially on guard, are likely to allow their subservience to technology to outrun their moral sense.

Besides the mechanical model, there are two other currently popular paradigms in psychology that are, in my opinion, only slightly less inept in guiding significant research or theory concerning the foundations of social morality. I refer to the phylogenic model and to the infant mind. Although both these patterns during the past two generations have brought new insights and correctives into our work, they have not proved adequate to the needs of clinical, personnel, and social psychology.

The Current Appeal to Psychology

Public officials, confronted by post-war dilemmas, are urgently seeking the aid of psychologists. Many of us who have been approached are embarrassed by the scarcity of scientific findings, and even of serviceable concepts and well-formulated problems, that psychology has to offer *of the type that is being sought.* What is asked for is instant help in discovering the sources and conditions of man's moral sense in order that this sense may be enlarged and brought into focus. What is asked for is aid from a science of human relationships whose assistance Franklin D. Roosevelt likewise invoked in his last speech before his death.[2] Yet we may comb the entire file of the *Psychological Abstracts* and find very little that has any bearing upon the improvement of human relationships on an international scale.

Why have we so relatively little to offer? Is it that we are young and need to follow the machine model for a thousand years? Or have we gotten off to a thoroughly bad start through our adoption of root-metaphors that lead away from, rather than toward, the problem at hand? Three generations ago psychology was commonly classified as a "moral science." Though we may not favor the aura of this term, how can we expect anything other than a science *of* moral conduct to discover conditions that will bring the needed counterpoise to technology run wild?

When any one of us undertakes a piece of research he inevitably adopts, according to his preference, one or another of the fundamental models available to psychologists. My thesis is that now if ever we need

---

[2] "Today we are faced with the pre-eminent fact that, if civilization is to survive, we must cultivate the science of human relationships—the ability of all peoples, of all kinds, to live together and work together, in the same world, at peace."

to test our preferred model for its capacity to yield discoveries that have some sure relevance to moral nature and to social skills.

Expectancy and Intention

If I interpret the matter correctly, American psychology naturally adopted mechanical models because our culture has always been action-oriented and technological. By and large our psychology is a motorized psychology, and is only now widening its concept of action to include the ego-involved participation of the human organism in matters affecting its own destiny (Allport, 1945). The earlier extreme position, represented by E. B. Holt and J. B. Watson, held personality to be essentially a battery of trigger-release mechanisms. This view paid no attention to the sustained directions of striving characteristic of moral behavior, to what in this paper I shall call "intentions."

This trigger-model, still preferred by a few, gave way gradually to a more purposive behaviorism. The concept of "sign-Gestalt expectancy" was introduced by Tolman, and mercifully shortened by Hilgard and Marquis to "expectancy" (1940). It is an interesting fact that these authors seem to regard the principle of expectancy as the most purposive of all the essentially mechanical theories derived from the multitudinous experiments on the conditioned reflex (1940, p. 101). In other words, some version of the principle of expectancy is as far as many psychologists have come in their conception of the nature of personal and social conduct.

The principle holds that in the presence of certain signs the organism expects a certain goal to appear if it follows the customary behavior route. If the goal is reached, the expectation is confirmed; if not, the organism may vary its behavior (Hilgard and Marquis, 1940, p. 88). The principle, while allowing for the importance of attitude, is essentially stimulus-bound. We behave according to the cues we have learned, according to our expectancies.

In order not to complicate my argument I shall leave out of consideration the law of effect, which, it would be easy to show, likewise ascribes behavior wholly to past experience, to learned cues, and to mechanical reinforcements (Allport, 1946[a]). Both principles, so far as I can see, accord nothing to the *un*rewarded, *un*realized, yet persistive, intentions of man's moral nature.

The trouble with these currently fashionable concepts, drawn from the phylogenetic model, is that while they seem to apply aptly enough to animal behavior whence they were derived, they have only a limited or else a remote analogical bearing on the activities of human beings. We may know a person's expectancies and even his past rewards, and yet be singularly unable to predict or control his future behavior, unless at the same time we know also his basic intentions which are by no means a stencilled copy of his previous expectancies and rewards (All-port, 1946ᵇ).

To take an example, the sign-Gestalten today are such that we may now reasonably expect future trouble with Russia. Does this fact tell in any degree what we can, should, or will do about it? This precise area of conflict is a novel one (as indeed all important situations are). The best predictive basis we have lies in our own national and personal *intentions* regarding Russia. It is our purposes, not our expectancies, that are now the issue.

As if aware of the scantiness of the expectancy principle, Tolman advises us to embrace also a "need-cathexis psychology" (1945). But the situation here turns out to be parallel. Need-cathexis psychology—of course I oversimplify—holds essentially that a handful of physiological drives get attached to this, that, or the other object. A man who, in Tolman's pleasing vernacular, is "raised right" meshes his drive into a socially acceptable gear. A man "raised wrong" does not. But what is so striking about human motivation is that so often a desire or aspiration is meshed into no gear. It simply reaches forward hungrily into the future like the tip of a scarlet-runner bean groping for a goal that it does not know about.

The embarrassment of the need-cathexis type of psychology is reflected in the apologetic language it uses when referring to this expansive aspect of human motivation. Accustomed to work with animals or with infants, need-cathexis psychology labels adult human intentions "secondary drives," "derived drives," or "drive conversions." With such depreciating concepts both the mechanical and the phylogenetic psychologists apparently seek to dispose of those morally relevant desires and aspirations that are in fact so different from the drive-impelled excursions of the cozy robot or cozy rodent.[3]

---

[3] It is instructive to read the perorations of two recent presidential addresses by psychologists, one preferring the machine model, the other the rat model. Though good-humored and witty, both authors candidly acknowledge their own escapist motives. To paraphrase Carlson's quip concerning Cannon's theory of emotions: the authors seem to entertain their models because the models entertain them.

"I believe that robotic thinking helps precision of psychological thought, and will continue to help it until psychophysiology is so far advanced that an image is nothing other than a neural event, and object constancy is obviously just something that happens in the brain. That time is still a long way off, and in the interval I choose to sit cozily with my robot, squeezing his hand and feeling a thrill—a scientist's thrill—when he squeezes mine back again" (Boring, 1946, p. 192).

"And, as a final peroration, let it be noted that rats live in cages; they do not go on binges the night before one has planned an experiment; they do not kill each other

My objection to the animal paradigm for personality and for social psychology is not so much that animals lack culture—a fact which Mr. Tolman in his sparkling paper first frankly admits and then amiably represses. My objection is rather that the motivational structure of man and of lower animals seems to be in only a slight degree similar. In this respect as with his evolutionary brain development, "Man," to quote Julian Huxley's conclusion, "stands alone" (1941). Animals are demonstrably creatures of stimulus-expectancy and need-cathexis. Man, in all that is distinctive of his species, is a creature of his intentions. We may well doubt that the basic equation for intentional morality, or that for intentional learning, can be written from a study of organisms that lack propositional symbols. To this point I shall return.

While I am disapproving of current models I shall state my final grievance, this time against the rigid ontogenetic stencils that derive from Freudianism. Odd as it may appear, Freud resembles the mechanical and phylogenetic psychologists in wanting his doctrine of motivation anchored to neuro-anatomy. I assume that this is his desire because of his refusal to see anything at all in the co-operative, socialized, affiliative, undertakings of mankind excepting goal-inhibited sexuality. To the sex drive he adds principally the impulses of aggression, destruction, and death. It seems obvious that Freudianism, even though eagerly adopted by many who have found the mechanical and animal models inadequate, offers an equally meagre basis for a serviceable study of man's moral conduct.

The trouble lies chiefly in the excessive emphasis upon infantile experience. We are asked to believe that an individual's character-structure is, in all essentials, determined by the time his last diaper is changed. Even Suttie, who postulates as the foundation of morality an original and embracing instinct of tenderness, affection, and social symbiosis, believes its fate is sealed according to the manner in which the mother handles this affiliative impulse before and after weaning (1935). If the chances for peace in the world depend to such a degree upon infant fixations ought we not disband this Division and register as wet nurses to the mewling citizens of tomorrow?

---

off in war; they do not invent engines of destruction, and if they did, they would not be so dumb about controlling such engines; they do not go in for either class conflicts or race conflicts; they avoid politics, economics and papers on psychology. They are marvelous, pure and delightful. And, as soon as I possibly can, I am going to climb back again out on that good old philogenetic limb and sit there, this time right side up and unashamed, wiggling my whiskers at all the dumb, yet at the same time far too complicated, specimens of *homo sapiens*, whom I shall see strutting and fighting and messing things up, down there on the ground below me" (Tolman, 1945, p. 166).

The concept of intention, which I am here opposing to reactivity, expectancy, and infantile fixation, is not immediately congenial to American psychology. Yet its adoption in some form or another, I argue, is necessary. With some malice aforethought I have selected the term *intention*—spiced, as it is, by an aggravating flavor of mentalism—to signify those aspects of thought and of motivation that play a leading, but now neglected, part in the complex, affiliative, moral conduct of men. I believe it is precisely the "private" worlds of desire, aspiration, and conscience that must be studied if we are to succeed in the task of social engineering.

In using the term intention, however, I am not arguing surreptitiously for phenomenology, though in order to improve our grasp on the subtleties of man's intentions we would do well to emulate the refinement of its descriptive method.[4] Nor am I arguing for a revival of Brentano, though we have neglected unduly the central proposition of Act Psychology: that at every moment man's mind is directed by some intention, be it loving, hating, comparing, understanding, desiring, rejecting, planning, or some similar mental act.

Let us define intention simply as *what the individual is trying to do*. Naïve as this definition may sound it is in reality the product of decades of sophisticated wrestling with the problems of human motivation. In this concept influences as diversified as Brentano, Darwin, Freud, Cannon, and Wertheimer are brought into focus. In essence it no longer draws the sharp distinction, advanced by both Kant and Schopenhauer, between will (or drive) on the one hand, and intellect on the other. The machine, rat, and infant models we have been following (though I am sure they'd be surprised and grieved to know it) preserve this irreconcilable Kantian dichotomy. They side somewhat more, however, with Schopenhauer in regarding the functions of the intellect as wholly instrumental and secondary. Without forgetting for a moment what we have learned about rationalizing and about the untrustworthiness of introspective reports on motives, we may safely declare that the opposing of motive and thought-process has gone much too far. Usually the individual is trying to do something in which his wants and his plans easily co-operate. Instead of being at opposite poles his emotion and his reason canalize into a single endeavor. The direction of his endeavor I designate as the intention, and

---

[4] An excellent example is Bertocci's analysis of man's sense of moral obligation (1945). He shows that when we study the *ought-consciousness* phenomenologically we discover how entirely different it is from the *must-consciousness*. This discovery leads to a justifiable suspicion that, whatever conscience may be, it does not derive merely from fear of punishment or from social coercion. Too hastily and heedlessly have psychologists accepted Freud's identification of the Super-ego with threat of parental punishment.

offer this concept as an improvement upon the one-sided irrationalistic doctrines of drive, need, instinct, and cathexis.

In deference to the discoveries of psychoanalysis we readily admit that an individual does not always know precisely what his own intentions are. *Consciously* he may misinterpret the line of his own endeavor. A neurotic frequently does so. In such cases insight is either lacking or partially lacking. But as a rule, the "posture or lay of consciousness" reflects accurately enough that inextricable fusion of driving and planning which we find in the dynamics of mature human conduct.[5]

It is the mark of an intention that it is directed toward the future. Yet it is typical of the models we have followed that they lead to preoccupation with adjustments in the past. While people are living their lives forward, psychologists are busy tracing them backward. The model we need for our investigations of human relationships will escape from our present excessive dependence on geneticism in all its forms (Allport, 1946[b]).

A geneticist, for example one who places great weight on the expectancy-principle, is inclined to define personality as a peculiar set of reaction-tendencies. An intentionist, on the other hand, sees personality as a peculiar set of subjective values. There is a difference. The one learns at best only about moral *accomplishment;* the other gains additional light on moral *potential.*

It may be argued that the models I am presuming to criticize do deal both with "goal reactions" and with "anticipatory goal reactions." Dr. Hull, for example, offers "anticipatory goal reaction" as a "physical mechanism" which he says he regards as equivalent to the concept of "guiding ideas," or what I am calling *intention* (1931). The difficulty with "anticipatory goal reaction" as with "expectancy" is that men often have values without having any specific goal in mind. They may have a consistent direction of striving, but their goals are either transient or else undefinable. All of a rat's, but only a small bit of human, behavior can be

---

[5] McDougall specifically objected to the concept of intention on the grounds that conscious intention merely obscures the instinctive motive at work (1923, pp. 121 f.). He had in mind the indubitable fact that men's verbal reports of their intentions may be rationalizations. But in my use of the term I do not confine intention to reportable purpose. Sometimes the essential direction of an intention is understood well enough by the subject, sometimes not. If the term, as I propose, is taken to mean *both* the understood and non-understood direction of an act I maintain that it can serve as a proper designation for "ultimate motives" and not merely for proximate or rationalized motives.

To my mind it is unnecessary to have recourse to a doctrine of underlying needs or instincts. McDougall, for example, allowed far too little for the ever-changing panorama of man's intentions which, as they evolve from an original genetic equipment, undergo complete change of form and functional significance (Allport, 1940).

characterized in terms of concrete goals whose attainment will de-tension specific drives. For the most part the course of man's behavior runs according to certain schemata, or in prolonged channels. Only now and then are these channels marked by lights or buoys that represent specific goals.

A simple example may be borrowed from Lecky's analysis of childhood thumbsucking. The following statement distinguishes neatly between expectancy and what I am here calling intention; that is, between behavior regulated by habit and behavior ordered to non-specific schemata.

> Certainly the child who sucks his thumb gives the act plenty of exercise and gets enough satisfaction from it to fix it indelibly. Therefore if the habit theory is true, we should be able to predict absolutely that the child will continue to suck his thumb for the rest of his life. But what really happens? Every year millions of children who have industriously sucked their thumbs since birth, and who have successfully resisted every effort to force them to change their behavior, quit the practice spontaneously when they are five or six years old. The reason is that they are beginning at this age to think of themselves as big boys or girls, and they recognize that thumb-sucking is inconsistent with the effort to maintain this new idea (1945, pp. 122 f.).

An intention often takes the form of a self-image as in the case of Lecky's reformed thumbsucker. Having adopted a conception of what we want to be we are constrained to make good in the role we have assumed. The specific goals we set for ourselves are almost always subsidiary to our long-range intentions. A good parent, a good neighbor, a good citizen, is not good because his specific goals are acceptable, but because his successive goals are ordered to a dependable and socially desirable set of values. We now know that juvenile delinquency and adult criminality were sadly misconceived so long as they were regarded as a matter of bad habit-formations. For years reformatories have trained habits, but have achieved few reformations. Only a radical shift of outlook and intention remakes a criminal, alcoholic or neurotic character.

The models we have been following lack the long-range orientation which is the essence of morality. Infant and rodent have immediate goals and indulge in anticipatory goal reactions, but have no directive schemata. By contrast, a child in puberty develops a desire to become a successful and respected man of affairs, and acquires this generalized objective long before he knows what concrete goals he has to work for. Thus, customarily, image and intention seem to antedate and to define goal-reactions. The essence of moral behavior is of this sort. It presupposes long-range purposes whose directions precede their specifications.

When President Roosevelt enunciated the Four Freedoms he was speaking of certain common intentions of the human race. An important feature of his historic formulation lies in his assumption that *all* men, in *all* cultures, intend (that is, long for) freedom from want, freedom from fear, freedom of speech and of worship. Note how this assumption contrasts with the prevailing creed of modern social science. Cultural relativity, really a doctrine of stimulus-expectancy, has laid such a heavy hand upon us that we have overlooked the possibility of universal intentions. Yet unless Roosevelt's bold assumption is found justified, we can scarcely hope to find a psychological basis for effective world organization.

In all probability Roosevelt's formulation is psychologically not the best that can be made; nor dare we underestimate the incompatibility of nationalistic intentions and rivalries. What I am saying is that the psychologists' perspective should be equally bold. It is up to us to find out whether there are in fact common purposes that might provide ground for international solidarity. To do so, social psychologists in all lands might well join in a search, through modern instruments of polling, clinical interviewing, child study, and life-histories, for existent moral bases on which international co-operation can be built.

It is conceivable—I think probable—that such research would discover the ruthless pursuit of personal and national power to be a result of the frustration of basically affiliative intentions. In clinical practice we know how often the clamorous manifestations of egotism gain the upper hand when men are denied a proper continuation of the originally friendly and symbiotic relationship with family, friends, and neighbors. It seems probable that every child in every nation, the world over, at a time when he is most plastic, wants security, affection, and an affiliative and comprehending relation to the surrounding world. It is conceivable that the same basic intentions exist in most adults, although thwarting and perversion of this relationship have engendered a vast amount of hatred, emotional instability, and warlike impulse.

Basic research would discover why the taboo on tenderness, on nurturant desires, has grown so excessive that the development of co-operative and affiliative behavior outside one's own family is, at least in our culture, generally disapproved. It would seek to discover under what conditions the impulse to love and to be loved is turned to the impulse to hate and to invite hatred. If it is the child's nature to trust everyone, why is it the nature of national or ethnic groups to distrust nearly everyone? The models we have been following tend to deflect our attention from problems of human affection and the conditions for its development. When a bit of human friendliness is discovered—and it can be discovered only accidentally with models now current—it is likely to be labeled "goal inhibited sexuality," and thus tagged, forgotten. Up to now the sexual activity of rat and man has received incomparably more attention from psychologists than has the co-operative activity of men and nations.

Besides the study of affection and hatred, the possibilities for peace require research into many other strictly human capacities—among them the use of humor, the function of creeds, the processes of communication. For moral development depends on many factors other than root-desires and intentions. But every aspect of moral conduct that one can name depends intricately upon the employment of symbols.

Signs and Symbols

Perhaps the clearest symptom of the present conceptual confusion in our field is the extent to which we confound symbols with signs, or—if one prefers Morris's terminology—symbols with signals.

We know that all animals, as well as men, respond to signals. The principle of expectancy says so, and in this respect is right. A signal is something that exists in the physical world; it is an identifiable stimulus. But even the most behavioristically inclined theorists cannot, and do not, claim that animals can handle propositional symbols—those self-produced signs *of* signs which are man's prized and troublesome possession. An animal, says Thorndike, can "think things," but it cannot "think about things" (1911, p. 119). And Yerkes asserts that symbolic processes in chimpanzees are rare and difficult to observe. One may, he says, fairly continue to question their existence, though it may be that signal responses can be regarded in some way as "antecedents of human symbolic processes" (1943, p. 189). Surveying relevant investigations and opinions, Cassirer concludes: "In all literature of the subject there does not seem to be a single conclusive proof of the fact that any animal ever made the decisive step from subjective to objective, from affective to propositional, language" (1945, p. 30).

Cassirer argues, reasonably enough, that the symbolic system creates a wholly new dimension of reality for man. Instead of dealing directly with things themselves or with their visible signals, man deals with their ideational surrogates,[6] "He has so enveloped himself in linguistic forms,

---

[6] Even in human beings we occasionally encounter a sharp break between symbols and signs. Some of Goldstein's aphasic patients, for example, seem capable of responding to signs but not to symbols, as in the case of the man who could understand the word-signs "Drink it," when a glass full of water was presented to him, but was unable to go through the symbolic motions of drinking it if the glass was empty (1940, p. 44).

Without symbols we could not make-believe, dissimulate, or lie; we could not form plans for our future; nor hold those schemata in mind that make possible consistency in moral conduct.

in artistic images, in mythical symbols or religious rites, that he cannot see or know anything except by the interposition of this artificial medium" (1945, p. 25).

Even so behavioristic a writer as Morris admits that the theory of sign-response as developed by himself carries over with difficulty to the human sphere. These are his words:

> . . . non-human beings seldom produce the signs which influence their behavior, while human individuals in their language and post-language symbols characteristically do this and to a surprising degree. Here is a basic difference between men and animals, and until behavioral theory develops a semiotic adequate to this difference it will remain what it is today: a careful study of animals and a pious hope for a science of the human person (1946, p. 198).

In this passage Morris seems to be saying with fine candor that there is a world of difference between signal and symbol; and that even his own careful system of semiotic fails adequately to bridge the gap. Though I have not actually counted the illustrations in his recent book I have the impression that a majority of them refer to animal responses to signals, and that relatively few deal with human responses to symbols. In any case it is clear that Morris, like many psychologists, is enamored of the phylogenetic model.

I venture to cite another brilliant and candid passage from his book. He writes of the fact that a sign may be *iconic*, that is to say, it may itself resemble the properties of its denotatum. Thus a motion picture is highly iconic; an onomatopoeic word less so; a wholly arbitrary sign not at all iconic. He then goes on to make this highly significant remark: "One of the dangers of the use of models in science, for instance, arises out of the temptation to ascribe to the subject matter of a theory properties of the model illustrating the theory which are not involved in the theory itself" (1946, p. 23).

From this warning would it not follow that an adequate theory of symbols can hardly be derived from the animal model in which *signals* alone predominate? How can we expect to understand human symbolism in terms of the phylogenetic type when, as Morris himself asserts, we are tempted to over-extend the properties of our type-model and force them to serve in place of the independent theory that we need to develop?

The Model We Need

To sum up: the designs we have been using in our studies of motivation, of symbol, and hence of the foundations of moral behavior, are not —to borrow Morris's crisp term—sufficiently iconic with our subject matter. Addiction to machines, rats, or infants leads us to overplay those features of human behavior that are peripheral, signal-oriented, or genetic.

Correspondingly it causes us to underplay those features that are central, future-oriented, and symbolic.

What sort of a model then do we need? This question opens systematic vistas that lie beyond the scope of this paper. Yet, lest my numerous criticisms indicate a despair that I do not actually feel, I shall mention a few recent signs and portents that signify a newer—and, to my mind—more wholesome outlook.

Most noteworthy is the fact that the war led many psychologists to deal directly with the integrated behavior of GI Joe, of the factory worker, of the civilian. We then learned that the interests of morale, psychotherapy, personnel placement, psychological warfare, could not be pursued successfully by clinging to our threadbare models. Our inadequate root-metaphors went into the ash can for the duration. It is because of this conceptual discard, with its resultant wartime success in the promotion of social engineering, that I have presumed at this time to bring into the open a conflict that many, perhaps most of us, have secretly felt. Must we now resume the tattered stencils that we so recently abandoned with such good effect?

There are various indicators of improvement in theoretical outlook. I have in mind the new and vital conception of the ego that has come into psychotherapy in recent years (Allport, 1946[a]); the discovery and application of psychological principles involved in bringing the worker into a participant relation with his job (Allport, 1945); the discovery and application of procedures leading to successful administration (Leighton, 1945). We discern an accelerated movement toward the development of such theories as can have their acid test here and now, not one thousand years hence. These theories neither strain the credulity, nor stretch an inappropriate model some distance beyond its logical breaking point.

We happily find more emphasis than before on the structuring activities of the person, on the importance of centrally initiated motive patterns, on cognitive dynamisms—including ideology, schemata of meaning, frames of reference. We find the contemporaneity of motives stressed, as well as the important functions of self-esteem and ego-involvement. Though symbols are still confused with signals, we are beginning, through content-analysis and interviewing, to study symbols both in their own right, and as the basic ingredients that they are in all complex conduct, including all morally relevant thought and behavior. We have learned, through improved polls and other methods of inquiry, to ascertain the direction of social purpose as it resides in individual minds. From such knowledge it should be possible to fashion a domestic and international social policy that will be sufficiently realistic to succeed.

All these and many more signs indicate the growing dependence of modern theories upon a model that is none the less scientific for being humane. As this design for personality and social psychology gradually becomes better tempered to our subject matter we shall cease borrowing false notes—whether squeaks, squeals, or squalls. We shall read the score of human personality more accurately, and for the benefit of the world audience that waits to listen.

References

Allport, G. W. Motivation in personality: Reply to Mr. Bertocci. *Psychol. Rev.*, 1940, *47*, 533–554.

———. The psychology of participation. *Psychol. Rev.*, 1945, *53*, 117–132.

———. Effect: A secondary condition of learning. *Psychol. Rev.*, 1946, *54*, 335–347(a).

———. Geneticism *versus* ego-structure in theories of personality. *Brit. J. Educ. Psychol.*, 1946, *16*, II, 57–68(b).

Bertocci, P. A reinterpretation of moral obligation. *Phil. & Phenomenol. Res.*, 1945, *6*, 270–283.

Boring, E. G. Mind and mechanism. *Amer. J. Psychol.*, 1946, *54*, 173–192.

Cassirer, E. *An essay on man.* New Haven: Yale Univ. Press, 1945.

Goldstein, K. *Human nature in the light of psychopathology.* Cambridge, Mass.: Harvard Univ. Press, 1940.

Hilgard, E. R., and Marquis, D. G. *Conditioning and learning.* New York: D. Appleton-Century, 1940.

Hoslett, S. D. (ed.). *Human factors in management.* Parkville, Mo.: The Park College Press, 1946.

Hull, C. L. Goal attraction and directing ideas conceived as habit phenomena. *Psychol. Rev.*, 1931, *38*, 487–506.

Huxley, J. *Man stands alone.* New York: Harpers, 1941.

Lecky, P. *Self-consistency: a theory of personality.* New York: The Island Press, 1945.

Leighton, A. H. *The governing of men.* Princeton, N.J.: Princeton Univ. Press, 1945.

McDougall, W. *Outline of psychology.* New York: Scribners, 1923.

Morris, C. W. *Signs, language and behavior.* New York: Prentice-Hall, 1946.

Suttie, I. D. *The origins of love and hate.* London: Kegan Paul, 1935.

Thorndike, E. L. *Animal intelligence.* New York: Macmillan, 1911.

Tolman, E. C. A stimulus-expectancy need-cathexis psychology. *Science*, 1945, *101*, 160–166.

Yerkes, R. M. *Chimpanzees: a laboratory colony.* New Haven: Yale Univ. Press, 1943.

19 | *The Emphasis on Basic Functions*[1]

KENNETH W. SPENCE

There was a time when the term "behaviorism" in the title of a speech required no further specification. Every psychologist at least knew the referent to be that new brand of psychology, introduced by Watson, which proposed to break with tradition and deny that psychology had anything to do either with a mentalistic entity called consciousness or a method known as introspection. Today the situation is not so simple. The term "behaviorism" may, on the one hand, merely imply a very general point of view which has come to be accepted by almost all psychologists and thus does not point to any particular group or theoretical position. Or, on the other hand, it may refer to any one of several varieties of behaviorism which have been offered as supplementations or modifications of the original formulation of Watson (e.g., molecular behaviorism, molar behaviorism, operational behaviorism, purposive behaviorism, logical behaviorism—to mention only some of the varieties). While these current formulations usually acknowledge some debt to Watson, for various reasons which we cannot stop to discuss they almost invariably take great pains to differentiate themselves from what has come to be known as "Watsonian Behaviorism" or "Watsonianism." In fact, so far as I know, there are no proponents today of the original Watsonian version. Proper care should be taken to note, however, that this statement holds true only for the particular pattern of assumptions that Watson advanced. Many of the basic postulates of his formulation are to be found in the present-day varieties of behaviorism and, what is more important, probably, in the

From K. W. Spence, The methods and postulates of "behaviorism," *Psychol. Rev.*, 1948, 55, 67–78. Reprinted by permission of the author, the *Psychological Review*, and the American Psychological Association.

[1] This article was an address given at the Symposium on "The Postulates and Methods of Gestalt Psychology, Behaviorism and Psychoanalysis" given at the Conference on Methods in Philosophy and the Sciences in New York City, November, 1946. Some minor changes have been made in the paper itself and a list of references has been added.

underlying working assumptions of the great majority of present-day American psychologists.

Now that I have taken the precaution to differentiate the behaviorisms of today from the original version of behaviorism, I should like to call attention to the further interesting fact that with the exception possibly of Tolman very few, if any, current psychologists ever seem to think of themselves, or at least explicitly refer to themselves, as behaviorists. Such labeling, when it occurs, is usually the contribution of psychologists who consider themselves opposed to behaviorism. Undoubtedly, one of the reasons underlying this absence or lack of "old-school-tie" spirit is that a large majority of present-day American psychologists just take for granted many of the behavioristic assumptions and, occupied as they have been with the details of developing and applying their specific research tools, they have had little time or inclination to give much thought to the more general methodological and systematic problems of their science.

Even the more theoretical-minded of the behavioristically-oriented psychologists seem to have been too preoccupied with matters of detail to get around to the consideration of a more general theoretical framework. Instead of attempting to formulate a complete system of psychology, these theorists have been more concerned with the elaboration of relatively specific hypotheses concerning rather limited realms of data—e.g., theories of simple learning phenomena, motivational theories, theories of personality development, etc. As a consequence we find that instead of being built up around the symbol "behaviorism," allegiances tend to become attached to such labels as associationism, conditioning, reinforcement theory, frustration hypothesis, etc. It seems, in other words, that these psychologists have outgrown the stage of schools.

Under these circumstances, I cannot and I shall not undertake to present a fixed set of articles of faith, articulately and self-consciously held by a group of men calling themselves behaviorists. Instead, I shall attempt to formulate a few methodological principles that are, I believe, exemplified in the work of certain contemporary psychologists who would undoubtedly acknowledge a heavy historical debt to that earlier formulation known as the school of behaviorism.

The first problem that I shall discuss has to do with the behavior scientist's conception of the nature of psychological events. In the older, classical psychologies, whether of the structural or act varieties, the point of view taken was that psychology, if it was a natural science, was, to say the least, a somewhat unique one. Instead of being conceived like physics, for example, as concerning itself with events mediated by or occurring in the consciousness or immediate experience of the observing scientist, psychology was said to observe and analyze by a kind of inner sense immediate experience per se. Sensations, emotions, thoughts were regarded as observable aspects of direct experience rather than systematic constructs which, like the physicist's atoms and electrons, were inferred from immediate experience.

Fortunately, the relationship of immediate experience (consciousness) to the data and constructs of science has been considerably clarified in recent years by the writings of several different groups of thinkers. The philosophers of science, particularly the logical positivists (Bergmann, 1940; Carnap, 1935, 1936–37; Feigl, 1945), philosophically-minded scientists such as Bridgman (1928) and, within psychology, such writers as Boring (1933), Pratt (1939), and Stevens (1935) have succeeded, I believe, in making the point that the data of all sciences have the same origin —namely, the immediate experience of an observing person, the scientist himself. That is to say, immediate experience, the initial matrix out of which all sciences develop, is no longer considered a matter of concern for the scientist qua scientist. He simply takes it for granted and then proceeds to his task of describing the events occurring in it and discovering and formulating the nature of the relationships holding among them.

Boring stated this matter very clearly for psychologists in his book of some years ago, *The Physical Dimensions of Consciousness*. He wrote: "Thus the events of physics, as Wundt said, are mediate to experience, which stands in the background as the dator of scientific data, unrealizable as reality except inductively. In the same way psychology must deal with existential reals which are similarly mediate to experience. There is no way of getting at 'direct experience' because experience gives itself up to science indirectly, inferentially, by the experimental method" (1933, p. 6).

More recently Pratt, in his *Logic of Modern Psychology* (1939), has hammered home this same point with considerable effectiveness. As he points out, the subject matter of psychology is exactly the same in kind as all other sciences; any differentiation among the sciences is merely a matter of convenience, a division of scientific labor resorted to as the amount of detailed knowledge increases beyond the capacity of a single person's grasp.

I think that it is of some historical interest to note in connection with this point that in the first of his articles introducing the behavioristic position, Watson took essentially the same stand. He wrote: "It [psychology] can dispense with consciousness in a psychological sense. The separate observation of 'states of consciousness' is, on this assumption, no more a part of the task of the psychologist than of the physicist. We might call this the return to a nonreflective and naïve use of consciousness. In this sense consciousness may be said to be the instrument or tool with which all scientists work" (1913, p. 176).

Acknowledging, then, that the psychologist conceives his task as that of bringing order and meaning into the realm of certain events provided by immediate experience, we now turn to the question of what these particular observed events are. In attempting to answer this question, attention should first be directed to the fact that the sense events in the experience of the observing scientist may depend upon or result from two different classes of conditions, intra-organic and extra-organic, the former exciting the interoceptors and the latter, the exteroceptors. The physical sciences, it should be noted, moreover, deal only with events of an extra-organic origin—i.e., those received through the exteroceptors. The data of classical psychology, on the other hand, were regarded as involving primarily sense events initiated through the interoceptors. These latter were regarded as being stimulated by such internal mental activities as thinking, desiring, emotional reactions, perceiving, etc., and hence were thought of as providing primary data concerning them.

It is apparent, however, that these internally initiated experiences differ rather markedly from the externally aroused ones in the extent to which they are publicly controllable and communicable. At least, if we can judge from the interminable disagreements of the introspective psychologists themselves, this class of experiences does not meet too well the requirements of social verification and acceptance demanded by the scientist. It was in the face of this difficulty that Watson made his suggestion that the psychologist, like all other scientists, should confine himself to those segments of his experience which have their origin in extra-organic conditions. In other words, the events studied by the psychologist, Watson held, should consist in observations of the overt behavior of *other* organisms, other persons than the observing scientist himself, and not in the observation of the scientist's own internal activities.

As everyone knows, however, most behavior scientists have continued more or less to make use of this latter type of material in the form of the objectively recordable verbal reports of their subjects. Indeed, the scientist himself, in certain circumstances, may assume a dual role and serve as both subject and experimenter. In this event his own introspective report is recorded as a linguistic response and becomes a part of the objective data. To some critics of the behavioristic viewpoint, this acceptance of the verbal reports of their subjects as a part of the data has seemed to represent an abandonment of the strict behavioristic position and a return to the conception that psychology studies *experiential* events as well as overt behavior.

Such a contention, it seems to me, fails to note a very important difference in the two positions. The introspectionist, it should be recalled, assumed a strict one-to-one relationship between the verbal responses of his subjects and the inner mental processes. Accordingly, he accepted these introspective reports as *facts* or *data* about the inner mental events which they represented. The behavior scientist takes a very different position. He accepts verbal response as just one more form of behavior and he proposes to use this type of data in exactly the same manner as he does other types of behavior variables. Thus he attempts to discover laws relating verbal responses to environmental events of the past or present, and he seeks to find what relations they have to other types of response variables. He also makes use of them as a 'basis for making inferences as to certain hypothetical or theoretical constructs which he employs. In contrast, then, to the introspectionist's conception of these verbal reports as mirroring directly inner mental events, i.e., facts, the behaviorist uses them either as data in their own right to be related to other data, or as a base from which to infer theoretical constructs which presumably represent internal or covert activities of their subjects. We shall return later to the use made of such language responses in the theorizing of the behaviorist.

From this all too cursory discussion of the initial data of the behavioristic psychologist, I should like now to turn to a consideration of the nature of the concepts which he employs to record and describe these events. I do not believe it is necessary for me to discuss at any length the position of the behaviorist with respect to the movement known as operationism. The insistence of the early behaviorists on a thoroughgoing operational analysis of the traditional mentalistic concepts was really nothing more than an anticipation of this somewhat overemphasized program. That a body of empirical knowledge cannot be built up without providing for verifiability of the terms in use is simply taken for granted by the behaviorist. Instead, then, of talking about operational definition of psychological concepts, I should like to discuss certain matters related to a second criterion of acceptability of a scientific concept—namely, its *significance*.

One often hears criticisms to the effect that behavioristic concepts are too elementaristic, too atomistic, or that they fail to portray the real essence or true meaning of man's behavior. These latter critics often complain bitterly about the impoverishment of the mind, and of the lack of warmth and glowing particulars in the behaviorist's picture of psychological events. Some of these criticisms merely reflect, of course, a lack of appreciation on the part of some "psychologists" as to the difference between scientific knowledge of an event on the one hand and everyday knowledge, or the kind of knowledge the novelist or poet portrays, on the other. Either by reason of training or because of their basically nonscientific interests, these critics have never really understood the abstract character of the scientific account of any phenomenon. The only reply that can be made to such a critic is to point out that the scientist's interests are quite different from his. There are, of course, other legitimate interpretations of nature and man than the scientific one and each has its right to be pursued. The behavior scientist merely asks that he be given the same opportunity to develop a scientific account of his phenomena that his colleagues in the physical and biological fields have had. If there are aspects of human or animal behavior for which such an account cannot ever be developed, there are not, so far as I know, any means of finding this out without a try. Unfortunately, the attitudes of too many psychologists with regard to this matter are not such as are likely to lead them to the discovery of such knowledge. The difficulty, I fear, is that too many persons whose interests are non-scientific have become psychologists under the mistaken impression that psychology is one of the arts.

As to the criticisms that the behaviorist's concepts are too elementaristic, I must confess to the belief that the term "elementarism" is merely one of those stereotypes, or "rally-round-the-flag" words which the Gestalt psychologist has used in the defense and exposition of his holistic doctrines. However fervently the Gestalt psychologist may claim that he deals only with wholes, with total situations, the fact remains that if he is interested in discovering uniformities or scientific laws he must, of necessity, fractionate or abstract out certain features of the total events he observes. Such uniformities or laws describe ways in which events repeat themselves. Total concrete events, however, are seldom if ever repeated. Only certain features of events are repeated and since this is the case science must always abstract.

The problem here is really one of the size of the "units of description" that the scientist is to employ and this brings us back to the criterion of acceptability of a scientific term which we referred to as *significance*. By the *significance* of a scientific concept is here meant the extent to which a concept or variable aids or enters into the formulation of laws. Significant concepts in science are those which are discovered to have functional relations with other concepts. Unfortunately, there are few if any rules for deciding a priori which concepts will and which ones will not be significant. Whether elementaristic concepts or units of description which, like the Gestaltists, are nearer the "meaningful" common sense level, are to be chosen is entirely a pragmatic matter of which ones are most successful— i.e., which ones lead to the discovery of laws. This can be ascertained only by trying them out.

Attention might also be called here to the further fact that it is entirely conceivable that different sizes or levels of descriptive units may be employed for the same set of events. The physical sciences provide us with numerous instances of this sort of thing and we see examples of it in psychology both in the description of behavior and stimulus events. Thus, employing the terms of Brunswik (1939) and Heider (1939), we may make use of either a proximal or distal account of the stimulus situation, and behavior may be described either in terms of movements (muscular patterns) or in terms of gross achievements. The particular alternative chosen, molecular or molar, depends upon the interest and purpose of the scientist, the kind of law he expects to find or use. As Hull (1943ª) has pointed out in discussing this matter, some of the seeming disagreements among current psychologists are merely that one prefers to use more molar concepts than another.

Such different descriptions, however, do not necessarily represent fundamental disagreements. If two systems of concepts should each be successful in leading to the discovery and formulation of laws, it should also be possible to discover co-ordinating definitions which will reveal the interrelations of the two systems. Or, as Hull (1943ª) suggests, the postulates or primary assumptions of those working at a more molar level may ultimately appear as theorems in a more molecular description.

To sum up, then, the position which the behavior scientist takes with respect to the selection of the descriptive concepts to be employed in his science, recognizes 1) that the *significance* of a concept is to be measured in terms of the extent to which it leads to the formulation of laws about the phenomena; 2) that a scientific law is always, in some greater or lesser degree, abstract in the sense that it refers only to certain properties of the events or sequence of events it describes and ignores other properties which are irrelevant to the particular momentary purpose; 3) that the method of elementary abstraction or analysis has been highly successful in all fields of science. While the disentanglement of the great complexes of properties and relations (sequences) among psychological events is undoubtedly much more difficult than in the case of physical phenomena, the difference between them need not be regarded as more than one of degree. On the basis of this assumption there would seem to be little reason for abandoning the method of abstraction or analysis.

We have said that the primary aim of the behavior scientist is to bring order and meaning into the particular realm of events he studies. Ordering a set of observable events for the scientist consists in discovering relationships between the events or, as we say, in the finding of empirical laws. The scientist seeks to establish laws relating his concepts or variables because they make possible explanation and prediction.

In the case of such areas of science as physics, the finding of empirical laws has involved chiefly the process of inductive generalization from observation and experimentation. In other words, in physics it has been possible to isolate sufficiently simple systems of observation to arrive at such laws in this manner. The situation in psychology and the other behavior sciences is quite different. Primarily because of the greater complexity of psychological as compared with physical phenomena, the psychologist has either been unable to isolate, experimentally, simple systems, or he has not found satisfactory means of measuring all of the relevant variables in the system under observation. In this circumstance he has resorted to guesses or postulations as to the uncontrolled or as yet un-measurable factors. As a result of this difference the term "theory" has, as I have pointed out elsewhere (1944), come to have a very different con-notation in psychology from that which it has in physics. Theories in physics are constructions which serve primarily to integrate or organize into a single deductive system sets of empirical laws which previously were unrelated. The classical example is, of course, the Newtonian in-tegration of the previously unconnected areas of mechanics and astronomy by the gravitational theory. Other well-known examples are the electro-magnetic theory of light and the kinetic theory of gases.

In psychology, on the other hand, theories serve primarily as a device to aid in the formulation of the empirical laws. They consist in guesses as to how the uncontrolled or unknown factors in the system under study are related to the experimentally-known variables. To these hypothetical constructs Tolman (1938) has applied the very appropriate term "inter-vening variable" because they are assumed to intervene between the measurable environmental and organic variables, on the one hand, and the measurable behavior properties on the other.

The manner in which the behavior scientist has used these hypothetical, intervening constructs may be shown by considering the various kinds of laws which the psychologist seeks to discover. Confining ourselves for the moment to laws which do not involve any hypothetical components, we find that the variables studied by the behavioristic psychologist fall into two, or possibly three main groups:

1. Response variables: measurements of behavior properties.
2. Stimulus variables: measurements of properties of the physical and social environment.
3. Organic variables: measurements of neuroanatomical or neurophys-iological properties of the organism.

The different types of empirical relationships or laws in which psy-chologists have been interested are as follows:

1. $R = f(R)$
2. $R = f(S)$
3. $R = f(O)$
4. $O = f(S)$

Type 1 laws are laws of association of behavior properties. A great deal of use is made of the statistical constant, the coefficient of correlation, in the formulation of these laws and, as is well known, this type of law is investigated extensively in the field of psychological testing.

Type 2 laws may be concerned with the present environment or with past environmental events. Thus in the case of the typical perception experiments, we are interested in the effects of variation of aspects or features of the environmental stimulus on the perceptual or discrimination responses of the subject. Best examples of laws relating behavior to past events in the environment are laws of learning, laws of secondary motivation, etc.

For the most part the present-day behavioristic psychologists tend to concentrate their energies on these two classes of laws and to a very considerable extent they have favored the use of the molar rather than molecular concepts. A few psychologists whose interests have been in mediational problems have concerned themselves with type 3 and type 4 laws. These latter are obviously in the field of neurophysiological psychology and have in the main been concerned only with the simplest kinds of behavior phenomena—e.g., sensory responses. Indeed, our inability to develop measures of this class of events (i.e., organic variables) in the case of the more complex behavior phenomena has been one of the factors underlying the substitution of the hypothetical intervening constructs in their place.

Figure 1 continues this analysis of the laws of psychology. In this dia-

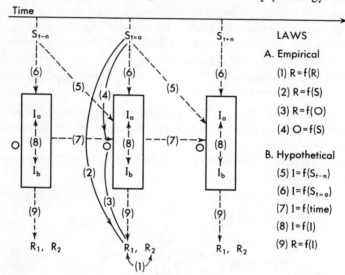

Figure 1.   Showing different kinds of laws.

gram I have attempted to portray, in addition to the four types of empirical laws which we have been discussing, the new hypothetical or guessed-at types of relationships which are involved in the introduction of the hypothetical intervening constructs. These latter are indicated as I_a and I_b and are represented as *hypothetical state variables* (enclosed within the rectangle). The environment or world situation at three different time intervals is represented by $S_t - n$ (past), $S_t = 0$ (present), $S_t + n$ (future). These S's and also the R's represent empirical variables. I have also represented the class of experimental neurophysiological variables of the first figure by the symbol O, to the left of the rectangle. The four classes of empirical laws, listed at the right side of the figure, are represented by the solid curved lines. The guessed-at or postulated laws relating the hypothetical state variables (I_a, I_b, etc.) to the various experimental variables are represented by the dotted lines. Thus No. 5 type of "law" defines or introduces the intervening variables in terms of past events; No. 6 type relates them to the present environmental variables and No. 7 to time; No. 8 "laws" present interrelations assumed between these intervening variables, and, finally, the relations represented by No. 9 relate the intervening variables to the response variables. That is to say, these dotted lines should be thought of as representative of different classes of postulated relationships, not the usual notion of an S-R connection.

Those who are acquainted with the theoretical constructs of Hull (1943a) will recognize specific examples of these hypothetical laws. Thus his postulate or definition of the construct habit strength, or $_sH_R$, as a function of the number of past reinforcements is a good example of Class No. 5 "law." His assumption of the nature of the manner in which H and D interact to determine E falls in Class No. 8 and his postulate as to how the construct of reactive inhibition (I_R) is assumed to change (disintegrate) with time is an instance of No. 7 type of "law." Incidentally, it will be noted that this last relationship is the only one which is similar to the so-called dynamic or process laws of physics. This type of law states or describes the laws governing the changes that occur within a system in time.

A question concerning these theoretical constructs that invariably seems to arise is whether they represent some kind of internal, presumably neurophysiological, process or state. The persistence with which misunderstanding arises on this point is truly surprising. It is probably to be explained in terms of the difficulty and resistance we have in shedding old, familiar meanings of words. In this connection it is not a little amusing to note that whereas Hull is usually accused of stuffing the organism with mythological brain states, Tolman, whose theoretical concepts have exactly the same formal structure as those of Hull—i.e., intervening variables defined in terms of independent environmental events—is often charged with the guilt of dreaming up mentalistic ghosts. The explanation of this situation is readily seen when we recall the terms employed by these two men to designate their intervening variables. Thus Hull used such words as habit, drive, excitatory potential and inhibitory potential while Tolman named his theoretical constructs, demands, sign-Gestalt-expectations, hypotheses, etc.

The only meanings that these theoretical intervening constructs have *at the present time* is provided by the equations which relate them to the known experimental variables—the environmental measurements on the one hand and the behavior measures on the other. Such equations constitute the definitions of these terms.

The present role of these theoretical constructs we have said is to aid the psychologist in his search for the empirical laws relating behavior to the conditions determining it. In this sense they are a kind of calculational device which helps us to write the complete law describing the interrelations between all of the relevant experimental variables. In a recent article (1944) on this problem of theory construction in contemporary psychology I called attention to the point that it is possible in the case of the theoretical formulation of simple learning behavior developed by Hull to substitute in the successive equations introducing the intervening theoretical constructs and obtain a single equation which states the response measure as a function of the several antecedent environmental variables. In this equation the intervening theoretical variables are represented among the parameters of the equation.

While both Tolman and I have emphasized the heuristic value of this type of theoretical construction in the formulation of the complete form of the laws, Hull (1943b) has called attention to another use which these constructs serve. Such constructs as habit and excitatory potential also provide, he claims, convenient, quantitative representations or indices of the particular complex of experimental variables for which they stand. Thus instead of having to state that the subject has had so many reinforcements in the situation under conditions in which the goal was of such-and-such a magnitude and was delayed for such-and-such a period, it is possible to substitute the calculated value of habit strength.

Finally, there remains the possibility, at least, that these intervening constructs may turn out to have their counterparts somewhere under the skin of the organism. Hull in particular has been quite prone to accept this possibility and has not hesitated to add further statements about these constructs which suggest their possible locus and functioning in the nervous system. His justification, however, has always been that such conjectures provide experimental hints to persons interested in making such co-ordinations of our knowledge. His main theoretical efforts have been primarily at the molar-behavioral level.

In concluding this discussion of the theoretical framework of the behavioristic psychologist, I should like to emphasize that it is as yet only in a very primitive state of development, a fact which has unfortunately been lost sight of by many of the current critics of this position. The theorist in this field apparently has to choose between attempting to lay down the general theoretical framework of the whole range of behavior phenomena or working out the detailed nature of one small realm of data. Tolman has, for the most part, chosen the former alternative with the consequence that his treatment is characterized by an obvious lack of detailed specification of his theoretical constructs. Hull, on the other hand, has elected to follow the second method. His recent book, *Principles of Behavior*, dealt only with the most *simple* instances of laboratory learning phenomena, classical and instrumental conditioning, and he and his students are now engaged in extending the fundamental laws there discovered to the major phenomena of individual behavior.

So far as theoretical constructs are concerned, it is obvious that the simple behavior phenomena dealt with by Hull and other behavioristic-oriented psychologists have not required (to any great extent) a whole class of hypothetical intervening variables that must ultimately be postulated. Thus the theoretical constructs in Hull's recent book—habit, excitatory and inhibitory potential, drive, etc.—are what might be referred to as *state variables*. Each of these constructs represents a hypothetical condition or state of the organism which is assumed to have resulted from and is defined in terms of the past interactions of the organism and its environment. In contrast the new theoretical constructs referred to above will represent, not states, but hypothetical, non-observable responses, implicit processes, occurring in the individual. Thus, in dealing with the more complex types of animal and human behavior, implicit emotional responses, covert verbal responses and not easily observable receptor-exposure and postural adjustments will have to be postulated in addition to these state variables. As yet only a bare beginning has been made in the use of such theoretical constructs—e.g., anxiety reactions and their secondary reinforcing effects (Mowrer, 1939), fractional anticipatory goal reactions as the basis of purposive behavior (Hull, 1930, 1931).

It is in this realm of theorizing that the verbal reports of human subjects are likely to be of most use to the behavior theorist, for presumably these reports can be made the basis on which to postulate the occurrence of these inferred activities. There are, of course, many pitfalls in the use of such verbal reports and considerable caution needs to be exercised in their use. However, careful control and checking in terms of other, non-verbal responses should provide a means of detecting distortions, both deliberate and otherwise, in this source of data (Skinner, 1945).

A discussion of behaviorism, especially when it occurs in conjunction with a symposium which includes Gestalt psychology, requires at least some comment on the distinction often made between field and non-field theories in psychology. The Gestalt psychologists, in particular, have been very fond of this contrast and they have not hesitated to imply that their theoretical structures are similar in some respect to the type of field theory in physics represented by the Maxwell electromagnetic theory and

Einstein's gravitational theory. In some instances the further implication has been made that behavioristic theories are a mechanical type of theory and as such are just as outmoded as the mechanistic theories of physics. Now I have often wondered what our theoretical brethren from the field of physics would think of these claims if perchance they were ever to take a serious look at these two groups of theories. Certainly the behavioristic theoretical structure I have been talking about uses neither the mechanical models—i.e., particles with their attracting forces—nor the type of mathematical equations that characterize a mechanical theory. Nor do I believe that there is anything even remotely resembling the field equations of Maxwell and Einstein in the theoretical formulations of the Gestalt psychologists. In the sense, then, in which the theoretical physicist understands, the dichotomy, mechanical versus field theory, no such distinction, in my opinion, exists in psychology today.

If, on the other hand, the concept of field refers in psychology essentially to the notion of a system of interdependent variables, with its implication that the behavior of an organism at any moment is a resultant of the totality of relevant variables, then there is not to my knowledge any behavioristic theory today which would not also be a field theory. Furthermore, if we accept the additional notion that it is the pattern of interrelationships between the determining variables that is the crucial factor differentiating psychological field theories from non-field theories, I do not believe that the behavior theories which I have been describing would fail to qualify as field theories. The hypothetical equations which Hull (1943a) postulates in the introduction of his theoretical constructs provide in precise mathematical form these very patterns of interrelationship. Finally, as to the characteristic of field theory emphasized by Lewin (1943) under the principle of contemporaneity—namely, that the behavior at any moment is a function of the situation *at that moment only* and not a function of past or future situations—I find it difficult to believe that any present-day psychologist believes that other conditions than those of the present moment determine the behavior of this moment. Even the psychoanalyst never held, as Lewin sometimes seems to imply, that past events somehow jump through time to determine the present behavior, but, instead, conceived of these past events leaving their effects in the organism and through them determining the behavior of the moment. The behaviorist takes exactly the same view of the matter.

The development of our science has not been helped, in my opinion, by such distinctions as field and non-field theory. A much more useful procedure would be to examine in detail these differing theoretical positions with a view to ascertaining to what extent they differ in the particular variables they believe to be relevant in a particular instance and what differences, if any, exist in their postulation as to the pattern of the inter-relationships involved—i.e., in the form of the hypothetical laws they assume. It is my personal belief that if this procedure were followed there would be much less in the way of specific disagreements to settle than is usually thought. I base this prediction not only on the well-known fact that the Gestaltists, psychoanalysts and behaviorists have to a considerable extent been interested in very different realms of psychological phenomena and that hence their theories are not in competition with one another, but also on the fact that very little real theorizing, particularly in the matter of specifying the precise form of the interrelations between the variables, has actually been done. It is most imperative that psychologists attempt to formulate their theories in as precise and articulate a manner as possible, for it is only by means of such theorizing that psychology can hope, finally, to attain full-fledged scientific statehood.

References

Bergmann, G. The subject matter of psychology. *Phil. Sci.*, 1940, 7, 415–433.

Boring, E. G. *The physical dimensions of consciousness.* New York: Century, 1933.

Bridgman, P. W. *The logic of modern physics.* New York: Macmillan, 1928.

Brunswik, E. The conceptual focus of some psychological systems. *J. Unif. Sci. (Erkenntnis)*, 1939, 8, 36–49.

Carnap, R. *Philosophy and logical syntax.* London: Kegan Paul, Trench, Trubner, 1935.

———. Testability and meaning. *Phil. Sci.*, 1936, 3, 419–471; 1937, 4, 1–40.

Feigl, H. Operationism and scientific method. *Psychol. Rev.*, 1945, 52, 243–246.

Heider, F. Environmental determinants in psychological theories. *Psychol. Rev.*, 1939, 46, 383–410.

Hull, C. L. Knowledge and purpose as habit mechanisms. *Psychol. Rev.*, 1930, 37, 511–525.

———. Goal attraction and directing ideas conceived as habit phenomena. *Psychol. Rev.*, 1931, 38, 487–506.

———. *Principles of behavior.* New York: Appleton-Century-Crofts, 1943(a).

———. The problem of intervening variables in molar behavior theory. *Psychol. Rev.*, 1943, 50, 273–291(b).

Lewin, K. Defining the "field" at a given time. *Psychol. Rev.*, 1943, 50, 292–310.

Mowrer, O. H. A stimulus-response analysis of anxiety and its role as a reinforcing agent. *Psychol. Rev.*, 1939, 46, 553–565.

Pratt, C. C. *The logic of modern psychology.* New York: Macmillan, 1939.

Skinner, B. F. The operational analysis of psychological terms. *Psychol. Rev.*, 1945, 52, 270–278.

Spence, K. W. The nature of theory construction in contemporary psychology. *Psychol. Rev.*, 1944, 51, 47–68.

Stevens, S. S. The operational definition of psychological concepts. *Psychol. Rev.*, 1935, 42, 517–527.

Tolman, E. C. *Purposive behavior in animals and men.* New York: Century, 1932.

———. The determiners of behavior at a choice point. *Psychol. Rev.*, 1938, *45*, 1–41.

Watson, J. B. Psychology as the behaviorist views it. *Psychol. Rev.*, 1913, *20*, 158–177.

20 | *The Principle of Gradualness*[1]

ROBERT S. MORISON

Before reading the text from which the title of this sermon is derived, let me, as gracefully as one can, lay the blame for it on your President-elect. For it is due to his mastery of the principle of gradualness that I am here at all. Away back last spring when Labor Day seemed co-distant with dooms-day, your President, a shrewd Nova Scotian and a practical psychologist, telephoned from Montreal to say that he was going to write me a letter. The telephone call was but a preliminary step in a subversion. He then embarked on a long explanation of APA Day as a sort of interlude between theory and practice. The applied scientists who have been talking to each other for three days have mostly gone home, and the pure psychologists have not yet arrived. Something is obviously needed to fill the gap. Fifteen years of experience in the foundation apparatus leave one with certain unextinguishable conditioned reflexes; and I quickly responded that I was very sympathetic with his problem, but unfortunately requests for money to fill gaps between theory and practice fall entirely outside our usual program.

Gradualist Hebb was waiting for this moment, and he immediately came up with the punch line he had been so carefully preparing: "Oh! It's not your money we want; just talk to us." No wonder your society has chosen him as Mr. Psychology for 1959–60. Let us analyze the situation a little further. Clearly, Hebb was using his knowledge of conditioned reflex

From R. S. Morison, "Gradualness, gradualness, gradualness". (I. P. Pavlov), *Amer. Psychologist*, 1960, *15*, 187–197. Reprinted by permission of the author, the *American Psychologist*, and the American Psychological Association.

[1] Invited Address delivered at the sixty-seventh Annual Convention of the American Psychological Association, Cincinnati, Ohio, September 6, 1959.

theory to deduce that I would first think of money. His familiarity with Freudian psychodynamics had equipped him with the knowledge that I would be suffering a momentary twinge of guilt at having to turn down an old friend and that I would want to expiate this by responding positively to the next stimulus. As a student of Stephen Potter and W. C. Allee, he deftly established his superior spot in the peck order by catching me in a misinterpretation of his initial purpose, thus potentiating my suggestibility. And finally, his well-known common sense and wide clinical experience had taught him that philanthropoids love to talk.

It so happened that that very afternoon I attended a seminar on the relation of the frontal lobes to the delayed response—the first psychological meeting I had been to for some years. As a onetime neurophysiologist, I recalled the original studies done by Carlyle Jacobson in Fulton's laboratory nearly 30 years ago. Naturally, one expected to find that 30 years of work would have brought us precise identification of the variables involved in this obviously simple phenomenon, if not indeed a general theory of frontal lobe function. What then was my surprise to discover that three decades of the most painstaking and intelligent investigation by the best minds in psychology had served only to convince us that we have but the foggiest notion of what goes on in the cell assemblies of the frontal lobes between the moment a monkey sees a peanut covered by a small tin can and the time he reaches for it 30 seconds later. Ladies and gentlemen, let us think on this before we set forth to tell mothers how to bring up children, industrial leaders how to choose junior executives, social workers how to abolish delinquency, the staff of the State Department how to negotiate with the Russians, or foundation officers how to detect genius.

And so we come to our text which is lifted from a letter written by Pavlov in the eighty-eighth year of his life:

What can I wish to the youth of my country who devote themselves to science?

Firstly, gradualness. About this most important condition of fruitful scientific work I never can speak without emotion. Gradualness, gradualness, and gradualness. From the very beginning of your work, school yourselves to severe gradualness in the accumulation of knowledge.

Learn the ABC of science before you try to ascend to its summit. Never begin the subsequent without mastering the preceding. Never attempt to screen an insufficiency of knowledge even by the most audacious surmise and hypothesis. Howsoever this soap-bubble will rejoice your eyes by its play, it inevitably will burst and you will have nothing except shame.

School yourselves to demureness and patience. Learn to inure yourselves to drudgery in science. Learn, compare, collect the facts!

But learning, experimenting, observing, try not to stay on the surface of the facts. Do not become the archivists of facts. Try to penetrate to the secret of their occurrence, persistently search for the laws which govern them.

The injunction to observe the principle of gradualness is important for any scientist, but it is particularly relevant for those who deal primarily with human beings. I speak to you today from a platform provided by a basic training in medicine, and I am going to try to tell you how psychology looks to one perhaps somewhat aberrant medical man. There will be no pretense of a thorough review of the data or a careful weighing of evidence. If any of you are looking for some sort of utility or relevance in these remarks, I hope you will find it as the kind of help one occasionally gets from a frank brother or sister, prompted by a mixture of love, sympathy, and sibling rivalry, to give improving advice to other members of his family.

Theory and Practice

We can now get back to explaining why the principle of gradualness is especially important for those who deal primarily with human beings. Hippocrates, who was both a good medical man and an equally good psychologist, summed the situation up very neatly when he said that life is short, the art long, experiment perilous, and decision difficult. The fact that life is short is one of the primary conditions of human existence. The realization of the transitoriness of human beings and their affairs seems to give those who deal with human problems a sense of urgency which interferes with the principle of gradualness. This tendency to deprecate the steady plodder progressing slowly but constantly to a distant unseen goal has been given a sort of flippant dignity by John Maynard Keynes, the most influential economist of the depression years: "Speaking of long run analysis," he said, "this *long run* is a misleading guide to human affairs. In the long run we are all dead."

And so it is that experts in human behavior, from economists to physicians, from sociologists to psychologists, from parents to politicians, all seem obsessed by the necessity of doing something right here and now to ameliorate the state of man. In this sense, the behavioral sciences would for the most part have to be classified, at least until very recent times, as applied research.

By now one must suppose that everyone has heard of the conversation between the engineer and the scientist in which the former inquires of the latter: "Are you doing pure research or do you have something in mind?" How many behavioral scientists can you name who have not had something in mind?

Plutarch, who gave us those extraordinary clinical studies of greatness, was primarily interested in stimulating his readers to lead better lives and emphasized the "applied" nature of his work when he said: "Moral good is a practical stimulus; it is no sooner seen, than it inspires an impulse to practice. . . . And so we have thought fit to spend our time and pains in writing of the lives of famous persons."

Students of the seamier side of life have been no less interested in putting their observations to practical use. Machiavelli published his penetrating observations not as a theoretical treatise on evil but as a handbook of practical instructions for contemporary' princes. Even Freud, whose permanent contributions have probably been more theoretical than practical and whose own attitude toward his work was that of the scholar rather than the practitioner, felt it necessary to define psychoanalysis in the third sentence of his *General Introduction* as "a method of medical treatment for those suffering from mental disorders." And John B. Watson, if memory serves, offered to end the shortage of stenographers if only he could be supplied with an appropriate number of young girls unconditioned by previous circumstances.

How different has been the tradition in the natural sciences! Archimedes thought so little of his practical inventions that he left no written record of them among the 15 treatises that have come down to us. Isaac Newton displayed his devotion to pure science and his awareness of the principle of gradualness in his celebrated statement:

I do not know what I may appear to the world; but to myself I seem to have been only like a boy playing on the seashore, and diverting myself in now and then finding a smoother pebble or a prettier shell than ordinary, whilst the great ocean of truth lay all undiscovered before me.

Apparently, physicists and astronomers have faith that the solar system will be around for a long time and are thus content to study its laws step by step. If one generation does not succeed with the whole problem, somebody else will come along later to add a few more shining pebbles.

The founders of the life sciences, even though many of them were practicing physicians and knew that "life is short," were willing to give more emphasis to the length of the art. William Harvey described the circulation of the blood without bothering to mention more than one rather minor practical application and spent his later years investigating problems of embryology which did not reach the clinic for 300 years.

These and others set the tone for the natural or, if you will, "subhuman" sciences. From time to time this tone has wavered as when Pasteur set out to make French beer better than German beer, but on the whole the natural sciences have remained basic and have contented themselves with a long time-scale.

This is the tradition of gradualness in which the modern medical man has grown up; and it is worth noting that Pavlov, the supplier of the text, was trained in medicine long before he became a psychologist. But what does today's medical man see as he peeps over the fence into the backyard of his neighboring science, psychology? In the first place he finds to his astonishment that psychology has existed as a separate discipline for only slightly more than a century. Before that time, all the work which we would now regard as psychological in content was carried on either by speculative philosophers or by physicists and physiologists. Indeed most of the people whom we regard as the founders of modern psychology—Wundt, Weber, Fechner, Helmholtz, and the like—had received their basic training as medical men or physicists. Admirably gradualistic in their approach, they confined themselves for the most part to measuring stimuli and analyzing the responses of various sensory end organs of the soul. It was only towards the end of the nineteenth century that psychologists turned their attention to the soul or psyche as such.

At this point we encounter a strange paradox. For it is just when psychology begins to tackle the most difficult problems of all—perception, learning, motivation, consciousness, unconsciousness, individual intelligence, and social interaction—that it abandons the principle of gradualness and begins to jump at conclusions.

From about 1890 to the present, at least every decade has seen some general theory put forward to explain why we behave like human beings. Acting on the prevalent notion that the simplest theory is the best, psychologists have attempted to show that the continuum of human personality could be divided into two parts: introverts and extroverts. Introverts tend to get schizophrenia; and extroverts, manic depressive disorder. A little later on, three categories were described: cerebrotonic, viscerotonic, and somatotonic. Others, less interested in taxonomy, became "dynamic" and traced all behavior to the elaboration or repression of sexual impulses, or the feeling of inferiority. Still others took the view that behavior was nothing but conditioned reflexes. Those who objected to the atomistic approach sought satisfaction in contemplating the individual as a whole and delighted in the fact that the Germans had a word for it.

Now one should admit right off that there is nothing wrong with proposing theories. As a matter of fact some sort of theory is always necessary to guide the intelligent collection of facts. As Darwin said: "How odd it is that anyone should not see that all observation must be for or against some view if it is to be of any service." Nor can anyone nowadays believe that enough facts carefully collected and lined up side by side will inevitably and almost automatically arrange themselves into a neat and illuminating generalization as Francis Bacon seemed to hope. Somewhere along the line somebody has to make a poetic guess about how things might be arranged so as to make sense.

Why then are so many people concerned about the present state of psychological theories? In the first place, as suggested above, there are probably too many of them. It is difficult for the newcomer to find his way through the luxuriant growth. In the second place, although many of the theoretical formulations appear to overlap in the sense that they claim to be explaining the same set of phenomena, relatively little effort is actually made to bring them into effective congruence. Each school differs from the other not only in its theoretical outlook but in the kinds of facts it collects and the methods used for their collection. In the third place and pretty much as a result of the foregoing considerations, there is no one psychological theory which has achieved the same sort of beauty and elegance that is such a characteristic feature of the classical sciences and such a source of satisfaction to their pursuers.

I will assume the first of these propositions to be self-evident and will not discuss it further. Let us look at the other two to see how far they are true, to make some guesses as to why the field has developed in the way it has, and finally to suggest some possible ways of improving matters.

The claim of each school to explain a broad range of psychological phenomena is frequently more implicit than explicit. Frequently enough to prove our point, however, a particularly courageous theoretician will explicitly lay claim to the whole field, as when Watson wrote his book to show how the phenomena discussed by Freud could be subsumed under the Pavlovian aegis, or Miller and Dollard claimed the same area for Clark Hull.

Brilliant intellectual efforts though these productions are, they are too often directed at bringing the schools together from the top down, rather than from the bottom up. The authors sit in their studies and attempt to reduce the "Unconscious" to "associative learning" in broad general terms. They may even go so far as to show how evidence gleaned from human beings lying on the couch is consistent with experimental evidence culled from dogs in a soundproof room. But for really critical testing of their own theory they almost always return to their laboratories and repeat with minor variations the experiments on which it was originally based.

Even within a single field this tendency to repeat the classical experiment delays progress toward greater generality and completeness. Ever since the learning people discovered that rats could find their way through a maze, hecatombs have run faster and faster through more and more ·complex patterns, like so many red queens hoping that, if they only ran fast enough, learning theory would stay in the same place, and everyone would have his reward. Other rats have jumped to avoid punishment, pigeons have pecked at levers for random rewards, sheep have developed neuroses, and psychologists have got professorships. The cumulative record is impressively large, but somehow we are left unsatisfied.

Perhaps our dissatisfaction stems from the lack of clear relationships between the laboratory situations and what we experience in everyday life. The great bulk of the well controlled work has for good reasons been concentrated on relatively simple stimulus-response situations. Knowledge of "classical" and "operant conditioning" has an obvious relevance to certain limited real life situations encountered in child rearing or the design of slot machines, but both categories are perceived by most of us as special cases. When most of us think of learning in the everyday sense, we are much more likely to refer to the "multiple response learning" involved in skills like playing the piano or the "cognitive" learning which leads, say, to a mastery of physics. These categories have been singularly resistant to laboratory analysis, perhaps because no one has been sufficiently resourceful in developing appropriate techniques for their investigation.

What are the reasons for this rapid proliferation of theory and for the intensity with which the followers of particular theories defend their limited positions? Three rather closely related considerations present themselves. The first is the natural wish of any young science to find a dignified place for itself in the intellectual world. Second is the sense of urgency to get on with the solution of human problems. As discussed above this sense of urgency grows naturally from our poignant awareness of the shortness of human life. Third is the need to allay the anxieties of those who must practice the arts of psychotherapy and management. And under management let us include a wide range of activity from bringing up children to the governing of a great nation.

There is no need to belabor the first point. It is common knowledge that there is a hierarchy among the sciences, based in large part on the generality and rigor of their principal theories. Physics leads the procession with $E = MC^2$ emblazoned on its banner, chemistry follows in the van holding aloft the Mendeleeff table and the theory of the chemical bond, biology proudly gathers around the standard set by evolution. Even anthropology hopes that the forces latent in the concept of culture will gain it at least a modest place in the parade of the hard sciences. Nobody likes to be thought of as soft. No wonder psychology continues to search for some overarching generalization which will bring all the vagaries of man into a single explanatory pattern.

It would be foolish to attempt to cure psychology of its wish to generalize. This entirely normal appetite is bound to be good for the organism in the long run. But it may allay unnecessary suffering along the way if we bear in mind two points. The hard sciences needed about 3,000 years to get where they are today, and they dealt with much simpler material. If psychology, which is only 100 years old, compares itself with physics before Galileo or biology before Darwin, it should feel more than satisfied with its status. So long as it takes precautions to follow sound scientific means, the principle of gradualness insures the ends.

Our second and third explanations of the tendency to premature theorizing are closely related to one another, and in turn grow out of a close relationship between theory and practice. Such relationships are common in science, but there are certain peculiarities in the relationship as it exists in psychology which deserve special comment. Medicine has had a long experience in combining a theoretical science with a practical art, and this experience may help us in identifying certain dangers and prescribing appropriate precautions.

But first, in order to clarify a point which may be worrying you, let me say that I am not one of those who is concerned about competition between psychology and medicine for the right to take care of patients with personality disorders—aside, of course, from those strictly biological abnormalities in which medicine has demonstrated competence. After all, there is nothing in the record to show that medicine is any better than anybody else in dealing with functional neurotics.

Medicine does demonstrate, moreover, that there are great advantages in a close association between those who do pure or basic research and those who practice the art based on such research. The spectacular advances of modern medicine largely date from the time that the basic sciences became incorporated in medical schools as full-time disciplines. Numerous examples can be given of how the empirical findings of practitioners have become food for theoretical reflection and vice versa. Without the opportunity to test the value of its newly developed instruments against the realities of mental disturbance, psychology could never find the measure of its strengths and weaknesses. Furthermore, the growing association between medical psychiatry and clinical psychology can hardly fail to widen the outlook and sharpen the experience of each side.

Let no one cast doubt on the value of this association by asking whether clinical psychology is really useful in the sense that it does more "good" than harm. For one thing it is too early to say, and in any case its existence can be thoroughly justified by the traditional relationship between other practical arts and their related sciences. As the astronomer Kepler said 400 years ago: "Nature which has given to every animal the means of subsistence, has given astrology to astronomy." Several years ago a distinguished psychologist pointed out to me that medicine was allowed a dignified place in society for thousands of years before it could demonstrate that its ministrations really did much good. In his opinion the long history of excessive bleedings, purgings, and counter-irritations was amply justified by the support they gave the few inquiring minds who together finally built the medical edifice we profit from today. Enlightened by these sobering reflections no conscientious medical man would wish to deny the sister profession of psychology its right to try its hand at practical problems.

What worries one are the quantitative aspects of the recent *drang nach klinik*. So many have gone so far so fast that one wonders if there is anyone left to do basic work. Even most of the professors one knows seem to spend at least half their time advising some industrial outfit or government service on how to handle its practical problems.

In addition to this drawing off of talent from more basic matters, overemphasis of the practical operates in other more subtle ways to inhibit the advance of knowledge. Medicine in its occasional moments of soul searching has become aware of the dangers of being sought after. When the whole world knocks on your door, it is difficult to avoid the impression that you have something very special on the ball. "Power corrupts," but the flattered illusion of power corrupts even more completely. Why bother to seek out the weaknesses and ineptitudes of your techniques if everyone else thinks they are wonderful? And this in turn brings us back to one of our explanations for the intensity with which the various schools of psychology defend their particular theories.

The will to believe in a new hypothesis which appears to explain a whole area of behavior is very great. It may become an uncontrollable faith when the theory forms the background for practical intervention in human affairs. If we may allow ourselves to become Freudian for a moment, we may say that the subconscious anxieties of those who have to make decisions regarding other people are almost overwhelming. No one has ever given a satisfactory answer to Cain's famous question. There is, therefore, an element of presumption in all psychotherapy and in all political action. The conscientious therapist and all but the most cynical governors *must* feel that their methods have some sort of theoretical validity. Thus it has probably been a considerable misfortune that Freudian psychology was swept so soon into therapeutic practice and that the ideas of Pavlov fitted so neatly into the Communist thesis that all the troubles of man are the result of a pernicious social system. For so it came to pass that in America any attempt at disinterested exploration of the Freudian hypothesis is a threat to the personal security of a large number of therapists, teachers, and other practicing experts. In Russia, similar attempts to explore the limitations of conditioned reflex theory have become crimes against the state. In both instances, research has for the most part become a matter of confirming the Master's theory by repeating with minor and inconsequential modifications the Master's original observations.

Overemphasis of the practical may also contribute to the splitting of psychology into competing schools by encouraging premature attention to differences between individuals and to frank abnormalities of behavior. The scientific method, if it is a method, was devised to detect regularities in nature. Its triumphs have almost all been made by focusing on what a given set of events has in common and rigorously rejecting everything else. But as we seek to apply the scientific method to human beings, it often turns out that we are more interested in knowing how men differ from one another than in determining their uniformities. This tempts us to use the scientific method in ad hoc interpretations for which it was not designed.

Medicine has been familiar with this problem for some time, and the dichotomy between uniformity and individual difference is what underlies the frequently heard cliché that medicine is both a science and an art. So far, however, the great triumphs of medicine have all been in the scientific part. The art has shown little change from the time of Hippocrates. But we need not despair. Although it may be wrong to look to science for *immediate* help with the problem of individuality, the development of modern scientific medicine shows that an intensive search for the regularities and uniformities in human biology ultimately does provide us with means for describing and understanding individual differences. Knowledge of normal biochemistry, for example, provides the *ground* against which the various *figures* of abnormal variation stand out clearly. Modern bacteriology, which began on the assumption that all men were more or less equal in their responses to invading organisms, finally provides the tools for discovering why some children come down with every infection in the community, while others escape with the usual quota of the childhood exanthemas and a cold or two a year. As an entirely unexpected dividend, the science of immunology, by asking itself why organs cannot be easily transplanted from one individual to another except in the case of identical twins, has given us an extraordinarily precise means of describing individual differences in terms of protein chemistry.

Psychology has made similar advances in limited areas like learning, sensation, and perception by looking for uniformity in normal populations; but it remains difficult to talk for any length of time about personality without referring to abnormality. In other words, most of our knowledge of personality structure comes from contemplation of individual differences rather than from a search for regularity. Indeed there seems no good explanation of why most people function as well as they do. All of them have had less than perfect mothers and fathers, and all of them are subjected from time to time to severe psychological stress. Feelings of hostility, inferiority, and dependency are the lot of every one of us. Why do most people bear them so well and others succumb so easily? Nobody knows. Worse than that, nobody, except a few middle-aged psychiatrists, disillusioned with the neat formulas of their training days, seems to care.

One is reminded here of Judge Coates in Cozzens' *The Just and the Unjust.* "Every day is a miracle," he said to his son, "[To keep the world running] is on the face of it, impossible. Well, every day we do it." Perhaps the psychology of personality would be further along if it knew more about Judge Coates even at the cost of knowing somewhat less about Little Hans.

Antidotes

Having welcomed the advantages of a close relationship between theory and practice and identified some of its dangers, what can we prescribe as an antidote to the latter? In the first place one may suggest some simple precautions to protect the basic science of psychology. Medicine had to learn them the hard way, since it had been a practical profession for millennia before it became a science. As pointed out above, its recent period of real progress began a hundred years ago when the basic medical sciences acquired institutional form with the establishment of full-time chairs in anatomy and physiology. Since then the trend has been towards the greater and greater detachment of teachers and research workers from the practical art, so that now every branch of the profession has its cadre of academic people giving essentially full time to the advancement of knowledge.

Psychology appears to have gone at the thing the other way around. It began with the pure science and waited until very recent times to become a profession. Soon it must protect itself from the danger that the practical side may overgrow the basic or theoretical, as a result of the enormous momentum gained in the past two decades. The pure of heart should think twice before accepting that attractive consulting position with industry or the interesting committee just formed to consider the psychological aspects of the design of space ships. If they do not, the profession may soon find itself where medicine was in 1750 with little basic science and scant progress.

In the second place, those psychologists who are earnestly and quite properly bent on developing the practical art should give up looking to theory to secure them against personal anxiety. Such self-denial would have two salutary effects. It would take the pressure off the theorists and allow them more freedom to question, alter, or extend existing formulations. And on the other hand it would turn the attention of practical people to seeking their proper sanction in practical results.

In spite of the large amount of practical clinical psychology now being done, there is astonishingly little in the literature to show that real practical results are actually achieved. It almost seems as if psychology had become "applied" without becoming "pragmatic" in the sense of adapting pragmatic criteria for the establishment of the truth of its propositions.

And this thought brings us to a few words about the utility of naïveté. It can be demonstrated that medicine, most notably perhaps in the case of the infectious diseases, has made astonishing progress by adopting an over-simplified view of causality. Perhaps it was simply lucky to grow up in an unsophisticated era when no one took David Hume's billiard balls very seriously, questioned the validity of the inductive method, or reflected on the proposition that everything is probably related to everything else in some multivariable system with lots of feedback. Maybe the explanation lies in the fact that most medical men have been relatively simple minded souls anxious to do something to help mankind.

Whatever the reason, medical men have found it congenial to assume that they could find something called *The Cause* of a particular disease. If one looks at the history of any particular disease, one finds that the notion of its cause has varied with the state of the art. In general the procedure has been to select as *The Cause* that element in the situation which one could do the most about. In many cases it turned out that, if one could take away this element or reduce its influence, the disease simply disappeared or was reduced in severity. This was certainly desirable, and it seemed sensible enough to say that one had got at the cause of the condition. Thus in ancient and medieval times malaria as its name implies was thought to be due to the bad air of the lowlands. As a result, towns were built on the tops of hills, as one notices in much of Italy today. The disease did not disappear, but its incidence and severity were reduced to a level consistent with productive community life.

At this stage it seemed reasonable enough to regard bad air as the cause of malaria, but soon the introduction of quinine to Europe from South America suggested another approach. Apparently quinine acted on some situation within the patient to relieve and often to cure him completely. Toward the end of the last century the malarial parasite was discovered in the blood of patients suffering from the disease. The effectiveness of quinine was explained by its ability to eliminate this parasite from the blood. The parasite now became *The Cause*, and those who could afford the cost of quinine and were reasonably regular in their habits were enabled to escape the most serious ravages of the disease. It did not disappear as a public health problem, however; and further study was given to the chain of causality. These studies were shortly rewarded by the discovery that the parasite was transmitted by certain species of mosquitoes. For practical purposes *The Cause* of epidemic malaria became the Mosquito, and attention was directed to control of its activities.

Entertainingly enough, however, malaria has disappeared from large parts of the world without anyone doing much about it at all. The fens of Boston and other northern cities still produce mosquitoes capable of transmitting the parasite, and people carrying the organism still come to these areas from time to time; but it has been many decades since the last case of the disease occurred locally. Observations such as this point to the probability that epidemic malaria is the result of a nicely balanced set of social and economic, as well as biological, factors, each one of which has to be present at the appropriate level. We are still completely unable to describe these sufficient conditions with any degree of accuracy, but we know what to do in an epidemic area because we have focused attention on three or four of the most necessary ones.

It may have been naive to regard these necessary conditions as *causes*. It might have been wiser in some philosophical sense to have perceived epidemic malaria as the result of a complex interaction of unidentified social, economic, and biological factors. But there are times when it is well to remember Santayana's penetrating line: "It is not wisdom to be only wise."

Has not this brief analogy a bearing on some of the situations encountered in psychology? Take the problem of delinquency, for example. There is a general impression, presumably quite true, that delinquency is the result of a number of social, economic, and biological factors. But no one has been able to describe in any detail what they are or how they work together to produce the deplorable situation which is observed. Even if we could describe them, it is not obvious that such a description would help much in solving the problem. Complex social and economic situations are notoriously difficult to alter very quickly.

But there are other more basic reasons for not encouraging practical people to become too preoccupied with the overall complexity of human situations. As Warren Weaver has pointed out, science has not yet developed effective ways of dealing with organized complexity. For some time to come it will probably have to confine itself to breaking down complex wholes into constituent parts which can be dealt with separately. Preoccupation with complexity tends to distract attention from the search for the one or more necessary conditions which might be controlled or eliminated to bring about a marked improvement in the total situation of which they are a part. Worse than this, the holistic approach may actually offer a refuge or escape to those who are reluctant to get down to the hard work characteristic of more gradual attitudes.

It is not my business to propose solutions for delinquency or for any other psychological problem. It does, however, seem reasonable to recommend that attention be given to following up whatever concrete leads there now are with primary emphasis on variables that can be manipulated in some way. One of the drawbacks to the disproportionate amount of attention given to early parental influences, broken homes, and the like is that so little can be done about them. Such hypotheses not only contribute little to practical control but they may actually inhibit more potentially productive research. Attention is directed away from the delinquent subject who is here in our hands to shadowy characters from the past who often enough cannot be identified, let alone manipulated in any way.

And it should be emphasized that this regard for getting one's hands on a manipulatable variable is not exclusively or even primarily based on immediate practical considerations. The best way of getting what L. J. Henderson used to call "an intuitive feel for one's material" is to follow what happens when one pushes an important variable one way or another. And without this intuitive feel neither practice nor theory can get very far.

Those of you who have remained alert through all this may recall our third reason for being concerned about the present state of psychological theory. It was said, somewhat flatfootedly perhaps, that, so far, psychology seems unable to produce theories of the same beauty and elegance as those of the natural sciences. This handicap, if indeed there is one, operates in two ways. It reduces the pleasure of being a psychologist, and it tends to reduce the attractiveness of the field for those who might be capable of making better theories.

Now beauty and elegance are a matter of opinion; and there may be those who find learning theory, or Gestalt, or Freudian psychodynamics just as beautiful and elegant as $F = MA$, $E = mc^2$, or the rules of Mendelian genetics. But such views are not widely held. Nor is the difficulty solely because the classical theories are mathematical in form, whereas most psychological theories are not. There have been theories of great generality and power which have never been reduced to mathematics and which do possess a certain beauty—a bit roughhewn perhaps, but still very satisfying to the beholder. Evolution may be the most notable example.

The beauty of scientific theories is in large part due to a blend of simplicity and completeness, and it is undeniable that the mathematical formula is the easiest way to express simplicity and completeness. But one does not have to be all that simple in order to produce esthetic pleasure. It *is* necessary, however, to be reasonably complete. To use an older expression, a theory has to "save" the phenomena with which it purports to deal or it is not much of a theory.

By and large, psychological theories do not leave the beholder with a sense of satisfaction over the extent to which they save the phenomena. There is usually an element of tour de force in the salvation achieved. Classical learning theory, for example, seems discouragingly incomplete, partly because it is so utilitarian. Animals never do anything except when motivated by a base desire for food, or sex, or a craven wish to avoid pain. There is no obvious place for play activities or for maneuvers which increase, rather than decrease, elemental drives—courtship for example.

True, all these matters including even neurotic aberrations can be brought to fit the Procrustian bed, but there is an element of pulling and hauling about these demonstrations which is inconsistent with the beauty of good theories.

Freudian theory obtains a greater comprehensiveness but only at the expense of suggesting that the whole thing is done with wires and mirrors. If a given act is inconsistent with a sound ego adjusting itself to reality, it can easily be palmed off as the expression of an unconscious id or the over-compensation of the conscientious superego. The brilliant comprehensiveness and internal consistency may have been gained at too great a sacrifice of rigor.

I must confess that I have no ready therapy at hand for this defect. Medicine does teach us, however, that it is possible to live for long periods of time, and reasonably happily, without theories of great elegance and beauty. In trying to meet this situation let us paraphrase Thucydides and do what we can while suffering what we must. After all, even the classical hard sciences are not all theoretical elegance and beauty. Physics has its strange particles, and biology has lots of pretty messy areas like lipoid chemistry or blood clotting.

Most scientists in other fields can compensate for a lack of theoretical elegance by immediate sensory satisfactions derived from their daily work of fact gathering. It seems harder for psychologists to do so. The elementary facts in the physical sciences are concrete entities which present themselves immediately to the senses. In many cases the work involved in gathering such facts has not been work at all. At the very least it has been fun; often it has been a deep esthetic satisfaction. The laboratory of the early astronomers was one of the most beautiful sights known to man. The early map makers of the skies combined natural history with poetry and mysticism to draw the constellations which aid the navigator and delight the soul. Ever since, the astronomer has enjoyed the same sense of charm and wonder "when a new planet swims into his ken"; even the earthbound discoverers, the geographers, cartographers, and geologists—Stout Cortez and all his men—"have gazed at each other with a wild surmise" as they stared at each new Pacific. How interesting it is in these days, when scientists are striving to convince a skeptical public that science is an art as well as a craft, that Keats, 150 years ago, should have turned to science for the metaphor which revealed his deep feeling for the power of poetry.

Biologists have always delighted in the beauty of the materials with which they have dealt, and the profession is still largely recruited from boys and girls who collect butterflies, watch birds, or press flowers for the sheer pleasure of it. The early anatomists of the Renaissance were half painter or sculptor, and the artist was half anatomist.

Psychology, insofar as it is different from biology and ascends from sensory physiology to that obscure realm in which bits of data are put together into perceptions, memories, and complex motor acts, does not present itself immediately to the senses of the observer. The mind is after all an inference, and it is hard to study the morphology of an inference. By the very nature of its material, psychology has been deprived of the morphological phase which has provided such a solid groundwork for the other sciences and, let us add, so much satisfaction to the born morphologists.

The elementary facts of psychology are for the most part happenings or outputs. They can be observed, recorded, and perhaps even counted; but they ordinarily cannot be felt, or smelled, or enjoyed for themselves. Worse than this, single psychological facts are rarely very interesting or significant by themselves. There needs to be a lot of them, and they have to be treated statistically. Whatever may be said about statistics—and lots of things have been said which I will not repeat—reliance on statistics tends to separate the scientist from an intuitive sense of his material. Instead of giving us a direct sense of cause and effect, they express such relationships by backhandedly remarking how unlikely it is that A was related to B by pure chance.

All the sciences have their portion of drudgery and frustration, but in most the drudgery and frustration are mitigated by the incidental sensory pleasures provided by the elementary data. Stars shine with a lovely blue light, magnetic fields produce intriguing patterns in iron filings, hematoxylin and eosin blend beautifully on the microscopic slide. The rat requires a thousand trials to reach criterion. Where is the compensating reward for the drudgery implied by such experiments?

Perhaps some psychologists are showing the way to a happier life by becoming more biological in outlook and method. One notes here with particular satisfaction the growing liaison between psychology and ethology. The ethologists have certainly had a lot of fun with the birds and the bees, while the learning theorists have submitted themselves to punishments, deprivations, drive reductions, and the cutting edge of controlled experiment. One thinks of these schools as the cavaliers and roundheads of the behavioral sciences. Clearly each has a lot to give to the other. Let us bless this marriage with *King Solomon's Ring* and look for hybrid vigor among the F_1s.

Less dramatic and colorful perhaps, but just as promising, is the growing relationship between the learning and conditioning people on the one hand and the neurophysiologists on the other. Here there is austerity and a certain classicism on both sides. Neurophysiologists bring a rich offering of a prestigeful technology replete with multiple channels, controlled parameters, and microsecond rise times—the whole illuminated by re-splendent cathode rays. Psychology brings its awareness that the brain is the organ of the mind and is thus something more than an exaggerated synapse. Already, cooperation between the two groups has produced two items which look suspiciously like breakthroughs: the production of motivation and avoidance by direct stimulation of the brain (a discovery in large part due to the fertile imagination of Hebb) and the identification of electrical signs of conditioning and extinction. To earthy types like me, both of these discoveries have the merit of giving some sort of material substance to what have hitherto been rather misty and abstract concepts. Perhaps the expression "material substance" is too strong a one for the context. It may well be more accurate, and more to the point, to say that both of these discoveries have brought basic elements of the learning process under much more direct observation and control than they ever were before. How nice it is that these developments promise to make psychology more fun at the same time that they make it more productive.

As I have wandered through this hour ruminating here and there on such portions of your large, complicated, and exciting field as have for one reason or another brought themselves to the attention of an observer from across the interdisciplinary fence, I hope I have not sounded captious or too critical. A medical man, especially one trained as a neurophysiologist, has every reason to be humble and sympathetic as he stands before those with the courage to take on the mind and all its foibles as a subject of serious study. If I have mentioned what appears to me as a lack of beauty or elegance in the facts or theories of psychology, it was only to express sympathy and encouragement for those who must trudge along so difficult a path unrelieved by the wild flowers and lovely views which so often have helped the pursuers of the sister sciences.

If I have stressed the principle of gradualness and naivete, it is only in the knowledge that the art is long. The brilliant beacon lights of physics, or of philosophical speculation on the wholeness of wholes, may be less certain guides than the series of inconspicuous and often not very neatly painted buoys by which biology has guided itself to some understanding of the body if not yet of the soul of man.

Finally it should be said that it makes no sense to criticize a science for not knowing more than it does. This would seem to be particularly true of psychology. Everybody else, prophets, priests, philosophers, doctors, lawyers, the man in the street—ever since the time when there were no streets—has tried to understand the behavior of man. And it is now more true than it ever was that man's greatest mystery is man himself. Why should not science have its chance? May it pursue it free from pressure for quick results.

And just in case you feel like brushing off these comments as those of a philanthropoid who should never have been allowed out of his Ivory Tower, let me quote a practical politician, Theodore Heuss, President of the German Republic: "We have the obligation to free the scientist from the nervousness of this era and to put the gift of time again at his disposal."

21 | *The Social Indifference of Psychology*[1]

RICHARD A. LITTMAN

I wish to analyze the following problem. When colleagues in other disciplines (mainly sociology, anthropology, political science, and economics) turn to psychology for help they are disappointed and, indeed, often aggrieved. What they begin to read with enthusiasm they put down with depression. What seemed promising turns out to be sterile, palpably trivial, or false and, in any case, a waste of time. Nor is this reaction restricted only to persons in other disciplines; it is also to be found in psychologists. In any case, there usually ensues a loud complaint either in the form of a remedy or an epitaph.

The search for help and enlightenment frequently arises when there is some practical need to be met in industry, education, or public affairs: "See the psychologist, he deals with people." As the penetration of psychology into practical affairs increases, as psychological engineering extends beyond clinical, educational, and man-machine problems we can only expect that more demands for aid will be addressed to psychologists. However, I do not want to deal here with problems having an engineering focus. I am more concerned about the vaguer but, in the long run, more important problem of understanding or, rather, lack of understanding and appreciation of the thoughtways of psychologists. At some point or other,

From R. A. Littman, Psychology: The socially indifferent science, *Amer. Psychologist*, 1961, *16*, 232–236. Reprinted by permission of the author, the *American Psychologist*, and the American Psychological Association.

[1] This paper is a revision of a talk given at the University of Oregon. The talk, in its turn, was based upon portions of an uncompleted manuscript devoted to the analysis of psychological concepts. I am grateful for the suggestions of D. Peabody and E. Rosen.

even the most sociologically or culturally oriented psychologist comes a cropper on this score; there is an undefinable, "*je ne sais quoi*" quality to his judgments or formulations which proves distasteful to his "foreign" colleagues (and even himself) and which leads to some form of rejection.

Commonly, the criticism or rejection takes the following form: "But you (I) have left out the person, his culture, and his social context." In recent years there have been attempts to remedy this (Asch, 1952; Heider, 1958; Sears, 1951; Sullivan, 1953) and there will surely be many more such efforts. The interpersonal approach to psychology is ascendent in much of psychology today and is likely to remain so indefinitely. So, it seems that we are on the road to quieting and, even, seducing our critics. Nevertheless, I predict that underneath the rosy glow of future intellectual camaraderie our relations are likely to be as disappointing as they now appear to be. I do not believe that we are presently correcting a flaw by studying social behavior more intensively; we have always studied social behavior and are only doing more of it now. We are, to be sure, more aware of studying it but that seems to have brought exhilaration rather than insight. In general, I have not been able to get any sense that matters are more satisfactory beyond the fact that psychologists now seem able to co-operate more effectively with people from other disciplines.

The reason for all this is a simple one, I believe, but it is one that psychologists, as well as persons who come to us for help and enlightenment, have not understood. It is that psychology is a *science without social content*. I am not saying without social significance, just content. The distinction is straightforward, I believe. The social significance of a science or body of knowledge and belief depends on the extent to which it influences the web of contemporary cultural practices. Twenty-one years ago nuclear physics was socially significant only within the framework of the employment and communication of physicists, pulp makers, printers, post offices, librarians, and science fictionists. Twenty years ago it was no longer a parochial matter. In general, I would think that every science has some social significance though what it is has to be under continual review.

Social content is another matter. What do I mean by it? I refer to the concrete social facts of relations between individuals who have social statuses and roles, e.g., father-mother, employer-employee, citizen-representative, teacher-pupil, thief-policeman, scientist-layman, and the many complicated structures that have been developed to regulate or to otherwise influence the course of these relations. In trying to understand them as social meanings the interests of many persons focus upon these matters. There could not be, for example, a political science unless there were the equivalents of state and law; there could be no anthropology or sociology were there no patterning of interaction, e.g., custom, kinships, institutions and offices, and the complex items of material culture. The important thing, therefore, for our sister sciences who are also devoted to the study of social behavior, is that theories and hypotheses dealing with these social facts are themselves couched in language which contains or refers directly to such social items. The social facts are the main ingredients of inquiry, and interest stems from and toward them, in and of themselves.

I believe the picture is very different for much, if not all, of psychology. Our theoretical expressions need not contain nor refer in any essential way to the concrete "substances" of social activity. In other words, expressions such as the following are not particularly psychological: "drinking from a milk bottle," "kissing one's mother," "farmer," "playing saxophone in a dance band," "going to the football game," "complaining to one's Congressman," "answering 'Yes' to questionnaire Item 68 ('The father should have the main responsibility for punishing children')," "seeing a devil on a mountain top," "saying a prayer for a newly-married couple," "having a tantrum over a broken balloon," "getting drunk with one's boss," "fishing from a Cajun punt," "being worried about your cousin's opinion," and "wearing a breech clout." The content of each of these expressions is culturally determined in some way. Each one refers to some sort of institutionalized characteristic so that it can be understood only from a social or cultural vantage point. And yet, there is something psychological about them all. If we can come to understand what this "something" is it may reduce, if not resolve, the ambiguity of our relations with other disciplines and hence their attitudes toward us. Such an understanding is likely to free the thinking of psychologists, too.

In view of my expressed interest in having a psychology that deals with complex forms of behavior, is not such a proposal a paradoxical one? Indeed, since it is my view that an effective psychology *should* be applicable to social behavior, is it not contradictory to characterize psychology in a way that appears to exclude such matters?

Now, there is no question that for certain purposes almost every action of people *must* be regarded from a social or cultural point of view. There is almost nothing about an intact human or domesticated animal that makes much sense unless we see the way that it is tied to how his companions or masters behave. Insofar as there are analogous species consistencies (Beach, 1959) it is probably true in a rather similar way for every vertebrate and many invertebrates. It is, indeed, almost illogical to speak of animals in any other way.

How then can psychology be indifferent with respect to social or cultural content? This is a rhetorical question, intended to convey my opinion that psychology has been and is now in such a condition, and my belief that it will and should remain so. What I am proposing could be called a thesis of methodological individualism. I believe that psychology has been and ought to be mainly interested in the properties and processes of individual organisms. On the other hand, I also believe that many of these properties and processes cannot be discovered or understood if organisms are studied in pure solitude. It is unfortunate that psychologists once believed that studying an isolated organism would yield all the significant things there are to know about him. But it is equally unfortunate if psychologists come to believe that because they study the organism in a social setting—which is the kind of setting for which biological and social evolution have selected almost all forms of animal life—that they are therefore necessarily studying social content in the sense that I am using the term.

Now, since I am trying to be brief I am sure there will be much misunderstanding. So let me point to an outcome of the predicament I believe many psychologists are getting into. They appear to believe that as they work more and more intensively in the realm of social behavior, that sociology and anthropology will wither away or coalesce with psychology; they seem less sure of political science and economics. Now, such a withering away can come about only by showing that either the facts dealt with by these disciplines are really not facts or else by offering a radically different explanation of them. I do not believe the former is true and, in the event of the latter, then these psychologists are really doing anthropology or sociology. What then is their psychology to be like?

Let me now state why I believe that psychology not only can, but in fact must, have this indifference. The reason is that "socially" characteristic and determined features differ from society to society; indeed, sociologists and anthropologists speak of subcultures and subsocieties, which they pursue right down to the level of the family or some one of the many significant dyadic units of social behavior. In their fine detail—which is the level at which scientists have to work because research, experimentation, and analysis are always in terms of particulars even though the goal may be generalization—the social and cultural contents are therefore very different in different places throughout the world. They are also different under different circumstances in any particular society. Yet there they are, patterned, regularly established in each member of each generation, and, in many cases, predictable as to their changes.

People in different societies are therefore really different from one another in many fundamental ways in the sense that the content of their behavior is radically divergent. *Eating?* Some people eat with their fingers, others with utensils; some people eat no meat, others eat only meat; some people eat openly and in groups, while others eat only in withdrawn solitude. Some people will eat only what they produce, others will eat only if others procure and prepare their food. Some people will starve to death for a principle or cause, others will kill and even eat human flesh to survive. *Social graces?* Some people are expected to be polite and greet strange women, others must avoid strange (or, in some cases, familiar) women, on penalty of death; one must shake hands with a stranger, one must not do so; one must not covet his friend's wife, one must accept a friend's offer of his wife for sexual relations; one must stand erect to greet a personage, one must prostrate himself before such an individual; to be presentable one's teeth should be clean and even, one must file his teeth so they resemble a comb; one must smile when sad, one must be inert or ranting when bereft; and so on.

How can organisms who differ so radically in the gross and fine details of their behavior all be members of the same species? If the social content of behavior alone were used this would indeed be a difficult judgment to make. Yet, immediately one asks such questions as: "Even though languages that are learned are vastly different, do the same principles underlly their acquisition?" "Though people in different societies have different visions and dreams (including that they have them at all with any frequency) are there similarities in the factors producing them?" "Why do people in different parts of the world form groups?" "Whether their parents beat them or fondle them, ignore them or regulate every aspect of their lives, why do children remain attached to them for as long as they do or why do they not remain attached as long in one society as in another?" "Why do people gamble?" And so on. As soon as one asks such questions, it is clear that there must be some common, universal characteristics of men that are involved in cultural behavior and which all cultures utilize, so to speak, in transmitting their own peculiar contents; *but, these universal characteristics do not determine the contents in their cultural detail.* It is obvious that all these differences that we have outlined among people are less radical than the differences that exist among various species and phyla. Yet it is clear that these different organisms also are, in many respects, like one another psychologically; and, for the most part, *these are exactly the same respects in which culturally different people are also alike.*

The sorts of things we have pointed to above are usually treated under such labels as "the psychology of Oriental peoples," ". . . of the proper Bostonian," ". . . the Frenchman," ". . . the Arab," "the criminal," "the physician," "wife," "athlete," "racing horse," "bird," "spaniel," "cockroach," etc. In this usage, the expression "the psychology of" refers either to the distinctive cultural features that distinguish each ethnic group or social role type, or the distinctive species characteristics. In similar fashion, the geneticist may speak of "the genetics of" the fly, the dog, the bacterium, and the naturalist may speak of "the mating behavior of" the stickleback, the finch, or the loon; they will both indicate, by so doing, that there are very important details in which the genetics or mating behaviors are similar within groups and different between them. But they also mean that there is something about genetics or mating behavior which transcends these differences.

I do not mean anything mysterious by the term transcending; it refers only to the fact that there are certain features in genetical or mating processes which are very much alike in spite of obvious and, in some respects, important species differences. Hence, the geneticist will speak of the ratios holding between certain dominant and recessive characteristics though, in the one case, he may refer to the eye color of a fly and, in another case, to the roughness of coat of a guinea pig. The naturalist will study the sort of activities that occur before, during, or after fertilization —the very term "fertilization," for example, is introduced because the mode of fertilization (the species content, so to speak) varies so markedly. But it would be a mistake to say that the task of genetics is to study flies or guinea pigs; that is what naturalists and sanitarians do.

In the same way, the psychologist studies speech (but to do so properly, he must deal with different tongues), learning (though he must always study something being learned), perception (and there are many different things to be seen), fear (so many things to be afraid of), love (so many ways of love), beliefs (so many kinds), or motives (like dragon's teeth). Every member of every society displays certain characteristic ways of behaving, shows an ability to do certain sorts of things, has various beliefs and opinions, knows certain sorts of things, cannot conceive of matters that come easily to people in other societies, and so on. Each opinion, belief, item of knowledge, movement of limb, utterance, fear, desire, problematic situation, standard, preference, and gait is, in some sense, culturally "labeled" or "tagged." There is no mistaking it and it is likely that psychologists (particularly those concerned with psychometric and scaling problems) should pay more attention to such cultural definitions. But each of these culturally tagged items has some general characteristic or property that is not so tagged. Regardless of cultural content, every attitude is like every other; as I understand the term, every attitude has some degree of strength, each attitude is directed at an object, and each one is favorable or unfavorable toward its object. Similarly, beliefs have certain culturally contentless features that are true of all beliefs, anywhere, any time. The psychologist has concentrated on discovering these properties and working out their "behavior."

If this could not be done, it would not be possible to speak of, or identify, such things as attitudes, beliefs, memories, habits, motives, or, indeed, personality structure, in different societies. We would have only specialized cultural meanings which could not be compared. But as apples and oranges are both regarded as fruits, so praying to a spirit and pressing an electric switch reveal a belief (in this case, of the efficacy of a certain course of action). Psychology, I suggest, has been so far the science which deals with the abstract, universal, culturally contentless features of behavior which in almost all cases—and surely all the most interesting cases—are socially tagged, but which are best analyzed as properties of individual organisms.[2]

An interesting aspect of this problem is the fact that only through the study of diversified behavior has the psychologist come to appreciate the many dimensions of psychological activity. At one time, the notion of a universal human mind, the "psychic unity of mankind" (Bastian, Wundt) was a postulate of thinkers interested in man. But the version of mind they professed resembled far too much the mind of an eighteenth century German university professor; other thinkers who looked at people, at home and abroad, could not be satisfied with it for very long. Psychologists are now freed from this provincial view; for that, we have to thank the anthropologist, the sociologist, and the naturalist. For awhile, indeed, we were so impressed by the enormous differences among societies that a complete psychological relativism seemed to own the field. Now, however, balance has been restored, and we can see that relativism was with respect to cultural contents; we have salvaged for our study the rather abstract, general, psychological properties that characterize all humans, just as we have begun to find those which are characteristic of mammals and of vertebrates.

There should be no misunderstanding of the point I am making. Psychologists do study and must study things and activities possessing social content. There is no other way; even if we were to progress to the point where behavioral simulation techniques (Simon and Newhall, 1956) were as effective for human behavior as they appear to be for delivering the means to obliterate human behavior, the behavior to be simulated would bear cultural labels. It is only that psychology has been a science that abstracts out of all these content-characterized behaviors the concepts which form the jargons of its subdisciplines. I see no reason why psychology should change in this respect though, to be sure, I foresee the time (though not the date) when it will be subsumed under a broader reaching, general theory.

There is a moral to all this, though it is perhaps more for people outside

---

[2] It is worth noting that my account resembles "the other side of the coin" that Durkheim (1926) advocated. His point was that since man is everywhere the same and culture and society everywhere different, we cannot look to the nature of man to explain social phenomena. I believe his view too stringent, and I do not intend my argument, which is focused on psychology as a theoretical discipline, to imply that I feel psychology is therefore irrelevant to social behavior.

of psychology than for us in it. If someone is interested in social behavior he ought not rely upon or even trust the analysis that a psychologist makes of most of it. I am impressed with how naive and conventional my colleagues and I are when confronted with most social phenomena. We are ignorant of the historical dimensions of most social activity, we do not see the complex interweaving of institutions and arrangements, when we think of social meanings and facts we tend to deal with them in terms of their possessors, we substitute fancy for fact, preference for actuality— not, to be sure, that political scientists and sociologists do not do this too often, too. In general, psychologists tend to be like laymen when they confront social phenomena, particularly those that involve large scale patterns. And the reason for all of this is that the main areas of social activity are only the *place* where psychologists study interesting sorts of things, rather than being the *focus of inquiry*.

On the other hand, I believe it is true that most analysts of social phenomena posit incorrect or weak laws about individual humans. They seek out the ones which are couched in familiar, social, or cultural labels. They fail to recognize the potential of many concepts precisely because the psychologist deals with them in a parochial way—as, I know, I do—deals with them as sterilized, centrifuged preparations. In other words, much of the responsibility for finding out what the implications of psychological thinking for social phenomena are probably has to be done by nonpsychologists. With the exception of a small band, the applications that psychologists make are mainly technological and conservative (except for the area of race relations I believe that this is the case) and often trivial, if not foolish.

I do not want what I am saying to be construed as an argument against the search for, or application of, psychological knowledge in cultural or social behavior. Indeed, I hope and believe that psychological knowledge will be sought in, and applied to, social behavior. I am arguing that the formulations which psychologists have made and ought to continue making do not and need not contain explicit social or cultural terms to satisfy the relevance of psychology for understanding social behavior. In contrast, sociologists and anthropologists, who also study these same activities, try to formulate principles which do cover, or are couched in terms of, these contents; they, of course, seek to generalize them in their own peculiar ways. We differ from them in the properties we have elected to study and I see no way to ignore these differences as a source of the fundamental friction that our relations seem to generate. If we can insert as a heat conductor a suitable view of these differences in objectives and interests we ought, surely, to be able to render unto them what they want and to ourselves what we need.

References

Asch, S. E. *Social psychology*. Englewood Cliffs, N.J.: Prentice-Hall, 1952.
Beach, F. A. Experimental investigations of species-specific behavior. *Amer. Psychologist*, 1959, *15*, 1–19.
Durkheim, E. *The elementary forms of the religious life*. New York: Macmillan, 1926.
Heider, F. *The psychology of interpersonal relations*. New York: Wiley, 1958.
Sears, R. R. Social behavior and personality development. In T. Parsons and E. A. Shills (eds.), *Toward a general theory of action*. Cambridge, Mass.: Harvard Univ. Press, 1951, pp. 465–478.
Simon, H. A., and Newell, A. Models, their uses and limitations. In L. D. White (ed.), *The state of the social sciences*. Chicago: Univ. of Chicago Press, 1956, pp. 66–83. [Selection 4 in this volume.]
Sullivan, H. S. *The interpersonal theory of psychiatry*. New York: Norton, 1953.

22 | *Confusion in Attitudes Toward Clinical Theory*[1]

MELVIN H. MARX

A. The Dual Rôle of the Clinician

Certain basic difficulties in relation to problems of theory construction in clinical psychology seem to have arisen, in large part at least, from a failure to keep clearly separate the two functions of the clinician—practice and research (cf. Raimy, 1950). Stated more bluntly, they are the result of the clinician's tending to act as practitioner rather than scientist in regard to the problems of theory construction. It is the purpose of the present paper to point out and analyze several such sources of confusion in attitudes toward clinical theory and to make certain suggestions for resolution of the basic issues thus revealed. Consideration will be given to these

From M. H. Marx, Sources of confusion in attitudes toward clinical theory, *J. Gen. Psychol.*, 1956, *55*, 19–30. Reprinted by permission of the author, the *Journal of General Psychology*, and the Journal Press.

[1] The major part of this paper was presented in a symposium on the rôle of theory in the training of clinical psychologists at the Cleveland meetings of the Midwestern Psychological Association in April, 1952.

problems: *a*) nomothetic vs. idiographic activities, *b*) control of variables in observations, and *c*) levels of explanation in theory construction.

Before taking up these problems, some qualifying remarks need to be made. It is recognized that the dual scientist and practitioner rôle of the clinician is by no means the only important factor contributing to the problems to be discussed. It is also recognized that the points stressed, while fundamentally rather simple, nevertheless have implications which are neither simple nor easily resolved. They are advanced, at the risk of offending the scientific sensibilities of those clinicians who do not need to be reminded of them, on the basis of the fact that they seem to be so often lacking in clinical attitudes toward theory. Finally, the desirability of clinical theory construction is simply assumed, for the purposes of this paper, and no invidious comparisons with other clinical functions are intended.

B. The Nomothetic-Idiographic Issue

In many respects the issue raised by the opposition of nomothetic to idiographic objectives most clearly reveals the differential operation of the two major interests of the clinician. If one assumes the methodological continuity of clinical and non-clinical scientist, as seems necessary, then this apparent issue is easily resolved. This does not mean that it is necessary to question the importance of the individual in clinical work, nor the fact of his uniqueness, nor the value of idiographic techniques. The resolution depends instead upon a simple recognition that in clinical psychology both kinds of activities are necessary and useful, and that they serve different functions.

There does not seem to be any way around the proposition that science is concerned with *generalities* and *abstractions*, and that these depend upon comparisons of many cases. However, it may be suggested that more attention be paid to *nomothetic* problems involving *intra-organismic* development and organization. Principles of this nature are necessarily based upon similarities among individuals discovered as a result of intensive study of a number of individual subjects. They may be considered as complementary to the more common laws of general behavior functions, which are ordinarily based upon a large number of less intensive observations.

The best known examples of this type of nomothetic interest in intra-organismic development have been provided by Freud and other psychoanalysts (cf. Hartmann and Kris, 1945; Kris, 1947), although by no means all psychoanalytic propositions can be so classified. Another more recent example is Harlow's research on the orderly development of learning sets (1949). It is apparent that this kind of research not only involves a significantly more fundamental interest in the individual subject as such than is ordinarily present in learning studies but also requires a marked shift in the techniques of observation. In this respect it may be contrasted with the typical discrimination-learning experiment, in which the size of the sample is usually considered of more importance than the degree to which investigation of any one individual is carried.

A somewhat more complex example of the nomothetic interest in behavior development is provided by the interpretations of food hoarding in terms of the fusion of independently learned habits, developed by the writer after intensive observations of individual rats (Marx, 1950[a], 1950[b], 1951[a]). This kind of investigation differs from that exemplified by Harlow's learning-set study in that it more definitely attempts to describe the interrelations of general behavior principles as components in the development of more complex patterns of behavior. Fuller recognition of this type of nomothetic interest as complementary to the more commonly emphasized general function type of law would help to satisfy the clinical demand for more adequate scientific appreciation of the developmental factors in behavior.

Predictions about specific individuals, as such, are essential for the clinical practitioner, and for this reason the nomothetic-idiographic distinction has strongly appealed to practically-oriented clinicians. It is of course quite true that an adequate understanding of any one individual, or personality, depends upon a high degree of knowledge about that individual. However, it is impossible to see how, apart from its potential usefulness in relation to the nomothetic interest in personality development and organization, any basic scientific value can attach to such individualized knowledge. Scientific interests do not require information on any one case, per se, but on a type of case, or, in practically all instances, a relatively large group of such cases. As Hunt (1951) has clearly pointed out in connection with the application of probability theory to clinical practice, evaluation of a clinician is dependent not upon his ability to predict satisfactorily in any one case but rather upon his continuing efforts in a number of cases. Failure to make a clear distinction between the scientific objective of generalized understanding from this sort of "group" prediction and the practical clinical objective of particularized understanding from individual prediction has resulted in the acceptance and perpetuation of this pseudo issue.

C. The Problem of Controlled Observation

Perhaps the most important single factor acting to retard clinical theory is the lack of recognition of the necessity, in so far as the scientific phase of clinical activity is concerned, for controlled observations in determination of the answers to scientific questions.

The difficulty here arises largely because of a confusion between scientifically legitimate *sources* of hypotheses and *tests* of hypotheses. There are no scientific restrictions on the source of hypotheses. These may arise from uncontrolled observations—such as clinical insights—or controlled observations—such as scientific experiments. Furthermore, they may be mediated through exposure to reports of either type of observations—psychoanalytic reconstructions or literary masterpieces, on the one hand, and orthodox scientific papers, on the other. However, it is necessary to recognize that in regard to tests of scientific hypotheses only controlled observations are permissible. It is on this latter point, unfortunately, that many clinicians seem to disagree, if one is to judge them by their actions.

It must be emphasized that this distinction follows from the premise that the most important and irreducible distinction between science and non-science is the presence of some degree of control of relevant variables in observations. If this premise is disputed then obviously the arguments based upon it will not be acceptable. It is very difficult to see any alternative, however, if the term science is to be used in a meaningful sense—or to describe the essential activities of persons conventionally called scientists. Inquiry is scientific to the extent to which it successfully employs the method of controlled observation, and thus is able to reduce the natural ambiguity of events so as to permit more reliable assignment of observed consequences to selected antecedent conditions. This seems to be the criterion of science at bedrock level.

The fact that scientific activity also necessarily involves ingenuity in discovering critical problems and relevant variables, and in formulating testable hypotheses, must not be allowed to confuse this issue. None of these important functions is so conspicuously peculiar to the scientific method as the formal and deliberate attempt to isolate the influence of particular variables.

It must be stressed that controlled observation is by no means confined to the experiment, which approximates the ideal situation with deliberate and systematic manipulation of selected variables and effective neutralization—"control," or "holding constant"—of other presumably relevant ones. Naturalistic types of observation can be controlled, sometimes to a fairly satisfactory degree. After-the-fact analyses of data, with control achieved through purely statistical techniques, can also be made. Here it should be noted that the degree of confidence that is placed in interpretations of data so analyzed is in direct proportion to the extent to which particular predictions are successfully made in advance of the analysis. Finally, it is a reasonable hypothesis that some degree of control can be achieved in the psychoanalytic interview and similar clinical situations, although it must be admitted that this is an extremely difficult task and that the progress made to date in this respect has been disappointing.

If the clinical practitioner is seriously motivated to combine his service function with the collection of controlled data, he is confronted with almost insurmountable obstacles. His primary concern is the welfare of his client. This means that he will almost certainly need to entertain a succession of hypotheses concerning the particular problems of the client, and should be ready to modify these as the development of the case indicates. Thus faced with the problem of constantly shifting hypotheses to adjust to the changes in the counseling situation, the practicing clinician is in an excellent position to continue to formulate potentially fruitful hypotheses through a combination of inference and intuition; but he is in an especially poor position to stop and make an adequately controlled test of any single hypothesis. Unless special steps are taken to institute more effective controls through a more or less formalized research program within the clinical situation the practitioner is unlikely to make significant contributions to scientific evidence.

Apart from the difficulty of making controlled observations, there is a more general attitudinal influence that the practitioner rôle seems to have on the clinician as scientist. The inertia of his hypothetical manner of thinking has serious consequences if this manner of thinking is transferred *without corrective* to problems of basic theory. Hypotheses long entertained but inadequately tested come to be regarded as supported, and may be used as premises upon which further hypotheses, even more remote from their empirical referents, are based. The dangers of this situation should be apparent.

The fact that so many clinicians do attempt to test scientific hypotheses with evidence from uncontrolled observations is again largely a reflection of the confusion between the rôle of practitioner and that of scientist. This is apparently because of the very great utility that such sources of evidence—e.g., the literary masterpieces—have in helping to impart the intuitive sort of understanding that is so important to practicing clinicians. It is also apparently due to the fact that the requirements of the scientifically controlled situation are, in one important respect, almost diametrically opposed to those involved in the practical clinical situation. This is in regard to the scientific need for personal detachment and objectivity —for taking oneself and one's biases out of the experimental situation, once the hypothesis to be tested has been set up and the relevant observations are to be made. Great resistance to this requirement is found among clinical practitioners. This is understandable in view of the necessity in clinical practice to make decisions frankly based on the kind of value judgments that are fundamental in applied research, and of the importance in clinical practice of personal relations and subjective evaluations. But it is necessary for practitioners to realize that valuable as these highly personalized factors are under some circumstances they must be set aside once the testing aspect of scientific investigation begins.

The distinction between clinical practitioner and clinical scientist is particularly evident in the part played by intuition, as contrasted with more overt cognitive processes, in theory construction. However labeled, intuition seems to be an integral part of the skill acquired by the experienced and successful interviewer, psychotherapist, or counselor. Similar kinds of abilities largely based upon unrecognized cues and complex perceptual-motor and intellectual habits are found in varying degrees in many other technical fields. By contrast, the rôle that intuition plays in the scientific phase of the clinician's activities is clearly circumscribed. Here intuition is restricted to the formulation of pertinent questions and relevant hypotheses. Such questions and hypotheses may of course be formulated at any time and during any phase of the scientific process— but they cannot be permitted to enter into the determination of their own correctness. That is, it is not scientifically permissible to offer intuitively-based observations as evidence for questions posed upon the same kind of intuitive basis. Intuition in science is thus restricted to the raising of questions and the *suggestion* of the direction in which answers may be sought —and cannot be used in answering its own questions.

An apparent exception to this generalization may arise if intuitive processes are utilized by clinicians as a part of the experimental, or controlled empirical, procedure. Here it is the intuitive process itself that is being investigated, directly or indirectly. The ordinary scientific precautions against bias in the collection of data are of course required and no exception to the above generalization actually occurs. The highly individualized nature of some particular clinical techniques cannot be accepted as an excuse for the failure to use adequate controls in the collection of data to test theory.

The attempt to test hypotheses with new evidence from uncontrolled sources is thus no better than the more obviously circular tendency to continue to answer such questions with old information from uncontrolled sources. Both types of activity, while useful for other purposes in clinical practice, must be clearly delimited from the recourse to new controlled observations, without which scientific progress cannot occur.

Dependence upon uncontrolled sources for scientific evidence is not only unproductive but may also be extremely dangerous. It may be objected that such sources are often correct, and are subsequently shown to be so by more objective scientific investigations. How often? And in which cases? Premature acceptance of hypotheses in the absence of scientifically controlled evidence is simply not the way of science—although it may often be necessary under practical pressure in clinical work.

One particularly widespread source of confusion in this respect deserves special mention. The fact that any given technique seems to "work" in practice—and thus appears to provide the clinician with a certain amount of practical prediction of and control over events—must not be accepted as evidence in support of the special theory that is propounded in connection with the technique. The lack of any necessary relationship between theory and practice is exemplified by all of the special practitioner techniques, ranging from psychoanalysis and other more or less orthodox clinical tools to the great variety of religious and cultist practices. In regard to the latter, it has long been recognized that much of the improvement found is explainable on the basis of certain general factors, for example, "suggestibility." The operation of these factors is not formally recognized in the official dogma regardless of the extent to which it may be suspected by the active practitioners. Recognition by clinicians of the same basic looseness of relation between theory and practical results seems to be considerably more difficult in regard to the more orthodox clinical procedures. It is essential for clinicians to realize that "clinical validation," however useful it may be under some practical conditions, is not acceptable as a substitute for controlled evidence in relation to problems of a theoretical nature.

D. Levels of Theory Construction

A major and especially unfortunate source of confusion that is often evident in attitudes toward theory in clinical psychology concerns the failure of many psychologists to recognize the existence of the different levels of explanation, or theory construction, at which scientific research is legitimately and usefully conducted. Again, in the case of the clinician, this difficulty may be in large part traced to the important differences between the practitioner and the scientist rôles. It involves the relatively greater emphasis necessarily placed by the clinical practitioner upon the "applied" rather than the "pure" aspects of scientific research. The consequence is that many clinicians tend to accept the glib dismissal of experimental research and theory construction as hopelessly remote from real people and real problems.

This attitude constitutes a serious problem in view of the fact that scientific theory generally develops in the direction of increasing degrees of abstraction. It is of course true that complex real-life problems initiate scientific inquiry and that the early theoretical developments in a given area tend to deal with such phenomena. However, this must be recognized as a transitory stage in the growth of theory (Marx, 1951[b]). A continuing effort is made to abstract essential variables from the welter of interacting factors. Basic research involves the disentanglement and realignment of this complex of factors. His simplification through analysis for purposes of more convenient study—that is, control of variables—does not mean that the scientist is unaware of the complexities of the everyday interactions. But his search is for underlying uniformities, and these simply cannot be effectively studied without some kind of simplification.

Now it is apparent that as the scientific investigator turns away from the real-life complexities of the world of practical affairs he is forsaking the arena in which the clinical practitioner must of necessity operate. Too many clinical practitioners, faced with immediate and pressing problems, and too many clinically-oriented psychologists with practitioner points of view, are consequently unimpressed by the long-range promise that this kind of behavioral research offers, and by the fact that in essentially similar situations other scientific researchers have provided consistent and often spectacular pay-offs in terms of practical applications (e.g., those contributed to medicine by means of basic discoveries in physiology and biochemistry, or to engineering by physics and chemistry). The kind of principles that such psychologists want is, obviously, the kind that they need in connection with the immediate requirements of clinical work. No one need quarrel with this motive. What may be regretted, however, is the lack of perspective so often found in clinical practitioners with regard to the objectives and methods of those interested in research and theory development on a more abstract level.

The relationship between purely practical interests and more basic scientific objectives may be pointed up by consideration of other, better established research areas. For centuries preceding the research of Mendel, animal breeders had been successfully applying certain principles of genetics. Theirs was a rough sort of "theory," judged by what we know today, but it was a highly useful one. A radically different approach was used by Mendel, who was blessed with an unusual degree of intellectual curiosity and was fortunately uninhibited by any practical considerations. His construction and empirical verification of the two-factor or gene theory of inheritance was made possible by the deliberate choice of a very simple plant material, the garden pea, and selection of single characteristics for analysis. In terms of the practical problems of the animal breeders, this was about as artificial and impractical a piece of research as could have been devised. It is certainly doubtful that it would ever have been performed by a scientific investigator who was also something of a cattle breeder and whose interests were therefore largely applied in nature. Yet today few will deny that this research and the enormously refined further researches which it ultimately stimulated have produced theoretical principles which are in a very real sense basic to the rule-of-thumb principles long utilized by the animal breeders.

Similar examples may be taken from a variety of other scientific fields.

The relationship between practical problems and basic research is especially well recognized, now, in the field of medicine, as is demonstrated by the extensive financial support of a wide range of extremely basic research projects in connection with the very practical problem of cancer control.

Medical research offers, also, a good illustration of the futility of attempting to differentiate between so-called "pure" and "applied" research in any other way than in terms of the researcher's objectives. Research is applied to the extent to which it is undertaken with more or less explicit intention of utilizing results in practical situations. The distinction between pure and applied research is thus a highly relative one and is often hard to draw in actual practice. Furthermore, it is important to discourage the notion that "pure" and "basic" are necessarily equivalent terms. Good basic research can be done in applied as well as pure frameworks, although it is no doubt true that it is more directly encouraged and more readily performed without commitment to practical objectives. It should also be emphasized, as noted earlier, that the execution of frankly applied research does not excuse the investigator from the ordinary rules of scientific investigation, particularly from the need for controlled observations.

The argument that psychology is "different" from the older natural sciences and therefore cannot be bound to ordinary scientific conventions makes some sense in regard to the particular techniques that are necessary for research but hardly in regard to the fundamental method that is shared by all scientific enterprises. Begging the question by arbitrary naming of one's own activities as "science," without regard for orthodox meanings of the term, only tends to worsen the already snarled lines of communication. The real test of the ingenuity of the clinician involves his ability to translate clinical insights into verified propositions that *can* meet the usual rigorous tests of scientific adequacy. This is a challenge that must be squarely faced by those clinicians who profess scientific interests and wish to claim scientific status. It is necessary for all clinicians to recognize that from a scientific point of view clinical theory *is* general behavior theory, and that it can be specifically further identified as "clinical" only in so far as it relates to the particular variables that are held to be significant in clinical situations.

The practical consequences of the frequent failure of the clinician to recognize the varying levels at which research and theory construction can be performed may now be considered. Perhaps the most serious consequence is represented by the simple failure to appreciate or acknowledge the need for any further research or theoretical development. This is most frequently apparent, probably, in connection with the defense of the theoretical adequacy of certain clinical techniques, and as the Rorschach, on the basis of "clinical validation," or their presumed diagnostic accuracy (cf. Thurstone, 1948). This is a strange attitude indeed, and there does not seem to be any scientific excuse for it. The obvious room for improvement in all clinical techniques and the equally obvious need for effective new techniques provide abundant justification for the attempt to develop general explanatory principles which point up the relevant variables and their relationships.

A less extreme but perhaps more common consequence is the attitude that psychologists should concentrate their research and theory construction at a practical level of investigation. Basic investigations are, more or less explicitly, disapproved. Any such attempt to legislate the particular type of investigation that psychologists "ought" to do is to be strongly deprecated (Marx, 1951c). In its most extreme form this attitude is close to the one previously considered. More frequently, however, the disapproval of basic research is more moderate, and in some cases the issue may revolve around the question of the degree of analysis that is most fruitful, or that is possible without too radical a change in the variables being studied. Here the issue of "reductionism" (e.g., Sloane, 1945) is often raised, especially in connection with a criticism of animal experimentation. This must be clearly recognized as a pseudo issue, and one not to be seriously considered, since the degree to which complex human behavioral functions can ultimately be explained in terms of relatively simpler principles, such as those deduced from infrahuman experimentation, is strictly a matter for future investigations to decide (Marx, 1951c; Spence, 1948).

The potential clinical value of animal experimentation, at least in so far as it offers useful leads for related investigations on human problems, is suggested by the large number of recent experiments dealing with clinically-derived or clinically-related problems (e.g., Farber, 1948; Goodson and Marx, 1953; Hunt and Schlosberg, 1950; Maier, 1949; Marx and Van Spanckeren, 1952; Masserman, 1943; Miller, 1944, 1948a, 1948b; Mowrer, 1950). Moreover, the very attempt to test the degree of applicability of simpler principles should result in the accumulation of a certain amount of data which will be valuable in helping to establish meaningful relationships among the relevant variables, regardless of the extent to which the original hypotheses need to be modified or supplemented. The success of this effort will depend upon how satisfactorily the clinicians are able to improve their own nonexperimental observational processes, in the direction of increased control and sharpened conceptualizations, as well as how closely the essential variables of clinical phenomena can be reproduced and experimentally manipulated in the laboratory. Prejudging the question by the dogmatic assertion that either one of these two objectives cannot be accomplished is scarcely the kind of attitude that stems from scientific interests or encourages scientific research.

E. Summary and Conclusions

Consideration has been given to a number of problems concerning clinical theory construction that have arisen in large part as a result of the dual rôle—as practitioner and scientist—of the psychological clinician. Several sources of confusion in attitudes toward clinical theory have been critically examined.

In summary, it is held that for the most effective scientific advance clinical theories must:

1. Develop in a *nomothetic* direction, since scientific objectives demand laws of the highest generality and abstractness. Apart from its scientific usefulness in the building of laws of personality development and organization, individual prediction is regarded as strictly a matter for the clinical practitioner.

2. Be constructed so as to be testable in terms of empirical—preferably experimental—observations under *controlled* conditions. Recourse to uncontrolled sources of observations, such as clinical insights and literary masterpieces, is seen as a legitimate source for the suggestion of hypotheses but not for their test.

3. Be encouraged at *all levels* of explanation from the most basic to the most practical. Emphasis on basic research is especially necessary in view of the natural orientation of the clinical practitioner in the other direction.

In conclusion, it is hoped that clarification of these fundamental issues such as has been attempted in this survey will help to improve the theoretical orientation of many who are primarily interested in the practitioner rôle of the clinician. It is also hoped that such clarification will provide an improved appreciation of experimental methodology, particularly of the so-called stimulus-response variety (MacCorquodale and Meehl, 1948; Marx, 1951[b], 1952), in those who are primarily concerned with conceptualization and theoretical systematization of clinical variables. Satisfactory development of clinical theory seems to depend upon the finding of a middle ground between the practical operating principles that are the immediate concern of the practitioner and the grand conceptual schemes that appear to be the major objective of many clinical theorists. It is in this middle ground that most of the actual theoretical advance will come, since it depends upon the careful experimental verification of hypotheses stating systematic relationships among constructs that describe the stimulus manipulations and response measurements of the investigator rather than his speculations.

How quickly adequate constructs are developed and lawfully related in theory will largely depend upon the experimental ingenuity of the investigators. The situation presents a challenge to the practicing clinician, who can most readily supply the rich experiential background necessary for fruitful insights, as well as the theoretical experimentalist (whether or not he is also a clinician), who can most readily supply the conceptual and experimental tools. Acceptance of the latter's methodological rigor, and modification of the conceptual rigidity that so often seems to deter the clinician, are necessary if clinical theory construction is to make significant headway.

References

Farber, I. E. Response fixation under anxiety and non-anxiety conditions. *J. Exp. Psychol.*, 1948, *38*, 111–131.

Goodson, F. E., and Marx, M. H. Increased resistance to audiogenic seizure in rats trained on an instrumental wheel-turning response. *J. Comp. and Physiol. Psychol.*, 1953, *46*, 225–230.

Harlow, H. F. The formation of learning sets. *Psychol. Rev.*, 1949, *56*, 51–65.

Hartmann, H., and Kris, E. The genetic approach in psychoanalysis. *Psychoanal. Study Child*, 1945, *1*, 11–30.

Hunt, J. McV., and Schlosberg, H. Behavior of rats in continuous conflict. *J. Comp. and Physiol. Psychol.*, 1950, *43*, 351–357.

Hunt, W. A. Clinical psychology—science or superstition. *Amer. Psychol.*, 1951, *6*, 683–687.

Kris, E. The nature of psychoanalytic propositions and their validation. In S. Hook and M. R. Konvitz (eds.), *Freedom and experience: essays presented to Horace Kellem.* Ithaca, N.Y.: Cornell Univ. Press, 1947.

MacCorquodale, K., and Meehl, P. E. On a distinction between hypothetical constructs and intervening variables. *Psychol. Rev.*, 1948, *55*, 95–107.

Maier, N. R. F. *Frustration: the study of behavior without a goal.* New York: McGraw-Hill, 1949.

Marx, M. H. A stimulus-response analysis of the hoarding habit in the rat. *Psychol. Rev.*, 1950, *57*, 80–93 (a).

——. Experimental analysis of the hoarding habit in the rat: I. Preliminary observations. *J. Comp. and Physiol. Psychol.*, 1950, *43*, 295–308 (b).

——. Experimental analysis of the hoarding habit in the rat: II. Terminal reinforcement. *J. Comp. and Physiol. Psychol.*, 1951, *44*, 168–177 (a).

——. Intervening variable or hypothetical construct? *Psychol. Rev.*, 1951, *58*, 235–247 (b). [Selection 10 in this volume.]

——. The general nature of theory construction. In M. H. Marx (ed.), *Psychological Theory.* New York: Macmillan, 1951(c).

——. Some suggestions for the stimulus-response analysis of complex intervening variables. Paper read before U. Minn. Psi Chi chapter, Oct., 1952.

Marx, M. H., and Van Spanckeren, W. J. Control of the audiogenic seizure by the rat. *J. Comp. and Physiol. Psychol.*, 1952, *45*.

Masserman, J. H. *Behavior and neurosis.* Chicago: Univ. of Chicago Press, 1943.

Miller, N. E. Experimental studies of conflict. In J. McV. Hunt (ed.), *Personality and the behavior disorders.* New York: Ronald Press, 1944.

———. Studies of fear as an acquirable drive: I. Fear as motivation and fear-reduction as reinforcement in the learning of new responses. *J. Exp. Psychol.*, 1948, *38*, 89–101 (a).

———. Theory and experiment relating psychoanalytic displacement to stimulus response generalization. *J. Abn. and Soc. Psychol.*, 1948, *43*, 155–178 (b).

Mowrer, O. H. *Learning theory and personality dynamics.* New York: Ronald Press, 1950.

Raimy, V. C. (ed.). *Training in clinical psychology.* Englewood Cliffs, N.J.: Prentice-Hall, 1950.

Sloane, E. H. Reductionism. *Psychol. Rev.*, 1945, *52*, 214–223.

Spence, K. W. The postulates and methods of "behaviorism." *Psychol. Rev.*, 1948, *55*, 67–78. [Selection 19 in this volume.]

Thurstone, L. L. The Rorschach in psychological science. *J. Abn. and Soc. Psychol.*, 1948, *43*, 471–475.

23 | *The Flight from the Laboratory*

B. F. SKINNER

An experimental psychologist sometimes invites a man into a laboratory, asks him to memorize a list of nonsense syllables or learn to keep a pointer on a moving target, and sends him on his way quite unaware that he will be asked to come back later for a second series of observations. The experiment will not succeed unless he is ignorant of the future test. I do not know whether the originator of these conferences was conducting such an experiment ten years ago, but I can now report what it feels like to be invited back for the second session. It is mainly a feeling of regret. If, when I was preparing my earlier paper (1947), I had known that I would be asked to compare my prediction of trends in experimental psychology with a decade of actual historical fact, I would have confined myself to statements which could have been more easily twisted to accommodate the eventualities. I would have prepared a much more palatable dish of humble pie.

It is obvious now, after the fact, that the trends I described were scarcely more than my hopes for the future of experimental psychology. Possibly my behavior could be defended as a gesture appropriate to the intellectual

From *Current trends in psychological theory.* Pittsburgh: University of Pittsburgh Press, 1961, pp. 50–69. Reprinted by permission of the author and the University of Pittsburgh Press.

climate of 1947. Experimental psychology was then at the nadir of its popularity. Graduate students were turning to social, personal, clinical, and applied psychology in ever increasing numbers, and defections from the ranks among older men were common. The practical contributions which experimental psychologists had made during World War II had not offset a growing impatience with their stubborn dedication to seemingly unimportant aspects of human behavior. But was there not a bright spot on this murky horizon? If the history of science were any guide, an effective psychology would eventually develop a central conception of human behavior which not only would be fundamentally "right" in the sense of enabling us to *understand* behavior, whatever that might mean, but would generate powerful techniques having important applications in every field of human affairs. No theory of behavior had yet come close to that achievement. Psychoanalysis was the only discipline which had spread beyond its original boundaries, and it had gone no further than some of the social sciences and literary criticism. Elsewhere—in government, economics, religion, education, and all the natural sciences—provincial theories of human behavior were eked out by the tattered theory which had been bequeathed to the English language by a long line of outmoded philosophies. It was as if each of the technologies of physical science had its own scientific conception of nature—as if specialists in synthetic fibers used one theory of molecular structure, pharmacologists another, and biochemists still another, while the layman carried on with a common-sense view of the structure of matter untouched by any of these technical treatments. Such a state of affairs was far from satisfactory. After all, it was the same man who was of interest to psychologists, political scientists, theologians, psychotherapists, economists, educators, literary critics, and scientific methodologists. Why should there be a different theory of human behavior in each case?

Into this power vacuum, it seemed to me, experimental psychology must eventually move. A general theory of human behavior was needed, and only an experimental science could supply it. Separate technologies of behavior could temporize with particular theories, but the special control of variables attainable only in laboratory experimentation would ultimately supply the account which, being in closest accord with the actual properties of the human organism, would be most useful in every field of human affairs. The close check with reality characteristic of experimental analysis would be most likely to expose the fictional entities which had played so devastating a role in what passed for psychological explanation and would permit us to escape from the inaccessible, hypothetical constructs emerging from statistical analyses. This extrapolation of the history of science was intended to give the experimental psychologist a broader horizon. In pointing out the potential significance of an effective theory of human behavior and the special place of a laboratory science in developing such a theory, I was trying to alter the contingencies of reinforcement of my colleagues in the hope of stemming what seemed to be a perpetually ebbing tide.

It is tempting to argue that this proved, indeed, to be an actual trend. It is possible that theories of behavior derived from the clinic or from field studies, rather than from the laboratory, are on the wane. A strict Freudian psychology, for example, is no longer stoutly defended. Certain general points have been made—in some sense we are all Freudians—but the facts and principles which have been salvaged can be stated in relatively nontechnical language. Even the patient under therapy is no longer likely to be burdened with technical references to the structure and function of the psyche. Experimental psychologists are not responsible for this change, but if the common heritage of psychoanalysis is to be put in good scientific order, if an effective technology is to be more than a general understanding of the motives and emotions of oneself and one's fellow men, experimental psychologists will play an important role. The Freudian dynamisms can be subjected to experimental analysis, and the resulting changes in definition reveal the experimental method at work (Skinner, 1953). The Freudian explanatory system seldom traces the causal linkage far enough. We do not really explain "disturbed behavior" by attributing it to "anxiety" until we have also explained the anxiety. The extra step required is in the spirit of an experimental science: it is a search for a manipulable variable rather than a verbal explanation. Psychoanalysis itself has identified some of the conditions which must be changed in order to modify behavior in psychotherapy, and to bring about other behavioral effects, but its methodology is not adapted to the manipulation and control of these conditions. In contrast, experimental psychology is becoming more and more successful in dealing with the variables to which one must eventually turn for a full account of behavior and for effective control.

There are other signs of a change. The layman's way of talking about behavior, deeply entrenched in our everyday vocabulary though it is, has lost ground. It is viewed with greater uneasiness by those who use it. Ten years ago the physiologist, neurologist, or pharmacologist whose research involved behavior was likely to set up his own experiments and to describe his results in nontechnical terms. He now accepts the experimental psychologist as a specialist to whom he must turn for help. To take a very different example, the lay terminology is now more often used with apologies (or in quotation marks) by political scientists. The ultimate danger of arguing from historical analogy, and of predicting or recommending courses of action by deducing theorems from axiomatic principles or governmental stereotypes, is more likely to be recognized. The ideological use of the work of Pavlov by Soviet propagandists has little to recommend it, but we probably make the same mistake when we counter by expressing contempt for techniques of government based upon "conditioned reflexes." In the long run all this will have a salutary effect if it leads us to ask whether a more adequate science of behavior may not be relevant to the design of governmental practices. A conception of human behavior will eventually prove workable, not because it fits a momentary predilection for a philosophy of government, but because it survives the test of experimental analysis.

Somewhere between the extremes of physiology and government lies a third bit of evidence for a possible trend. Educational psychologists have long been devotees of research, but the pattern of a laboratory science has not been closely followed. Their experiments have seldom come to grips with the behavior of the individual student in the act of learning. On the other hand, the experimental psychology of learning, though once a staple in textbooks on education, has been receiving less and less attention. But we have learned a great deal about learning in the past decade. [A proposal to put this to use in education was made at an earlier conference in this series (Skinner, 1954)]. The principles of an experimental analysis are now being extended to the field of verbal behavior (Skinner, 1957), and it is inconceivable that the results will not be used to improve instructional procedures. And with fabulous results. Enough has already been done to justify the prediction that what is now learned by the average college student will someday be learned in half the time with half the effort.

There is, then, evidence of a renaissance in experimental psychology which might be attributed in part to a realization of the potential contribution of the experimental method. But it does not warrant the claim that I correctly predicted a major trend. A general theory of human behavior in this sense has appealed to only a "happy few." As one can easily discover by glancing at the tables of contents of our journals, experimental psychology as a whole has not shown much change. Very little current research is reported in the frame of reference of a comprehensive theory. Nor has the point of view of an experimental analysis yet reached far afield. Many social sciences remain untouched, and among natural scientists there is almost complete ignorance of the promise and achievement of the scientific study of behavior. Dr. Neils Bohr, one of the most distinguished living physicists, recently discussed certain issues in psychology.

Quite apart from the extent to which the use of words like "instinct" and "reason" in the description of animal behavior is necessary and justifiable, the word "consciousness," applied to oneself as well as to others, is indispensable when describing the human situation. The use of words like "thought" and "feeling" does not refer to a firmly connected causal chain, but to experiences which exclude each other because of different distinctions between the conscious content and the background which we loosely term ourselves. . . . We must recognize that psychical experience cannot be subjected to physical measurements and that the very concept of volition does not refer to a generalization of a deterministic description, but from the outset points to characteristics of human life. Without entering into the old philosophical discussion of freedom of the will, I shall only mention that in an objective description of our situation the use of the word "volition" corresponds closely to that of words like "hope" and "responsibility," which are equally indispensable to human communication (1958).

These terms and issues would have been at home in psychological discussions fifty years ago. How shocked Dr. Bohr would be if a distinguished psychologist were to discuss current problems in physical science in the terms which were current at the beginning of the century! Psychology in general, and experimental psychology in particular, is still a long way from providing a conception of human behavior which is as readily accepted by those who deal with men as the views of physics are accepted by those who deal with the physical world. And psychologists themselves are not doing much about it.

I therefore return to the attack. [In doing so I assert my membership in a species distinguished by the fact that, at least when psychotic, its members sometimes fail to show extinction (Lindsley).] But I shall not doggedly repeat my exhortations or promises of a decade ago. It is evidently not enough to strengthen the scientific behavior of psychologists by giving them a glimpse of an exciting future.

Fortunately, as one achievement of the intervening decade, the problem can now be attacked with a better brand of behavioral engineering. I propose to analyze the behavior of psychologists. Why are they not currently developing the pure science of human behavior from which such tremendous technological advances would certainly flow? How are we to explain the continuing flight from the experimental field? Where have the experimental psychologists gone, and what are they doing instead? And why? And, above all, what steps can be taken to remedy the situation? Such questions clarify the engineering task which faces us if we are to *produce* the trend in experimental psychology which I insist upon predicting.

So stated, the problem has an analogy in a type of experiment which is growing in importance in the experimental analysis of behavior. When we have studied the performances generated by various contingencies of reinforcement in a single arbitrary response, we can move on to two or more concurrent responses. Instead of one lever to be pressed by a rat or one key to be pecked by a pigeon, our experimental space now frequently contains two or three levers or keys, each with its own set of reinforcing contingencies (Ferster and Skinner, 1957). In the present experiment, we are to account for the fact that psychologists have stopped pressing the experimental lever and have turned to other available manipulanda. To explain this two questions must be asked: 1) What has happened to the reinforcing contingencies on the experimental lever? and 2) What contingencies compete so effectively elsewhere? Once these questions have been answered, we can proceed to the engineering task of increasing the relative effectiveness of the experimental contingencies. It would probably be unfair to do this by attacking competing conditions, for any source of scientific zeal should be respected, but it is possible that some of the reinforcements responsible for activity on other levers can be made contingent upon the response in which we are primarily interested.

Some deficiencies in the rewards of the experimental psychologist were analyzed in my earlier paper. All sciences undergo changes in fashion. Problems lose interest even though they remain unsolved. In psychology many green pastures have been glimpsed on the other side of the experimental fence. The very success of a science may force it to become preoccupied with smaller and smaller details, which cannot compete with broad new issues. The philosophical motivation of the pioneers of a "mental science" has been lost. Although idealism is evidently still a fighting word in some parts of the world, dualism is no longer a challenging issue in American psychology. Classical research on the relation between the psychic and the physical has been transmuted into the study of the physiological and physical actions of end organs. This is a scientific step forward, but an important source of inspiration has been left behind.

Some of the most effective rewards contingent upon experimental practice have been inadvertently destroyed in another way. We owe most of our scientific knowledge to methods of inquiry which have never been formally analyzed or expressed in normative rules. For more than a generation, however, our graduate schools have been building psychologists on a different pattern of Man Thinking. They have taught statistics in lieu of scientific method. Unfortunately, the statistical pattern is incompatible with some major features of laboratory research. As now taught, statistics plays down the direct manipulation of variables and emphasizes the treatment of variation after the fact. If the graduate student's first result is not significant, statistics tells him to increase the size of his sample; it does not tell him (and, because of self-imposed restrictions on method, it cannot tell him) how to achieve the same result by improving his instruments and his methods of observation. Bigger samples mean more work, the brunt of which the young psychologist may have to bear. When he gets his degree (and a grant), he may pass the labor on to someone else, but in doing so he himself loses contact with the experimental organism he is studying. What statisticians call experimental design (I have pointed out elsewhere that this means design which yields data to which the methods of statistics are appropriate) usually generates a much more intimate acquaintance with a calculating machine than with a behaving organism.

One result is a damaging delay in reinforcement. An experiment may "pay off" only after weeks of routine computation. A graduate student who designs an experiment according to accepted statistical methods may survive the ordeal of the calculating room by virtue of his youthful zeal, but his ultimate reinforcement as a scientist may be so long deferred that he will never begin another experiment. Other levers then beckon.

The psychologist who adopts the commoner statistical methods has at best an indirect acquaintance with the "facts" he discovers—with the vectors, factors, and hypothetical processes secreted by the statistical machine. He is inclined to rest content with rough measures of behavior because statistics shows him how to "do something about them." He is likely to continue with fundamentally unproductive methods, because squeezing something of significance out of questionable data discourages the possibly more profitable step of scrapping the experiment and starting again.

Statistics offers its own brand of reinforcement, of course, but this is often not contingent upon behavior which is most productive in the laboratory. One destructive effect is to supply a sort of busy work for the compulsive. In the early stages of any inquiry the investigator often has to weather a period of ignorance and chaos during which apparent progress is slight, if not lacking altogether. This is something he must be taught to endure. He must acquire a kind of faith in the ultimate value of ostensibly undirected exploration. He must also learn to be indifferent to the criticism that he is not getting anywhere. If he has accepted funds in support of his research, he must learn to tolerate a gnawing anxiety about the annual report. At such times statistics offers consoling comfort and, what is worse, an all-too-convenient escape hatch. How simple it is to match groups of subjects, devise a crude measure of the behavior at issue, arrange for tests to be administered, and punch the scores into IBM cards! No matter what comes of it all, no one can say that work has not been done. Statistics will even see to it that the result will be "significant" even if it is proved to mean nothing.

The intention of the statistician is honorable and generous. He wants the experimental scientist to be sure of his results and to get the most out of them. But, whether or not he understands the essence of laboratory practice, his recommendations are often inimical to it. Perhaps against his will, he has made certain essential activities in good laboratory research no longer respectable. The very instrument which might have made an experimental science more rewarding has, instead, all but destroyed its basic features. In the long run the psychologist has been deprived of some of his most profitable, and hence eventually most reinforcing, achievements.

The resulting flight from the laboratory can be stopped by pointing to alternative methods of research. If all psychologists are to be required to take courses in statistics, they should also be made familiar with laboratory practices and given the chance to behave as scientists rather than as the robots described by scientific methodologists. In particular, young psychologists should learn how to work with single organisms rather than with large groups. Possibly with that one step alone, we could restore experimental psychology to the vigorous health it deserves.

But it will be worth while to examine the competing contingencies. Psychologists have fled from the laboratory, and perhaps for good reason. Where have they gone?

The Flight to Real People

Laboratories can be dull places, and not only when furnished with calculating machines. It is not surprising that psychologists have been attracted by the human interest of real life. The experimental subject in the laboratory is only part of a man, and frequently an uninteresting part, while the whole individual is a fascinating source of reinforcement. Literature flourishes for that reason. Psychologists have long since learned to borrow from the literary domain. If a lecture flags, or a chapter seems dull, one has only to bring in a case history and everything literally "comes to life." The recipe is so foolproof that the lecture or text which consists of nothing but case histories has been closely approximated. But in resorting to this device for pedagogical or therapeutic effect psychologists have themselves been influenced by these reinforcers; their courses of action as scientists have been deflected. They often recognize this and from time to time have felt the need for a special theory of scientific knowledge (based, for example, on empathy or intuition) to justify themselves. They seldom seem to feel secure, however, in the belief that they have regained full citizenship in the scientific commonwealth.

The reinforcements which flow from real people are not all related to, on the one hand, an intellectual conviction that the proper study of mankind is man or, on the other, the insatiable curiosity of a Paul Pry. In a world in which ethical training is widespread, most men are reinforced when they succeed in reinforcing others. In such a world personal gratitude is a powerful generalized reinforcer. We can scarcely hold it against psychologists that, like other men of good will, they want to help their fellow men—either one by one in the clinic or nation by nation in, say, studies of international good will. We may agree that the world would be a better place if more men would concern themselves with personal and political problems. But we must not forget that the remedial step is necessarily a short-term measure and that it is not the only step leading to the same goal. The lively prosecution of a science of behavior, applied to the broad problem of cultural design, could have more sweeping consequences.

If such a promising alternative is actually feasible, any one who is capable of making a long-term contribution may wisely resist the effect of other consequences which, no matter how important they may be to him personally, are irrelevant to the scientific process and confine him to short-term remedial action. A classical example from another field is Albert Schweitzer. Here is a brilliant man who, for reasons we need not examine, dedicated his life to helping his fellow men—one by one. He has earned the gratitude of thousands, but we must not forget what he might have done instead. If he had worked as energetically for as many years in a laboratory of tropical medicine, he would almost certainly have made discoveries which in the long run would help—not thousands—but literally *billions* of people. We do not know enough about Schweitzer to say why he took the short-term course. Could he not resist the blandishments of gratitude? Was he freeing himself from feelings of guilt? Whatever his reasons, his story warns us of the danger of a cultural design which does not harness some personal reinforcement in the interests of pure science. The young psychologist who wants above all to help his fellow men should be made to see the tremendous potential consequences of even a small contribution to the scientific understanding of human behavior. It is possibly this understanding alone, with the improved cultural patterns which will flow from it, which will eventually alleviate the anxieties and miseries of mankind.

The Flight to Mathematical Models

The flight from the experimental method has sometimes gone in the other direction. If the human being studied in the laboratory has been too drab and unreal for some, he has been just the opposite for others. In spite of our vaunted control of variables, the experimental subject too often remains capricious. Sometimes he is not only warm but, as baseball players say, too hot to handle. Even the "average man," when captured in the statistical net, may be unpleasantly refractory. Some psychologists have therefore fled to an ivory image of their own sculpturing, mounted on a mathematical pedestal. These Pygmalions have constructed a Galatea who always behaves as she is supposed to behave, whose processes are orderly and relatively simple, and to whose behavior the most elegant of mathematical procedures may be applied. She is a creature whose slightest blemish can be erased by the simple expedient of changing an assumption. Just as political scientists used to simplify their problems by talking about an abstract Political Man, and the economists theirs by talking about Economic Man, so psychologists have built the ideal experimental organism—the Mathematical Model.

The effect of this practice on so-called learning theory has been pointed out elsewhere (Skinner, 1950). Early techniques available for the study of learning—from the nonsense syllables of Ebbinghaus, through the problem boxes of Thorndike and the mazes of Watson, to the discrimination apparatuses of Yerkes and Lashley—always yielded learning curves of disturbing irregularity. In experiments with these instruments an orderly change in the behavior of a single organism was seldom seen. Orderly processes had to be generated by averaging data, either for many trials or many organisms. Even so, the resulting "learning curves" varied in a disturbing way from experiment to experiment. The theoretical solution to this problem was to assume that an orderly learning process, which had the same properties regardless of the particular features of a given experiment, took place somewhere inside the organism. A given result was accounted for by making a distinction between learning and performance. Though the performance might be chaotic, the psychologist could continue to cherish the belief that learning was always orderly. Indeed, the mathematical organism seemed so orderly that model builders remained faithful to techniques which consistently yielded disorderly data. An examination of mathematical models in learning theory will show that no degree of disorder in the facts has placed any restriction on the elegance of the mathematical treatment.

The properties which (to drop to a two-dimensional figure of speech) make a paper doll more amenable than a living organism are crucial in a scientific account of behavior. No matter how many of the formulations derived from the study of a model eventually prove useful in describing reality (remember wave-mechanics!), the questions to which answers are most urgently needed concern the correspondence between the two realms. How can we be sure that a model is a model of *behavior?* What *is* behavior, and how is it to be analyzed and measured? What are the relevant features of the environment, and how are they to be measured and controlled? How are these two sets of variables related? The answers to these questions cannot be found by constructing models. (Nor is a model likely to be helpful in furthering the necessary empirical inquiry. It is often argued that some model, hypothesis, or theory is essential because the scientist cannot otherwise choose among the facts to be studied. But there are presumably as many models, hypotheses, or theories as facts. If the scientific methodologist will explain how he proposes to choose among them, his answer will serve as well to explain how one may choose among empirical facts.)

What sort of behavioral engineering will reduce the rate of responding to the mathematical lever and induce distinguished psychologists to get back to the laboratory? Two steps seem to be needed. First, it must be made clear that the formal properties of a system of variables can be profitably treated only after the dimensional problems have been solved. The detached and essentially tautological nature of mathematical models is usually frankly admitted by their authors, particularly those who come into experimental psychology from mathematics, but for the psychologist these disclaimers are often lost among the integral signs. Secondly, the opportunity to be mathematical in dealing with factual material should be clarified. To return to the example of learning theory, the psychologist should recognize that with proper techniques one can *see learning take place*, not in some inner recess far removed from the observable performance of an organism, but as a change in that performance itself. Techniques are now available for the experimental analysis of very subtle behavioral processes, and this work is ready for the kind of mathematical theory which has always been productive at the proper stage in the history of science. What is needed is not a mathematical model, constructed with little regard for the fundamental dimensions of behavior, but a mathematical treatment of experimental data. Mathematics will come into its own in the analysis of behavior when appropriate methods yield data which are so orderly that there is no longer any need to escape to a dream world.

The Flight to the Inner Man

Experimental psychology has suffered perhaps its greatest loss of manpower because competent investigators, beginning with a *descriptive* interest in behavior, have passed almost immediately to an *explanatory* preoccupation with what is going on inside the organism. In discussing this flight to the inner man I should like to believe that I am whipping a dead horse, but the fact remains that human behavior is still most commonly discussed in terms of psychic or physiological processes. A dualistic philosophy is not necessarily implied in either case for it may be argued, on the one hand, that the data of physics reduce at last to the direct experience of the physicist or, on the other, that behavior is only a highly organized set of biological facts. The nature of any real or fancied inner cause of behavior is not at issue; investigative practices suffer the same damage in any case.

Sometimes, especially among psychoanalysts, the inner men are said to be organized personalities whose activities lead at last to the behavior of the organism we observe. The commoner practice is to dissect the inner man and deal separately with his traits, perceptions, experiences, habits, ideas, and so on. In this way an observable subject matter is abandoned in favor of an inferred. It was Freud himself who insisted that mental processes could occur without "conscious participation," and that since they could not always be directly observed, our knowledge of them must be inferential. Much of the machinery of psychoanalysis is concerned with the process of inference. In the analysis of behavior we may deal with *all* mental processes as inferences, whether or not they are said to be conscious. The resulting redefinition (call it operational if you like) conveniently omits the mentalistic dimension. At the same time, however, the explanatory force is lost. Inner entities or events do not "cause" behavior, nor does behavior "express" them. At best they are mediators, but the causal relations between the terminal events which are mediated are inadequately represented by traditional devices. Mentalistic concepts may have had some heuristic value at one stage in the analysis of behavior, but it has long since been more profitable to abandon them. In an acceptable explanatory scheme the ultimate causes of behavior must be found *outside* the organism.

The *physiological* inner man is, of course, no longer wholly inferential. New methods and instruments have brought the nervous system and other mechanisms under direct observation. The new data have their own dimensions and require their own formulations. The behavioral facts in the field of learning, for example, are dealt with in terms appropriate to behavior, while electrical or chemical activities occurring at the same time demand a different conceptual framework. Similarly, the effects of deprivation and satiation on behavior are not the same as the events seen through a gastric fistula. Nor is emotion, studied as behavioral predisposition, capable of being analyzed in terms appropriate to pneumographs and electrocardiographs. Both sets of facts, and their appropriate concepts, are important—but they are *equally* important, not dependent one upon the other. Under the influence of a contrary philosophy of explanation, which insists upon the reductive priority of the inner event, many brilliant men who began with an interest in behavior, and might have advanced our knowledge of that field in many ways, have turned instead to the study of physiology. We cannot dispute the importance of their contributions; we can only imagine with regret what they might have done instead.

If we are to make a study of behavior sufficiently reinforcing to hold the interest of young men in competition with inner mechanisms, we must make clear that behavior is an acceptable subject matter in its own right, and that it can be studied with acceptable methods and without an eye to reductive explanation. The responses of an organism to a given environment are physical events. Modern methods of analysis reveal a degree of order in such a subject matter which compares favorably with that of any phenomena of comparable complexity. Behavior is not simply the result of more fundamental activities, to which our research must therefore be addressed, but an end in itself, the substance and importance of which are demonstrated in the practical results of an experimental analysis. We can predict and control behavior, we can modify it, we can construct it according to specifications—and all without answering the explanatory questions which have driven investigators into the study of the inner man. The young psychologist may contemplate a true science of behavior without anxiety.

The Flight to Laymanship

Experimental psychology has also had to contend with what is in essence a rejection of the whole scientific enterprise. In a recent review of a study of the psychological problems of aging, the reviewer comments upon "a tendency in psychological thought which is returning to prominence after some years of relative disfavor. The statements have a certain refreshing directness and 'elegance' in their approach to the study of human behavior. The sterile arguments of so-called 'learning theory,' the doctrinaire half-truths of the 'schools,' the panacea treatments of 'systems,' and the high-sounding, empty technical terms often found in psychological writings are conspicuous by their absence." No one will want to defend "*sterile* arguments," "half-truths," "panaceas," or "*empty* technical terms," no matter what their sources, but the force of the passage is more than this. The author is rejecting all efforts to improve upon the psychology of the layman in approaching the problems of the aging. And many psychologists agree with him. "Enough of the lingo of the laboratory!" the argument runs. "Enough of clinical jargon! Enough of frightening equations! A plague on all your houses! Let us go back to common sense! Let us say what we want to say about human behavior in the well-worn but still useful vocabulary of the layman!" Whether this is a gesture of fatigue or impatience, or the expression of a desire to get on with practical matters at the expense of a basic understanding, it must be answered by any one who defends a pure science. It would be easier to find the answer if experimental psychology had moved more rapidly toward a helpful conception of human behavior.

Some progress has been made in proving the superiority of scientific concepts over those of traditional usage. Consider, for example, two psychological accounts written in the vulgar tongue. First, a sample in the field of emotional behavior:

The emotional temper of the type of juvenile delinquent just mentioned is as extraordinary as it is well known. Far from being naturally peaceful, sympathetic, or generous, men who are excluded from the society of their fellow men become savage, cruel, and morose. The wanton destructiveness of the delinquent is not due to sudden bursts of fury, but to a deliberate and brooding resolve to wage war on everything.

The second has to do with intellect. It is an explanation of how a child learns to open a door by depressing a thumb-latch and pushing against the door with his legs.

Of course the child may have observed that doors are opened by grownups placing their hands on the handles, and having observed this the child may act by what is termed imitation. But the process as a whole is something more than imitative. Observation alone would be scarcely enough to enable the child to discover that the essential thing is not to grasp the handle but to depress the latch. Moreover, the child certainly never saw any grownup push the door with his legs as it is necessary for the child to do. This pushing action must be due to an originally deliberate intention to open the door, not to accidentally having found this action to have this effect.

Both passages make intelligible points and would conceivably be helpful in discussing juvenile delinquency or the teaching of children. But there is a trap. Actually, the heroes of these pieces were not human at all. The quotations are slightly altered passages from Romanes' *Animal Intelligence*, published about seventy-five years ago. The first describes the behavior of the prototype of all delinquents—the Rogue elephant. The "child" of the second was a cat—possibly the very cat which set Thorndike to work to discover how animals do, indeed, learn to press latches.

The experimental analysis of behavior has clearly shown the practical and theoretical value of abandoning a common-sense way of talking about behavior and has demonstrated the advantages of an alternative account of emotion and intelligence. That is to say, it has done this for cats, rats, pigeons, and monkeys. Its successes are only slowly reaching into the field of human behavior—not because we any longer assume that man is fundamentally different but in part because an alternative method of analysis is felt to be available because of the scientist's membership in the human species. But the special knowledge resulting from self-observation can be given a formulation which preserves intact the notion of the continuity of species. Experimental methods can be applied first to the behavior of the Other One, and only later to the analysis of the behavior of the scientist himself. The value of this practice is demonstrated in the consistency of the resulting account and the effectiveness of the resulting technological control.

It is not difficult to explain the strength of traditional concepts. Many of those who discuss human behavior are speaking to laymen and must adapt their terms to their audience. The immediate effect of the lay vocabulary also gains strength from its deep intrenchment in the language. Our legal system is based on it, and the literature of ideas is couched in it. Moreover, from time to time efforts are made to rejuvenate the philosophical systems from which it came. Aristotle, through Thomas Aquinas, still speaks to the same students of behavior. The very fact that Aristotle's psychology, scarcely modified, can be seriously championed in behavioral science today shows how little it has done to advance our understanding. Aristotelian physics, chemistry, and biology have enjoyed no such longevity. We may look forward to the early demise of this sole survivor of Greek science.

A return to the lay vocabulary of behavior cannot be justified. The move is a matter of motivation, competence, or the accessibility of goals. These are all irrelevant to the long-term achievement of a scientific account of behavior. No doubt, many pressing needs can still be most readily satisfied by casual discussion. In the long run, however, we shall need an effective understanding of human behavior—so that, in the example cited, we shall know the nature of the changes which take place as men and women grow old and shall, therefore, be in the most favorable position to do something about them. To reach that understanding we must recognize the limitations of the remedial patchwork which emerges from common-sense discussion and must be willing to resort to experiments which quite possibly involve complicated techniques and to theoretical treatments quite possibly expressed in difficult terms.

Conclusion

We have glanced briefly at four *divertissements* in the growth of a science of human behavior. Real Men, Mathematical Men, Inner Men, and Everyday Men—it would be a mistake to underestimate their seductive power. Together they constitute a formidable array of rival suitors, and to groom the Experimental Organism for this race may seem a hopeless enterprise. But he has a chance, for in the long run he offers the greatest net reinforcement to the scientist engaged in the study of behavior. I doubt whether this fact will affect many of those who have already flown from the laboratory, but I am not speaking to them. A story about William James is appropriate. James was much in demand as a lecturer and one day discovered that he was scheduled to address a ladies' literary society in a suburb of Boston. He set off to keep his appointment after having picked up from his desk the first lecture which came to hand. It happened to be a lecture he had prepared for one of his Radcliffe classes. His audience, in contrast, was composed of elderly New England matrons. James was reading his paper, possibly thinking of other things, when to his horror he heard himself saying, ". . . and so, my fair young friends. . . ." He looked out upon a sea of startled faces and—failing utterly in this pragmatic test of a psychologist—blurted out, "I should explain that this lecture was written for a very different audience."

I wish I could say, and also with more tact, what audience *this* lecture was prepared for. No matter how strong my conviction that we are close to an effective science of human behavior, with all which such a science implies, I do not expect to recapture the interest and enthusiasm of those who have fled from the laboratory to pleasurable dalliance elsewhere. But some of you, I hope, are not yet committed. For you the possibility of an adequate theory of behavior, in the sense in which any empirical science leads eventually to a theoretical formulation, together with its enormous technical potential, may be enough to tip the balance. And if such of you there be, I look to you to restore to experimental psychology the energy, enthusiasm, and productivity which characterized it in an earlier epoch.

We are living in an age in which science fiction is coming true. The thrilling spectacle of man-made satellites has turned our eyes toward outer space. What we shall find there only time will tell. Meanwhile, we are confronted by far more important problems on the surface of the earth. A possible solution is in the spirit of another kind of science fiction: the eighteenth-century Utopian dream of Perfectionism with its basic contention that, if human nature is determined by environment and if environment can be changed, human nature can be changed. Like an artificial satellite or a rocket to the moon, this was once a foolish dream. But science moves forward at a breathless pace. We may shortly be designing the world in which men will henceforth live. But how is it to be designed, and to what end? These are difficult questions, to which nothing short of an effective science of man will provide the answers. The methods of science no longer need verbal defense; one cannot throw a moon around the earth with dialectic. Applied to human behavior, the same methods promise even more thrilling achievements. That prospect will, I still believe, determine the trend in experimental psychology in the years to come.

References

Bohr, Neils. *Atomic physics and human knowledge.* New York: Wiley, 1958.
Ferster, C. B., and Skinner, B. F. *Schedules of reinforcement.* New York: Appleton-Century-Crofts, 1957.
Lindsley, Ogden R. Operant conditioning trends applied to research in chronic schizophrenia. *Psychiatric Research Reports 5.*
Skinner, B. F. Experimental psychology. In *Current trends in psychology.* Pittsburgh: University of Pittsburgh Press, 1947.
———. Are theories of learning necessary? *Psych. Rev.,* 1950, 57, 193–216.
———. *Science and human behavior.* New York: Macmillan, 1953.
———. The science of learning and the art of teaching. In *Current trends in psychology and the behavioral sciences.* Pittsburgh: University of Pittsburgh Press, 1954.
———. *Verbal behavior.* New York: Appleton-Century-Crofts, 1957.

PART THREE

Fields
of Study

CHAPTER VII

Developmental and Social Functions

THE TWO PAPERS IN THIS CHAPTER *survey meta-theoretical problems in the areas of developmental and social psychology. Edward Zigler offers a searching examination of the status of theoretical efforts in developmental psychology, and in so doing treats a wide variety of methodological problems in that field. His treatment is particularly provocative because of the numerous constructive suggestions made for necessary improvements in the field if effective theory is to be developed. The paper by Leonard Berkowitz on theory in social psychology also offers a broad treatment of metatheoretical problems, emphasizing historical factors and singling out Festinger's cognitive-dissonance theory for examination as a contemporary specimen in the field.*

24 | *Metatheoretical Issues in Developmental Psychology*[1]

EDWARD ZIGLER

This paper shall deal with the problems involved in defining developmental psychology, a discussion of the goals and methods appropriate to this area, and a brief overview of certain of the major approaches or frameworks which have been employed by developmentalists. The

---

[1] The writer is much indebted to Irvin Child, Lawrence Kohlberg, William Kessen, and June Chance for their critical reading of an earlier version of this paper. The present manuscript owes much to their insightful comments.

writer's penchant for the dialectic method of presentation may result in the reader's experiencing a certain sense of ambiguity with respect to the writer's own position. It is therefore only proper that the writer's views and biases be put on display at the outset.

He feels that relatively little progress has been made towards formal theory construction in this area. What have passed for "theories" in developmental psychology are actually little more than grand designs or frames of reference which attempt to explain everything and hence succeed in explaining very little. While such frameworks would constitute a legitimate first stage in theory construction, there has been a reluctance to move on to more circumscribed and refined theoretical efforts. Many of the systems presently being employed in developmental psychology are heavily populated with two types of constructs. The first type is closely tied to observables and represents little more than shorthand expressions for the empirical observations they encompass. The second type is so far removed from observables that the empirical operations which give these constructs meaning cannot be delineated. One would have no quarrel with these latter-type concepts if the user treated them as assumptive or given and then went on to provide constructs of the middle range, which would then constitute the necessary bridge between the assumptive constructs and lower-level constructs, finally terminating in the empirical content which the system is directed towards illuminating. Such constructs of the middle range are rare, just as are theories of the middle range, i.e., an articulated set of related concepts dealing with the development of a relatively limited aspect of behavior, e.g., smiling or dependency.

The writer's view is that the relatively slow progress in theory construction in developmental psychology is in part due to an over-reliance on natural observation and an under-use of the experimental method. By experimentation we are not referring to that usage of the term which permits the inclusion of almost any type of research, but rather we are referring to the random-assignment type experiment in which independent variables are manipulated. Some investigators have stated that the problems and content of developmental psychology are such that they can only be investigated through natural observation, with the experimental method being simply inapplicable. The writer shall reject this position. Although he has the profoundest respect for the method of natural observation and is well aware of the theoretical gains which may accrue from it, he will argue not only that the content of developmental psychology is open to the experimental method, but that the use of this method is intimately related to the problems of theory construction, validation, and refinement. This is not to assert that natural observations must invariably result in inadequate theorizing. One need only examine the history of astronomy to refute such a view. Furthermore, we are not asserting that a simple commitment to the experimental method must invariably lead to sound theory. We are saying that the experimental method has a unique role to play in developmental psychology and that the failure of many developmentalists to utilize this tool adequately has retarded progress in theory construction.

One final statement of bias is in order. The writer is committed to the view that theories are valuable and therefore tends to place high value on those efforts related to sound theory construction. He is well aware of the controversy surrounding such a view and out of respect to it will present in one of the following sections an argument favoring an atheoretical approach to developmental psychology. This argument and certain others which will be raised for didactic reasons should not be misconstrued as reflecting the writer's personal views. This brief introduction will give the reader some insight into the writer's particular orientation. Hopefully, much of the remainder of this paper will constitute a defense of his particular biases.

The Problem of Definition

In any discussion of developmental psychology, one is initially faced with the perplexing task of definition. The boundaries delimiting this area are indeed vague and have often been the subject of disputation (Ausubel, 1958; Harris, 1957; Inhelder, 1957). Although developmental psychology has often been equated with child development, certain leading developmentalists (Inhelder, 1957; Werner, 1957[b]) have objected to such a usage. Werner (1957[b]) has been especially outspoken in his criticism of drawing such a parallel, insisting that development be conceived as a concept applicable to all of behavior. Others have argued against equating child and developmental psychology on the grounds that the type or age of the subject is not what determines whether a study is developmental. What then is the criterion by which we can identify a theory as being developmental in nature?

There is, of course, agreement that developmental psychology involves the study of the change in behavior as a function of time. But the issue again becomes confused when one notes that developmentalists also agree that time is not itself a psychological variable nor one which readily fits into behavioral equations. No developmentalist—nor any other psychologist, for that matter—would be so foolhardy as to assert that a particular behavior was a function of a minute or an hour or a year. Depending upon his orientation, the developmentalist would not hazard a prediction of behavior as a function of time unless he were allowed to specify where in the life cycle this particular segment of time was situated, what environmental factors were influencing the person at that point in time, what the person had experienced prior to that segment of time, or some combination of these factors.

Perhaps the essence of developmental theorizing is the assertion that behavior is a function of chronological age. Such a shift allows us to rephrase our statement that behavior is a function of two years to behavior is a function of being two years old. But even this equation, though often used, does not reflect the essence of developmental thinking. Actually, as Ausubel (1958) has noted, it has been the source of considerable confusion. Being two years old simply means that two years have passed since the birth of the organism, and one again finds himself predicting change in behavior as a function of the passage of time. What is added when we designate when in the life cycle this particular passage of time occurs? Such a designation suggests that time to the developmentalist is nothing more than a convenient backdrop on which behaviors can be chronologically ordered and changes noted.

The developmentalist is interested in change, not as a function of time, but rather as a group of organismic processes which take place over time. The developmentally-oriented psychologist has always been struck by the phenomena of growth and change and the orderliness, sequentiality, and apparent lawfulness of the transition taking place from the birth or conception of the organism to the attainment of maturity. The developmentalist's theoretical task has been one of constructing principles or constructs making such change comprehensible. Such principles clearly have little to do with time and much to do with those processes, involving the person and his environment, which give rise to changes in behavior.

Stated in this way, developmental psychology becomes an extremely arbitrary subdivision of psychology. For if the concept of process is divorced from any particular theory, all of psychology is concerned with change in behavior as a function of process. Thus, when defined in terms of an interest in change, developmental theory is reducible to general behavior theory, since such theory, regardless of its orientation, must deal with the problem of change in behavior, regardless of when in the life cycle such change occurs.

While the fact remains that other subdivisions of theoretical psychology are also ultimately reducible to general behavior theory, they nevertheless have defining features which act as a rationale for the existence of the subdivisions and, more importantly for our discussion, guide and delimit the theory construction one encounters in these areas. Such delimitations have value, for psychologists are ill-equipped to construct theories capable of subsuming behavior in its entirety. Smaller domains are needed which permit the abstraction or imposition of theoretical superstructures which make the behavior found in these domains under-standable and predictable.

But what are the defining features which make developmental psy-chology such a domain? To the extent that it is equated with an interest in change as a function of process, it has no defining features and be-comes one with all of the subdivisions of psychology taken in toto. The breadth of behavioral content often included in its subject matter attests to this undifferentiated usage. Congruent with this broad inclusion, one can find all of psychology's commonly-held theoretical positions being employed to deal with the contents of developmental psychology. If this branch of psychology is treated in this way, then little value accrues in continuing to treat it as a unique field, and any discussion of theory con-struction in this area becomes superfluous.

Developmental psychology does appear to contain unique interests and concerns which make it a delimited domain demanding approaches, methodologies, and theories having particular characteristics. What is re-quired for such delimitation is not the definition that developmental psychology is concerned with change as a function of process, but rather that it is concerned with the changes in the form or organization of re-sponses over time as contrasted with the change in the strength or ac-curacy of the response. What happens to a response after a prescribed number of trials is "learning." What happens over five years is "devel-opment." Thus, the developmentalist focuses on structural changes in a response, changes which cannot be defined simply in terms of changes which occur with single trials or stimulus presentations. Again contrast-ing developmental psychology with the psychology of learning, the orthodox learning theorist would handle observed changes in the effec-tiveness of his variables at different ages by introducing into his equations or predictions different values for the parameters of interest. The de-velopmentalist is interested in a super-ordinate explanation of all such substitutions of values. While the learning theorist may change the values of his parameters from age to age, the developmentalist is concerned with discovering the transition rules for these changes, making the change itself, rather than the content of change, the central issue.

In principle the developmentalist can study such change during any segment or all of the life span. In practice the developmentalist's investi-gation has been facilitated by concentrating on those periods in the life span during which the responses of the person are characterized by con-tinuous and striking change, rather than those periods in the life cycle where one is impressed by the stability of the person, his sameness from day to day and from year to year. Certainly, even in such stable states change does occur, but our interest is in the behavioral content of the change rather than in the structural change in responses. During such a period, change as a phenomenon in itself is of little concern, nor does there appear to be much need during this stable state for different parameters or concepts at different times to deal with observed changes in behavior.

This division of the life span into periods of either striking change or stability appears to do little injustice to what we actually observe. The periods of infancy, childhood, and adolescence are those during which change in behavior is both continuous and striking. During these periods non-developmental theories of behavior apply only with great difficulty. We then have the rather lengthy and stable adulthood of the individual, and it is certainly this period which is the concern of most state theories dealing with human behavior. Following this adulthood we have a period of old age or decline, where we again are struck by the phenomenon of change. This view of the life span is reflected in the myriad of physical and intellectual growth curves in which the individual ascends to an asymptote, remains at this asymptote for a number of years, and then descends from it.

The periods defined by this ascension and, more recently, the descension have been the fertile areas of investigation for developmentalists. The fact that many developmental psychologists, e.g., John Anderson and Nancy Bayley, who early in their careers focused on child development, are now attending to the problems of aging, is more than coincidental. One can immediately see the constancy of these efforts when they are conceptualized in terms of an interest in the deviation from the asymptote mentioned above. This increased concern of developmentalists with the changes of old age is of rather recent vintage. Developmental psychology, therefore, remains most identified with the ascending portion of our curve, namely, child development.

Thus, for the purposes of our analysis, we shall treat developmental theory as being concerned with that most obvious period of change, childhood. Such a delimitation will be criticized by a number of developmentalists who have continually asserted that the developmental principles or concepts which have been advanced to explain changes in behavior, e.g., accommodation, assimilation, equilibration (Piaget), differentiation (Lewin and Werner), permeability of boundaries in the life space (Lewin and Kounin), psychosexual stages (Freud), and nuclear conflicts of the ego (Erikson), are principles operative throughout the life span.

However, the efforts of such developmentalists fall far short of supporting their premise concerning the generality of developmental principles. Freud and his more orthodox followers were content to deal with the psychosexual stages up to the point in adolescence where the genital stage was attained. Erikson, though postulating nuclear conflicts of the ego throughout the life span of the individual, dealt at length only with the earlier-appearing conflicts and suggested that if the earlier conflicts are successfully navigated, the later conflicts pose little difficulty. Piaget has no hesitancy in locating the ultimate stage of cognitive development characterized by logical thinking in early adolescence. The concept of differentiation has little meaning when extended beyond adolescence. To the extent that this concept has been given operational meaning by equating it with MA, the defining operations themselves limit the applicability of this concept to approximately the onset of adulthood.

In Werner's efforts such methodological procedures as tachistoscopic presentation of stimuli to investigate microgenesis and developmental Rorschach scoring are meaningful only to the extent that the measures obtained are reminiscent of the behaviors of children. The concept of regression, so often used by developmentalists, is a further case in point. Regardless of its theoretical underpinnings, the statement that an individual of 25 is manifesting behaviors characteristic of a 10-year-old or a 5-year-old conveys some meaning. But what meaning could be attributed to the statement that a 45-year-old is acting like a 35- or 30-year-old? Such statements are rare in the writings of developmentalists and, when used, have little to do with issues central to developmental theorizing.

The point being made here involves more than a defense of our somewhat arbitrary delimitation of developmental psychology. We can only conclude that while certain developmentalists have asserted the applicability of developmental principles to all of human behavior, the bulk of their efforts has belied their assertion. The application of developmental principles to the asymptotic portion of the life span of the normal individual is probably the single most demanding, yet most under-attacked problem in developmental psychology. Thus, given the present status of developmental theorizing, developmental theories are best assessed in terms of how adequately they handle that particular domain represented by child development. Therefore, for the purposes of this paper, only those efforts will be considered whose central concern is the structural changes in behavior observed during childhood.

Methods and Goals

The foregoing analysis has served to identify the general content area of developmental psychology; we shall now move on to the problem of methodology. As Anderson (1954) has so well pointed out, there is a natural sequence from content to methodology to theory. In the premethodological period we find an interest, a concern, or a curiosity about a particular set of phenomena. Questions are asked and problems are established. Such a process requires neither method nor formal theory.

As noted, in developmental psychology this concern has been with certain progressive changes in behavior. Neither theory nor methodology was required to arouse man's interest in human growth and development. How does the person change from the tiny, pre-linguistic, motorically incompetent organism which we encounter in infancy to that larger, verbal, motorically skilled organism represented in adulthood? How does the dependent, asocial, and amoral infant develop into the independent, socialized, moralistic adult? How do the non-veridical perceptions, the egocentric and illogical thought processes develop into the veridical perception, the reality-oriented and logical cognitive functioning encountered in maturity? These and related problems are the content of developmental psychology.

Is some one particular methodology especially appropriate for unraveling the mysteries of this content? Some have argued (cf. Ausubel, 1958) that developmental problems are so complex and involve phenomena which are spatially so gross and of such long duration that a naturalistic methodology is the only appropriate one. Thus Ausubel (1958) asserts that, given this particular content area, the developmentalist "has no other choice but to describe, measure, and relate phenomena as they occur naturally in uncontrived situations." The experimental method is viewed as being not only inapplicable but also as being slightly dangerous, on the grounds that the phenomena under investigation cannot be replicated or manipulated in the experimental setting. Efforts to do so must by necessity introduce artificial components which can only result in an erroneous conclusion concerning the relationship of the particular independent and dependent variables being investigated. While the naturalistic approach appears more amenable to atheoretical than to theoretical efforts, Ausubel has argued that it does not preclude the construction of theory. Indeed he has argued that unless the investigator abstracts principles from the data obtained through naturalistic methods and theoretically relates these principles, he cannot qualify as a developmental psychologist. To Ausubel, purely normative or empirical investigations involve an interest in a discrete series of unrelated contemporaneous events and have little to do with any concern with change as a phenomenon.

The view that the methodology of developmental psychology is exclusively naturalistic and non-experimental and that adequate theorizing can be built upon such a limited methodology has been basic to much of the effort in this area and therefore deserves our closest scrutiny. As indicated earlier, theory and methodology are closely interwoven, and therefore a commitment to a particular methodology must result in the construction of particular kinds of theories. The author's view is that scientific efforts in psychology which have no recourse to experimental investigations can only result in inadequate theorizing, and that those who argue against employing experimental methods in developmental psychology have an erroneous conception of the role of experiments in our efforts after understanding.

Clearly, no amount of normative investigation or naturalistic observation guarantees the emergence of theoretical concepts which relate or explain the phenomena which have been observed. Such concepts are constructions of the observer and do not flow unerringly from the observations. The observer alone determines the amount of empirical data required to induce or construct those principles or concepts which, when welded together, form for the observer his explanatory edifice. The reward for this effort is the theoretician's feeling that he now understands the phenomena in question, and the disorganized and mysterious content becomes orderly and meaningful.

The conceptual distance between the theoretical constructs and the empirical data from which they were derived is also determined by the theory constructor. One can closely scrutinize the motoric development of the infant and on the basis of his observations induce the principle that such development is cephalo-caudal in nature. Such a concept is not far removed from the data from which it was derived. On the other hand, the observer may be impressed with the lack of smoothness in physical and social growth, noting periods of physiological and psychological spurts interspersed with periods of relative quiescence. When faced with such observations, the theoretician may construct a concept of developmental disequilibrium (Ausubel, 1958), a conceptual entity quite removed from the natural observations which gave rise to it.

Note that both concepts only have meaning to the extent that they are tied to observables or to other concepts in the theoretical matrix which are themselves tied to some behavioral referents. Such collections of concepts gained through naturalistic observations have a striking characteristic—they are quite refractory to disproof. To the extent that the concepts are of a low order of inference, they represent shorthand expressions for the observations from which they were derived, and thus they unquestionably encompass the data on which they were constructed. Concepts of a higher level of inference are also induced from observables and must therefore by necessity subsume these observables, making it difficult to designate what conditions will be necessary to demonstrate the lack of validity of the concept. The more rarefied the concept, the more difficult to disprove it.

These rarefied concepts also appear to have greater "explanatory" power than lower-order concepts, due to their more minimal tie to the observations from which they were derived. Actually, such concepts lack definitional rigor and allow the systematizer to place quite divergent behaviors within their rubric. Thus, the systematizer can attribute both resistiveness and ultra-conformity in behavior to developmental disequilibrium (Ausubel, 1958). In this same vein, the developmentalist may subsume the quite different observations concerning the genesis of motor behavior made by Coghill (1929) and Windle (1937) under the "orthogenetic principle of differentiation and hierarchic integration" (Werner, 1957[b]).

The systematizer is aware of the ambiguity of concepts which are viewed as underlying such diverse phenomena and makes a case for their retention by taking refuge in such extra-theoretical views as that a single genotype gives rise to diverse phenotypes (Ausubel, 1958) or that a uniform principle underlies a multiformity of specific developmental changes (Werner, 1957[b]). But this is to beg the issue. What the systematizer must do is not merely attach labels or concepts to behaviors, but rather use his explanatory edifice to clarify why and under what conditions a particular behavior occurs rather than another. We would like to know why one child displays conformity while another is resistive. We would like to know when differentiation will occur and when hierarchization will occur. Here we are damning neither conceptual entities nor assumptive principles. We are simply asserting that such entities must be explicitly related to other concepts, usually of the middle range, within a system before either inter- or intra-individual changes or differences in behavior become theoretically comprehensible.

This, of course, demands continuous expansion and refinement of the explanatory matrix, model, or theory. The history of developmental psychology indicates that the naturalistic method provides little impetus for such refinement. It results in the construction of explanatory concepts so little removed from the phenomena that they are merely shorthand expressions of them. This method also appears to have resulted in the construction of concepts so far removed from the phenomena that they permit the systematizer to encompass verbally vast collections of empirical observations while actually explaining very little. Again, what appear to be missing are constructs which relate these two types of concepts to one another. We are here obviously referring to the grand systems which have appeared in developmental psychology, the efforts of a Freud, a Piaget, a Gesell, or a Werner. It is enlightening to note that, with the exception of Werner, these systems were built upon an observational base, and the essence of the systems was never submitted to experimental investigation.

Indeed, when faced with such grand systems, one is hard pressed to discover what constitutes an adequate test of them. When the concepts are translated into experimental data language and a test attempted, the effort may be repudiated by the system builder or his adherents on the grounds that this experimental effort does not reflect the natural appearing phenomena or does some injustice to the system itself. Those who defend systems on this latter ground fail to realize that they are indicting the system as well as the experimenter, for a system must eventually be judged in terms of how clearly it permits tests of the propositions advanced therein. Without such tests the system must forever remain an encapsulated conceptual entity which by the very nature of its construction can "explain" the phenomena on which it was constructed.

But how does one ever choose between two such systems when no criterion of validity exists independent of the system? There is no way to do so; all such systems are equally "true." As a result such systems proliferate, and they exist side by side. They are defended vigorously, and the suggestion that perhaps Freud, Piaget, or Gesell may have erred in the conceptual extrapolations made from their observations is met with vehement response.

What we have been saying does not appear to do an injustice to the history of developmental psychology. With perhaps the exception of the most primitive predeterministic or homuncular views, the grand systems are still with us. What is missing in developmental psychology is the steady increase in knowledge resulting from the cumulative effects of data collection interspersed with ever-changing theoretical formulations. We see no theoretical efforts built solidly upon, and thereby replacing, earlier efforts. We do not profit by the errors of our predecessors, because of the lack of ground rules whereby one investigator's extrapolations from his observations demonstrate that another investigator's extrapolations are in error. Thus, the developmental psychology of the grand systems becomes a personal, rather than a public, effort, with each generation awaiting that truly sensitive observer who will bring order to the vast complexity which is our content area. Observation is not what is at fault, but the failure of developmentalists to appreciate the importance of maximizing the stability of observation. Such stability and objectivity are maximally provided by the experiment. In addition to providing such observational stability, the experiment may also perform certain validating functions.

Only to the extent that we introduce some external criterion of validity can we choose or synthesize what is useful in those conceptual principles or constructs induced from naturalistic observation. To the author such a criterion is provided by the experimental method. As indicated earlier, many developmentalists have not fully comprehended the role of experiment in the validation process. In order to illuminate this relationship, a clear distinction must be drawn between two types of experiments. One type of experiment unquestionably represents an effort to mimic nature. That is, nature is brought into the laboratory, and a number of controls are exerted to discover the relationship between particular variables. This type of experiment falls on the same continuum with natural observation, its superiority lying in its efficiency. Thus, armed with a thermometer and the knowledge of how far above sea level various locations were, we could through naturalistic observations discover the temperature at which water boils and how air pressure affects this boiling point. But how much easier can we discover these relationships in the controlled situations provided by the experiment. However, many developmentalists find this type of experiment inapplicable to developmental psychology, and their view is probably partially correct. Much of the nature in which we are interested either cannot or should not be mimicked in the laboratory. But note that such nature-mimicking experiments have more to do with validating low-order laws or even empirical relationships than they do with demonstrating the merit of broad theoretical systems. Indeed, such experiments, rather than validating systems, are employed in much the same way as are naturalistic observations, namely, as the data from which concepts are extrapolated and systems are built (cf. Werner, 1957ᵃ).

A second type of experiment is more related to the problem of validating theoretical systems. This type of experiment does not mimic, but rather creates, nature. Here the phenomena of nature are not brought into the laboratory, but instead phenomena are created which have little or no chance of being found outside of the laboratory. At this point the experimenter can be conceptualized as dealing with two distinct worlds, the world at large and the "world" which he has created. Explanatory systems which are advanced, be they in physics or developmental psychology, are established to explain the real world. How then are they related to the artificial world created by the experimentalist? Such explanatory systems appear to contain theoretical givens, concepts both closely and loosely tied to observables, principles relating these one to the other, and specific hypotheses designating relationships derivable from such a nomological network. Again, this network is constructed to explain the real world, but what characterizes such systems is that the processes suggested or the principles specified somehow transcend the world for which they were constructed and are applicable to other worlds as well.

Experiments do not test theories in their entirety, because of that portion of theories which is given, assumed, and untestable. However, the elemental principles or processes are tested, and the outcome of such tests determines the validity of the system. Thus, experiments of the second type are invariably of the theory-testing variety and involve the "if such—then such" paradigm. What the experimenter is saying is that if such and such holds in the real world because of the principles expounded in the particular theory under investigation, then such and such should hold in the world which the experimenter has created. This translatability is what gives theoretical import to experiments which involve phenomena which, taken in isolation, not only appear picayune but seem to have little relationship with what one observes in nature. These experiments have tremendous practical import. If the translation is confirmed, the experiment is a go-ahead signal; its results suggest that we would be wise to apply our explanatory system to the real world. If the translation fails, then the system stands indicted, and we are informed that employing such an explanatory system may lead us into error. In the early stages of a science some translations are confirmed, while others are not. But this is exactly how the science grows and the explanatory edifice is refined.

A clear example of an experiment of the second type in developmental psychology is provided in the work of Werner on microgenesis. Basic to Werner's position is the view that the ontogenesis of any human activity is characterized by an orderly sequence of stages. For instance, in the ontogenesis of perception, stages can be identified: first, a global stage, in which whole-qualities are dominant; a later analytic stage, in which perception is selectively directed toward parts; and a final stage, in which parts become increasingly more articulated and integrated with respect to the whole. Such ontogenetic development can be verified by examining the perceptions of children at various ages. However, Werner's clear statement that ". . . a comprehensive comparative psychology of development cannot be achieved without the aid of a general experimental psychology . . ." (1957b, p. 128) suggests that merely noting developmental changes in children's perceptions does not constitute an adequate test of his ontogenetic principle of development. He has attempted to confirm his ontogenetic principle by employing an experiment of the second type.

Underlying this experimental effort is the assumption that if the ontogenetic principle of development is true, then it should also hold in situations involving the unfolding of perceptions over seconds as well as over years. Thus, using a tachistoscope, studies were done on developmental changes in perception which occurred when the time of exposure was increased from trial to trial. Investigators discovered that changes in percepts with increasing time exposures were similar to those found with increasing age in children. Such changes with increased exposure time (microgenesis) were then employed as evidence supporting Werner's developmental theory of the ontogenesis of perception. What should be noted is that very little in this theory relates ontogenesis to microgenesis, nor is the theory seriously concerned with what happens to a percept in that extremely artificial situation in which a tachistoscopic exposure time is changed from .01 to .10 seconds. The goal of the microgenetic work was to demonstrate experimentally that a particular principle held in the laboratory situation, which in turn indicates that the principle so verified was applicable to the natural world as well.

We have, of course, painted a much too simple picture. Certain experiments have some characteristics of both the first and second types discussed above. We have also not attended to the fact that if the translation is not confirmed, an error may have been committed by the experimenter when translating from the system to his laboratory domain. On this last point, the clearer and more rigorous the system becomes, the more direct and free from error should be the translation efforts of the experimenter. Thus, even errors in logical translation have a useful purpose in forcing the systematizer to make his system more explicit. The impetus for such effort is always with the systematizer, provided the system is built with exactly this type of testing in mind.

What is needed in a science is not only experiments which efficiently mimic nature, but experiments specifically designed to test explanatory systems. That we cannot move the cosmos into our laboratory has not dissuaded the astrophysicist from employing experimental methods. One finds in nature neither certain of the phenomena produced in the cyclotron nor some of those in experimental embryology, but these phenomena have been of tremendous theoretical import to those who, early in the history of their science, were forced to depend on natural observation. Those who argue against the experimental method in developmental psychology are arguing against the refinement of our theoretical efforts. The only requirements lacking to make developmental psychology experimental are theories explicit enough to allow the logical translations discussed above and investigators willing to employ experimental investigation.

While experimental efforts have been relatively rare in developmental psychology, developmentalists currently appear to be employing such a methodology to a greater extent than ever before. Werner (1957[b]) has continually insisted that his system be tested experimentally, and one can point to the recent efforts of Kohlberg (1958) on the development of morality, Smedslund (1961) on the development of conservation, the efforts of the behavior geneticists (cf. Fuller and Thompson, 1960), the work of Wolff (1959), Gewirtz and Baer's (1958[a], 1958[b]) experimental investigation of social deprivation and satiation, the work of the Kendlers (1962) on problem solving, the efforts of Stevenson and Weir (1959) on probability learning, and Gibson's (1961) work on the development of perception. We must conclude with Anderson (1954) that no methods of investigation are unique to the study of development and that any and all methods are legitimate in illuminating this content area.

Related to the above discussion is the problem of the goals of developmental psychology. Although many developmentalists have taken the conventional view that our goal is the prediction of behavior in specified situations, others have argued against the view that prediction and control are the legitimate aims of developmental psychology. For instance, Martin (1959), one of developmental psychology's most articulate spokesmen, has stated that understanding, rather than prediction and control, is what we are after. He bolsters this argument by noting Scriven's (1959) point that we can have prediction without having understanding. This is unquestionably true and is adequately illustrated in the plethora of normative studies that have been conducted in developmental psychology. Many of our predictions concerning behavior are derived from solely empirical, actuarial, or correlational methods; no pretense is made that an explanation for the behavior is being offered. Granting that our aim is understanding rather than prediction of this type, what constitutes understanding? As suggested earlier, we shall take a position in this paper contrary to that of Scriven (1959) and Brown (1936) and assert that while prediction without explanation is possible, explanation without some predictability is impossible, and that this very predictability is what defines explanation or understanding.

To this point we have been content to treat understanding in terms of the personal feelings of the individual concerning his explanation of phenomena in question. However, such a definition appears to be grossly inadequate. For several centuries man was content with the belief that the sun revolved around the earth. But can we say that men who were content with this belief understood the nature of the movement of these two heavenly bodies? We are arguing here that understanding must be defined in terms of criteria other than the personal satisfaction of individuals. But let us move our discussion into the sphere of developmental psychology. We have long been concerned with the development of morality, and a number of explanations of this phenomenon have been offered. Some explanations have involved the flowering or maturation of the individual. Others have explained it in terms of instincts, the pleasure and reality principles, castration anxieties, the Oedipus complex, and identification. Others see the development of morality as depending on general cognitive abilities. Still others have explained moral behavior in terms of learning, with major emphasis being given to reinforcement, in what is considered a shaping process.

All of these explanations contain a certain degree of inherent logic, and all appear capable of explaining the behavioral phenomena with which they deal. But the student of developmental psychology has a right to inquire which explanation is "true." A moment's thought indicates that "truth" is an illusive commodity. All the general systems are true if one stays completely within the confines of each system and defines truth in terms of being able to explain the phenomena. All are wrong if one examines them from the vantage point of an opposing position. For, from such a vantage point, alternative explanations always appear inadequate and disquieting and therefore erroneous. If one stands outside all the systems, then there is no way of deciding which is right and which is wrong. In evaluating systems, right must not be viewed as an absolute but, instead, must be approached pragmatically. The question must be raised about the consequences of believing one system rather than another. Or, stated somewhat differently, what can the system do for you beyond supplying you with somewhat questionable feelings of omniscience?

In this presentation, we shall assert that if a system allows you to make predictions and exert controls, broadly defined, it is right. We shall further assert that if the system generates erroneous predictions and thereby causes you to act inappropriately in terms of certain goals, then it is wrong. We shall further assert that if a system does not allow for testable predictions, thus allowing you a test of the adequacy of your own actions, it is useless. Thus, we are asserting that the real criterion of understanding phenomena is not a personal but a public one, and one can only claim understanding when the legitimate predictions he makes about phenomena are confirmed.

Such an assertion appears to be an inescapable outcome of the argument that has been advanced. The writer, however, would like to go beyond this conclusion and express some views based more on his value system than on any inherent validity. He feels that the value of theories does not lie in the comfort they provide the user but rather in the things that the user can now do which he would not be able to do in the absence of a theory. What is of major importance is not the validation of a prediction but rather the implication that such validation has for human action. Thus, a good theory directs us to appropriate actions as opposed to inappropriate ones. This is true whether our goals are navigating between celestial spheres or raising children. Thus, theories must be evaluated not in terms of their inherent "trueness" but rather in terms of their usefulness as described above.

This is not to assert that a good theory can or must predict everything. We are essentially in agreement with the argument that much of human behavior, and non-behavioral phenomena as well, is unpredictable. With Scriven (1956) we accept the probability that our ultimate ability to predict will fall far short of perfection. But this does not negate the importance of prediction as a criterion of understanding. Indeed, as noted earlier, the most important predictions from the point of view of theoretical validation may be those that are made in the artificial world of the laboratory. While Brown (1936) argues that we cannot predict earthquakes, we can certainly test certain principles of seismology in the laboratory and thus confirm the heuristic values of the explanation of earthquakes advanced by the seismologist.

Let us now turn our attention to the problem of control. This has been an especially troublesome concept in the field of developmental psychology, since developmentalists are so centrally concerned with children. When the concept of control is raised, developmentalists have a tendency to think of Skinner's pigeons, and the spectre of an artificial and unhealthy method of shaping behavior is raised. As intimated above, the author feels that the concept of control has been too narrowly defined in psychology in general and developmental psychology in particular. When we speak of prediction and control, we do not necessarily mean that we can control the phenomena which we are predicting. While control may involve this, it should be defined more broadly and more pragmatically: we may wish to predict the movements of heavenly bodies, not to control these objects but rather to control the behavior of the individual capable of making the prediction.

Certainly, the ability to predict a hurricane does not mean that we can bring about or stop such a happening. But we are in a position to exercise some control over human action that we could not exercise prior to our ability to make the prediction. We know when to clear the streets, how much protective preparation will be necessary, etc. When control is defined in this way, it invariably accompanies the ability to predict, and this wider definition seems much more appropriate to the nature of the scientific enterprise than does the narrower definition. We may thus conclude that understanding always involves the ability to predict, that this ability to predict always involves the ability to control, and that the legitimate goal of theory in developmental psychology is understanding defined in terms of such prediction and control.

The Theoretical Efforts: An Overview

The foregoing discussion should make clear that many of the grand designs employed as explanatory edifices by developmental psychologists are actually pre-theoretic in nature. They are steps towards theories rather than theories themselves. When miniature theories are carved from them for purposes of experimental investigation, as in the work of Werner, the concepts in the system employed are homogeneous in nature without the hierarchical quality of more rigorous hypothetico-deductive systems. Taken as a group, developmental psychologists, until very recently, have been little concerned with the requirements of theory construction and have been not in the least self-conscious about the explanatory efforts advanced to subsume the content with which they were dealing. This lack of concern with metatheoretical problems is in part attributable to two factors: 1) the peculiar history of developmental psychology and 2) the atheoretical nature of the bulk of the empirical efforts in this area. As Baldwin (1960) has noted, much of the history of developmental psychology is characterized by a separation from academic psychology in general and behavior theory in particular.

This separation was certainly facilitated by the growth of the child institutes which were in their ascendency during that epoch in psychology which Koch (1959) has referred to as the Age of Theory. Thus, while departments of psychology were actively concerned with problems of theory, developmental psychologists were insulated from this concern by their actual physical separation from departments of psychology. This isolation no longer exists. Developmental psychology certainly appears to have escaped the now somewhat abated demands for overly-formalized theory construction. The second factor giving rise to the lack of concern with theory was the atheoretical and practical nature of much of the empirical work in this area, best characterized by the normative and longitudinal studies which were so popular with developmental psychologists. This is not to imply that such studies are by their very nature atheoretical. Whether such studies are theoretical or not depends solely on the willingness of the investigator to assert that they represent a test of some particular view, or his willingness to extrapolate from his findings and advance some explanation for them. However, many of these investigations neither began with theory nor eventuated in theory, and this theoretical sterility has certainly come under attack (cf. Ausubel, 1958).

Such attacks strike the author as somewhat arbitrary. These studies have certainly resulted in the collection of a sound body of empirical facts concerning the development of a multitude of abilities and age-related behaviors. The importance and further need of this type of data have been emphasized by some of our more thoughtful developmentalists (cf. Anderson, 1960; Kessen, 1960). The value of this work for evaluating the growth of any particular child and for making better predictions certainly needs no defense. One further point concerning such investigations does appear to be in order. The author is obviously committed to the view that theories are both useful and necessary. However, the view that the total field of developmental psychology is amenable to what would be considered adequate theorizing is, in the present state of knowledge, an assumption.

It can and has been argued that efforts after theory can only blind us to behavioral givens and thus lead us away from knowledge; this position is difficult to refute. The success that theories have enjoyed in other sciences or areas is no guarantee that such success will automatically be forthcoming in developmental psychology. In the last analysis, the pre-

requisites and upper limits of our explanatory efforts will be determined
by the nature of our content rather than the desires of those investigating this content. Thus, the methodological problems of developmental
psychology may be more akin to those presented by the study of geography than they are to the science of physics. As in geography, what
may be required are not postulates but rather the careful point-by-point
exploration and mapping of human development. Such a map would then
be our ultimate explanatory device in ordering the phenomena we are
interested in and in directing us in our own interactions with this phenomena. In this respect it is interesting to note that Shuttleworth's classic
normative work for the adolescent period was presented in a publication entitled *Graphic Atlas* (1951). Thus an individual's commitment
either to theory or to purely empirical investigations appears to be a
matter of personal predilection rather than a matter of the inherent
superiority of either approach.

As indicated earlier, a large number of normative studies have emanated
either implicitly or explicitly from a particular theoretical orientation.
Such studies are most clearly represented in the work of Gesell and his
co-workers. The orientation here was quite similar to earlier predeterministic views. The growth and change in physiological and psychological processes were attributed almost entirely to endogenous regulatory
mechanisms. This rather extreme maturational position has come in for
severe criticism (Ausubel, 1958; Hunt, 1961), and the fine points of its
content need not concern us here. For the purposes of this paper we
shall only concern ourselves with the question of how such an orientation gave rise to the particular empirical methodology which accompanied it and with an assessment of its formal qualities as a theory.

If the behavioral potentialities of the individual are predetermined at
the moment of conception, and human growth and development are primarily a flowering or an unfolding process during which these behavioral
givens manifest themselves, clearly the most appropriate type of investigation is the normative one, in which we carefully chart the sequentiality
of this process and the particular times during which such a developmental morphology results in particular behaviors. Within such a system, any differences in the timetable of development are simply attributed to differences in genetic inheritance. While such a view has been
and continues to be an influential one, it is difficult to refer to as a
theory. It appears rather to be a grand view having but a single construct, maturation. Every behavior that is seen is simply attributed to
this construct, and explanation is thus reduced to a labeling process.
Within such a framework, no other choice exists than to make the norms
discovered through empirical investigations into explanatory devices.
Thus, one discovers that at a certain age children manifest negative be-

haviors, and one "explains" these behaviors by saying that children of this age are in the negative stage. The vacuousness and conceptual inadequacy of such a procedure has frequently been noted (cf. Kessen, 1960; Lewin, 1936).

This is not to assert that an explanatory system is to be evaluated in terms of the number of concepts available to the user, nor does it mean that a commitment to a predeterministic orientation invariably had to lead to an inadequate system. Explaining the negativism observed in children with a more complex conceptual schema involving libidinal attachments and withdrawals, instinctual gratifications and their frustration, ego development, etc., has little to recommend it over the predeterministic view, if in both instances the explanation is nothing more than an exercise in verbal circumlocution. What is required of theory is that it have a sufficient number of concepts to encompass adequately the empirical phenomena that are grossly observable and that these concepts be at least minimally defined and related one to the other so that the system generates certain testable hypotheses concerning the phenomena subsumed by the theory. If negativistic behaviors could be demonstrated to be invariate both in terms of the actual behaviors observed and the time of their occurrence, then the predeterministic position would have much to recommend it. However, the observed differences, both in particular behaviors and in stimuli eliciting such behaviors, and differences in the timetable of their occurrence led many developmentalists to discount the predeterministic position. On the other hand, having a collection of verbal labels at your disposal to explain such differences in any particular observed instance constitutes little improvement over such a position. While such systems suggest great explanatory ability, as indicated in the preceding section, they have not been formalized to the extent required to test their validity.

A system of this type, which has also employed normative investigations, is that of Piaget and his co-workers. This system has recently become the focal point of attention for many developmentalists. Again, our purpose is not to discuss the content of the system but rather to assess its theoretical sophistication. The popularity of this system is in part attributable to the fact that it includes all of the possible factors which could conceivably be advanced to account for human development. While the maturationist may stress endogenous factors and the environmentalist emphasizes learning, both can feel comfortable with at least some aspects of Piaget's conceptual rubric. To Piaget, development is a function of an internal process, equilibration, which in turn is dependent on activity and experience. Development to Piaget is conceptualized as something quite different from Gesell's maturation, since it is highly influenced by the experiences of the individual which bring out latent contradictions and gaps in the mental structure and thus act as a catalyst for inner reorganization. We thus have here an interactionist position, with the continued interaction between organism and environment being subsumed within Piaget's concepts of accommodation and assimilation. Piaget presents us with a grand scheme which seems to contain the necessary concepts for explaining not only the sequentiality in cognitive development but also the individual differences observed in such development. Again the methodological emphasis is on the normative investigation to demonstrate the differences in cognitive functioning with age.

But beyond such demonstrations, Piaget's system is difficult to apply. One must conclude with Rapaport (1959) that the actual application of the genetic point of view contained in the work of Werner and Piaget is far from solved. Again the difficulty in application appears to rest in the failure to translate a point of view into a theory containing testable propositions involving the phenomena of interest. On this point, Stevenson's succinct evaluation of Piaget's explanatory effort is interesting. Stevenson (in press) writes:

Actually, it is questionable whether Piaget has really developed more than a conceptual framework for discussing intellective development. If Piaget's writings are to be assessed in terms of their ability to produce new synthetic statements which involve more than relating a type of behavior to a developmental stage, they must be judged to constitute an unsatisfactory theory. As is true in most developmental points of view, the most that can be predicted is that the subject will show certain types of behavior if he is at a particular developmental level.

While some interesting hypotheses (cf. Hunt, 1961) have been derived from Piaget's schema, such derivations are more a product of the translation made by the deriver than anything explicit in Piaget. Piaget, though offering a conceptually more satisfactory explanation than Gesell, deserts us at that point at which sequentiality and age norms are demonstrated. For all of the talk concerning the importance of the individual, the environment, and the interaction between the two, both the individual and the environment are treated as constant. As even serious students of Piaget must note (Hunt, 1961; Wolff, 1960), nothing in Piaget allows one to assess the effects of either the state of the organism or differences in the environment that give rise to individual differences in development.

Piaget's supporters have failed to appreciate the importance of those studies which have demonstrated that Piaget's age norms do not fit children in other cultures. To stress that Piaget is more interested in demonstrating the sequence of such development, rather than the age at which certain behaviors become manifest, is to miss the point of such critical studies. In psychology we are most intimately concerned with the issue of what conditions give rise to what behaviors and why. This concern is manifested in the study of individual differences, and a system that addresses itself to cognitive development but makes no allowances for such differences can make no pretense of being an adequate psychology of human behavior. And here we come to the crux of the matter. As has frequently been noted (cf. Martin, 1959), Piaget has been more interested in developing an epistemology than a psychology. Or as Kessen (in press) has stated, "It should be noted that Piaget has little interest in individual variation among children in the rate at which they achieve a stage or their over-all capacity during it; he is a student of the development of thinking more than he is a student of children."

Thus, the actual difference between Gesell and Piaget is not as great as one might initially imagine. The predictions derived from either system are limited almost entirely to sequential behaviors. Neither system has explicit concepts relating particular environmental factors to the nature of the sequence or to the content observed. This is true for Gesell because he is a maturationist, and, his notion of reciprocal interweaving to the contrary notwithstanding, such issues are viewed by him as pseudo-issues. It is true for Piaget because he is more interested in the general epistemological implication of the sequences than he is in the psychology of human behavior. However, we do not mean to imply that Piaget has not given us an extremely provocative system. Its prime value appears to rest not on its merit as a finished theory but rather on its susceptibility to translation, either in whole or in part, into more formally adequate theories or propositions. Representative of such translations are the works of Stevenson (in press), Hunt (1961), Berlyne (1960), Kohlberg (1958), and Wolff (1960). That Piaget's efforts lend themselves to such translations is a tribute to his system.

Another provocative system constructed in the grand manner is that of Freud. Since the theoretical development of this system is at approximately the same level as that of Piaget's, i.e., a pre-theoretic collection of concepts, and since the metatheoretic aspects of this system have so frequently been discussed and are being treated again in this volume, we shall confine ourselves to a few remarks related to central issues in developmental psychology. Although Freud's conceptualization of the psychosexual stages clearly earmarks him as a developmentalist, he occupies a rather odd position in the developmental firmament. While Freud's system has led to certain proselytizing efforts in the area of child rearing and has served to direct general behavior theorists to apply their principles to particular age periods or content areas, the system has had less impact on developmental psychology than is generally believed. The reason for this, in addition to historical ones, seems to be related to certain basic assumptions of the system rather than to the nature of its construction or its formal characteristics.

A brief examination of these features should not only illuminate the inadequacies of Freud's developmental psychology but also should make clear to the reader both a distinguishing feature of developmental theorizing and one felt to be indispensable by most developmentalists. We are referring here to the commitment to the view that development, both initially and in its later stages, is a positive process. Growth is conceptualized as the continuous emergence of ever greater adaptive abilities, with the growing organism demonstrating and fulfilling this greater potential at successive stages in his development. The developmentalist has always been concerned with the self-actualizing features of growth and has shied away from those views which characterize man as inherently base and negative in nature. The tension-reduction, hedonistic approach to man, whether it stems from the Freudian or classic behavioral systems, has always been unacceptable to the developmentalist, for such a view simply does not reflect what developmentalists have grossly observed in the child's development. That Harlow's (1953) attack on this negativistic emphasis was prefaced by his common sense observations of his own children is illuminating in this regard. Indeed, the behavioral achievements demonstrated by the child in the course of his development have not been and cannot be placed within a theoretic rubric which employs the quiescence of a few base drives as the ultimate explanation of behavior.

Developmentalists can only smile at the fairly recent "discovery" and emphasis in general psychology of such adaptive aspects of behavior as curiosity, manipulation, and the general motive of effectance. This emphasis on the positive, the adaptive, and the self-fulfilling has always been accepted by the developmentally oriented, and one finds it either implicitly or explicitly in such diverse efforts as the atheoretical normative work, the maturational view of Gesell, and the equilibration positions of Piaget and Werner. What identifies the developmentalist is this commitment to growth in the most positive sense, and the lack of such a commitment makes the Freudian system both inapplicable and unpalatable to those most intimately involved in the observation of the developing child. In a classical Freudian system, most of the content of developmental psychology as defined earlier in this chapter has no place. The effort to explain the continually emerging adaptive and creative potentialities of the person in terms of basic hedonistic instincts and their gratification, frustration, and sublimation simply strikes one as being labored.

As Wolff (1960) has noted, Freud is the only classical stage theorist who has given no attention to the concept of structure, emphasizing instead the instincts and their vicissitudes. (Although Freud's id, ego, and superego are "structures," they have little in common with the concepts involving structure found elsewhere in developmental psychology.) This omission on Freud's part is quite in keeping with his negativistic orientation, for the concept of developing structures has invariably been employed by other developmental thinkers as the theoretical mechanisms underlying the ever-increasing . adaptive adequacy of the growing organism. This lack of concern with the characteristics of developing structures and the insistence on reducing or explaining the behaviors that emerge with age to primitive hedonistic factors have led even analytically oriented developmentalists to conclude that "Freud's position shows a profound disbelief in the phenomenon of change and development . . ." (Schachtel, 1959). The implication that "either Freud had no real developmental psychology or that he had a wrong one" (Scheerer, 1961), which can be derived from Schachtel's critique, is certainly consistent with the view being espoused here. While ego psychology with its emphasis on the conflict-free sphere of adaptive ego-functioning is more amenable to developmental thought, the present theoretical status of ego psychology represents little more than a belated confession that the classical maladaptive and negative emphasis of Freud is inadequate to the task of dealing with the developmental process. Such a confession does not in itself constitute a developmental theory but simply indicates the possibility of initiating the construction of such a theory within this revised analytic framework.

We shall conclude this overview with a brief look at that body of work in developmental psychology which has been done within a learning-theory framework. For the most part this work has emanated from the theoretical positions of Hull, the neo-Hullians, and Skinner. Again, since the metatheoretical aspects of these theories are being discussed in other chapters of this volume, we shall address ourselves only to certain general issues of interest to the student of developmental psychology.

That the classical S-R tension-reduction model has never been warmly received by most developmentalists should be immediately noted. As suggested earlier, one reason for this apathy was the negative orientation of tension-reduction or extrinsic-reinforcement models, an orientation that has never been acceptable to developmentalists. Another cause of this rejection was the fact that although learning theorists viewed their principles as being applicable across species, the theories were contructed on work done with animals. The early form of such theories thus had no place within their theoretical matrices for cognitive development and other central processes. The rigor and parsimony of such theories thus resulted in the exclusion of phenomena that were of the most immediate concern to developmentalists. Furthermore, the asserted generality of the theoretical principles not only across species but across age levels within any one species was completely antithetical to the gross observations of the developmental psychologists. The learning theorist attempted to bridge this gap between the assertion of generality and the empirical evidence to the contrary by invoking the concept of maturation. Thus, the learning theorist treated maturation as some sort of biological given, whereas to the developmentalist it has always been an extremely complex process requiring theoretical illumination in its own right. Stated somewhat differently, to the learning theorist growth simply required changing parametric values, whereas to the developmentalist growth had to be treated as the central content of the theory. The learning theorist, committed to the study of general processes that relate the organism to its environment through its past history, has continued to remain indifferent to the repeated demonstration of striking changes in behavior that are relatively uninfluenced and unmodifiable by the organism's experiences. This indifference has understandably annoyed the developmentalist. On the other hand the classical developmental psychologist has been slow to appreciate the importance in the developmental process of the principles emphasized by learning theorists. Piaget's view that external reinforcers are only influential early in life represents a striking disregard for considerable evidence.

Non-learning-theory-oriented developmentalists of even the interactionist persuasion, though giving considerable lip service to the importance of the experiences of the organism, nevertheless treat experience and learning as a constant, giving their primary theoretic attention to the autochthonous factors in the developmental process. Furthermore, the developmentalists seemed to be forever attacking Watson, Hull, and Skinner, refusing to accept the fact that the new emphasis on positive motivational factors provided in the work of Sheffield, Harlow, Butler, and Montgomery (cf. White, 1959, for a review of this work), and the inclusion and emphasis of mediational variables in the theoretical efforts of Miller, Dollard, Mowrer, and Osgood have given considerable new breadth to learning theory, making it capable of handling many phenomena of central concern to the developmentalist.

Another factor that has made developmentalists wary of investigators with a learning theory approach has been the reluctance of many of these investigators to become truly involved with and receptive to the total behavioral picture presented by the developing child. Such investigators appear much more committed to a particular learning theory than they are to the content area of developmental psychology. Their efforts have appeared to be directed more towards the demonstration of the applicability of a learning theory principle than to the unraveling of the central problems of growth and development. Such efforts are best exemplified in the numerous demonstrations that the Law of Effect does indeed hold for children and in that plethora of studies that attempt nothing more than the mechanical application to children of research designs originally employed with animal populations. Such investigations do little to refine the learning theories from which they were derived, nor are they of much assistance to the developmentalist attempting to illumine the mysteries of human development.

This criticism, though a justifiable one, appears to have been overextended by many developmentalists. For many years a group of developmental psychologists, though beginning with classical learning theory, have been genuinely committed to the investigation of children's behavior and have been primarily concerned with the development of a learning theory capable of encompassing this behavior, rather than with the demonstration that the original theoretical efforts were valid. In almost every instance, the efforts of such investigators have resulted in the enrichment of the original theory employed, as well as adding to our understanding of children's behavior. Though the following listing is far from inclusive, such effort can be seen in the earlier work of Child, Whiting, the Nowlises, and the Searses, and in the more recent work of Berlyne, Gewirtz, Stevenson, Kessen, and the Kendlers.

A clear example of a development-sensitive learning-theory approach is contained in the recent work of the Kendlers (cf. 1962). These investigators have dealt with the problem of when in development children shift from responding in a manner consistent with a single unit S-R theory to responding in a mediational manner. They have gone on to investigate the relationships among hypothesized mediational processes, the verbalizations of the child, and his problem-solving behavior, an area of long-standing concern to developmentalists.

Any adequate theory of human behavior must include both classic developmental and learning constructs. As for the long-standing antipathy between developmentalists and learning theorists, the author can only conclude with Kendler (in press) that:

The fact is that if the principles generated by research with laboratory animals are applicable to higher-level human behavior, then research directed at understanding the changes that take place with increasing maturity can extend the range and the vitality of behavior theory. If some of the knowledge derived from learning experiments can give direction to developmental research and can help to explain and organize its findings, behavior theorists may yet convert a potential enemy into a valuable ally.

In view of the over-all purpose of this chapter, one final point concerning the importance of the efforts of learning theorists in this area is in order. A view that has permeated this paper is that theory construction in developmental psychology is not only at an extremely primitive level, but also that there has been relatively little concern with even the minimal requirements of formal theory construction. One need not unduly lament such a state of affairs, since it has permitted the developmentalist complete freedom in exploring his content area, isolating key issues, and developing promising conceptual entities. This activity unquestionably constitutes the first stage in theory construction. However, such efforts must remain theoretically inadequate unless developmentalists move on to higher levels of theory construction, including at least minimal definitions of concepts, the explicit designation of the relationship between the concepts employed, and the experimental validation of these relationships within the limitations noted earlier in this paper.

What is disturbing is not the primitive stage of theorizing in developmental psychology, but the fact that there is rather little impetus within the area to move on to more sophisticated theoretical efforts. Many have mistakenly viewed the grand designs which have populated this area as ultimate explanatory devices, while others have continued to argue that much more empirical investigation must be conducted before any theoretical efforts can be made. This latter argument suffers from a confusion between theory as an arbitrarily constructed tool, aiding the investigator in the knowledge-gathering process, and theory construed as some final explanatory achievement capable of encompassing all the phenomena with which we are concerned. Developmental psychology is not only ready but badly in need of theories of the former sort, if for no other reason than to move us beyond our present state of knowledge. The construction of such theories is insured to the extent that we have investigators within developmental psychology who are imbued with a heritage which emphasizes the importance and value of theory construction and who are sophisticated as to the rigorous requirements of such an undertaking. The developmental psychologists with a learning-theory orientation appear to represent just such a heritage, and the infusion of their thinking in this area should result in a greater concern with and a more sophisticated effort after theory construction. Any real assessment of the effects of this infusion must await future developments in this area.

References

Anderson, J. Methods of child psychology. In L. Carmichael (ed.), *Manual of child psychology* (2nd ed.). New York: Wiley, 1954.
———. Child development research: the next twenty-five years. *Child Develpm.*, 1960, *31*, 191–199.
Ausubel, D. *Theories and problems of child development.* New York: Grune and Stratton, 1958.

Baldwin, A. The study of child behavior and development. In P. Mussen (ed.), *Handbook of research methods in child development.* New York: Wiley, 1960.

Berlyne, D. *Conflict, arousal, and curiosity.* New York: McGraw-Hill, 1960.

Brown, W. Facing the facts. In *Proc. 25th Anniv. Celebr. Inaug. Grad. Stud.* Los Angeles: Univ. of South. Calif. Press, 1936, pp. 116–121.

Coghill, G. *Anatomy and the problem of behavior.* New York: Macmillan, 1929.

Fuller, J., and Thompson, W. *Behavior genetics.* New York: Wiley, 1960.

Gewirtz, J., and Baer, D. The effect of brief social deprivation on behaviors for a social reinforcer. *J. Abnorm. Soc. Psychol.*, 1958[a], 56, 49–56.

———. Deprivation and satiation of social reinforcers as drive states. *J. Abnorm. Soc. Psychol.*, 1958[b], 57, 165–172.

Gibson, E. Differentiation and association in perceptual development. Paper read at SRCD meetings, University Park, Pa., March 1961.

Harlow, H. Mice, monkeys, men, and motives. *Psychol. Rev.*, 1953, 60, 23–32.

Harris, D. (ed.). *The concept of development: an issue in the study of human behavior.* Minneapolis: Univ. of Minnesota Press, 1957.

Hunt, J. *Intelligence and experience.* New York: Ronald, 1961.

Inhelder, Bärbel. Developmental psychology. *Ann. Rev. Psychol.*, 1957, 8, 139–162.

Kendler, H., and Kendler, Tracy. Vertical and horizontal processes in problem solving. *Psychol. Rev.*, 1962, 69, 1–16.

Kendler, Tracy. The development of mediating responses in children. In J. Wright, J. Kagan, and H. Stevenson (eds.), *Basic processes in cognitive development. Monogr. Soc. Res. Child Develpm.* (in press).

Kessen, W. Research design in the study of developmental problems. In P. Mussen (ed.), *Handbook of research methods in child development.* New York: Wiley, 1960.

———. Stage and structure in the study of children. In W. Kessen and Clementina Kuhlman (eds.), *The thought of the child. Monogr. Soc. Res. Child Develpm.* (in press).

Koch, S. Epilogue. In S. Koch (ed.), *Psychology: a study of a science,* Vol. 3. New York: McGraw-Hill, 1959.

Kohlberg, L. The development of modes of moral thinking and choice in the years 10–16. Unpublished doctoral dissertation, University of Chicago, 1958.

Lewin, K. *A dynamic theory of personality.* New York: McGraw-Hill, 1936.

Martin, W. Rediscovering the mind of the child: a significant trend in research in child development. *Merrill-Palmer Quart. Behav. Develpm.*, 1959, 6, 67–76.

Rapaport, D. The structure of psychoanalytic theory: a systematizing attempt. In S. Koch (ed.), *Psychology: a study of a science,* Vol. 1. New York: McGraw-Hill, 1959.

Schachtel, E. *Metamorphosis: on the development of affect, perception, attention, and memory.* New York: Basic Books, 1959.

Scheerer, M. Review of Schachtel's *Metamorphosis. Contemp. Psychol.*, 1961, 6, 1–4.

Scriven, M. A possible distinction between traditional scientific disciplines and the study of human behavior. In H. Feigl and M. Scriven (eds.), *Minnesota Studies in the Philosophy of Science,* Vol. 1. Minneapolis: Univ. of Minnesota Press, 1956.

————. Explanation and prediction in evolutionary theory. *Science*, 1959, *130*, 477–482.

Shuttleworth, F. *The adolescent period: a graphic atlas. Monogr. Soc. Res. Child Develpm.*, Volume 14, No. 1, Serial No. 49.

Smedslund, J. The acquisition of conservation of substance and weight in children. I. Introduction. *Scand. J. Psychol.*, 1961, 2, 11–20.

Stevenson, H. Piaget, behavior theory, and intelligence. In W. Kessen and Clementina Kuhlman (eds.), *The thought of the child. Monogr. Soc. Res. Child Develpm.* (in press).

Stevenson, H., and Weir, M. Variables affecting children's performance in a probability learning task. *J. Exp. Psychol.*, 1959, *57*, 403–412.

Werner, H. *Comparative psychology of mental development* (2nd ed.). New York: International Universities Press, Inc., 1957[a].

————. The concept of development from a comparative and organismic point of view. In D. Harris (ed.), *The concept of development: an issue in the study of human behavior.* Minneapolis: Univ. of Minnesota Press, 1957[b].

White, R. Motivation reconsidered: the concept of competence. *Psychol. Rev.*, 1959, *66*, 297–333.

Windle, W., and Fitzgerald, J. Development of the spinal reflex mechanism in human embryos. *J. Comp. Neurol.*, 1937, 67, 493–509.

Wolff, P. Observations on newborn infants. *Psychosomat. Med.*, 1959, *21*, 110–118.

————. The developmental psychologies of Jean Piaget and psychoanalysis. *Psychol. Issues*, 1960, 2 (entire).

25 | *Social Psychological Theorizing*

LEONARD BERKOWITZ

Historical Background

The history of modern social psychology can conveniently be divided in three phases. We can say, admittedly oversimplifying somewhat, that the century began with wide-ranging theoretical speculations based upon uncontrolled, if not haphazard, observations. This was followed by a time of empiricist rebellion that was largely devoted to the collection of facts. Most recently, attention has again been focused on theory development, although now in conjunction with the controlled testing of theoretically-relevant hypotheses. First we shall review some of the dominant modes of thought in social psychology prior to the late 1940s, i.e., the first two stages. This discussion will provide a context for a consideration of the theoretical methodology in social psychology in these periods. We shall pay particular attention to some of the general theoretical assumptions (metatheories) guiding the research and thinking of the times. Following this, the more prominent theoretical approaches in present-day social psychology will be summarized and analyzed.

SPECULATIVE APPROACHES   During the first phase, which actually dates back to the earliest social philosophers, writers spread their speculative nets over wide areas of human behavior. They typically attempted to explain almost all forms of human endeavor, from courtship and family living to commercial activities, politics, and war. But despite this broad scope of attention, not a few of these observers erected their theoretical systems on the foundation of a very small number of explanatory principles. Psychoanalysis of course provides an excellent illustration of such an all-embracing system resting on a relatively small number of concepts, but other broad, although less detailed, formulations also have attracted attention. These include the various forms of economic determinism, McDougall's (1908) conception of instincts as the mainspring of behavior, Tarde's (1903) analysis of society in terms of imitation, and Ross' (1908) application of the concepts of suggestion and imitation to fashions, customs, and social conformity.

Since the present paper cannot devote too much space to the historical origins of contemporary theories (the interested reader should consult Gordon Allport's [1954] excellent survey), we will consider only two relevant aspects of early twentieth-century social psychological thought: the predilection to explain by applying a label, and the view of man as basically irrational.

Most of the theoretical accounts of the period emphasized three supposedly basic processes: sympathy, imitation, and suggestion. If a man did not steal an attractive object from another person, or if he sought to protect someone, this was because of his sympathy for this individual. He obeyed a leader, accepted a politician's opinions, and bought an advertised product because he was suggestible; he followed the customs, fads, and fashions of his day because of his imitative tendencies (cf. Allport, 1954, pp. 18–29). All too many discussions of the period, whether they employed this classic triad or other conjectured processes, were basically tautological in nature. Given actions were said to be instances of a certain category of behavior, and the category name was then invoked as the explanation for the behavior. Many cases of conformity to social codes, for example, supposedly were imitative actions—and these occurrences presumably arose because of man's inclination to imitate. The argument may have varied somewhat from one writer to another, but stripped to its essentials this type of reasoning often said little more than that a person imitated because he imitated.

To cite another illustration, let us simplify (for the purposes of exposition) McDougall's (1908) analysis of *suggestion*. This psychologist defined suggestion as the adoption of some communicated opinion "in the absence of logically adequate grounds" and contended that the un-critical acceptance of the stated proposition was due to the operation of the instinct of submission. Note that we have two concepts here, *suggestion* and *instinct of submission*. But are they really different? If we knew nothing else about the "instinct" but what has just been stated, it would be an hypothesized mechanism observed only through the action it theoretically impels. We might as well say suggestibility (the response) is produced by suggestibility (an assumed internal process). However, to be fair to McDougall, his formulation was not quite this circular. He did define the antecedent organismic condition, submissiveness, somewhat independently of the consequent behavior, suggestibility. Submissiveness for him was a tendency (supposedly innate—but this is another prob-lem) set into operation by the presence of a prestigeful person or symbol, and *prestige* can be coordinated to such notions as "having a history of successful accomplishments."

The summary presented so far also documents another important aspect of social psychological thought at the turn of the century. Interpretations of particular phenomena were guided primarily by meta-theories concerning the nature of man rather than by more limited hypotheses dealing with relatively precisely defined variables. Tarde (1903), along with others in France and elsewhere, viewed man as a being in a semi-hypnotic state who automatically accepted the sugges-tions of dominant models. If socially inferior groups imitated their social superiors (one of Tarde's "laws" of imitation), this was virtually a semi-hypnotic reaction having little to do with problem-solving or the attempt to attain certain goals. The other prevailing analyses of imitation and suggestion, including McDougall's instinct doctrine, also were based upon a general conception of human nature. As Gordon Allport has pointed out (1954, p. 16), the role of the intellect was confined largely to inventing after-the-fact explanations and rationalizations for behavior motivated by non-intellectual determinants. We shall see later that present-day social psychology has given the intellect a much more im-portant position. Thinking and reasoning, so goes the current argument, instigate and steer behavior in addition to providing *post hoc* excuses for it.

EMPIRICISM AND SCHOOLS OF PSYCHOLOGY   Social psychologists had en-tered the laboratory by the time of the First World War. Conceiving of their field as dealing with the individual's responses to stimuli associated with other people, their first·experiments were almost exclusively concerned with the effects of the presence of others upon a person's activity: for example, how did the performance of subjects working alone compare with their performance while working together? (The typical answer obtained was that quantity and rate of output increased in the presence of others, while quality tended to decrease.) Floyd Allport undoubtedly is the best-known member of this group of investigators, but other researchers, such as Triplett and Moede, had preceded him, and still others (e.g., Dashiell, 1935) also made significant contributions.

Floyd Allport's (1924) writings were couched in stimulus-response terminology, but· he was by no means a Watsonian. Where he thought necessary, he employed peripheral, rather than central, nervous-system constructs in his theorizing, as did the more orthodox behaviorists of the day. The accelerated performance by·people working side-by-side (i.e., in "co-acting groups") was largely due to peripheral phenomena, according to Allport. He contended that an increased social stimulation, ·stemming from the sight and sound of others engaged in the same activity, was engendered.

But, unlike these latter psychologists, he also readily made inferences about cognitive reactions; he believed some forms of social activity were strongly influenced by cognitive processes. Such cognitive concepts can clearly be seen in his analysis of crowd behavior. Along with other writers, he was faced with the question of why people in crowds did things they would not do when alone. Why, for example, do crowds sometimes act so extremely aggressively? Where French sociologists (e.g., LeBon) and other psychiatrically influenced authorities spoke simply (and glibly) of a "release of repressed impulses" perhaps aided by the anonymity of the individual in the mob, Allport attributed the emotions largely to the frustrations which confronted the mob members and which they were struggling to overcome. These emotions could be expressed in the crowd situation, he went on, at least in part because the individual members had an "impression of universality." Everyone about them was engaged in the same behavior, and this consensus defined the action .as socially proper. As a consequence, many of the mob members presumably believed it was not morally wrong to attack their victim. Allport's analysis here anticipates more recent research demonstrating the importance of perceived consensus in social definitions of reality: in the absence of more objective tests of the validity of a belief, we tend to believe the opinions shared by all or most of the people about us are probably correct (Asch, 1951; Festinger, 1950).

George Herbert Mead (1934), a philosopher and disciple of John Dewey, stressed the role of symbolic activity in social interaction. Calling himself a "social behaviorist," but insisting that symbolic response processes were integral to distinctively human behavior, Mead advanced some conceptions which have influenced sociologists more than psychologists. Shared group experiences play an important part in a person's thinking, he pointed out. Because of these common experiences, the individual's verbal gestures evoke in him much the same responses which are aroused in his listeners, and consequently, by holding an internal conversation with himself (thinking), he is able to anticipate the actions of others. But as suggestive as Mead's notions were, they apparently have not, in themselves, led to specific empirical investigations.

His followers make frequent use of the concept of *role*, generally trying to explain everything from the behavior of the psychopath to the actions of the school superintendent in these terms. With such a breadth of coverage, the role concept not surprisingly is far from precise, and little agreement exists as to exactly how a role should be defined (cf. Neiman and Hughes, 1951).

Most of the research conducted in this middle period was oriented toward empirical data collection rather than the resolution of broader theoretical problems. Indeed, we can even say that much of the research was concerned with questions having immediate practical relevance. Are groups better at problem-solving than an equal number of individuals working separately? How might attributes toward important social issues, such as Prohibition, Communism, the Church, protective tariffs, etc., be assessed? Can movies portraying a particular group in an unfavorable light increase the audience's dislike for this group? Such were some of the typical problems investigated during the '20s and '30s.

As empirically focused as these studies tended to be, many of them were influenced by metatheoretical conceptions. They were guided by assumptions concerning the functioning of the central nervous system and the part played by the intellect in human behavior. By and large, they were based on the image of man as an automaton. Habits and stimulus-response connections had replaced instincts and hypnotic states in the thinking of most American psychologists, but human beings were still not regarded as motivated by intellectual processes. A person imitated the actions of another because he had been conditioned to do so. In previous situations when he had not been able to discriminate the relevant cues, he had obtained rewards through following the actions of some leader who had been able to detect these cues, and thus he had developed the acquired tendency to imitate at least in similar situations (Miller and Dollard, 1941).

Suggestion also operated in an automatic fashion, "relatively uninfluenced by thought" (Allport, 1924, p. 251). A typical study of prestige suggestion, conducted by Lorge (1936), is relevant here. Subjects were shown statements such as, "I hold it that a little rebellion, now and then, is a good thing . . ." and were told that a particular public figure (e.g., Thomas Jefferson) was the author of each statement. The subjects' ratings of their degree of liking for each statement was found to be correlated with previously obtained ratings of the authors. According to Lorge, the affective responses evoked by a given public figure automatically generalized to influence the reactions to the statement attributed to him.

THE RISE OF PHENOMENOLOGY IN SOCIAL PSYCHOLOGY   World War II marked the end of the behavioristic dominance over social psychological theorizing. Influenced primarily by the thinking and imaginative studies of Kurt Lewin and other Gestalt-oriented researchers, a tide of phenomenological analyses all but engulfed social psychology by the late 1940s. The emphasis now—and remaining so to the present—was upon the subject's understanding of his situation. How did objective stimulus conditions influence the individual's cognitions (of course, as assessed by verbal reports), and what were the effects of these (inferred) cognitions upon his behavior?

But where all phenomenological analyses stress the importance of considering interpretations, beliefs, and understanding, all do not necessarily agree in picturing man as frequently acting in a rational, i.e., objectively intelligent, manner. Several Gestalt psychologists, including Solomon Asch (1948), insisting that man's intellect cannot be denied, have criticized the associationistic conceptions of suggestion, prestige, and imitation for neglecting the operation of rational processes. According to Asch, the associationistic interpretation of prestige-suggestion assumes that a fixed object of judgment has experienced only a change in evaluation. The proposition advanced by the prestige figure supposedly is "understood" the same way whether his name is connected with the statement or not. But, Asch argued, providing the subject with the name of the author may actually establish a context affecting the statement's interpretation. To illustrate, Asch read to a group of college students a number of statements, including the previously mentioned proposition regarding rebellion. In some cases the subjects were told that Jefferson was the author of this particular assertion, while other students were informed that Lenin was the author. Brief essays composed by the subjects demonstrated that the identification of the author had affected the judgment of the proposition. Thomas Jefferson's advocacy of rebellion meant one thing; Lenin's urging periodic rebellions meant something altogether different. Changing the authorship had altered the cognitive content of the statement. A greater acceptance of the proposition when it was attributed to the highly prestigeful figure, Jefferson, presumably was then due to the altered meaning rather than the automatic generalization of affect from the author to the assertion.

Asch's theme can be extended to explain many instances of apparent imitation or other prestige effects. Copying the actions of a prestigeful figure or otherwise adopting his opinions may be a rational attempt at problem-solving. If a person does not know what response to make in an ambiguous situation, he might do well to copy the actions of someone else who has a history of success on similar tasks. Since this latter individual had been correct frequently in the past, a good probability obtains that his present behavior is correct (Mausner, 1954).

An emphasis upon individual experience and cognition, of course, does not necessarily entail such assumptions of rationality. The dominant theoretical conceptions in present-day social psychology stress, if anything, defensive reactions which, by distorting objective reality, may actually interfere with intelligent problem-solving. Further, these defensive, tension-reducing reactions presumably operate just as automatically as the stimulus generalization assumed by associationists to produce prestige-suggestion. Some contemporary theoretical formulations (e.g., Osgood and Tannenbaum, 1955) even postulate what is essentially a spread of affect from an author to an assertion attributed to him —but as the supposed result of cognitive imbalance rather than because of a stimulus generalization.

Before proceeding to these contemporary formulations, however, a few general remarks regarding the earlier theorizing are appropriate. With only a few exceptions (such as psychoanalysis), the theories of the period are "theories" only in the most general meaning of the term. Some of the writers advanced broad, usually imprecise statements of empirical relationships, e.g., Tarde's previously cited "law" that inferior social groups imitate their superiors, rather than vice versa. In the terms of Chapter I, these were more or less primitive *inductive theories*. Such formulations were comparatively rare, however. Most of the theories consisted only of gross assumptions (e.g., man is rational, man is irrational, behavior is innately determined, etc.) and made use of particular classes of constructs (instincts, imitation, suggestion, stimulus-response connections, life-space, social facilitation, etc.), but, generally, they did not yield specific behavioral predictions. Their sole utility as a research tool was to suggest general types of investigations which might be carried out or comparatively wide areas of behavior to be studied. By and large (Asch's explanation of prestige-suggestion is relatively unusual in this regard), they did not necessarily lead to specific, testable hypotheses.[1]

---

[1] Because of space limitations, I have not discussed many important studies in this period, such as Sherif's (1936) demonstration that judgments learned in a group situation can operate later when the person is alone, and the Chapman and Volkmann (1939) experiment showing that an individual's level of aspiration is often affected by comparisons he makes with the performance of particular groups. While

Contemporary Theorizing

SIMILARITIES AND DIFFERENCES WITH OTHER THEORETICAL APPROACHES
Much of the controversy in social psychology stemming from the opposing claims of psychological schools has now vanished from the scene.
Two trends appear to be primarily responsible for such a change. For
one, largely because of the demise of the extreme positivism of the 1930s,
there is relatively little insistence nowadays that cognitive constructs are
in themselves philosophically unrespectable. Many social and experimental psychologists are willing to make inferences about internal processes, so long as these inferences are based upon objective observations
and employ carefully defined terms. They no longer maintain that every
construct must be denotable. Consequently, most psychologists seem to
treat the situation-person relation in a surprisingly similar fashion. As
Koch (1959) has pointed out, stimulus-response theorists such as Guthrie
and Miller no longer define a "stimulus" in terms of physical energy.
Stimuli to them (but not to Estes and the Skinnerians) are "constructions
or discriminations made by the observer" which have a "stable referent"
to some consequent condition (p. 757). These antecedent conditions, furthermore, frequently involve implicit language responses. A person's behavior in some situation, in other words, often depends upon his thoughts
about the situation, i.e., the "meaning" it has for him.

By making use of such subjective reactions to external objects (inner
responses which establish mediated generalization gradients), S-R concepts can be applied to a wide variety of phenomena, such as hostility displacement (Miller, 1948) and the "scapegoat theory of prejudice"
(Berkowitz, 1962). Clearly, to use Koch's words (1959, pp. 762–763),
"the treatment of environment-variables" by many S-R theorists has
moved toward the position taken by most personality and social psychologists.

Controversy has also been stilled under the force of empirical evidence concerning the functioning of the central nervous system. The old
"telephone switchboard" conception of the brain, implicit in the S-R
hypotheses of the second of our historical periods, is now obviously outmoded. Here, too, the metatheory adopted by S-R psychologists such as

---

many of the findings obtained in these investigations will have to be integrated into
any theoretical system claiming to be really comprehensive, the experiments typically were not derived from a set of interrelated hypotheses. The hypotheses they
dealt with generally were relatively narrow in scope. The occasional wider-ranging
exceptions, such as "reference group theory," were limited by their primitive state;
they could not adequately specify the operative conditions and could be applied
only after the fact to explain what had been found, rather than permitting
unequivocal predictions (cf. Merton and Kitt, 1950).

Miller has come closer to the implicit general model favored by contemporary social psychology. "The brain," Miller has written recently (1961), "is an active organ which exerts considerable control over its own sensory input." Many social psychologists have been saying just this since the 1940s.

But although they typically recognize the importance of cognitive processes and are no longer so exclusively restricted to peripheralistic constructs, S-R psychologists still prefer to explain man's behavior by means of non-cognitive mechanisms (Miller, cited in Koch, 1959, p. 765). Here we have perhaps the major difference between the dominant contemporary social psychological theories and the neo-behavioristic points of view more prevalent in other areas of psychology. The formulations gaining the most attention in social psychology today emphasize cognitive processes. More than this, in violation of Watsonian precepts, these formulations propose that many actions are directly instigated by cognitive reactions.

PERCEPTIONS, HYPOTHESES, AND JUDGMENTS   Some of the current emphasis upon cognitive functioning in social psychology can be traced to the so-called "New Look" experiments of the 1940s and earlier. These studies, in a sense, sought to demonstrate what textbook writers and clinicians had long believed to be true: that needs influenced perception, that what a person saw in a situation was often governed by his motives, wishes, and defenses. Although some of the researchers undoubtedly did not begin with any particular global conception of the human personality, I think it fair to say that the first studies in this area were based upon the classic psychoanalytic model of personality functioning. Psychological processes, whether they involved thought, perception, or purposive behavior, were regarded as primarily autistic in nature, supposedly always going in the direction of tension reduction. For Sigmund Freud and for his followers, it seemed to be a truism that every psychological process was motivationally determined and, furthermore, would ultimately result in less internal excitement unless blocked by inhibitions.

The first uncritical enthusiasm for the doctrine of autistic influences upon perception gave way to a more sober skepticism within a few short years. Often contradictory findings had first led to a multiplication of explanatory concepts (e.g., "perceptual defense," "perceptual vigilance") in an effort to reconcile the opposing results. Then, in the face of continued difficulties came the recognition that motives have a minor and probably non-existent role in the determination of visual thresholds— although they could affect the person's memory (cf. Allport, 1955). Motives lost their primary role as influences upon perception. Instead of glibly invoking magical and ill-understood processes as explanations for what a person sees in a situation, the psychologist must now rely chiefly upon the more traditional, although less dramatic, concepts of the experimental laboratory: e.g., set, learning, and concept identification and formation.

Bruner and Postman, who had been among the leaders of the "New Look" movement, were also among the first to return the study of perception to the familiar traditions of experimental psychology. Beginning in the early years of the 1950s, they suggested that all cognitive processes—perceiving, thinking, or remembering—were governed by the "hypotheses" elicited by a particular situation, i.e., the set the individual had developed. As inferred internal processes, hypotheses were anchored at the antecedent end by such objective (or potentially objective) observations as frequency of prior confirmation and consensual validation and by observations of their consequences regarding the amount of information necessary to evoke, confirm, or change them. (For an excellent discussion of hypothesis-theory and related issues, see Allport, 1955).

Again we can see changes making for a lessening of controversy within psychology. But now (regarding Bruner and Postman as more or less representative of many social psychologists) social psychology seems to have moved toward experimental psychology. Even though some writers have argued that "person perception" is different from "thing perception" in important respects, we still can contend that many of the hypotheses and theories developed in the experimental or psychophysics laboratory are applicable to social phenomena (Berkowitz, 1960). Thus, Bruner has extended his studies of thinking carried out with inanimate stimuli to more usual social situations (Bruner, 1958), while Sherif and Hovland (1961) and others (e.g., Berkowitz, 1960) have suggested that adaptation-level formulations dealing with judgments made along physical dimensions can be generalized to social judgments. Social psychological principles may indeed turn out to be only special cases of more general psychological laws.

Such a rapprochement between experimental and social psychology is encouraging for several reasons. Most obviously, scientific progress is facilitated if communication is easier among the different fields of psychology. Each can contribute to the others' development. But in addition, I might also point out, experimental psychological theorizing can accelerate a trend of vital importance to social psychology: the trend away from an excessive reliance upon motivational constructs. We cannot neglect the pervasive influence of motivational factors, but we also should not assume that *every* response is carried out in the interests of satisfying some hypothesized need. For example, if we are asked to judge the opinion position of a communicator who has expressed views considerably different from our own, we probably would exaggerate the discrepancy between his and our beliefs (cf. Sherif and Hovland, 1961, Ch. 7). This exaggeration is not necessarily the result of a "need" to regard the communicator as being altogether different from ourselves; it may well arise as a consequence of motivationally neutral judgmental processes.

Social psychologists (and personality theorists and clinicians as well) have too readily made inferences about motives or needs in explaining their empirical data. Reasoning from the basis of an implicit and all-embracing motivational determinism, they all too frequently have postulated that a need was the cause of a particular response. The "need" in this case may be nothing more than word magic—a label is employed as an explanation.

THE THEORIES OF LEON FESTINGER The first really systematic argument for the cognitive instigation of behavior (in contrast to previous, less precise armchair speculations, such as that put forth by Cantril [1941] and others) was advanced by Leon Festinger. Discussing informal social communications arising from "pressures toward uniformity (of opinion) in a group," Festinger (1950) advanced two major reasons why group members would want such opinion uniformity: 1) for group locomotion, i.e., in order to reach some goal, and 2) in order to achieve a social definition of reality. This latter pressure toward uniformity is obviously entirely cognitively-based.

If a person wanted to determine the validity of his beliefs, but had no objective, physical means for doing so, he had to rely on social definitions of reality. He could feel confident that a belief was correct only if it was shared by all or most of the people in the group "to which he refers this opinion or attitude." As Festinger has commented, the difficulty is to define in a non-circular fashion which groups are appropriate reference groups for a particular individual on a particular opinion or attitude. He proposed that a group's likelihood of serving as a referent for a person on a given opinion was a direct function of 1) the group's attractiveness to him (i.e., its cohesiveness) and 2) the relevance of the opinion to the group's functioning. Employing these propositions as the basic axioms, Festinger then advanced a set of interrelated hypotheses which are close to comprising a deductive theory. The hypotheses deal with a) the magnitude of the pressures to communicate, b) the choice of the recipient for the communications, c) determinants of opinion change in the communication recipient, and d) the magnitude of tendencies to reject nonconformers.

Festinger's conceptualizations have stimulated an impressive series of investigations, both in the field and in the laboratory, and many of them have resulted in findings consistent with his hypotheses. However, that this 1950 formulation is far from complete is now clear. The postulated relationships apparently hold, for example, only when the communicator believes the majority of other group members share his views (cf., Festinger et al., 1952).

But more important for our present purposes is Festinger's basic reasoning regarding the striving for social reality. He assumed that most people have a drive to know the truth, i.e., to ascertain the correctness of some belief. They seek consensus within their reference groups, not necessarily to obtain support for their own opinions but presumably in order to be fairly confident that *some* belief is right. Needless to say, the existence of such a drive has not been demonstrated unequivocally, and some experimental results (e.g., Festinger et al., 1952) cast doubt on the ubiquitousness of this instigation. Whether such an instigation really exists or not, the inferred drive was employed as an explanatory mechanism too frequently and with too much certainty, considering its shaky empirical foundation.

A later theoretical statement by Festinger (1954) paid particular attention to the basis of this conjectured striving after the truth. But here Festinger argued that the individual possessed a drive to evaluate his own opinions and abilities. If he did not have an objective, non-social means for evaluating himself, he supposedly would try to assess his opinions and/or abilities by comparing himself with others. However, Festinger suggested, since comparisons made with other people who were greatly different in opinions and/or abilities would be relatively imprecise, the person theoretically would want to compare himself only with people who were fairly close to him on the given evaluation dimension. Going on from these postulates, Festinger proposed that the individual would try to reduce opinion and/or ability discrepancies in his groups in order to achieve the subjectively more precise self-evaluation and that he would be relatively strongly attracted to groups having members fairly similar to him on the evaluation dimension because of the satisfaction of his yearning to assess himself.

The interrelated hypotheses presented in the 1954 paper again form a deductive system of "hypotheses," "corollaries," and "derivations." Some of these "derivations," however, represent fairly broad and speculative jumps. Suppose we grant, for example, that comparisons we make with people who are greatly different from ourselves in opinions or abilities would be relatively imprecise; do we necessarily cease communicating with them because we 1) know the comparisons are imprecise and 2) are looking elsewhere for more accurate comparisons?

Festinger has always excelled in the necessary scientific task of formulating general theoretical principles that are capable of integrating apparently diverse phenomena. Nevertheless, his brilliant pursuit of the general theoretical statement has at times led him to offer relatively un-parsimonious hypotheses where simpler, alternative explanations might suffice. Some obvious illustrations of this lack of parsimony can be seen in his 1954 paper. For example, Festinger reported an experiment by Hochbaum in which half of the subjects were led to believe they were good at making judgments on the issues they were to discuss. When the issues were taken up later, these subjects were found to be comparatively unlikely to change their opinions in spite of disagreement with the other group members. According to Festinger, the preliminary information telling these subjects that they were good at the assigned task had given them an objective, non-social basis for evaluating their ability, and there-fore they supposedly did not have to conform to the others' views in order to be able to use these other people as a comparison group. A sim-pler explanation, of course, is that the preliminary information had given them confidence in the correctness of their later opinions and so they were less likely to believe the other group members were probably correct.

A few years later, Festinger embarked on a new line of theoretical development which was both less and more ambitious than his previous conceptualizations. Less ambitious in that he no longer couched his hypotheses in the form of a deductive theory, he at the same time set a very high level of aspiration for his new formulation by extending it to cover an extremely wide range of behaviors—and species. His book (1957) introducing dissonance theory took up such varied topics as rumor transmission, communication in small group settings, the effects of decision-making, and the effects of voluntary and involuntary ex-posure to belief-relevant information, while more recent research brings dissonance theory to rat behavior (1961).

Festinger was now concerned with man's attempts at achieving self-consistency—a concern which had simultaneously attracted the attention of several other prominent psychologists. His basic notion is a simple one. If a person had elements of knowledge about himself and/or his sur-roundings that were inconsistent with each other (i.e., if one element of knowledge implied the psychological opposite of another knowledge ele-ment he possessed), a state of cognitive dissonance supposedly existed which, because it presumably was uncomfortable, would motivate at-tempts to reduce this dissonance by altering the knowledge elements.

Several critics of dissonance theory have attempted to minimize Fest-inger's formulation by saying it merely deals with intra-organismic con-flicts. Instead of coining new constructs, they claim, Festinger should have spoken about conflict. The present writer cannot agree. Other analyses of psychological conflict (e.g., Miller, 1948) have to do with opposing response tendencies, not opposing elements of knowledge. Perhaps more important, dissonance theory has provided insights not anticipated by the other formulations. Decision-making offers a good illustration. The typical conflict analysis of decision-making deals only with events leading up to the final choice. Dissonance theory, however, suggests that the individual is not necessarily at peace once he has made a decision; his knowledge of the alternative he has chosen is inconsistent with his knowledge of the attractive features of the rejected choice, and a state of cognitive dissonance would exist. As one of Festinger's students, Brehm (1956), had demonstrated, the consequence apparently is a dissonance-reducing change in the attractiveness of the previously competing alternatives; the chosen alternative becomes more attractive and the rejected choice less attractive.

Festinger's theory has been extremely valuable as a stimulant to research, at times even predicting "non-obvious" outcomes. Such otherwise unexpected predictions can be seen in the dissonance-theory analysis of role playing. Previous investigators, e.g., Kelman (1956), had generally interpreted the attitude change resulting from role playing as stemming from the rehearsal of particular ideational responses. Contrary to this approach, Festinger (1957) maintained that at least some of these cases of attitude change could be due to cognitive dissonance. The individual arguing in favor of a viewpoint opposite to the belief he actually held might be bothered by the knowledge that he was voluntarily expressing beliefs entirely inconsistent with his real opinions. The less he could justify his inconsistent statements (for example, by thinking of the financial rewards to be gained through this behavior), the greater would be the dissonance and, consequently, the likelihood of opinion change to reduce this dissonance. In accord with his analysis, Festinger and Carlsmith (1959) demonstrated that subjects receiving a small reward for expressing opinions counter to their initial beliefs tended to have a greater attitude change toward the beliefs they had expressed than did subjects getting a substantial reward for making these statements.

But in spite of this empirical fruitfulness,[2] dissonance theory is still in a relatively primitive state. In the terms of Chapter I, it is a *functional*,

---

[2] Dissonance theory can dispose of some of the troublesome "gaps" in Festinger's 1950 formulation. Thus, where the earlier theory had maintained that subjects would tend to direct their first communications to the other group members whose views were furthest from their own, later research (Festinger et al., 1952) indicated that people whose beliefs were in the minority tended to communicate primarily to others holding somewhat similar beliefs. These opinion deviates, we now can say, probably were experiencing great cognitive dissonance and thus sought to eliminate their discomfort by gaining support from the group members most likely to give them this support.

rather than a deductive, theory, serving primarily as a tool to suggest the types of situations in which cognitive dissonance-reducing reactions might occur, rather than deductively to generate specific hypotheses. Indeed, most of the studies carried out under the banner of dissonance theory have really demonstrated only that Festinger's formulation can be applied to a tremendous variety of apparently diverse phenomena. The theory, as it now exists, consists of only one hypothetical construct, cognitive dissonance (which also can be regarded as essentially referring to a relationship between antecedent elements of "knowledge"), and there are few, if any, other formally defined concepts. Not surprisingly, then, the present form of the theory cannot specify just what modes of dissonance reduction are particularly likely to occur in specific situations or, for that matter, satisfactorily explain *within the terms of the theory* why some dissonant states are tolerated (Mills et al., 1959) or even sought after (Zajonc, 1960, p. 295).

Further development of dissonance theory undoubtedly requires a closer and more detailed specification of the instigating conditions. Researchers must be able to state the dimensions along which knowledge-sets differ and should be able to quantify the degree of discrepancy between these sets on these dimensions. If the investigators are to predict outcomes, furthermore, they must be able to specify the relations between the discrepant knowledge-sets and the other kinds of knowledge available and/or responses that are possible in a situation. Clearly, advocates of dissonance theory must now go beyond mere demonstrations of the applicability of their formulations.

Dissonance-theory research can also benefit from the introduction of dissonance measures that are independent, operationally, of the chief dependent variables. The experimenters typically create certain conditions experimentally, infer that dissonance exists, and, then, maintain that the obtained results are due to the subjects' attempts at dissonance reduction. Their argument would be stronger if they could show, independently of the outcome, that dissonance had indeed been established. (It is, of course, particularly important to have such independent measures when the theory rests so heavily on inferred internal states.) A case in point can be found in the study by Aronson and Mills (1959). College women who had volunteered to participate in group discussions "on the psychology of sex" were given either a severe or a mild initiation experience. The women in the former condition presumably were subjected to great embarrassment as the result of such activities as reading aloud vivid descriptions of sexual activity, while the "mild initiation" women only had to read words such as "prostitute" and "virgin." Afterwards, the subjects listened to a somewhat boring discussion held by the group which they were to join, and the "severe initiation" women were found to regard the group more favorably than did the women in the "mild initiation" condition. This difference arose, say Aronson and Mills, because the former subjects had been in a stronger state of dissonance. However, another interpretation is also possible. Since the women had volunteered to join in a discussion of sex, they probably were fairly strongly attracted to sexual material. The so-called embarrassing passages in the "severe initiation" condition may actually have been regarded as a sample of the fascinating things to come (whether to read the passages aloud was embarrassing), and so, the women conceivably could have rated the group favorably in anticipation of future enjoyable discussions.

BALANCE, SYMMETRY, AND CONGRUITY   Several writers working independently of Festinger have also discussed the operation of a trend toward consistency, but in a more limited context. Heider (1946), a follower of the Gestalt school, was the first to conceptualize this trend. He limited his analysis to two people, P (the perceiver) and O (another person), and some object, idea, or issue, X. In his formalization Heider distinguished between two types of relations, *liking* and *unit* (e.g., possession, similarity, cause) relations, and proposed the occurrence of a trend toward *balance* in P's perception of these relations. A balanced state would exist if all three relations among P, O, and X were positive, or if two were negative and one positive. For example, cognitive balance exists when P likes O, P dislikes X, and O dislikes X. Cartwright and Harary (1956) have established a formal model employing the mathematics of graph theory which generalized Heider's theory to n-person groups and which also, for the first time, treated balance as a matter of degree.

Newcomb (1953) also extended the Heider thesis to deal with communication between two people, A and B, about some issue, X. Using many of the same studies cited by Festinger in 1950 as evidence for his position, Newcomb postulated a *strain toward symmetry* of orientations which, to the extent that A and B are attracted to each other, would result in shared attitudes (a "co-orientation") about X. Unlike the Gestalters, Newcomb suggested that this strain toward symmetry is an acquired, rather than an intrinsic, characteristic of cognitive processes; we presumably have learned the advantages of symmetry from past experience: ready calculability of another's behavior and increased confidence in one's own orientations.

Osgood and Tannenbaum (1955) based their *congruity principle* on the assumption that "judgmental frames of reference tend toward maximal simplicity." One finds it simpler to hold the same evaluation of both a communicator and an assertion made by him than to discriminate between these two. Accordingly, they argued, attitudes toward the source and object of a communication tend to become congruent with each other. There would be an incongruity, for example, if an extremely highly regarded communicator is seen making a positive assertion about some negatively evaluated object or issue. In order to reduce this incongruity, the communication recipient presumably will alter his evaluation of both the source and object of the communication.[3] Some of the factors affecting the degree and direction of these attitude changes were specified in quantitative terms. Thus, the total pressure towards congruity operating on the judgmental object is supposedly equal to the difference between its initial location on the evaluation dimension and the location at which congruence would be maximum. But, the more extreme the initial evaluation, the less would be the change; extreme evaluations are held with great conviction. However, the greater the incongruity, the stronger is the "incredulity" reaction, and this failure to believe decreases attitude change.

Whether these trends are described in terms of balance, symmetry of orientations, or congruity, their existence has been corroborated by empirical research. As an example, Berkowitz (1957) has shown that subjects who were induced to have strong liking for their partners generally evaluated their partners' opinions more highly than did other subjects led to have lower liking for their fellow group members. Similarly, Kogan and Tagiuri (1958) found a greater-than-chance occurrence of balanced states in the liking relationships actually existing among groups of sailors and an even greater frequency of balanced states in the relationships which the sailors thought existed. To cite one final bit of evidence, Newcomb (1961) studied two groups of college students living in a rooming house and demonstrated that their *A-B* re *X* orientation systems tended to be balanced. The house members' attitudes on important issues generally remained fairly stable over the period investigated. As they acquired more information about each others' attitudes with prolonged acquaintance, they increasingly came to prefer the members with whom they were more closely in agreement. Estimates of others' orientations also changed in ways that were balance-producing without necessarily becoming more accurate.

With this type of supporting evidence, the simplicity of the balance-congruity formulations is appealing. *Balance* can be defined mathemati-

---

[3] The congruity formulation is similar to the S-R analysis of prestige-suggestion described earlier and is also subject to the type of criticism employed by Asch (1948) in attacking that analysis. Instead of a fixed object of judgment experiencing a change in evaluation, as the congruity notion implies, the communicator may provide a context altering the interpretation of his message. Similarly, his message may mean the communicator is interpreted differently.

cally, and formal models (cf. Cartwright and Harary, 1956) capable of generating specific predictions can be developed. Yet, clearly, balance tendencies are frequently overriden by other factors. Festinger is credited with citing two exceptions that point up the serious incompleteness of balance formulations. "If I like chicken," he asked, "and a chicken likes chicken feed, do I also have to like chicken feed?" (quoted in Zajonc, 1960, p. 285). "Liking" apparently has to be differentiated more precisely than is customary. Also, to paraphrase another question, would two women necessarily like each other if each was in love with the same man? Balance conceptualizations obviously do not yet constitute a deductive theory that can be applied to more than a limited range of situations. They do not even state (in conceptual terms coherent with the main body of the theory) what conditions counter the operation of balancing tendencies.

CONCEPTUALIZATIONS NOT BASED ON CONSISTENCY NOTIONS   The present essay has been somewhat one-sided in emphasizing the social psychological theories based upon some conjectured trend toward self-consistency. Other theoretical approaches have been employed in this field, needless to say, and many contemporary social psychological investigations have been concerned with testing relatively limited hypotheses rather than broader generalizations. One well-known formulation, the theory of the authoritarian personality (Adorno et al., 1950), deals with a particular type of individual, the ethnically prejudiced person with a predisposition to fascistic attitudes. The theory is an amalgam of interrelated psychoanalytic and cognitive hypotheses describing how this kind of person presumably thinks and feels in certain situations (e.g., in highly ambiguous, stressful conditions, or in interaction with members of minority groups). Much more detailed and complicated than, say, Festinger's conceptualizations, the theory is still more functional than deductive. All in all, there has been an impressive accumulation of corroborative evidence.

Two recent books (Homans, 1961; Thibaut and Kelley, 1959) have taken an approach altogether different from the other formulations described in this paper. Clearly functional rather than deductive in their present state, both conceptualizations analyze a broad variety of social situations in terms of the rewards and costs incurred by the people in these settings. Cognitive constructs have an important place in these approaches; Thibaut and Kelley say, for example, that the attractiveness of a certain course of action is affected by comparisons with the attractiveness of the available alternative actions. Nevertheless, both are in line with traditional psychological formulations, and Homans even bases many of his analyses upon analogies with pigeons in a Skinner box.

References

Adorno, T., Frenkel-Brunswik, E., Levinson, D., and Sanford, R. *The authoritarian personality.* New York: Harper, 1950.

Allport, F. H. *Social psychology.* Boston: Houghton-Mifflin, 1924.

———. *Theories of perception and the concept of structure.* New York: Wiley, 1955.

Allport, G. W. The historical background of modern social psychology. In G. Lindzey (ed.), *Handbook of social psychology.* Cambridge, Mass.: Addison-Wesley, 1954.

Aronson, E., and Mills, J. The effect of severity of initiation on liking for a group. *J. Abnorm. Soc. Psychol.,* 1959, *59,* 177–181.

Asch, S. E. The doctrine of suggestion, prestige and imitation in social psychology. *Psychol. Rev.,* 1948, *55,* 250–276.

———. Effects of group pressure upon the modification and distortion of judgments. In H. Guetzkow (ed.), *Groups, leadership, and men.* Pittsburgh: Carnegie Press, 1951.

Berkowitz, L. Liking for the group and the perceived merit of the group's behavior. *J. Abnorm. Soc. Psychol.,* 1957, *54,* 353–357.

———. The judgmental process in personality functioning. *Psychol. Rev.,* 1960, *67,* 130–142.

———. *Aggression: a social psychological analysis.* New York: McGraw-Hill, 1962.

Brehm, J. Post-decision changes in the desirability of alternatives. *J. Abnorm. Soc. Psychol.,* 1956, *52,* 384–389.

Bruner, J. S. Social psychology and perception. In Eleanor Maccoby, T. Newcomb, and E. Hartley (eds.), *Readings in social psychology* (3rd ed.). New York: Holt, 1958.

Cantril, H. *Psychology of social movements.* New York: Wiley, 1941.

Cartwright, D., and Harary, F. Structural balance: a generalization of Heider's theory. *Psychol. Rev.,* 1956, *63,* 277–293.

Chapman, D. E., and Volkmann, J. A social determinant of the level of aspiration. *J. Abnorm. Soc. Psychol.,* 1939, *34,* 225–238.

Dashiell, J. F. Experimental studies of the influence of social situations on the behavior of individual human adults. In C. Murchison (ed.), *Handbook of social psychology.* Worcester, Mass.: Clark Univ. Press, 1935.

Festinger, L. Informal social communication. *Psychol. Rev.,* 1950, *57,* 271–282.

———. A theory of social comparison processes. *Hum. Relat.,* 1954, 7, 117–140.

———. *A theory of cognitive dissonance.* Evanston, Ill.: Row, Peterson, 1957.

———. The psychological effects of insufficient rewards. *Amer. Psychologist,* 1961, *16,* 1–11.

Festinger, L., and Carlsmith, J. M. Cognitive consequences of forced compliance. *J. Abnorm. Soc. Psychol.,* 1959, *58,* 203–210.

Festinger, L., Gerard, H. B., Hymovitch, B., Kelley, H. H., and Raven, B. The influence process in the presence of extreme deviates. *Hum. Relat.,* 1952, *5,* 327–346.

Heider, F. Attitudes and cognitive organization. *J. Psychol.,* 1946, *21,* 107–112.

Homans, G. C. *Social behavior: its elementary forms.* New York: Harcourt, Brace & World, 1961.

Kelman, H. Attitude change as a function of response restriction. *Hum. Relat.*, 1956, *9*, 177–186.

Koch, S. Epilogue. In S. Koch (ed.), *Psychology: a study of a science. Vol. 3: Formulations of the person and the social context.* New York: McGraw-Hill, 1959.

Kogan, N., and Tagiuri, R. Interpersonal preference and cognitive organization. *J. Abnorm. Soc. Psychol.*, 1958, *56*, 113–116.

Lorge, I. Prestige, suggestion and attitudes. *J. Soc. Psychol.*, 1936, 7, 386–402.

Mausner, B. The effect of one partner's success in a relevant task on the interaction of observer pairs. *J. Abnorm. Soc. Psychol.*, 1954, *49*, 557–560.

McDougall, W. *Introduction to social psychology.* London: Methuen, 1908.

Mead, G. H. *Mind, self, and society.* Chicago: Univ. of Chicago Press, 1934.

Merton, R. K., and Kitt, Alice S. Contributions to the theory of reference group behavior. In R. K. Merton and P. F. Lazarsfeld (eds.), *Continuities in social research: studies in the scope and method of "The American soldier."* Glencoe, Ill.: Free Press, 1950.

Miller, N. Theory and experiment relating psychoanalytic displacement to stimulus-response generalization. *J. Abnorm. Soc. Psychol.*, 1948, *43*, 155–178.

———. Analytical studies of drive and reward. *Amer. Psychologist*, 1961, *16*, 739–754.

Miller, N., and Dollard, J. *Social learning and imitation.* New Haven: Yale Univ. Press, 1941.

Mills, J., Aronson, E., and Robinson, H. Selectivity in exposure to information. *J. Abnorm. Soc. Psychol.*, 1959, *58*, 250–253.

Neiman, L. J., and Hughes, J. W. The problem of the concept of role: a re-survey of the literature. *Social Forces*, 1951, *30*, 141–149.

Newcomb, T. M. An approach to the study of communicative acts. *Psychol. Rev.*, 1953, *60*, 393–404.

———. *The acquaintance process.* New York: Holt, Rinehart and Winston, 1961.

Osgood, C. E., and Tannenbaum, P. H. The principle of congruity in the prediction of attitude change. *Psychol. Rev.*, 1955, *62*, 42–55.

Ross, E. A. *Social psychology.* New York: Macmillan, 1908.

Sherif, M. *The psychology of social norms.* New York: Harper, 1936.

Sherif, M., and Hovland, C. *Social judgment.* New Haven: Yale Univ. Press, 1961.

Tarde, G. *The laws of imitation.* Transl., New York: Henry Holt, 1903. Cited in G. W. Allport, The historical background of modern social psychology. In G. Lindzey (ed.) *Handbook of social psychology.* Cambridge, Mass.: Addison-Wesley, 1954.

Thibaut, J. W., and Kelley, H. H. *The social psychology of groups.* New York: Wiley, 1959.

Zajonc, R. B. Balance, congruity, and dissonance. *Pub. Opin. Quart.*, 1960, *24*, 280–296.

CHAPTER VIII

Personality and Psychodynamics

THIS CHAPTER INCLUDES THREE PAPERS reviewing theoretical efforts in the areas of personality, psychoanalysis, and emotion. The paper by Robert Leeper on personality theory examines a number of fundamental methodological questions which need to be thoroughly considered; in essence, it may be considered an attempt to achieve some of the richness of literary and similar treatments of personality, while at the same time maintaining at least a moderate amount of scientific rigor. In the second paper, Leonard Horwitz offers a methodological critique of psychoanalytic theory from an essentially sympathetic but critical point of view. Finally, Henry N. Peters, a long-time functionalist of the Chicago school, provides a distinctly functionalistic examination of the traditional interpretations of affective and emotional processes.

26 | *Theoretical Methodology in the Psychology of Personality*

ROBERT W. LEEPER

When we speak about the *psychology* of personality, we are speaking about a field of relatively technical observation and highly abstract theorizing. However, we are also speaking about a field which deals with matters of great interest to people generally. The number of words which refer to personality indicate this fact; in English, for example, Allport and Odbert (1936) found almost 18,000 terms concerned with personality, and most of these originated centuries ago. Consider, for example, such words as affectionate, ambitious, timid, selfish, surly, petulant, kindly, persistent, despondent, morose, sarcastic, jovial, vain, modest, daring, reckless, and aimless. If we can assume that the richness of vocabulary in any field is an indication of the interest which people have had in that field of thought, it must be assumed that personality is something that has long been of great importance and interest in the lives of people rather generally.

The same conclusion is suggested by a consideration of literature. The plays of Sophocles, Shakespeare, and Eugene O'Neill, the novels of Victor Hugo, Tolstoi, and Dostoevski, or for that matter the Canterbury Tales of Chaucer—all are merely outstanding examples from a huge number of cases that might be cited as evidence that writers have had a tremendous interest in the description and interpretation of personality. It is worth noting, too, that one of the main bases on which people have judged the greatness of novels and dramatic productions has been the "soundness" of these as portrayals of human life. The question is, "Would a person who felt and thought and did such and such things also have done these other things, too? Would a person who had gone through such and such experiences, and who had reacted to them in such and such ways, also have felt and done these other things, or does the account simply not 'hold together'?" People do not turn to literature just for accounts of adventure. They have valued those writers who seemed to have achieved some unusually valid understanding of those phases of human life which we might speak of as personality.

Why people have had so much interest in personality is not hard to find. It is a part of the natural world which can take vastly different forms. In a sense, it is not more important than our mechanisms for breathing, swallowing, and maintaining a proper bodily temperature; it is not more important, perhaps, than a child's learning to speak or learning to perceive accurately the shapes and distances of things around him. But these other things, one might say, generally take care of themselves. A parent needs to have no understanding of how a child swallows or how he learns to speak. Barring some relatively rare cases, children typically breathe, swallow, perspire, acquire the accent of their native tongue, and develop the simpler perceptual skills in much the same fashion that virtually all other children do. But the development and operation of personality takes no such standardized course—witness the range of adjectives we suggested above. Furthermore, one can profit greatly from the ability to recognize personality differences and to deal with them, whether a person is kindly or sarcastic, aimless or well-organized, ruthless or considerate, cheerful or despondent—not to mention the question of whether he is psychotic or handicapped by some other severe disorder of personality. Such differences of personality develop within different persons in the same economic and educational level, in the same vocational and professional groups, and even in the same family. Not merely intellectual curiosity, therefore, has led people over the ages to take an interest in personality. People had plenty of basis for realizing that personality is something that they themselves have to try to assess and deal with in responsible ways, rather than being able to turn over most of such problems to experts or specialists.

As an area susceptible to systematic technical work, however, the field of personality is of very recent development. Particularly is this true if we are thinking about the psychology of personality as a research- or theoretically-oriented field. Technical work on personality did not begin in this form. It began as a part of the practical work of physicians (and more particularly of neurologists and psychiatrists). It began because such medical workers were obliged to try to deal with persons with serious personality disorders. Not only did this early medical work, through the first half of the nineteenth century, have a strongly practical orientation, but most of it took the form of searching for possible organic factors that might be responsible (factors such as, indeed, have been found in cases of senile disorders, alcoholic psychoses, pellagra psychoses, and paresis as a consequence of one form of syphilis). This work, therefore, was not adapted to make many contributions to the type of understanding of personality that would apply to the great majority of individuals.

A more general theory started to develop when medical workers became concerned with the rather less severe personality disturbances called neuroses. Even at that, significantly, this latter work developed first with cases of hysteria, where the symptoms—such as blindness, paralysis, or loss of feeling in some part of the body—suggested the occurrence of some injury to the sense organs or nerves of the person. Persons with hysterical symptoms came to neurologists because they believed they had neurological problems. However, the neurologists were forced to recognize that many of such symptoms could not possibly be explained in terms of bodily injuries, but would have to be explained instead—if they could be explained at all—in terms of the thoughts and feelings and past experiences of the patients. Out of such work were developed the theories not only of early workers such as Charcot, Morton Prince, Boris Sidis, and Pierre Janet, but also of Sigmund Freud, whose psychoanalytic theory remains one of the most important of current theories of personality. When Freud first started to develop the ideas and methods for which he has become famous, he saw these as suited solely for work with cases of hysteria. He had no anticipation, it seems, of the scope of the inquiry on which he was launching.

In their work with such patients, the medical workers could see little reason to turn for help to the field of psychology. What they found in their patients seemed much more complex than the phenomena with which the newly-developing field of psychology was starting to work. So, the development of personality theory in the field of psychiatry generally, and in psychoanalysis more particularly, went on in virtual isolation from the work and theorizing of psychology (and of other fields like physiology and neurology). This is important to note. One of the principal current questions in the field of personality is whether such practically-oriented theorizing about personality ought to continue to be based almost solely on data from psychotherapeutic work, or whether such theorizing ought to seek to utilize a broader base of observation and theoretical concepts.

As a parallel and independent stream, a more theoretically-oriented or pure-science type of approach to psychological phenomena also was developing during the 1800s. It started, however, with matters quite different from personality. It started from speculative discussions of learning by philosophers, in laboratory research on sensory processes and reaction-time by physiologists and physicists, and in studies of animal behavior by biologists interested in the concept of evolution which Darwin had presented in 1859. Some of these strands were pulled together in the work of the new psychological institutes established in Germany from about 1880 on, in the new psychological laboratories in the United States from about 1890 on, and in other countries following them.

These new workers were under no pressure to deal with urgent practical problems such as confronted psychiatrists. Instead, the psychologists started with those problems which offered the possibility, by using careful experimental methods, of obtaining findings which could readily be duplicated by other investigators. Somewhat as Freud started with hysteria because it was the most tangible neurotic disturbance, so the experimental psychologists started—as any science tends to start—with what was most tangible, most readily controlled, and most clearly a matter of close time-relationships between observable causes and effects (Leeper, 1951). The new research field of psychology, therefore, started with the relatively simple problems of rote memorizing, color vision, space perception, and the like. Small wonder that psychiatrists like Freud could see no relationships between such phenomena and those they were trying to understand. Freud realized that personality disturbances might depend on earlier learning and that personality disorders perhaps might be described as partly matters of how patients perceived things. But personality learning did not seem at all analogous to the learning of nonsense syllables, nor did the perceptions vital to personality appear to be related to the perceptions being studied in psychological laboratories.

In the period since the 1880s and 1890s, however, the field of psychology has been greatly broadened. From the work of biologists like Lloyd Morgan and Hobhouse, psychologists came to see the possibility of research on trial-and-error learning. From the work of the Russian physiologist, Pavlov, they came to appreciate that learning might affect autonomic functioning rather than merely ordinary muscular reactions. From Pavlov, furthermore, they accepted a whole series of concepts—of initial generalization, differentiation, experimental extinction, and experimental neurosis, for instance—which had not been developed by other workers. From workers in biology and physiology, psychologists came to realize the possibility and value of psychological studies of human infants. Various practical pressures induced psychologists to develop means of trying to measure intelligence, educational aptitudes, and even personality. Under the influence of anthropology and sociology, psychologists were encouraged to investigate relatively complex social processes.

This sketch of the expanding interests of psychology is very incomplete, of course. It may be sufficient, however, to suggest this point: psychology worked first with what could be dealt with in very circumscribed situations, ones where the crucial independent variables were relatively easy to control and where the resulting effects could be measured in relatively simple and direct ways. Out of this early work, however, and out of the contributions from other fields, psychologists obtained the means of appreciating more and more factors and more and more relationships which they had not been able to appreciate originally. Psychologists were laying the basis, therefore, for an eventual interest in the field of personality, which previously had been accepted as a responsibility by medical workers.

The growth of interest in personality on the part of psychologists came partly because other disciplines, recognizing the broadening interests of psychologists, put psychologists under pressure to accept practical clinical responsibilities analogous to those previously accepted by psychiatrists. Even without this practical pressure, however, it was inevitable that psychologists would begin to concern themselves with phenomena of personality. The problems involved in research on personality are terribly complex; the theoretical problems of the field are tremendous. But the study obviously is of great potential significance, both practically and theoretically. Increasingly, therefore, from about 1920 on, the field of personality has become one of the half-dozen main areas of research and theory of psychology.

As might have been expected, however, this new discipline has presented great difficulties. These are not solely on the side of how to secure good empirical observations. They are difficulties also of very basic theoretical sorts. The phenomena of personality are so complex and are frequently related to such subtle environmental influences and to such complex expressions in the life of each individual that it is exceedingly difficult to develop an adequate understanding of personality. Perhaps because of this, the differences between alternative theories seem to cut deeper in the field of personality than in any other portion of psychology.

In this situation, a good deal of thought ought to be given not just to details of asserted empirical observations but to background questions of the theoretical methodology of the field. In all probability, the formulations which might be arrived at on such matters cannot be as specific and as demonstrably useful as the special procedures of statistics as aids in handling bodies of quantitative data. Nevertheless, in some degree the same sort of value may be attainable. Some real advantages may accrue by establishing some abstract formulations about theoretical methodology of work on personality and by examining various personality theories in the light of such formulations. To this task, then, the present paper is devoted.

In our discussion, we will have opportunity to indicate some main features of the half-dozen chief types of theory which have been developed to explain personality. Our main attention, however, will be focused on some key issues of theoretical methodology. The discussion of particular personality theories will be incidental to the discussion of these.

All the questions that we will consider are highly controversial. Any student should be warned, therefore, that the following account may have some very serious blind spots in it. However, perhaps we can eliminate a bit of the confusion which now prevails in the theorizing about personality.

Is the Psychology of Personality a Study of *Unique* Characteristics of Persons?

In the definitions of personality given in many books, some reference appears over and over again to the conception of personality as a matter of *unique* characteristics. Guilford's book on personality, for example, summed up his definition in these words: *"An individual's personality, then, is his unique pattern of traits"* (1959, p. 5, italics his). Not only do various authors speak in this way, but at least one very influential psychologist in this field—Gordon Allport (1937)—really meant it. At least in his earlier discussions, he was very explicit in his suggestion that the basic distinction between the psychology of personality and the psychology of other phases of life is that the psychology of personality is dealing with what is truly unique in each person—what exists in him but in no other persons. Many other authors, such as Stagner (1937), Guilford (1959), Hilgard (1962), and Lundin (1961), apparently have accepted this terminology from Allport, even though the research procedures and methods of theorizing they favor are basically not concerned with unique characteristics.

Some reasons for advocating Allport's view are easily seen, since, in anything as complex as a human personality, each personality probably is unique in some respects. Furthermore, the generalized principles of psychology no doubt have encompassed only a limited part of what is important in personality, thus leaving a lot of room for psychologists to make very intensive studies of individual persons.

To say all this, however, is not equivalent to saying that the psychology of personality ought to be conceived as a study of unique characteristics. Such a definition can hardly be used in actual practice. We could determine what characteristics are relatively *rare*. But to determine what characteristics are really unique—found only in the given person out of the two billion or more of people on the face of the earth—that is simply impossible. Furthermore, if we want to make a penetrating study of any given individual, we have to bring to that task many skills and understandings derived from knowledge of other persons. Otherwise we could recognize little that is meaningful in the life of the new individual we are trying to understand. The case is like that of listening to a piece of music. We may well want to hear any unique features of the particular performance. But, to do this, we must bring to this listening as much as we possibly can of skills derived from previous listening to other pieces of music. Otherwise we will hear nothing more than the simplest aspects of what is played. Of the two very important reasons for intensive studies of individual personalities, neither one of them justifies the conclusion that psychological research on personality should be conceived as a study of unique features.

Within the psychology of personality, the main reason for making intensive studies of single individuals is that such research, even though it may seem to be dealing only with what is found in that one person, is likely to reveal factors, processes, and relationships which will prove important in other persons as well, but which we may not be able to recognize in other persons until we have studied some one particular person in whom these things were manifested in some unusually striking form. The situation is like that in astronomy, geology, meteorology, and any other science which deals with complex systems. All of such sciences are dealing with unique things, and all such sciences make intensive studies of individual cases. But when geologists make such studies, they are not trying to learn about the unique features of the particular earthquake or particular volcanic eruption. They are trying to get light on additional *general* factors which they can identify only by the most careful study and measurement of single cases.

There are some practical reasons for interest in individual cases. With complex systems, it is more or less inevitable that there will be some predictions which people can learn to make about the particular case and which are worthwhile for practical reasons, but which cannot be made with the help of any generalized principles available to date. Studies of the weather of any particular region, for instance, are apt to yield some means of prediction of this sort. The same is true of earthquake records in a particular area and of medical records on individual patients. Such knowledge can be of great value. But, aside from the possibility, mentioned in the preceding paragraph, that studies like these can help in the recognition of what is *not* unique, the value of such studies is merely a practical one. I think we can conclude, therefore, that psychologists have no more reason to speak about personality as something unique than geologists have to dwell on the uniqueness of mountains or astronomers to rhapsodize about the uniqueness of stars.

Should the Psychology of Personality Be Defined at Least as the Study of *Distinctive* Characteristics?

Even though various current books continue to echo the earlier discussion by Allport about unique qualities, other psychological discussions, including Allport's (1961) revision of his book on personality, have started to speak instead about the idea that the psychology of personality should be conceived as the field which is dealing with individual characteristics which are somewhat distinctive, even though not unique. This view is well expressed by McGuigan as follows: ". . . personality consists of what we need to know about a person in order to improve our predictions, control, and understanding of his behavior above the level afforded by knowledge of people in general" (Calvin et al., 1961, p. 402). From many angles, this proposal seems very plausible. Certainly, when we think about personality, we are thinking, or *may* be thinking, about respects in which people are different—witness the list of adjectives mentioned in the second paragraph of this paper.

However, this proposal also involves serious difficulties. The fundamental trouble is that every field of psychology, because of the basic nature of scientific method, has to deal both with differences and with common features. We find that one thing is the crucial causal factor in relation to another by observing differences of effects in different cases and relating these to differences of antecedent condition. We start, for instance, with the fact that some people have malaria and other people do not. Then, working with such different persons, we try to find the generalized law that can account for such differences of state of health. But in such work in medicine, it would be pointless to identify one part of medicine as concerned with the differences between people and other parts of medicine as concerned with "knowledge about people in general." The whole field of medicine is trying to find the things about human beings that make them get malaria and which makes the attacks more severe in some cases than others.

The same thing holds true of all fields of psychology. Research on conditioned responses, for example, tries to cast light on the question of why a conditioned response is harder to extinguish in one animal than in another. From what has been learned, for instance, we can say that the dog which has been trained with intermittent reinforcements would take longer to extinguish than the dog which has been trained with invariable reinforcements. To know how long a person would retain his knowledge of a list of nonsense syllables which he could recite perfectly, we would have to know about the kind and amount of training he had had on that list. But we do not want to define personality so that it will include all of such features which help us to make more accurate predictions. If we did, the psychology of personality would be co-extensive with the whole field of psychology. All fields of psychology have to deal with differences between individuals.

In the other direction, we must recognize too that personality is just as truly a matter of those respects in which organisms are similar as of those respects in which they differ. For example, suppose the psychoanalysts are right in saying that a series of constitutionally determined stages of personality development occurs in the human infant, with an oral-dependent phase first, an oral-aggressive phase next, and so on. If this is true, it is important in the field of personality. It belongs in the field of personality not a whit less through the fact (if it be a fact) that the proposition holds true of all children. Or, suppose Harlow (1958, 1962) is right in claiming that certain conditions of contact with their mothers or with mother-surrogates are decisive in producing certain effects in infant monkeys. This is an important fact about the psychology of personality of monkeys, even though it concerns the emotional needs of all monkeys.

It does seem necessary to distinguish between personality and other phases of the life of the individual. When we pick up a book on the psychology of personality, we expect it to be dealing with a special part of the field of psychology, rather than with the whole field. But the distinction must be found along some line other than defining personality as the distinctive characteristics of the individual. Any such conception is too broad in some respects, too narrow in others.

In Research on Personality, Should the Determination
of Abstract Categories Precede Attempts to
Determine Functional Relationships?

If we agree that the psychology of personality must deal in terms of generalized factors and generalized principles, rather than in terms of unique characteristics, we must face the question of when, in general, the psychological research on personality should focus on trying to classify what it studies (the "taxonomic" problem) and when on trying to determine the relationships between different factors.

On this problem, a distinctive view has been urged by a number of academic psychologists who favor what they call the "factor analytic" method of research on personality. This is a viewpoint urged in the writings of R. B. Cattell (1959), Eysenck (1953), and Guilford (1959). These men agree that the psychology of personality will need to study the functional relations (they might well say the "causal relations") between different types of factors in human life, as between various personal qualities and the environmental conditions which tend to produce them. But, they say, the effort to determine such relationships ought to be postponed until after we have determined the classes or categories or dimensions or traits that will need to be studied as related to such-and-such other things. If research on personality is to be efficient, they say, we should undertake the taxonomic work first. First, they maintain, we should find what abstract terms are justified in speaking about the personality characteristics of people. Not to proceed in this way would be to fail to recognize the essential fact that scientific work needs to be highly abstract.

To implement this proposal, the factor analysts have developed various rather elaborate statistical procedures for taking measurements on very large groups of persons (at least three to four hundred for careful work) and for analyzing the correlations of such data to find the statistically or mathematically simplest ways of describing the main features of such data. In this work, the factor analysts have performed a valuable service in showing that appreciable economies may be made in description by this procedure of statistical distillation.

This procedure is quite different, of course, from that which has been used by psychoanalysts and other psychotherapeutic theorists. Such psychotherapists have depended on intensive studies of relatively very small numbers of persons. They have depended on observations which could hardly be expressed in quantitative terms except in the very rough terms of presence or absence of some effect or very rough differences of degree, as in statements that a given individual has a very high degree of anxiety, hostility, or what not. The factor analysts, in contrast, in order to get the kind of data they need for their statistical work, have had to get data which could be put in more detailed quantitative form. They had to get data on large numbers of persons. Consequently, even though the factor analysts would be happy to use data from intensive investigations on each individual, they have had to settle for much less. Because of their pressure for data on large numbers of persons measured under comparable conditions, they have had to depend on data that could be secured by rather brief observations of each person involved.

When we are trying to evaluate the proposal of these factor analysts, we need to make clear that, contrary to the impression which the factor-analysts often state or imply, the factor-analytic approach has by no means a monopoly on interest in learning to identify the fundamental factors involved in personality or other phases of behavior. In fact, the effort to identify fundamental factors is something that runs through all phases of scientific work. The research workers in nutrition, for instance, have tried to identify the fundamental factors that are responsible for the prevention of rickets, scurvy, beri-beri, and so on. They are not interested merely in listing all the specific foods, prepared under such and such specific conditions, which would prevent such disorders. Their quest has been for fundamental vitamins, mineral salts, enzymes, and so on.

Yet, we may note, even though all other sciences are basically concerned with identifying fundamental factors in their particular fields, none of these other fields use methods analogous to those which are employed by the factor-analysts in their studies of personality. In these other fields, the discovery of causal relations comes *first*, and the categorizing or classifying is a later step. One wonders therefore whether some fundamental difference between personality and the subject matters studied in these other fields would make other methods of research so profitable elsewhere but would suggest that in research on personality the order of procedure should be reversed.

The situation is the more puzzling when we recall that in a science the fundamental basis for grouping things together is evidence that such and such different concrete things all have similar functional properties or that all may be described by the same laws. This would indicate that research on functional relationships should precede and be the means for grouping different things together, rather than our having an order which would be the reverse of this!

We may note, too, that the statistical methods of factor analysis are adapted only for securing relatively economical descriptions of things which already have been recognized as worth studying. Statistical methods cannot reach out and provide data which the research worker did not realize that he needed to include. Except in relatively minor cases, they cannot point to things that the research worker had not yet suspected.

To learn to recognize new factors and new processes is important. But how is this ordinarily to be accomplished? Is it to be accomplished by taking measurements at random of every conceivable and measurable thing and then attempting to distill out the consistent relationships within the whole mass of material? In anything as complicated as human life, this is hardly a feasible procedure. There are vastly too many factors to permit us to proceed in this way. Instead, the work of science is more a matter of sleuthing, of getting clues by making deductions or analogies from other things that are known or by picking them up from circumstances in which some relationship has happened to be manifested in an unusually clear way. It is frequently a matter of getting hunches and then of devising or locating other peculiarly simplified situations to see whether, in fact, the observed relationship was anything more than a chance configuration of factors.

For instance, the fact that fluorides can be a fundamental factor in preventing tooth decay did not come (and could hardly have come) from some statistical analysis of the diets of people taken at random. It came because dentists in a few small areas of the United States noted and were curious about the fact that the children who grew up in those regions had very few cavities. The discovery by Semmelweiss of the fundamental factor involved in puerperal (child-bed) fever, which in some months claimed the lives of up to 30 per cent of the women who came to the obstetrical ward in which he worked, came only after he had observed that one of his colleagues died of the typical symptoms of this disease four days after cutting his hand while conducting a post-mortem examination on a woman who had died of this disorder. Innumerable other examples could be cited from the history of medicine, genetics, physiology, and other sciences.

Many of the correlations with which factor-analysis works are merely the chance products of given cultural conditions. This still does not vitiate the fact that factor-analytic studies are useful for some purposes. But it does mean that their service is primarily a narrowly practical one, rather than a fundamental scientific one (Wishner, 1960). They make contributions through the business of providing more economical descriptions and means of measurement of particular groups. But they hardly do more than that, and most of the task of achieving a better scientific understanding of personality lies in this "more than that"—in the discovery of factors and relationships which, up to that point, no research worker would have thought important to measure.

So, even though the factor-analysts have made strong claims about the fundamental scientific significance of their proposal to proceed with taxonomic work first, these claims hardly seem justified. The main hope of developing a better knowledge of personality depends, not on those methods which seek to classify first, but on those methods, with which the rest of our discussion will concern itself, which seek first and foremost to develop and test new hypotheses in specific cases and pursue the work of classification as a secondary development from this.

Should the Psychology of Personality Be Stated Partly in Inferential Terms or Solely as a Matter of Relationships between Directly Observable Factors?

Another distinctive methodological principle has been urged by a number of experimental psychologists, most effectively by B. F. Skinner (1950, 1956). They have urged that much of the theorizing of psychologists, especially in the field of personality, gets bogged down in hopeless confusion because the findings and observations of the field are stated in reference to hypothesized or inferred factors, rather than in terms of relationships between directly observable factors. Skinner has claimed that the more mature sciences do not think in terms of factors and processes that lie back of what can directly be observed, but content themselves merely with mathematical statements of the relationships between different parts of what is directly measured.

If Skinner is correct in this description of other sciences, and if no basic difference exists between them and the psychology of personality, then indeed the psychology of personality seemingly ought to be developed on basically different theoretical lines than commonly are employed. However, especially at the present time, it is difficult to believe that anyone familiar with other scientific fields would speak seriously of them as dealing merely in terms of direct relationships between observables, rather than as using inferential terms to help them organize and manipulate the empirical observations of their fields. In molecular biology, for example, the work concerning DNA and RNA molecules as mechanisms of heredity, as means of resistance to disease, and as factors in bodily development, seems to have tremendous value. But the concepts about such molecular structures are not matters of direct observation; they are concepts obtained by piecing together a great host of specific observations and building an elaborate inferential model which might account for these. The same is true of atomic physics, most of chemistry, most of recent neurological research, and various other fields.

Why do scientific workers deal in terms of constructs about factors and processes which they cannot observe? Why don't they keep their feet on the ground, as Skinner believes they should do? Are all of these other workers somehow suffering from some self-deceptions in believing that they profit by such inferences? If they are not deceived, wherein does the gain arise? Certainly, as Skinner says, such inferences do not as such constitute any additions to the empirical observations but merely add a more or less precarious theoretical superstructure. What could be the use of such?

Note that Skinner has not been questioning the value of abstract terms. All of his key terms are highly abstract. When he speaks about "reinforcements," he intends that the term should cover thousands of different factors of the most diverse kinds. When he speaks of "schedules of reinforcement," he intends, again, that this should be understood as an extremely comprehensive abstract term. Nor is Skinner unappreciative of the value of extrapolations from what is known to what is unknown. But such extrapolations or hypotheses, he insists, should be to the effect that, since certain relationships had been observed between such and such specific observable factors, possibly this same relationship may exist and would be worth checking between such and such other observable factors which seem analogous to those already studied.

That such formulations and extrapolations as Skinner advocates often are made and often are valuable is unquestionable. Particularly from the standpoint of serving short-range practical interests, often all that is important is that one factor is related to some other factor. It is sufficient, for some of the purposes of automobile insurance agencies, for example, to learn that teen-agers who have taken driver-training courses are worth insuring at lower rates than teen-agers who have not had such courses, and it is not necessary to ask why. But for longer-range practical interests, such as those which medical research serves, and for more basic theoretical purposes, is the approach which Skinner recommends the preferable approach to use? Is anything else to be gained, even though inferential concepts do not, as such, increase our observational data?

A considerable change in the philosophy of science on this question has developed since the 1930s. The change lies in more than just an acceptance of the idea that some inferential terms can be of value. Instead, the view which has been developing is that, in a field which deals with very complex phenomena and which has a wealth of empirical evidence to use in trying to interpret those phenomena, organization of the knowledge of the field by complex *nomological nets* (Feigl, 1956) is necessary. This term refers to complex inferential systems where only some of the inferential terms are directly tied to observable factors and where, to achieve an efficient intellectual device, many other terms should be tied (admittedly in careful ways) to other inferred factors. Such an intellectual device permits breaking down the whole intellectual activity into a series of shorter propositions connected by transitional terms. It does not add data, but it does add an indispensable aid for dealing with complex data.

Of course, we must recognize when we are using concepts about factors we infer rather than observe. Our language and our logic need to be as clear and careful as possible. We need to realize that we need to develop and test out predictive implications of our inferences, lest otherwise we fall into the error of using fictions that are worthless or worse than worthless. But though the whole procedure is a risky and precarious one, it seems the only means of getting the intellectual simplicity which is needed for much of the development of scientific work in relatively complex fields.

How Broad Should the Area Be on Which the Concepts of Personality Are Based?

If we have not somehow gone astray in our discussion of the issues considered thus far, it follows that the work of theory construction in the psychology of personality will need particularly to take the form of a highly abstract inferential system or nomological net. Especially will this be true if we think of the psychology of personality as trying to develop a basic scientific understanding of personality, rather than attempting to achieve merely the short-range objectives of a narrowly technological sort.

To say this, however, does not narrow the field of personality theory to merely one approach, even as far as already-developed personality theories are concerned. A number of those that already exist are such complex inferential theories as the preceding discussion has suggested. Among these are some significant differences, however. Very important differences occur, for instance, between psychoanalytic theory, neo-Freudian types of theory, S-R personality theory, and perceptual or organizational theories which are based both on clinical and on experimental data.

To discuss these four types of theory, it is worth developing the idea that the character of an inferential system is likely to be influenced greatly by these three factors: 1) the concrete descriptive knowledge that the system uses, 2) the model or analogical system which it uses as a help to its thinking, and 3) the breadth of material which it uses as a help in generating its hypotheses and in testing them.

THE PSYCHOANALYTIC OR FREUDIAN THEORY   The Freudian theory has been revised a good deal in the course of its history and is continuing to be revised. Consequently, it is hard to know what one should accept as psychoanalytic theory and what he should see as deviating markedly enough so that he should regard it as the Freudian group generally has regarded the ideas of Adler and Horney—as being such drastic changes that they no longer are forms of psychoanalytic theory. For clarity, let me speak somewhat conservatively, rather than taking one of the most recent variations of Freudian theory.

If we take the main body of psychoanalytic writing as the basis for our discussion, several main features in the psychoanalytic theory of personality can be described (see Jones, 1953, 1955, 1957). In the first place, the data on which it is based are almost solely data from within the field of personality itself, and even more narrowly they are data from psychotherapeutic work. The use of this limited area of observation is defended by the psychoanalysts on the grounds that only in this type of situation can a really intensive and careful body of concrete descriptive knowledge about personality be secured. Personality is complicated enough, and the individual learns so strenuously to defend himself against recognizing and giving expression to some of the most important and powerful processes within himself, that any observational situation which does not have the special features of the intensive psychoanalytic-therapy situation cannot reveal many of the concrete phenomena from which an adequate theory of personality can be generated. Even more narrowly, psychoanalytic theory seems to be based particularly on observations on certain sorts of psychopathological effects. Psychoanalytic concepts seem derived particularly from observations on compulsive, obsessive, and phobic cases, cases of paranoid distortion, and phenomena of dreams. All of these are cases where what seems important in personality is intra-psychic conflict and where repressed motivational processes seem able frequently to distort intellectual processes from the form which they otherwise would have (Madison, 1961; Progoff, 1956).

The model which the psychoanalysts have found useful in thinking about such cases is that of a physical device utilizing a very diffuse energy which can be harnessed to operate some mechanical devices within the system, but which also presses for escape through any weak spots in the confining structures. Partly from the influence of this model, and partly from the nature of the psychopathological effects with which psychoanalysts have been most concerned, their theoretical emphasis has led to their picturing motivational and cognitive processes in quite different terms. A sharp distinction is drawn between the ego as one part of the individual and the id and superego as other parts.

The ego is portrayed as being able to profit by experience and tending to be realistic and adaptive, except when it is overwhelmed by difficulties of dealing with the superego or with the id, which is the repository of the main instinctual energies or motivational forces of the personality. The basic motivational forces of the personality are pictured as welling up from within, from constitutional sources, rather than as being modes of reaction that depend a great deal on circumstances and on past learning as determinants of the degree to which these basic forces will press for expression within the individual's life. Training can change the reaction to these forces—e.g., how much anxiety their stirrings will arouse, and how effectively they will be used in constructive activities in the individual's life—but not their strength or basic character (S. Freud, 1930; Anna Freud, 1951; Munroe, 1955; White, 1959).

CONCEPTUAL AND NEO-FREUDIAN THEORIES   A second type of personality theory has also been developed almost entirely from psychotherapeutic material but has emphasized a different type of observation. This is the type of theory developed first by Alfred Adler (Ansbacher and Ansbacher, 1956) and later by such other workers as Karen Horney (1939, 1950), Harry Stack Sullivan (Mullahy, 1952), and Erich Fromm (1947).[1] This type of theory has paid most attention to the reactions of maladjusted persons to other persons in their social environments. Adler, for example, sought to get data on the personalities and behavior of other members of the family who surrounded the individual in his childhood. Chief emphasis was placed on the capacity of the individual, even as a small child, to develop highly generalized concepts of what he was likely to meet in life, what techniques would be available to him to try to cope with these situations, and what objectives he would be likely to achieve with such different techniques. These concepts were not envisaged as conscious and necessarily rational or realistic appraisals of life situations. On the contrary, Adler and all of these other workers insisted that the individual would typically not merely lack insight into his own key concepts but would have strong resistances against accepting even the most logical and valid interpretations which might be given him by other persons who had tried to figure out what patterns he must be living by. Motivational factors also have been stressed by such theorists, but the motivational forces are seen as determined very heavily by learning and by current circumstances. According to these theorists, the individual does not differ merely in how he expresses his motives but also in what motives he is under pressure to express.

---

[1] On all of these theories, as well as on the regular psychoanalytic theory, an invaluable summary and set of critical notes is given by Munroe (1955).

What model such theorists have used is unclear. Some physical analogies now are available, such as cybernetic devices which might have helped to clarify ideas about the goal-directedness of activity and electronic computers which might have illustrated the development of programs for processing the particular information from different situations. Furthermore, some use might have been made of various examples from experimental psychology as models for thinking about such personality phenomena. However, at least to the best of my knowledge, this group of theorists tended to think of their material only in terms rather directly related to what they felt were significant factual materials. One might have expected that, at least, they could have found some convenient models from experimental-psychological research on concept formation and perceptual processes. However, there was apparently very little tendency toward such borrowing from or drawing parallels with any problems studied by experimental psychologists.

Somewhat the same trends have been seen more recently in the personality theorizing of Carl Rogers (1959, 1961) and George Kelly (1955). Both of these men have had their professional training in the field of psychology rather than in psychiatry. However, both of them have preferred to develop their concepts almost solely from data derived from psychotherapeutic work. They have not felt that they had much to gain through trying to relate such material to other types of observation and theory within psychology (see, however, the recent development of Kelly's approach by Harvey, Hunt, and Schroder, 1961, as an attempt to relate Kelly's concepts to a much larger background).

At least in one respect, one can sympathize with the separatist spirit of such workers and feel grateful for the fact that they developed their concepts independently. The data from which experimental psychologists have worked are data from a very restricted range of situations. Quite possibly, therefore, the hypotheses from experimental psychologists would have been misleading in the field of more complex processes that the psychotherapists were exploring.

As time has passed, however, and as more psychologists have become interested in personality, two main types of theorizing have arisen which have sought to work both from experimental data and from such other data as the Freudians and neo-Freudians had used.

S-R PERSONALITY THEORIES   One of these further developments has come through efforts to interrelate observations of personality with the field of learning as studied and interpreted by that particular school of learning theory known as S-R reinforcement theory. A number of important books on personality have been written from this standpoint, including the volumes by Bagby (1929), Shaffer (1936, 2nd edition with Shoben, 1960), Stagner (1937, 1961), Guthrie (1938), Dollard and Miller (1950), and Wolpe (1958). Pavlov had started this type of discussion with what seemed to him very legitimate extensions of his research on conditioned responses. Many different efforts have been made to reinterpret therapeutic work in these terms (see Bandura, 1961).

Because of this extension of their thinking to a new field of observation, these theorists have sought to use a broader base and, correspondingly, more highly abstract concepts than those employed by therapeutically-based theories. However, this type of theory has used only some portions of psychological research. No attempt was made to relate phenomena of personality to phenomena from research on perception, and few efforts to relate personality phenomena to phenomena of concept formation. Even Dollard and Miller, good Hullians though they have been, did not mention the famous experiment by Hull (1920) which set the basic methodology for subsequent research on concept formation (by presenting learning materials which could be dealt with either by rote memorizing or by concept formation, and by giving the subjects no intimation of the fact that the situation could be dealt with by concept formation).

In some respects, the use of S-R learning theory has led to basically different principles from those involved in either of the therapeutically-based types of theory mentioned above. Even Dollard and Miller, though expressing a strong kinship with the Freudian theory, have changed the idea of motivation to one which places great stress on habits as determining what motives will be dominant in any person's life. Furthermore, S-R personality theories show much less tendency to speak about the infant and child as having the elaborate and bizarre phantasy activities which the Freudians described.

The chief question of theoretical methodology which is worth raising with reference to such S-R theories is whether, even within the field of research on learning, from which they derive so large a part of their interpretation, their conclusions have been based on really broad-area research. After all, even if a person believes, as Hull did, that all principles should be based directly or indirectly on objectively observable factors of stimulation and effector activity, this still does not justify the description of habit-linkages in one sort of terms or another. Since habits are inferred entities, not something directly observed, their properties can legitimately be inferred only by studying their effects under as wide a diversity of situations as may be needed to get a complete picture of their influences. For example, if one is tempted to say that habits are something that operate as rather specific S-R connections rather than as though they were concepts, this proposition must be established by testing the learner under conditions that would give the opportunity for demonstrating whether or not the learner had acquired some very generalized means of processing afferent material.

PERCEPTUAL OR ORGANIZATIONAL THEORIES OF PERSONALITY   Another type of theory of personality has sought to base its interpretations on experimental psychology as well as on non-experimental studies of personality. This is a type of theory which is likely to be spoken of as cognitive or perceptual. It has been developed by such workers as Allport (1936, 1961), Murphy (1947), Lecky (1951), Diamond (1957), Leeper and Madison (1959), and McCurdy (1961), and Leeper (1963). Like the S-R theory, it places considerable reliance on experimental work on learning, but the concepts stressed from that field are not the concepts peculiar to Pavlov, Thorndike, or Hull, but more importantly the concepts from such workers as Tolman, Köhler, Lashley, and Maier. Furthermore, the experimental studies which are used as a paradigm are not merely those in the field of conditioning and problem-solving learning, but also experiments in concept formation and perception, as well as research in comparative psychology by ethologists like Tinbergen and Lorenz.

Several different models or analogies have been used in this type of approach to help envisage and organize ideas. One is the sort of model which Köhler employed in his discussions of brain processes as dynamically organized events—models such as those of distribution of electric currents in a complex conduction system. Another model, to illustrate the goal-directed quality which this approach emphasizes in much of psychological activity, is the type of cybernetic device now becoming so well-known in connection with automation in industrial equipment and as the controlling mechanisms in guided missiles. Electronic computers are a third model for certain other purposes, especially to express the idea that, where a system has limited storage capacity, a great deal of what is stored would not be concrete and specific material but programs for processing specific material fed into it.

The view sometimes is expressed that no basic differences of empirical hypotheses exist between S-R theory and perceptual theory and that the spokesmen for the two viewpoints ought to realize that their differences are almost entirely differences merely of terminology. Undoubtedly the two theories have been changing and developing and, in this process have become more akin to each other. Despite such developments, however, some profound differences of interpretation remain. At any rate, let me indicate some main propositions relative to personality which would characterize such a perceptual type of theory. If these concepts are acceptable to S-R theory, the differences between the two viewpoints are minimal.

The first point in a perceptual type of theory is a shift in primary attention from effector responses to activities of the brain. The main processes which are studied are those whereby the organism perceives or represents its situation as one which has such and such a character.

Second, the brain mechanism is seen as something that needs to become greatly modified, both in character and degree of complexity, by the learning of the organism. There are no "biologically adequate stimuli" for most of the brain processes which the individual needs to develop. Learning develops much more complex functional units in the brain, and primarily the psychological activity of the individual is to be understood in terms of the nature and functioning of these.

Third, these complex brain processes are dynamically organized processes. They operate selectively and abstractively, stressing merely certain aspects of afferent material and neglecting or even obstructing the use of other aspects. When a person has been badly injured, for instance, the amount of pain felt cannot be predicted from the intensity of peripheral stimulation. The painfulness of the experience will be determined by a host of factors that come both from the cultural background of the individual and from the particular circumstances of the injury, as has been shown in studies of the reactions of soldiers as compared with civilians (Melzack, 1961).

Fourth, this dynamically organized character of brain processes means that once some mechanism has developed, it tends to obstruct the reorganization of the brain activity into some other form which, save for the earlier learning, might very naturally have been the more probable perceptual reaction to the same situation. There is considerable importance to primacy effects.

Fifth, the brain processes of the individual are by no means merely short-time processes that disappear soon after the cessation of the afferent activity which arouses them. The representational processes of the brain can continue for long periods (of hours or more) as a continuing background stream that determines the main effects which will be aroused by the many details of stimulation met during that time.

Sixth, these perceptual processes are not to be interpreted as matters merely of what the person "knows" to be the case, in the sense of our ordinary meaning of this word. They are not all rational or intelligent or realistic processes. Whether so or not depends on the conditions under which they were developed. The small child, particularly, can have bizarre ideas about his world such as some which the psychoanalysts have described—but these still are regular perceptual processes, not processes of some qualitatively different id.

Seventh, the perceptual processes of the individual are not to be seen as "merely intellectual" or "merely cognitive" processes. All motivational processes constitute a part of the larger category of perceptual or cognitive processes. Most perceptual research, it is true, has been conducted with motivationally neutral perceptual processes, but this has been merely for reasons of convenience. Our basic conception of cognitive processes should recognize, for example, that the process aroused by a foul-smelling substance is truly a perceptual process, even though it also is a process that puts the organism under pressure to try to escape from the offending stimulation. The motivational processes of the individual, therefore, are not something given as unalterable instincts of the id, as portrayed in psychoanalytic theory (Anna Freud, 1951; Gill, 1959), nor merely as processes which can operate as innate drives attached to new stimuli. Instead, motivation is subject to enormous potential changes in the life of the individual. This is more the case with some motives than with others, but all motives are subject to at least considerable changes through modifications of the neural mechanisms involved in the perceptual-motivational processes of the individual. The cheeses that are rejected violently by most Chinese, for instance, as impossibly offensive in odor and taste are viewed as delicacies by certain groups with other training and background. The situations which arouse tremendous exploratory interest in some individuals, such as scientists, are unable to produce any motivationally powerful perceptions in most other persons.

Such an experimentally-related personality theory has much in common with the sort of interpretation of personality given by such theorists as Adler, Horney, Sullivan, Rogers, and Kelly, who have worked almost solely from therapeutic data. Do gains come from seeking to get more generalized concepts of this sort—ones which can apply both to personality material and to experiments on learning, perception, and other material which this last group of theorists also would like to use for their possible heuristic advantages? This remains to be seen.

Conclusions

The field of personality theory includes a number of different approaches, all of which agree that the psychology of personality should attempt to deal not merely with the differences between individuals but with generalized principles seeking to account for those differences, and should seek to account for them by the development of complicated inferential systems. A great deal of work needs to be done to evaluate these systems and find means of more adequate development of them. Part of this work will have to be a matter of getting much more adequate empirical evidence, of course. But the problem seems to be more complex than merely this. It is a problem also of becoming more skillful with technical methods of theory construction.

In this last section we have been speaking mainly about differences in area of the empirical material on which these four different personality theories have built. In general, many advantages seem to obtain in trying to base our theories of personality not merely on data from within that specific field but also on studies of other parts of psychology which, at first thought, may seem quite different from the psychology of personality. As time passes, our personality theories likely will have more and more of this broadened character. On the other hand, though, it is worth recognizing that when psychologists broaden their field of observation and data in the fields of experimental psychology, they may be reducing the adequacy of their contacts with the phenomena of personality. One of the important points that the psychoanalysts have made is that, for work in the field of personality, part of the equipment that is needed is a kind of emotional adaptation which will permit honest and effective facing of data which an investigator might otherwise find too disquieting to deal with. We have not spoken of this type of problem in this discussion, but it is important. The task of adequate theorizing in the field of personality, therefore, is an extremely complex one in more ways than one. This is such a significant area for modern man, however, that we must make all the progress we can in developing and using the means of really effective technical work in this very old field.

References

Allport, G. W. *Personality*. New York: Holt, 1937.

———. *Pattern and growth in personality*. New York: Holt, 1961.

Allport, G. W., and Odbert, H. S. Trait-names: a psycho-lexical study. *Psychol. Monog.*, 1936, 47, No. 211.

Ansbacher, H. L., and Ansbacher, Rowena (eds.). *The individual psychology of Alfred Adler*. New York: Basic Books, 1956.

Bagby, E. *Psychology of personality*. New York: Holt, 1928.

Bandura, A. Psychotherapy as a learning process. *Psychol. Bull.*, 1961, 58, 145–159.

Calvin, A., et al. *Psychology*. Boston: Allyn and Bacon, 1961.

Cattell, R. B. Personality theory growing from multivariate quantitative research. In S. Koch (ed.), *Psychology: a study of a science*, Vol. 3. New York: McGraw-Hill, 1959, pp. 257–327.

Diamond, S. *Personality and temperament*. New York: McGraw-Hill, 1957.

Dollard, J., and Miller, N. E. *Personality and psychotherapy*. New York: McGraw-Hill, 1950.

Eysenck, H. *The structure of human personality*. New York: Wiley, 1953.

Feigl, H. Some major issues and developments in the philosophy of science of logical empiricism. *Minn. Studies in the Philos. of Science*, 1956, 1, 3–37.

Freud, Anna. The contributions of psychoanalysis to genetic psychology. *Amer. J. Orthopsychiat.*, 1951, *21*, 476–497.

Freud, S. *Civilization and its discontents.* London: Hogarth Press, 1930.

Fromm, E. *Man for himself.* New York: Rinehart, 1947.

Gill, M. The present state of psychoanalytic theory. *J. Abnorm. Soc. Psychol.*, 1959, *58*, 1–8.

Guilford, J. P. *Personality.* New York: McGraw-Hill, 1959.

Guthrie, E. R. *Psychology of human conflict.* New York: Harper, 1938.

Harlow, H. F. The nature of love. *Amer. Psychologist*, 1958, *13*, 673–685.

————. The heterosexual affectional system in monkeys. *Amer. Psychologist*, 1962, *17*, 1–9.

Harvey, O. J., Hunt, D. E., and Schroder, H. M. *Conceptual systems and personality organization.* New York: Wiley, 1961.

Hilgard, E. R. *Psychology* (3d ed.). New York: Harcourt, 1962.

Horney, Karen. *New ways in psychoanalysis.* New York: Norton, 1939.

————. *Neurosis and human growth.* New York: Norton, 1950.

Hull, C. L. Quantitative aspects of the evolution of concepts: an experimental study. *Psychol. Monog.*, 1920, *28*, No. 123.

Jones, E. *The life and work of Sigmund Freud.* (3 vols.) New York: Basic Books, 1953, 1955, 1957.

Kelly, G. *The psychology of personal constructs.* (2 vols.) New York: W. W. Norton, 1955.

Lecky, P. *Self-consistency: a theory of personality* (2d ed.), New York: Island Press, 1951.

Leeper, R. Current trends in theories of personality. In Wayne Dennis et al., *Current trends in psychological theory.* Pittsburgh: Univ. of Pittsburgh Press, 1951, pp. 21–56.

————. Learning in relation to perception, motivation, and personality. In S. Koch (ed.), *Psychology: a study of a science*, Vol. 5. New York: McGraw-Hill, 1963.

Leeper, R., and Madison, P. *Toward understanding human personalities.* New York: Appleton-Century-Crofts, 1959.

McCurdy, H. G. *The personal world.* New York: Harcourt, 1961.

Madison, P. *Freud's concepts of repression and defense.* Minneapolis: Univ. of Minnesota Press, 1961.

Melzack, R. The perception of pain. *Sci. Am.*, 1961, *204*, 41–49.

Mullahy, P. (ed.). *The contributions of Harry Stack Sullivan.* New York: Hermitage House, 1952.

Munroe, Ruth L. *Schools of psychoanalytic thought.* New York: Dryden, 1955.

Murphy, G. *Personality.* New York: Harper, 1947.

Progoff, I. *The death and rebirth of psychology.* New York: Julian Press, 1956.

Rogers, C. R. A theory of therapy, personality, and interpersonal relationships, as developed in the client-centered framework. In S. Koch (ed.), *Psychology: a study of a science*, Vol. 3. New York: McGraw-Hill, 1959, 184–256.

————. *On becoming a person: a therapist's view of psychotherapy.* Boston: Houghton Mifflin, 1961.

Shaffer, L. F., and Shoben, E. J. *Psychology of adjustment.* Boston: Houghton Mifflin, 1936, 1956.

Skinner, B. F. Are theories of learning necessary? *Psychol. Rev.*, 1950, *57*, 193–216.

———. Critique of psychoanalytic concepts and theories. *Minn. Studies in the Philos. of Science*, 1956, *1*, 77–87.
Stagner, R. *Psychology of personality*. New York: McGraw-Hill, 1937, 1961.
White, R. W. Review of S. Hook (ed.), *Psychoanalysis, scientific method, and philosophy*, and P. Rieff, *Freud: the mind of the moralist*. *Sci. Am.*, 1959, *201*, 267–276.
Wishner, J. Review of J. P. Guilford's *Personality*. *Amer. J. Psychol.*, 1960, *73*, 650–651.
Wolpe, J. *Psychotherapy by reciprocal inhibition*. Palo Alto, Calif.: Stanford Univ. Press, 1958.

27 | Theory Construction and Validation in Psychoanalysis[1]

LEONARD HORWITZ

Psychoanalysts, in contrast to academic psychologists, have not been particularly concerned with problems of theoretical methodology. This trend is beginning to change as the psychoanalytic movement in the past two decades has made increasing contact with the other behavioral sciences and has begun to see itself through the lenses of other disciplines. Contrary to the view of most psychologists, Freud was actually quite sophisticated about problems of theory construction and kept in mind more carefully than did many of his disciples the distinction between theorizing which was close and that which was distant from empirical data (Frenkel-Brunswik, 1954). Until relatively recently, academic psychologists have been fairly unanimous in viewing psychoanalysis as a kind of demonology, given to all of the sins of metaphysical and anti-scientific speculation (dogmatism, vague concepts, reification, etc.). These views have been considerably tempered in recent years with the result that many psychologists now look upon psychoanalytic theory as a legitimate scientific discipline, though perhaps still not quite respectable.

Many persons interested in problems of methodology now hold that academic psychology was burdened down by an overly severe scientific "superego" which placed excessive demands for precision both upon itself and upon the findings and theories of psychoanalysis. The academicians

[1] The suggestions and comments of Drs. Gardner Murphy, Robert S. Wallerstein, Richard S. Siegal, and Harold M. Voth are gratefully acknowledged.

have been accused of attempting to strait-jacket prematurely all psychological research in a model of science where methods tend to determine problems rather than vice versa. The procedural tail has tended to wag the substantive dog. The handicap of such approaches, claim the analysts, is suggested in the contrast between the bodies of knowledge about human behavior accumulated by academic psychology on the one hand and psychoanalysis on the other. Clinicians usually cannot conceive of understanding their patients without using the concept of unconscious motivation; experimental psychology has only recently begun to incorporate this concept into its studies, as in the areas of unconscious and preconscious perception. In its long struggle over the admissibility of introspective data, psychology has cut off from its observational base some extremely rich and valuable data concerning the determinants of human behavior and therefore has understandably lagged far behind Freud and his followers, who did not shut their eyes on philosophical grounds to certain simple facts of observation.

The trend toward the relaxation of unrealistically rigid standards of scientific procedure has occurred both in psychology and in the philosophy of science. The shift in philosophy is largely exemplified by the modification of the requirement, originally proposed by the logical positivists, that *all* concepts used in scientific discourse be operationally defined. Most philosophers now recognize that rigid operationism leads to an undue narrowness and sterility in science and that only through the use of "fictitious concepts" (Hempel, 1952) or "hypothetical constructs" which may have but a tenuous tie with the level of observation can the creative scientist construct the theories which will ultimately clarify the unknowns in nature. The requirement that concepts be defined by operations upon observables has been replaced by the more reasonable caution that one be aware of the extent of the connections between observation and theory. This shift away from radical operationism now allows for hypotheses if they are *indirectly* confirmable and for theoretical constructs if they are part of a network which connects them with terms designating data of direct observation (Feigl, 1956). The rationale of this point of view has been expressed by Scriven (1956, p. 113): "A term is fruitful only if it encourages changes in its own meaning; and, to some considerable extent, this is incompatible with operational definition." The challenge posed by psychoanalytic theory to be admitted into the household of the respectable sciences has possibly at least partly contributed to the demise of the strictly operationist approach.

A parallel shift has started to occur during the last decade within academic psychology itself and is best exemplified by the introduction of the conception of "construct validity." Cronbach and Meehl (1955), in one of the most important methodological papers in psychology in recent years, have proposed that psychologists begin to accommodate their tests and measurements to the fact that many of the concepts in psychology are as yet incompletely defined. The so-called independent criterion in the measurement of such significant concepts as anxiety or aggression is an ideal which we can only approach slowly by a system of successive approximations. The rationale for this approach was stated as follows (p. 294):

Since the meaning of theoretical constructs is set forth by stating the laws in which they occur, our incomplete knowledge of the laws of nature produces a vagueness in our constructs. We will be able to say "what anxiety is" when we know all the laws involving it; meanwhile, since we are in the process of discovering these laws, we do not yet know precisely what anxiety is.

This methodological conception represents a radical departure from the conventional view of validity, which disallowed any test which was not linked to a fully defined criterion measure. The authors have demonstrated, for example, the operation of a "bootstraps effect," by which a test and its independent criterion, after a period of refinement, may ultimately find their positions reversed. This has occurred with regard to intelligence test measures and teachers' ratings, where the tests have now become the criterion measure against which teachers' ratings are "validated." The introduction of the construct-validity idea into academic psychology may have two salutary effects. It may help to bring psychoanalytic studies and research, with their un-operationist concepts, within the purview of its respectable scientific confreres. Second, it emphasizes the importance of doing research upon concepts embedded in a "nomological network" in which the various links between theoretical constructs and observables are spelled out as clearly as possible and the relationship between the construct at hand and related constructs is defined. This suggestion may help to curb the numerous piecemeal studies, unrelated to any kind of comprehensive theory, from flooding the literature—studies which often add little to the advancement of psychological science.

Structure of the Theory

Rapaport (1960) has suggested that psychoanalysis contains the potential for a systematic, hypothetico-deductive structure, although it has not achieved this form as yet. This kind of systematic treatment was regarded by Freud as an ideal (Frenkel-Brunswik, 1954) and had been started by Rapaport shortly before his untimely death (Rapaport, 1960; Rapaport and Gill, 1959). Largely based upon Freud's theorizing and supplemented by Hartmann's contributions in ego psychology as well as Erikson's psychosocial emphasis, Rapaport and Gill have suggested some of the broad outlines of the kind of theory which may eventually emerge.

They dealt primarily with the "metapsychology," a term which undoubtedly conjures up images of mysticism, armchair theorizing, and an anti-empirical approach. But metapsychology is not intended as transcendent psychology, as is true of metaphysics in relation to the science of physics. Rather, it is the study of the assumptions upon which the system of psychoanalytic theory is based. Like any good theory, it takes speculative leaps, but, its critics to the contrary, it is also reasonably responsive to empirical investigations (Gill, 1959). The beginning systematizing efforts of Rapaport and Gill consisted of designating the five "points of view" in psychoanalysis, referring to those aspects of a mental event which must be described in order to present a complete psychoanalytic explanation of the phenomenon. The five "points of view" consist of the dynamic, economic, structural, genetic, and adaptive.

Under each of these rubrics is a set of assumptions which have been abstracted from a related set of psychoanalytic propositions. The structural point of view, for example, contains the following assumptions: "a) There are psychological structures. b) Structures are configurations of a slow rate of change. c) Structures are configurations within which, between which, and by means of which mental processes take place. d) Structures are hierarchically ordered" (Rapaport and Gill, 1959, p. 157–158). These assumptions underlie a series of propositions which move toward an empirical base. Thus, the assumption about the existence of psychological structures would include the propositions from the general psychoanalytic theory concerning ego, id, and superego as well as the more recent propositions concerning "apparatuses" (Hartmann) and "modes" (Erikson). These would then subsume the propositions from the special theory of psychoanalysis (referring to pathological developments). Such statements, in turn, would subsume empirical propositions. Rapaport and Gill (1959, p. 157) illustrate these distinctions as follows:

Empirical proposition: around the fourth year of life boys regard their fathers as rivals; *specific psychoanalytic proposition:* the solution of the oedipal situation is a decisive determinant of character formation and pathology; *general psychoanalytic proposition:* structure formation by means of identifications and anti-cathexes explains theoretically the consequences of the "decline of the oedipal complex"; *metapsychological proposition:* the propositions of the general psychoanalytic theory which explain the oedipal situation and the decline of the Oedipus complex involve dynamic, economic, structural, genetic, and adaptive assumptions.

Several points need to be made about the hierarchical structure described above. Although the system would appear to be of a hypothetico-deductive form, it is by no means a tightly-knit axiomatic system in which, as in Euclidean geometry, all of the propositions are ultimately derived from the basic givens, or axioms. Axiomatization is an ideal in every science which none, not even physics, has yet achieved. Indeed, the outline presented above is hardly even a system; it is little more than a program, a beginning effort towards systematizing and integrating the assumptions in the metapsychology with the many diverse propositions at different levels of the hierarchy.

The major shortcoming in achieving a more adequate systematization of the theory is the lack of precision of its concepts. This point is acknowledged by Rapaport and Gill (1959, p. 11) when they state: "We are not yet in a position to present formal definitions of the terms used in stating these assumptions. We are, however, aware that without such definitions a set of assumptions is of limited value and that, indeed, some of the assumptions presented here are little more than covert definitions. Thus the formulation of the definitions will probably modify this statement of the assumptions." At the level of the observation language, even such a key clinical concept like ego strength is as yet only vaguely defined. Barron's (1953) definition in terms of selected MMPI items is considered by most clinicians to be incomplete, narrow, and restricting. On the other hand, the recent efforts by Karush et al. (1962) to construct an ego-strength scale seemed to err in the opposite direction by including practically every significant aspect of personality functioning. This latter effort was a distinct contribution toward defining the concept insofar as it pointed up the complexity of the variable; optimal ego strength was viewed as a balance which avoided the extremes of excessive inhibition on the one hand and lack of control on the other. One large-scale psychoanalytic study (Wallerstein, Robbins, et al., 1956) attempts to avoid the pitfalls of excessive narrowness and over-inclusiveness by defining the concept as only one of a score of significant personality variables. But no clinician would contend that an adequate conceptualization of this variable has yet been achieved. This reservation applies to all of the currently used intrapsychic variables, such as self-concept, anxiety tolerance, psychological mindedness, etc. They are viewed by clinicians as highly significant but still not adequately conceptualized. This is not to say, however, that we are unable to achieve reliable judgments about them which can be used to formulate predictions and thus test hypotheses. But these concepts are highly complex and are not in a one-to-one relationship with observable behavior. The judgments, therefore, must be derived from a wide range of observational data which are not always easy to specify in advance.

If we take the notion of construct validity seriously, we should not be too alarmed by the lack of precise operational definitions, even for the more empirical propositions. The definitions of concepts should be regarded as tentative working definitions which must gradually be sharpened and clarified. The only cause for concern should be a sense of complacency about the acceptability of inadequate formulations.

The danger of rigidification of theoretical constructs is also raised by the hypothetico-deductive form into which the system appears to be moving. Marx, in this volume, mentions several objections to the premature formalization of theory that was typified by the Hullian system. In essence he pointed to the excessive narrowing, both in methodology and in theorizing, which such systematizing may encourage, particularly in the more immature sciences like psychology. Similarly, critics of psychoanalysis have levelled charges of dogmatism, orthodoxy, and inflexibility against analytic theory. While every branch of science has its fanatic adherents to the status quo, evidence exists that the system is responsive to new discoveries and modifications at every level of its structure. Gill (1959) particularly addressed himself to this problem in a recent paper and has cogently documented the shift in the past two to three decades from an id psychology to an ego psychology: a greater concern for overt behavior as opposed to an exclusive preoccupation with depth psychology, a shift in emphasis from primary to secondary process thinking, and an increased attention to environmental factors as opposed to the purely internal psychological processes. These developments have been reflected in the inclusion of the "adaptive point of view" as a major rubric of psychoanalytic assumptions.

One of the safeguards against a self-contained and sterile system is its openness to a broad range of psychological phenomena. Insofar as its main observational base had been the psychoanalytic treatment situation, psychoanalytic theory has tended to emphasize the intrapsychic, the irrational, and the pathological. To some extent the danger of excluding from its range of study certain phenomena, particularly conflict-free functioning, remains a hazard. At the same time psychoanalysis, in contrast to many of the other systems of psychology, significantly includes within its sphere a wide array of human behavior ranging from experimental observations of the laboratory to naturalistic, cross-cultural studies.

Special Problems of Theory Construction in Psychoanalysis

Before delving into the particular methods of research in psychoanalysis and the issues associated with them, we would do well to examine some of the special problems with which a theory of human behavior is confronted. The complexity and variability of the human organism, plus the uniqueness found in every individual, presents the behavioral scientist with problems which the physical scientist need never consider.

The problem of exercising adequate controls, particularly with regard to matching subjects, is enormously difficult and may only be solved by some method of approximation. This is particularly true when the researcher is investigating the larger, molar segments of behavior (like a patient's response to psychotherapy), as usually occurs in psychoanalytic studies. In attempting to match pairs of subjects for control purposes, the clinician is immediately struck by the lack of congruence between people. Despite similarities along many dimensions, the subtle uniqueness of every individual when studied as a unitary functioning organism makes it well nigh impossible to conceive of matching individuals over a broad spectrum of personality variables. A solution which is now being tried (Wallerstein, Robbins, et al., 1958) and which appears to be more satisfactory than matching pairs, but is far from being a final answer to this problem, is the use of the subject as his own control. As used in studies of psychotherapy, this method is based upon the assumption that the person, at least the adult patient, is unlikely to manifest substantial personality changes over a period of time and the changes which he shows during treatment will be the result of psychiatric intervention. While the assumption is far from correct and does not, for example, take into consideration the phenomenon of spontaneous remissions, it has enough of a core of validity to warrant application. This is particularly true when, as in certain studies (Wallerstein, Robbins, et al., 1958), an effort is made to assess the patient's life situation as a possible contributing factor to the change or lack of change in the patient.

Another complexity is the problem of the relationship between surface and depth, or between phenotype and genotype. Psychoanalytic constructs are such that there is a considerable distance between the levels of overt, observable behavior and its related intrapsychic variables. Basic clinical concepts like anxiety tolerance or ego strength are still vaguely defined in their own right and are weakly linked to behavioral phenomena. Also, identical-appearing surface behavior may be based upon widely different, or even opposite, motives. Generosity or altruism may be the result of a genuine, tender concern for another human being, or it may be a defense against less benevolent wishes. The necessity to see beyond, or behind, the superficial aspects of behavior impinges upon the whole problem of objectivity of observation. Academic psychologists have often recoiled from the highly speculative and inferential interpretations which the depth psychologist feels he must make. While no one can deny that psychoanalysts have often been guilty of "wild analysis" and an over-readiness to engage in unfettered intuitive guesses, neither can one assert that the solution to the problem is to restrict oneself to a narrow range of observational data for the sake of exactness and objectivity. In a very significant contribution to the methodology of psychoanalytic research, Sargent (1961) has proposed that clinical judgments by well-trained observers be used as the primary data of clinical research. Elaborating a basic postulate of a long-term research project on psychotherapy at The

Menninger Foundation, she suggested that objectivity be attained by inter-subjective agreement among judges rather than at the level of the behavioral data themselves.

Another complicating feature of behavioral research is found in an underlying principle of psychoanalytic theory, e.g., multiple determination. Based upon the observation that human behavior is complexly determined and emerges as a final common pathway for multiple impulses and defenses, this state of affairs enormously complicates psychoanalytic research methodology as compared with the physical sciences. The classical experimental situation in which everything is held constant except for the single experimental variable is a model which is usually inapplicable to behavioral research. Escalona (1950) has described the futility of studying the effects of breast feeding vs. cup feeding, for example, in a research which assumes everything else is equal. The context in which the feeding occurs, particularly the mother-child relationship, is an integral part of the hypotheses regarding oral gratification and frustration and therefore must be studied concomitantly in any investigation of infant feeding. This kind of failure to recognize the complexity of psychoanalytic theory on the part of many experimental psychologists attempting to evaluate the validity of its hypotheses is what has contributed to the jaundiced eye which many clinicians cast upon experimental approaches to psychoanalysis.

Over-determination also leads to major problems in evaluating the relative weights of the multiple factors leading to a given behavior at any given time. The same act may be determined by a combination of A, B, C, and D, and may look superficially the same when A is the dominant factor and when D is the dominant factor. Not only are identical overt behaviors produced by a variety of different motives, but the configuration of motive and defense within the same individual leading to identical behaviors may vary from time to time. This phenomenon is a commonplace observation in the analytic situation. The appearance of a given symptom, although determined by several factors, can best be understood in terms of a shifting hierarchy of causes: now it may be understood in terms of a resurgence of oral conflicts, and later it may result primarily from a struggle with hostile impulses.

We have mentioned some of the major problems with which psychoanalysis must cope in attempting to devise more adequate methods of research. Related problems, like the difficulties inherent in being both a participant and observer in certain kinds of research enterprises, will be discussed at greater length below. Suffice it to say that the complexity of the subject matter of psychoanalysis has made the diagnosis of difficulties easier than the prescription of solutions.

The Psychoanalytic Interview as a Research Method

Freud believed that the major tool of psychoanalytic research was the interview method and, more particularly, the procedure of free association by a patient upon a couch. His tremendous discoveries, almost exclusively based upon the case study method, have set a model of "research" in psychoanalysis which continues to this day. Only in recent years have any notable attempts been made to broaden the base of psychoanalytic study to include a variety of controlled observational methods as well as laboratory experimentation. Benjamin (1950) has expressed the opinion that the psychoanalytic interview is still "our most powerful weapon of psychological research" but is not capable alone of solving, for example, the problems of the differential etiology of personality development. His own intensive long-range studies of personality development in children is a model of psychoanalytic research which is not confined simply to the analytic interview. As will be shown later, a number of controlled experimental studies have been undertaken in recent years in the attempt to validate and extend psychoanalytic theory.

Before discussing the issues raised by the use of the psychoanalytic interview as a research method, we would do well to consider the importance of accumulating simple facts and observations about human behavior which pertain to psychoanalytic hypotheses. Psychoanalysis has emphasized the importance of the experiences and modes of thinking which occur in childhood. Only since the recent "cultural revolution" induced by psychoanalysis have we become aware of the importance of creating an atmosphere of freedom from shame and embarrassment as a way of eliciting from children the wishes and fears which constitute an important fabric of the human personality. The rich nuggets of information that can be easily elicited from children contain material about personality functioning which can be understood with a minimum of interpretation and which do not seem to the analysts to require elaborate confirmation. The observations of Piaget (1929) and the writings of Werner (1957) are filled with data concerning primary process modes of thinking which need to be extended rather than merely confirmed. Kubie (1952) has argued against the uselessness of making "pallid facsimiles in the laboratory of the data which are already manifest in nature, merely to get around the human reluctance to look human nature in the eye."

Although the psychoanalytic situation alone is not a suitable vehicle with which to test theory, it has no peer in uncovering many important facets of personality functioning. We shall be dealing here, however, with the phase of verification, as well as the phase of discovery in scientific research. The psychoanalytic situation obviously is a locus par excellence for the generation of hypotheses. But less obvious is the extent to which this method can be used in the process of confirming or disconfirming theory.

The psychoanalytic situation has certain unique characteristics in contributing to our understanding of the intrapsychic mental life of the patient. We are enabled to observe, or at least infer, the dominant unconscious motivations and defenses which the person is forced to conceal, under other circumstances, both from himself and from others. If one accepts the existence and the importance of unconscious motivation in shaping human behavior, one is hard put to find a situation which is comparable to this one for the investigation of the relationships between the conscious and unconscious life of the individual. Thus, all of the hypotheses concerning the arousal of anxiety as a function of a breakdown of repression, the heightening of defensive and adaptive efforts in dealing with increments of anxiety, and other phenomena which are dependent upon the understanding of intrapsychic functions are relatively inaccessible to us without this kind of investigation in depth.

One objection frequently raised about the use of this method is the fact that the data with which we are presented are derived from pathological states. But experience with patients suffering from psychic distress has explained the apparent paradox of attempting to understand the human personality through the use of a relatively restricted sample of subjects. Only under the pressure of considerable discomfort and the hope of finding relief is a person willing to undergo the painful process of attempting to uncover thoughts and feelings which ordinarily remain inaccessible. Furthermore, the fact is now accepted fairly widely that the principles of personality functioning are broadly applicable across the whole spectrum of human behavior, normal as well as abnormal. Particularly with the advent of psychoanalytic ego psychology with its emphasis upon conflict-free spheres of functioning and of adaptive processes which are relatively autonomous from drives and instincts, psychoanalysis has increasingly been moving in the direction of becoming a general psychology as opposed merely to being a special theory of psychopathology or of therapy (Hartmann, 1958).

But despite the potential value of findings in the psychoanalytic situation and its broad applicability, a researcher using this method is confronted with serious methodological problems which may be summarized under the heading of the participant-observer. On the one hand, we are unable to gather certain essential information except via psychoanalytic therapy, and on the other hand, inevitable distortions occur by virtue of the fact that the analyst-researcher is combining several functions at once: he is attempting to observe and record the patient's behavior; he is attempting to evaluate his own reaction to the patient; and he must act in order to induce change in the person who has come for help (Kris, 1951). The therapist's observations are affected and distorted by his own involvement in the process of attempting to induce change, and the patient's productions are inevitably biased by the therapist's interventions and suggestions, however minimal.

These are serious obstacles to research efforts using such a tool. Is it necessary to discard the method, despite its uniquely fruitful data, because of its inherent sources of error, contamination, and subjectivity? The reluctance of psychologists to attempt controlled studies within the context of the psychoanalytic situation has resulted in protests by psychoanalysts and others that proofs are demanded of them by persons who refuse to use their instruments.[2] Kubie (1952) has likened this attitude to the objections in Leeuwenhoek's day to his findings while at the same time refusing to look through his microscope. A similar point was made by Ruth Tolman (1953, p. 276), who reported the reaction of a prominent physicist to the demand for independent confirmation of psychoanalytic findings.

Does anyone not trained in experimental physics ever say to Carl Anderson: "Look, I will not believe there is such a thing as a positron unless I can discover it for myself by some other independent method"? . . . In any other science, no one expects to step in without training in the specific method and verify or refute a finding.

It is generally agreed that the analyst is not able to be both researcher and therapist at the same time without distorting each function. The reconciliation has been suggested by Shakow (1960). The pitfalls of subjectivity and conflict of interest can be avoided by 1) divorcing the therapist from any but the purely therapeutic function, the research duties falling upon others, 2) having data collection depend primarily upon recorded psychoanalytic interviews, preferably motion pictures, and 3) getting additional pertinent data regarding the therapist's reactions to the patient in post-session reactions.

This point of view is obviously a shift from the notion, held by some, that every analyst is performing a "research study" upon each case he treats. The contention is that controls are introduced by means of the minimal participation of the analyst and by the therapeutic method of maintaining the analytic incognito. Furthermore, this view holds that the therapist is able to test his hypotheses via the patient's reactions to the analyst's interpretations. The now famous Cordelia story (Frenkel-Brunswik, 1940) is often quoted to illustrate the manner in which an interpreta-

---

[2] It is true, of course, that analysts have been guilty of the converse attitude. On the grounds that research into their methods by a third party would interfere with the therapeutic process, many analysts have objected to the study of their work.

tion leads to a recovery of a buried memory and to the confirmation of an analytic hypothesis concerning a daughter's relationship to her father. Such incidents, however convincing to the practitioner, lack the controls necessary for scientific confirmation or disconfirmation. The systematic investigation of hypotheses requires greater objectivity than can be attained in the consulting room, and repetitions of such testing under comparable circumstances is necessary to raise the level of probability of the proposition. Without the introduction of the kind of controls suggested by Shakow, the analytic situation is of only limited value for hypothesis-testing.

A further difficulty, not confined to the interview method but highlighted in this context, is the dearth of canons of interpretation of clinical observations. No definite rules for the inference process have been established. The analyst must call upon his theoretical understanding, his empathy, his clinical acumen, and his observational skills to interpret the significance of a given piece of behavior, to translate the covert or unconscious meanings. This process is obviously fraught with possibilities for error and subjectivity, part of which the analyst has conceptualized as "countertransference." This problem harks back to the dilemma of the objective molecular observation versus the more adequate molar observation which is also more subjective. Until a more adequate method has been devised, control by means of intersubjective agreement among trained observers must be the solution to the dilemma. Obviously, this method does not solve the problem of smuggling in the confirmation of the theory by means of the interpretation. If the interpretation is based upon a working theory, whether or not used by more than one judge, the danger of circularity is a distinct possibility. This danger is particularly great when validation is attempted by persons who are trained within a given frame of reference and are affectively disposed toward finding confirmation. Ideally, the investigator should have no personal commitment to validate or invalidate the propositions under study.

Experimental Approaches

Despite the fact that the psychoanalytic interview provides a unique situation for the study of the relationship between conscious and unconscious phenomena, and despite the controls which may be applied in such a study, this method cannot be relied upon exclusively for either the discovery or testing of propositions. A major set of hypotheses in analytic theory concerns psychosexual development during the first few years of life. These findings were mainly inferred from the productions of adults in treatment and obviously must be investigated more directly in longitudinal and cross-sectional studies of children. While much important information can be gained from the patient's reconstructions in treatment concerning his early experiences, we can only know the patient's psychic reality, not the actual situation. The checking of hypotheses regarding parent-child relationships should ideally be done by direct observations of such situations.

In addition to the incomplete base of observations provided by the psychoanalytic situation is a need for the control and manipulation of experimental variables which is not possible in the analytic setting. Recent studies on dream deprivation (Fisher and Dement, 1961), by means of interruption of sleep when the subject begins to dream or by drugs to inhibit dreaming, have been used to explore the adaptive function of dreaming. The McGill studies of sensory deprivation have contributed to a generalization concerning the need for sensory input as a means of maintaining adequate autonomy of reality testing and other executive functions of the ego (Rapaport, 1958). Hilgard (1952) has suggested that projective instruments enable the experimenter to test psychoanalytic hypotheses more adequately than does the therapeutic situation because of the use of standard stimuli in contrast to the more uncontrolled situation in relationship to the analyst.

The relative lack of interest of psychoanalysts in experimental approaches may be understood in terms of several factors. First, many of the experimental efforts have consisted only of attempts to establish the existence of well-known and widely accepted clinical phenomena. It is of no interest to the clinician to learn that the mechanism of repression exists. But it is very much to the heart of the matter to learn more about its operation, why certain individuals use it more heavily than others, its relationship to other defenses, and a host of other questions. The lack of fertility of most experimental attempts, observed by analyst and experimentalist alike (Kubie, 1952; Hilgard, 1952), has served as a deterrent to extensive experimentation.

Even more discouraging to the analyst have been the studies which have shown a remarkable neglect of the actual content of the theory. Propositions have been ripped out of context and translated into naively oversimplified experimental tests. The series of studies on the recall of pleasant and unpleasant words are an instance of this abuse. Some experimentalists have innocently believed that their finding of the superior recall of words like "sugar" over "quinine" test the psychoanalytic hypothesis concerning the repression of unacceptable impulses. There is no substitute for the thorough understanding of psychoanalytic concepts in any effort to study them experimentally.

But even given a mastery of the theory and a sophistication about the pertinent problems needing investigation, the experimentalist must steer an uneasy course between oversimplification and unwieldy complexity. It is now well accepted that the traditional method of manipulating one independent variable while observing its effect upon another (dependent) variable and keeping all other conditions constant is not suitable to psychoanalytic investigation. Rather, it is usually necessary to observe and manipulate a number of pertinent variables at both ends of the observational base. Any study which arbitrarily focuses upon a single set of independent and dependent variables while arbitrarily neglecting other factors known to be important is fated to be unproductive. The studies on subception which originally related only the factors of traumatic content and perceptual threshold failed to yield consistent results because of their neglect of the factor of individual differences in dealing with stressful material. When the experimenters began to introduce the additional variable of characterological differences and separated the "sensitizers," who tend to become hyper-alert in the presence of danger, from the repressers, who tend to blind themselves to danger, the results began to fit with the predictions (Stein, 1953).

This is not to say, of course, that every study requires the consideration of the total and infinite complexity of all possible factors in order to do justice to the phenomenon. Naturally one must ignore or neglect certain variables in order to focus upon others. There appear to be no definite rules of procedure for the optimal restriction or inclusion of pertinent variables. As Benjamin (1959) has pointed out, the hallmark of the gifted researcher is to know which factors can be excluded, or set aside temporarily, while other factors are being investigated. He suggests that a rule of thumb might be that "formulations which ignore parameters known to be relevant are oversimplified" (p. 72).

One method of avoiding the exclusion of pertinent variables is to engage in naturalistic studies where the phenomenon being investigated is not experimentally manipulated. Controls are imposed by means of the conceptualization and study of the pertinent variables. This is the major method used in such fields as astronomy and geology, where the "laboratory" is generally some part of the natural world. As a result of catastrophe, war, or other crises, situations have arisen which provide excellent bases for the study of variables which could not have been studied otherwise, primarily because humane considerations would have precluded the experimental induction of such changes. The best-known of these are the now-classic investigations by Spitz (1945) on hospitalism in infants raised in orphanages and by A. Freud and Burlingham (1944) on children separated from their families during the bombings in Britain. The "controls" introduced into these studies depended upon the kinds of variables the investigator deemed important: the length of separation from the natural mother, the age at which a stable figure becomes essential, the effect of changes in mother surrogates, as well as the variety of behavioral deviations which result from these situations.

Projective techniques also offer opportunities for controlled observation which at the same time do not excessively narrow the field of study. On the one hand, a standard stimulus is presented to the subject, and his responses are recorded verbatim. On the other hand, a broad spectrum of responses is possible, which enables the subject to reveal behavioral reactions from the points of view both of surface and depth. As in the use of the psychoanalytic interview, the controls over subjectivity of interpretation must be introduced at some point, and the use of independent judges or some other control is necessary. The use of projective testing has been fruitful, for example, in Holt's (1956) studies of the primary process as it relates to individual differences in reacting to altered states of consciousness.

The applicability of animal studies to psychoanalytic propositions appear to be at best somewhat limited. Benjamin (1950) holds that the sole contribution of such experiments has been their confirmatory effect of fairly well-accepted hypotheses, such as the importance of crucial early life experiences or the effect of oral deprivation upon later behavior. Recent studies by Harlow (1958), however, on cloth-and-wire mother surrogates may prove to be valuable in elucidating the major variables leading to normal sexual and maternal behavior. Despite the advantages afforded by the control and manipulation of the environment which is possible among animal subjects, the major shortcoming such studies have in relation to humans is the absence of language and verbal behavior, a crucial determinant in human development.

The Prediction Method

One of the most promising methods of analytic research, be it used in psychoanalytic therapy or on other kinds of observational data, is that of predicting future developments on the basis of analytic theory. During the past decade several studies have been reported in which the prediction method is the major approach to validating and extending the theory. This is in contrast to Freud's method, which was essentially post-dictive (Rapaport, 1959). In the course of his investigations in depth on an individual case or a series of cases, Freud reconstructed the genesis of personality development and set forth certain generalizations about crucial life experiences which molded the person. Philosophical support for this position is supplied by the contention that satisfactory explanations of the past are possible even when prediction of the future is not possible. Scriven (1959) points to Darwin's theory of the survival of the fittest, which has very weak predictive value but which is a potent explanatory principle. Rapaport (1959) asserts that post-diction is theoretically as valid as prediction, provided care is taken not to invoke *ex post facto* explanation.

But we should mention that post-dictive explanation does not have the explanatory power of a prediction, which must be based upon a universal law in which both necessary and sufficient conditions are elucidated. Although the theory of evolution is not readily subject to test by prediction, psychoanalytic theory should be. Psychoanalytic phenomena only encompass some portion of an individual's life span, in contrast to hypotheses about eons of time such as occur in evolution. Also, the post-dictive method appears to be useful in the early phases of science and is appropriate to the process of formulating hypotheses, as Freud did. The validation of propositions, however, is more effectively done through efforts to forecast future developments than by explaining past events.

The primary method still being used in psychoanalytic study is that of post-diction. Psychoanalytic literature abounds in detailed case studies in which, following Freud, hypotheses are formulated after a patient has been studied intensively by the analyst. Several reasons may be at the basis of the reluctance of analytic researchers to use the more stringent method of prediction. One of these is the difficulty of formulating predictions about situations in which a variety of unforeseeable events or situations, not within the realm of what is being predicted but capable of affecting the outcome, have to be considered. The vicissitudes of life circumstances which impinge upon the person, including the birth of a sibling, the death of a parent, a divorce—all constitute potential environmental changes which are often unforeseeable and could alter the expected course of events in a person's life. Benjamin (1959) has attempted to deal with these contingencies by formulating his predictions concerning personality development in children to include at least some of these events, although obviously it is impossible to predict for the infinite variety of important life circumstances. They are special contingency predictions, and they have the form of "if this, then that."

The predictive method is also faced with the problem of the relative immaturity and incompleteness of the theory. Psychoanalysis has formulated a number of necessary conditions for the development of certain behaviors but has not begun to approach a delineation of sufficient conditions. Benjamin (1950) suggests that the discovery of sufficient conditions may be a "possibly unattainable ideal." We know, for example, that personality variables like anxiety tolerance, impulse control, capacity for the development of a transference neurosis, and freedom from strong regressive trends contribute to a prediction concerning successful resolution of intrapsychic conflict in a psychoanalytic procedure. But no one claims that these personality factors constitute all of the pertinent variables. Similarly, M. Kris (1957) has pointed out that our knowledge and competence in certain areas are still quite deficient, as demonstrated by the Yale longitudinal studies of child development. Their predictions were fairly accurate in designating areas of difficulty for the developing child, but they were not nearly as successful in designating the particular form or manifestation of the difficulty. Similarly, they were much better at predicting the occurrence of pathology than conflict-free functioning and the use of normal defenses. But these deficiencies in our understanding should not be a deterrent to prediction studies. Predictions not only test theory but have a heuristic value as well. Whether or not psychoanalysis will ever arrive at a formulation of sufficient causes, the prediction method undoubtedly is capable of helping to validate, refine, and extend its present causal explanations. Increasing efforts to use and perfect this method in a variety of contexts, mainly in research upon psychotherapy and upon longitudinal studies of children, is one of the brighter lights in the horizon of research in psychoanalysis.

Perhaps the main source of reluctance to engage in prediction studies has been what Rapaport (1959) refers to as the lack of "critical tests" in psychoanalysis. This is also the major criticism that has been leveled against psychoanalysis in discussions of its scientific status. Proponents of psychoanalysis say that it is not possible to formulate a clear-cut set of alternatives one of which would eventuate from one theoretical formulation and another tending to confirm an alternative and mutually exclusive postulate. This apparent lack of alternative hypotheses to explain the same observations is based upon two different factors. First, no alternative theory, or set of theories, attempts to deal comprehensively with the scope of human behavior in the way that psychoanalysis does. The Neo-Freudian theories do not appear to constitute definite alternatives; rather they constitute changes in emphasis, such as the Sullivanian focusing upon interpersonal relations rather than intrapsychic conflict. These conceptions are gradually being incorporated into the mainstream of analytic theory, particularly through the work of Erikson (Rapaport, 1959). Learning theory has not actually joined the issue with psychoanalytic theory, partly because psychoanalysis itself lacks an explicit theory of learning.[3] One is tempted to add that the dearth of alternative theories is probably the basis for the feeling of clinicians, more implicit than explicit, that psychoanalysis is not the best theory of human behavior; it is the *only* theory.

The second aspect of the problem of no critical tests being available refers more to the nature of the theory itself. The theory contains propo-

---

[3] Rapaport (1959) believes that the scientific struggles will eventually occur in this arena, and not around the psychoanalytic theories of motivation which are its present core.

sitions which embrace a wide range of alternative possibilities, any one of which may emerge and yet be compatible with the theory. This point is made, for example, in relation to the use of reaction formation to explain the appearance of one form of behavior or its opposite. Thus, psychoanalysts claim that the presence of marked anal conflicts may lead either to stinginess or to extravagance. The analyst is often unable to predict the form of the behavior, since the final emergence of the instinctual derivatives is extremely complex. Hence the reliance upon post-dictive explanation. Such a state of affairs is naturally the bane of the experimentalist, who not only fails to see operational definitions but is confronted with propositions which appear to be disconfirmable. Although there may be shifting fashions of scientific canons, the one requirement of a scientific proposition which is not likely to be altered is that the generalization be subject, now or in the future, to empirical test (Richfield, 1954).

It is surprising, therefore, that a leading psychoanalytic methodologist like Rapaport (1959, p. 120) should have expressed pessimism about ever being able to confirm the special (clinical) theory of psychoanalysis via prediction and even wondered about confirmation of the general (psychological) theory of psychoanalysis:

Clinical predictions are always fraught with the fact that all motivations have multiple, equivalent means and goals. Thus, such predictions usually cannot specify which of these alternatives are to be expected and therefore, the results of experimental tests on predictions must first be interpreted before their bearing on the theory can be established.

This pessimism does not appear to be entirely justified. In the first place, even a prediction about areas of difficulty or change, provided the area is specified, is a legitimate prediction, though perhaps not the most satisfactory. Predictions made in the Psychotherapy Research Project of The Menninger Foundation (Wallerstein, Robbins, et al., 1956), for example, range all the way from highly specific behavioral outcomes (the patient will not return to the family business) to very non-specific changes (the patient will show increased impulse control) requiring clinical judgment and interpretation to confirm. The latter prediction is similar in some respects to a prediction stating that the person will evidence difficulties in managing anal conflicts. Such predictions pose methodological problems in confirmation but are not devoid of important content which bears on the theory.

Furthermore, there is no *a priori* reason to assume that simply because psychoanalytic predictions so far have not been able to attain the highest possible level of specificity, they will not be able to do so in the future. Of course, we may have to settle ultimately for a more general, rather than a more specific, prediction, because we may never derive the sufficient, as well as necessary, causes of behavior. This point of view has been expressed by those who describe certain parts of psychoanalysis as only capable of formulating "tendency statements" (Farrell, 1961). These are statements which are neither universal nor statistical in character and therefore are incapable of being verified or, at best, are capable of only partial verification. To predict that a person will show a tendency toward stinginess, for example, means that such behavior will occur only under certain conditions which may not be entirely specified. But such statements appear to be a reflection of our *current* inability to specify the circumstances of the appearance of this behavior. Such a prediction is not worthless, although it has a limited value in attempting to prognosticate for specific instances. Similarly, whether stinginess or its opposite or both in alternation will appear may not always be possible to predict. But these approximations toward increased specificity are signs of an immature science and do not necessarily mean that critical tests will never be possible. Frenkel-Brunswik (1954) has demonstrated experimentally that the same genotype may give rise to behaviors that are often in opposition to each other. Thus, irritability and exuberance were correlated negatively with each other, but both were correlated with a drive for aggression. The intervening factors giving rise to one manifestation as opposed to the other still remain as a problem for study in order to increase predictive power.

Despite these barriers to prediction studies, they are gaining in popularity and in refinement. One reason for this development is the relatively simple but cogent observation that all clinical work actually involves prediction, implicit or explicit (Sargent, 1961; Kris, 1957). When we say that a patient is suffering from an anaclitic depression, we are in effect predicting that he should respond favorably to treatment in which his dependency needs find gratification. The decision of the therapist to emphasize supportive rather than expressive techniques is based upon the prediction that the patient will react to such treatment with more effective and adaptive behavior in his environment. The treatment situation, long the subject of post-dictive study, is now becoming the locus of predictive studies. Bellak and Smith (1956) have reported a carefully controlled study of short-term predictions concerning the expected developments in the analytic treatment of patients whose preceding hours had been carefully studied by a group of analyst-predictors who were not themselves treating the patient. Robbins and Wallerstein (1956, 1958, 1960) have initiated a long-range study of both process and outcome in which a major method is the formulation of predictions prior to beginning treatment. A key feature of this investigation is the formulation of the theoretical assumptive base for each prediction in an effort to validate and extend psychoanalytic theory.

Summary and Conclusions

1. The trend in both philosophy of science and in academic psychology has been towards a de-emphasis upon strict operationism. Philosophers now regard radical operationism as excessively restricting to creative scientific work and stress the importance of hypothetical constructs in any growing science. Similarly, psychologists are beginning to adopt the point of view that the adequate definition of many psychological concepts can only be approached gradually by a system of successive approximations (construct validity).

2. Recent efforts to systematize psychoanalytic theory suggest that it may be formulated as a hypothetico-deductive system. The "metapsychological" rubrics embrace the higher order assumptions which subsume, in decreasing hierarchical order, the general psychoanalytic propositions, special psychoanalytic propositions, and empirical propositions.

3. The major unsolved problems in theory validation consist of the difficulty in matching subjects over a broad range of personality variables, the distance between the intrapsychic variable and its behavioral manifestations, and the fact that multiply-patterned factors usually underlie a given behavior.

4. The psychoanalytic interview is still the major, but not the only, observational method in psychoanalysis. While invaluable in hypotheses-finding, it can be used for hypothesis-testing only insofar as the therapeutic and research functions are carefully separated from each other.

5. For purposes of broadening the base of psychoanalytic observations and in the interest of increased control and manipulation of variables, controlled experimentation is necessary. The major pitfall in this approach has been the danger of oversimplification of complex theoretical constructs.

6. The traditional methodological approach in psychoanalysis has been that of post-diction, formulating explanations and theoretical constructs after the observations have been collected. An increasing number of psychoanalytic studies based upon a prediction method are now appearing, and these should eventually answer the question whether sufficient, as well as necessary, causes for behavior will ultimately be discovered. The lack of "critical tests" in psychoanalysis is seen as a problem relating both to a dearth of rival theories and to the lack of specificity in the propositions themselves, perhaps related to the immaturity of the science.

References

Barron, F. An ego-strength scale which predicts response to psychotherapy. *J. Cons. Psychol.*, 1953, 17, 327–333.

Bellak, L., and Smith, M. B. An experimental exploration of the psychoanalytic process. *Psychoanal. Quart.*, 1956, *25*, 385–414.

Benjamin, John. Methodological considerations in the validation and elaboration of psychoanalytic personality theory. *Amer. J. Ortho.*, 1950, *20*, 139–156.

———. Prediction and psychopathological theory. In L. Jessner and E. Pavenstedt (eds.), *Dynamic psychopathology in childhood.* New York: Grune and Stratton, 1959.

Cronbach, L. J., and Meehl, P. E. Construct validity in psychological tests. *Psychol. Bull.*, 1955, *52*, 281–302.

Escalona, S. K. (Roundtable 1949). Approaches to a dynamic theory of development. III. Discussion. *Amer. J. Orthopsychiat.*, 1950, *20*, 157–160.

———. Problems of psychoanalytic research. *Int. J. Psa.*, 1952, *33*, 11–21.

Ezriel, H. The scientific testing of psychoanalytic findings and theory. *Brit. J. Med. Psychol.*, 1951, *24*, 30–34.

Farrell, B. A. Symposium of psychoanalysis and validation. II. On the character of psychodynamic discourse. *Brit. J. Med. Psychol.*, 1961, *34*, 7–13.

Fisher, C., and Dement, W. C. Dreaming and psychosis. Unpublished paper, 1961.

Feigl, H. Some major issues and developments in the philosophy of science and logical empiricism. In Feigl, H., and Scriven, M. (eds.), *The foundation of science and the concepts of psychology and psychoanalysis*, Vol. I. Minneapolis: University of Minnesota Press, 1956.

Frenkel-Brunswik, E. Psychoanalysis and personality research. *J. Abnorm. Soc. Psychol.*, 1940, *35*, 176–197.

———. Motivation and behavior. *Genetic Psychology Monograph.* 1942.

———. Psychoanalysis and the unity of science. *Proceedings, Amer. Acad. of Arts and Sci.*, 1954, *80*, 271–350.

Freud, A., and Burlingham, D. *Infants without families.* New York: International Universities Press, 1944.

Gill, M. M. The present state of psychoanalytic theory. *J. Abnorm. Soc. Psychol.*, 1959, *58*, 1–8.

Harlow, H. F. The nature of love. *Amer. Psychologist*, 1958, *13*, 673–685.

Hartmann, H. *Ego psychology and the problem of adaptation.* New York: International Universities Press, 1958.

Hempel, C. G. Fundamentals of concept formation in empirical science. *Intern. Encycl. Unified Sci.*, Vol. II, No. 7. Chicago: Univ. of Chicago Press, 1952.

Hilgard, E. Experimental approaches to psychoanalysis. In E. Pumpian-Mindlin (ed.), *Psychoanalysis as science.* Stanford, Calif.: Stanford Univ. Press, 1952.

Holt, R. R. Gauging primary and secondary processes in Rorschach responses. *J. Proj. Tech.*, 1956, *20*, 14–25.

Karush, A., et al. The evaluation of ego strength: a scale of adaptive balance. Unpublished paper, 1962.

Kris, E. Psychoanalytic propositions. In Marx, M. H. (ed.), *Psychological theory.* New York: Macmillan, 1951.

Kris, M. The use of prediction in a longitudinal study. *Psa. Study of the Child*, 1957, *12*, 175–189.

Kubie, L. S. Problems and techniques in psychoanalytic validation and progress. In E. Pumpian-Mindlin (ed.), *Psychoanalysis as science.* Stanford, Calif.: Stanford Univ. Press, 1952.

Murphy, G. The current impact of Freud upon psychology. *Amer. Psychologist*, 1956, *11*, 663–672.

Piaget, J. *The child's conception of the world*. New York: Harcourt, Brace, 1929.

Rapaport, D. The theory of ego autonomy: a generalization. *Bull. Menninger Clin.*, 1958, *22*, 13–35.

———. The structure of psychoanalytic theory: a systematizing attempt. *Psychological Issues*, 1960, No. 6.

Rapaport, D., and Gill, M. M. The points of view and assumptions of meta-psychology. *Int. J. Psychoanal.*, 1959, *40*, 153–162.

Richfield, J. On the scientific status of psychoanalysis. *Sci. Mon.*, 1954, *79*, 306–309.

Sargent, H. D. Intrapsychic change: methodological problems in psychotherapy research. *Psychiatry*, 1961, *24*, 93–108.

Scriven, M. A study of radical behaviorism. In H. Feigl and M. Scriven (eds.), *The foundations of science and the concepts of psychology and psychoanalysis*, Vol. I. Minneapolis: Univ. of Minnesota Press, 1956.

———. Explanation and prediction in evolutionary theory. *Science*, 1959, *130*, 577–482.

Sears, R. R. *Survey of objective studies of psychoanalytic concepts*. New York: Social Science Research Council, Bulletin No. 51, 1943.

Shakow, D. The recorded psychoanalytic interview as an objective approach to research in psychoanalysis. *Psa. Quart.*, 1960, *29*, 82–97.

Spitz, R. A. Hospitalism. *Psa. Study of the Child*, 1945, *1*, 53–74.

Stein, K. B. Perceptual defense and perceptual sensitization under neutral and involved conditions. *J. Pers.*, 1953, *21*, 467–478.

Tolman, Ruth S. Virtue rewarded and vice punished. *Amer. Psychologist*, 1953, *8*, 721–733.

Wallerstein, R. S., Robbins, L. L., et al. The psychotherapy research project of the Menninger foundation. *Bull. Menninger Clin.*, 1956, *20*, 221–276.

———. The psychotherapy research project of the Menninger foundation: 2nd report. *Bull. Menninger Clin.*, 1958, *22*, 115–166.

———. The psychotherapy research project of the Menninger foundation: 3rd report. *Bull. Menninger Clin.*, 1960, *24*, 157–216.

Werner, H. *Comparative psychology of mental development* (3rd ed.). New York: International Universities Press, 1957.

White, R. W. Motivation reconsidered: the concept of competence. *Psychol. Rev.*, 1959, 297–333.

28 | *Affect and Emotion*

HENRY N. PETERS

Sources of Confusion

Thinking in this field has shown more confusion than in most fields of science. This is evidenced by a multiplicity of views, many apparently contradictory theories, and a paucity of clean-cut hypotheses. As a result, there has been a tendency, prevalent in American psychology in the last decade or two, to solve the problem by ignoring it. The best way to begin a discussion of the subject is by bringing the sources of confusion out into the open, so that there will be some prospect of avoiding them.

1. The term "emotion" is used to refer to three different levels, or categories, of behavior. Writings on the subject have often left the reader in the dark as to which referent was intended.

a. One of these is the "felt emotion," which is private to the individual, like redness or any other state of awareness, but which is not projected to the world outside the skin. This is probably the most subjective of all experiences. We often try to communicate thoughts; seldom, if ever, do we consciously intend to communicate a felt emotion. The confusion here is compounded by sometimes using "felt emotion" to refer to a very general emotional state (excitement) and at other times to any one of the many specific emotions—anger, fear, love, rage, shame, etc.—each supposedly having a quite different feeling.

b. The visceral response is another category of behavior which is often the intended referent for the word "emotion." These responses form a unique class, structurally (smooth muscles), functionally (vegetative), and in innervation (autonomic nervous system). There is no question about the activation of these responses during states described as emotional. The correlation is so high that they offer an obvious operational measure of emotion.

c. Third are the overt responses (skeletal muscles), which include reflexes and the visible, global adjustment of the organism to the environment. In addition to the running, fighting, dodging kind of behavior, this category includes a sub-class of responses usually referred to as "expression"—facial, postural, and gestural reactions.

The picture with respect to this last category is complicated by two additional factors. One is the fact that many of the visible signs of emotion are the result of autonomic nervous system (visceral) activation. Coloration changes, rising hackles in the dog or cat, pupillary responses, and enlarged veins in the neck and face are among these visible visceral reactions. Yet these reactions are often described as "expressive" and lumped with the third category.

A second complicating factor is that many of the responses of the expressional type are also used for communication purposes. Thus, one is never certain, in the case of his own behavior or that of others, whether an expressional response is genuine emotional behavior, a communication response, or, as is probably true with the great majority of adult emotions, a mixture of both.

2. Another serious source of confusion has been the ignoring or slighting of the cognitive-perceptual aspect of emotional behavior. Certainly almost every emotional experience must also be classed as a perceptual one. Something in the environment or the body (e.g., a loud heartbeat) is perceived and interpreted. Without perception—e.g., the smell plus interpretation of smoke in the attic—the great majority of adult human emotions would not really take place.

Also evident is that many emotional experiences may originate in thinking or imagining activity. An individual may voluntarily imagine an experience (say falling out of a twentieth-story window) and accordingly generate a relatively weak emotional reaction. In the case of daydreaming, the emotion can of course be much more intense. And probably even more intense is the emotion created by recalling certain of our past experiences. Dreams, which are certainly symbolic, cognitive reactions, are sometimes the source of our most intense emotions, often leaving a residue which can last for a day or more. Any adequate theory of emotion must take into account this apparent cause-effect (cognition-emotion) relationship and at the same time avoid setting emotional behavior up as a unique, separate kind of activity.

3. The multiplicity of names for different emotions is another factor contributing to confusion. We have the concept of a general state of emotional excitement, plus hundreds of words ostensibly referring to certain sub-categories in the wealth of emotional experiences. Most students in this area have distinguished, for one, a set of *primary emotions,* usually including anger, fear, and love, assumed to be more intimately connected with the instinctive side of human nature; a second category distinguished has been a set of fairly universal but derived emotions, such as disgust, shame, and surprise. In addition, some have recognized a third set which

are milder and more subject to social conditioning, sometimes referred to as "sentiments," such as reverence, admiration, sympathy, etc.; a fourth category, the "moods," are relatively mild and long-lasting emotional states. And lastly, a pair of special feelings or "affections," usually assumed to be the same in kind as emotion, has been designated; these are referred to as pleasure and pain, or more often as pleasantness and unpleasantness. Since the days of the structuralists, this pair has been considered a special type of primitive experience, more like sensations than the other emotional feelings. They are also distinguished by being bi-polar and by being somehow mixed in with the other emotions. Thus, anger is usually considered to be mixed with unpleasantness, and love with pleasantness.

A question not often faced squarely by psychologists of emotion is: do all of these 50 or more named emotions actually feel different? This is hardly plausible. More likely, the majority of these emotions are merely names for emotional behavior in certain perceived situations. Most of the derived mild and socially conditioned emotions are primarily descriptions of behavior situations, not distinct feelings at all.

Some students have attempted to solve this multiplicity problem by conceiving of a limited number of dimensions which can be used to locate all of the many emotions. This is a purely conceptual scheme, after the analogy of the color solid with visual sensations. Wundt's (1922) *Tridimensional Theory*—pleasantness-unpleasantness, tension-relaxation, excitement-quiescence—is the best-known example. Such schemes may make the chaos of emotions more easy to deal with rationally, but each of the unlimited number of points in such an "emotional space" is still assumed to be uniquely felt, and this taxes the evidence of introspection.

4. A fourth source of confusion is the close tie that has existed in the literature between emotion and the instinct doctrine. This is a connection which has been maintained even to the present day. Darwin (1873) is usually given credit for starting this, although his real emphasis was on instinct, of which the emotions were merely the feeling or awareness side. Consequently, some of the confused thinking about heredity and environment as separate agents, which developed during the discourses over the instinct idea, has rubbed off on emotions. And granted the invariable connection between emotion and instinct, how is one to conceive of a list of instincts as long as the prevalent list of emotions?

5. Probably the basic source of confusion is in the fallacy of the reification of concepts. This is the same error which has infested so many of the concepts in psychology, including that of "mind" itself. Specifically, the error consists in assuming that, because we have a single noun-word, "emotion," something in nature must correspond to it, something as independent, as unique and unchanging, and as readily capable of entering subject-predicate relations with other things. This has led to treating

emotion as a separate category or part of behavior, a force and an agent—
it is still at the present day spoken of in this way in psychological literature. The actual data with which we are concerned are *emotional behaviors*, which are eventful, process-like in nature; this is crucial to keep
in mind. It is certainly not always evident that these emotional behaviors
differ in any obvious way from other forms of behavior.

A parallel here between emotion and sensation should lend some clarification to the basic issue underlying the confusion. When John says he sees
"blue," does he see the same quality which I see and call "blue"? How
do I know that to him what I call blue actually looks like what I call red?
As long as we make corresponding verbal reactions to the same physical
objects, I will never know. Now students of human behavior today seldom
spend much time on this problem. The focus of attention rather has shifted
to what can be known with certainty, namely, overt, discriminatory reactions.

The same basic problem, with the same kind of solution available, exists
in the field of emotion. When John says he feels "angry," does he experience the same conscious quality I feel? Here, as in the field of sensation,
the solution lies in the control (and manipulation) of physical variables
with the recording of overt (including vocal) responses. An important
difference should be noted between the two statements, that an object is
blue and that a person is angry. In the one he assumes that he is telling us
of something outside of his body, whereas in the statement "I am angry,"
he is referring to something within his body. In the case of a judgment,
"John is angry," the inference is of a condition private to John, not observable to just anyone who will look.

Theoretical Conceptions of Emotion

EMOTION AS THE FEELING OR AWARENESS SIDE OF INSTINCTS   The essential
feature of this view is that whenever an inherited behavior mechanism is
aroused, an emotion characteristic of it is felt. "Emotion" and "instinct"
are really the awareness and behavior sides of instincts. Treatment of the
causal relation between the two is somewhat ambiguous, but the usual implication is that the emotion causes the instinctive behavior. The writers
who have held this view have also implied that a separate inherited mechanism (in the brain) underlies each distinct emotion.

This view of emotion, which numbers Darwin (1873) and McDougall
(1910) among its prominent early supporters, has practically no adherents
among present-day American psychologists. It has survived, however,
among European psychologists, particularly the comparative ethologists
(Fletcher, 1957). McDougall's famous definition of an instinct is a good

summary of this theory: "An inherited or innate psychophysical disposition which determine its possessor to perceive, and to pay attention to, objects of a certain class, to experience an emotional excitement of a particular quality upon perceiving such an object, and to act in regard to it in a particular manner, or at least, to experience an impulse to such action." The main concern of these writers has been with the adaptive behavior of organisms, not with the "emotion," which they sometimes seem to treat as a separate event and at other times as synonymous with behavior.

This view postulates a series of distinct feeling states of indefinite length. While our language does have a long series of feeling-words, we cannot assume an innate basis, or a distinct feeling state, for all of them. Any attempt to limit the list is arbitrary and has little pragmatic value outside of the classroom. Another weakness is the treatment of the emotional state as an agent distinct from other mental states and behavior and capable of entering cause-effect relations with them.

This view of instinct-emotion fails to take adequate account of learning, although the definition of instinct, such as McDougall's, clearly fits some behavioral processes which are learned. The trouble here probably stems from treating the subject on a schematic abstract plane, where it is divorced from actual observations of behavior. The modern comparative ethologist school has improved on this theoretical view by introducing the concept of the inner releasing mechanism which is activated by stimuli, conditioned or unconditioned, and which triggers modifiable behavior patterns. This approach has proven most fruitful in the study of innate behavior of animals. Little attempt has been made to transfer the method to human beings. With this approach, however, the problem of "emotion" recedes into the forest of behavior, and the center of absorption is with *instincts*.

We would do well to remember that what exists in an introspecting human being is perception of a situation, which is interpreted promptly as "danger," "insulting," "love-receptive," etc., and a becoming-aware of impulses, overt behavior, and autonomic reactions. These latter, the impulses and reactions, are a series of events which may spread over an extended time span. At some point in time, later than the original situation, the whole experience is labeled "emotional." Little good for scientific understanding, to try and fit this congeries of events into the pigeon holes of sensation, perception, cognition, emotion, motor reactions, etc.

EMOTION AS AWARENESS OF BODILY CHANGES   This is usually considered exclusively a theory of felt emotion. According to this theory, it is not necessary to postulate a series of specific conscious states corresponding to a series of named emotions. The reactions made during an emotional experience are felt by the individual—through proprioceptive feedback—

and this makes up what is identified as the "feeling" of the emotion. In any particular experience, say the famous bear-in-woods, is first the perception of the situation; next, the widespread bodily reactions, including both skeletal and vegetative; and, lastly, the awareness of the bodily changes. It should be realized, however, that this neat temporal scheme of events occurs only in an abstract discussion of emotion. In actual concrete experience in the laboratory or in every-day life, the sequence of events is much more complicated. Some sort of perception is probably primary, but it may change several times in a few seconds. And the bodily reactions do not occur as a unit, to be subsequently felt *en masse*. The responses occur at different points in the total duration of the experience, and each is felt almost simultaneously with its occurrence. Changes in tension of skeletal muscles take place almost simultaneously with the first perception. The vegetative reactions are probably the slowest of all.

William James is usually given credit for originating this theory (1884). Although he did not limit the felt reactions to the vegetative, he did place emphasis on them, and subsequent treatises by other writers have tended to make the theory one of felt visceral changes only. On this basis, two criticisms have been leveled against this theory; both of these are the result of experimental observation. One is that visceral reactions are too slow to be the felt basis of emotions. This criticism recognizes that some felt emotions, like the fright at a sudden loud noise, occur within a small fraction of a second of the stimulus, certainly before the stimulus is perceived (identified) as a sonic boom. Visceral responses have a longer latent period. The other criticism follows from the fact of failure in repeated experimental studies to identify distinct patterns of visceral reactions which correlate with what are considered obviously different emotions (anger, fear, lust, etc.).

The force of these criticisms is lessened when skeletal muscle reactions, as well as the visceral, are included in the felt bodily changes. Some of them, e.g., the startle reactions, do follow the stimulus with very short latency. This form of the theory, which takes into account a manifold of responses of varied latencies, accounts for the fact that many emotional experiences build up to a climax, are often felt after considerable delay, or change drastically with passing moments.

The inclusion of skeletal muscles also reduces the relevance of the more or less diffuse, undifferentiated nature of visceral reactions, assuming that the various named emotions feel differently. There is a good deal of evidence that the skeletal-muscle reaction patterns do tend to vary with the reported felt emotion. And different patterns certainly exist from the time of infancy. The fact that the slow welling-up of visceral responses is pretty much the same in all strong emotions agrees with the introspective evidence, at least as it appears to many of us, that all strong emotions have much in common.

This view of emotion has suffered from abstract oversimplification, which has involved limitation of the bodily reactions to the vegetative, a tendency to ignore the cognitive (including perceptual) elements in the total experience, and failure to make explicit some of the implications for the total science of behavior. The improvement which goes with including skeletal-muscle responses has been discussed. Emphasis on the perceptual aspect of emotional experience is probably even more important to the completion of this theory. At the beginning of the majority of emotional experiences is an alerting reaction, which is experienced as a sudden re-orientation and a narrowing of the focus of attention. This is followed, sometimes immediately, by awareness of a distinct Gestalt, or meaning-of-object-for-self. In the adult human being are several of these Gestalts, undoubtedly largely the product of training, which will vary with the "emotion." Examples of these stereotyped meanings are: 1) danger-to-be-avoided (fear); 2) obstruction-to-be-destroyed (anger); and 3) living-thing-to-be-enjoyed (love). This aspect of emotion has not been sufficiently explored. The stereotyped meaning, which is a sort of framework to many of the "secondary" emotions, such as reverence, shame, anxiety, etc., could undoubtedly be spelled out clearly. This is the cognitive aspect of emotional experience which should be central to any conceptual treatment of the subject.

The implications of this theory, including all categories of reactions, for psychology in general are gratifying to the behavioristically-oriented experimentalist. If emotion is the awareness of bodily reactions, then whenever the situation is defined as an emotional one, the experimentalist needs only to record observations of behavior. This is pretty much what has happened in American psychology. Parameters of behavior are measured in cognitively defined situations which attempt to identify and control the critical variables.

One consequence of this approach has been a haziness or loss of the boundary between emotion and non-emotion. Yet our direct experience of sometimes feeling emotional at some times and not at other times continues to support the conviction that emotion is a distinct kind of awareness. Can we sort out those reactions which give rise to this emotional experience and are distinct from other reactions which arise in non-emotional experience? The answer to this question can be an affirmation, and the distinguishing feature found by identifying what is usually stressed as the prime characteristic of the visceral responses, namely, their independence of our active choosing, their non-voluntary nature.

The question of the possibility of operationally defining "voluntary" (or its opposite) immediately arises, since unless this can be done, the concept is of little value to the experimental psychologist. In any particular stimulus-response situation, the experimenter isolates and measures certain parameters (intensity, latency, frequency) of one or more responses. The dependence of measurements on two major classes of conditions is studied: 1) conditions *external* to the organism—usually referred to as the "stimulus," and 2) factors or conditions *internal* to the organism—which include many sub-classes of conditions (e.g., glandular, chemical) and which are usually lumped under the label "motivation." Now, the essence of volition is the exercise, on the part of the subject, of choice or discrimination of external factors. It follows that insofar as a parameter measurement can be shown to depend on an external stimulus variable, the response may be considered non-emotional. And conversely, the response may be classed as emotional to the extent that the behavior parameter is shown to change with internal variables.

According to this extension of the James theory into the laboratory context, it is a fallacy to judge any particular response as *either* emotional *or* not emotional. Any molar response (e.g., reading a word presented in a tachistoscope) is both involuntary and voluntary, emotional and non-emotional, to the extent that one of its parameters can be shown to have a functional relationship with internal and with external variables.

It is interesting to note that when the implications of this felt emotion theory are followed into actual behavior, as observed in the experimental laboratory or in everyday life, it comes very close to the same conceptual scheme outlined above as the instinct theory. All overt behavior, emotional or otherwise, has a feedback in the awareness of the individual. If this awareness is identified with the feeling side of the experience, it becomes somewhat tautologous to mention the tandem relation of the behavior and the feeling. There is, of course, one important difference between the two, a difference which points up the potential fruitfulness of the James theory, as well as the sterility of the instinct theory. The behavioral basis of the James theory can be wholly or in part the product of training (learning or experience), whereas the other theory is restricted to innate patterns of behavior and is thus unlikely to prove useful, at least with human beings.

One group of behaviorally oriented psychologists (Carr, 1928; Dunlap, 1928; Watson, 1930) have followed the implications of the narrow form of the James theory, in which the felt responses are limited to the visceral, into the science of behavior as a whole. These theorists have simply identified the emotions with visceral reactions. They have ignored the conscious data of emotional experiences, consequently overlooking the critical role of cognitive functions. As an attempt at operational definition of emotion, this form of the James theory is acceptable as long as one recognizes that the concept so defined really includes only a part of the total emotional experience as conceived by the majority of specialists, as well as the man-on-the-street.

CONFLICT THEORY In outline, this theory of emotion runs as follows: first is the arousal of an internal state in the form of an attitude, urge, or impulse. When this state goes over directly into an appropriate adaptive reaction, the behavior is non-emotional. When its expression in action is blocked, the behavior is emotional. The obstruction may be either external (environment) or internal (inhibition). The latter type of obstruction causes what is usually referred to by the term "conflict." This term infers that the primary conative state is actually blocked by an opposing, incompatible impulse or attitude.

This theory has been presented as a general theory of all emotional behavior by some (Dewey, 1894; Angier, 1927), and as an explanation of only certain emotions by others (Washburn, 1928; Ruckmick, 1936). However, the central concept "conflict" has been most thoroughly developed by Freud (1920), whose major concern was with neuroses and the doctrine of instincts. Clearly, conflict is an inference from behavior observed and has been inferred from two kinds of behavior observation: 1) One of these is applicable to both animals and men and has been used in the experimental laboratory (with varying degrees of adequate variable control). Here it is objectively established that the organism has two incompatible responses, one to S_1 and the other to S_2. When both stimuli are given simultaneously, the organism is said to be in a state of conflict. However, with both animals and men, the actual presence and nature of an inner condition of conflict is inferred from the responses observed. In actual observations the results are variable, from subject to subject and from time to time in the same subject. One of the Rs may appear, unchanged; one may appear, but with a modified latency, intensity, or form; under some conditions, neither R takes place. An inner state of conflict can be inferred directly from the behavior, but what good is a concept which is the product entirely of one-way inferences from behavior? And the temporary-choice sort of behavior is not what most students mean by conflict. They mean an inner state of which the subject is aware as a condition of tension (Dewey, 1894) and which is of prolonged duration, unpleasant, and usually accompanied by a manifold of visceral responses. 2) A second method of observation has yielded the concept of conflict which is the widely accepted one. The behavior observed here is the spontaneous verbal communication of an individual in the psychotherapeutic setting. The subject (usually considered neurotic) is undoubtedly motivated to understand and to do something about himself, this, of course, with the therapist's help. A great part of the therapist's behavior, regardless of the particular form of psychotherapy, consists of passively listening and making inferences, which he keeps mostly to himself. This kind of unique observation is usually done in weekly one-hour sessions and, for any one subject (patient), may continue for years. There is probably no other type of situation in modern life in which one human being gathers so much information about the inner thoughts, desires, etc., of another human being.

The subjects of this type of observation report a generalized awareness of "tension" and material from which the therapist infers the nature of two or more incompatible conative patterns (drives, attitudes, desires, motives). Psychoanalysis and related psychopathologies are attempts to erect a conceptual scheme which will serve as a rationale for this type of data.

While the conception of the doctrine of conflict (in the sense implied in the second of these procedures) has enriched our understanding of the emotional experience of introspective modern man (of Western civilization), it does not serve as a complete, general theory of emotion, as do the other two previously discussed ones. Some experiences which are universally considered as emotional obviously do involve a direct discharge in behavior. The second, and most productive, of the methods used by conflict theorists is of no help with infants and animals.

The two chief general criticisms of the conflict theory of emotion can be stated as follows: 1) This theory takes a condition (obstruction) of one type of emotional experience and makes of it a *sine qua non* of all emotions. 2) A satisfactory operational definition of a state of conflict has not emerged. We have no way of telling when a person is or is not in this condition. When is a modern man *not* in a state of conflict? This theory is inadequate to explain the behavioral crises, usually involving rather explosive reactions, which are at the focus of interest in a theory of emotion.

On the favorable side, this theory is adequate to, and has satisfactorily explained, one kind of experience which everyone considers emotional and which does seem to involve a conflict of impulses, namely, *anxiety*. This is a prolonged state of the organism, experienced as tension and akin to fear, but with no overt, rapid withdrawal pattern of behavior. Anxiety is probably the most common emotion in modern, civilized man, who is subjected to so many contradictory (biological and social) forces. Strong evidence that conflict is basic to anxiety is to be found in the observation that chronic anxiety is uncommon among prisoners. It begins to appear, however, as their parole date approaches, and they know that they must again face decisions. A similar phenomenon is to be observed in the behavior of incarcerated mental patients. The newly admitted patient commonly is observed in a state of acute anxiety, which disappears after a few weeks when he has become habituated to the regimented environment.

Episodes of anxiety tend to reappear, however, when he is given privileges and is required to resume some degree of decision-making.

In any systematic treatise or experimental study of emotion, account should be taken of the functional relation between intensity of reaction and obstruction. That under some conditions response-intensity is enhanced by obstruction can hardly be doubted. For example, a common observation is an increased loudness of voice with delayed auditory feedback, which is subjectively experienced as a blocking phenomenon. Another similar experience, and evidence for a conflict or blocking condition of emotion, is the intense struggle which first follows the thwarting of body movement by being wrapped in a sheet.

EMOTION AS ENERGY OR FORCE   Many students of human behavior, particularly those with a strong philosophical bent, have postulated a mental energy of some kind. In some instances, the idea has obviously referred to a neural energy (Piéron, 1928); in others, it has been treated as purely conceptual, with no reference to any physical aspect (Freud, 1920). A complete analysis of this concept of energy, which would take this paper too far afield, should take into consideration the status of basic conceptions of the physical sciences at present. If this were done, we would arrive at the conclusion that the concept of a simple energy is outmoded.

In brief, the theory is that affect, or feeling, is the form which mental energy takes when it is expressed in behavior. When this energy is at a high level, the behavior becomes emotional. Piéron (1928) held that when adaptive behavior is inadequate to handle the energy aroused, some of the energy overflows into visceral reactions.

The nature of this theory, like all others, is clarified when we focus attention on the behavior-observation level. Two aspects of the behavior in emotional situations are obviously relevant to this concept of energy. 1) One of these is the observed varying intensity of response. Usually the intensity of response is greater in emotional conditions. For example, most people probably squeeze a dynamometer with greater force when angry; under emotion, the voice gets louder, one runs faster, etc. However, this relationship is not an invariable one in the same or in different people. One emotion, namely depression, is obviously an exception to any general rule here. 2) The other observation is the persistence of behavior under conditions, usually classed as emotional, known to involve factors internal to the organism, such as hunger, sex, etc. This is simply the motivational aspect of behavior.

The concept of mental (or neural) energy is a highly abstract idea. It can be operationally defined only in terms of one of these two types of observational material. It actually adds nothing useful to the treatment of intensity as a parameter of response or to the study of behavior as dependent on variables internal to the organism (motivation). A concept such as mental energy is resorted to only when the student enters a realm of abstract concepts and loses his bearings in observational behavior.

DISRUPTION OR DISORGANIZATION THEORY   Ample evidence in everyday observation shows that at times the occurrence of an emotion seems to interfere with the efficiency of an on-going performance or adaptive behavior. For example, a sudden fright while driving a car at high speed may be followed by the trembling of hands and feet to such an extent that to continue driving is difficult. A similar experience is that of awareness of performance decrement when for some reason one's desire to succeed is greater than usual. Then there are the occasions when behavior is described as "explosive" (usually anger), and the on-going behavior is clearly maladaptive. Many students of emotion consider the epileptic convulsion as the extreme form of this explosive, undifferentiated release of emotion.

The disruption theory identifies emotion with this maladaptive aspect to the extent of holding that emotion occurs only in a state of no adaptation (Claparede, 1928; Young, 1943). The proponents of this view prefer the term "feeling" for the awareness of milder forms of motivation or attitude of the whole organism which are not accompanied by disorganization.

Leeper (1948), who obviously does not have such a restricted referent for the term emotion, has stressed just the opposite feature, namely, its organizing character. On the one hand, he points out that any strong motivation toward one direction (behavior pattern) is obviously going to interfere with other, incompatible lines of action. On the more positive side, he has made a strong case for the conception of emotions as organizing (selecting, unifying) factors in behavior. For example, if a person is inordinately motivated by a fear of failure, this fear colors most of his perceptions, directs his thinking and planning, and can be used to explain the major activities he exhibits over a period of years.

Both of these extreme views have some validity; it is a matter of which aspect one wishes to stress (if either one must be chosen) and which referent is preferred for the term emotion. To most people, expert or otherwise, "emotion" has a meaning broad enough to include both views. The critical question is: As the internal, motivating state of an organism is increased in intensity or amount, what is the correlative change in performance—as measured by time, errors, or other parameters of behavior? This problem has been attacked by several experimenters, and a fairly consistent functional relationship, the Yerkes-Dodson Law, has emerged (Eysenck, 1955). The dependence of performance on level of motivation takes an inverted U shape, with the maximum of behavior efficiency located somewhere in the middle range of drive intensities.

An Experimentalist's View of Emotion

In the above discussion of five theories, each has been to some extent supplemented or expanded, especially in view of an emphasis on the kind of behavior actually observed in any particular instance of emotion. This is really the emphasis or viewpoint of the experimentalist. He is concerned with identifying and measuring a behavior variable, observing under controlled conditions, and discovering functional relations between behavior variables and conditions.

Two basic concepts seem to emerge from considering emotion from this viewpoint. One of these is the concept of *perceptual pattern* (Gestalt), a more or less fixed picture of self-in-relation-to-world. Everybody has several of these patterns, which exist somehow at the threshold of awareness, ready to be triggered into action. When activated, they tend to dominate awareness and behavior. This concept is quite similar to the familiar ones of *attitude* and *complex*, except that with these concepts the emphasis is not usually placed on the perceptual aspect. When some stimulus situation arouses one of these patterns, the person interprets the environment in a more or less stereotyped (for him) fashion and has an urge to behave in a certain manner. For example, when the authority-threat pattern is aroused in an individual who has it available, he interprets the social situation as dangerous to his welfare and most commonly has a destructive-aggressive urge. Other examples of perceptual patterns are insecurity, miserliness, respect for human dignity, subjection to public humiliation. These, and probably all the personality traits identified thus far, can be interpreted as instances of such patterns. In considering these items as perceptual patterns, instead of attitudes or traits, the emphasis is shifted from the obviously variable, overt behavior and abstract interpersonal relations to the fairly rigid picture which enters the subject's awareness when one of them is aroused.

Individuals certainly differ widely in the nature, number, and readiness of arousal of their perceptual patterns. This, of course, supports the view that these patterns are products of experience or training. Some of them are undoubtedly culturally determined, such as the Gestalt of a world-full-of-dangerous-people, which fosters a readiness for hostility to strangers and a reluctance to enter friendly relations. This pattern is not as common in some cultures as it is in the Western European. Fear of death is another culturally determined pattern. While the problem of determining to what extent, and in which patterns, heredity plays a role is an interesting one, determination of the exact nature, prevalence, and methods of identifying (and modifying) them are far more pressing.

The second basic concept is the distinction between two sets of variables which condition behavior, the *external* and the *internal*. The first of these, of course, includes all of what are ordinarily called the environmental stimuli. Operationally, members of this set of variables are identified, and functional relations with behavior measured, by the various sensory discrimination procedures.

The internal variables include urges, drives, impulses, motives, etc. When activity is recognized as being determined to any extent by a variable of this set, it is to this extent considered independent of the environment and therefore internally determined.

Some of these factors, the so-called biological motives, are built into the organism (nervous system) and developed under genetic control. Others are probably developed entirely through training, especially social and cultural conditioning. And some are probably the product of cultural modification of biological motives.

One group of modern behavioral scientists who stress this distinction between external and internal behavior regulators is that of the comparative ethologists (Fletcher, 1957). The following quotation of N. Tinbergen, cited by Fletcher (p. 348), is typical of their position. "Behavior is reaction in so far as it is, to a certain extent, dependent on external stimulation. It is spontaneous in so far as it is also dependent on internal causal factors, or motivational factors, responsible for the activation of an urge or drive."

Is the internal set to be limited to central nervous system regulations? If so, the classification problem posed by the demonstrations that animals clearly can discriminate visceral afferent reverberations would be avoided. However, the internal-external distinction need not be identified with the old theoretical problem of the relative importance of central and peripheral controls of behavior. One could just as well make the dividing line the skin of the subject or, with human beings, the boundary of his self-concept.

What is really important is that, with a clear operational definition of internal, an experimenter can vary his position as to the meaning of the term and do significant work from several different positions. Internal, for example, may be defined as control by any bodily mechanisms (central nervous system or stomach sensations). One can define the term in a negative manner as what is left (of response determination) when all evidence of sensory discrimination is removed. Another positive position is to define internal in terms of demonstration of dependency on nervous system mechanisms, as is done in extirpation and electrode-implantation studies.

This is a rather academic problem when the interest of the experimenter is centered on the motives (including values) of men. Patriotism, miserliness, romantic love, respect for human dignity, fear of mushroom clouds—all such motives are certainly primarily under control of central nervous system mechanisms. The essence of the experimenter's view of emotion is that to the extent that a behavioral process is under control of factors which he defines as internal, it is emotional. This view recognizes that all behavior, even a simple reflex, is to some degree determined by both internal and external factors. Since the external stimulus conditions are easier to control, especially with animal subjects, estimate of the internal (emotional) influence is usually made by elimination, i.e., as that part of the behavior which is not stimulus-determined. However, the deprivation technique is often used with both animals and men to vary the strength of internal controls directly.

Some internal factors are temporary and relatively unimportant in regulating the behavior of (civilized) men. These are the biological motives —hunger, thirst, sex, maternal affection, etc.—which dominate the behavior of animals. More important internal factors in the regulation of men are the relatively permanent social motives, e.g., religious and economic attitudes and prejudices.

While the external-internal distinction may be a rather difficult one to hold rigidly on a high-level abstract plane of thought, on the concrete level of direct observation of a particular animal qr man, it is an obvious distinction and is made in all experimental studies, although the terms "external" and "internal" may not be used. The important thing to hold in mind is that there are several operational, workable definitions of the distinction. As long as these different ways can be rationalized in a single conceptual scheme of some sort of c.n.s. mechanisms, which, though triggered by external stimuli, go into operation with relative independence and introduce a spontaneous element in behavior, it will be satisfactory to hold a concept of one class of internal factors. Future work may require erection of a schema of several classes of such factors.

These two basic concepts are of course not unrelated. The perceptual patterns are not static mind pictures. In addition to an intense arousal of alertness and focusing of attention, each has some strong implications for overt behavior. For example, if one has the culturally determined pattern of a world-inhabited-by-dangerous-people, his behavior will tend toward avoidance of strangers and a reluctance to enter friendship relations. Thus, the perceptual pattern is one of the class of internal factors which condition behavior. In any short temporal segment of behavior, it is clear that they are not "produced," but rather are "triggered" by, the objective stimulus situation.

Methods of identifying and measuring this type of internal factor in any one person are rather crude but are adequate for many experimental purposes. These methods include the various techniques for scaling attitudes and the rating scales for evaluating self or others. More refined techniques for measuring these patterns undoubtedly will be developed, probably through analysis of communication responses.

The technique of sensory deprivation may be employed in this respect, if it can be proved that the intense states of awareness (delusions, anxieties, fixed ideas) which arise during deprivation correspond to the patterns (attitudes, complexes) identified in the person prior to entering the deprivation state.

The findings of the sensory deprivation studies (Heron, 1957; Vernon *et al*, 1961) clearly point to some role of external stimulation in maintenance of "emotional control." If this method should prove valuable in identifying a subject's perceptual patterns, it would clarify this role somewhat by indicating that this role is one of inhibition. The prime importance of external stimulation in the establishment and development of stable emotional responses has been demonstrated by the work with scotties reared in isolation (Thompson and Melzack, 1956). Some evidence of a similar dependence of healthy emotional responses on external stimulation has been found in human infants (Gesell and Amatruda, 1947). Studies of the importance of imprinting on the tracking response of ducks and chicks is another line of evidence supporting the view that the formation of internal regulators of behavior, including fixed perceptual patterns, is dependent on early external stimulation (Hess, 1958; Levine, 1960). Now, the sensory deprivation findings imply that in later life the role of external stimulation *vis-a-vis* the internal controls is more than simply a triggering function.

According to this view, emotion is not a separate category of behavior; it is an aspect of all activity to some extent, no matter how small. It is the name for part of the causal matrix, the internal regulators, determining any and all behavior. This view amounts to identifying emotion and motivation. This is not a new view, since Duffy (1934) was stressing the identity of the two categories almost 30 years ago. However, Bindra clearly sees the need for stressing the identity of emotion and motivation in his book on motivation (1959, p. 29). Recognition of this identity requires a more general, less rigid meaning for both terms. They both reduce, for the experimenter, to the study of functional relations between performance and internal control.

The wealth of work on the function of central nervous system mechanisms and emotion has, of course, a direct bearing on this view, since these mechanisms are by definition internal regulators. The work of many investigators in the tradition set by Cannon (1927) and Bard (1934 and 1939), using techniques of extirpation and electrical stimulation of nervous tissue, has proved that strong emotion is dependent on mechanisms in the hypothalamus. Another line of work points up the function of the reticular alerting system in emotional responses (Lindsley, 1951). The internal causation of behavior is most dramatically shown in the studies which used electrodes implanted in the brains of animals (Olds, 1956; von Holst, 1962).

The uselessness of a taxonomy of behavior, from the viewpoint of an experimentalist, is shown by the inadequacy and artificiality of the distinction between emotion and learning, as well as that between emotion and motivation. Under the very general meaning of learning as any influence of past experience on present performance, two kinds of functional relations have been studied. In stimulus discrimination studies, the focus of attention is on functional relations between physical stimulation variables and some response (approach or avoidance) which the animal has "learned." In investigations of the second kind of relation, the focus has been on building into the nervous system of the subject, through practice, a determining, response-regulating pattern or mechanism. This is true in the case of the sequence of vocal responses established in serial verbal learning, as well as with the muscle coordination built up in pursuit-rotar learning.

A result of learning of this second type obviously is that internal response-determining factors are established within the subject. Evidence of this establishment of internal control is usually cited as evidence of "learning," or retention. It can also, according to the present view, be cited as evidence of "emotion," since it is a demonstration of the operation of internal factors on behavior.

FELT EMOTION It has never been demonstrated that there is a unique conscious content for either emotion in general or for the different named emotions. Certainly, introspection testifies to no distinctions between emotions as forceful and convincing as those between different colors and between different pitches. We must seek something in awareness of a kind similar to the imageless thoughts, such as feelings of "as if," "if . . . , then . . . ," or almost any awareness of relationship, particularly *causality*.

When a person describes an emotional experience, the chief thing he stresses, in addition to his cognition of the environmental situation, is his awareness of bodily changes, plus awareness of strong urges and impulses to action. A likely hypothesis is that the one unique thing about experiences described as emotional is that the subject is aware that his responses are to some degree nonvoluntary, that they are caused by something other than his "self." Reactions, including ideas, are taking place without his choice or decision and are to some degree "beyond his control."

A cataloguing of the situations into which subjects are put in experimental studies of emotion would reveal a list of stimuli calculated to call forth strong reactions. Typical of stimuli which have been used are a loud noise, loss of support, pornographic pictures, disgusting odors, and the sudden presentation of a large snake. The only thing common to such situations and which sets them off from all others is the likelihood of arousal of involuntary impulses.

It should be noticed that the objective analysis of emotional behavior led to the concept of internal determination of action. Now, consideration of the subjective aspect points to *awareness* of such determinants (urges) on the part of the subject. Thus, the two sides of this experimentalist's view of emotion supplement each other.

The terms "affect" and "feeling" are useful only from the subjective approach. They may be considered merely names for the milder forms of emotional experience. On the objective side, they should correlate with responses which have only a small degree of internal determination.

At one time in psychology, the prevalent tendency was to identify "feelings" with experiences of pleasantness and unpleasantness. Now, it is generally recognized that, operationally, the latter two terms signify judgmental reactions (Peters, 1935) and should not be classed as emotional reactions. Only when the terms pleasantness and unpleasantness are operationally defined in terms of overt evidence of approach or avoidance reactions should they be considered emotional experiences. And since the reactions are usually rather mild, they can appropriately be distinguished by the milder terms, affects or feelings.

Any experience in which the subject is aware of an element of *spontaneity* in his behavior is also a feeling experience. This is true of any highly skilled performance, in which the subject often is aware of his body moving independently of his self-control. He may have to initiate the global performance with a conscious decision, but once started, the part acts follow with a high degree of autonomy. Another type of feeling experience, creative activity, can be explained on the basis of spontaneity. A large part of the thrill of invention or creativity occurs in a condition of conscious passivity in which the subject experiences (to him) novel ideas which seem to occur spontaneously without awareness of willing or decision on his part. When one is trying to solve a challenging geometry problem, say the division of the area of a square into eight acute triangles, the creativity thrills (insights) seem to occur when the subject reaches a sort of compromise between decision-making, with attention focused on the problem, and a state of passively submitting to ideas which emerge, as it were, on their own.

Spontaneity, of course, can vary over a wide range. At one extreme is manic behavior, which can be beyond all apparent self-control. At the other extreme are milder experiences in which the subject is aware that he is turning some determination of his behavior over to impulses, yet is still maintaining a degree of "control."

References

Angier, R. P. The conflict theory of emotion. *Amer. J. Psychol.,* 1927, *39,* 390–401.

Bard, P. On emotional expression after decortication with some remarks on certain theoretical views. Parts I and II. *Psychol. Rev.,* 1934, *41,* 309–329, 424–449.

———. Central nervous mechanisms for emotional behavior patterns in animals. *Res. Publ. Ass. Nerv. Mental. Dis.,* 1939, *19,* 190–218.

Bindra, D. *Motivation: a systematic reinterpretation.* New York: Ronald Press, 1959.

Bull, Nina. Towards a clarification of the concept of emotion. *Psychosom. Med.,* 1945, 7, 210.

Cannon, W. B. *Bodily changes in pain, hunger, fear and rage* (2nd ed.) New York: Appleton-Century-Crofts, 1927.

Carr, H. A. *Psychology: a study of mental activity.* New York: Longmans, Green, 1925, Ch. XIII.

———. The differentia of an emotion. *Feelings and emotions: the Wittenberg symposium,* Ch. 19 [see Reymert (1928)].

Claparede, E. Feelings and emotions. *Feelings and emotions: the Wittenberg symposium,* Ch. 9 [see Reymert (1928)].

Darwin, C. R. *The expression of emotion in man and animals.* New York: Appleton, 1873.

Dewey, J. The theory of emotion. *Psychol. Rev.,* 1894, *1,* 553–569; 1895, *2,* 13–32.

Duffy, E. Emotion: an example of the need for reorientation in psychology. *Psychol. Rev.,* 1934, *41,* 184–198.

———. An explanation of "emotional" phenomena without the use of the concept "emotion." *J. Gen. Psy.,* 1941, *25,* 283–293.

Dunlap, K. Emotion as a dynamic background. *Feelings and emotions: the Wittenberg symposium,* Ch. 11 [see Reymert (1928)].

Eysenck, H. J. A dynamic theory of anxiety and hysteria. *J. Ment. Science,* 1955, *101,* 28–51.

Fletcher, R. *Instinct in man, in the light of recent work in comparative psychology.* New York: International Universities Press, 1957.

Freud, S. *A general introduction to psychoanalysis.* New York: Boni and Liveright, 1920.

Gesell, A., and Amatruda, C. S. *Developmental diagnosis. Normal and abnormal child development. Clinical methods and pediatric applications.* New York: Hoeber, 1947.

Goodenough, F. L. Expression of emotions in a deaf-blind child. *J. Abnorm. Soc. Psychol.,* 1932, 27, 428–433.

Heron, W. The pathology of boredom. *Sci. Am.,* 1957, *196,* 52–56.

Hess, E. H. "Imprinting" in animals. *Sci. Am.,* 1958, *198,* 81–90.

James, W. "What is an emotion?" *Mind,* 1884, *9,* 188–205.

Leeper, R. W. A motivational theory of emotion to replace "emotion as disorganized response." *Psychol. Rev.,* 1948, *55,* 5–21.

Levine, S. Stimulation in infancy. *Sci. Am.,* 1960, *202,* 80–86.

Lindsley, D. B. Emotion. In S. S. Stevens (ed.), *Handbook of experimental psychol.* New York: Wiley, 1951.

MacCurdy, J. T. *Psychology of emotion, morbid and normal*. New York: Harcourt, 1925, 549–571.

McDougall, W. *Introduction to social psychology*. Boston: Luce, 1910, pp. 46 ff.

Olds, J. Pleasure centers in the brain. *Sci. Am.*, 1956, *195*, 105–116.

Peters, H. N. The judgmental theory of pleasantness and unpleasantness. *Psychol. Rev.*, 1935, *42*, 354–386.

Pierón, H. Emotion in animals and man. *Feelings and emotions: the Wittenberg symposium*, Ch. 24 [see Reymert (1928)].

Prince, M. Can emotion be regarded as energy? *Feelings and emotions: the Wittenberg symposium*, Ch. 12 [see Reymert (1928)].

Reymert, M. L. (ed.). *Feelings and emotions: the Wittenberg symposium*. Worcester, Mass.: Clark Univ. Press, 1928.

————. *Feelings and emotions: the Mooseheart symposium in cooperation with the University of Chicago*. New York: McGraw-Hill, 1950.

Ruckmick, C. A. *The psychology of feeling and emotion*. New York: McGraw-Hill, 1936.

Thompson, W. R., and Melzack, R. Early environment. *Sci. Am.*, 1956, *194*, 38–42.

Vernon, J., Marton, T. and Peterson E. Sensory deprivation and hallucinations. *Science*, 1961, *133*, 1808–1812.

Von Holst, E. Electrically controlled behavior. *Sci. Am.*, 1962, *206*, 50–59.

Washburn, Margaret F. Emotion and thought: a motor theory of their relations. *Feelings and emotions: the Wittenberg symposium*, Ch. 7 [see Reymert (1928)].

Watson, J. B. *The new behaviorism*. New York: Norton, 1930.

Wenger, M. A. Emotion as visceral action: An extension of Lange's theory. *Feelings and emotions: the Mooseheart symposium*, Ch. 1 [see Reymert (1950)].

Wundt, W. *Principles of physiological psychology*. New York: Macmillan, 1922.

Young, P. T. *Emotion in man and animal*. New York: Wiley, 1943.

CHAPTER IX

Complex Processes

THIS CHAPTER IS CONCERNED WITH behavioral functions of a relatively complex variety. The paper by Philip B. Gough and James J. Jenkins is a wide-ranging treatment of the role of theory in verbal learning and psycholinguistics, two domains with independent, and quite different, origins but at least superficial relationships. As they show, verbal-learning research has a clear line of descent from classical experimental psychology, while what is called psycholinguistics has a more motley and recent ancestry. The second selection, by Donald W. Taylor, is a comprehensive overview of theoretical problems in the realm of "thinking." As the author indicates, he means to include under that term such apparently diverse processes as problem-solving, decision-making, and creativity. The treatment of Piaget's work is especially useful in view of the relative scarcity of clear, detailed descriptions in English. (Piaget's theory is also discussed by Zigler in Selection 24. In relation to the other topics emphasized by Taylor, see Selection 4 for a paper by Simon and Newell on the computer model.)

29 | *Verbal Learning and Psycholinguistics*

PHILIP B. GOUGH AND JAMES J. JENKINS

Verbal learning and psycholinguistics share a concern with the verbal behavior of the human organism. Both are intimately involved with the
acquisition and retention of verbal habits. They differ most markedly in
that the study of verbal learning has focused on the rote learning of such
habits under a set of standard controlled experimental procedures, while
psycholinguistics has as its domain of inquiry the development of such
habits in the natural language and their role in other behaviors. This is not
to say that they are independent fields of inquiry. In recent years students
of verbal learning have become increasingly concerned with the role of
natural language habits in rote learning, and students of the psychology
of language have often turned to rote learning situations for tests of
psycholinguistic theories.

Yet the two areas have developed independently. The study of verbal
learning has its roots in associationism and the classic work of Ebbinghaus;
it has developed in the Ebbinghaus tradition, nurtured by the functionalist
school. The study of verbal learning has not led to the study of verbal
behavior in general, to the psychology of language. That discipline, psycholinguistics, has but recently sprung from other sources: descriptive
linguistics, information theory, and learning theory.

Given these differences in empirical domain and historical development,
that the disciplines boast relatively independent theoretical positions is
not surprising. Accordingly, they will be treated separately here.

Verbal Learning

Verbal learning, more than any area of psychology, has been dominated
by a single methodology, a single approach to theory construction (cf.
Irion, 1959). That approach is functionalism. Indeed, the domain of verbal
learning has been the principal source of examples of the functionalist
approach (e.g., Hilgard, 1956, Ch. 10).

The functional approach to theory construction is modest. It does not encourage systematic theory. With one exception, no systematic theories of the verbal learning process have been formulated; the exception, the *Mathematico-deductive Theory of Rote Learning* of Hull *et al.* (1940), has had no impact on the field. The typical theory in verbal learning is a situational one, a special set of hypotheses designed to explain a limited range of phenomena. For example, a number of theories have been generated to account for phenomena as specific as the differential effects of massed and distributed practice (cf. Hilgard, *loc. cit.*).

The functional approach to theory construction is cautious. Just as the typical theory in verbal learning does not venture to encompass a broad range of data, so the theory does not venture far beyond the data at hand. The typical student of verbal learning prefers descriptive laws to theories; symptomatically, he is apt to evaluate theories not so much in the light of their truth value as with regard to their heuristic aspect. Thus, when Postman dismisses the trace theory of Gestalt psychology as a serious alternative to an interference theory of forgetting, he does so on grounds that the former "has thus far proved experimentally sterile and resistant to rigorous test" (1961, p. 152). Or when Underwood is discussing the Ebbinghaus tradition in the study of forgetting, his reaction to the "periodic verbal revolts" against this tradition is that "nothing much ever happens in the laboratory as a consequence of these revolts" (1957, p. 49).

Moreover, when a theoretical statement is ventured in verbal learning, its proponent is likely to play down its theoretical aspect. Thus, when Underwood, Runquist, and Schulz (1959) propose that verbal learning be conceptualized as a two-stage process (a first stage in which responses are integrated and a response pool is formed, and a second, associative stage in which these responses are attached to specific stimuli), they refer to their conception as a two-stage *analysis* of verbal learning; this despite the fact that the conception is clearly theoretical and of considerable generality.

The emphasis in verbal learning is clearly empiricistic. In other areas of psychology, the influential non-experimental contributions, the "classics" of an area, are customarily theoretical statements. In verbal learning such contributions tend to be analytical summaries of existent data. Such is the case, for example, of Osgood's "The Similarity Paradox" (1949), in which Osgood attempts to state a set of descriptive laws which would subsume the welter of data concerning the relationship between degree of similarity and the amount and direction of transfer and retroaction. So too with Underwood's "Interference and Forgetting" (1957), a re-examination of the data which had led to the conclusion that forgetting of materials learned in the laboratory is massive and largely attributable to interference from materials learned subsequently outside the laboratory. Underwood's analysis demonstrated, without recourse to theory, that the magnitude of forgetting is a function of the number of lists learned in the laboratory prior to the test list, and that forgetting is to a large degree a function of proactive interference. In such papers—and they are typical—theory plays little part.

This is not to imply that theory has played no role in verbal learning. On the contrary, theory has played a definite and significant role. But the theory is of a particular sort; theory in which the inferential component is minimal. More ambitious, speculative theory has not been welcomed, while descriptive analysis of the sort exemplified by the papers of Osgood and Underwood is as fully respected as theory construction.

In point of fact, theory in verbal learning tends toward this kind of analysis as a limit, and the border is not always distinct. (Indeed, writers like Underwood and Postman tend to use the terms "theory" and "analysis" interchangeably.) The typical theory in verbal learning is close to description. Its terms, where they are not descriptive concepts, tend to be tightly anchored to specified operations, reducible to the observation language without mediate inference. In MacCorquodale and Meehl's (1948) distinction, they tend to be intervening variables, with clear referents outside the organism. They tend not to be hypothetical constructs, and physiological speculation is, in the mainstream of verbal learning, almost unheard of.

The closeness of such theory to the observation language, together with the respect accorded experimentation by students of verbal learning, encourages the experimental test of theory and its consequent modifications. A close and continuous interplay between data and theory characterizes the methodology of verbal learning to such an extent that to illustrate the development of a theory in verbal learning is more appropriate than to describe its present status.

The homogeneity of theory construction in verbal learning allows us to convey its character with a single example. A noteworthy instance of the characteristic interplay between data and theory is found in the development of the interference theory of forgetting, and we will take it as our example.

INTERFERENCE THEORY OF FORGETTING   Contemporary interference theory stems from the competition-of-response theory of McGeoch (1942). McGeoch's theory was advanced to account for the phenomenon of retroactive inhibition, a decrement in the retention of some learned material attributable to the interpolation of another learning task between the original learning and recall of the test material. The theory reduces retroactive inhibition to *reproductive* inhibition (McGeoch, 1932). It assumes that the responses from both original and interpolated learning are available to the subject at the point of recall. If those responses are attached to similar or identical stimuli, competition between the responses will occur, and the stronger response will be produced; if the responses are of equal strength, they will block each other, and no response will be emitted. If the stronger of the two responses is one from the interpolated task, or if no response is emitted, the recorded result is an error in recall, and decrement will occur in the measured retention of the original learning. Retroactive inhibition is, then, due to *interference*, in the attempt to reproduce the responses of the original task from responses acquired in the interpolated task.

Typical of those of verbal learning, McGeoch's is a low-order theory. Its domain of application is limited; the data with which it deals come, generally speaking, from a single experimental paradigm. Its central concept, response competition, is a low-order theoretical construct, linked directly to observable antecedents and consequents. It is assumed to be a direct function of the degree of interpolated learning and the degree of similarity between original and interpolated learning, and therefore an inverse function of the degree of original learning. On the consequent side, response competition is manifested as a decrement in recall or relearning, i.e., as retroactive inhibition.

McGeoch's theory is typical, too, in that it led to the collection of new data in test of the theory, which data, in turn, led to the modification of the theory. If retroactive inhibition (RI) is attributable to interference from responses learned in the interpolated task, then a clear implication of the theory is that the number of overt intrusions of those competing responses in recall should vary with the amount of RI. (The test of this prediction requires that the experimenter record not only the occurrence of errors in recall but also their nature; that the recording and analysis of error data has become part of the standard experimental methodology of verbal learning has been an important consequence of McGeoch's theory.) But Melton and Irwin (1940) found that while RI increases steadily as a function of degree of interpolated learning, the predicted overt inter-list intrusions rise to a maximum and then decline. At high degrees of interpolated learning (IL), RI attributable to overt intrusions constitutes only a slight fraction of the total amount of RI.

Evidently RI and overt intrusions do not co-vary in the direct manner seemingly predicted by McGeoch's theory. This is not decisive evidence against the theory, for it states that competition is manifested in response blocking as well as overt intrusion. But Melton and Irwin argued that it is reasonable to expect, on the basis of McGeoch's theory, that overt intrusions should account for a constant proportion of RI, and that at high degrees of IL the amount of RI not attributable to overt intrusions is too great to be accounted for by response blocking.

This reasoning led Melton and Irwin to conclude that some factor other than reproductive inhibition must contribute to RI, its contribution increasing with degree of IL. With characteristic caution, they labeled this unknown *Factor X* and tentatively suggested that it might be identified as the *unlearning* of first-list responses during IL, in analogy to experimental extinction in classical conditioning. Direct evidence on the unlearning hypothesis was not immediately forthcoming, but this *two-factor theory* generated new research and received indirect support when an important prediction derived from the theory was confirmed.

The two-factor theory yields the prediction that the retention of the original material will be less than that of the interpolated, for the original material is subjected both to unlearning during interpolated learning and to competition during recall, while the interpolated material is subject only to the latter. The theory thus implies that retroactive inhibition will be greater than proactive inhibition, and a test of this prediction (Melton and Von Lackum, 1941) yielded clear evidence of the predicted difference.

Interference theory was further enriched with the introduction of the concept of *differentiation* (Thune and Underwood, 1943; Underwood, 1945). Its authors argued, against Melton and Irwin, that, in maintaining the competition-of-response theory, we need not assume that overt intrusions should account for a constant proportion of RI as it increases with the degree of IL. Admittedly, the theory demands that responses from the interpolated list become increasingly dominant and successfully compete with the correct responses as degree of IL is increased, but these competing responses are not necessarily manifested as *overt* intrusions. We can assume that increasing dominance of competing responses from interpolated learning is accompanied by increasing *differentiation* between the lists, that is, by an increasing ability on the part of the subject to discriminate the list membership of the responses. At high levels of IL, when the difference in strength of the competing responses is great, intrusions are readily identified as incorrect responses and rejected, and few overt intrusions ensue. Since differentiation is assumed to be a function of the degree of IL relative to that of original learning, it follows that as a function of degree of interpolated learning, overt intrusions should increase to a maximum (when degree of IL is approximately equal to that of original learning) and then decrease. And this is, of course, what Melton and Irwin had demonstrated.

Differentiation is another low-order construct, assumed to be a function of the degree of IL with respect to the degree of original learning and to result in an increase in the percentage of recorded errors of omission. It has been a heuristic construct, leading to research like that of Underwood (1945), who demonstrated that if amount of IL is increased under circumstances such that differentiation cannot develop (by varying, rather than the number of trials on a single interpolated list, the number of interpolated lists), the frequency of overt inter-list intrusions does not vary. Moreover, the construct broadened the systematic scope of interference theory by coordinating with it a previously unrelated variable, the time interval between the end of IL and the beginning of recall, with which differentiation is assumed to vary (inversely).

The unlearning and differentiation hypotheses constitute modifications of McGeoch's theory, introduced to account for the discrepancy between that theory and the data (of Melton and Irwin) generated by it. They exemplify different (but equally legitimate) strategies in the modification of theory. The differentiation hypothesis attempts to preserve the theory by adding to it a further concept; the unlearning hypothesis modifies the theory by revising one of its assumptions, the assumption that the strength of the responses in the first list is not altered during IL.

Both appear to be fruitful hypotheses, adequately accounting for the problematic data and, in addition, generating further research and confirming data. But they constitute alternative explanations of the same phenomenon, and while the differentiation hypothesis is not contradictory to that of unlearning (for unlearning might be assumed to reduce the strength of first-list responses relative to that of responses from IL, thus influencing differentiation), its acceptance weakens the original argument for unlearning. The attempt to provide stronger evidence for unlearning, in the face of these considerations, led to still further new techniques and new data.

Firm evidence regarding the unlearning hypothesis necessitates a technique which eliminates the possible confounding effects of both differentiation and response competition. A procedure which eliminates the first of these, the technique of *modified free recall* (MFR), was introduced by Underwood (1948). In MFR the subject is asked to produce, in the presence of a stimulus common to the original and interpolated lists, a response from *either* list, without regard to list membership. Using this technique, Underwood found that as degree of IL is increased, the frequency of responses from the first list declines, while that of responses from the interpolated list increases. This is not, of course, crucial evidence for the unlearning hypothesis, for the results can be attributed to increasing response competition. But if the temporal interval between IL and recall is manipulated (a variation suggested by the differentiation hypothesis), the relative frequency of first-list responses can be shown to increase over a 24-hour period. Underwood suggested that the first-list responses were indeed, unlearned, or extinguished, and then exhibited spontaneous recovery; his suggestion furthers the analogy of unlearning to the experimental extinction of conditioned responses and additionally amplifies interference theory.

Crucial evidence for the unlearning hypothesis was finally provided with the introduction of a technique which eliminates response competition as well as differentiation. Barnes and Underwood (1959) asked their subjects to recall, following IL, the responses from *both* lists. Under these circumstances differentiation is not a factor, for the subject is not required to discriminate list membership prior to producing the response. Response competition is not a factor, for both responses are to be produced. The Barnes and Underwood technique, then, provides a pure measure of response availability, and their data provide clear support for the unlearning hypothesis. As IL is increased, there is a steady decline in the number of first-list responses recalled and a steady increase in the number of responses from IL. As IL is increased, first-list responses become increasingly unavailable; they are unlearned.

These results of Barnes and Underwood, added to their further finding that subjects are able to identify the list membership of their responses with a high degree of accuracy immediately after IL, have led to further modification and refinement of the interference theory of retroactive inhibition. Postman (1961, pp. 156–157) has provided a succinct summary of these refinements:

Barnes and Underwood conclude that "the present results would strongly suggest that nearly all RI could be accounted for by unlearning or extinction if unlimited recall time is given immediately after interpolated learning" (p. 103). Lack of differentiation would develop after an interval of time and add response competition as a further source of interference. If and when the responses extinguished during IL recover fully, response competition would remain as the only source of interference. This argument constitutes a restatement of two-factor theory, with the important additional assumption that the contribution of the two components varies systematically with the length of the retention interval. Thus, the known experimental facts about temporal changes in the amount and manifestations of interference are incorporated into the theory. . . . There is every reason to believe that the extension of two-factor theory proposed by Barnes and Underwood will adequately account for the course of interference when intertask transfer is negative.

This sketch of the development of interference theory does not constitute a complete picture of that development; nor does it provide an adequate representation of the current status of that theory. (Postman's 1961 paper admirably serves both of these functions.) But the sketch serves to illustrate the theory's characteristic methodological features, and these features are common to most theories in verbal learning.[1] The theory is

---

[1] There are salient exceptions to this homogeneity. Eleanor Gibson's extremely influential theory of verbal learning (1940) was patterned after the hypothetico-deductive approach of Hull, with formally stated postulates and operational definitions. But a recent evaluation of her theory (Underwood, 1961) concludes that "the usefulness of the Gibson theory, as originally conceived, has ended" (p. 198).

A definitely viable alternative methodology, the approach of the advocates of

formulated to account for a restricted set of data deriving from a standard experimental paradigm. The theory is modest in inference as well as in scope. It stands close to known descriptive laws and uses low-order constructs rigorously defined in terms of standard experimental operations. It is continuously subjected to test and modified accordingly. It is an exemplary instance of one methodology of theory construction in science.

Psycholinguistics

Psycholinguistics, or the psychology of language, has, in contrast to verbal learning, no clear line of descent. It was hybridized (circa 1950) from diverse parental strains (cf. Osgood and Sebeok, 1954). It has drawn most heavily from descriptive linguistics, information theory, and learning theory. Each of these sources has provided a distinctive vocabulary for the description of behavioral phenomena involving language and an implicit conceptual system detectable in the work of psycholinguists impressed with it. Each has served as a source of orienting attitudes toward the psychology of language, which have suggested the research problems and strategies of a number of psycholinguists. Only one has provided explicit psycholinguistic theory.

Modern descriptive linguistics has not provided behavior theory; it does not profess to this aim. To be sure, there are "theories" in linguistics in the sense of sets of explanatory premises or postulates from which theorems are then derived (cf. Chomsky, 1957), but the explananda of such theories are not behavioral phenomena. The linguist (cf. Gleason, 1961) is careful to distinguish between language as an abstract system, a code, and that code in its physical expression as speech, as behavior; he is equally careful in restricting his concern to language as system, not as behavior. The linguist's aim is to isolate the structure of a language and to describe the units (e.g., the phoneme and the morpheme) and their rules of combination which constitute a linguistic system. Behavior falls within the linguist's domain only as an expression of such a system, the basis from which he constructs the system.

The psychologist intimate with the linguistic viewpoint (e.g., Brown, 1958) is apt to concern himself with phenomena reflecting the linguistic concern, such as the acquisition of grammar (e.g., Berko, 1958) or the Whorfian hypothesis that a language molds the thought of its speakers (e.g., Brown and Lenneberg, 1954). But while the linguistic frame of ref-

---

mathematical models, has recently made itself felt in the verbal learning area (e.g., Estes, 1960; Bower, 1962). Since mathematical models are given separate treatment elsewhere (Selection 33) this approach will not be treated here.

erence may influence his choice of research problems (and the terms in which he deals with them), it offers him no help in explaining what that research produces.

Information theory similarly has been barren of theoretical fruit. Information theory is not itself a substantive theory (cf. Frick, 1959); it is a set of statistics. It provides a mathematical vocabulary for characterizing inputs and outputs in terms of probabilities and conditional probabilities and the capacities of men and machines in transforming inputs into outputs. It provides a mode of description, not explanation.

The psycholinguist who holds information theory in esteem (cf. Rubenstein and Aborn, 1960) is apt to select for manipulation variables which can be translated into its vocabulary. Thus his research is focused on such characteristics of verbal stimulus materials as their relative frequency of occurrence in the natural language (Pierce and Karlin, 1957) and their sequential organization (Miller and Selfridge, 1953), which can be directly coordinated to the terms of information theory. Moreover, he is likely to abstract from his subjects' responses properties which can be dealt with in the same terms (e.g., Miller, Bruner, and Postman, 1954). With the concepts of information theory, he is able to describe in the same terms both stimuli and responses of widely diverse natures, but information theory neither predicts nor is disconfirmed by the functional relationships which are found to obtain between those stimuli and responses. Information theory does not explain; with only few exceptions (e.g., Miller, 1956), it has not led to explanatory theory.

The prominent systematic positions in psycholinguistics (if any may be so called in such a young area) have been drawn from learning theory, specifically from S-R learning theory. Osgood's theory of meaning (Osgood, 1952; Osgood, Suci, and Tannenbaum, 1957) derives from Hull; Skinner's analysis of verbal behavior (1957) stems from his analysis of animal behavior. A third position, built around the concept of verbal association and identified with no single theorist but claiming a number of recent adherents, arises from the general tradition of functional associationism. Accordingly, these three represent the same types of theory construction as their antecedents, in rough correspondence to the major positions outlined in Chapter 1.

Osgood   Unlike many influential theorists in the S-R tradition, Osgood has shown little interest in formal methodology; he has written *about* theory only infrequently and then informally (e.g., Osgood, 1956). Nevertheless, his attitudes toward controversial issues of theory construction are manifest. His own theory is explicit, rigorous, and extensively elaborated. He readily indulges in physiological speculation in the exposition of that theory (e.g., Osgood, 1957). And the pivotal concept of his theory is, we will argue, a full-blown hypothetical construct.

That concept is the *representational mediation process*. Osgood's theory is concerned with meaning, and in the theory, meaning is identified with a mediating response, the r_m-s_m. An r_m-s_m is learned, and meaning is acquired when a sign is paired with a significate, "any stimulus which . . . regularly and reliably produces a predictable pattern of behavior" (Osgood, Suci, and Tannenbaum, 1957, p. 6). Some fraction of the total response to the significate is conditioned to the sign as its meaning. This fractional response, an r_m-s_m, is then a representational mediation process. It is representational because it is part of the same behavior produced by the significate itself, and mediational because the self-stimulation it produces can become associated with overt, instrumental responses. The r_m-s_m is assumed to function as a response to a sign, as stimulus to overt behavior. Both of these habits are assumed to obey the laws which govern observable *S-R* contingencies.

Such an implicit mediating response can be conceptualized as an *inferred* response, differing from observable responses only in that it is covert rather than overt. Descriptive *S-R* laws are simply extrapolated to include *S-R* relations which are not, at present, capable of being directly confirmed, but the lack of direct testability is a result of the inadequacy of present techniques. Such would seem to be the methodological conception of the implicit response espoused by Watson (1914) in his motor theory of thought and by Skinner (see below).

This is not Osgood's conception. He rejects any identification of the r_m-s_m with a specifiable physiological locus; he chooses the term "mediation *process*" rather than "mediating *response*" to "leave explicitly open the questions of the underlying nature of such representational mediators" (Osgood, Suci, and Tannenbaum, 1957, p. 7). Given Osgood's conception, we have no way of identifying an r_m-s_m in direct observation, and direct confirmation of his hypotheses regarding that concept is in principle, not just in practice, impossible.

The r_m-s_m is a *hypothetical*, not an *hypothesized*, event. The descriptive *S-R* laws are not simply hypothesized to hold in a domain where they have not yet been tested; rather, they are taken as a convenient source of postulates concerning a theoretical construct. This becomes apparent when we realize that should the descriptive *S-R* laws be modified, Osgood would find no *necessity* to change any of his statements regarding the r_m-s_m.[2] Osgood's theory, as he puts it, simply transfers all of the conceptual machinery of single-stage *S-R* psychology into a two stage model inside

---

[2] That is, of course, provided that the derivations from those postulates are not falsified by the revised laws.

the organism, but in this relocation what were inductive descriptive laws become the postulates of a deductive theory, testable only indirectly via the derivation of predictions of observable behavioral events.

Osgood's theory consists of a series of statements, amounting to postulates, about a theoretical construct. That construct, the r_m-s_m, is not introduced by operational definition. This does not imply that it is devoid of empirical meaning. It is introduced in a set of hypothetical laws or postulates, some of which (e.g., Osgood's statements as to how meaning is acquired) indirectly relate the construct to observable events, and its meaning is conferred upon it by the propositions in which it occurs. It is thus defined by a *nomological network* (cf. Cronbach and Meehl, 1955) in which it is embedded, and only after the construct is so presented does Osgood turn to the problem of its measurement. And significantly, in the classification of r_m-s_m as a hypothetical construct rather than an intervening variable, Osgood treats the problem of measurement as one of finding *indices* of meaning, not of defining it.

The construct is not defined by an operation; it is held to be indexed by a measuring instrument, the *semantic differential*. A semantic differential consists of a set of bi-polar adjectival scales (e.g., HOT-COLD, GOOD-BAD), on each of which the subject is asked to locate the concept the meaning of which is being measured. The subject's ratings are assumed to provide an index of the r_m-s_m evoked by the concept. The direction of his ratings (e.g., toward HOT or COLD from neutral) is assumed to reflect the nature of the r_m-s_m; the distance of the rating from neutral is assumed to reflect its intensity. A comparison of a subject's ratings of two different concepts provides an index of the similarity of the r_m-s_m's which they evoke.

The semantic differential provides an index of the character of the r_m-s_m evoked by a sign. Given that character, the theory generates predictions concerning behavioral phenomena involving that sign.[3] For example, the theory asserts that whenever a sign is presented to a subject, the sign evokes the representational mediation process associated with it. If some overt response R is paired under appropriate circumstances with the presentation of some sign S_1, an association will be formed between the stimulus consequences of the representational mediation process (s_m) evoked by S_1 and the response R. Suppose another sign S_2, physically different from S_1 but having a meaning (r_m-s_m) similar to that of S_1 (as indexed by the semantic differential) is now presented. The sign S_2 will evoke that r_m-s_m; s_m will, in turn, evoke R. The response R will occur to the sign S_2 despite the fact that it has not been learned to that stimulus.

---

[3] With emphasis shifted from the theory to the measuring instrument, Osgood's program constitutes an exemplary instance of the investigation of *construct validity* (cf. Cronbach and Meehl, 1955).

Thus Osgood derives the phenomenon of semantic generalization (cf. Cofer and Foley, 1942), in which a response learned to a given word can be shown to generalize to its synonyms.

Osgood's theory derives from Hull and his concept of the pure stimulus act (Hull, 1930, 1931). Like Hull's, his theory consists of a set of propositions from which testable predictions are derived. (Unlike Hull's, Osgood's propositions are not presented as formal postulates; his theory might be characterized as an *in*formal hypothetico-deductive system.) Like Hull's, Osgood's theory has generated a substantial number of predictions, an impressive number of which have been experimentally confirmed (e.g., Solarz, 1960; Staats and Staats, 1957). Finally, like Hull's, the theory has aroused much theoretical controversy, a controversy engendered by the proponents of the verbal association position.

VERBAL ASSOCIATION Each of these prominent psycholinguistic theories stems from *S-R* learning theory. The central construct of such theory is the habit or associative bond which is held to connect stimulus and response. In traditional *S-R* learning theory, based largely on laboratory experimentation in which the learning history of the organism is tightly controlled, the existence of habits or bonds is inferred largely on the basis of that learning history. The enormous complexity of the human organism's learning history with respect to language has been prohibitively difficult of description; lacking this, the psycholinguistic *S-R* theorist has been forced to substitute for the historical inferential base. Osgood's course is to postulate that every stimulus (sign) is connected, by habit, to a hypothetical response (its representational mediation process), and then to infer the nature of that response on the basis of the semantic differential. Skinner, on whom the lack of a known learning history wreaks the greatest methodological hardship (since his aim is to analyze present behavior *in terms of* past history), chooses to hypothesize the stimuli controlling a response and, assuming these, to infer a learning history. The verbal association position is defined by its solution of this problem; its use of word association techniques to assess verbal habits.

The verbal association position is not a formal systematic theory; it is not, for that matter, *a* theory. It is a set of informal theoretical assumptions about verbal habits, elaborated and developed by individual psycholinguists into distinct theoretical conceptions (e.g., Bousfield, 1961; Deese, 1962) but shared as the common property of a number of investigators.

The central assumption is that word associations function as habits, that the responses given to words in free association are connected by habits to those words as stimuli. No assumption is made as to the origin of these habits; this is a topic of current experimental interest (cf. Osgood and Sebeok, 1954). The assumption is that the strength of such a habit can be inferred from the relative frequency of occurrence of the response among the free associations of a standard population (cf. Russell, 1961).

Using only these assumptions, the association position amounts to little more than a working hypothesis, one which suggests that a given empirical variable is important in the determination of behavior and is, consequently, a fruitful variable to manipulate experimentally. The affinity of the verbal association position with functionalism is apparent here, for the principal function of the low-level theoretical assumptions adopted is to guide research. This is exemplified by Jenkins and Russell, who, with their students, have centered a program of research on a single theorem derivable from the stated assumptions alone (Jenkins and Russell, 1952). The theorem—that the presence of a stimulus word will tend to evoke its popular associates as responses in any situation—has been confirmed in situations ranging from recall (Jenkins, Mink, and Russell, 1958) to tachistoscopic recognition (O'Neil, 1953).

In such applications, the association position is not saliently a theoretical position. Word associations themselves are observable stimulus-response contingencies; the theorem investigated by Jenkins and Russell takes the form of a descriptive law. Only the hypothetical habit inferred to link those stimuli and responses and to mediate the results of Jenkins and Russell raises the formulation from the descriptive to the theoretical level.

At this level, the association position does not controvert Osgood's theory. But the associative assumptions are not limited to observable stimuli and responses. They are extended, by most proponents of the position, to include implicit stimulus and response events. The assumption is made that verbal stimuli elicit their associates as implicit responses, and that those responses can serve as stimuli, either to their own associates as further implicit responses or to overt behavior. And here the opposition to Osgood's system is formed. With Osgood, the proponents of the verbal association position expands the basic *S-R* conception into a two-stage model, the stages of which are bridged by an inferred mediating event. But where Osgood makes that event a *representational mediation process,* the associationist assumes that the mediating function is served by implicit verbal responses.

The assumptions of the verbal association position thus resemble, in form, those of Osgood, but the nature of the mediating event hypothesized by the opposing positions is different. The disputed event is a theoretical construct; the dispute cannot be settled by direct observation. But the disagreement is not merely verbal and devoid of empirical implications. The two theoretical positions, including their differing modes of tapping the mediation construct, lead to contrary predictions, and tests of those predictions have constituted a sizable body of research.

The theories provide, for example, differing accounts of the phenomenon of semantic generalization. Osgood's theory, as we have seen, explains the phenomenon by postulating a representational mediation process common to the training and test stimuli; the phenomenon is asserted to depend on the similarity of meaning of the two words. The association position argues that the meaning of the words is irrelevant and that the phenomenon is dependent on the existence of an association between the stimulus words themselves. If, for example, an overt response R were trained to one word of a pair of synonyms, that word would, during training, evoke the synonym as an implicit mediating response; the stimulus consequences of that mediating response would become attached to the response R. When the synonym is subsequently presented as the test stimulus, it will evoke the response R, and semantic generalization will be demonstrated.

Osgood's theory thus makes semantic generalization depend on similarity of meaning between the training and test stimuli; the association position rests the phenomenon on the existence of an association between the stimulus words themselves. The adequacy of these differing conceptions can be compared by contrasting the amount of semantic generalization obtained between pairs of meaningfully similar but non-associated words with that obtained between pairs of associated but dissimilar words.

Experimental comparisons of this sort have found substantial amounts of semantic generalization in both instances (e.g., Bastian, 1961; Ryan, 1960). Thus evidence exists for the independent operation of both processes (and cf. Staats and Staats, 1957). No theoretical controversy is settled so simply and harmoniously, for no theoretical controversy *is* simple, and the controversy between the associationists and Osgood is no exception (cf. Bousfield, 1961). But the associationists are increasingly foregoing polemical experimentation in favor of investigation of the empirical determinants of phenomena exemplifying the processes common to both theories of mediation (cf. Horton and Kjeldergaard, 1961).

The verbal-association position thus comes full circle, from data to theory to data; in so doing, it clearly reflects its functional orientation. It originated in the empirical hypothesis that word associations are important determinants of behavior. The success of the hypothesis at this level encouraged its extension as a theoretical statement, one embodying implicit as well as explicit word associations. The theory thus proposed is not elaborate or formal. Neither is it highly speculative; it is limited to the extension of descriptive laws to include unobservable events. At this level, it found itself embracing in its explanatory domain phenomena with an alternative explanation in terms of another theory. Comparative tests of the opposing explanations suggest a convergence on common explanatory principles, and the association position has turned to the investigation of those principles.

SKINNER   In the psychology of language, as in general, Skinner is firmly anti-theoretical: "The 'understanding of verbal behavior' . . . is not to be confused with the confirmation of any set of theoretical principles" (1957, p. 3). What he argues for is a *functional analysis* of verbal behavior, an identification of the variables of which that behavior is a function. This is, for Skinner, explanation, and he would have it in terms of variables to be found outside the organism, for the "traditional practice" of appealing to events taking place inside the organism has led only to the creation of explanatory fictions like "ideas," "meaning," and "information."

The explanandum is verbal behavior, a subdivision of human behavior to be topographically described. Skinner's account of this behavior is devotedly positivistic. The unit of analysis is identified as the verbal operant, "a response of identifiable form functionally related to one or more independent variables" (Skinner, 1957, p. 20). (This unit is not to be identified with the word or any one linguistic unit; it may vary in size and complexity from the single phoneme to a whole phrase or sentence.) Every verbal operant may be thought of as having a specified strength; the notion of strength is held to be related to several response variables, such as energy, speed, and repetition. But the strength of a verbal operant should not be construed to be, like habit strength, an intervening variable, defined in terms of and relating several disparate operational measures. Rather, Skinner selects a "basic datum," probability of emission under specified circumstances, and it is to this single datum that strength is equated. The other response measures are held to be useful, if not wholly reliable, indicators of strength, related to but not definitive of strength.

The probability that a verbal response of given form will occur at a given time is the independent variable of Skinner's functional analysis. The independent variables, the causes of behavior, are descriptive concepts: reinforcement, stimulus control, deprivation, aversive stimulation. These are the terms of Skinner's operant conditioning paradigm, and that paradigm is taken to apply, without significant modification, to verbal behavior. A verbal operant acquires strength when an utterance is frequently followed by reinforcement; the acquisition of language by a child is a process of shaping through the reinforcement of successive approximations to the language of the reinforcing community. A verbal response may be brought under stimulus control when the language community reinforces that response only in the presence of a specified stimulus, and so forth. The functional analysis of verbal behavior can be accomplished in the terms of the operant conditioning paradigm; no new explanatory concepts are required.

To be sure, Skinner's *Verbal Behavior* (1957) introduces new terminology. The *mand* is "a verbal operant in which the response is reinforced by a characteristic consequence and is therefore under the functional control of relevant conditions of deprivation or aversive stimulation" (pp. 35–36). The *tact* is "a verbal operant in which a response of given form is evoked (or at least strengthened) by a particular object or event or property of an object or event" (pp. 81–82). *Echoic, textual,* and *intraverbal* operants are responses under the control of verbal stimuli. But these novel terms are not new explanatory concepts. They simply amount to a taxonomy of verbal operants according to the antecedent conditions controlling the response; those operants themselves are not different from any other operants. The operant conditioning paradigm is taken to apply, without significant modification, to verbal behavior.

In short, Skinner holds that the laws of verbal behavior are the laws of behavior as they have been isolated in the experimental animal laboratory; language requires no new laws, no new concepts. The verbal responses of men are determined by their past history and present circumstances, and a satisfactory explanation of that behavior is achieved by describing that behavior and its antecedents, and without recourse to theoretical constructs.

Skinner's approach to verbal behavior thus exemplifies the general Skinnerian methodological approach. Skinner eschews theoretical construction in favor of descriptive analysis, deduction in favor of induction. But his aversion to deductive theory is not, as his *Verbal Behavior* amply testifies, extended to inference. While his account of verbal behavior is descriptive in that it avoids the use of theoretical constructs, it is not descriptive of demonstrated empirical relationships. That verbal behavior is acquired and maintained in the manner asserted by Skinner is not a matter of established empirical fact but, rather, a bold extrapolation from the principles demonstrated in the laboratory with other organisms and other responses. Skinner does not *describe* the learning history of the organism with respect to verbal behavior; he *prescribes* that history (cf. Chomsky, 1959). His account of verbal behavior is not a theoretical construction, but neither is it an inductive summary of established empirical principles; it is a plausible, but clearly hypothetical, reconstruction of verbal behavior in accord with principles isolated in the empirical investigation of other behavior.

Skinner's *Verbal Behavior* thus makes apparent the fact that his positivism does not prohibit hypothesis formation, even bold hypothesis formation, if the hypothesis is formulated in descriptive terms. Moreover, it is equally clear that, while Skinner is vociferously opposed to the postulation of intra-organismic theoretical constructs, he is *not* opposed to the formation of hypotheses about intra-organismic events. Skinner's account of verbal behavior relies heavily upon such hypotheses: verbal behavior is often held to be under the control of *private* stimuli (e.g., Skinner, 1957, pp. 130–146); one source of such stimuli is *covert* behavior (pp. 141–142).

One detects here, in the framework of a descriptive, positivistic account of verbal behavior, a hypothesis very like that of the mediation hypotheses of Osgood and the verbal associationists. But Skinner's conception of that hypothesis is subtly and importantly different. The covert responses hypothesized by Skinner are not some fractional component of a total response like those of Osgood, nor are they implicit associates which, according to association theory, are always evoked by verbal stimuli. Covert behavior is, according to Skinner, overt behavior which has receded, and this process itself is open to description. Covert behavior, its antecedents, and its controlling conditions are describable in exactly the same terms as overt behavior. That behavior is unobservable does not exclude it from a descriptive account. Covert behavior, like overt behavior, is to be subjected to functional analysis, accounted for in terms of its past history and present circumstances.

References

Barnes, J. M., and Underwood, B. J. Fate of first-list associations in transfer theory. *J. Exp. Psychol.*, 1959, *58*, 97–105.

Bastian, J. Associative factors in verbal transfer. *J. Exp. Psychol.*, 1961, *62*, 70–79.

Berko, J. The child's learning of English morphology. *Word*, 1958, *14*, 150–177.

Bousfield, W. A. The problem of meaning in verbal learning. In C. N. Cofer (ed.), *Verbal learning and verbal behavior.* New York: McGraw-Hill, 1961, pp. 81–91.

Bower, G. H. An association model for response and training variables in paired-associate learning. *Psychol. Rev.*, 1962, *69*, 34–53.

Brown, R. W. *Words and things.* Glencoe, Ill.: The Free Press, 1958.

Brown, R. W., and Lenneberg, E. H. A study in language and cognition. *J. Abnorm. Soc. Psychol.*, 1954, *49*, 454–462.

Chomsky, N. *Syntactic structures.* The Hague: Mouton, 1957.

———. Review of *Verbal behavior* by B. F. Skinner. *Language*, 1959, *35*, 26–58.

Cofer, C. N., and Foley, J. P. Mediated generalization and the interpretation of verbal behavior: I. Prolegomena. *Psychol. Rev.*, 1942, *49*, 513–540.

Cronbach, L. J., and Meehl, P. E. Construct validity in psychological tests. *Psychol. Bull.*, 1955, *52*, 281–302.

Deese, J. On the structure of associative meaning. *Psychol. Rev.*, 1962, *69*, 161–175.

Estes, W. K. Learning theory and the new "mental chemistry." *Psychol. Rev.*, 1960, *67*, 207–223.

Frick, F. C. Information theory. In S. Koch (ed.), *Psychology: a study of a science*, Vol. 2. New York: McGraw-Hill, 1959, pp. 611–636.

Gibson, E. J. A systematic application of the concepts of generalization and differentiation to verbal learning. *Psychol. Rev.*, 1940, *47*, 196–229.

Gleason, H. A., Jr. *An introduction to descriptive linguistics* (rev. ed.). New York: Holt, Rinehart and Winston, 1961.

Hilgard, Ernest, R. *Theories of learning* (2nd ed.). New York: Appleton-Century-Crofts, 1956.

Horton, D. L., & Kjeldergaard, P. M. An experimental analysis of associative factors in mediated generalizations. *Psychol. Monogr.*, 1961, *75* (11, Whole No. 515).

Hull, C. L. Knowledge and purpose as habit mechanisms. *Psychol. Rev.*, 1930, *37*, 511–525.

———. Goal attraction and directing ideas conceived as habit phenomena. *Psychol. Rev.*, 1931, *38*, 487–506.

Hull, C. L., Hovland, C. I., Ross, R. T., Hall, M. Perkins, D. T., and Fitch, F. B. *Mathematico-deductive theory of rote learning*. New Haven, Conn.: Yale University Press, 1940.

Irion, A. L. Rote learning. In S. Koch (ed.), *Psychology: a study of a science*, Vol. 2. New York: McGraw-Hill, 1959, pp. 538–560.

Jenkins, J. J., Mink, W. D., and Russell, W. A. Associative clustering as a function of verbal association strength. *Psychol. Rep.*, 1958, *4*, 127–136.

Jenkins, J. J., and Russell, W. A. Associative clustering during recall. *J. Abn. Soc. Psychol.*, 1952, *47*, 818–821.

MacCorquodale, K., and Meehl, P. E. On a distinction between hypothetical constructs and intervening variables. *Psychol. Rev.*, 1948, *55*, 95–107.

McGeoch, J. A. The influence of degree of interpolated learning upon retroactive inhibition. *Amer. J. Psychol.*, 1932, *44*, 695–708.

———. *The psychology of human learning: an introduction*. New York: Longmans, 1942.

Melton, A. W., and Irwin, J. McQ. The influence of degree of interpolated learning upon retroactive inhibition and the overt transfer of specific responses. *Amer. J. Psychol.*, 1940, *53*, 173–203.

Melton, A. W., and Von Lackum, W. J. Retroactive and proactive inhibition in retention: evidence for a two-factor theory of retroactive inhibition. *Amer. J. Psychol.*, 1941, *54*, 157–173.

Miller, G. A. Human memory and the storage of information. *IRE Trans. on Inform. Theory*, 1956, *IT–2*, 129–137.

Miller, G. A., Bruner, J. S., and Postman, L. Familiarity of letter sequences and tachistoscopic identification. *J. Gen. Psychol.*, 1954, *50*, 129–139.

Miller, G. A., and Selfridge, J. A. Verbal context and the recall of meaningful material. *Amer. J. Psychol.*, 1953, *63*, 176–185.

O'Neil, W. M. The effect of verbal association on tachistoscopic recognition. *Aust. J. Psychol.*, 1953, *5*, 42–45.

Osgood, C. E. The similarity paradox in human learning: A resolution. *Psychol. Rev.*, 1949, *56*, 132–143.

———. The nature and measurement of meaning. *Psychol. Bull.*, 1952, *49*, 197–237.

———. Behavior theory and the social sciences. *Behav. Sci.*, 1956, *1*, 167–185.

———. A behavioristic analysis of perception and language as cognitive phenomena. In Bruner et al., *Contemporary approaches to cognition*. Cambridge, Mass.: Harvard University Press, 1957.

Osgood, C. E., and Sebeok, T. A. Psycholinguistics: a survey of theory and research. *J. Abnorm. Soc. Psychol.*, 1954, *49*, Suppl. to No. 4.

Osgood, C. E., Suci, G. J., and Tannenbaum, P. H. *The measurement of meaning*. Urbana, Ill.: University of Illinois Press, 1957.

Pierce, J. R., and Karlin, J. E. Reading rates and the information rate of a human channel. *Bell System Tech. J.*, 1957, *36*, 497–516.

Postman, L. The present status of interference theory. In C. N. Cofer (ed.), *Verbal learning and verbal behavior*. New York: McGraw-Hill, 1961, pp. 152–179.

Rubenstein, H., and Aborn, M. Psycholinguistics. *Ann. Rev. Psychol.*, 1960, *11*, 291–322.

Russell, W. A. Assessment versus experimental acquisition of verbal habits. In C. N. Cofer (ed.), *Verbal learning and verbal behavior*. New York: McGraw-Hill, 1961, pp. 110–123.

Russell, W. A., and Storms, L. H. Implicit verbal chaining in paired-associate learning. *J. Exp. Psychol.*, 1955, *49*, 287–293.

Ryan, J. J. Comparison of verbal response transfer mediated by meaningfully similar and associated stimuli. *J. Exp. Psychol.*, 1960, *60*, 408–415.

Skinner, B. F. *Verbal behavior*. New York: Appleton-Century-Crofts, 1957.

Solarz, A. K. Latency of instrumental responses as a function of compatibility with the meaning of eliciting verbal signs. *J. Exp. Psychol.*, 1960, *59*, 239–245.

Staats, A. W., and Staats, C. K. Meaning and *m*: Correlated but separate. *Psychol. Rev.*, 1959, *66*, 136–144.

Staats, C. K., and Staats, A. W. Meaning established by classical conditioning. *J. Exp. Psychol.*, 1957, *54*, 74–80.

Thune, L. E., and Underwood, B. J. Retroactive inhibition as a function of degree of interpolated learning. *J. Exp. Psychol.*, 1943, *32*, 185–200.

Underwood, B. J. The effect of successive interpolations on retroactive and proactive inhibition. *Psychol. Monogr.*, 1945, *59*, No. 3.

———. Proactive and retroactive inhibition after five and forty-eight hours. *J. Exp. Psychol.*, 1948, *38*, 29–38.

———. Interference and forgetting. *Psychol. Rev.*, 1957, *64*, 49–60.

———. An evaluation of the Gibson theory of verbal learning. In C. N. Cofer (ed.), *Verbal learning and verbal behavior*. New York: McGraw-Hill, 1961.

Underwood, B. J., Runquist, W. N., and Schulz, R. W. Response learning in paired-associate lists as a function of intralist similarity. *J. Exp. Psychol.*, 1959, *52*, 119–126.

Watson, J. B. *Behavior: an introduction to comparative psychology*. New York: Holt, 1914.

30 | *Thinking*[1]

DONALD W. TAYLOR

The first systematic experimental investigation of thinking was carried out during the first decade of this century by a group of men associated with Kulpe at the University of Würzburg in Germany (Humphrey, 1951). The central question with which the Würzburg group was concerned was whether thinking is possible without the occurrence of images. Their work, and also that of Binet (1903) and Woodworth (1906), led to the conclusion that imageless thought is indeed common. It also resulted in a number of other contributions, including the introduction of such concepts as "set" (Einstellung), "task" (Aufgabe), and "determining tendency," in attempting to account for the processes which occur during thinking.

During the next four decades, the investigation of thinking was continued by individuals such as Wertheimer (1945), Duncker (1945), Spearman (1923), Vygotsky (1962), Maier (1930, 1940), and Piaget (1929). Much less attention, however, was devoted to this area than to other areas of psychology, such as perception, learning, motivation, or personality. This relative neglect of thinking was probably in part the result of the dominant position held by behaviorism, particularly among psychologists in the United States. But probably it was also in considerable measure the result of the complexity of problems encountered in the study of thinking, combined with a lack of adequate methods or tools for dealing with such problems.

Within the most recent decade, however, an important increase has occurred in the amount of time being devoted to the study of decision

[1] This paper was prepared during the year in which the author held an appointment as Research Fellow in the Center for Cognitive Studies at Harvard University and also simultaneously one as Senior Faculty Fellow at Yale University. Appreciation is due to Dr. Herbert Wells for assistance in the preparation of the pages dealing with Piaget. The author's program of research on thinking, of which the preparation of this paper was a part, is supported by Contract Nonr 609(20) between Yale and the Office of Naval Research and by a grant from the Ford Foundation.

475

making (Edwards, 1954, 1961), of problem solving (Taylor and Mc-Nemar, 1956; Gagne, 1959), and of creative thinking (Taylor 1960). These activities and others, as for example, the attainment of concepts (Bruner, Goodnow, and Austin, 1956), are all included within the concept of thinking. The task of a general theory of thinking is to specify the processes which account for the behavior observed in such varied activities.

Reference is often made to "the decision-making process," "the problem-solving process," or "the creative process." These terms would suggest that these activities can be clearly distinguished in terms of the processes involved. In fact, the view is sometimes taken explicitly that creativity, for example, is to be defined in terms of some unique process (Stein, 1956). Although this possibility cannot be excluded, present evidence would not appear to support such a view. Instead, creative thinking appears to be best defined not in terms of process, for it involves a variety of processes, but in terms of product: creativity is that thinking which results in the production of ideas (or other products) that are both novel and worthwhile (Taylor, 1960). Similarly, problem solving is that thinking which results in the solution of problems; decision making is that thinking which results in choice among alternative courses of action. From this view, decision making, problem solving, and creativity are all to be regarded as kinds of thinking. The question of the degree to which these and other kinds of thinking involve the same or different processes is a question to be solved by empirical investigation, not by definition. It may be appropriate at this point to recall Guilford's warning (1960) of the danger of assuming that one name means one process.

The task of a general theory of thinking is a very complex one. Marx noted earlier (see Chapter I) that difficulties encountered in attempts to construct general theories in other areas of psychology have led in recent years to more emphasis on the use of miniature theories or of models. Nothing in the preceding paragraph should be taken to question the desirability of similar emphasis on more limited theories or models in the study of thinking. Indeed, at this time, the optimal strategy may well be to attempt construction not of a general theory of thinking, but of a more limited theory of some particular kind of thinking—for example, of a theory of problem solving, or even perhaps a theory of the problem solving (or would it be decision making?) involved in playing chess.

Three different approaches to a theory of thinking will be discussed in the remainder of this chapter. These three were selected for discussion primarily because each has resulted in extended empirical work during the past ten years. They were selected also because the three differ markedly from one another in the way in which their concepts were developed and in the methods by which data are obtained to test their predictions.

Hence, they should serve well to illustrate the problems of theory construction in this area.

In the first chapter of this book, several different modes of theory construction were distinguished. It is of interest to note that although the three theoretical approaches to thinking to be discussed here differ markedly from one another, all three represent the same mode of theory construction. None of the three represents the classical position and none the positivistic position; all three would be described as functionalist in terms of the classification presented earlier.

The Structure of Intellect

The tool of factor analysis is central to the first approach to be described. Although this tool has been available since the late 1930s, its use has been greatly facilitated during the past ten years by the development of another tool, the high-speed electronic computer. Because factor analysis is mathematically complex, no adequate description of it can be given here. (For a more complete description, see Harmon, 1960.) The purpose of this technique, however, may perhaps be made clear by the following hypothetical example.

Assume that 24 different tests, which may be referred to as "Test A," "Test B," . . . "Test X," respectively, have been administered to each of 200 individuals. The question may be raised as to whether what is measured by Test A is the same as what is measured by Test B or by any of the remainder of the 24 tests. Or the question may be raised as to how many different basic variables are required to account for the variations in performance observed in the 24 tests. The first step in answering such questions is to compute the correlation of every test with every other test. The resulting correlation coefficients form a table which is referred to as a correlational matrix. By a factor analysis of the matrix, one can then determine how many independent (uncorrelated) factors are needed to account for the observed intercorrelations among the 24 tests and also how heavily each of the tests is loaded (weighted) with each of these factors. For example, only five different factors might be necessary to account for the intercorrelations among the 24 tests; thus, Tests A, B, H, and M might all be found to be loaded rather heavily by Factor I, Tests B, D, J, W, and X by Factor II, etc. Ordinarily, each test will be loaded with more than one factor; in other words, only rarely will a test be a pure measure of a single factor. If two or more tests have essentially the same loadings on the same factors, then what is measured by one is essentially the same as what is measured by the other(s). The nature of each factor is inferred from the properties which are common to the tests on which it loads heavily; disagreement sometimes occurs as to just how a particular factor is to be interpreted.

Thurstone was among those who contributed most to the early development of the technique of factor analysis (1935). He also made important contributions employing this technique in investigating thinking (1938). Additional important contributions resulted from the wartime research of psychologists in the United States Air Force. Within recent years, Guilford and his associates at the University of Southern California have been the most active in pursuing this approach. The questions with which they have been concerned are: "What are the phenomena that exist in the domain of human thinking? What are the different kinds of operations or processes?" (Guilford, 1960).

At least as proposed by Guilford (1960, p. 8), the psychologist's first step in the factor analytic investigation of a particular domain is the formulation of hypotheses:

In some area of behavior, such as that of visual perception for example, he might hypothesize that seeing visual depth is a function separate and distinct from all other visual-perception functions. According to the hypothesis, individuals should be expected to differ from one another in ability to deal with tasks involving depth perception.

The investigator then sets about developing three or more tests, each of which he thinks should indicate such individual differences and each of which is sufficiently different from others in this group of tests to justify believing that they are not just alternate forms of the same test. At this stage, he has no basis for knowing whether all of the tests do indeed indicate individual differences in the same attribute and, if they do, to what extent they succeed. The investigator will think of other perceptual functions that he thinks are distinct from depth perception and from one another and will develop a few tests for each additional hypothesized factor. He will expect the pattern of intercorrelations among all the tests so developed to tell him, through the operations of factor analysis, which of his hypotheses are supported and which are not.

Thus far, more than 50 different intellectual factors have been discovered, a number so large that we cannot discuss them individually here. Guilford (1959), however, has suggested that these factors can themselves be classified with respect to at least three major fundamental ways in which they differ. Figure 1 presents the model which he proposes for representing "the structure of intellect." The concept of information plays a central role in this model; this fact becomes apparent from an examination of the bases of classification proposed.

One dimension of the model divides factors in terms of the kinds of processes or operations involved. Two of the five classes represented on this dimension would not ordinarily be included within the concept of thinking; these two are memory, involving storage of information, and cognition, involving discovery, comprehension, or understanding, in other

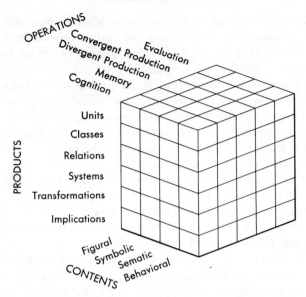

Figure 1.   Model for the structure of intellect. (Reprinted by permission of the author and publisher from J. P. Guilford, "Basic Conceptual Problems in the Psychology of Thinking" in E. Harms (ed.), *Fundamentals of Psychology: The Psychology of Thinking.* Annals of the New York Academy of Sciences, *91,* 1960, p. 10.)

words, awareness of information. Divergent production involves the generation of new information from perceived and remembered information, as does convergent production; in divergent thinking, however, a variety of answers is produced, whereas convergent thinking leads to one right answer or to a recognized best answer. Evaluation involves operations for determining whether information which is perceived, remembered, or produced meets certain criteria.

The second dimension of the model divides factors in terms of the kinds of products which result from thinking, or from cognizing or remembering (Guilford, 1960): "Units of information are relatively segregated items with 'thing' character. Classes are sets of items of information the members of which have certain common properties. Relations are various kinds of connections between items. Systems are organized groups of interacting items. Transformations are changes, shifts, or reinterpretations. Implications are extrapolations of information to antecedents, concomitants, and consequents."

The third way of classifying intellectual factors is in terms of kinds of contents. The factors known thus far involve three kinds of material or content: figural, symbolic, and semantic. The latter two categories include abilities involved in dealing with abstract material; symbolic material is composed of letters, digits, and other conventional signs, and semantic material is in the form of verbal meanings or ideas. Figural content is concrete material, information perceived directly through the senses, such as that resulting from visual perception of form or color. The behavioral category is included in the model purely on theoretical grounds to represent the general area sometimes called "social intelligence." Although no factor yet discovered falls within this category, the suggestion is made that "empathy," for example, probably belongs in the area of cognition of behavioral content.

It should be emphasized that the model includes many cells for which no factors have yet been identified. This is apparent from the fact that, even excluding the behavioral category, the model includes 90 (5 × 6 × 3) cells, many more than the some 55 factors discovered thus far. Moreover, more than one factor is found in some cells.

What Guilford's proposal involves may perhaps be somewhat clarified by giving examples (taken from Guilford, 1959) of specific factors and indicating where they fit in the model. Thus, the well-known ability of word fluency would represent the cell in the model involving the divergent production of symbolic units. The nature of this factor is suggested by the fact that one may test for it by items which ask the individual to list words satisfying a specified letter requirement, such as words beginning with the letter "s" or words ending in "-ion." The divergent production of semantic units is illustrated by the factor called ideational fluency; a typical test item calls for listing objects which are round and edible.

Convergent production of relations is represented by three factors, all involving what Spearman calls the "eduction of correlates." This kind of ability is illustrated by analogies tests which call for completion; with symbolic content, an item might read:

pots   stop   bard   drab   rats   ?
                                                                       ―

A semantic item which measures the eduction of correlates is:

The absence of sound is _____.

One final example may be given. Convergent production of semantic implications might be measured by an item of the following type:

Charles is younger than Robert.
Charles is older than Frank.
Who is older: Robert or Frank?

Further comment on this approach to thinking will be delayed until the other two approaches have been presented.

Steps in the Development of Thinking

The second approach to thinking to be described is that of Piaget and his collaborators at the University of Geneva, including particularly Inhelder. The reports of Piaget's early work, translated in the late 1920s and the early 1930s (e.g., 1929, 1930), received much attention in the United States. Paradoxically, however, the extensive more recent work of the 1940s and 1950s has been largely ignored (Wallach, 1963). Only within the past few years have psychologists in this country begun to give major attention to this approach (e.g., Bruner, 1960; Flavell, 1962; Wallach, 1963).

Probably at least two reasons account for this neglect. One is that Piaget's approach to theory construction is that of the philosophically-oriented European and is more speculative than is ordinarily congenial to American psychologists. His work is clearly influenced by two aspects of philosophy. The first is epistemology, the problem of knowledge, what it is and how it is acquired by the mind. The second is modern logic, whose influence is apparent in the psychological concepts which he employs; moreover, the relation between logic and thinking is in itself of interest to him. Also worth noting is that his early training was as a biologist and that he entered psychology intending to demonstrate continuity between biological and psychological development and functioning. The impact of this background upon his theory will be seen later.

A second reason for the relative neglect of Piaget's work is the nature of the method which he has largely used in collecting data, together with the way in which he presents this data. What Piaget calls the "clinical" method is characterized by somewhat flexible questions put to the subject in an attempt to probe his understanding of concrete situations with which he is presented. If the subject does not reach the correct answer initially, the experimenter may try to elicit it by additional questions, a kind of "testing of the limits" by which one can judge whether the unsuccessful subject is truly incapable of formulating the correct answer. In describing his results, Piaget presents sample protocols to illustrate conclusions reached. But with few exceptions, he does not present quantitative data. Indeed, he often does not indicate even the number of subjects or nature of the sample upon which the conclusions are based. It is hardly surprising that psychologists accustomed to seek rigor in theory construction, to emphasize control in experimental procedures, to value measurement, and to be concerned with statistical inference, should find much to question in Piaget's work and hence tend to ignore it. Nevertheless, much in that work demands attention if one is concerned with understanding thinking.

Piaget distinguishes five general stages from birth to adolescence in the development of thinking. His conceptualization of each of these is so complex that no adequate summary can be presented here. Instead, only a brief description of the nature of each will be given.

The *Sensori-motor Stage* (birth to 18 months or 2 years) precedes the appearance of true thinking. During this period the infant operates on a pre-verbal level; he is unable to produce mentally any linguistic or non-linguistic images or representations of external events, and as a result there is no cognitive activity which is purely internal. This period is one of rapid change. In fact, Piaget distinguishes some six substages within it (for a summary of most of his work on pre-adolescent children, see Piaget, 1950). During the first month of life, the infant has available only innate reflexes. The first habits, e.g., thumbsucking, are acquired during the second substage, from one to three months. Subsequently, the infant develops in turn the capacity for repeated manipulation of objects, for putting together means-end sequences, and for producing new-found phenomena in different ways, exploring various possibilities in them. The sixth substage, from about 18 to 24 months, is one of transition and involves rudimentary beginnings of thinking. The achievement that marks the transition is internalization of motor acts, thus making possible the testing of the results of such acts without actually carrying them out (internal trial and error). Two other forms of behavior which become possible with the advent of motor images are imitation after delay and symbolic play (make believe), both of which are important in the following period.

The *Pre-conceptual Stage* (2 to 4 years) involves the beginning of fully internalized, representational activity. At this time, the child develops the capacity to respond to symbols and signs; for Piaget this capacity is fundamental to the development of both thought and language. Symbols are generally prelinguistic and personal, whereas signs are arbitrary, based on social convention, in other words, linguistic forms. The symbols and signs which now become available do not permit true conceptual activity. Rather, the child can employ only what Piaget calls "pre-concepts," something midway between a class concept and the individual members of the class. The child at this stage cannot decide whether successively-encountered instances are the same or different members of a class. An example is that of a child who sees several cats while taking a walk and says of each: "Oh, there's the cat." He is as likely to say "cat" as "cats." The form of thinking of the child who can use only pre-concepts is called "transduction" by Piaget. Transduction involves jumping from particular to particular without the mediation of generalities at any point. Piaget gives an example of the child who was told that the local hunchback had been sick with the flu but was now recovered, and who concluded that the hunchback would no longer have his hump (1951, p. 231).

The *Intuitive Stage* (4 to 7 years) is a time of transition in that several developments during it come to fruition only in the stage which follows. One clear improvement at this stage, however, is that the child can now grasp the notion of a class with several similar members. But he cannot yet manipulate or coordinate classes in thought dealing with the relationships among them. The child cannot see a situation as a set of causal relations but only as a perceptual configuration, together with the possible modifications which he could produce by his own actions of pushing, picking up, etc. He can carry out simultaneously in thought only those manipulations which could be performed simultaneously in overt action. His thought, therefore, lacks a very important characteristic which will develop only in the next stage, that of *reversibility:* "the permanent possibility of returning to the starting point of the operation in question" (Inhelder and Piaget, 1958, p. 272). Inability to de-center is important in explaining some reasoning at this level. For example, the child may be asked to place the same amount of liquid in each of two glasses of the same size and shape. The liquid from one of the two is then poured into another taller and narrower glass. When asked which of the two glasses now holding liquid contains the more, children in the early intuitive stage reply that the taller and narrower glass contains more (because it is taller) or less (because it is narrower) but not that the two contain the same. They do this because they consider only the present perceptual configuration and because they center on height to the exclusion of width, or vice versa. The increasing ability to *de-center*, to be less and less dependent upon immediate perception, plays an important part in Piaget's explanation of the development of thinking. Among the developments during this stage which reach completion only in the following stage is that of the notion of abstract number and with it the closely related notions of class inclusion and of ordering or seriation. Piaget has devoted one volume (1952) to exploring these closely related developments in detail.

The *Stage of Concrete Operations* (7 or 8 to 11 or 12 years) is characterized by the appearance of true operations. Operations are actions which are "internalizable, reversible, and coordinated into systems which are characterized by laws which apply to the system as a whole" (1957, p. 8). Operations are to be distinguished from non-operational actions primarily on the basis of reversibility. The pre-operational child can put two objects together and later take them apart, but Piaget maintains that if he does, he does not find his starting point unchanged. The only reversible actions which the pre-operational child can achieve are those of performing (and perceiving) displacements in space (1950, p. 112). An operation may be reversed either by negation (undoing the action) or by compensation (performing an equivalent action). Among the laws or rules which characterize the system at this level are, for example: 1) Two successive operations may be combined into one to yield a new operation; 2) The same point may be reached by two different paths or series of operations. Eight separate groupings of operations exist at the level of concrete operations (Piaget, 1949). Of the eight, four concern classes and four relations. An example of the latter would be the grouping of operations involving the simple ordering of a number of classes. An example of the former would be the grouping involving multiplicative classification, i.e., classification by two or more criteria simultaneously. As implied by the name of the stage, the available operations can be performed only on concrete data, not on verbal propositions. Or more precisely, the child can work with perceptual data or with verbal data which can be easily visualized but is unable to handle data which is not amenable to representation by images.

The *Stage of Formal Operations* (11 or 12 to 14 or 15) continues the trend, important in earlier stages, of the subordination of reality to possibility, and, for the first time, possibility becomes more important in thinking than reality: "The most distinctive property of formal thought is this reversal of direction between *reality* and *possibility* . . . . [Thinking now] proceeds *from* what is possible *to* what is empirically real . . ." (Inhelder and Piaget, 1958, p. 251). Thinking at this stage is characterized by the fact that the individual now deals not only with objects, classes, and simple relations, but with verbal statements about these elements, with propositions and relations between propositions. The model which Piaget proposes to represent formal thinking draws heavily on the language of logic and is much too complex even to summarize here. We may note briefly that it employs propositional logic to symbolize the individual's thinking, it is based on a "combinational system" which allows the systematic expression of all the possible combinations of observable events in a situation, and it is organized under the rules of a comparatively complex "group" which brings together the two distinct forms of reversibility. For further information, the reader may find Inhelder and Piaget (1958) and Piaget (1949) most helpful.

Elsewhere in this volume, attention is given to Piaget's theory as a theory of development and to its limitations (see Selection 24). Hence, the emphasis in this present discussion has been upon Piaget's account of the nature of the processes involved in thinking at each of the five stages and not upon his explanation of just what processes lead to change from one stage to another. Indeed, this latter aspect of his theorizing seems most subject to criticism. At least brief mention, however, should be made of certain other concepts which are central to his work. Basic to his theorizing and reflecting his biological training is the concept of *adaptation*. Adaptation consists of two complementary processes, *assimilation* and *accommodation*, psychological analogies of the biological processes with the same names. Assimilation refers to the process of incorporating environmental stimuli into the existing cognitive structure; accommodation is the modification of cognitive structure by new stimuli impinging upon the organism. Although Piaget makes extensive use of these concepts and also of the concept of *equilibrium*, whose meaning is even less clear (Bruner, 1959), their lack of clarity seriously limits their explanatory value.

Information Processing System

The newest approach to a theory of thinking is that initiated by Newell, Shaw, and Simon of Carnegie Institute of Technology and the Rand Corporation. What they propose essentially is that the individual solving problems be regarded as an information processing system. Such a system includes (Newell, Shaw, and Simon, 1958[b]):

1. A control system consisting of a number of *memories*, which contain symbolized information and are interconnected by various ordering relations. . . .

2. A number of *primitive information processes*, which operate on the information in the memories. Each primitive process is a perfectly definite operation for which known physical mechanisms exist. . . .

3. A perfectly definite set of rules for combining these processes into whole *programs* of processing. From a program it is possible to deduce unequivocally what externally observable behaviors will be generated.

At this level of theorizing, *an explanation of an observed behavior of the organism is provided by a program of primitive information processes that generates this behavior.*

Newell, Shaw, and Simon point out that, viewed as a theory of behavior, a program is highly specific in that it represents only the behavior of one individual in one set of situations. If either the individual or the class of situations is changed, the program must be changed. (An important resulting advantage is that precise predictions may be made concerning the behavior of single subjects.) However, important similarities may be expected among the programs which represent the behavior of the same individual in different situations, or among those which represent the behavior of different individuals in the same situations. On the basis of these similarities, a more general theory of the kind of behavior under study may be developed. Eventually this process should be able to produce a quite general program representing behavior in a wide variety of situations.

In employing this approach to the study of problem solving, or of some other kind of thinking, one begins by attempting to identify the processes involved in the particular kind of thinking under study. Thus, for example, one interested in chess would begin by attempting to identify the processes by which the individual chooses one from among the many alternative moves available to him. When some hypotheses have been formulated as to the processes involved, one next attempts to write the program which employs these processes and which simulates the thinking of the human individual. The objective in writing the program is not only to achieve the result which the human thinker achieves, but also to employ the same processes in doing so.

Such programs are written not in English, or in any other language in common use, for all such languages are imprecise. Instead, the program is written in a special language—a fully precise language especially constructed for this purpose. By using one of these fully precise languages, one may write an unambiguous program for simulating whatever behavior is under study. Moreover, because the program is written in a precise language, an important additional advantage is gained. Such a program may be run on any large high-speed electronic computer by supplying the computer with the appropriate "interpretive deck." The computer translates and carries out in machine language the instructions which it receives in information processing language (Green, 1963). We should emphasize that the purpose is not to make the computer think, but simply to use the computer to determine whether the program when carried out simulates adequately the behavior of the human subject.

The question of whether a given simulation is adequate represents an important unsolved methodological problem. One possible test is that proposed by Turing (1956). To carry out Turing's test, one first suitably records several performances of the human subject and of the computer program in some common code. The coded records, one performance to a sheet, are then placed in a container, mixed up, and drawn at random. If an expert cannot reliably tell which performances were produced by the human subject and which by the computer, the simulation is judged to be adequate. This test is useful; however, some are disturbed by the dependence of the test upon the skill of the expert or the lack of it. This methodological problem is not peculiar to the study of thinking, but arises wherever simulation is employed. A similar problem is involved whenever one is concerned with the fit of any model. If any simulation or model is to be more than an *ex post facto* explanation, it must, of course, be useful in predicting the effect on behavior of changing experimental conditions.

For some kinds of problems, processes are known which have the very valuable property that if the problem has a solution, the process will, sooner or later, produce it. Such a process is called an algorithm. A simple example of an algorithm would be the process of opening a safe by trying all possible combinations, testing each in turn to see if it unlocks the safe. Formal education involves the acquisition of a variety of algorithms. If, for example, one wishes to find the maximum for a function, knowing the equation and being familiar with calculus, he takes the first derivative, sets it equal to zero, solves for x, and then continues with one of three alternative procedures.

A heuristic is a process for solving a problem which, if followed, may aid in solution but offers no guarantee of doing so. The eminent mathematician Polya has dealt at length with the use of heuristics in problem solving at the level of high school mathematics (1945). For example, one heuristic that he describes is "working backwards." One begins with the result that one wishes to achieve and attempts to work backwards step by step toward that which is given. In using the "make-a-plan" heuristic, the individual thinks of another problem similar to but simpler than the one he is trying to solve, solves that other problem, and then uses the successful procedure as a plan for attacking the more difficult original problem. In employing the "means-end" heuristic, the individual compares that which he has with that which he wishes to obtain, finds a difference between the two, and seeks an operation that will reduce this difference, repeating this procedure as often as necessary. In his two-volume work, *Mathematics and Plausible Reasoning*, Polya (1954) deals at greater length with the role of heuristic procedures in mathematical problem solving.

Only recently has the importance of heuristic procedures in human problem solving become fully evident. For those problems for which algorithms are known, such procedures are of course preferred. They guarantee solution if the problems have solutions. But for many important classes of problems, no algorithms are known. And for some types of problems for which algorithms are known, the time required to carry out such procedures is prohibitive. Chess, for example, is a finite game. An algorithm for playing chess is to consider all possible continuations of the game from the existing position to termination and then to select the move which would lead to checkmate of the opposing king. The mathematician Shannon has estimated that if this procedure were employed, it is unlikely that a single game would be completed within a lifetime, even if the players worked at the speed of the fastest electronic computers (Newell, Shaw, and Simon, 1958[a]). Instead, chess is played by employing such heuristics as "Protect your king," "Develop your pawns," "Try to control the center of the board," etc.

Within the past few years, programs have been written employing heuristic processes and simulating important kinds of human thinking. One of the first was the Logic Theorist, a program capable of discovering proofs for theorems in elementary symbolic logic (Newell, Shaw, and Simon, 1958[b]). A variety of experiments were carried out in which this program was run upon the Johnniac, a high-speed digital computer. The results were impressive. *Principia Mathematica* by Whitehead and Russell is, of course, a classic of modern symbolic logic. In one experiment, the Logic Theorist, employing the same axioms, definitions, and rules used in the *Principia*, was presented with the problem of constructing in turn a valid proof of each of the first 52 theorems in Chapter 2 of the *Principia* in the order in which they appear there. Whenever a theorem was proved, it was stored in memory and was available, together with the original axioms, for use in proving subsequent theorems. Under these conditions, the Logic Theorist succeeded in proving 38 of the 52 theorems and did so in times ranging from less than a minute to more than 15 minutes. We should emphasize that the Logic Theorist does not carry out exhaustive searches of all possibilities. Instead, like human thinkers, it employs heuristic methods in conducting selective searches leading to the discovery of proofs. To discover a proof requires what is ordinarily called "ingenuity," "imagination," or "good intuitive judgment." In one instance, the Logic Theorist actually produced a proof more elegant than that originally discovered by Whitehead and Russell (Newell, Shaw, and Simon, 1958c).

More recently, the Logic Theorist has been superseded by the General Problem Solver (Newell, Shaw, and Simon, 1959; Newell and Simon, 1961). Although originally devised to simulate the behavior of specific human subjects solving problems in symbolic logic, it is called "general" because available evidence indicates that this newer program can also do trigonometric identities, perform formal integration, and solve algebraic equations; moreover, there is reason to hope that it can be extended to an even wider range of tasks (Newell and Simon, 1959). What is noteworthy is that the General Problem Solver employs only two principal heuristics, the "means-end" heuristic and the "make-a-plan" heuristic, both of which were described above. One clear result of the use of simulation thus far has been to provide rigorous evidence of the power of heuristic processes in solving problems, procedures which were often previously considered as rather trivial, if indeed they were considered at all.

Programs have also been written for simulating recognition of patterns and rote learning (Feigenbaum, 1961), binary choice (Feldman, 1961), attainment of concepts (Hovland and Hunt, 1961; Hunt, 1962), discovering proofs of theorems in plane geometry (Gelernter and Rochester, 1958), and playing chess (Newell, Shaw, and Simon, 1958[a]). For information concerning this and other work on simulation, the reader must refer to the original papers or to books by Miller, Galanter, and Pribram (1960), Green (1962), and Borko (1962).

Conclusions

Certain brief comments concerning these three quite different approaches to a theory of thinking may be appropriate at this point.

The factor analytic approach meets well several of the criteria of scientific theory construction described in the first chapter. The search for the smallest number of factors which will account for the intercorrelations among the empirically-measured variables exemplifies the principle of parsimony. Empirical data are obtained by carefully constructed and administered tests, hence, under well-controlled conditions. The operations defining the constructs are, though complex, clearly specified. The hypotheses are testable.

This approach, nevertheless, has limitations some of which should be mentioned. One limitation stems from the fact that a single investigation involves the administration of a fairly large number of tests to each of a large number of subjects. As a result, the time which can be allotted for each test is small. To be reliable, a test ordinarily must be composed of a number of items. Hence, the time available per item is very small. The result is that the problems included in such tests are very short, typically of the kinds given as examples above. For this reason, processes important in solving longer and more complex kinds of problems may escape discovery by the factor analytic investigator. At this point, at least, the possibility seems doubtful that this approach would lead to the identification of other processes comparable to the "means-end" or the "make-a-plan" heuristics.

The model presented in Figure 1 is very useful for aiding comprehension of the numerous intellectual factors thus far discovered. Two kinds of questions, however, may be raised concerning it as a "model for the structure of intellect." The first has to do with the way in which the model was constructed. Whereas factors are identified by the application of factor analysis to empirical data, the three dimensions of the model result simply from a logical analysis of known factors. Since the factors are described as independent or uncorrelated, a factor analysis of known factors would presumably yield no basis for classifying them as in the proposed model. What then is the empirical justification for the model? Note also that the order of the classes on each dimension, though logically plausible, is subject to question.

Question may also be raised concerning the use of the term "structure." Factor analysis provides a list of what may be considered to be elementary processes in thinking. It may also be used to determine the relative importance of these processes in solving complex problems (Guilford, 1960). But it provides no account of how these processes fit together in solving a problem or making a decision. At least some psychologists would prefer to use the term "structure" in referring to this general problem, one perhaps better attacked by other approaches.

Piaget's work, if examined only in terms of the various criteria of theory construction alluded to above, must be evaluated less favorably than that of Guilford. Piaget's "clinical" method of obtaining data is not well controlled. The empirical referents of his constructs are not clearly specified. In fact, his writing is often difficult to understand or interpret. Moreover, just how some of his hypotheses—those, for example, involving accommodation, assimilation, or equilibrium—would be tested is not clear.

Perhaps the most important fact, however, about Piaget's theory is that it has resulted in extensive additions to empirical knowledge. Thus, Wallach (1963) writes that when one disentangles empirical description from speculative theory, "there emerges an awareness that Piaget and others doing related work . . . have made an unparalleled contribution to the task of observing and describing the development of thinking from birth through adolescence." Wallach (1963) provides a thorough summary of that contribution.

The concept of "stage" plays a central role for Piaget. Kessen (1962) points out that this concept can be employed as a theoretical construct in several fundamentally different ways, at least three of which are represented in Piaget's work: that in which stage is used as a descriptive concept emphasizing sequence in development; that in which stages are taken "as parametric variations of a fundamental set of theoretical statements" (variation in mental structure as a function of assimilation and accommodation); that in which successive stages are seen as involving "operation of different rule-systems." It is the last which is of most interest. In a sense, Piaget has not one but several theories of thinking, one for each of the stages he describes. That fact implies that a program written to simulate thinking at one stage would be essentially different from one written to simulate thinking at another stage (Kessen, 1962), an interesting implication which remains to be tested.

Of the three approaches to thinking, the one that regards the thinker as an information processing system and employs simulation is the one which appears to offer the most promise; this promise, however, remains to be justified. The use of simulation by programming a computer is, of course, not limited to the study of thinking. One may undertake to simulate almost any behavior of individuals or of groups. In fact, in all of the social sciences, simulation promises to be one of the most useful tools available.

The use of simulation by writing programs for a computer has several advantages. A model or theory expressed in the form of a computer program is fully precise. By employing a computer, one may determine quickly and rigorously the consequences of models or theories of a complexity which would otherwise be unmanageable. Within the model expressed in an information processing language many more variables can be included than could be handled within a model employing the familiar methods of mathematics. Whereas mathematical models must often be limited to linear relations among variables, the model expressed in this kind of computer program may easily include nonlinear relations.

Any of a number of theories of thinking may be expressed in a program written in an information processing language. The Logic Theorist is a miniature theory of one particular kind of thinking. The General Problem Solver is still a limited theory, but one of a wider range of thinking. If a particular program of this kind turns out to be inadequate to simulate human thinking even in a limited area, this failure in no sense will invalidate the general approach. Indeed, progress will require the replacement both of less adequate by more adequate simulations of given kinds of thinking and of programs which are quite limited by those which are more general in the kinds of thinking which they simulate.

References

Binet, A. *L'etude Experimentale de l'intelligence*. Paris, 1903.

Borko, H. (ed.). *Computer applications in the behavioral sciences*. Englewood Cliffs, N.J.: Prentice-Hall, 1962.

Bruner, J. S. Inhelder and Piaget's *The growth of logical thinking*. I: A psychologist's viewpoint. *British J. Psychol.*, 1959, *50*, 363–370.

———. Individual and collective problems in the study of thinking. In E. Harms (ed.), *Fundamentals of psychology: the psychology of thinking*. Annals of the New York Academy of Sciences, 1960, *91*, Art. 1, pp. 22–37.

Bruner, J. S., Goodnow, Jacqueline J., and Austin, G. A. *A study of thinking*. New York: Wiley, 1956.

Duncker, K. On problem-solving (trans. by Lynne S. Lees). *Psychol. Monogr.*, 1945, *58*, No. 5 (No. 270 entire).

Edwards, W. The theory of decision making. *Psychol. Bull.*, 1954, *51*, 380–417.

———. Behavioral decision theory. In P. R. Farnsworth (ed.), *Annual review of psychology*. Palo Alto, Calif.: Annual Reviews, Inc., 1961, *12*, pp. 473–498.

Feigenbaum, E. The simulation of verbal learning behavior. *Proc. Western Joint Computer Conf.*, 1961, *19*, 121–132.

Feldman, J. Simulation of behavior in the binary choice experiment. *Proc. Western Joint Computer Conf.*, 1961, *19*, 133–144.

Flavell, J. *The developmental psychology of Jean Piaget*. 1962 (in press).

Gagné, R. M. Problem solving and thinking. In P. R. Farnsworth (ed.), *Annual review of psychology*. Palo Alto, Calif.: Annual Reviews, Inc., 1959, *10*, pp. 147–172.

Gelernter, H. L., and Rochester, N. Intelligent behavior in problem-solving machines. *IBM J. Res. Develop.*, 1958, *2*, 336–345.

Green, B. F. *Digital computers in research.* 1963 (in press).

Guilford, J. P. Three faces of intellect. *Amer. Psychologist*, 1959, *14*, 469–479.

———. Basic conceptual problems in the psychology of thinking. In E. Harms (ed.), *Fundamentals of psychology: the psychology of thinking.* Annals of the New York Academy of Sciences, 1960, *91*, Art. 1, pp. 6–21.

Harmon, H. H. *Modern factor analysis.* Chicago: Univ. of Chicago Press, 1960.

Hovland, C. I., and Hunt, E. B. Programming a model of human concept formulation. *Proc. Western Joint Computer Conf.*, 1961, *19*, 145–155.

Humphrey, G. *Thinking.* New York: Wiley, 1951.

Hunt, E. B. *Concept learning.* New York: Wiley, 1962.

Inhelder, Bärbel, and Piaget, J. *The growth of logical thinking from childhood to adolescence.* New York: Basic Books, 1958.

Kessen, W. Stage and structure in the study of children. In W. Kessen and Clementina Kuhlman (eds.), *The thought of the child. Monogr. Soc. Res. Child Develpm.* 1962.

Maier, N. R. F. Reasoning in humans. *J. Comp. Psychol.*, 1930, *10*, 115–143.

———. The behavior mechanisms concerned with problem solving. *Psychol. Rev.*, 1940, *47*, 43–58.

Miller, G. A., Galanter, E., and Pribram, K. H. *Plans and the structure of behavior.* New York: Holt, 1960.

Newell, A., Shaw, J. C., and Simon, H. A. Chess-playing programs and the problem of complexity. *IBM J. Res. Develop.*, 1958, *2*, 320–335. (a)

———. Elements of a theory of human problem solving. *Psychol. Rev.*, 1958, *65*, 151–166 (b).

———. The processes of creative thinking. The RAND Corporation, Paper P–1320, August, 1958 (c).

———. Report on a general problem-solving program. The RAND Corporation, Paper P–1584, February, 1959.

Newell, A., and Simon, H. A. The simulation of human thought. The RAND Corporation, Paper P–1734, June, 1959.

———. Computer simulation of human thinking. *Science*, 1961, *134*, 2011–2017.

Piaget, J. *The child's conception of the world.* New York: Harcourt, Brace, 1929.

———. *The child's conception of physical causality.* New York: Harcourt, Brace, 1930.

———. *Traité de logique.* Paris: Librarie Armand Colin, 1949.

———. *The psychology of intelligence.* London: Routledge and Kegan Paul, 1950.

———. *Play, dreams and imitation in childhood.* New York: Norton, 1951.

———. *The child's conception of number.* London: Routledge and Kegan Paul, 1952.

———. *Logic and psychology.* New York: Basic Books, 1957.

Polya, G. *How to solve it.* Princeton: Princeton Univ. Press, 1945.

———. *Mathematics and plausible reasoning.* Princeton: Princeton Univ. Press, 1954.

Spearman, C. *The nature of "intelligence" and the principles of cognition.* London: Macmillan, 1923.

Stein, M. I. A transactional approach to creativity. In C. W. Taylor (ed.),

Research conference on the identification of creative scientific talent. Salt Lake City, Utah: Univ. of Utah Press, 1956, pp. 171–181.

Taylor, D. W. Thinking and creativity. In E. Harms (ed.), *Fundamentals of psychology: the psychology of thinking.* Annals of the New York Academy of Sciences, 1960, *91,* Art. 1, pp. 108–127.

Taylor, D. W., and McNemar, Olga W. *Problem solving and thinking.* In C. P. Stone (ed.), *Annual Review of Psychology.* Stanford, Calif.: Annual Review, Inc., 1955, *6,* pp. 455–482.

Thurstone, L. L. *The vectors of mind.* Chicago: Univ. of Chicago Press, 1935, p. 266.

——. Primary mental abilities. *Psychometric Monogr.,* 1938, *1,* 1–121.

Turing, A. M. Can a machine think? In J. R. Newman (ed.), *The World of Mathematics,* Vol. 4. New York: Simon and Schuster, 1956, pp. 2099–2123.

Vygotsky, L. S. *Thought and language.* New York: Wiley, 1962.

Wallach, M. A. Research on children's thinking. In *1963 Yearbook of the National Society for the Study of Education: Child psychology.* 1963 (in press).

Wertheimer, M. *Productive thinking.* New York: Harper, 1945.

Woodworth, R. S. Imageless thought. *J. Phil.,* 1906, *3,* 701–708.

CHAPTER X

Learning Processes

THIS CHAPTER INCLUDES two very thorough reviews of theory construction and one specimen development of a mathematical model of learning. In the first selection, William W. Grings offers a comprehensive treatment of theory in classical conditioning. He analyzes in particular the theories of Spence, Razran, Woodworth, and current Russian workers. The second selection, by John W. Cotton, is a detailed examination of some of the major theoretical efforts and problems in the area of instrumental learning. The scope and depth of Cotton's analysis lends credence to his opening contention that learning theories are among the best-developed theories in psychology. The final selection in the chapter is Richard C. Atkinson's exposition of the development of a specific mathematical model with perceptual as well as learning aspects. (The reader also is referred to Selection 6, a more general treatment of mathematical models of learning by William K. Estes, and to Selection 35, in which Mueller and McGill consider signal detection theory.)

31 | *Classical Conditioning*

WILLIAM W. GRINGS

The distinguishing feature of classical conditioning is a particular set of experimental conditions or operations. Two stimuli are presented in a temporal relation (pairing), and changes in behavior with reference to one of the stimuli are produced. The first stimulus, the conditioned stimulus (CS), is, at the outset, relatively incapable of bringing about the learned behavior, the conditioned response (CR). The second stimulus, the unconditioned stimulus (UCS), is initially adequate to elicit the unconditioned response (UCR), which is in some definable way related to the learned behavior (the CR).

Temporal pairing of the stimuli is described in terms of a CS-UCS interval, referring usually to the time from onset of the CS to the onset of the UCS. When the CS is followed by the UCS, the term *forward* conditioning is applied; when the CS is preceded by the UCS, the term *backward* conditioning is used. If the CS remains on until the UCS comes on, the situation is described as *delay* conditioning, whereas if the CS ceases prior to the onset of the UCS, *trace* conditioning results.

The best-known arrangement for illustrating these events is that of salivary conditioning, where a dog is observed in an environment in which controlled stimuli can be presented and the amount of saliva secreted can be measured. The CS may be some sound or light and the UCS the insertion of meat powder into the dog's mouth. The responses (UCR and CR) are secretions of saliva measured in volume or by weight. The other important parameter in the situation is the number of trials (i.e., the number of paired presentations of the CS and UCS). The important experimental observation is the development of salivation secretion (CR) as a response to the previously inadequate stimulus (CS).

Psychologists generally agree that the term *classical* conditioning refers to one aspect of a more general term, *conditioning*. The emphasis in classical conditioning is upon various forms of the basic temporal arrangement (CS paired with UCS) through a sequence of trials in which the occurrence of the UCS is not contingent upon the occurrence of a particular response. The implications of this last definitional limitation can be seen by noting other common modifiers of the general term, "conditioning."

The distinction above focuses upon the difference between *classical* conditioning and *instrumental* conditioning, as suggested by the following quotation. "In the first type the occurrence of the CR results in no change in the procedure; the UCS is presented invariably at a fixed interval after the CS. In the instrumental training, however, the CS is followed by a reward (or an avoidance of punishment) only when the appropriate response is made to it" (Hilgard and Marquis, 1940, pp. 27–28). For further discussion of this distinction, see Kimble (1961) and Mowrer (1960).

The above quotation introduces other distinctive notions when it implies that *avoidance* conditioning might be different from *reward* conditioning. Then, too, the organism might not completely avoid the noxious UCS but might escape from it by some appropriate response, at which time *escape* conditioning would occur. Still another modifier to the term "conditioning" comes from consideration of how the conditioned response comes about. Some responses of the organism appear to be elicited by stimuli, whereas others appear to be emitted by the organism. The situation involving behavior elicited by a stimulus came to be called *respondent* conditioning in order to differentiate it from that involving behavior not correlated with specific eliciting stimuli, called *operant* conditioning (Skinner, 1938, pp. 18–21).

These distinctions point out the fact that the concept "conditioning" has expanded in scope since the early description of the Pavlovian paradigm. What was originally a very limited domain has been extended to encompass most of behavior modification under the one term, "conditioning." At the extreme, from the standpoint of theoretical methodology, the concept of conditioning cannot be differentiated from the concept "learning."

To stay within the space limitations of this review, arbitrary restriction to the scope of the term "classical conditioning" must be made. Only the simplest examples of the concept will be included: those where the necessary elements are an originally inadequate stimulus (a CS), an adequate stimulus (the UCS, which by definition elicits a UCR), some form of paired presentation of these events (CS, UCS, UCR), and the consequent appearance of a response (the CR), elicited by the CS and bearing specified properties of the UCR. The occurrence of the UCS is not contingent upon a response of the organism.

Two major sub-classes of events will depend upon whether the UCS implies administration of pain to the organism (noxious conditioning) or positive stimulation (reward conditioning). These sub-classes are not exhaustive, even in this restricted definition, for situations exist which do not readily fit into either (e.g., conditioning of passive movements; cf. Doehring, 1957).

Some of the major areas which will be omitted from further discussion are instrumental conditioning, avoidance conditioning, and escape conditioning. Concentration on situations where the CR is made in response to a specific cue (CS) will lead to omission of operant conditioning. One further omission will be the circumstance where the problem involves the learning of choice response. The above limitations are made at the sacrifice of vast empirical-theoretical areas, like those of Skinner (1938, 1959) and Estes (1959).

Origins of Theory

Theory in the subject-matter area of classical conditioning has many quite different roots. In the present section an attempt will be made to sketch briefly some of these as an introduction to a later discussion of representative modern points of view. Among the origins of theory which will be noted are those where emphasis is upon physiological explanation, those where the goal is prediction of behavior by deductions from higher-order concepts which are essentially behavioral, and those where the emphasis is on the definition and manipulation of empirical parameters determining the amount and retention of conditioning.

Because Pavlov was a physiologist, it is not surprising to find that his theoretical constructs rested heavily on biological structure and function. His principal concepts were those of cortical excitation and cortical inhibition. The basic fact of conditioning was explained by assuming that stimulation (by either CS or UCS) is accompanied by excitation in the cerebral cortex. This excitation was assumed to be localized or focused on the cortex but to irradiate to other points. In this way the excitation from the CS could reach the points of excitation of the UCS and its resulting UCR. Repetition (i.e., a succession of paired presentations) presumably increases the opportunity for excitation from the two loci to irradiate and overlap. Inhibition as well as excitation could occur as a result of interaction of cortical activity, i.e., inhibition of the activity of one locus would be brought about as the result of activity of some other locus in a manner basically similar to irradiation of excitation.

Time and space do not permit elaboration, or even enumeration, of the concepts from Pavlov's early theory which have contributed to the present-day status of knowledge in the area of classical conditioning. However, one point requires review at this time. That is the question of how Pavlov developed his theory and how he related the theory to his experimental research work.

First of all, the concepts involved in the theory were generated from ideas about how the brain functions. Concepts like excitation, inhibition, and irradiation were current neurological concepts of the period. The "behavioral" aspects of the situation were not of primary importance in themselves. They provided a novel way to get at the study of the nervous system. To put this more simply, Pavlov was interested in explaining the function of the nervous system in controlling bodily processes; he discovered that the observations of stimuli and related reflexes provided regularities which seemed to reflect some of his notions about how the nervous system works. Thereupon, he began to postulate some hypothetical concepts of nervous system function, relating these concepts to subclasses of observable (stimulus and response) events. The labels for the observable events were either taken from neurophysiology (e.g., positive and negative induction) or chosen to describe the observations themselves (e.g., secondary conditioned reflexes).

In this simple identification of behavioral events with cortical events lies the main weakness of Pavlov's theory. The cortical events are entirely inferred entities and are used to predict behavior events. The observed behavior events come to require new explanatory concepts which are achieved by hypothesizing more specific cortico-neural events. As long as this approach is used, two major alternatives for continued development exist. One is eventually to find direct and independent evidence to support the neurological concepts. The other is to continue to use the cortical tie-in for purposes of reasoning by analogy, as one would proceed in constructing a formal model. Here the significance of the model would eventually be judged in terms of the success with which objective operations could be developed for proceeding from the formal (hypothetical) to the observable systems. It is probably safe to assume that Pavlov had no intention of following the latter path. Therefore, his theory must ultimately be evaluated in terms of the extent to which certain neurological concepts are validated.

From the standpoint of theoretical methodology, the earliest American workers were predominantly impressed by another feature of classical conditioning. Instead of seeing the phenomenon of classical conditioning as a way to the nervous system, they saw it as a neat method for objectifying behavior study. In a period where empirical studies of behavior were plagued with "private experience" and "phenomenal givens," the simple operations of stimulus pairing provided an effective tool for the behaviorists. The work of Watson (1916, 1919) is probably the best-known example of this phase of theoretical development.

With the rapid rise of interest in conditioning that occurred in the United States in the late 1920s and 1930s, the theoretical methodological picture became quite complex. There remained those persons who worked predominantly with neurological concepts. The bulk of researchers, however, turned to behavior concepts. Since this was also the period of increased influence of logical positivism (see Pratt, 1938), theories showed increasing concern for relating general explanatory concepts to observable events which could be deduced directly from the concepts. A striking increase occurred in the relations of theory development to formal logic.

Three major theoretical efforts of the period are of particular relevance here, because all rested their major arguments upon certain essential or fundamental behavior concepts. Hull (1943, 1951) was very much concerned with the concept "motivation" and its related concept "reinforcement" as necessary and sufficient conditions to learning. Many originally physiological concepts were taken over from Pavlov and given more strictly behavioral definitions. Notable examples are "cortical excitation," which became an intervening behavior variable "excitatory potential," defined operationally in terms of stimulus and response events; and "cortical inhibition," redefined as "inhibitory potential," also an intervening variable. The extent to which the concepts required neurophysiological specification was a point of disagreement between Hull and some of his associates (e.g., Spence, 1956, p. 55). Hull originally stressed a strict hypothetico-deductive approach specifying axioms, postulates, and corollaries. However, as his system developed further, he came eventually to an intervening-variable approach. His higher-order concepts were developed from empirical events as intervening variables defined in terms of stimulus variables or response variables (Bergmann and Spence, 1941).

While Hull was emphasizing the concept of reinforcement, Guthrie (1932, 1935) was developing persuasive arguments for the sufficiency of the concept of contiguity. He stressed, particularly, the importance of the temporal coincidence of a movement or a response and the termination of the signalling stimulus (the CS). A recent re-emphasis of this argument has been made (Guthrie, 1959).

Another major behavioral emphasis of the period was upon cognitive factors (Tolman, 1932). Conditioning was viewed as the establishment of a relationship between two stimuli, the sign and the significate. "The acquisition of a conditioned response is in reality the building up of a sign-gestalt-expectation" (p. 330). In other words, the organism was assumed to learn that the UCS follows the CS, with the CS providing a signal to produce an expectation of the UCS to follow.

The theories which will be considered in more detail later show clearly the influence of these earlier conceptual developments. Spence emphasizes motivation and reinforcement concepts, Razran stresses contiguity, and Woodworth re-emphasizes expectations. In each of the above cases, the theoretical emphasis is upon fairly general behavioral concepts (reinforcement, contiguity, and expectation).

In contrast with this stress upon general behavior concepts as a basis for deduction is the approach which developed general terms primarily to summarize and organize empirical events. As a basis for considering the empirical origin of manipulable parameters, a brief review of the experimental paradigm will be made. Note Figure 1. In diagram (a), a brief CS is followed immediately by a brief UCS. The CS-UCS interval is generally defined as the time period between the onset of the CS and the onset of the UCS. The major difference, then, between (a) and (b) is that the CS-UCS interval has changed; (b) would be called a longer delay conditioning than (a). Discussion is currently active as to the existence of a simple monotonic function showing differences in the amount of conditioning with variation in the delay interval. A few years ago, this question was felt to have been answered. However, this function has been found to depend upon the nature of the response being conditioned, with the possibility still remaining that it is in part a function of the natural latency of the responses at issue (particularly as to a possible

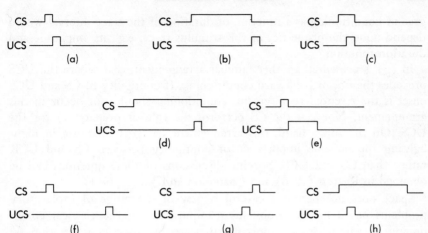

Figure 1.   Some simple experimental manipulations of the Pavlovian paradigm.

difference between skeletal and autonomic responses; cf. Mowrer, 1960; Kimble, 1961).

Compare diagrams (a) and (b) with diagrams (c) and (d). In the latter pair, note that the UCS comes on before the CS goes off. The temporal coincidence, then, is between the CS offset and the UCS offset. In positive reward conditioning, we might hypothesize that a maximum change in motivation is brought about by the UCS at its onset through maximum drive induction. In noxious conditioning, we might argue that the release of the shock would provide drive reduction and that cessation of the UCS is the important aspect. This leads to a family of questions concerning the contiguity of the CS with either the onset or the offset of the UCS (for examples, see Solomon and Brush, 1956).

If stimulus offset is the important determiner, the duration of the UCS becomes an important parameter. Note example (e). A difference might be predicted between (a) and (e) since the cessation of the UCS is farther removed in time from the CS in (e) than in (a). This might be attributed to a greater delay in drive reduction in (e), a line of reasoning which has been followed by a number of persons. For a concise summary of the role which this distinction has played in discussions of reinforcement in classical conditioning theory, see Brown (1961, pp. 339–348).

Note example (f), which illustrates the trace conditioning situation, i.e., the CS is off before the UCS comes on. Strict temporal contiguity of stimuli would not appear to be obtained, yet conditioning does occur. Explanation of this result usually introduces the assumption of a stimulus trace which persists for a period after the physical stimulus ceases. Degree of conditioning as a function of duration of the trace interval would depend upon the properties of this stimulus trace, e.g., its amplitude and duration function.

In (g) is presented another familiar arrangement, that where the UCS precedes the CS, or backward conditioning. If contiguity of CS and UCS onset is the essential requirement, conditioning should not occur in this arrangement. Nor can the CS perform the role of preparation for the UCS. On the other hand, this arrangement has particular use in highlighting the possible importance of contiguity between CS and UCR rather than CS and UCS. Specific discussions of these questions can be obtained in Razran (1956) and Champion and Jones (1961).

Space does not permit a careful review of the range of explanatory problems posed by these obvious manipulations of the classical conditioning paradigm. It is important to note that such concentration on manipulations of stimulus onsets and offsets leaves untouched large classes of important parameters, such as stimulus intensities and schedules of reinforcement. Another point which is not so obvious is that stimulus manipulations for operational definition of higher-level concepts lead to problems of experimental confounding. As one example of this problem, consider the explanation of an observed difference in performance from situation (a) to situation (b) in Figure 1. The observed difference might be "explained" as due to a longer delay interval (longer CS-UCS interval). However, we can just as reasonably attribute it to a longer duration of the CS, a situation for which a control comparison might be sought, as in example (h). But, equating stimulus duration while varying CS-UCS interval (defined as time between onsets) introduces the kind of "overlap" variation discussed in connection with example (d).

Much work must be done in the area of classical conditioning before multifold empirical arrangements and higher-order explanatory constructs can be brought into the kind of agreement which is the ideal of behavioral science.

Some Contemporary Theories

Several brief summaries of contemporary theories will now be presented. Some conjectures about their points of origin will be made, and their principal orienting predispositions toward theory will be noted. The specific examples were chosen because they are representative of the present-day state of theory and because they differ in well-defined ways with respect to the manner in which theory is developed and used. The examples are identified with Spence, Razran, Woodworth, and present-day Russian workers.

The first of these (Spence) is representative of the American trend toward conceptual or constructive theories, where an effort is made to develop a total system eventually capable of covering all behavior within a particular class. The theory of Spence, in this respect, is a systematic attempt, characterized by strong efforts to tie higher-level constructs to observable data, to keep surplus meaning to a minimum, and to emphasize an intervening-variable approach to the explanation of relations between stimuli and responses. Little tendency toward neurologizing is shown, the theory remaining behavioral throughout. The tradition in which it is set has generally been called a "reinforcement" tradition, in the sense that variables beyond simple temporal conjunction of stimuli and responses are implied and these extra elements are related to the general behavior concept of "motivation."

The second example (Razran) is characterized by constructs built from empirical events. A preference for some grounding in the nervous system is quite evident. Explanatory efforts are focused upon the particular phenomena at issue here—classical conditioning—with the result that the concepts are defined in terms of events of the Pavlovian paradigm. The relations postulated are predominantly empirical, and the higher-order notions provide supplemental reductive explanation through the use of hypothetical neural constructs. A major influence on this theory has been the empirical data of the Russian laboratories with their emphasis upon empirical study rather than theorizing.

An illustrative preliminary comparison between Spence and Razran can be made in terms of the concepts which are of central importance to them as far as explanation is concerned. Spence emphasized the development of higher-order behavioral constructs, chief among which are mediating response mechanisms. These are hypothesized responses occurring inside the organism in the form of motivational (emotional) responses, goal anticipatory responses, or frustration responses. For Razran, on the other hand, emphasis is upon stimulus and response magnitudes, with higher-order explanations dependent upon concepts which refer to hypothetical neural states to which properties correlated with stimulus and response magnitudes can be attached.

The third example (Woodworth) is chosen because it represents a much different line of development. It has roots in phenomenal methods of description and deals with classes of variables which are not emphasized in the other approaches. These are perceptual and cognitive variables, and the theory can be classed as representative of "expectancy" explanations of conditioning phenomena. One point of striking difference between the third example and the other two is the lack of emphasis on the empirical basis for the concepts. That is, concepts are introduced freely for explanatory purposes, but the logical relations between the concepts and the observable events on which they are based are not specified in as much detail as in the other two examples.

SPENCE The present theory of Spence is identified historically with the theory of Hull. Their common goal is a network of concepts or a theoretical structure which will quantitatively relate performance variables and determining variables in the conditioning situation. The observable conditions are environmental manipulations or individual differences on the independent-variable side and denotable characteristics of response on the performance side. Intervening variables are of two main classes: excitatory, tending to increase probability of response, and inhibitory, tending to reduce likelihood of response.

Neither Hull nor Spence has sought to develop a theory devoted exclusively to classical conditioning, for both have been interested in broader aspects of learning—instrumental conditioning, selective learning, and serial learning. Published discussions shift frequently from classical to instrumental conditioning situations, giving rise to difficulty in determining specific reference for particular concepts in one learning situation as separate from the other.

What is even more important is the extent to which assumptions about classical conditioning are basic to the development of concepts occupying important theoretical positions in explaining other forms of learning. In accounting for performance in instrumental learning situations, for example, motivational concepts, such as "drive" and "incentive motivation," are very important. Definitions of these concepts have rested upon prior assumptions about classical conditioning. "Incentive motivation" is a form of learned motivation, and the process by which it is learned may be classical conditioning. In describing Spence on this point, Mowrer asserts "that all learning is in the nature of classical conditioning and that so-called instrumental conditioning is derived therefrom" (1960, p. 266).

Without further background discussion of concepts of instrumental conditioning *per se*, we cannot profitably pursue these issues in greater detail here. In the summary of Spence's theory which follows, an attempt will be made to concentrate on those issues most specific to classical conditioning.

For both Spence and Hull, the main excitatory tendency in classical conditioning derives from an associative concept (habit) and a motivational concept (drive). The habit variable (H) is defined chiefly in terms of (N), the number of conditioning trials. This immediately gives rise to the question of the necessary condition for defining a trial. Is it the paired presentation of a CS and a UCS in some particular time relation? Apparently this is not a sufficient condition unless the UCS meets certain reinforcing requirements (for in aversive conditioning, at least, conditioning is dependent on intensity of UCS). Spence strives to hold to an "empirical" concept of reinforcement; e.g., "It is not necessary to decide the question as to whether an increment in habit strength is contingent in any manner on the action of a reinforcer, or whether it results merely as a consequence of the occurrence of a response" (1956, p. 94). Decision on this point (the meaning of "trial" in the definition of N) is further complicated by situational differences in definition of the "response" involved, as can be seen by a further quotation: "Habit strength is assumed to be related only to N, the number of response occurrences, whether goal responses or not. N is the number of classical conditioning trials, i.e., the number of times the animal enters the goal box and responds to (consumes or sees) the goal object" (1956, p. 136).

In general, then, the increment of H is interpreted as being a function of the occurrence and properties of the reinforcing UCS (Spence, 1960). N is defined as the number of paired presentations of the CS and UCS within a set of boundary conditions still not completely specified. One of the boundary conditions relates to time (CS-UCS interval, etc.), and another is tied to UCS variables such as intensity and possibly duration.

The main excitatory motivational concept in classical conditioning is drive (D). It reflects the general appetitional and emotional condition of the organism at the time. It has been most extensively discussed by Spence in terms of aversive conditioning. Drive "in the case of aversive situations, at least, is a function of the magnitude or strength of a hypothetical response mechanism—a persisting emotional response in the organism designated as r_e, that is aroused by any form of aversive stimulation" (1958, p. 132).

Three major properties of the hypothetical drive mechanism are discussed: 1) r_e will vary with the intensity or degree of noxiousness of the stimulus. Hence, level of D in classical defense conditioning will be a positive function of the intensity of the UCS, and performance will vary positively with UCS intensity. 2) r_e will adapt or become weakened by repeated stimulation. Therefore, if a series of UCS presentations were given prior to conditioning, a lower level of D would result during subsequent conditioning (and hence a lower level of conditioning performance), as compared to the situation with no adaptation trials. 3) Individuals will differ characteristically in the magnitude of their r_e to the same intensity of stressful situation. This leads to the assumption that highly emotional subjects should exhibit a higher level of performance than less emotional subjects in aversive forms of conditioning.

The habit and drive variables in this theory have received most of the experimental attention. They are presumed to combine in a multiplicative fashion to form the excitatory potential (E).

The excitatory potential may be reduced by inhibitory factors, the most common of which would be a hypothetical response mechanism in many ways similar to the previously mentioned r_e. For positive conditioning, at least, this response mechanism would operate not as a work or fatigue phenomenon (as was suggested by Hull) but rather as a frustration phenomenon. An inhibitory variable (I_n) develops as a function of n, the number of non-reinforced trials (CS not followed by UCS), and involves a hypothetical frustration response r_f. In other words, I_n is a symbol representing the quantitative inhibitory effects of n on E. The mechanism by which this occurs is assumed to be r_f. Spence states that "the nature of the mechanism lying behind inhibition (I_n) in the case of aversive conditioning is very different from that in learning situations involving appetitional needs and reward situations" (1960, p. 110). Other inhibitory variables, such as I_t, which is a form of delay-of-reinforcement variable, are discussed more frequently in connection with application of the theory to instrumental conditioning than in connection with classical conditioning. One might assume that in the classical conditioning situation, I_t operates similarly to early concepts of "inhibition of delay." Inhibition also operates through an oscillatory process. When excitatory factors and inhibitory factors combine to form a momentary value which exceeds the threshold for responding, the response occurs.

The main response variables for Spence are the probability of occurrence of a given response (R_p) following a given stimulus, the amplitude of the response (R_a), and the speed of the response (R_s). To these Hull would probably add an extinction measure, such as number of trials to reach a given reduced level of performance (R_m). At a given moment, the observable response in any of its first three mentioned forms is a direct result of the state in the organism referred to as the momentary excitatory potential. A diagrammatic summary of the concepts just discussed is given in Figure 2.

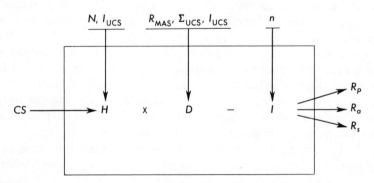

Figure 2.   Diagrammatic summary of major concepts in Spence's
theory.

It will be noted in review that a great deal of stress in Spence's theory is placed on concepts which hypothesize some form of mediating response mechanism (e.g., r_e, r_f, etc.). One would thus expect that a major emphasis in recent empirical studies would be the testing of implications of these constructs. That this is the case will be illustrated by brief reference to a few experiments designed to test the implications of the mediating response r_e.

A few paragraphs back, three major properties of r_e were listed. The third of these assumed that highly emotional subjects would exhibit a higher level of performance than less emotional subjects in aversive conditioning. At least two classes of operations have been used for specifying these individual differences as the independent variable in experiments. The best-known involves a psychometric definition in terms of the Manifest Anxiety Scale (Taylor, 1951). A number of studies with confirmatory results are summarized by Spence (1956), and an extensive empirical literature has developed. A closely related approach defines individual differences in emotionality from psychophysiological measurements of Ss prior to conditioning. In an example of this type, Runquist and Ross (1959) measured pulse rate and skin conductance changes upon presentation of an air puff and then used standard scores to separate out "emotional" and "non-emotional" groups; these were found on subsequent eyelid conditioning to perform in the direction predicted by assumptions about drive level as a determiner of performance in the conditioning situation.

A second empirical example relates to the question of whether habit strength (H) is a function of the intensity of the UCS in classical aversive (eyelid) conditioning. Recall that the implication had been made earlier that the increment in H in this situation was a function of the occurrence and *properties* of the UCS. If, with level of D held constant, conditioning could be shown to be a function of the intensity of the UCS on reinforced trials, this result might be interpreted as lending support to a reinforcement-type theory.

In an eyeblink conditioning study (Spence, Haggard, and Ross, 1958), one group (high reinforcement) was trained with a strong UCS, and another group (low reinforcement) was trained with a weak UCS. Average drive was equated by interspersing among the acquisition trials an equal number of presentations of the "other" UCS after a cue but with a nonoptimum CS-UCS interval. In both cases, the high-reinforcement group gave a greater number of CRs than the low-reinforcement group. This was interpreted as confirming the prediction that habit strength is a function of the intensity of the UCS (Spence, 1960).

Spence's theory and its related empirical studies form a clear example of the use of theoretical constructs as a basis for classical-conditioning research. Experimental studies set out to test an empirical proposition which has been derived by deduction from the system. In this way a body of knowledge is built up which relates closely to the central constructs of the theory. One effect of this is a high concentration of effort upon relations among a few critical concepts and a necessary concern for the boundary conditions of the system. Theoretical-empirical issues tend to be restricted to certain classes of responses or certain levels of organism behavior.

RAZRAN In his recent writings on classical conditioning, Razran has shown concern for a variety of problems. One is the specification of the necessary and sufficient conditions to the learning process. Another is the relation of the data and concepts of classical conditioning to broader issues of human behavior (e.g., unconscious behavior). A third is the assertion that present-day American conditioning theory should cope with the important problems receiving attention in Russia.

Considerable attention has been given to the methodology underlying development of conditioning theory. Razran (1957) asserts that his general intent is to present a comprehensive "inductive account of classical conditioning" with its emphasis upon the organization of observable events. He points out that this is not done with the notion of implying "that theories of learning are unnecessary (Skinner, 1950), or at least that classical conditioning need not resort to anything beyond its own level of direct observables to be fully systematized" (1957, p. 11). He defines his position on theory as "somewhere between that of Skinner and Hull" and holds "that the primary task of the psychology of learning is to discover low-level (directly observable) facts and to array them into low-level functional relationships (parameters, laws) with a use of low-level concepts, and that this task may be—and often is—hampered and misled by 'transcendent' theories and concepts that are only loosely and fragmentarily anchored to empirical bases" (p. 13). In carrying his analysis through, Razran makes direct comparisons of his theory to those of Pavlov, Guthrie, Hull and Tolman.

He states that his strictly empirical account can be supplemented profitably by explanatory efforts employing constructs relating to unobservables. To illustrate this point, he presents and defends an account of conditioning involving assumptions regarding neural action and conditioning "somewhere between that of Pavlov and of Bergmann and Spence" (p. 13). In introducing the theory, below, the "neural" account will be presented first, followed by the more strictly empirical-behavioral account.

According to Razran, for learning to take place by classical conditioning, two general classes of neural events must occur under certain limiting circumstances. These events are observable through the CS and the

UCS (or its attendant UCR). Contiguity (of the CS and UCR) is a necessary but not a sufficient condition for the acquisition of conditioning. In other words, the mere occurrence of a UCR in conjunction with a CS will not ensure learning by conditioning; yet learning will not occur without such a temporal conjunction. In this theory, reinforcement, in the sense of drive reduction, is neither a sufficient nor a necessary condition for conditioning, since drive strength is viewed only as a general energizer or indirect indicator of the events attendant to the UCR.

The effectiveness of conditioning is explained in terms of the concept of *dominance*. Dominance implies certain relations between central factors (CS attensity and UCR affectivity) and peripheral factors (CS intensity and UCR magnitude), operating under the limitation of a specific threshold of conditionability. At a strictly empirical level, dominance may be defined in terms of stimulus intensities (CS and UCS intensity) and response-inferred concepts of CS attensity (attention value of a CS), UCR magnitude, and UCR affectivity. Efficient conditioning depends upon optimum relations (dominance ratios) among these variables.

In describing Razran's theory in neural terms, two concepts are emphasized. One is the concept of "neural event"; the other is the concept of "neural dominance." The former of these implies that the CS and the UCS initiate neural events about which three major properties may be assumed: a) that the two neural events resulting from the CS and the UCS are the basis (the "immediate antecedents") of conditioned response acquisition; b) that the values of the CS-initiated neural event vary directly with the values of CS intensity and CS attensity, and the values of the UCS-initiated event vary directly with the values of UCR magnitude and UCS affectivity; and c) that the two neural events have common characteristics and common points of interaction.

Neural dominance is then defined as a ratio between the UCS-initiated neural events and the CS-initiated events (UCS_N/CS_N ratio) which is greater than 1.00. Conditioning depends upon contiguity and dominance, with four major relations specified: 1) Minimal dominance: conditioning will occur only when the ratio of UCS-initiated neural events to CS-initiated events equals a value K, where K is considerably greater than 1.00; 2) Optimal dominance: conditioning increases as the dominance ratio increases from value K to some value M; 3) Overdominance: conditioning effectiveness decreases as the dominance ratio further increases from the value M to the value W; 4) General action level: conditioning also varies directly with the absolute values of the UCS- and CS-initiated neural events.

The empirical-behavioral account of the theory is made possible by the definition of seven observable parameters, with relations among them specified and tied into the main concept of dominance. These empirical concepts and relations will be reviewed briefly.

CS intensity is defined in terms of physical or psychophysical measures. Conditioning is assumed to become better as CS intensity increases up to a high level of CS intensity, where a reverse relationship sets in. Both an upper and a lower threshold are predicted for these CS intensity effects. That is, conditioning will not occur for CS intensities which are either too low or too high.

Evidence for these relations comes largely from reports of Russian experiments. Directly relevant data in the United States literature are sparse, due to such facts as an emphasis on extinction measures in tests of the CS-intensity parameter (e.g., Grant and Schneider, 1948, 1949), whereas, in this theory, predictions are stated in terms of speed or effectiveness of acquisition. One experiment designed to explore the relation (Kimmel, 1959) yielded confirmatory evidence; another (Passey, 1959) was inconclusive.

Magnitude of UCR is typified by the measurement of amount of unconditioned salivation. Except for special conditions, the larger UCR is accompanied by faster conditioning and a greater magnitude of CR. No reversal occurs with higher magnitude levels, nor is there any upper threshold of conditionability. On the other hand, a lower threshold does exist, i.e., conditioning does not occur when the UCR is comparatively small in magnitude. Again, the data from which this relation is taken are predominantly Russian. However, American experiments upon other theoretical issues (e.g., effect of intensity of UCS on conditioning; Spence, 1960; Gantt, 1938) contain data lending confirmatory support, due to the very high correlation which exists between UCS intensity and UCR magnitude.

The effectiveness of conditioning is determined by the *ratio of the UCR magnitude and the CS intensity*. Measures of conditioning for a wide range of values of UCR magnitude and CS intensity should show an ascending gradient followed by a descending gradient. The higher the fixed value of one variable, while the other is permitted to vary through its range, the farther along the other variable will the reversal of gradients occur. Generally, the higher the value of the fixed variable, the higher the conditioning effectiveness of the series of values for the other variable. Another way to state this is that acquisition is limited by two thresholds, an upper one of CS intensity and a lower one of UCR magnitude. Between the thresholds, conditioning varies directly with absolute values of UCR magnitude, then inversely with absolute values of CS intensity. Effectiveness of conditioning varies with the ratios of the UCR and CS values, there being an optimum ratio, with the gradient of decreasing effectiveness being steeper for ratios above the optimum ratio value than for ratios below the optimum value.

The *interval between the two stimuli* (CS and UCS) determines the course of conditioning. For positive delays (CS preceding UCS), the effect of lengthening the interval is likened to the weakening of the CS intensity, resulting in a steep rise in conditioning up to delays of a few seconds and then a gradual decline, or, under other conditions of absolute stimulus intensities, a gradual decline throughout. For backward conditioning, the effect of lengthening the interval (UCS preceding CS) is likened to decreasing the UCR magnitude. Empirical data related to this point are too extensive to review here. However, recent discussions relevant to this context have been provided by Kimble (1961, p. 156) and Champion and Jones (1961).

The last three empirical concepts are *CS attensity*, *UCR affectivity*, and the *UCR affectivity/CS attensity ratio*. The first of these refers to the attention value of the CS. It might be measured in terms of amount of attention paid to the CS, as indicated, for example, by a test of recognition of stimuli at the conclusion of the experiment. And UCR affectivity refers to the amount of pleasantness or unpleasantness associated with the UCS-UCR complex. This might be evaluated by means of a rating by S of such matters as the enjoyment of eating the food in a salivation conditioning experiment or the unpleasantness of a noxious stimulus, such as electric shock, used as a UCS.

As one would expect from the discussion above, CS attensity is correlated with CS intensity, and UCR affectivity is correlated with UCR magnitude. The gradients relating these variables and efficiency of conditioning are also similar. However, through the use of partial correlations, Razran demonstrates that the attensity and affectivity parameters contribute significant variance to the conditioning situation beyond that predictable from CS intensity and UCR magnitude variables. The ratio of UCR affectivity to CS attensity is predicted to determine effectiveness of conditioning in terms of a function similar to that for the UCR magnitude to CS intensity ratio. Conditioning increases as the ratio increases up to a maximum point, and then a decrease sets in.

The experimental example in terms of which Razran discusses these last three parameters (UCR affectivity, CS attensity, and the ratio between them) is that of human salivary conditioning, where Ss are presented conditioned stimuli while eating pretzels, sandwiches, or candy, and saliva is measured by absorption devices. In this setting, correlations between amount of conditioning and scores on a CS-recognition test (CS attensity) were curvilinear, with values of .51 to .58 for positive slopes and -.41 to -.43 for negative slopes (computed separately by dividing CS attensity scores at the 75-per-cent point). UCR affectivity scores (ratings on a

5-point scale of enjoyment of the food consumed) correlated .56 with amount of conditioning. When the effect of UCR magnitude was partialed out, the correlation remained significant (.30 with an N of 150).

If one keeps in mind the relation of what Razran calls his "psycho-central" parameters (UCR affectivity, CS attensity, etc.) and his "physico-peripheral" parameters (UCR magnitude, CS intensity, etc.), the main empirical relations in the theory can be reviewed in terms of four basic predictions: 1) acquisition is limited by two thresholds, an upper threshold of CS properties and a lower threshold of UCR properties; 2) between these limits conditioning varies directly with UCR properties and at first directly then inversely with absolute values of the CS properties; 3) conditioning varies with the ratio of the UCR-CS properties, there being an optimum ratio with decreasing amounts of conditioning above the optimum ratio and below that value; and 4) the decreasing gradient above the optimum ratio is steeper than the decreasing gradient below the optimum point.

So far, this review shows only Razran's concern for the major determining conditions of classical conditioning. It does not include some of the important collateral concepts, only one or two of which can be touched upon in the space allowed. For example, he puts forth numerous empirical propositions resulting from classical conditioning involving interoceptive and proprioceptive stimulation. Among these are the findings that interoceptive conditioning is readily obtainable (whether the internal stimuli are CSs or UCSs) and, unlike exteroceptive stimulation, leads largely to unconscious reactions. Further, because interoceptive stimulation is organism-bound, it is constantly generated and regenerated in the process of living, which makes it probably more recurrent and pervasive than exteroceptive stimulation. The examination of propositions like these (1961, pp. 97–99) permits him to tie classical conditioning with Freudian theory and to suggest quite novel approaches to unconscious processes.

Further, by emphasizing the importance of the study of classical conditioning of responses to the sense or meaning of signs (semantic conditioning) and the importance of configural conditioning, Razran has stressed a concept of levels of learning. This is accompanied by the notion of a phylogenetic development of learning. Here the emphasis is not on different "types" of learning (e.g., one for lower animals and one for man, etc.). Instead, the concept of levels implies that some learning is occurring at a more primitive level than other learning. With human subjects this is seen in the possibility of learning occurring at different levels at the same time, e.g., what Razran calls "unknowing" conditioning can occur at the same time that "knowing" conditioning takes place. These matters are closely tied to the question of perception as related to classical conditioning

(Razran, 1955) and particularly to the questions of conditioning involving "meaningful" stimuli. The theoretical importance of such "extensions" is obvious when it is recognized that the use of complex and symbolic stimuli is the commonplace rather than the exception with human subjects. Perception of stimuli, as well as perception of relations between stimuli (CS and UCS), are important constituents of the human conditioning process.

WOODWORTH   The theory of Woodworth places an emphasis on the perceptual factor in conditioning. The perception (sometimes referred to as registration) involves a sequence of events which becomes learned through a process termed "reinforcement of perception" (Woodworth, 1947). The conditioning experiment is viewed as the establishment of a new perception, i.e., the change in the subject during conditioning is viewed as a "change in S's way of receiving or perceiving the sequence of stimuli, especially the CS" (p. 122).

When a sequence of stimuli (CS-UCS) occurs repeatedly, the CS may serve as a signal that the UCS is coming, with the result that the subject responds to the CS by "getting ready" for the UCS. Conditioning in this sense develops a readiness for one stimulus to follow another. This readiness takes the form of a preparatory set or an expectancy.

In elaborating upon the process of conditioning, an S_1, R_1, S_2, R_2 sequence is introduced. The subject "learns to take S_1 as a signal of the coming S_2 and to make preparations accordingly. If S_2 is something good, his preparation R_1 is some form of approach; if S_2 is something bad, he prepares to avoid it or at least 'take it'; if S_2 is something of no importance to him, he prepares to disregard it, etc." (1958, p. 239).

This emphasis on R_1 as a preparatory or anticipatory response is in essential agreement with Tolman's (1932, 1960) notion of expectancy. The learning of the sequence is considered as involving at least two steps: first, a readiness for "something" to follow the CS; second, a readiness for the specific stimulus (UCS) to follow the CS. Originally, the investigatory response to the novel CS gives rise to an indefinite expectancy. The UCS subsequently "transforms the indefinite into something definite." The perception is "driven by a direct, inherent motive which might be called a will to perceive" (1947, p. 123). Exploratory behavior is viewed as a questioning process seeking a significant answer.

At this point we might assume that the emphasis on stimulus sequences would imply the sufficiency of contiguity as the essential condition to learning. This is not the case, for "sequence learning" does not occur automatically; in order for learning to occur, reinforcement must take place. This reinforcement may be likened to the confirmation of an expectancy, i.e., the occurrence of the anticipated stimulation. In contrasting his view of reinforcement with drive-reduction views, Woodworth likens the situation to a question and answer (trial-and-check) process. The CS puts the question, and the UCS gives the answer. The CS arouses a questioning set or a readiness for the UCS. Some attention is given to the properties a CS must have in order to "raise a question" (e.g., largely properties of "standing out from the environment"). However, Woodworth never quite specifies what properties S_2 must have in order to provide the "answer." Presumably, S_2 must lead to an "appropriate" R_2, which in the case of reward conditioning might be a consummatory act.

To paraphrase what has been said so far, Woodworth's explanation of conditioning is as follows. A stimulus occurs which has characteristics which cause it to stand out in the environment. This stimulus elicits an investigatory (or What is it?) response from the organism. The occurrence of this S_1, R_1 sequence in conjunction with a "consequent" stimulus S_2 has the effect of changing (shaping) R_1 from a reaction of exploration to a reaction with new characteristics (those of preparing for the S_2). In order for S_2 to meet the necessary conditions for modifying R_1, it must have certain properties, vested largely in the response which it elicits (R_2). One might say that the S_2 must have some kind of incentive value and that R_1 modification is in the form of adient or abient behavior. In this form of explanation, the CR is viewed as a response preparatory to the UCR and not identical with it.

When viewed in this way, Woodworth's notions can be related to current empirical study by Russian workers. These persons (particularly Sokolov, 1957, 1958) have emphasized the relation between perception and the orienting reaction. The implication again is that certain properties of stimuli (novelty, intensity, etc.) make these stimuli adequate to elicit responses of orientation. These orienting responses are modified in the process of conditioning. For a more extensive reference to Woodworth's concepts in this context, see Berlyne (1960), where R_1 is identified with an increase in arousal. It is also relevant to note in passing that Broadbent (1953) similarly attempted to integrate the concepts of conditioning with those of perceptual vigilance.

Extinction is viewed by Woodworth as the learning of a new sequence, CS followed by no-UCS. Such extinction does not erase the previous sequence learning; it simply places the CS in a new sequence; then, under certain circumstances, either sequence might be called forth. Stimulus generalization is treated as a failure to distinguish or differentiate similar stimuli. And some of the observed differences between continuous and other pairing situations (100-per-cent and partial reinforcement) are explained in terms of the relative ease with which the new (extinction) sequence can be differentiated from the old (acquisition) sequence.

Woodworth's position has many of the characteristics of some of the "early" theories (e.g., of Guthrie and Tolman) which make it difficult to define variables operationally or to specify relations at the empirical level. This may be the reason that there is little direct empirical tie-in, i.e., experiments generated by the theory, at least in traditional classical conditioning situations. The writer (Grings, 1960) has tried to develop operations which would define a preparatory "R_1" in a classical conditioning situation. White and Schlosberg (1952) interpret observed differences in degree of conditioning as a function of the period of delay as support for a stimulus-stimulus conception of conditioning. On a formal level, at least one Russian theorist (Anokhin, 1955) subscribes to a "learned preparatory state" notion of conditioning based on neurological constructs (for a summary, see Grings, 1960).

In reviewing Woodworth's most recent statements concerning learning, Mowrer (1959) attacks the unsystematic state of the theory and its conceptual inconsistency. Another reviewer chose the term "presystematic" rather than unsystematic and felt that the main conceptual confusion rests in the definition of reinforcement (e.g., "Does he mean learning by reward or by confirmation?" (Seward, 1959, p. 134). The most recent extensive discussion incorporating the basic notions of this theory is in a book on perceptual learning (Solley and Murphy, 1960). From the standpoint of theoretical methodology, that treatment only amplifies the problems already discussed.

OTHER POINTS OF VIEW   No review of theory in classical conditioning would be complete if it left out completely one of its "champions," persons who gave to classical conditioning the status of central concept in the general explanation of behavior. Such a person is Mowrer, who, by his own admission, has passed through several "versions" of theoretical interpretations of learning. In early versions, conditioning was one of two types of learning. For example, the term "conditioning" was restricted to sign learning involving responses (emotions, meanings, attitudes, etc.) largely mediated by the autonomic nervous system, with the term "solution learning" applied to those situations involving instrumental habit formation. "Conditioned responses, as we thus see, are intimately related to physiology as distinct from problem-solving behavior, which is mediated by the central nervous system and the skeletal musculature" (1951, p. 354).

In the current version of his theory, all learning is conditioning or sign learning (Mowrer, 1960). The earlier two factors are now replaced by two new ones. One, conditioned fear, is based on incremental reinforcement (drive induction, punishment). The second, conditioned hope, is based on decremental reinforcement (drive reduction, reward). The concept of "habit" is essentially similar to that of other reinforcement theorists, and what is learned involves a mediating response mechanism (conditioned fear or conditioned hope).

Another point of view has been labeled the "sensory integration" interpretation of conditioning (Birch and Bitterman, 1949, 1951). This interpretation can be sensed from the quotation (1951, p. 358):

When two afferent centers are contiguously activated, a functional relation is established between them such that the subsequent innervation of one will arouse the other. Here we postulate a purely afferent process of modification which may operate not only in the absence of concurrent motor activity but in the absence of need-reduction as well. This process is revealed most directly in the development of stimulus-equivalence which occurs in conditioning— when two stimuli are presented contiguously, the first acquires some of the functional properties of the second.

This is not only a contiguity theory but an afferent contiguity theory.

The main criticism of the "sensory integration" theorists is again leveled at their theoretical methodology. In the words of Kendler, the term "sensory integration" has rich connotative meaning but a "lack of objective reference." The proponents of the theory "have committed an error which is common to many physiologically-oriented psychologists. They have failed to appreciate the fact that physiological speculation is not equivalent to scientific explanation. Adequate explanatory systems, involving either physiological or behavioral mechanisms, must have deductive components" (1951, p. 370).

CURRENT RUSSIAN ORIENTATION   As has been suggested earlier, present-day Russian workers in the area of classical conditioning are not much concerned with the development of conceptual theories. Their emphasis is empirical, with more of an "acknowledgment" to the theories of men like Pavlov than of deductions from and formal extensions upon those theories (Razran, 1958). However, certain empirical constructs are quite dominant, and the major orienting attitudes are physiological rather than behavioral. Three major areas of emphasis have recently been reviewed at length by Razran (1961). They are interoceptive conditioning, semantic conditioning, and the orienting reflex. These he extends by discussions of proprioceptive and operant conditioning, compound and configural conditioning, verbal conditioning, and phylogenetic and ontogenetic determiners of conditioning.

As an illustration of the explanatory potential of the concepts being employed in the Russian laboratories, two of the concepts will be touched on a bit more extensively. One is the orienting response as it relates to classical conditioning. The other is the concept of the second signal system.

Just how an extensive study of orienting responses can affect interpretations of classical conditioning can be seen from the fact that such orienting responses are intimately related to conditions of attention (Sokolov, 1957; Berlyne, 1960; Razran, 1961). And even casual study of theoretical arguments in this country will show that a most crucial condition (e.g., with reference to effectiveness of "reinforcement") is whether or not the organism attends to, "sees," or responds to the conditioned stimulus. One empirical phenomenon on which extensive theoretical arguments have hinged is the phenomenon of sensory preconditioning. To date, explanations of this phenomenon have relied on hypothetical conditions of "sensory integration" or have postulated a mediating response mechanism for linking of the two relevant cue stimuli (Wickens and Briggs, 1951). To date, the weakest aspect of the latter explanation has been the lack of a clear-cut basis for deducing the nature of the mediating response. The orienting response provides such a mechanism (see Berlyne, 1960, p. 226, for further discussion).

The concept of different signalling systems[1] has a wide spectrum of implications. One is the relation it poses between classical conditioning as a general class and verbal conditioning as a specific class. What may be more important than this is the point that the concept of a second signal system orients explanatory attempts away from the oversimplification which results from attention only to nonverbalizing organisms (Razran, 1961). The implication here may be one of a phylogenetic theory, where organisms at the lowest level operate with a very simple communication relation to their environment. Learning in this circumstance is of the "lowest" level. As one proceeds through the phylogenetic scale where symbolic processes become the potentially dominant processes, one must face the issue as to whether learning remains founded on the same single concept or whether the symbolic processes which develop with man provide the opportunity for superior forms of learning to develop. The concept of the second signal system does not repudiate the idea of simple or elementary learning concepts. It does, however, demand the extensions upon such learning to account adequately for behavior in a verbally signalizing organism (e.g., Platanov, 1959).

In summary, the present status of Russian theory and related work on classical conditioning would highlight two major features. One is the tremendous amount of empirical work in the area. Research in the U.S.S.R. on classical conditioning is considerably more extensive than work in the

---

[1] Pavlov defines signal systems in terms of levels of nervous function. The most primitive level of nervous function consists of inborn reflexes and instincts and is the basis for initial interaction with the environment. These reflexes and instincts, when modified by concrete sensory experience, form the first signal system. The second signal system, which is possessed presumably only by humans, builds upon the inborn reflexes and includes the responses of speech, complex symbolic processes, and the capacity for conceptual learning.

U.S.A. Witness to this fact is the existence of experimental journals (e.g., the *Pavlov Journal of Higher Nervous Activity*) and books (e.g., Bykov, 1957) devoted almost exclusively to this work (and available in English). A second feature is the large number of concepts employed by the Russians and missing from American theory. These concepts take the Russian thinkers into avenues of human behavior and potential explanation (e.g., internal stimulus cueing of behavior and unconscious processes) relatively untapped in this country. What is perhaps even more important is the possibility that American theorists, with their preoccupation with certain types of questions (e.g., the reinforcement issue) and situations (e.g., mazes and Skinner boxes) have failed to keep abreast of the foreign contributions. That this is a real possibility is suggested by the fact that the most recent book on the subject of "conditioning" (Kimble, 1961) makes almost no reference to present Russian contributions. Razran refers to this state of affairs as going beyond the language barrier to "a systemocentricity of one affluent group ignoring the wealth of the other" (1961, p. 126).

Some of this isolation is due, no doubt, to the fact that the Russian work does not follow American methodological standards. With respect to scientific reporting, for example, it is generally accepted in the U.S. that a research report should be sufficiently unambiguous that another investigator could repeat the study. Russian reporting is most scanty by these standards, for techniques and procedures are quite incompletely recorded. Similarly, the Russians have little concern for the methodology of inference, particularly for the use of statistical methods in evaluating the test of an experimental hypothesis. Single or "selected" case data are sometimes extended to group generalizations without specification of any inferential criteria.

From the standpoint of theoretical methodology, the Russian work shares with some of the earlier-mentioned American work the lack of a clearly specified logic for relating concept labels to the essential operational definitions of the concepts. That is, concepts are introduced into an experimental investigation without careful written attention being paid to operational definition of the concepts. This fact, in turn, makes it hard for an American worker to make maximum use of either the data or the concepts involved in such experimentation.

A recent example may be helpful in illustrating some of the above points. At the present time, the Russians exhibit considerable concern over the separation of "conditioned responses" from other behavior in the conditioning situation, such as attention and "orienting responses." Merlin (1960) reported a study which, from its title, implied a definitive investigation of just that problem. Perusal of the study, however, leaves the reader quite unsure of essential requirements for "the CR with an orienting component present" and "the CR with the orienting component absent."

Some Current Issues

In conclusion, brief note will be taken of some of the problems in classical conditioning which are receiving experimental attention at the time of this writing. Several of these have already been mentioned—for example, the work on interoceptive conditioning, semantic conditioning, and the orienting reflex (Razran, 1961).

One outstanding feature of the present period is a re-emphasis upon conditioning in the study of the central nervous system as it relates to behavior (Brazier, 1958, 1959, 1960). Recent developments in neuroanatomy and neurophysiology have used conditioned responses as behavior indices accompanying manipulations of the brain by mechanical, electrical, and chemical means (Galambos and Morgan, 1960). Electrical potentials from the brain (EEGs) are being used extensively in evaluating the neural basis for conditioning. For a historical review, see Morgan and Stellar (1950); for recent examples, see Jasper and Shmirnov (1960) and John (1961).

Behavior studies may be divided into three or four arbitrary classes of events: tests of deductions from behavioral theories; observation of functional relations between conditioning, the dependent variable, and important independent variables; and demonstrations or explorations of conditioning phenomena comprising limited sub-theories. A few of these will be mentioned.

Among tests of deductions from theory, those stimulated by Spence's theory have probably been most numerous. Already cited were one or two examples evaluating the effect of general drive level on conditioning (Spence, 1958; Runquist and Ross, 1959). Typical later studies manipulating general drive level include Spence and Weyant (1960), Baron and Connor (1960), and Spence and Goldstein (1961). Closely related is the problem of demonstrating UCS intensity as a determiner of conditioning over and above its effect upon general drive level (Spence, Haggard, and Ross, 1958), which has more recently been expanded to partial-reinforcement situations (Ross and Spence, 1960) and tied in more closely to the UCS as a reinforcing stimulus capable of influencing habit (Trapold and Spence, 1960). Other properties of the UCS have been studied (e.g., UCS duration; Runquist and Spence, 1959). And the possibility that an anticipatory motivational-emotional response (conditioned fear) develops to the CS and occurs before the UCS comes on has been studied by means of a probe-stimulus procedure (Spence and Runquist, 1958; Ross, 1961).

One deduction about conditioning thus far unmentioned in this review proceeds from individual differences observed in developing a general theory of personality. It links Pavlov's concepts of excitation and inhibition with personality dimensions of introversion and extraversion and predicts that extraverted subjects will condition less well than introverted Ss. A summary discussion of both the theory and results to date is given by Franks (1961). Others (e.g., Warren and Grant, 1955) have made limited predictions about conditioning from behaviors associated with specific traits of personality.

Increasing concern has been shown for the difficulties involved in isolating and defining a specific conditioned response. Examples include the confusion of conditioned cardiac responses with processes like respiration (e.g., Westcott and Huttenlocker, 1961); the difficulty in differentiating orienting responses from conditioned responses (Merlin, 1960); and the involvement of the conditioned pupillary response in the total emotional-response complex (Young, 1958; Gerall, Sampson, and Boslov, 1957). Related efforts with the eyeblink CR have extended upon the earlier procedures for removing beta responses (Grant and Norris, 1947) to use corrections for voluntary responding (Spence and Ross, 1959; Hartman and Ross, 1961). Closely related to this are such procedural determiners as whether or not a ready signal is used (e.g., McAllister and McAllister, 1960; Dufort and Kimble, 1958).

Parametric studies have explored variations of UCS intensity (e.g., Prokasy, Grant, and Myers, 1958), CS intensity (Kimmel, 1959) and related characteristics of the CS (Wickens and Cochran, 1960). Both CS and UCS intensities have been varied in a factorial arrangement to explore their joint effect (Walker, 1960). The interstimulus interval remains an important matter for investigation, with results differing for different responses (e.g., Gerall and Woodward, 1958; Boneau, 1958; Jones 1961). A related study found that offset of a CS could serve the same function as onset of the same stimulus in determining conditioning (Hansche and Grant, 1960). Schedules of reinforcement have been widely studied, both as they relate to acquisition and to extinction (e.g., Hartman and Grant, 1960, 1962). Prokasy and Whaley (1961) relate intertrial-interval variations to Hull's concepts of response-produced inhibition. To compare classical with instrumental conditioning of the same response, a "yoked subjects" procedure has been used (Moore and Gormezano, 1961).

Many familiar phenomena are under continued study. These include sensory preconditioning (Coppock, 1958), compound stimulus conditioning (Wickens, 1959; Grings and Shmelev, 1959), the effects of instructions upon extinction (Silverman, 1960; Lindley and Moyer, 1961) and mediated generalization (Phillips, 1958). Among the newer phenomena is a proposed conditioned inhibitory process inferred from a reduction in the UCS following conditioning and associated with the presence of the CS (Kimble and Ost, 1961). Extension of the classical-conditioning methodology has been made to the conditioning of verbal meaning (Staats, Staats, and Heard, 1961), and in the past two decades conditioning procedures have been extended into such applied areas as clinical audiology with humans (Grings, Lowell, and Rushford, 1959). The relation of conditioning to psychiatry continues to be emphasized (Dykman, Gantt, and Whitehorn, 1958).

Unfortunately, a detailed summary of the literature in classical conditioning is not presently available. In the space allotted here, it has been possible only to touch upon a few of the high spots of an area of theory and empirical investigation which is very basic to the understanding and explanation of many behavior events ranging from the simplest acts of "learning to fear the hot stove" to the objectification of processes that are vaguely labeled "the unconscious."

References

Anokhin, P. K. Characteristics of the afferent apparatus of a conditioned reflex and its importance for psychology. *Voprosy Psikhologii*, 1955, No. 6, 16–38.

Baron, M., and Connor, J. P. Eyelid conditioned responses with various levels of anxiety. *J. Exp. Psychol.*, 1960, 60, 310–313.

Bergmann, G., and Spence, K. W. Operationism and theory in psychology. *Psychol. Rev.*, 1941, 48, 1–14.

Berlyne, D. E. *Conflict, arousal and curiosity.* New York: McGraw-Hill, 1960.

Birch, H. G., and Bitterman, M. E. Reinforcement and learning: The process of sensory integration. *Psychol. Rev.*, 1949, 56, 292–307.

———. Sensory integration and cognitive theory. *Psychol. Rev.*, 1951, 58, 355–361.

Boneau, C. A. The interstimulus interval and the latency of the conditioned eyelid response. *J. Exp. Psychol.*, 1958, 56, 464–471.

Brazier, M. A. B. (ed.). *The central nervous system and behavior.* New York: Josiah Macy Found. 1st Conf., 1958, 2nd Conf., 1959, 3rd Conf., 1960.

Broadbent, D. E. Classical conditioning and human watch keeping. *Psychol. Rev.*, 1953, 60, 331–339.

Brown, J. S. *The motivation of behavior.* New York: McGraw-Hill, 1961.

Bykov, K. M. *The cerebral cortex and the internal organs.* (Trans. W. H. Gantt.) New York: Chemical Publishing Co., 1957.

Champion, R. A., and Jones, J. E. Forward, backward, and pseudoconditioning of the GSR. *J. Exp. Psychol.*, 1961, 62, 58–61.

Coppock, W. J. Pre-extinction in sensory preconditioning. *J. Exp. Psychol.*, 1958, 55, 213–219.

Doehring, D. G. Conditioning of muscle action potential responses resulting from passive hand movement. *J. Exp. Psychol.*, 1957, 54, 292–296.

Dufort, R. H., and Kimble, G. A. Ready signals and the effect of interpolated UCS presentations in eyelid conditioning. *J. Exp. Psychol.*, 1958, 56, 1–7.

Dykman, R. A., Gantt, W. H., and Whitehorn, J. C. Conditioning as emotional sensitization and differentiation. In W. H. Gantt (ed.), *Physiological bases of psychiatry.* Springfield, Mass.: C. C. Thomas, 1958.

Estes, W. K. The statistical approach to learning theory. In S. Koch (ed.), *Psychology: a study of a science,* Vol. 2. New York: McGraw-Hill, 1959.

Estes, W. K., Koch, S., MacCorquodale, D., Meehl, P., Mueller, C. G. Jr., Schoenfeld, W. N., and Verplanck, W. S. *Modern learning theory.* New York: Appleton-Century-Crofts, 1954.

Franks, C. M. Conditioning and abnormal behavior. In H. Eysenck (ed.), *Handbook of abnormal psychology.* New York: Basic Books, 1961.

Galambos, R., and Morgan, C. T. The neural basis of learning. In J. Field (ed.), *Handbook of physiology,* Vol. 3, Section 1: Neurophysiology. Washington: Amer. Physiol. Soc., 1960.

Gantt, W. H. The nervous secretion of saliva: the relation of the conditioned reflex to the intensity of the unconditioned stimulus. *Amer. J. Physiol.,* 1938, *124,* 1–70.

Gerall, A., Sampson, P. B., and Boslov, G. L. Classical conditioning of human pupillary dilation. *J. Exp. Psychol.,* 1957, *54,* 467–474.

Gerall, A., and Woodward, J. K. Conditioning of the human pupillary dilation response as a function of the CS–UCS interval. *J. Exp. Psychol.,* 1958, *55,* 501–507.

Grant, D. A., and Schneider, D. E. Intensity of the conditioned stimulus and strength of conditioning. I. The conditioned eyelid response to light. *J. Exp. Psychol.,* 1948, *38,* 690–696.

———. Intensity of the conditioned stimulus and strength of conditioning. II. The conditioned galvanic skin response to an auditory stimulus. *J. Exp. Psychol.,* 1949, *39,* 35–40.

Grant, D. A., and Norris, E. B. Eyelid conditioning as influenced by the presence of sensitized beta-responses. *J. Exp. Psychol.,* 1947, *37,* 423–433.

Grings, W. W. Preparatory set variables in the classical conditioning of autonomic variables. *Psychol. Rev.,* 1960, *67,* 243–252.

Grings, W. W., Lowell, E. L., and Rushford, G. N. The role of conditioning of GSR audiometry with children. *J. Speech Hear. Dis.,* 1959, *24,* 380–390.

Grings, W. W., and Shmelev, V. Changes in GSR to a single stimulus as a result of training on a compound stimulus. *J. Exp. Psychol.,* 1959, *58,* 129–133.

Guthrie, E. R. *The psychology of learning.* New York: Harper, 1935. (2nd ed., 1952).

———. Association by contiguity. In S. Koch (ed.), *Psychology: a study of a science,* Vol. 2. New York: McGraw-Hill, 1959.

Hansche, W. J., and Grant, D. A. Onset versus termination of a stimulus as the CS in eyelid conditioning. *J. Exp. Psychol.,* 1960, *59,* 19–26.

Hartman, T. F., and Grant, D. A. Effect of intermittent reinforcement on acquisition, extinction, and spontaneous recovery of the conditioned eyelid response. *J. Exp. Psychol.,* 1960, *60,* 89–96.

———. Effects of pattern of reinforcement and verbal information on acquisition, extinction, and spontaneous recovery of the eyelid CR. *J. Exp. Psychol.,* 1962, *63,* 217–226.

Hartman, T. F., and Ross, L. E. An alternative criterion for the elimination of "voluntary" responses in eyelid conditioning. *J. Exp. Psychol.,* 1961, *61,* 334–338.

Hilgard, E. R. *Theories of learning* (2nd ed.). New York: Appleton-Century-Crofts, 1956.

Hilgard, E. R., and Marquis, D. G. *Conditioning and learning.* New York: Appleton-Century-Crofts, 1940.

Hull, C. L. The factor of the conditioned reflex. In C. Murchison (ed.), *A handbook of general experimental psychology.* Worcester, Mass.: Clark Univ. Press, 1934.

———. *Principles of behavior.* New York: Appleton-Century-Crofts, 1943.

———. *Essentials of behavior.* New Haven, Conn.: Yale Univ. Press, 1951.

Jasper, H. H., and Smirnov, G. D. (eds.). The Moscow colloquium on electroencephalography of higher nervous activity. *Electroencephalog. and Clin. Neurophysiol.*, 1960, Suppl. No. 13.

John, E. R. Higher nervous functions (brain function and learning). *Am. Rev. Physiol.*, 1961, 23, 451–484.

Jones, J. E. The CS–UCS interval in conditioning short- and long-latency responses. *J. Exp. Psychol.*, 1961, 62, 612–617.

Kendler, H. H. Reflections and confessions of a reinforcement theorist. *Psychol. Rev.*, 1951, 58, 368–374.

Kimble, G. A. *Conditioning and learning*, a revision of Hilgard and Marquis. New York: Appleton-Century-Crofts, 1961.

Kimble, G. A., and Ost, J. W. P. A conditioned inhibitory process in eyelid conditioning. *J. Exp. Psychol.*, 1961, 61, 150–156.

Kimmel, H. D. Amount of conditioning and intensity of conditioned stimulus. *J. Exp. Psychol.*, 1959, 58, 283–288.

Konorski, J. Mechanisms of learning. In *Soc. Exp. Biol., Symposium on physiological mechanisms in animal behavior* Vol. 4. New York: Academic Press, 1950.

Lindley, R. H., and Moyer, K. E. Effects of instructions of the extinction of a conditioned finger-withdrawal response. *J. Exp. Psychol.*, 1961, 61, 82–88.

Logan, F. A. The Hull-Spence approach. In S. Koch (ed.), *Psychology: a study of a science* Vol. 2. New York: McGraw-Hill, 1959.

McAllister, R., and McAllister, D. E. The influence of the ready signal and unpaired UCS presentations on eyelid conditioning. *J. Exp. Psychol.*, 1960, 60, 30–35.

Merlin, V. S. Specific features of the skin-galvanic component of the conditioned reflex in the presence and absence of an orienting component. *Pavlov J. Higher Nerv. Activ.*, 1960, 10, 713–720.

Moore, J. W., and Gormezano, I. Yoked comparisons of instrumental and classical eyelid conditioning. *J. Exp. Psychol.*, 1961, 62, 552–559.

Morgan, C. T., and Stellar, E. *Physiological psychology.* New York: McGraw-Hill, 1950.

Mowrer, O. H. Two-factor learning theory: Summary and comment. *Psychol. Rev.*, 1951, 58, 350–354.

———. Review of R. S. Woodworth's *Dynamics of Behavior. Contemp. Psychol.*, 1959, 4, 129–133.

———. *Learning theory and behavior.* New York: Wiley, 1960.

Passey, G. E. On Razran's favorable ratios of excitation. *J. Psychol.*, 1959, 48, 341–356.

Pavlov, I. P. *Conditioned reflexes.* (Trans. Anrep.). New York: Oxford Univ. Press, 1927.

———. *Lectures on conditioned reflexes.* (Trans. W. H. Gantt.) New York: International Publ., 1928.

Phillips, L. W. Mediated verbal similarity as a determinant of the generalization of a conditioned GSR. *J. Exp. Psychol.*, 1958, *55*, 56–62.

Platonov, K. *The word as a physiological and therapeutic factor.* Moscow: Foreign Lang. Publ., 1959.

Pratt, C. C. *The logic of modern psychology.* New York: Macmillan, 1939.

Prokasy, W. F., Jr., Grant, D. A., and Myers, N. A. Eyelid conditioning as a function of unconditioned stimulus intensity and intertrial interval. *J. Exp. Psychol.*, 1958, *55*, 242–246.

Prokasy, W. F., and Whaley, F. L. The intertrial interval in classical conditioning. *J. Exp. Psychol.*, 1961, *62*, 560–564.

Razran, G. H. S. Theory of conditioning and related phenomena. *Psychol. Rev.*, 1930, *37*, 25–43.

———. Conditioned responses: a classified bibliography. *Psychol. Bull.*, 1937, *34*, 191–265.

———. Studies in configural conditioning: I. Historical and preliminary experimentation. *J. Gen. Psychol.*, 1939, *21*, 307–330.

———. Conditioning and perception. *Psychol. Rev.*, 1955, *62*, 83–95.

———. Backward conditioning. *Psychol. Bull.*, 1956, *53*, 55–69.

———. The dominance-contiguity theory of the acquisition of classical conditioning. *Psychol. Bull.*, 1957, *54*, 1–46.

———. Soviet psychology and psychophysiology. *Science*, 1958, *128*, 1187–1194.

———. The observable unconscious and the inferable conscious in current Soviet psychophysiology: Interoceptive conditioning, semantic conditioning and the orienting reflex. *Psychol. Rev.*, 1961, *68*, 81–147.

Ross, L. E. Conditioned fear as a function of CS–UCS and probe stimulus intervals. *J. Exp. Psychol.*, 1961, *61*, 265–273.

Ross, L. E., and Spence, K. W. Eyelid conditioning performance under partial reinforcement as a function of UCS intensity. *J. Exp. Psychol.*, 1960, *59*, 379–382.

Runquist, W. N., and Ross, L. E. The relation between physiological measures of emotionality and performance in eyelid conditioning. *J. Exp. Psychol.*, 1959, *57*, 329–332.

Runquist, W. N., and Spence, K. W. Performance in eyelid conditioning as a function of UCS duration. *J. Exp. Psychol.*, 1959, *57*, 249–252.

Seward, J. P. Review of R. S. Woodworth's *Dynamics of behavior. Contemp. Psychol.*, 1959, *4*, 133–134.

Silverman, R. E. Eliminating a conditioned GSR by the reduction of experimental anxiety. *J. Exp. Psychol.*, 1960, *59*, 122–125.

Skinner, B. F. *The behavior of organisms.* New York: Appleton-Century-Crofts, 1938.

———. Are theories of learning necessary? *Psychol. Rev.*, 1950, *57*, 193–216.

———. *Cumulative record.* New York: Appleton-Century-Crofts, 1959.

Sokolov, E. N. Higher nervous activity and the problem of perception. In B. Simon (ed.), *Psychology in the Soviet Union.* Stanford, Calif.: Stanford Univ. Press, 1957.

———. *Perception and the conditioned reflex.* Moscow: Univ. of Moscow, 1958.

Solley, C. M., and Murphy, G. *Development of the perceptual world.* New York: Basic Books, 1960.

Solomon, R. L., and Brush, Elinor S. Experimentally derived conceptions of anxiety and aversion. In *Nebraska symposium on motivation.* Lincoln: Univ. of Nebraska Press, 1956.

Spence, K. W. *Behavior theory and conditioning.* New Haven: Yale Univ. Press, 1956.

———. A theory of emotionally based drive (D) and its relation to performance in simple learning situations. *Amer. Psychologist,* 1958, *13,* 131–141.

———. *Behavior theory and learning.* Englewood Cliffs, N.J.: Prentice-Hall, 1960.

Spence, K. W., and Goldstein, H. Eyelid conditioning performance as a function of emotion-producing instructions. *J. Exp. Psychol.,* 1961, *62,* 291–294.

Spence, K. W., Haggard, D. F., and Ross, L. E. UCS intensity and the associative (habit) strength of the eyelid CR. *J. Exp. Psychol.,* 1958, *55,* 404–411.

Spence, K. W., and Ross, L. E. A methodological study of the form and latency of eyelid responses in conditioning. *J. Exp. Psychol.,* 1959, *58,* 376–381.

Spence, K. W., and Runquist, W. N. Temporal effects of conditioned fear on the eyelid reflex. *J. Exp. Psychol.,* 1958, *55,* 613–616.

Spence, K. W., and Weyant, R. G. Conditioning performance of high-and-low-anxious Ss in the absence of a warning signal. *J. Exp. Psychol.,* 1960, *60,* 146–149.

Staats, A. W., Staats, C. K., and Heard, W. G. Denotative meaning established by classical conditioning. *J. Exp. Psychol.,* 1961, *61,* 300–303.

Taylor, J. A. The relationship of anxiety to the conditioned eyelid response. *J. Exp. Psychol.,* 1951, *41,* 81–92.

Tolman, E. C. *Purposive behavior in animals and men.* New York: Century, 1932.

———. Principles of purposive behavior. In S. Koch (ed.), *Psychology: a study of a science,* Vol. 2. New York: McGraw-Hill, 1959.

Trapold, M. A., and Spence, K. W. Performance changes in eyelid conditioning as related to the motivational and reinforcing properties of the UCS. *J. Exp. Psychol.,* 1960, *59,* 209–213.

Voeks, V. W. Acquisition of S-R connections: a test of Hull's and Guthrie's theories. *J. Exp. Psychol.,* 1954, *47,* 137–147.

Walker, E. G. Eyelid conditioning as a function of intensity of conditioned and unconditioned stimuli. *J. Exp. Psychol.,* 1960, *59,* 303–311.

Warren, A. B., and Grant, D. A. The relation of conditioned discrimination to the MMPI Pd personality variable. *J. Exp. Psychol.,* 1955, *49,* 23–27.

Watson, J. B. The place of the conditioned reflex in psychology. *Psychol. Rev.,* 1916, *23,* 89–116.

———. *Psychology from the standpoint of a behaviorist.* Philadelphia: Lippincott, 1919.

Westcott, M. R., and Huttenlocher, J. Cardiac conditioning: the effects and implications of controlled and uncontrolled respiration. *J. Exp. Psychol.,* 1961, *61,* 353–359.

White, C. T., and Schlosberg, H. Degree of conditioning of the GSR as a function of the period of delay. *J. Exp. Psychol.,* 1952, *43,* 357–362.

Wickens, D. D. Conditioning to complex stimuli. *Amer. Psychologist,* 1959, *14,* 180–188.

Wickens, D. D., and Briggs, G. E. Mediated stimulus generalization as a factor in sensory preconditioning. *J. Exp. Psychol.*, 1951, *42*, 197–200.

Wickens, D. D., and Cochran, S. W. Conditioned stimulus flash rate and efficiency of conditioning. *J. Comp. Physiol. Psychol.*, 1960, *53*, 341–345.

Wickens, D. D., Gehman, R. S., and Sullivan, S. N. The effect of differential onset time on the conditioned response strength to elements of a stimulus complex. *J. Exp. Psychol.*, 1959, *58*, 85–93. '

Woodworth, R. S. Reinforcement of perception. *Amer. J. Psychol.*, 1947, *60*, 119–124.

———. *Dynamics of behavior.* New York: Holt, 1958.

Young, F. A. Studies of pupillary conditioning. *J. Exp. Psychol.*, 1958, *55*, 97–110.

Zeaman, D., and Wegner, Norma. The role of drive reduction in the classical conditioning of an autonomically mediated response. *J. Exp. Psychol.*, 1954, *48*, 349–354.

32 | *Theory Construction and Instrumental Learning*

JOHN W. COTTON

Except perhaps for certain areas of sensory psychology, the best-developed psychological theories are those devoted to learning and related behaviors. Because the major learning theorists have either invoked identical processes to treat classical and instrumental learning (as in Hull, Guthrie, and Estes' work) or have given parallel, closely related treatment to the two types of learning (Skinner and, to a lesser degree, Tolman), this paper, though emphasizing instrumental conditioning, has implications for classical conditioning as well.

I assume some acquaintance by the reader with representative statements by the five theorists just mentioned. (Some question exists whether Skinner should be called a theorist; if desired, the reader may interpret "theorist" to mean "systematist" in his case.) Four aspects of theory construction are to be emphasized in this paper. The first two are formal matters: how theoretical constructs are defined and how these constructs are used in the statement of behavior laws. The other two are at least quasi-empirical: the supra-definitional connotations of the constructs and the specific behavior laws hypothesized in each system. A fifth category, the use and content of the postulates of each theory, will receive only incidental mention.

Definition of Theoretical Concepts

CLASSIFICATION

We shall presume that many terms, such as *book, table, length, weight, rat*, and *luminosity*, belong to the physical thing language (Carnap, 1938, p. 52) and are not theoretical terms for psychologists. We shall further presume that some primitive, undefined terms can be used in this chapter. Now consider five approaches to the definition of theoretical concepts.

TYPE 1. NON-SPECIFIC DEFINITIONS   A theoretical term such as "hunger-drive level" may be defined non-specifically in a way like this: "Hunger drive level is the degree of *food-seeking tendency existing in an animal at a given time.*" This definition might easily appear in a dictionary of pre-behavioristic psychology. Though it gives hints as to how hunger-drive level is to be measured, it does not state the operations by which the measurement could be performed. Some psychologists might find the implications of this non-specific definition more or less appealing than the following: "Hunger-drive level is the degree of *food deficiency existing in an animal at a given time.*" However, neither definition permits the entry of *hunger-drive level* into a behavior law until the definition is objectified.

Guthrie (1952, p. 25) gives a definition of stimuli which falls in this category: "Stimuli are changes in the world order to which sense organs or receptors respond by exciting impulses in sensory nerves." In principle, one could eventually establish what "changes in the world order" are stimuli at any moment, but in practice this definition is clearly non-specific. As a matter of fact, "stimulus" and "response" are almost always non-specifically defined because theorists have hesitated to sacrifice breadth of meaning for specificity. It is my belief that these terms are better treated as primitive, undefined terms and that they should perhaps enter into postulates and high-level laws (discussed below) but—paradoxically—not into S-R laws stating the relation between operationally-defined stimulus (environmental) and response (behavioral) events.

TYPE 2. RESPONSE-TIED DEFINITIONS   This is the most popular device for defining theoretical constructs in psychology. Thus Skinner says, "In measuring the strength of a drive we are in reality only measuring strength of behavior" (1938, p. 368). Being chary of theoretical constructs, he adds on the same page: ". . . The 'drive' is a hypothetical state interpolated between operation and behavior and is not actually required in a descriptive system." Skinner seems to have mentioned drive only out of a sense of conventionality; he does not explicitly define it and so has not quite moved out of Type 1.

Tolman formulated for psychology the notion of intervening variables (1951, Chs. 10, 11, and 13), whose initial properties arise from response-tied definitions. In discussing what he calls D_1 (the demand for a given type of food), i.e., what other theorists call drive level, he says (Tolman, 1951, p. 123), "In other words, we must assume that we have chosen a setup such that the variations in the selected aspect of the behavior mirror directly those of the desired intervening variable and that we can there-fore re-score and re-label our curve. . . ." In a later article reprinted in the same book, Tolman (1951, pp. 158–159) exhibits how such re-labeling can be done with enough detail to permit us to find the approximate numerical values involved. He replaces a percentage incorrect (B, for behavior, it may be called) axis by a demand or D_1 axis. The numbers involved in the re-labeling are arbitrary; for explicitness, however, we note that the approximate transformation used was

$$D_1 = 100 - 2B \qquad (1)$$

Eq. (1) is a relatively simple example of a response-tied definition of a theoretical construct. In more complex cases the construct may be defined as a ratio between a dependent variable and an independent variable or a function of one or more dependent variables and previously-defined theoretical constructs. Hull has very frequently employed response-tied definitions of constructs, as for habit strength ($_sH_R$) in one book (Hull, 1943, p. 121), where habit strength is an explicit function of amplitude (A) of response, and for drive (D) in another (Hull, 1951, pp. 35–36).

Note that Tolman was not hesitant to give relatively objective defini-tions to concepts commonly classed as mentalistic. For example, though he later admitted (1951, p. 166), "I would hardly dare propose it now," he once (1932, p. 206) wrote, "We herewith define conscious awareness as consisting in the performance of a 'sampling' or 'running-back-and-forth' behavior."

TYPE 3. STIMULUS-TIED DEFINITIONS   Tolman (1951, p. 158) considered the response-tied definition of a theoretical construct only a temporary expedient on the way to stating a functional relation between the con-struct and antecedent events. Thus his re-labeled graph previously men-tioned states the relation between demand (D_1) and time-since-last-feeding (M). The equation describing that relation might prove of the order of

$$D_1 = 90 - .068 (M - 48)^2 \qquad (2)$$

for some part of the figure at least.

Eq. (2) is a *law*, or statement of functional relationship between D_1 (as originally response-defined) and M, and Tolman would so regard it. However, he also emphasized the importance of laws relating non-theoretical terms. Combination of Eqs. (1) and (2) provides such a law.

$$B = 5 + .034 (M - 48)^2 \qquad (3)$$

Despite the fact that Eq. (2) was established as an empirical relationship, one may choose to apply it in later experiments as a stimulus-tied definition. As such, it has the advantage of defining drive in terms of an antecedent condition (or "cause"). Now drive has gone through a cycle beginning with a response-tied definition, proceeding through an empirical relation with an antecedent condition, and continuing on to a stimulus-tied definition. The desirability of this stems from the fact that hunger-drive level may now be defined before the experiment, and its effects upon running speed, for example, tested. The relation between hunger-drive level and running speed could hardly be obtained so long as hunger-drive level was response-defined.

Hull has frequently followed the Tolman procedure of getting a functional relation between a previously response-defined construct and an antecedent event. In the case of habit strength previously mentioned (Hull, 1943, p. 121), an explicit equation relating $_sH_R$ to number of reinforced responses (N) results and becomes a stimulus-tied definition. A similar statement holds for drive (Hull, 1951, p. 37). Sometimes, however, this procedure is reversed by Hull. In his *Principles of Behavior* (1943, p. 255), D is given as $\frac{100}{120} h$, with h being the number of hours of food privation. This is an initial stimulus-tied definition of a theoretical construct. Use of the empirical equation relating h and n (the number of extinction responses) at the bottom of Hull's page 254 could, with our stimulus-tied definition, lead to a response-tied definition of D, completing the reverse of Tolman's procedure.

TYPE 4. EXCLUSION OF A THEORETICAL CONSTRUCT   We have seen that Skinner found little reason to introduce drive as a theoretical construct. With his more recent rejection of "reflex reserve"—the Skinnerian counterpart of habit strength (see Skinner, 1956, p. 227)—such constructs find almost no welcome within his system. By and large, Skinner presents the results of experiments as S-R laws comparable to Eq. (3), though often in graphic or verbal form. This position is also characteristic of experimenters less often viewed as systematists of instrumental behavior. (See Graham and Gagné, 1940, for example.)

TYPE 5. USE OF UNDEFINED THEORETICAL TERMS   A strongly axiomatic theory is likely to introduce undefined constructs at the beginning of the theory, making assumptions about their action and later coordinating new, theoretical terms arising in theorems to empirical terms. In such a case, the originally undefined constructs remain undefined, though they gain some implicit definition in the context of the theory. Estes' statistical learning theory (1950) gives to the term "stimulus elements" exactly the status just described.

EVALUATION OF THE FIVE POSITIONS

TYPE I   The five approaches to the definition of theoretical constructs all have counterparts in other sciences, and all have proved useful in theories of instrumental learning. Only the first, nonspecific definition, is unacceptable in a completed, formal theory. Propositions about constructs thus defined are not testable, so that the truth value of theories including them must remain in doubt. Nonetheless, in the context of discovery rather than verification, these nonspecific definitions have often been useful, perhaps even necessary. One suspects that they are the usual forerunners of more precise definitions.

TYPES II AND III   Hull (1943, p. 22) has set forth the requirement that constructs must invariably be anchored on each end, i.e., given both stimulus and response definitions. Though Tolman has presented a diagram much like that used by Hull in this argument, Hull seems more emphatic because he views the construct as literally *intervening* between the antecedent and consequent events, whereas for Tolman the construct may parallel behavior rather than being hypothesized to be a link between the stimulus and response. The usual course for a theoretical construct is that its functional relations to antecedent and consequent events will become known. However, exceptions are permissible, as will be noted in the case of Estes' and Hull's theories.

One should note that one, and only one, anchoring of the intervening variable will be arbitrary. For example, given Eq. (3) and either Eq. (1) or (2), the other is forced to hold. Since Eq. (3) is the stated empirical relationship, I will presume it unchangeable and remark that an entirely different version of Eq. (1) could have been made. For example,

$$D_1 = \frac{1}{B} \tag{1'}$$

would be permissible (though implausible) but would *force* revision of Eq. (2) to read

$$D_1 = \frac{1}{5 + .034 \, (P_1 - 48)^2} \tag{2'}$$

Alternatively one could have arbitrarily defined D_1 as any function of P_1, in which case the relation between D_1 and B would have been forced. It is irrelevant which statement is made the arbitrary one, since all that is required of a theory is internal logical consistency and conformity of its predictions to observed events. Beginning with either stimulus-tied or response-tied definitions is justifiable, then. However, as noted after Eq. (3), in order to state the effects of an intervening variable upon a *new* response measure, a stimulus definition of the variable (whether or not it is the original definition) seems preferable.

TYPE IV The completely atheoretical position seems almost unassailable, logically. Whenever a systematist like Skinner discovers a law relating antecedent and consequent events without invoking theoretical constructs, he has a concise single statement like Eq. (3) rather than the package like Eqs. (1–3) required by a theorist. He has the further advantage that all his terms refer to directly measurable quantities, making for greater clarity.

Why, then should one ever introduce intervening variables? Not, I should say, because of any belief in the ontological status of a construct like habit strength. The justification more likely is that given by Miller (1959), who reasons like this: If, for example, 3 antecedent variables control habit strength and habit strength controls 4 response measures, 7 equations involving habit strength describe the results of 12 possible experiments, which would otherwise require 12 equations to summarize them.

Having never seen a concrete example of saving 5 equations in this manner, I am not certain that this is a truly realistic argument. I would attest, however, to the *difficulty* of doing a wholly empirical job of stating the relation between several antecedent variables and several response measures. Those who find no such difficulty quite properly continue working without theoretical constructs.

TYPE V Underwood (1957, pp. 215–216) has objected to the fifth approach, the introduction of undefined theoretical constructs, because it fails to meet Hull's criterion of firm anchorage on either end. This objection can be applied to Estes' stimulus elements and also, alas, to Hull's concept (1943, Ch. 17) of behavioral oscillation ($_sO_R$). In disagreement with Underwood and with the "conservative" Hull, I defend Estes and the "radical" Hull: This fifth approach is logically acceptable insofar as it leads to testable propositions about behavior, even if not about stimulus elements or behavioral oscillation. These testable propositions or theorems do exist for both theories (Burke, 1949; Estes and Straughan, 1954; Estes and Burke, 1955); accordingly, the theories are logically acceptable, and the question of interest becomes, "Are the theoretical predictions correct?" Any attempt to require further pinning down of the constructs in question is to reify the constructs, rather than to use them as conveniences in organizing a system.

THE QUESTION OF SURPLUS MEANING

The above treatment of definitional problems may bespeak an extreme operational position (Bridgman, 1927) and indeed was intended to do so, except in discussion of the treatment of undefined constructs. For formalized behavior systems, I specifically reject a "triangulation theory" of definition, which speaks of drive or another concept as a "real entity" to be simultaneously defined by a multitude of imperfectly correlated measures which are to be combined in some vaguely specified way (Campbell, 1959, pp. 177–179). Such a procedure seems to reduce all empirical investigation to the search for definitions, with little effort reserved for the statement of laws between the terms so defined and events directly describable in the physical-thing language.

I now relax the operational criterion momentarily. *Hunger-drive level* has been defined operationally in foregoing sections, and this seems appropriate. *Hunger drive*, however, may be thought of as a state of the organism associated with the number given to hunger-drive level. The magnitude of the state is defined by the following reduction sentence a la Carnap (1938, pp. 50–52): If we place a rat in a Warden (1931) obstruction box, and he makes 10 crossings of the shock grid when food is provided in the other side of the grid, then the rat has a hunger-drive state whose magnitude is 10. This state is not fully defined, though we have a means of measuring its magnitude. The triangulation approach of Campbell as applied to drive would be an attempt to understand the state more fully by determining how much the animal eats, how long he was deprived, how many trials would be required to extinguish a lever-pressing response previously rewarded by food, etc. However, the state can never be fully understood; to define the drive magnitude and then state relations between it and each other variable separately seems much more precise. When emphasis is placed upon surplus meaning, such as the properties of the organism having the hunger-drive state in question, then we have stepped over the boundary from drive as an "intervening variable" to drive as a "hypothetical construct" (see Chapter I in this book).

PREFERENCES FOR DIFFERENT TYPES OF CONSTRUCTS

Theorists use constructs having three sorts of connotations: physiological, mental, and behavioral. "Afferent neural impulse," as used in Postulates 1 and 2 of Hull (1943, p. 47), is a typical example of a physiologically-oriented construct. "Expectation" in Tolman (1932, p. 444) has a mental connotation, while "movement-produced stimuli" in Guthrie

(1952, p. 47) and "habit strength" (Hull, 1943, pp. 108–109) have a behavioral flavor with physiological implications as well. Though Skinner tries to exclude mental constructs completely from his system, most theorists have accepted some constructs of each type. Even Hull, whose final emphasis was on physiological constructs (particularly with a peripheral rather than central nervous-system involvement) and behavioral constructs, devoted a great deal of time to the objectification of mental constructs such as "purpose" (Hull, 1930). Tolman, on the other hand, used mentalistic constructs most frequently.

This is not to say that Tolman thought of himself as a mentalist. A purposive behaviorist, he stated his view on mental processes as follows (1932, p. 3): " 'Mental processes' are, for the behaviorist, naught but inferred determinants of behavior, which ultimately are deducible from behavior." Since Tolman explicitly rejected philosophical dualism, it may seem inappropriate to call his concepts mentalistic. Note, however, that reference is being made to the *connotations* of his terms, not their intent when used by him.

To the extent that constructs are objectively defined, they are acceptable, more or less independently of their connotations. Thus the logical status of incentive motivation (K) in Spence's (1956) form of Hullian theory would not be changed if Spence called K "expectancy," in line with his half-offer (p. 152) to join Tolman in an S-R expectancy—half reinforcement, half contiguity—theory. Correspondingly, "pugnacity" in Tolman's system could be renamed "excess of bile," thereby gaining in Hippocratic fashion a physiological aura in place of its mentalistic one but without changing the implications of the theory qua theory.

Two objections, however, can be raised against the use of constructs with heavily mentalistic connotations. As Skinner (1938, p. 436) argues against Hull's early use of them, so many mentalistic terms or layman's terms are available for objectification that one hardly knows where to stop, rendering the parsimonious ideal of a minimal number of theoretical constructs almost impossible to attain. Secondly, although we have noted that the use of mentalistic terms does not necessarily come from or lead to philosophical dualism, it surely may do so.

Physiological constructs have a corresponding disadvantage reflected in the following quotation from Spence (1956, p. 56):

It is perhaps unnecessary to add that it was only the mathematical definitions of Hull's intervening variables that provided for the derivation of the empirical laws of conditioning. As so defined these constructs have no relation whatever to such issues as whether learning involves some kind of organization among sensory processes or whether it is to be conceived in terms of changes in the resistance of neural connections mediating between afferent and efferent processes. It is only by virtue of this quite superfluous neurophysiological speculation that Hull's theorizing ever got enmeshed in such issues.

Hilgard (1958), though not directly replying to this comment, would provide the counter-argument that, useful as intervening variables are as integrating devices, Hull was wise in wanting to infer physiological processes as well as establishing behavior laws, for there is something of substance and thus worth study behind the behavior. Nonetheless, Hilgard agrees that Hull's theory has suffered from lack of care in manipulating its theoretical constructs.

Construction of S-R Laws of Instrumental Learning

GUTHRIEAN LAWS   In this section let us examine those lawful statements whose terms are all objectively defined. Such a procedure admittedly excludes many of Guthrie's notions, because he has such a shortage of objective terms.

Now what shall a law be? Common usage is clear and acceptable: A law is a statement of the form, "If event X occurs, then event Y will also occur." One law discovered under the influence of Guthriean theory is that of Sheffield and Roby (1950): *If saccharine is given as a reward following a particular turn in a T-maze, a food-deprived rat will progressively increase its turns in that direction.* This is a very specific finding, for which the term "law" may seem pretentious. Regardless of its importance, however (and this finding is very important because it makes clear that *need* reduction is not necessary to learning, even though drive reduction may be necessary), an "*if . . . then*" relationship of this kind is considered fundamental enough to deserve the appellation "law." This of course leads to a great multiplicity of laws, making a later organization of them into a smaller number desirable.

Guthrie himself did relatively little experimentation, producing almost no laws at the level now being considered. We mention only one, the Guthrie and Horton finding (1946) of stereotypy in the positions of several cats, each bumping a pole to release a door mechanism permitting escape from a box. This finding was thought by Guthrie to reinforce his contention that specific movements are most characteristic of learning. Mueller and Schoenfeld (1954) have pointed out, however, that the interpretation is weak; stereotypy of position, being less than perfect, was not as great as the perfect stereotypy in the end result of bumping the pole.

TOLMANIAN LAWS   Behavioral-level laws of the type being discussed abound in Tolman's work and that of his associates. Consider, for example, Blodgett's (1929) finding that groups of rats trained in a 6-choice multiple T-maze for two days or six days (one trial per day) without food reward showed a reduction of less than one error per trial in that period, but then achieved a reduction of at least 1.5 errors on the average in the trial following the first food-rewarded trial, more than ever occurred in any single trial for an always-rewarded group. This finding of what is commonly called latent learning is an S-R law, a welcome one to Tolman because of his orientation to psychology, less welcome to Hull for the comparable reason. However, most learning theories make some attempt to accommodate the empirical finding, though not necessarily the interpretation (higher-level law) proposed by Tolman to account for the finding.

Tolman also reports some laws of an R-R (response-response) type: for example, he states (1932, p. 206) that running back and forth (which sometimes is equivalent to conscious awareness by his definition noted above) may accompany the learning of the correct choice in a discrimination box. Tolman relatively seldom ties such constructs as conscious awareness to antecedent events as we know he recommended—few laws are developed which correspond to Eq. (2). This is regrettable, since it reinforces a tendency in psychology to make definition the principal aim of research, with little emphasis upon lawful relations between the thing defined and other variables. Thus we spoke earlier of the effect of hunger-drive level upon running speed, an extremely hard issue to settle experimentally until hunger-drive level is stimulus-defined. An even more embarrassing situation is frustration: in some cases frustration is taken simply to be a stimulus operation, such as withholding reward. In others, however, the response measure, such as increased vigor, is taken to indicate the presence of frustration, in which case the effect of frustration and its definition are inseparable until a further study is done.

HULLIAN LAWS Hull's theory has led to a large number of S-R laws, which, like Blodgett's, can be stated verbally, and to mathematical expressions for many of them. As an example of the latter, consider Gladstone, Yamaguchi, Hull, and Felsinger's analysis (1947) of reaction latency ($_s t_R$) as a function of the number of reinforced trials (N). It deals with the following empirical relation obtained by them:

$$_s t_R \text{ median} = 74.05 \, N - 1.60 + .43 \qquad (4)$$

where $_s t_R$ median is the median reaction latency and N is 2 plus the number of reinforcements.

In this case, as in almost all others except behavioral oscillation (Hull, 1943, Postulate 10), Hull and his associates have taken seriously the requirement to anchor their constructs on both antecedent and consequent ends. However, their treatment of reaction potential ($_s E_R$) is subject to criticism. Though Hull realized that equations of the sort of Eqs. (1), (2), and (3) above must be mutually consistent (and Hull makes this consistency hold in at least one place [1943, p. 121]), the Gladstone,

Yamaguchi, Hull, and Felsinger equations do not satisfy this requirement. Thus, they stated the relation

$$_{s}t_{R} \text{ median} = \frac{8.71}{(_{s}E_{R} + .599)^{2.07}} \tag{5}$$

Since they also stated that

$$_{s}E_{R} = 3.55 \, (1 - 10^{-.0305\dot{N}}) \tag{6}$$

one would expect that substitution of the right-hand side of Eq. (6) for $_{s}E_{R}$ in Eq. (5) would yield Eq. (4). Comparison of Eqs. (4), (5), and (6) makes clear that this consistency is not achieved. Presuming that the combination of Eqs. (4) and (5) yields an acceptable statement of the relation between $_{s}t_{R}$ median and $\dot{N}$, then that combination equation would have both empirical and rational significance, whereas Eq. (4) would have empirical validity only. If it is intended that Eq. (4) should be part of the theory, however, the limitation mentioned in connection with Eqs. (1′) and (2′) must be noted. One anchoring of $_{s}E_{R}$ must be forced by the other. I have described other mathematical inconsistencies of Hull's theory in more detail elsewhere (Cotton, 1955). Koch (1954) has discussed a series of logical lapses in the theory. Both authors would admit that these criticisms are necessary only because Hull so closely approximates rigor in theory construction, whereas theories like those of Guthrie and Tolman are too informal to merit strict logical analysis.

ESTES-IAN LAWS   Estes presents a number of empirical generalizations, such as the *Probability Matching Law* (1957): "If the probabilities of reinforcement are constant throughout a series of trials, a subject's response probability will drift upward or downward until it reaches a value equal to its probability of reinforcement, then will continue indefinitely fluctuating around this matching value." Data by Gardner (1957) and others have led Estes most recently (1962, pp. 131–132) to defend the law only in the two-choice situation. I believe that slight restrictions upon its applicability in the two-choice situation will soon be necessary because of Edwards' (1961) finding of slight overshooting of the reinforcement probability by the response probability when 1000 trials are given.

Commonly, Estes' laws state the response probabilities for all trials, rather than for the asymptote alone. These laws are usually mathematical, as are Hull's. One notes, however, that Estes' deductions usually prove to be correct in a mathematical sense, a sign of growing maturity in psychological theorizing. It should be mentioned that Estes' postulates, being less obviously *post hoc* than Hull's, truly require certain empirical relations to hold if the theory is to be adequate. One of the great conveniences of Hullian theory, on the other hand, is its opportunism—if unexpected data arise, the postulates are easily changed. Compare the treatment of magnitude of reward in (1943) and (1951) and drive in the same years. Estes' theory is much neater because its postulates are not allowed such freedom; consequently, however, repeated modifications of the theory which preserve elegance are likely to be difficult. A much more complete treatment of Estes' position is given by Atkinson in Selection 33.

SKINNERIAN LAWS   At the behavioral level, Skinner presents laws relating such variables as amount eaten and time in the eating situation (1938, p. 344) or rate of lever-pressing and the delay of reinforcement (1938, p. 141). The former relationship is stated in an equation, but the latter is shown graphically, Skinner's favored means of summarizing data.

Occasionally a law takes a statistical form, as when Skinner reports (1938, pp. 68–69) that lever-pressing is acquired almost instantaneously: of 78 animals trained, 20 established a steady, high rate of lever-pressing immediately after the first reinforced lever press, 55 established such a rate after from 2 to 4 reinforced lever presses, and 3 did not establish it within 3 hours.

One expects the least differences between theorists at the level of S-R laws, since there can be less disagreement about observed relationships than about their interpretations. Yet Skinner has been more controversial than most. He finds that laws based on averaging data obtained from several animals are misleading in some instances; on both logical and empirical bases, others have at least partially agreed with him (Bakan, 1954; Estes, 1956; Sidman, 1952, 1960; Voeks, 1954, 1955). But some psychologists find reason to question the representativeness of data from a single organism or the degree of control over such factors as maturation or learning-to-learn when the same animal is tested under several experimental conditions. Note that Sidman (1960) has been well aware of these problems, devoting much effort to their solution within a Skinnerian framework. Skinner's reliance on a particular graphic method, the cumulative curve, has been criticized on the ground that irregularities in behavior are hidden by it (Battig, 1958).

Perhaps the most iconoclastic aspect of Skinner's approach to lawful behavior is his insistence that certain response measures are unacceptable. For example, he states (1938, p. 437), "The maze is not a suitable instrument for the investigation of the dynamic properties of behavior. Even when we consider a single 'choice-point' there remain two possible responses—turning right and turning left. No measure of the strength of either is provided by maze behavior, since a 'choice' reveals only the relatively greater strength of one." Though the fact is indisputable that a choice reveals only the greater strength of one response, the success of Hull and Estes in incorporating choice data into their systems would seem to disprove Skinner's contention of unsuitability.

On reflection, Skinner's system seems to gain its importance neither because of its paucity of theoretical constructs, nor because of its specific S-R laws, nor because of its rejection of certain statistical and experimental techniques. These matters are of some consequence, but the central characteristic of the system is Skinner's unshakeable conviction that operant behavior, as he differentiates it from respondent behavior (Skinner, 1938, p. 20), is subject to almost complete experimental control by appropriate scheduling of deprivation, reinforcement, and discriminative stimulation. This belief, held in moderation by most students of learning, is the basis for action by Skinnerians. While other theorists are like theologians telling the principles by which salvation is attainable, Skinnerians form a Salvation Army attempting to control schizophrenic behavior (Bullock, 1959; Lindsley, 1959), develop animal shows (Breland and Breland, 1951, 1961), build teaching machines (Skinner, 1954; Skinner, 1958), and, fictionally, reorganize society (Skinner, 1948).

Establishment of Higher-Level Laws

Logan (1959, pp. 299–301) has emphasized that general laws often subsume several specific laws. The making of general laws has often proceeded inductively, as when Jenkins and Stanley (1950) grouped several specific empirical relations together to conclude that resistance to extinction is greater following a partial reinforcement acquisition procedure than following a continuous reinforcement acquisition procedure. Such general laws are desirable in that they permit rapid transmission of information based on several studies. They should always be viewed with caution, however, and the limiting conditions on the generalization stated. At the risk of being over-skeptical, I am inclined to suspect that the search for regularities which hold across apparatuses, procedures, and species will be less successful than commonly thought by psychologists.

At an even higher level of generality, attempts are made to determine laws, such as that inhibition or interference is the primary contributor to response decrements in extinction. This is a case of two proposed high-level laws, either of which might arise inductively from certain bodies of data, deductively from theorists' axioms, or "spontaneously" as axioms. Their origin seems largely irrelevant; they must be judged by the theorems they produce.

Illustrative Theoretical Issues

LATENT EXTINCTION   The first of four theoretical issues taken to illustrate current thinking in the area of instrumental learning is that of latent extinction. First studied by Seward and Levy (1949), latent extinction is defined by Moltz (1957) as the "procedure whereby an animal is introduced directly into an unbaited goal location after having acquired a response instrumental in securing a reward object previously contained in that location." With a few exceptions (Bugelski, 1952; Scharlock, 1954), most investigations of latent extinction show that the following high-level law holds: If latent extinction precedes a test of the previously-acquired response, the animal will show a weaker response than control animals allowed to spend corresponding amounts of time in a non-goal location. Also, if latent extinction precedes testing with the goal location (formerly used in a straight alley) used as one end box of a T-maze, fewer turns to that side of the maze will be made than in a control group given corresponding amounts of time in a non-goal location.

Seward and Levy predicted the former half of the law just stated (and would agree that the latter half should also be predicted) from what they named the sign-learning theory of extinction, as stated by Tolman (1932, pp. 324–333) and Culler (1938). They describe its implications as follows: "During training the rats started sooner and ran faster largely because they developed a hypothesis that food was to be found on [the reward platform]. Before and between extinction trials the [experimental] rats had more time than the [control] rats to develop the contrary hypothesis. Essentially, then, it was the interference of one expectation with another that led to quicker extinction." Seward and Levy call this statement a free rendering of Tolman, but it seems clearly in the spirit of Tolman. The effects of latent extinction do follow from this theory, though not in a tightly reasoned way. "Hypothesis" in the sense used here seems equivalent to "expectation of food," which is defined by Tolman (1932, p. 74) on the response side, but not on the stimulus side, as needed for prediction of the Seward-Levy phenomenon. Something of this sort would be an example of the desired stimulus definition: The strength of the hypothesis that food is to be found on the reward platform is

$$
\left[\frac{\text{Number of previous experiences with food on the platform} - \text{Number of previous experiences without food on the platform}}{\text{Total number of experiences on the platform.}} \right]
$$

This definition is not proposed as the ideal one, for it has obvious defects. However, even as stated, it would give the objective meaning to "hypothesis" necessary for a serious theoretical statement. Similarly, postulates relating "hypothesis" to each of the response measures used by Seward and Levy would also be necessary in a formalization of the sign-learning theory of extinction. Regardless of these matters of rigor, the theory obviously has served the useful function of leading to successful prediction of a new phenomenon in psychology. An approach to formalization by Tolman's theory such as that given by MacCorquodale and Meehl (1953, 1954) might be a helpful refinement of this extinction theory.

As would be expected, other theories are able, after the fact, to predict the same phenomenon. Seward and Levy suggested that a Hullian explanation of the effect might use the r_g, or fractional antedating goal reaction, for a mechanism. This has been done, notably, but not exclusively, in the work of Moltz. He emphasizes that reactive inhibition (I_R) and conditioned inhibition ($_sI_R$) from Hull's theory do not have appropriate properties to lead to the latent-extinction phenomena in question, but that r_g does.

Very briefly, according to Moltz, r_g is evoked in the goal box, being extinguished if food is not presented. To the degree that cues in the goal box and at a choice-point in later testing are similar, r_g's at the choice-point will have reduced strength. Since s_g (a proprioceptive stimulus) is evoked by r_g and has strength which is a "direct function" of the strength of r_g, this implies a reduction in strength of s_g. But the magnitude of s_g and the K of Hull's theory are presumed to co-vary positively, so that K must decline with latent extinction. But K is positively related to reaction potential $_sE_R$, so that $_sE_R$ declines, and this leads to prediction of the performance decrements observed by Seward and Levy.

How shall we compare the Moltz analysis with that of Seward and Levy? Moltz comes closer to tying all constructs to antecedent and consequent conditions, but the theory would be much improved by clarification of terms like "direct function" and specification of exact relations between hypothesized variables. One also wonders whether s_g and r_g are necessary, in addition to K. Neglecting its relation to reward magnitude, one could readily define the magnitude of K independently of r_g and s_g so as to depend upon the number of experiences with and without food. In this case, K and "hypothesis" in Tolman's theory might prove to be equivalent concepts. This suggestion seems consistent with Spence's (1956, p. 135) indication that K must depend upon the number of rewarded trials in the goal box, a recommendation which has been followed with quantitative assumptions by Cotton, Jensen, and Lewis (1962).

Three reasons to retain r_g and s_g in addition to K are apparent: 1) Phenomena other than latent extinction may require their invocation (Kendler and Levine, 1951). 2) Some decrement in behavior can be produced by feeding instead of non-feeding in the goal box before extinction (Lewis and Cotton, 1958), though K as ordinarily defined should increase. Here an r_g, s_g interpretation has been made and seems a desirable intervening step before modification of the definition of K. 3) Though a less convincing reason, the use of r_g and s_g emphasizes the presumed muscular involvement associated with learning, a desirable feature to many Hullian theorists, even though irrelevant to the question of predictive adequacy. Despite these reasons, parsimony would dictate rejection of s_g and r_g if at all possible.

It may be remarked that the Lewis and Cotton finding, if replicable, is equally troublesome for Tolman's theory and for Hull's theory. Presumably, feeding in the goal box should have increased the hypothesis that food would be available.

One further comparison between Seward and Levy and Moltz seems relevant: Which position leads to the larger number of additional predictions related to latent extinction? Seward and Levy make only one: that overtraining preceding latent extinction should enhance the previously observed effect. Moltz makes at least three major predictions about effects of relevant and irrelevant drives and reward preceding latent extinction. Perhaps Seward and Levy's position would be as productive of predictions as Moltz's if given expression in a theoretical paper rather than an experimental one. I would guess, however, that Hullian theory, being more comprehensive in coverage of different psychological variables, might still come out in the lead.

SECONDARY REINFORCEMENT Hull and Skinner have held sharply different views regarding secondary reinforcement, with Hull (1943, p. 98) asserting that temporal contiguity of a stimulus and a response, plus close temporal association of both to drive reduction, leads to response-evoking power for that stimulus. Skinner (1938, pp. 244–257), on the other hand, asserts that secondary-reinforcement properties increase whenever a response is followed by a stimulus which functions as a positive discriminative stimulus (S^D) for some further response, such as eating. Hull's position does not really fit into his 1943 system, because secondary reinforcement effects are not explicitly tied to any construct such as $_sH_R$ and thus do not lead to prediction of behavior as a function of effective reaction potential ($_s\bar{E}_R$) or momentary effective reaction potential ($_s\dot{\bar{E}}_R$), as in the case of most other variables treated by Hull. Nonetheless, without entry into the postulate system, this analysis of secondary reinforcement led to the empirically correct but informal deduction that an animal given repeated sham feeding should eventually lead to refusal to eat the food provided (Hull, Livingston, Rouse, and Barker, 1951).

Hull later (1950) gave a corollary to his new Postulate 3 which could lead to inferences about the relation of secondary reinforcement to quantitatively-defined constructs in his theory: "A neutral receptor impulse which occurs repeatedly and consistently in close conjunction with a reinforcing state of affairs, whether primary or secondary, will itself acquire the power of acting as a reinforcing agent."

The implications of this corollary for habit strength ($_sH_R$) changes as a function of secondary reinforcements are clear enough to be unmentioned here; the effects on primary drive are more controversial. Though not a necessary consequence of this corollary, several investigators have noted that a natural hypothesis following from the corollary is that secondary reinforcements can reduce primary drive, so that consummatory behavior in a free-eating or free-drinking situation would be reduced by presenting secondary reinforcements immediately prior to the test condition. When these investigators (Simon, Wickens, Brown, and Pennock, 1951; Calvin, Bicknell, and Sperling, 1953; and Miles and Wickens, 1953) tested this prediction empirically, it was refuted.

Schoenfeld, Antonitis, and Bersh (1950) have tested the corollary just quoted (though as quoted it did not appear until after their study was published) by comparing an experimental group with a light presented only *during* eating following lever-pressing to a control group never presented with a light. After each group had experienced one hour of extinction without a light, members of each group received two more hours of extinction with a light following each lever press. Contrary to Hull's theory, no indication of a greater lever-pressing rate in the experimental group appeared. While this study is not completely definitive, since a third group with a light intervening between lever-pressing and eating was not run to demonstrate that ordinary secondary-reinforcement effects would appear with the existing test conditions, the experimental findings strongly suggest that Skinner's position is correct: Secondary reinforcers must have positive discriminative stimulus properties to be effective.

Dinsmoor (1950) has shown that a previously established positive discriminative stimulus for lever-pressing, when presented at all times except the three seconds immediately after a lever press, leads to a lever-pressing rate during extinction equal to that occurring if the stimulus is presented only for the three seconds immediately after the response. Both conditions led to higher response rates than when a negative discriminative stimulus was presented. Thus a discriminative stimulus has been shown also to have secondary reinforcing properties when delayed until after the response. Kimble (1960) attributes incentive properties to Dinsmoor's discriminative stimulus. This seems an acceptable interpretation within a Hullian framework which would tie magnitude of incentive motivation (K) to the response-evoking strength of the discriminative stimulus. This position goes beyond Skinner but seems not to deny his basic premise about the relation of discrimination to secondary reinforcement. Thus one Hullian analysis by Seward (1950) begins its summary paragraph with something Skinner could almost have said: "A reinforcer, in the case of positive cathexes, gains its potency through its ability, native or acquired, to arouse a consummatory response in the presence of the relevant need."

Work with chained responses gives results consistent with the experiments just cited. A response which produces a stimulus for a new response is secondarily reinforced by that stimulus (Ferster and Skinner, 1958, pp. 684–685).

ONE-TRIAL LEARNING VERSUS INCREMENTAL LEARNING We have seen Skinner reporting a low-level law that most of his rats achieved a maximal level of lever-pressing within the first four reinforced lever presses, often after only one. Guthrie has emphasized that learning occurs in a single pairing of stimulus and response. Estes, who had previously been Guthrian enough to assume that stimulus elements became conditioned and unconditioned in a single trial, has recently (1960) produced a one-element or pattern model which implies that appropriate research designs can show that associations between stimuli and responses are establishable in one trial. Tolman, on the whole, seems to presume that learning proceeds gradually, though not necessarily as a function of those variables emphasized by other theorists. Hullian theory has been most consistent in asserting that habit strength and, therefore (typically), direct-response measures of learning increase by incremental units. Even Hull's incremental point of view, however, has been used to predict one-trial learning at the phenotypic level (Spence, 1936).

Until very recently Hull's position on this point seemed very strong. Average learning curves for groups were typically quite gradual, and incremental-habit-strength assumptions predicted these curves admirably. Guthrian arguments as to the reasons one-trial learning was masked in real situations seemed plausible but unnecessary. However, a major controversy on this subject seems now in birth, for experimental as well as theoretical reasons. Voeks has shown that maze performance in human Ss is better predicted by assuming that the response just made will occur (prediction based on recency) than that the most frequent response (prediction based on frequency) hitherto will be made (1948). This finding is consistent with Guthrie's position, but similar findings in other studies, at least, can be predicted from an incremental theory.

For example, if one analyzes the report on 30 "stat-dogs" (i.e., sets of hypothetical Ss' data generated by a theory together with random sampling) reported for Bush and Mosteller's linear theory (1955, p. 252) as simulating data obtained by Solomon and Wynne (1953), one finds that only one animal's behavior is better predicted on the basis of frequency. Twenty-three dogs' responses are better predicted on the basis of recency, and the remainder are predicted equally well by each method. Voeks may have constructed a straw man in suggesting that theorists exist who would predict that the most frequent response of the past should be made in the future.

Two other Voeks' papers (1954, 1955) report that reduction of variability leads to increasing likelihood of an individual subject's jumping in a single trial from zero to 100 per cent probability of making a conditioned eyelid response.

More recently the stage has been shifted to verbal learning, where Rock (1957) and Rock and Heimer (1959) report that paired associates which are not paired correctly on one trial can be replaced by new pairs on the next trials without retarding learning of an n-pair list. Barring artifacts, this finding would suggest that a single incorrect trial has no beneficial effects whatever. In the 1957 paper, Rock himself raised the most serious objection to these findings, the possibility that the items dropped were on the average more difficult for the individual learner than those retained. Though Rock and Heimer performed two experiments designed to test this objection, their designs do not seem adequate to answer the question involved. Underwood, Rehula, and Keppel (1962) have shown that the dropped items are indeed generally more difficult. They also find some indication of inferior performance in groups using this drop-out procedure.

Estes, Hopkins, and Crothers (1960) and Estes (1961) have extended Rock's work by examining the effects of what they call an RTT design: one pairing of stimulus items and response items (reinforcement or R) upon two later tests (T's). They interpret the chance level of correct responses for previously incorrect items on the second test as evidence that items missed on the first test have not been partially learned.

Failure to produce correct responses (for previously correct items) on the second test in the first condition is attributed in part to chance successes on the first test and in part to retention losses between tests. Increases in correct response-frequency after two reinforcements, as compared with one, were attributed to the all-or-none conditioning of an increased number of items. A further experiment by Estes, Hopkins, and Crothers investigates the retention process. Several other experiments described by Estes (1960) also strengthen the case for one-trial learning. Estes (1960, p. 218) almost, but not quite, decides that an incremental theory cannot handle such data: "Interpretations which preserve the incremental conception of associative learning should certainly be sought with all vigor; at the time of writing, however, none has come to my attention that seems at all plausible."

Is Estes right? Does an all-or-none principle of learning almost force itself upon us? Despite his work, our answer would be "not yet," on two grounds. First, Estes' experimental findings must successfully meet attack on the empirical level. This challenge has already been begun by Underwood (1961), who argues very cogently that differences in item difficulty and individual differences of *S*s' learning ability contaminate the Estes, Hopkins, and Crothers analysis. He further points out that a reduction in length of the test during the second pairing of stimulus and response items should have reduced the difficulty of items tested after two pairings, making comparisons between once-paired and twice-paired items inappropriate. Additional objections are being raised in other quarters (Jones, 1962; Postman, 1961; Wollen, 1961).

Secondly, Estes' position gains much of its strength from the absence of a well-developed alternative theory. Hull's theory has never been put to the test of detailed quantitative predictions in verbal learning, despite the existence of *Mathematico-Deductive Theory of Rote Learning* (Hull et al., 1940). Verbal learning students such as Underwood (1961) and Wollen (1961) are beginning to make graphic arguments within the Hullian tradition as attempts to deduce the Estes, Hopkins, and Crothers findings noted above. On a qualitative level their arguments seem sound, but they are relatively vague when compared with Estes' predictions of specific probability values. Estes (1962, p. 125) offers some general objections to the Underwood model but nonetheless seems to imply that it may predict the results of RTT experiments. A proof or disproof of this implication seems not to be in the literature.

Estes has, however, demonstrated that a certain class of incremental models contradict the results of certain RTT experiments. Bower's demonstration (1961, 1962) that all-or-none theory predicts his results much better than the linear model of statistical learning theory, and Suppes and Ginsberg's finding (1962) of excellent and detailed correspondence between children's concept-formation data and all-or-none theory also strengthen the all-or-none position. Nonetheless, it seems possible in principle to find incremental models to account for these findings. I personally expect some such model to prove a satisfactory competitor to all-or-none theory. Clearly, however, such a competitor remains to be developed in detail.

ADDITIVE VERSUS MULTIPLICATIVE PROPERTIES OF DRIVE (D) AND INCENTIVE MOTIVATION (K)   The final illustration of specific theoretical issues is a point of disagreement wholly within the system espoused by Hull and his followers. Hull (1951, 1952) assumed that drive (D) and incentive motivation (K) are multiplied by each other in the formation of reaction potential ($_sE_R$), as in Postulate 8 of the 1952 reference. On the other hand, his close associate Spence (1956, p. 164) says that drive and incentive motivation add to each other in the formation of reaction potential. Hull seems simply to have guessed that D and K should be multiplied, but Spence holds his position because of indirect experimental evidence.

Reynolds, Marx, and Henderson (1952) studied the interaction of drive level and reward magnitude (controllers of D and K, respectively) even before the issue of additivity of D and K arose. The data from the training phase of their Skinner-box experiment provides some assessment of the Hull and Spence positions. An apparent but statistically untested interaction between drive and reward effects gives support to Hull. Unfortunately no indication is given that the high-drive condition yielded faster responses than the low-drive condition, as would be expected from both theories.

Seward, Shea, and Elkind (1958) also found an interaction between drive and reward magnitude effects. In addition, their high-drive animals, tested in a straight alley, ran faster than their low-drive animals, in conformity with both theories. Since Spence assumed (1956, p. 117) that speed of evocation of a response is linearly related to its reaction potential, these results imply that interaction existed for reaction potentials as well as for speeds, at least in the sample studied. This contradicts Spence's assumption of additivity of D and K effects.

Seward, Shea, and Elkind pointed out that their experiment employed zero values of drive and reward magnitude for the low-magnitude conditions, making it a special case of the general test for additivity. On the basis of related experiments, they indicated that interaction should not be present when non-zero magnitudes are used.

That inference is verified in recent reports by Weiss (1960) and by Reynolds and Pavlik (1960). In each case no interaction was found between deprivation level and magnitude of reinforcement effects upon mean starting speed and/or mean running speed in a straight alley. These findings are consistent with Spence's assumption that D and K add, for any non-additivity of D and K would have produced interaction in the population values of reaction potential and, therefore, of speed. Unless we have committed a Type II statistical error (concluding from sample data that no effect exists when it does exist in the population), additivity is the correct assumption to make within the Spence system for the drive and reward levels of these two studies.

Interestingly, because Spence's and Hull's systems differ in other respects than the question of the combination of D and K effects, these two studies make a very great deal of trouble for Hull: Hull's Postulate 14 (1952) implies that median speed is proportional to a non-unitary power of reaction potential. Therefore deprivation and reward magnitude effects on speed should interact regardless of whether D and K add or multiply. Thus these experiments weaken the credibility of his Postulate 14 without providing a crucial test of the multiplicative hypothesis within the framework of his system.

Conclusions

Four criteria commonly employed in the evaluation of competing theories are conformity of data and predictions, simplicity, internal consistency, and fruitfulness in stimulation of research. The last of these may be an unhappy result for a theory lacking other virtues. Thus an interest in dianetics, to choose an extreme example, may stimulate research. This does not make dianetics a good theory. At best it leads to well-designed studies yielding negative results; at worst it weds bad research to bad theory.

Reflection on the theories discussed above suggests one conclusion about the present state of psychology: search for a crucial experiment (e.g., on latent learning or all-or-none learning) whose findings will clearly conform to one theory, and to no other, is likely to be no more than temporarily successful. A wounded theory quickly is modified to account for those findings, and the battle goes on. Perhaps the focus of theoretical contests should shift from the attempt to predict S-R laws which are inexplicable by the opposition to the attempt to predict results which will surprise, rather than confound, the opposition. Indeed this form of fruitfulness would seem to have greater general applicability than the fourth criterion discussed above.

References

Bakan, D. A generalization of Sidman's results on group and individual functions, and a criterion. *Psychol. Bull.*, 1954, *51*, 63–64.

Battig, W. F. On the use of cumulative response curves in psychology. *Psychol. Rep.*, 1958, *4*, 731–741.

Blodgett, H. C. The effect of the introduction of reward upon the maze performance of rats. *Univ. Calif. Publ. Psychol.*, 1929, *4*, 113–134.

Bower, G. H. Application of a model to paired associate learning. *Psychometrika*, 1961, *26*, 255–280.

———. An association model for response and training variables in paired-associate learning. *Psychol. Rev.*, 1962, *69*, 34–53.

Breland, K., and Breland, Marian. A field of applied animal psychology. *Amer. Psychol.*, 1951, *6*, 202–204.

———. The misbehavior of organisms. *Amer. Psychol.*, 1961, *16*, 681–684.

Bridgman, P. W. *The logic of modern physics.* New York: Macmillan, 1927.

Bugelski, B. R., Coyer, R. A., and Rogers, W. A. A criticism of pre-acquisition and pre-extinction of expectancies. *J. Exp. Psychol.*, 1952, *44*, 27–30.

Bullock, D. H. Operant behavior in psychiatric patients. *J. Exp. Anal. Behav.*, 1959, *2*, 262.

Burke, C. J. A theory relating momentary effective reaction potential to response latency. *Psychol. Rev.*, 1949, *56*, 208–223.

Bush, R. R., and Mosteller, F. *Stochastic models for learning.* New York: Wiley, 1955.

Calvin, J. S., Bicknell, Elizabeth A., and Sperling, D. S. Effect of a secondary reinforcer on consummatory behavior. *J. Comp. Physiol. Psychol.*, 1953, *46*, 176–179.

Campbell, D. T. Methodological suggestions from a comparative psychology of knowledge processes. *Inquiry*, 1959, *2*, 152–182.

Carnap, R. Logical foundations of the unity of science. In O. Neurath, R. Carnap, and C. Morris (eds.), *International Encyclopedia of Unified Science*, Vol. 1, No. 1. Chicago: Univ. of Chicago, 1938, pp. 42–62.

Cotton, J. W. On making predictions from Hull's theory. *Psychol. Rev.*, 1955, *62*, 303–314.

Cotton, J. W., Jensen, G. D., and Lewis, D. J. Wide variation in spontaneous recovery interval as an influence on reacquisition of T-maze behavior. *J. Exp. Psychol.*, 1962, *63*, 555–562.

Culler, E. A. Recent advances in some concepts of conditioning. *Psychol. Rev.*, 1938, *45*, 134–153.

Dinsmoor, J. A. A quantitative comparison of the discriminative and reinforcing functions of a stimulus. *J. Exp. Psychol.*, 1950, *40*, 458–472.

Edwards, W. Probability learning in 1000 trials. *J. Exp. Psychol.*, 1961, *62*, 385–394.

Estes, W. K. Toward a statistical theory of learning. *Psychol. Rev.*, 1950, *57*, 94–107.

———. The problem of inference from curves based on group data. *Psychol. Bull.*, 1956, *53*, 134–140.

———. Of models and men. *Amer. Psychol.*, 1957, *12*, 609–617.

———. The statistical approach to learning theory. In S. Koch (ed.), *Psychology: a study of a science*, Vol. 2. New York: McGraw-Hill, 1959, pp. 380–491.

———. Learning theory and the new "mental chemistry." *Psychol. Rev.*, 1960, *67*, 207–223.

———. New developments in statistical behavior theory: differential tests of axioms for associative learning. *Psychometrika*, 1961, *26*, 73–84.

———. Learning theory. In P. R. Farnsworth (ed.), *Annual Rev. Psychol.* Palo Alto, Calif.: Annual Reviews, Inc., 1962, *13*, pp. 107–144.

Estes, W. K., and Burke, C. J. Application of a statistical model to simple discrimination learning in human subjects. *J. Exp. Psychol.*, 1955, *50*, 81–88.

Estes, W. K., Hopkins, B. L., and Crothers, E. J. All-or-none and conservation effects in the learning and retention of paired associates. *J. Exp. Psychol.*, 1960, *60*, 329–339.

Estes, W. K., and Straughan, J. H. Analysis of a verbal conditioning situation in terms of statistical learning theory. *J. Exp. Psychol.*, 1954, *47*, 225–234.

Ferster, C. B., and Skinner, B. F. *Schedules of reinforcement.* New York: Appleton-Century-Crofts, 1957.

Gardner, R. A. Probability-learning with two and three choices. *Amer. J Psychol.*, 1957, *70*, 174–185.

Gladstone, A. I., Yamaguchi, H. G., Hull, C. L., and Felsinger, J. M. Some functional relationships of reaction potential ($_sE_R$) and related phenomena. *J. Exp. Psychol.*, 1947, *37*, 510–526.

Graham, C. H., and Gagné, R. M. The acquisition, extinction, and spontaneous recovery of a conditioned operant response. *J. Exp. Psychol.*, 1940, *26*, 251–280.

Guthrie, E. R. *The psychology of learning* (rev. ed.). New York: Harper, 1952.

———. Association by contiguity. In S. Koch (ed.), *Psychology: a study of a science*, Vol. 2. New York: McGraw-Hill, 1959, pp. 158–195.

Guthrie, E. R., and Horton, G. P. *Cats in a puzzle box*. New York: Rinehart, 1946.

Hilgard, E. R. Intervening variables, hypothetical constructs, parameters, and constants. *Amer. J. Psychol.*, 1958, 71, 238–246.

Hull, C. L. Knowledge and purpose as habit mechanisms. *Psychol. Rev.*, 1930, 37, 511–525.

———. *Principles of behavior: an introduction to behavior theory*. New York: Appleton-Century-Crofts, 1943.

———. Behavior postulates and corollaries—1949. *Psychol. Rev.*, 1950, 57, 173–180.

———. *Essentials of behavior*. New Haven: Yale Univ. Press, 1951.

———. *A behavior system: an introduction to behavior theory concerning the individual organism*. New Haven: Yale Univ. Press, 1952.

Hull, C. L., Hovland, C. I., Ross, R. T., Hall, M., Perkins, D. T., and Fitch, F. B. *Mathematico-deductive theory of rote learning: a study in scientific methodology*. New Haven: Yale Univ. Press, 1940.

Hull, C. L., Livingston, J. R., Rouse, R. O., and Barker, A. N. True, sham, and esophageal feeding as reinforcements. *J. Comp. Physiol. Psychol.*, 1951, 44, 236–245.

Jenkins, W. O., and Stanley, J. C., Jr. Partial reinforcement: A review and critique. *Psychol. Bull.*, 1950, 47, 193–234.

Jones, Joan E. All-or-none versus incremental learning. *Psychol. Rev.*, 1962, 69, 156–160.

Kendler, H. H., and Levine, S. Studies of the effect of change of drive: I. From hunger to thirst in a T-maze. *J. Exp. Psychol.*, 1951, 41, 429–436.

Kimble, G. A. *Hilgard and Marquis' Conditioning and learning* (2nd ed.). New York: Appleton-Century-Crofts, 1961.

Koch, S. Clark L. Hull. In W. K. Estes, et al., *Modern learning theory: a critical analysis of five examples*. New York: Appleton-Century-Crofts, 1954, pp. 1–176.

Lewis, D. J., and Cotton, J. W. Partial reinforcement and non-response acquisition. *J. Comp. Physiol. Psychol.*, 1958, 51, 251–254.

Lindsley, O. R. Reduction in the rate of vocal psychotic symptoms by differential positive reinforcement. *J. Exp. Anal. Behav.*, 1959, 2, 269.

Logan, F. A. The Hull-Spence approach. In S. Koch (ed.), *Psychology: a study of a science*, Vol. 2. New York: McGraw-Hill, 1959, pp. 293–358.

MacCorquodale, K., and Meehl, P. E. On a distinction between hypothetical constructs and intervening variables. *Psychol. Rev.*, 1948, 55, 95–107.

———. Preliminary suggestions as to a formalization of expectancy theory. *Psychol. Rev.*, 1953, 60, 55–63.

———. Edward C. Tolman. In W. K. Estes et al., *Modern learning theory: a critical analysis of five examples*. New York: Appleton-Century-Crofts, 1954, pp. 177–266.

Miles, R. C., and Wickens, D. D. Effect of a secondary reinforcer on the primary hunger drive. *J. Comp. Physiol. Psychol.*, 1953, 46, 77–79.

Miller, N. E. Liberalization of basic S-R concepts: Extensions to conflict behavior, motivation, and social learning. In S. Koch (ed.), *Psychology: a study of a science*, Vol. 2. New York: McGraw-Hill, 1959, pp. 196–292.

Moltz, H. Latent extinction and the fractional anticipatory response mechanism. *Psychol. Rev.*, 1957, *64*, 229–241.

Mueller, C. G., Jr., and Schoenfeld, W. N. Edwin R. Guthrie. In W. K. Estes et al., *Modern learning theory: a critical analysis of five examples*. New York: Appleton-Century-Crofts, 1954, pp. 345–379.

Postman, L., One-trial learning. Paper presented at 2nd O.N.R. Conference on Verbal Learning, New York City, June 1961.

Reynolds, B., Marx, M. H., and Henderson, R. L. Resistance to extinction as a function of drive-reward interaction. *J. Comp. Physiol. Psychol.*, 1952, *45*, 36–42.

Reynolds, W. F., and Pavlik, W. B. Running speed as a function of deprivation period and reward magnitude. *J. Comp. Physiol. Psychol.*, 1960, *53*, 615–618.

Rock, I. The role of repetition in associative learning. *Amer. J. Psychol.*, 1957, *70*, 186–193.

Rock, I., and Heimer, W. Further evidence of one-trial associative learning. *Amer. J. Psychol.*, 1959, 72, 1–16.

Scharlock, D. P. The effects of a pre-extinction procedure on the extinction of place and response performance in a T-maze. *J. Exp. Psychol.*, 1954, *48*, 31–36.

Schoenfeld, W. N., Antonitis, J. J., and Bersh, P. J. A preliminary study of training conditions necessary for secondary reinforcement. *J. Exp. Psychol.*, 1950, *40*, 40–45.

Seward, J. P. Secondary reinforcement as tertiary motivation: a revision of Hull's revision. *Psychol. Rev.*, 1950, *57*, 362–374.

Seward, J. P., and Levy, N. Sign learning as a factor in extinction. *J. Exp. Psychol.*, 1949, *39*, 660–668.

Seward, J. P., Shea, R. A., and Elkind, D. Evidence for the interaction of drive and reward. *Amer. J. Psychol.*, 1958, *71*, 404–407.

Sheffield, F. D., and Roby, T. B. Reward value of a non-nutritive sweet taste. *J. Comp. Physiol. Psychol.*, 1950, *43*, 471–481.

Sidman, M. A note on functional relations obtained from group data. *Psychol. Bull.*, 1952, *49*, 263–269.

———. *Tactics of scientific research: Evaluating experimental data in psychology*. New York: Basic Books, 1960.

Simon, C. W., Wickens, D. D., Brown, Ursula, and Pennock, L. Effect of the secondary reinforcing agents on the primary thirst drive. *J. Comp. Physiol. Psychol.*, 1951, *44*, 67–70.

Skinner, B. F. *The behavior of organisms: an experimental analysis*. New York: D. Appleton-Century, 1938.

———. *Walden Two*. New York: Macmillan, 1948.

———. Are theories of learning necessary? *Psychol. Rev.*, 1950, *57*, 193–216.

———. The science of learning and the art of teaching. *Harvard Educ. Rev.*, 1954, *29*, 86–97.

———. A case history in scientific method. *Amer. Psychol.*, 1956, *11*, 221–233.

———. Teaching machines. *Science*, 1958, *128*, 969–977.

Solomon, R. L., and Wynne, L. C. Traumatic avoidance learning: acquisition in normal dogs. *Psychol. Monogr.*, 1953, *67*, No. 4.

Spence, K. W. The nature of discrimination learning in animals. *Psychol. Rev.*, 1936, *43*, 427–449.

———. *Behavior theory and conditioning.* New Haven: Yale Univ. Press, 1956.

Suppes, P., and Ginsberg, Rose. Application of a stimulus sampling model to children's concept formation with and without overt correction responses. *J. Exp. Psychol.,* 1962, *63,* 330–341.

Tolman, E. C. *Purposive behavior in animals and men.* New York: Century, 1932.

———. *Collected papers in psychology.* Berkeley, Calif.: Univ. of Calif. Press, 1951.

Underwood, B. J. *Psychological research.* New York: Appleton-Century-Crofts, 1957.

———. One-trial learning? Paper presented at Midwest. Psychol. Assoc., Chicago, Ill., May 6, 1961.

Underwood, B. J., Rehula, R., and Keppel, G. Item selection in paired-associate learning. *Amer. J. Psychol.,* 1962, *75,* 353–371.

Voeks, Virginia W. Postremity, recency, and frequency as bases for prediction in the maze situation. *J. Exp. Psychol.,* 1948, *38,* 495–510.

———. Acquisition of S-R connections: a test of Hull's and Guthrie's theories. *J. Exp. Psychol.,* 1954, 47, 137–147.

———. Gradual strengthening of S-R connections or increasing number of S-R connections. *J. Psychol.,* 1955, *39,* 289–299.

Warden, C. J. *Animal motivation: experimental studies on the albino rat.* New York: Columbia Univ. Press, 1931.

Weiss, R. F. Deprivation and reward magnitude effects on speed throughout the goal gradient. *J. Exp. Psychol.,* 1960, *60,* 384–390.

Wollen, K. A. One trial versus incremental paired-associate learning. Unpublished doctoral dissertation. State University of Iowa, 1961.

33 | *Mathematical Models in Research on Perception and Learning*[1]

RICHARD C. ATKINSON

The purpose of this paper is to examine the role of mathematical models in research on perception and learning. The reader, however, should be warned at the outset that we will not present a formal philosophical analysis of the function of models but, instead, will examine the development and application of a specific model. A formal analysis would lead

[1] The ideas presented in this paper have been much influenced by discussions with R. Kinchla and E. C. Carterette. The research was supported by the National Institute of Mental Health under Contract M-5184. Portions of the paper were presented at an International Colloquium on the concept and the role of models in mathematics and science held in Utrecht on January 4–8, 1960.

us into a great deal of abstract discussion and would not stress current developments in research techniques. The model which will be examined deals with a forced-choice signal-detection situation. It is particularly useful for illustrative purposes because it combines two quite distinct processes: a simple perceptual process and a learning process. As the theory is developed, we will be able to indicate the role of mathematical models in determining programs of psychological research and in specifying the types of empirical observations to be made.

Before turning to the example, a few general comments seem in order. The use of mathematical models is virtually synonymous with the construction of a quantitative theory of behavior. From a mathematical standpoint, it is logically possible to have a theory of behavior that leads only to qualitative predictions. However, in the history of science it is difficult to find theories of this sort that have had sustained empirical significance. From the systematic standpoint, a theory based only on qualitative distinctions leads to a relatively small number of testable predictions. Further, as the set of phenomena that we study expands in complexity, so also does the reasoning necessary for the design of experiments and the formulation of hypotheses. Ordinary logic becomes inadequate, and the elaboration of the theory requires the powerful tool of mathematical analysis.

In this regard, perhaps the most important role of mathematical models in recent psychological research has been to provide a framework within which the detailed sequential aspects of behavior can be scrutinized. An experiment designed only to establish the existence of a gross relation between two variables, such as response speed and reward magnitude, ignores the many sequential properties of psychological phenomena. Examination of these properties is a significant step forward in that it provides a source of behavioral information that cannot be obtained from an analysis of average-performance curves. Theories stated only in qualitative terms do not provide an adequate means for analyzing and interpreting such complex sequential phenomena.

Further, the absence of precise systematization often leads to pseudo-derivations from the theory, that is, derivations which require assumptions that are not part of the original theory. Some people claim to be unconcerned with whether the predictions tested by an experiment follow in a strictly logical sense from basic postulates. They maintain that the essential act is the making of the prediction, not its derivation from fundamental theory. The reply to this point of view seems obvious. The inability of a theory to yield significant predictions without additional *ad hoc* assumptions is an indication that the theory does not provide an objective analysis of behavior. An important function of the mathematical model is to clarify this aspect of a theory. Of course, many models can stem from the same fundamental theory. The important factor is whether the theory will yield at least one well-defined model in a non-arbitrary manner. The attempt to specify a model will in itself require an exact characterization of the theory and will frequently reveal unstated assumptions.

Experimental Situation

The psychophysical experiment that we shall analyze was conducted by Kinchla (1962), and he has kindly given us permission to present some of his data. He employed a forced-choice visual-detection situation involving a series of over 800 discrete trials; we shall only consider data from a subset of 600 trials. Two areas were outlined on a uniformly-illuminated milk-glass screen. Each trial began with an auditory signal. During the auditory signal one of the following events occurred: a) A fixed increment in radiant intensity occurred in one of the two areas of the visual display. A trial will be termed a T_1 or T_2 trial, depending upon which of the two signal areas had an increment in illumination. b) No change in the radiant character of either signal area occurred. Such *blank* trials will be denoted T_0.

Subjects were instructed that a change would occur in one of the two areas on each trial. Following the auditory signal, the subject was required to make either an A_1 or A_2 response to indicate which area he believed had changed in brightness; thus, the subject was *forced* to respond on every trial regardless of how confident he was of his choice. In this particular study by Kinchla, the subject was given no information at the end of the trial as to whether his response was correct. In summary, on a given trial one of three events occurred (T_1, T_2, or T_0), the subject made either an A_1 or A_2 response, and a short time later the next trial began.

For a fixed signal intensity, the experimenter has the option of specifying a schedule for presenting the T_i events. Kinchla selected a simple probabilistic procedure where the likelihood of presenting T_i on trial n was constant over all trials and independent of preceding responses and events; i.e., $\Pr(T_{i,n}) = \pi_i$, where $\pi_1 + \pi_2 + \pi_0 = 1$. Two groups of subjects were run: for Group I, $\pi_1 = \pi_2 = .4$ and $\pi_0 = .2$; for Group II, $\pi_1 = \pi_0 = .2$ and $\pi_2 = .6$.

MODEL The model which will be used to describe Kinchla's experiment is a generalization of stimulus sampling concepts as originally formulated by Estes (1950). Only those axioms relevant to the experiment will be presented. The reader interested in a more comprehensive formulation of stimulus sampling theory is referred to Estes (1959), Estes and Suppes (1959), or Atkinson and Estes (1962); for a discussion of signal

detection within the framework of stimulus sampling theory, see Atkinson (1961).

In this paper, the stimulus situation is represented in terms of two
sensory elements, s_1 and s_2, and a set S* of stimulus elements associated
with background stimulation. These stimulus elements are theoretical
constructs to which we assign certain properties. Although it is sometimes convenient and suggestive to speak in such terms, one should not
assume that the stimulus elements are to be identified with any simple
neurophysiological unit, as, for example, receptor cells. At the present
stage of theory construction, we mean to assume only that certain properties of the set-theoretical model represent certain properties of the
process of stimulation. If these assumptions prove to be adequately substantiated when the model is tested against a wide range of behavioral
data, then it will be in order to look for neurophysiological variables
which might underlie the correspondence.

On every trial the subject samples a single element from the background set S* and may or may not sample one of the sensory elements.
If the s_1 sensory element is sampled, an A_1 occurs; if s_2 is sampled, A_2
occurs. If neither sensory element is sampled, the subject makes the response to which the background element is conditioned. Conditioning of
elements in S* may change from trial to trial via a simple learning
process. As will become evident in the statement of the axioms, we have
a Fechner-type threshold model which interacts with a learning process
to generate the subjects' protocol of responses.

The axioms will be formulated verbally. It is not difficult to state them
in mathematical form, but for our purposes this will not be necessary.
The first group of axioms deals with the sampling of stimulus elements,
the second group with the conditioning process, and the third group
with responses.

Stimulus Axioms

*S1. If $T_i(i = 1, 2)$ occurs, then sensory element s_i will be sampled with
probability* h *(with probability* $1 - h$, *neither* S_1 *nor* S_2 *will be
sampled).*

S2. If T_0 occurs, then neither s_1 nor s_2 will be sampled.

S3. Exactly one element is sampled from set S on every trial. Given the
set S* of N elements, the probability of sampling a particular element is* $\frac{1}{N}$, *independently of the trial number and preceding events.*

Conditioning Axioms

C1. On every trial each element in S is conditioned to either A_1 or A_2.*
C2. If $s_i(i = 1, 2)$ is sampled on trial n, then with probability c' the ele-

ment sampled from S* on trial n *becomes conditioned to* A_i *at the end of trial* n.

C3. *If neither* s_1 *nor* s_2 *are sampled, then with probability* c *the element sampled from S* on trial* n *becomes conditioned with equal likelihood to either* A_1 *or* A_2 *at the end of trial* n.

Response Axioms

R1. *If sensory element* s_i *is sampled, then the* A_i *response will occur.*

R2. *If neither sensory element is sampled, then the response to which the sampled element from set S* is conditioned will occur.*

PREDICTED AND OBSERVED QUANTITIES   We begin our analysis of the model by deriving an expression for the proportion of elements in set S* conditioned to A_1 at the start of trial *n;* this quantity will be denoted as p_n. Once an expression for p_n has been obtained, we immediately can write an equation for the probability of response A_i, given event T_i on trial *n.* The expressions are obtained directly by applying axioms R1 and R2 and are as follows:

$$Pr(A_{1,n}|T_{1,n}) = h + (1 - h)p_n \qquad (1a)$$

$$Pr(A_{2,n}|T_{2,n}) = h + (1 - h)(1 - p_n) \qquad (1b)$$

$$Pr(A_{1,n}|T_{0,n}) = p_n \qquad (1c)$$

To obtain an expression for p_n, it is helpful to proceed in a series of steps. First assume that on trial *n* a T_1 event occurred, and an element conditioned to A_1 was sampled from set S*; the likelihood of this event is $\pi_1 p_n$. Given these events on trial *n*, the possible changes that can occur in p_n are specified by the tree in Figure 1. On the upper branch, an s_1 sensory element is sampled with probability h (see Axiom S1), and by Axiom C2 the element sampled from S* remains conditioned to A_1; hence on this

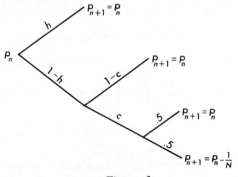

Figure 1

branch $p_{n+1} = p_n$. On the lower branch, neither sensory element is sampled with probability $1 - h$. By Axiom C3 there is a probability $\frac{c}{2}$ that the element sampled from S* will become conditioned to A_2 (and hence on this branch $p_{n+1} = p_n - \frac{1}{N}$), and a probability $1 - c + \frac{c}{2}$ that the element remains conditioned to A_1 (whence $p_{n+1} = p_n$). Thus, with probability $\pi_1 p_n$,

$$p_{n+1} = h\,p_n + (1 - h)\left[\left(1 - \frac{c}{2}\right)p_n + \frac{c}{2}\left(p_n - \frac{1}{N}\right)\right]$$

or more simply, $p_{n+1} = p_n - \frac{1}{N}(1 - h)\frac{c}{2}$.

Similarly, if on trial n a T_2 occurs, and an element conditioned to A_1 is sampled from S* (the probability of the joint event being $\pi_2 p_n$), then the possible changes in p_n are given by the tree in Figure 2. On the upper

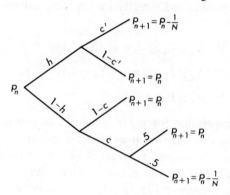

Figure 2

branch, an s_2 sensory element is sampled, and by Axiom C2 the element sampled from set S* will become conditioned with probability c' to A_2, whence $p_{n+1} = p_n - \frac{1}{N}$. The lower branches of the tree are derived by application of Axiom C3. Hence, with probability $\pi_2 p_n$, the value of p_{n+1} is

$$\left[p_n - \frac{1}{N}\right]\left[hc' + (1 - h)\frac{c}{2}\right] + p_n\left[h(1 - c') + (1 - h)\left(1 - \frac{c}{2}\right)\right]$$

or more simply, $p_{n+1} = p_n - \frac{1}{N}\left[hc' + (1 - h)\frac{c}{2}\right]$.

Following the same procedure, we may derive a comparable expression for p_{n+1}, given the joint occurrence of event T_0 and an element sampled from S^* conditioned to A_1; similarly, expressions for p_{n+1} may be obtained, given the joint occurrence of an element sampled from S^* conditioned to A_2 and event $T_i (i = 0, 1, 2)$. If these six results are combined, weighting each by its likelihood of occurrence, the following expression is obtained:

$$p_{n+1} = \pi_1 p_n \left[p_n - \frac{1}{N} (1-h) \frac{c}{2} \right] + \pi_2 p_n \left[p_n - \frac{1}{N} \right.$$

$$\left\{ hc' + (1-h) \frac{c}{2} \right\} \right] + \pi_0 p_n \left[p_n - \frac{1}{N} \frac{c}{2} \right]$$

$$+ \pi_1 (1 - p_n) \left[p_n + \frac{1}{N} \left\{ hc' + (1-h) \frac{c}{2} \right\} \right]$$

$$+ \pi_2 (1 - p_n) \left[p_n + \frac{1}{N} (1-h) \frac{c}{2} \right]$$

$$+ \pi_0 (1 - p_n) \left[p_n + \frac{1}{N} \frac{c}{2} \right].$$

Collecting terms and simplifying yields a recursive expression in p_n:

$$p_{n+1} = p_n \left[1 - \frac{1}{N} (a + b) \right] + \frac{1}{N} a \tag{2}$$

where $a = \pi_1 hc' + (1-h) \dfrac{c}{2} + \pi_0 h \dfrac{c}{2}$ and $b = \pi_2 hc' + (1-h) \dfrac{c}{2} + \pi_0 h$

$\dfrac{c}{2}$. This difference equation has the well-known solution (cf. Bush and Mosteller, 1955; Suppes and Atkinson, 1960)

$$p_n = p_\infty - (p_\infty - p_1) \left[1 - \frac{1}{N} (a + b) \right]^{n-1}, \tag{3}$$

where $p_\infty = \dfrac{a}{a+b}$. Dividing the numerator and denominator of p_∞ by c yields the expression

$$p_\infty = \frac{\pi_1 h\psi + \dfrac{1}{2} (1-h) + \pi_0 h \dfrac{1}{2}}{(1 - \pi_0)(1 - h + h\psi) + \pi_0} \tag{4}$$

where $\psi = \dfrac{c'}{c}$. Thus, the asymptotic expression for p_n does not depend on the actual values of c' and c but only on their ratio.

With this expression at hand, we can now look at part of Kinchla's data. Figures 3 and 4 present the observed mean proportions for an A_i

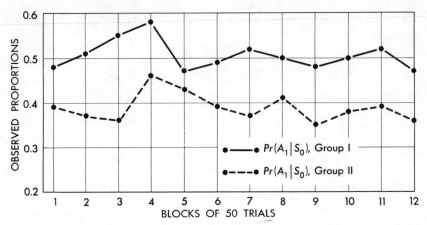

Figure 3.   Observed estimates of $Pr(A_1|T_1)$ and $Pr(A_2|T_2)$ in successive 50-trial blocks.

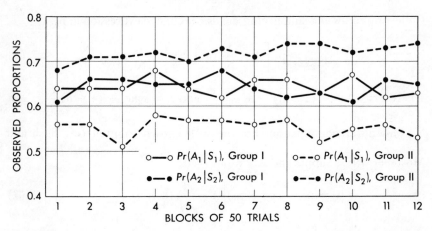

Figure 4.   Observed estimates for $Pr(A_1|T_0)$ in successive 50-trial blocks.

response, given a T_j event in successive blocks of 50 trials. An inspection of these curves indicates that all of the functions are quite stable over the last 400 trials. In view of this observation, we have estimated asymptotic response probabilities by averaging over the last 400 trials. Table 1 presents these observed values for the two groups. The corresponding asymptotic proportions are specified in terms of Eq. 1 and Eq. 4 and are simply

$$\lim_{n \to \infty} Pr(A_{1,n}|T_{1,n}) = h + (1-h)p_\infty \qquad (5a)$$

$$\lim_{n \to \infty} \text{Pr}(A_{2,n}|T_{2,n}) = h + (1 - h)(1 - p_\infty) \tag{5b}$$

$$\lim_{n \to \infty} \text{Pr}(A_{1,n}|T_{0,n}) = p_\infty \tag{5c}$$

In order to generate asymptotic predictions, we need values for h and ψ. We first note by inspection of Eq. 4 that $p_\infty = \frac{1}{2}$ for Group I; in fact, whenever $\pi_1 = \pi_2$, we have $p_\infty = \frac{1}{2}$, independent of the value of ψ. Hence, taking the observed asymptotic value for $\text{Pr}(A_1|T_1)$ in Group I (i.e., .645) and setting it equal to $h + (1 - h)\frac{1}{2}$ yields an estimate of $h = .289$. The physical stimuli and the increments in radiant intensity are the same for both experimental groups, and therefore we would require an estimate of h obtained from Group I to be applicable to Group II. In order to estimate ψ, we take the observed asymptotic value of $\text{Pr}(A_1|T_0)$ in Group II and set it equal to Eq. 4, with $h = .289$, $\pi_1 = \pi_0 = .2$, and $\pi_2 = .6$; solving for ψ, we obtain $\hat{\psi} = 2.8$. Using these estimates of h and ψ and Eqs. 4 and 5 yields the asymptotic predictions given in Table 1.

Table 1

Predicted and Observed Asymptotic Response Probabilities

	GROUP I		GROUP II	
	Observed	*Predicted*	*Observed*	*Predicted*
$\text{Pr}(A_1|T_1)$	.645	.645	.558	.565
$\text{Pr}(A_2|T_2)$	.643	.645	.730	.724
$\text{Pr}(A_1|T_0)$	.494	.500	.388	.388

Over-all, the equations give an excellent account of these particular response measures. However, the model provides a much richer analysis of the experiment than the above results indicate. For as we have said before, the model predicts not only average performance but also detailed sequential phenomena. In terms of our axioms, sequential effects are produced by the trial-to-trial fluctuations which occur in the conditioning of elements in set S^*; such fluctuations, of course, can take place on any trial and are not restricted to pre-asymptotic data. For example, even at asymptote, the likelihood of making a correct response to a T_1 event depends in a very definite way on whether an A_1 or A_2 response occurred on the preceding trial.

It should be emphasized that one of the important contributions of mathematics to behavior theory has been to provide a framework within which sequential phenomena can be analyzed. Prior to the development of mathematical models, relatively little attention was given to trial-to-trial events; at the present time, for many experimental problems (especially in learning) such phenomena are viewed as the most basic feature of the data. To indicate the type of sequential predictions which can be obtained, consider the probability of an A_1 response on a T_1 trial, given the various trial types and responses which can occur on the preceding trial; i.e.,

$$\Pr(A_{1, n+1} | T_{1, n+1} A_{i, n} T_{j, n})$$

where $i = 1, 2$ and $j = 0, 1, 2$. Explicit expressions for these quantities can be derived from the axioms. The actual derivations are quite lengthy and will not be presented here; the reader interested in the mathematical techniques involved should consult Atkinson and Estes (1962). Also, for purposes of this paper, the analysis of sequential statistics will be confined to asymptotic data. Therefore, only theoretical expressions for $\lim_{n \to \infty} \Pr(A_{1, n+1} | T_{1, n+1} A_{i, n} T_{j, n})$ will be given, and to simplify notation they will be written as $\Pr(A_1 | T_1 A_i T_j)$. The expressions for these quantities are as follows:

$$\Pr(A_1 | T_1 A_1 T_1) = \frac{[h + (1 - h)\delta]p_\infty + (1 - p_\infty)h\gamma'}{NX} + \frac{(N - 1)X}{N} \quad (6a)$$

$$\Pr(A_1 | T_1 A_2 T_1) = \frac{(1 - h)\delta'(1 - p_\infty)}{N(1 - X)} + \frac{(N - 1)X}{N} \quad (6b)$$

$$\Pr(A_1 | T_1 A_2 T_2) = \frac{h\gamma p_\infty + [h^2 + (1 - h)\delta'](1 - p_\infty)}{NY} + \frac{(N - 1)X}{N} \quad (6c)$$

$$\Pr(A_1 | T_1 A_1 T_2) = \frac{(1 - h)\delta p_\infty}{N(1 - Y)} + \frac{(N - 1)X}{N} \quad (6d)$$

$$\Pr(A_1 | T_1 A_1 T_0) = \frac{\delta}{N} + \frac{(N - 1)X}{N} \quad (6e)$$

$$\Pr(A_1 | T_1 A_2 T_0) = \frac{\delta'}{N} + \frac{(N - 1)X}{N} \quad (6f)$$

where $\gamma = c'h + (1 - c')$, $\gamma' = c' + (1 - c')h$, $\delta = \frac{c}{2} h + (1 - \frac{c}{2})$, $\delta' = \frac{c}{2} + (1 - \frac{c}{2})h$, $X = h + (1 - h)p_\infty$, and $Y = h + (1 - h)(1 - p_\infty)$. It is interesting to note that the asymptotic expressions for $\lim \Pr(A_{i, n} | T_{j, n})$ depend only on h and ψ, whereas the quantities in Eq. 6 are functions of all four parameters N, c, c' and h. Comparable sets of equations can be written for $Pr(A_2|T_2A_iT_j)$ and $Pr(A_1|T_0A_iT_j)$. We return to this point later.

The expressions in Eq. 6 are rather formidable, but numerical predictions can be easily calculated once values for the parameters have been obtained. Further, independent of the parameter values, certain relations among the sequential probabilities can be specified. As a simple example of such a relation, it can be shown that $Pr(A_1|T_1A_1T_0) \geqq Pr(A_1|T_1A_2T_0)$ for any stimulus schedule and any set of parameter values. To see this, simply subtract Eq. 6f from Eq. 6c and note that $\delta \geqq \delta'$.

In Table 2 the observed values for $Pr(A_i|T_jA_kT_1)$ are presented as reported by Kinchla. Estimates of these conditional probabilities were computed for individual subjects using the data over the last 400 trials; the average of these individual estimates are the quantities given in the table. Each entry is based on 24 subjects.

In order to generate theoretical predictions for the observed entries in Table 2, values for N, c, c' and h are needed. Of course, estimates of h and $\psi = \dfrac{c'}{c}$ already have been made for this set of data, and therefore we need only to estimate N and either c or c'. We obtain our estimates of N and c by a least-squares method, i.e., we select values of N and c (where $c' = c\hat{\psi}$) so that the sum of squared deviations between the 36 observed

Table 2

Predicted and Observed Sequential Response Probabilities at Asymptote

| | Group I | | Group II | |
	Observed	Predicted	Observed	Predicted
$Pr(A_2|T_2A_1T_1)$	.57	.58	.59	.64
$Pr(A_2|T_2A_2T_1)$	.65	.69	.70	.76
$Pr(A_2|T_2A_2T_2)$	.71	.71	.79	.77
$Pr(A_2|T_2A_1T_2)$	.61	.59	.69	.66
$Pr(A_2|T_2A_1T_0)$	.54	.59	.68	.66
$Pr(A_2|T_2A_2T_0)$	.66	.70	.71	.76
$Pr(A_1|T_1A_1T_1)$	.73	.71	.70	.65
$Pr(A_1|T_1A_2T_1)$	.62	.59	.59	.52
$Pr(A_1|T_1A_2T_2)$	.53	.58	.53	.51
$Pr(A_1|T_1A_1T_2)$	.66	.70	.64	.64
$Pr(A_1|T_1A_1T_0)$	.72	.70	.61	.63
$Pr(A_1|T_1A_2T_0)$	.61	.59	.48	.52
$Pr(A_2|T_0A_1T_1)$	.38	.40	.47	.49
$Pr(A_2|T_0A_2T_1)$	.56	.58	.59	.66
$Pr(A_2|T_0A_2T_2)$	.64	.60	.67	.68
$Pr(A_2|T_0A_1T_2)$	.47	.42	.51	.51
$Pr(A_2|T_0A_1T_0)$	.47	.42	.50	.51
$Pr(A_2|T_0A_2T_0)$	.60	.58	.65	.66

values in Table 2 and the corresponding theoretical quantities is minimized. The theoretical quantities for $\Pr(A_1|T_1A_iT_j)$ are computed from Eq. 6; theoretical expressions for $\Pr(A_2|T_2A_iT_j)$ and $\Pr(A_2|T_0A_iT_j)$ have not been presented in this paper but are of the same general form as those given in Eq. 6.

Using this technique, estimates of the parameters are as follows:

$$N = 4.23$$

$$c' = 1.00$$

$$c = .357 \tag{7}$$

$$h = .289$$

The predictions corresponding to these parameter values are presented in Table 2. When one considers that only four of the possible 36 degrees of freedom represented in Table 2 have been utilized in estimating parameters, the close correspondence between theoretical and observed quantities in Table 2 may be interpreted as giving considerable support to the assumptions of the model. Of course, for any given subject, N must be an integer. The fact that our estimation procedure yielded a non-integral value may signify that N varies somewhat between subjects, or it may reflect some contamination of the data by sources of experimental error not represented in the model. To answer these questions, a more detailed analysis of the data would be necessary in which estimates of the parameter values are made for individual subjects. Such analyses are too lengthy to discuss here.

Discussion

No model can be expected to give a perfect account of the fallible data arising from real experiments as distinguished from the idealized experiment to which the model should apply strictly. Consequently, it is difficult to know how to evaluate the goodness-of-fit of theoretical to observed values. In practice, investigators usually proceed on a largely intuitive basis, evaluating the fit in a given instance against that which it appears reasonable to expect in view of what is known about the precision of experimental control and measurement. Statistical tests of goodness-of-fit are sometimes possible (discussions of some tests that may be used in conjunction with stimulus sampling models are given by Suppes and Atkinson, 1960); however, statistical tests are not entirely satisfactory taken by themselves, for a sufficiently precise test will often indicate significant differences between theoretical and observed values even in cases where the agreement is as close as could reasonably be expected. Generally, once a degree of descriptive accuracy has been attained that appears satisfactory to investigators familiar with the given research area, further progress must come largely via differential tests of alternative models.

The problems involved in making differential tests among various models for signal detection are beyond the scope of this paper. However, it is clear that alternative models which deserve careful analysis can be formulated. For example, in this paper we have examined a very special Markovian conditioning process defined on the background stimuli; it would be important to determine whether other formulations of the learning process, such as those developed by Bush and Mosteller (1955), would provide as good or even better fits. Also, it would be valuable to consider variations in the scheme for sampling sensory elements along lines developed by Luce (1959) and Restle (1961).

Independent of further analysis, this particular model for signal detection appears to provide an impressive account of average response proportions and of various complex sequential events. Some readers may object to the model and argue that the axioms are unrealistic from a physiological viewpoint or in terms of a cognitive analysis. Such objections are important if they generate new ideas. However, in the absence of concrete suggestions that lead to testable models, it is doubtful whether this type of criticism is meaningful. For on that basis, one might just as well object to the kinetic theory of gases because it assumes that gas molecules behave as perfectly rigid spheres or to classical hydrodynamics because it postulates complete continuity of fluids. Certainly there is no single *true* theory. Rather, there is an infinite number of hypotheses and theories that can explain an array of phenomena, and we judge a particular theory not by some intuitive notion of reality but in terms of the theory's ability to account for the facts at hand and to generate new predictions.

In our concluding remarks, we should like to refer to a list of criteria or a decision rule that would evaluate the approach taken in this paper and tell us whether this specific development or related mathematical models are of genuine value in analyzing psychological phenomena. Of course, such decision procedures do not exist. Only the perspective gained by refinement and extension of these models with empirical verification at critical stages will permit us to make such an evaluation. Certainly within the last decade many behavioral phenomena have been examined with reference to one or more mathematical models, and these analyses have led to a deeper understanding of the empirical findings. In addition, many new lines of experimental research have been initiated by work on mathematical models. Despite these developments some behavioral scientists maintain that psychology has not yet reached a stage where mathematical analysis is appropriate; still others argue that the data of psychology are inherently different from those of the natural sciences and defy any type of rigorous systematization. There is no conclusive answer to these criticisms. Similar objections were raised against mathematical physics as recently as the late nineteenth century, and only the brilliant success of the approach silenced opposition. A convincing argument is yet to be made for the possibility that mathematical psychology will not enjoy similar success.

References

Atkinson, R. C. A variable threshold model for signal detection. Technical Report No. 42, Psychology Series, Institute for Mathematical Studies in the Social Sciences. Palo Alto, Calif.: Stanford Univ., 1961.

Atkinson, R. C., and Estes, W. K. Stimulus sampling theory. In R. R. Bush, E. Galanter, and R. D. Luce (eds.), *Handbook of mathematical psychology.* New York: Wiley (in preparation).

Bush, R. R., and Mosteller, F. *Stochastic models for learning.* New York: Wiley, 1955.

Estes, W. K. Toward a statistical theory of learning. *Psychol. Rev.,* 1950, 57, 94–107.

———. The statistical approach to learning theory. In S. Koch (ed.), *Psychology: a study of a science,* Vol. 2. New York: McGraw-Hill, 1959, pp. 383–491.

Estes, W. K., and Suppes, P. Foundations of statistical learning theory. II. The stimulus sampling model for simple learning. Technical Report No. 26, Psychology Series, Institute for Mathematical Studies in the Social Sciences. Palo Alto, Calif.: Stanford Univ., 1959.

Kinchla, R. A. Learned factors in visual discrimination. Unpublished doctoral dissertation, University of California, Los Angeles, 1962.

Luce, R. D. *Individual choice behavior: a theoretical analysis.* New York: Wiley, 1959.

Restle, F. *Psychology of judgment and choice: a theoretical essay.* New York: Wiley, 1961.

Suppes, P., and Atkinson, R. C. *Markov learning models for multiperson interactions.* Palo Alto, Calif.: Stanford Univ. Press, 1960.

CHAPTER XI

Sensory and Perceptual Functions

IN THIS FINAL CHAPTER, Hershel Leibowitz considers certain trends in perceptual theory. Leibowitz thoroughly documents his contention that established sensory mechanisms need to be considered as important contributory factors in interpretations of more complex "perceptual" processes, and that no simple dichotomy between sensation and perception can be justified. An important theme of this paper, to the effect that sound physiological knowledge should not be neglected by sensory theorists, is emphasized also in the last selection. There Conrad G. Mueller and William J. McGill present an intensive analysis of the theoretical substrate of current interpretations of color vision, pitch, and the threshold problem, with special reference to signal detection theory.

34 | *Some Trends in Perceptual Theory*

H . L E I B O W I T Z

Theory construction has played an active role in the history of psychology. Indeed, the development of a major system, *Gestalt* psychology, was concerned primarily with perceptual phenomena and perceptual theory. Later historical developments include a number of theoretical formulations in an attempt to account for the variety of interesting phenomena which are implied by the term "perception." In general, these theories have not proven to be adequate, as they fail to indicate specific tests whereby the

validity of their assumptions and implications can be experimentally verified. However, the purpose of the present account is not to examine existing theories of perception. Rather, it will attempt to identify a number of
current trends which, it is felt, have important implications for the development of more adequate theory in the future.

Classically, sensation and perception have been differentiated, sensation
being characterized as less "complex" and more "analyzable." The functional validity of this dichotomy has been attacked on a number of
grounds, and it is thought to be operationally untenable (Graham, 1952).
Nevertheless, the major theoretical approaches do reflect the historical
influence of this dichotomy. "Perceptual" theories are concerned with
phenomena such as the constancies, figural after effects, attention, and
space. "Sensory" theories deal with absolute threshold, color vision (see
Selection 35 by Mueller and McGill), intensity discrimination, visual
acuity, etc. Sensory theories tend to look for explanatory mechanisms in
the anatomy and physiology of the sense organs, while perceptual theories
are more concerned with central effects, learning, and motivation.

From the point of view of methodology, approaches to both "sensory"
and "perceptual" theory construction have been as varied as that of
psychological theory construction in general. Some approaches have
emerged as minor or major parts of psychological systems. The introspective method of Wundt, which provided the technique for the Structural
school of psychology, was designed to provide information regarding the
content of the mind in terms of elements, many of which could be
classified as sensory or perceptual. Thus, interest in perceptual phenomena
and theory followed naturally (and was restricted by) the more general
systematic approach advocated by the Structuralists. This method was
vigorously attacked by the Gestaltists primarily on the grounds that the
analytic method of introspection destroys critical features of perception.
The Gestalt movement, in addition to its general systematic implications
which were primarily, but not exclusively, concerned with perceptual
phenomena, has provided elaborate theoretical hypotheses regarding the
central correlates of perceptual processes. Other theoretical approaches to
both "sensory" and "perceptual" problems have been directed toward
more specific classes of phenomena such as color vision, audition, signal
detection (see Selection 35 by Mueller and McGill), space perception, and
the like. These approaches have strongly emphasized physiological and
mathematical principles when appropriate. The problems of space perception have been treated theoretically, both as part of the Gestalt movement
and in terms of more specific approaches. The analysis of some of the
phenomena of binocular vision by Luneberg (1947) is one of the most
mathematically sophisticated theories in the behavioral sciences. More
recently, the developing technologies associated with information process-

ing and computer design have suggested approaches to perceptual theory which are designed not only to provide a theoretical methodology, but to provide models that will permit the construction of electronic devices which will replace, to a limited extent, the human visual system (Attneave, 1954; Rosenblatt, 1958). Other theoretical approaches of interest emphasize the overlap between the study of the visual system, and related disciplines and systems. For example, there have been a number of attempts to integrate perception and personality which have generally followed the approaches of personality theorists (see, for example, Bruner and Krech, 1950). The close relation between perception and the vestibular and muscular systems of the body is treated in detail by Werner and Wapner (1952). The well-known theory of Hebb (1949), is an attempt to integrate some phenomena of perception and perceptual learning with neurophysiological principles.

It is clear however, even from a cursory survey of theoretical approaches, that they are deficient in a number of respects despite the fact that they may have admirably served the purposes for which they were originally intended. A dichotomy among various categories of phenomena is illogical at any level of analysis. Both peripheral and central mechanisms are necessarily activated, irrespective of the type of discrimination under consideration. A general criticism which can be made of all existing theories, both sensory or perceptual, is that they are too restrictive in terms of the range of phenomena to which they address themselves. Ultimately, we would hope to develop a comprehensive theoretical system which would treat a wide variety of phenomena regardless of their historical classification as sensory or perceptual. Admittedly, this goal will be difficult to attain and will require, at least, an empirical data base many times larger than that which is now available. However, there have been a number of trends, some of which will be outlined in this selection, which provide encouraging first steps on which a general approach encompassing both perceptual and sensory phenomena can be based. These trends, it is felt, are significant for theory construction in that their implications are testable and that they contribute to the all-important goal of providing the necessary concepts, techniques, and mechanisms on which a comprehensive theory can be developed.

The Reciprocity Law of Photochemistry

Because of the presence of photochemical substances in the visual end organs, it is reasonable to question the extent to which photochemical principles can account for visual behavior. In line with this approach, Hecht (1935) has proposed a photochemical theory of vision which accounts fairly adequately for a limited number of sensory phenomena.

An important principle of photochemistry is the Bunsen-Roscoe, or reciprocity, law. This relation states that the effect of photic stimulation is a function of the total quantity of energy, irrespective of the specific values of time or intensity. More precisely,

$$I \times T = C$$

where C is a constant, I is intensity, and T is time.

This law has been shown to be applicable to the visual system below a critical duration of 0.1 second, to the activation of single receptors in the horseshoe crab, *Limulus*, and, in human psychophysical studies, to absolute threshold, intensity discrimination, visual acuity, and movement perception.

More recently, Hunter and Sigler (1940) investigated the extent to which the reciprocity law is applicable to the visual span of attention. This phenomenon refers to the number of objects which can be perceived in a single brief glance. Historically, the span has been considered in a context which includes the categories of attention, cognition, and apprehension (Woodworth, 1938). By systematically varying the time and intensity of stimulation and determining the number of objects, i.e., dots, the subject could perceive correctly, Hunter and Sigler established that both time and intensity of stimulation are relevant variables affecting the span of attention. Further analysis revealed that below the critical duration of 0.1 second, and for eight dots or fewer, the reciprocity law predicts the number of dots the subject can perceive correctly. For a given number of dots, any combination of time and intensity which produces a constant amount of energy will result in equivalent behavioral effects. (Above eight objects, the concept of the span does not apply, and a different mechanism, perhaps counting, is operative.)

Thus, a phenomenon which has been historically considered as "perceptual" and has usually been treated theoretically in terms of central factors has been shown to be limited by the same initial photochemical events which are important determiners of a number of "sensory" phenomena. This demonstration is illustrative of the way in which the identification of a basic mechanism has improved our understanding of a number of phenomena, from both the sensory and perceptual domains, and as such has served to point the way to a more comprehensive theoretical treatment.

Neural Inhibition

A familiar principle of neurophysiology is that excitation of one part of the nervous system can inhibit or diminish activity in other parts

(Sherrington, 1906). Neural inhibition has been demonstrated at various levels, including the reflex activity of the spinal cord as well as the mammalian retina (Graham, 1934). Recently, experimental investigation of neural inhibition in the lateral eye of the horseshoe crab, *Limulus*, has identified basic characteristics which have important implications for understanding a number of visual phenomena.

Hartline and his co-workers, recording from the lateral eye of *Limulus*, have demonstrated that the frequency of discharge of a given receptor is diminished by the simultaneous excitation of neighboring sense cells. This inhibition effect has a number of characteristics of interest in the present analysis. The magnitude of the inhibition is increased the greater the difference in the excitation of the sense cells in question. The effect diminishes with increasing separation between the stimulated receptors. In addition, it can be shown that when a number of receptors are activated, the inhibition effect is mutual; each receptor inhibits, and at the same time is inhibited by, its neighbors. Another characteristic of the effect is that it is primarily unidirectional; the more intensely illuminated receptor exerts a stronger inhibition upon the less intensely illuminated units than the latter exert on the former.

The identification of these characteristics of neural inhibition has a number of implications for the understanding of visual phenomena. It is evident that neural inhibition accounts for the well-known effect of simultaneous contrast. Indeed, a number of human psychophysical studies have produced functional relations which are entirely in accord with the characteristics obtained in *Limulus* (Diamond, 1960). Historically, there has been some controversy as to the locus in the nervous system of the contrast relationship, Helmholtz having attributed it to "judgment," presumably implying a central locus (Graham, 1934). The demonstration of clearly defined mechanisms in *Limulus* which parallel the results of human studies would seem to establish that it is not necessary to invoke higher processes in order to understand simultaneous brightness contrast.

With the specifications of the conditions under which contrast is obtained available from independent studies, it has been possible to reinvestigate the role of simultaneous contrast in brightness constancy, a relationship first suggested by Hering (1878). If a gray test-object is viewed on a black background, very little if any contrast will be exhibited. Similarly, there is very little brightness constancy observed under these same conditions. If, however, the same gray test-object is seen against a white background, both contrast and brightness constancy are exhibited (Leibowitz, Myers, and Chinetti, 1955). Thus, brightness constancy is seen to follow from the introduction of contrast, the latter being defined in terms of the basic relationships of neural inhibition. This conclusion has been recently substantiated by an experiment in which the separation between two contrasting fields, a procedure which is known to reduce contrast, also produced a corresponding diminution in brightness constancy (Dunn and Leibowitz, 1961).

The neural studies of inhibition have also contributed to our understanding of a mechanism which can account for the perceived sharpness of borders. It is well known that the eye suffers from a variety of aberrations which, together with diffraction, result in considerable blurring of the retinal image. Despite this lack of definition, our perception of borders is sharp and well-defined. Ratliff and Hartline (1959, p. 1247) suggest an explanation of this effect as follows:

> On the basis of the diminution of the inhibitory interaction with increasing distance one can predict the general form of the patterns of response which will be elicited from the elements of the receptor mosaic by various spatial patterns of illumination. Contrast effects, for example, may be expected to be greatest at or near the boundary between a dimly illuminated region and a brightly illuminated region of the retina. A unit which is within the dimly illuminated region, but which is near this boundary, will be inhibited not only by dimly illuminated neighbors, but also by brightly illuminated ones. The total inhibition exerted on it will therefore be greater than that exerted upon other dimly illuminated elements that are farther from the boundary; consequently its frequency of response will be less than theirs. Similarly, a unit within but near the boundary of the brightly illuminated field will have a higher frequency of discharge than other equally illuminated units which are located well within the bright field but which are subject to stronger inhibition since all their immediate neighbors are also brightly illuminated. Thus the differences in the activity of elements on either side of the boundary will be exaggerated and the discontinuity in this pattern of illumination will be accentuated in the pattern of neural response.

Experimental verification of this prediction was obtained by recording the frequency of discharge of receptors in *Limulus* when the entire eye was exposed to a pattern containing an abrupt transition from dark to light. Receptors located within the light region but near the area of transition have a higher frequency of discharge than other fibers in the light region which are located at some distance from the region of transition. Similarly, fibers in the dark region have a lower frequency of discharge the nearer they are to the border. It is clear from this demonstration that neural inhibition not only accounts for contrast, but that the particular properties of this mechanism seem to provide a most reasonable explanation of one of the recurring problems of perception, the perceived sharpness of borders.

In a subsequent demonstration, Ratliff and Hartline experimentally manipulated the slope of the gradient between the dark and light areas of stimulation. The result, as would be predicted from their theory, was that maxima and minima, which do not exist in the retinal image, were produced by the neural response at the regions of transition. This demonstrates an analog of the familiar phenomenon of Mach bands, the dark and light bands observed at the edge of shadows. Thus, the identification of a basic, specifiable mechanism has been shown to account for a variety of perceptual phenomena which previous theoretical formulations have attempted to explain by invoking more complex "higher" processes, or by mechanisms which are neither as basic nor as simple as that represented by neural inhibition.

The Re-afference Principle

A number of insects exhibit marked orienting responses to light stimulation. This phenomenon, known as the optomotor reflex, can be experimentally investigated by surrounding an insect, such as the fly *Eristalis*, with a series of black and white vertical stripes affixed to the inside of a cylinder. As the cylinder is rotated, the animal follows the movement of the stripes, continually orienting his body so that the image of the stripes in his eyes remains motionless. However, if the cylinder is motionless, the animal is able to move about freely without invoking the optomotor reflex, despite the fact that each motion of the animal produces movement of the retinal image.

Von Holst and Mittelstaedt (1950) have suggested that the central nervous system is able to differentiate between afferent stimulation produced by the movement of external objects, such as the cylinder in the example above, and afference produced by movement initiated by the animal itself. They distinguish between these two types of afference, although both involve the same peripheral mechanisms and presumably the same patterns of excitation, by referring to the former as ex-afference and the latter as re-afference. According to their theoretical scheme, ex-afference is perceived directly by the organism. Re-afference is not normally perceived, because the animal, when initiating a voluntary movement, produces an hypothesized "efference copy," the purpose of which is to cancel the self-produced re-afference. In the example of the fly in the cylinder, the initiation of the voluntary movement produces simultaneously an efference copy of retinal motion as well as re-afference of retinal motion. The two cancel each other, and therefore no perception of moving stripes nor optomotor reflexes occur as a result of self-produced movement.

As a test of their theory, they have experimentally produced mismatches between the efference copy and the re-afference. One such test consists of rotating the head of *Eristalis* 180 degrees around its longitudinal axis, so that movement in a given direction will result in motion of the retinal image *opposite* from that which would normally obtain. Thus, although both the re-afference and the efference copy are produced, they would be of the same instead of opposite sign and would reinforce rather than cancel each other. The results are in agreement with theory; as soon as the fly initiates the slightest movement, it continues to spin until exhausted, presumably because the retinal-image motion is not canceled and the optomotor reflex is evoked. In a more subtle test of this theory, the statoliths of fish were experimentally made heavier by rotating the animals in a centrifuge. Under such conditions, the efference copy would be normal, but the re-afference would be greater by an amount proportional to the acceleration of the centrifuge. Under such conditions, the tilting behavior of the fish is predictable by assuming a graded mismatch between the efference copy and the re-afference. (For details, see von Holst and Mittelstaedt, 1950.)

The theory of re-afference is relevant to a number of problems in visual perception: for example, the question of vision during saccadic eye movements, which evoked so much vigorous discussion among psychologists at the turn of the century (Woodworth, 1938). Holt (1903) suggested that the absence of vision was due to "central anesthesia," while Woodworth preferred an explanation based on the blurring of the retinal image. Von Holst and Mittelstaedt would prefer an explanation more in line with Holt's, but couched in the more general terms of the re-afference theory. A further advantage of the re-afference principle is in relation to the false perceptions which occur when the extra-ocular muscles are anesthetized. Under such conditions, an intended eye movement which fails to be executed because of the anesthetic results in a subjective shift of the visual scene in the direction of the intended movement (Teuber, 1960). Under the re-afference scheme, this illusion is a result of the uncanceled efference copy, and the results of such experiments are presented in support of the theory. Other visual phenomena to which the re-afference theory seems to be applicable are size constancy (for near objects), the micropsia and macropsia which result from paralyzing the accommodation mechanism, and the projected size of the visual after-image.

The psychologist, while perhaps recognizing the applicability of the re-afference theory to a number of perceptual phenomena, will be interested in knowing more about the factors which contribute to the hypothesized efference copy. In a most interesting series of experiments involving disarrangement of the visual field by means of prisms, Held has concluded that re-afference is necessary for readaptation to the disarranged condition, and for the re-establishment of sensory motor coordination. Presumably, re-afference contributes to the formation of the efference copy during learning and as such may provide a useful concept in the analysis of perceptual and perceptual-motor learning effects (Held and Schlank, 1959).

Conclusions

The preceding examples have been chosen as representative of recent developments in visual science which have important implications for the development of theory. Specifically, they support the position that a dichotomy between sensation and perception is neither definitive nor useful and imply that future theories will encompass phenomena and mechanisms from, historically, sensation and perception. In addition, they illustrate the multidisciplinary approach to understanding of the visual system. It has been suggested that our knowledge of the span of attention is increased by a consideration of relatively simple photochemical relationships, that brightness constancy and contour formation, among other phenomena, can be re-interpreted with the aid of well-defined principles of neurophysiology, and that some aspects of space perception and several "abnormal" perceptual phenomena can be integrated into a meaningful formulation with the help of principles derived from study of the behavior of insects. It is gratifying to see that these mechanisms are not confined to the visual system but, in particular cases, are of relevance to the reflex behavior of the spinal cord, the function of the organs of equilibrium, and even, in the case of the reciprocity law, to non-biological systems.

This point of view does not imply that the problems of visual perception are ultimately reducible to simple laws of photochemistry or neural inhibition. It does imply that these mechanisms can in some cases limit the behavior of the visual system and, as such, cannot be ignored by any reasonably adequate formulation. In one sense, the identification of such mechanisms facilitates the task of the theorist and experimenter by providing the means for making explicit those relations which depend on known mechanisms and those which require further explanation. For example, studies of the span of attention have yielded discrepant numerical values. In view of the results of the Hunter-Sigler study, we should now ask how much of this variability was due to the factors of intensity and time which, prior to Hunter and Sigler, were not considered as relevant and were probably not controlled. After such a determination has been made, the remaining variance can more safely be attributed to other variables such as age, intelligence, and so forth. Similarly, the demonstration that neural inhibition is an important factor in brightness constancy does not negate the explanatory value of other variables such as pupil diameter, memory, and familiarity. It does mean that any investigation of brightness constancy must be careful to control for contrast, which is certainly a major mechanism contributing to the phenomenon. When the effect of major variables are controlled and specified, the task of identifying and assessing the role of secondary effects is made considerably less difficult.

Whether the developments referred to above are isolated examples, and the trend toward a comprehensive theory of vision will continue, is a question for the future. Theories are formulated to account for phenomena, and theory, in turn, suggests further tests which provide data for modification and improvement of theory. It is difficult to imagine that the identification of basic mechanisms, relevant to a number of phenomena, and capable of experimental verification or refutation, will not contribute to the growth of improved visual theory.

References

Attneave, F. Some informational aspects of visual perception. *Psych. Rev.*, 1954, *61*, 183–193.

Bruner, J. S., and Krech, D. *Perception and personality: a symposium.* Durham, N.C.: Duke University Press, 1950.

Diamond, A. L. A theory of depression and enhancement in the brightness response. *Psych. Rev.*, 1960, 67, 168–199.

Dunn, B., and Leibowitz, H. The effect of separation between test and inducing fields on brightness constancy. *J. Exp. Psych.*, 1961, *61*, 505–507.

Graham, C. H. Some neural correlations. In C. Murchison (ed.), *Handbook of general experimental psychology*. Worcester, Mass.: Clark University Press, 1934.

Graham, C. H. Behavior and the psychophysical methods: an analysis of some recent experiments. *Psych. Rev.*, 1952, *59*, 62–70.

Hebb, D. O. The organization of behavior. New York: John Wiley & Sons, 1949.

Hecht, S. A theory of visual intensity discrimination. *J. Gen. Physiol.*, 1935, *18*, 767–789.

Held, R., and Schlank, M. Adaptation to disarranged eye-hand coordination in the distance dimension. *Amer. J. Psych.*, 1959, 72, 603–605.

Hering, E. *Gründezuge der Lehre vom Lichsinn*. Berlin: Springer, 1920.

Holst, E. von, and Mittelstaedt, H. Das reafferenzprinzip. *Naturwissenschaften*, 1950, *37*, 464–476.

Holt, E. B. Eye movement and central anesthesia. I. The problem of anesthesia during eye movement. *Psych. Monogr.*, 1903, #17.

Hunter, W. S., and Sigler, M. The span of visual discrimination as a function of time and intensity of stimulation. *J. Exp. Psych.*, 1940, *26*, 160–179.

Leibowitz, H., Myers, N., and Chinetti, P. The role of simultaneous contrast in brightness constancy. *J. Exp. Psychol.*, 1955, *50*, 15–18.

Luneberg, R. Mathematical analysis of binocular vision. Princeton, N.J.: Princeton University Press, 1947 (for the Dartmouth Eye Institute).

Ratliff, F., and Hartline, H. K. The responses of *Limulus* optic nerve fibers to patterns of illumination on the receptor mosaic. *J. Gen. Physiol.*, 1959, *42*, 1241–1255.

Rosenblatt, F. The perceptron: a probalistic model for information storage and organization in the brain. *Psych. Rev.*, 1958, *65*, 386–408.

Sherrington, C. S. The integrative action of the nervous system. New York: Scribners, 1906.

Teuber, H. L. Perception. In J. Field, H. W. Magoun, and V. E. Hall (eds.), *Handbook of physiology*, Sect. I, Vol. III, Neurophysiology. Washington, D.C.: American Physiological Society, 1960.

Werner, H., and Wapner, S. Toward a general theory of perception. *Psych. Rev.*, 1952, *59*, 324–388.

Woodworth, R. S. *Experimental psychology*. New York: Holt, 1938.

35 | *Theories in Sensory Psychology*

CONRAD MUELLER AND WILLIAM MCGILL

The nature of psychological theory has been a topic of great interest both to psychologists and philosophers of science for many years. In the process of discussing this subject, many "do-and-don't" rules have been offered as prescriptions for progress. Many of these rules mirror the needs and attitudes prevailing in a particular area of psychology, and we will probably not be able to avoid adding to the list. The organization of this article is predicated on two assumptions: the first is that sensory psychology can make a definite, and perhaps unique, contribution to our understanding of psychological theory; the second is that, at this time, it is not fruitful to discuss the nature of sensory theory in the abstract, i.e., outside the context of the data in the area.

Sensory data are tied together by our understanding of the physics of the stimuli and by the mechanisms that are known to be available for transforming energy changes in the environment into a form that will be useful in the "elicitation" or "emission" of behavior. The study of the data of sensory psychology highlights several problems or processes in the behavioral sciences which we may be able to discuss only abstractly in other areas of psychology. The first of these is the intimate relation between the behavioral measurements we make and the manner in which we define the stimulus. This problem is certainly alluded to in the learning literature, but it is difficult to find good examples. Because of the concern with the stimulus in sensory experiments, it may be said that the whole rationale of many programs of research is a search for an appropriate descriptive language for the "critical information" in the stimulus that is operated on by the chain of events between stimulus presentation and response occurrence. For instance, a class of dimensions in vision involves the concept of "luminous" energy. These dimensions employ energy measurements as their starting point but apply to these physical measurements a weighting function, i.e., the photopic visibility curve. This is a behavioral function based on the measurement of thresholds at different wavelengths. We encounter the same type of process in our discussion of audition, where a number of alternative ways of describing auditory stimuli are outlined. The question of whether we should specify acoustic stimuli in terms of their frequency spectrum, their autocorrelation function, their envelope, or in some other terms cannot be decided outside of the context of the discrimination data. This interaction of the behavioral data and the stimulus description has been a part of experimental research activities and theory construction throughout the history of sensory psychology.

A second point that is highlighted in any examination of the field of sensory psychology is the role played by physiological data in influencing the kinds of experiments that are done, the forms of theory that are constructed, and the way in which the problems of stimulus definition, discussed above, are resolved. In no other area of psychology do we pay as much attention to the quantitative characteristics of the successive links in the chain of events that is started by stimulus manipulation and terminates in the measurement of the response of the organism. It is the nature of the subject matter that with comparable stimulus conditions it is possible not only to study the behavior of the intact organism but to study the response of the sense cell, of the sensory nerve fibers, and of fibers in the sensory areas of the central nervous system. The results of such experiments help us in at least two ways. They provide us with detailed data on what happens to the information that is available in the stimulus and thus provide us with ways of organizing and interpreting our behavioral data; they also suggest specific behavioral experiments that throw light on the problems of stimulus definition and on the form that sensory theories should take.

This is certainly not typical of theory in other psychological areas. Learning theory usually does not stress physiological details. The study of personality often produces large theoretical superstructures, but commonly these are loosely defined and designed to bridge the gap between observable behavior and the theorist's speculations as to what is really going on. Why should sensory theory place such unusual stress on the nature of the stimulus and the physiological details of sensory systems?

At once, we concede that we do not have to do things in this way. It is certainly possible to construct purely behavioral (i.e., "empty organism" or "black box") theories of sensory data, just as it is possible to construct them in learning and in other areas. The essential difference between theories about sensory data and theories in other areas of psychology is measured in terms of the relative simplicity of the systems involved and in terms of the amount of physiological detail available. The outlines of at least the major sensory systems (vision, audition) have been developed practically the whole way from the stimulus—to sense organ—to neural processing—to behavior, so that in fact we do have some conception of how they work. We do not now understand all of the details, but the outline can be sketched in a way that is not true of any other area of psychology.

Consequently the theoretical problems have taken the form of tracing sensory information as it passes up the chain, in much the same way that an electrical engineer traces a signal as it passes through a complex electronic network. If we know of a way to analyze the stimulus, we are led to check the sense organ to learn whether it is constructed to perform that particular analysis. Moreover, if we know something about the operation of the sense organ and can find psychophysical (i.e., behavioral) data reflecting this operation, we may use discrepancies between the two kinds of information in order to indicate important areas for study. Many examples of this type of cross-checking are provided in the sections that follow. In the study of color vision, we find that three different color processes are sufficient to account for color-matching data. We are then led to look for three types of cones or for physiological color processes behind the cones that have the form indicated by the behavioral data. This information is conveyed from the wavelength of the light stimulus, and eventually it leads to color discriminations. The problem is to determine how it happens.

In audition there is simply no point in trying to relate pitch phenomena to simple resonance in the cochlea, because we now know that the system does not work in this way.

These suggestions are developed more fully in succeeding pages. Here we are trying to set the stage by outlining the peculiar and unique character of sensory theory; its emphasis on the communication of information and on the physiological processes linking the stimulus to behavior. Moreover, most sensory theories are closely connected to the systems they serve, because they are theories about how the systems are built. It is not really appropriate to think of them as models and to discuss them in abstract terms. Sensory theories are models of course, and problems arise in relating them to data, but these issues are not vitally important. What is essential is that the models of successive steps in sensory chains are interlocked, and information from any given step is used to shape our thinking about remote steps. The major objective is to link the physical, physiological, and behavioral levels of discourse together by the constraints of a common interpretation. We believe this linkage is possible and worth attempting.

Theories of Color Vision

Theories encountered in the field of color vision may start from any one of several empirical bases, but eventually they must come to grips with a long list of color phenomena. Included in this list are such diverse topics as 1) color mixture, 2) wavelength discrimination, 3) color blindness, 4) saturation, and 5) complementary colors. The fact that stimuli with broad and continuous spectra seem to have the same appearance as certain other stimuli consisting of a few discrete spectral components suggests that the number of receptor processes must be fairly small. The problem is to work out the properties of a few simple hypothetical processes which are sufficient to account for most of the color phenomena with which the theory must deal.

TRICHROMATIC THEORY   Historically the strongest color theory has been the *trichromatic theory*. As its name implies, it assumes three basic receptor processes. The intuitive plausibility of this assumption derives from the fact that it is possible to match the color of any comparison stimulus by mixing three monochromatic stimuli in appropriate proportions. It is not literally true that the comparison stimulus can be matched by mixing three monochromatic stimuli *together*, and this detracts somewhat from the intuitive base of the theory. Color matches can, in the general case, be made only when one of the mixing stimuli is added to the comparison stimulus. The correct statement of the color mixture rule is that it is always possible to match two mixtures, each of which is composed of two (appropriately related) monochromatic stimuli. This is an empirical rule and does not depend on theory. In view of the rule, we can write an algebraic equation describing color mixtures,

$$a\,[\lambda_i] + b\,[\lambda_1] = c\,[\lambda_2] + d\,[\lambda_3], \qquad (1)$$

where λ_i is an arbitrary test wavelength and λ_1, λ_2, and λ_3 denote three fixed wavelengths; a, b, c, and d are numerical coefficients. The square bracket [ ] is used in order to indicate "unit" intensity of the quantity within the bracket. These units are not conventional luminous units such as millilamberts but are functions of the latter designed to give equation (1) its simple appearance. For example, a criterion which is often used involves calling $[\lambda_1]$, $[\lambda_2]$, and $[\lambda_3]$ equal when their photometric values (whatever they may be) combine to produce a mixture equivalent to a given white.

Equation (1) means that the mixtures on each side match one another in hue. The relation is important, because we really can fix the wavelengths λ_1, λ_2, and λ_3 and simply adjust the magnitudes a, b, c, and d in order to satisfy the equality for all test lengths, λ_i. Experiments performed to check on the mixture equation work out as claimed. The wavelengths λ_1, λ_2, and λ_3 are called primaries. One or the other will always appear on the left-hand side of equation (1) as λ_i changes over the range of wavelengths in the visible spectrum (approximately 400–700 millimicrons).

Figure 1 illustrates an empirical determination of the coefficients in (1).

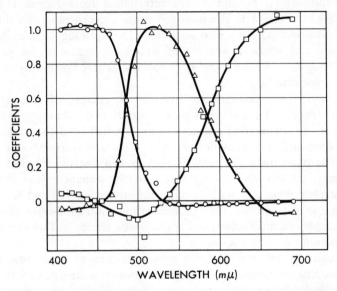

Figure 1. Relative intensities of three primary wavelengths that match unit intensity at each test wavelength given on the abscissa. Similar data are generated by all subjects with normal color vision. These subjects are called *trichromats* in view of this type of color matching. (Adapted from Graham and Hsia, 1958.)

The wavelengths corresponding to λ_i are plotted along the abscissa. The coefficients on the ordinate are the values of b, c, and d as they are determined experimentally. (Since these coefficients vary with wavelength, their values trace out three different curves.) At each wavelength (vertical slice), the three coefficients sum to 1, and one of them is always negative or zero. The data in Figure 1 were obtained by using primaries at:

$$\lambda_1 = 460 \text{ m}\mu \text{ (blue)}$$
$$\lambda_2 = 530 \text{ m}\mu \text{ (green)}$$
$$\lambda_3 = 650 \text{ m}\mu \text{ (red)}$$

Evidently, however, equation (1) can be solved for *any* of the three primaries in terms of the other two plus λ_i. Suppose, for example, we want to change the primary λ_1 from 460 mμ to 420 mμ (Call the latter λ_o.) We do not have to make another measurement. Instead we write equation (1) as follows:

$$[\lambda_1] = \frac{c_o}{b_o} [\lambda_2] + \frac{d_o}{b_o} [\lambda_3] - \frac{1}{b_o} [\lambda_0]. \tag{1a}$$

The values of c_o, b_o, and d_o are determined from Figure 1 at $\lambda_i = 420$ mμ. As before, $a = 1$. We now substitute the expression on the right side of equation (1a) back into equation (1), replacing $[\lambda_1]$, collect the coefficients, and obtain a new set of weights in terms of the primaries $\lambda_0 = 420$ mμ, $\lambda_2 = 530$ mμ, and $\lambda_3 = 650$ mμ. These coefficients will also generate color matches.

Stiles (1955) has pointed out two distinct usages of the term *trichromatic theory*. One use refers to no more than the descriptive analysis just outlined for generating a series of curves which will encompass color mixture data and will provide an algebra for transforming one set of primaries into another. The term is also used in a stronger sense. In the latter usage, trichromatic theory refers to the statement that there are three receptor processes with specific sensitivity curves and that these processes can account for the color discrimination of human observers. This is a theory of mechanism, and trichromatic theory in this strong sense is what we now wish to discuss.

Color mixture data tell us the relative intensities of λ_1, λ_2, and λ_3 that are required to match any given λ_i. If the primaries are assumed to stimulate three independent color processes, these color mixture data can be assumed to provide an expression for the relative contribution of each process to the color λ_i.

The selection of the primaries λ_1, λ_2, and λ_3 is evidently arbitrary; a great many sets of three wavelengths will satisfy equation (1). Primaries are usually chosen from the red, green, and blue portions of the spectrum, but many other sets are possible. The fact that primaries can be shifted algebraically attests to the generality of the color mixture equation, but it also means that, in principle, there is no limit to the number of such sets. This raises a very serious problem, because it means that we can generate an infinite number of curves like Figure 1, all of which satisfy the color mixture equation. Each set possesses the power of summarizing the color mixture data, and we do not know which one to choose.

The question then is whether we might impose additional constraints on the inferred "process" curves in order to arrive at a unique set. These constraints might be taken from other color discrimination data. A typical constraint assumes that the "process" curves must have shapes that will generate wavelength discrimination data. The threshold wavelength difference, $\Delta\lambda$, necessary to lead a normal observer to detect a difference in color depends on the reference wavelength, λ, as shown in Figure 2. Thus, we can restrict the class of admissible process curves to those that generate a wavelength discrimination function similar to the one actually found.

For example, suppose that the threshold change in wavelength is a function of the *rate of change* of the process curves. This assumption ex-

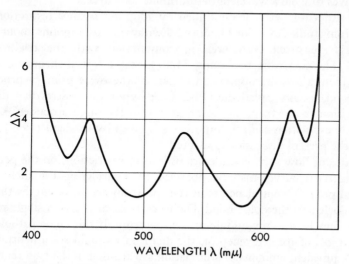

Figure 2.   Minimum detectable difference in wavelength as a function of the reference wavelength. (Adapted from Troland, 1930.)

presses the intuitive notion that we ought to be able to detect differences in wavelength easily if the component color processes change rapidly. Helmholtz (1896) assumed that a detectable change in wavelength requires a change in sensation (ΔS) due to changes in the R, G, and B processes (ΔS_R, ΔS_G, ΔS_B). According to the theory, the changes in the components combine to form ΔS via a simple relation:

$$(\Delta S)^2 = (\Delta S_R)^2 + (\Delta S_G)^2 + (\Delta S_B)^2. \tag{2}$$

We can see the logic of this assumption if we imagine a three-dimensional space in which the three (orthogonal) dimensions are the R, G, and B sensory processes. Helmholtz assumed that the eye could detect a difference in wavelength, if the latter represented a threshold distance in this space. The rule for combining the component effects in equation (2) is the length of the diagonal in a three-dimensional rectangle. Quantitative difficulties are encountered when we attempt to relate the hypothetical three-dimensional sensation space to empirical variables. No one supposes that a linear relation exists between stimulus intensity and "sensation." Hence, we find ourselves in complicated geometry when we try to translate equation (2) into an equivalent version involving the coefficients of the process curves in Figure 1. We will not go into the details of the transformation, but the approach exemplifies how constraints can be placed on the shape of the hypothetical process curves, forcing their derivatives to yield a wavelength discrimination curve.

This procedure may be continued by adopting further restrictions derived from studies of color blindness. Two major assumptions about color blindness are often considered in conjunction with the trichromatic theory. The first, due to Young (1807), states that dichromatic vision results from a loss or suppression of one of the three primary processes; the second, usually called the Leber-Fick hypothesis, asserts that dichromatic vision results from the fusion of two of the three processes. A more complete exposition of both hypotheses is given by Graham (1959), from which the present discussion is adapted.

An idea of how such considerations lead to restrictions on the permissible sensitivity curves may be obtained by considering the dichromat's "neutral point." Neutral points in the spectrum are wavelengths that appear colorless to the color blind. Dichromats usually have a single neutral point somewhere in the middle of the spectrum. If this color pathology is due to a loss of the red receptor, the dichromat should see a neutral gray where equivalent amounts of stimulation are aroused in the two remaining processes. Consequently the location of the neutral wavelength would reduce the possibilities to only those curves with crossing points at the required location.

ADDITIONAL FORMS OF COLOR THEORY   Although trichromatic theory in its many forms offers process curves of great generality, it is still changing to accommodate new data. In spite of its success, there have been suggestions that the general form of color theory must be changed. For example, Stiles (1959) has offered evidence suggesting that we should begin to think in terms of five or perhaps seven color receptive processes instead of three. Certain data, particularly increment threshold data for different wavelengths, are most easily organized by such a change in the form of theory.

Perhaps the most striking deviation from the strong trichromatic approach has been offered recently by Hurvich and Jameson (1957). Their work is modelled on the classical color theory developed by Hering (1880). Its intuitive base comes from the linkage of red and green on the one hand, and yellow and blue on the other, in color blindness, peripheral color vision fields, and certain other phenomena. Despite the fact that these color linkages have been known for a very long time, no quantitative version of the Hering theory was available for testing and no indication of its power was given until the work of Hurvich and Jameson.

A natural starting point for a quantitative approach to this type of theory is found in the area of complementary colors. Suppose, for example, a red wavelength is chosen, and we determine the intensities of certain other wavelengths (blue-green, green, yellow-green) required to erase the "redness" of the combined stimulus so that it looks neither red nor green. The experimental procedure provides us with a way to estimate the activity of two antagonistic systems, if we assume that we are measuring the ability of various wavelengths to activate a process that is opposed to the red system. At each wavelength the reciprocal of the intensity required to suppress the red primary in the mixture gives us a measure of the sensitivity curve for the opposing process, i.e., the green process.

Sensitivity curves for the red, yellow, and blue processes are developed in this same way. Typical curves are illustrated in Figure 3, adapted from

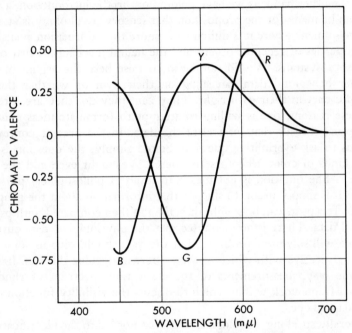

Figure 3. Color process curves. (Adapted from the data of Hurvich and Jameson, 1957.)

Hurvich and Jameson. These response curves can be converted into color mixture curves, and in view of this they meet the basic requirements for a color theory. In addition they can be used to interpret other color phenomena—hue discrimination data, the Bezold-Brücke phenomenon, and several types of discriminations in the color blind.

PHYSIOLOGICAL COLOR PROCESSES   It is our view that the success of the Hurvich and Jameson formulation crystallizes the essential dilemma that confronts a psychophysical color theory. As we have indicated, at least two types of process curves are capable of organizing substantial bodies of data on color discrimination. In fact, it is hard to find another area in psychology with an explicit algebra permitting so much quantitative manipulation in good agreement with the data. The problem is that several different versions of the theory work very well, and no easy way to converge on a unique theory has been found. We can of course continue to refine and evolve varieties of the existing theories until they approach some terminal stage of generality and to try to apply some criteria of parsimony in selecting the "best." We would then have to face the obvious questions of how to define what is meant by parsimony and how we know that the visual system is built in a parsimonious style.

On the other hand, as we have pointed out in the introduction, a strong case can be made for the proposition that sensory psychology is at a stage of development where it is difficult to ignore the information available on the properties of receptor organs and the neural mechanisms that operate in sensory systems. We do not mean to raise here the argument about whether behavioral data can stand on their own or whether they are scientific data in their own right. They can, they do, they are. Precisely for these reasons, one is willing to attempt to formulate ideas about the conceptual threads that interrelate the data. In the present context this leads us to ask a primitive question. Stated simply, the question is—how many kinds of color receptors are there? We might even add the word "really." The question is not meant to imply a philosophical pursuit of reality. It is simply meant to suggest that information about the properties of color receptors can be sought directly and then compared with psychophysical data. There is no guarantee that the physiological data currently available will solve our problems, but the data should give us some additional perspective with which to view alternative color theories. In much the same way, measurements of the absorption spectrum of rhodopsin give us a framework within which to discuss the visibility function of the dark-adapted eye.

Generally speaking, histological work has not led to the identification of different types of cones which could easily provide the base for theorizing about color vision. Nor is it clear at the present time that anyone has been able to record electrical activity in individual cone cells, although some reports suggest the possibility. However, certain electrical changes have been discovered in the vicinity of the bipolar and horizontal cells in the retina. Records from microelectrodes placed in this layer of the retina show a change in potential when a light is turned on and a restoration of the resting potential when the light is turned off. The potential change has a rise and decay time of the order of 50 milliseconds, and its magnitude is a function of the intensity of the stimulus.

One of the most provocative aspects of these potentials for the present discussion is the fact that the magnitude and direction of the potential changes are also functions of the wavelength of the stimulus. If we plot changes resulting from a stimulus of fixed energy but of varying wavelength, we obtain curve Y-B in Figure 4 from some cells. Other cells in

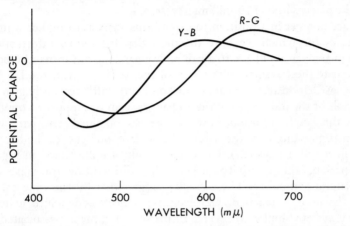

Figure 4.   **Magnitude of local potential changes measured in the vertebrate retina as a function of wavelength of the stimulus.** (Adapted from Svaetichin and MacNichol, 1958.)

the same layer of the retina respond as shown in curve R-G. The cellular activity in this layer of the retina seems to fall into three main categories, each cell yielding one of the two wavelength response curves shown in Figure 4 or a broad response which peaks in the middle regions of the visible spectrum. Figure 4 bears a striking resemblance to Figure 3, based on the Hurvich and Jameson procedure for measuring the response curves of opponent color processes. Regardless of the terminal form of color vision theory, it is clear now that there are retinal mechanisms yielding positive, negative, or zero electrical potentials, depending on the wavelength of the stimulus. More specifically there are at least three such systems, one with peaks in regions that we would call red and green, another with peaks in regions we would call yellow and blue, and a third with a broad sensitivity curve and a peak in the center of the visible spectrum.

We cannot rest on this physiological analysis, even with the suggestive similarity between the physiological measurements and the inferred processes derived by Hurvich and Jameson, for it is almost certain that these potentials are not conducted beyond the retina. If they are represented at all at higher levels, they must be recoded into impulsive form. A recent experiment by Wagner, MacNichol, and Wohlbarsh (1960) suggests how this might be accomplished. The variations in wavelength that produce the potential changes just described also seem to produce concomitant shifts from excitatory to inhibitory effects in optic-nerve responding, particularly from "on" to "off" responding. The shift from *on-responding* to *off-responding* is very sharply tuned to wavelengths and may take place within a 10-millimicron step.

We are not yet in a position to extend this analysis to higher centers in the species for which we have the most detailed retinal information. A thorough analysis will have to await additional data, but it may be possible to anticipate these results on the basis of the work on primates. De Valois (1960) has demonstrated changes in "on" and "off" responding in optic nerve cells of the monkey, and these changes seem to support an opponent-process theory. In addition, however, he has obtained sensitivity curves for "on-responding" in the lateral geniculate nucleus (a higher brain center in the visual system). De Valois' results are illustrated in Figure 5, which presents the sensitivity curves of five different neuron-types found in the lateral geniculate. These results suggest that by the time the level of the thalamus is reached, wavelength has been coded into a neuron-category system similar to several forms of color theory associated with the work of Stiles (1959) and others.

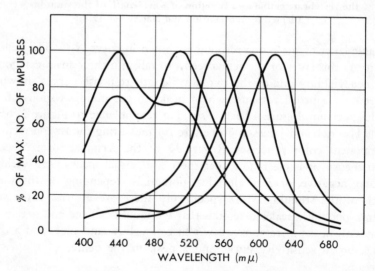

Figure 5. Average magnitude of "on" responses in the lateral geniculate nucleus as a function of the wavelength of the test stimulus. Responses of five different neuron-types are illustrated. (Adapted from De Valois, 1960.)

Electrical recording of color responses in the visual system is still in its early stages, although the work of Granit (1947) offers a substantial precursor of later research. At the present time we seem to be in the following position: 1) the *in vivo* experiments on photopigments suggest that there may be just three primary color systems at the level of the sense cell; 2) the microelectrode recording from retinal layers also suggests three processes, but quite different from those usually associated with strong trichromatic theory, the retinal data resembling the paired-opponent processes suggested by Hering and later by Hurvich and Jameson; 3) single-fiber recording from the lateral geniculate nucleus indicates that between three and five classes of elements may be available for coding color information. All of these results combine to suggest caution in thinking that a single class of theories can dominate the treatment of color discrimination data. Several of the different forms of psychophysical color theory may be essentially correct as descriptions of different stages in the analyzing process. The transformations which permit us to go from one of these theories to another may simply be describing the transformations imposed by the various stages of the visual sensory system.

Theories of Pitch Discrimination

Historically, theories of pitch discrimination have been classified into two main categories, place theories and frequency theories. The modern era probably began with the work of Helmholtz (1863), who proposed that the basilar membrane is essentially a series of resonators, each tuned to a different frequency. The frequency of a pure tone stimulus is transformed to a position on the basilar membrane determined by an appropriate resonator. Many other attempts to account for pitch discrimination have been placed in the literature since Helmholtz. These theories differ primarily in the conceptions they offer concerning physical characteristics of the inner ear. If we view the basilar membrane as having a variable width and being under transverse tension, we arrive at the Helmholtz notion of a bank of resonators. If we view the inner ear as a tube with an elastic membrane across it, we are led to consider either traveling waves or standing waves, depending on our assumptions about the damping constants. If the membrane is viewed as being very stiff, then it must vibrate more or less as a whole (like the diaphragm of a telephone), and we would make predictions similar to those offered by the frequency theories.

Such differences in viewpoint can persist only in the absence of good data on how the inner ear works. A most important step forward was taken when Békésy (1943), in an ingenious set of experiments, measured the vibration patterns of the basilar membrane in animals and in humans.

An example of his results is shown in Figure 6. It is quite evident from Békésy's observations that the basilar membrane does not vibrate uniformly to all frequencies and that some form of spatial representation of frequency must be a part of any theory of pitch discrimination. The position of maximum vibration depends on the frequency of the stimulus.

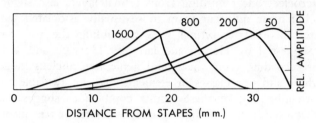

Figure 6.   Patterns of vibration of the basilar membrane for four different frequencies as measured by Békésy. (Adapted from Békésy, 1943.)

Other points emerge from Békésy's analysis of the mechanics of the inner ear. For instance, a phase lag occurs between the vibration at the stapes and the vibration at various points along the basilar membrane. This pattern of misalignment of the wave motions establishes that the spatial representation of frequency is not due to a simple resonance.

These observations become important when we think about alternative ways for describing auditory stimuli. The kinds of stimuli to which we are sensitive are changes in air pressure that occur relatively rapidly in time. The natural description of the stimulus would seem to be the amplitude-time function, i.e., a record of sound pressure taken as a function of time. In that case a sinusoid, a series of square waves, or a "sawtooth" function would appear to be relatively simple periodic stimuli. On the other hand, if we think of the ear as performing some kind of frequency analysis, we would be interested in describing a stimulus in terms of its frequency spectrum. The spectrum is a record of the frequency components of the waveform along with the magnitude of each component. In this analysis a sinusoidal waveform is simple. Its spectrum consists of a single line or weight, plotted over its frequency as illustrated in Figure 7. A square wave and a sawtooth pattern are complex stimuli, because their spectra contain many frequencies and each frequency component carries a different weight or amplitude loading. Time is entirely missing from the spectrum analysis. The notion that a waveform is periodic carries with it the implication that it has always been on and will never be turned off. Of course, in practice all auditory stimuli have finite durations. The frequency spectra of such finite stimuli must be expressed as combinations of sinusoids of infinite duration. Thus the effect of shortening the dura-

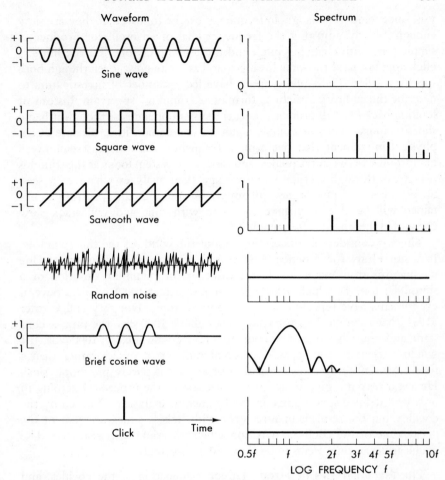

Figure 7. Two ways of representing the same acoustic stimuli. The waveforms on the left illustrate various amplitude-time functions. The spectrum representations on the right are the frequency components of each waveform. (Adapted from Licklider, 1951.)

tion of a stimulus shows up in the frequency representation as a fuzziness in the location of the spectral line. When the stimulus is radically shortened, the spectral line must be smeared over a broad band of frequencies that mutually cancel one another in accord with well-defined mathematical rules. Consequently, a brief stimulus, such as a click or a burst of a few cycles of tone, has a broad spectrum resembling noise.

It is useful to think of the ear as performing some form of frequency analysis, because a listener can pick out the spectral components of a complex tone. But it is equally clear that time *is* represented in the ear's analysis, since temporal changes in frequency can be followed, if they are slow enough. Slowly adjusting the frequency dial of an oscillator produces a simple tone with changing pitch and not a complex tone. Furthermore, a click does not have the same hissing sound as white noise, even though both spectra are flat. These observations have led a number of investigators to describe the auditory system as forming a "running" spectrum. Instead of looking back over all previous time, the system operates as though it had a short memory. This, of course, is not an uncommon idea, because every physical instrument that performs a frequency analysis must embody a compromise between frequency and time. The system looks at the stimulus waveform through a "time window" and then analyzes whatever it sees. Spectral lines for pure tones will appear blurred, but the spectrum so obtained will be able to change regularly with time and will track slow changes in the stimulus frequency.

There is considerable uncertainty about the width of the time-window. It is not clear, for instance, that it is independent of frequency. One method for studying it involves measuring the minimum duration of a sinusoidal tone at which a listener can just detect tonal quality. Several experiments have reported on this important topic. Doughty and Garner (1947) have shown that, for frequencies above 1000 cps, the time is constant and roughly equal to about 10 milliseconds. Below 1000 cps, the window seems to encompass a constant number of cycles rather than a fixed time. Of course, this estimation procedure is purely psychophysical. Hence, it may not give an accurate reflection of the process of zeroing in on a well-defined spectral line in the frequency analysis performed by the cochlea, but the result is in agreement with Békésy's measurement of the decay time of the cochlear partition when the stimulus is removed. The cochlear decay time seems to be about 10 milliseconds.

THE PSYCHOPHYSICS OF PITCH   Direct examination of the cochlea, and studies of the motion of the basilar membrane, indicate that pitch results from the frequency analysis performed by the inner ear. This analysis is carried out with short memory, so that the general effect produced in the cochlea is like a running spectrum or like a filter made up of resonators that are not very sharply tuned. The broad tuning of the basilar membrane observed by Békésy and illustrated in Figure 6 suggests that psychophysical studies of frequency sensitivity should turn up interactions between frequencies separated by many hundreds of cycles. This expectation is largely confirmed in studies of masked thresholds using pure tones and white noise. Data on loudness summation add further corroboration, but the expectation is completely confounded in studies of frequency discrimination. In the latter, astonishingly sharp sensitivity is encountered. Let us look briefly at these data.

Masking is an increase in the threshold intensity of a particular stimulus caused by the presence of another stimulus. Figure 8 shows a masking contour produced by a 1200-cps masking tone 44 decibels above the listener's threshold. Thresholds are affected over a very wide range of frequencies. In fact, the shift is 10 db or more over a range of about 400 cycles centered on 1200 cps.

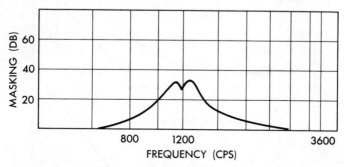

Figure 8.   Masking effects generated over surrounding frequencies by a 1200-cps pure tone at 44-db sensation level. The measure of masking is the change in threshold due to presence of the masking tone. (Adapted from Wegel and Lane, 1924.)

Similar broad-band masking can be seen with white noise. The masking effect is found in a band located near the frequency of the test tone. Fletcher (1940) called this noise band a "critical band" and suggested that its width is related to the range of excitation produced by the test tone along the basilar membrane.

The width of a critical band can be calculated from noise-masking data if we assume that at threshold the amount of power in the test tone and the noise power in the critical band stand in some fixed relation. Fletcher assumed that they were equal. The computation is based on the signal-to-noise ratio at threshold. If the noise is expressed in terms of power-per-cycle, the signal-to-noise ratio is dimensionally in cycles, i.e., it is a bandwidth. Suppose, for example, the threshold signal-to-noise ratio for a 1000-cps tone masked by white noise is 18 decibels. Then

$$10 \log W = 18,$$

where W is the width of the critical band, and

$$W = \text{antilog } 1.8,$$
$$W = 63 \text{ cycles.}$$

This value of W is given in Figure 9 as the width of the critical band at 1000 cps. The data are taken from the measurements and computations of

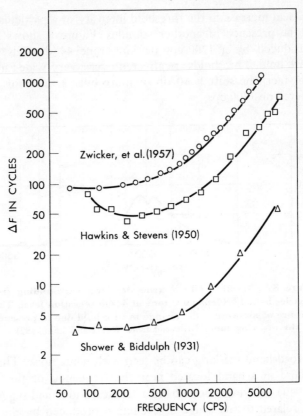

**Figure 9.   Three different measures of the sharpness
of auditory frequency analysis. The top curve (circles)
illustrates the width of frequency bands in which loudnesses fail to summate, plotted as a function of the
frequency at the center of the band. The middle curve
(squares) shows critical bands (critical ratios) computed from the thresholds of pure tones masked by
white noise. The lower curve (triangles) is the classical
difference limen for frequency with tones 15 db above
threshold. (Adapted from Zwicker, et al., 1957.)**

Hawkins and Stevens (1950). It is clear that the frequency interactions
suggested by critical bands are narrow in comparison with the data on the
motion of the basilar membrane. However, the actual values of the bandwidths depend on the assumption of equal power in the masked tone and
in the noise in a critical band. Schaefer et al. (1950) checked the assumption by studying the masking effect of a "noise" constructed with very precise frequency boundaries. They found that the critical band trailed off
slowly rather than sharply, as though it were not a band in the strictest

sense. Consequently, it is difficult to estimate the extent of the frequency interaction, although it is broader than the computed bandwidths.

Bandwidths that yield a function with the same general shape as the critical bands in Figure 9 (except that they are approximately 2.5 times wider), have been found in studies of loudness summation. Zwicker, Flottorp, and Stevens (1957) demonstrated that the total loudness of a set of four tones centered on a given frequency does not change until the spacing of the four tones exceeds a certain value. The four tones are (nearly) uniformly spaced, and the finding is that the loudness of the complex stimulus does not change until the spacing (measured by the frequency difference between the highest and lowest tone) passes some critical value, after which the loudness of the complex increases. Loudness changes were determined by measuring the intensity of a single pure tone that matched the loudness of the complex. At 1000 cps, the critical band measured in this way is about 150 cycles. Zwicker et al. suggest that we use the term "critical band" for the measurement based on loudness summation and "critical ratio" for the computed bandwidth derived from noise masking.

In sharp contrast to these wide-ranging frequency interactions, frequency discrimination is exceptionally acute. Figure 9 also shows the data of Shower and Biddulph (1931) on the minimum differences in frequency detectable by psychophysical methods. The difference limens are approximately 1/25 of the width of critical bands for loudness summation and 1/10 of the width of critical ratios for noise masking. The way in which all three measures vary with frequency suggests that they may have a common basis, but numerical comparisons raise a problem. It is very difficult to explain a frequency discrimination threshold of roughly 4–5 cycles at 1000 cps, in view of Békésy's observations of the motion of the basilar membrane. The resonance curves of 1000 and 1005 cps would be almost identical, differing by less than the width of a pencil point in Figure 6. Moreover, frequency discrimination gets *finer* as stimulus intensity increases. This is in direct contrast to the spread of activity on the basilar membrane inferred from the results obtained with pure-tone masking and with loudness summation.

Plainly, the very flat maxima of activity visible to direct observation of the basilar membrane must be sharpened in some way in order to account for this extraordinary sensitivity. Békésy (1957) has proposed a spatial contrast mechanism in which loci on the basilar membrane funnel their responses into the locus of the maximum, enhancing it at their own expense. This sharpening is presumed to be neurological and may be similar to the type of lateral inhibition demonstrated in the compound eye by Hartline, Wagner, and Ratliff (1956).

Huggins and Licklider (1952) have also discussed sharpening mechanisms. They consider a set of analyses of the motion of the basilar membrane utilizing the first four derivatives with respect to place and eventually achieve much sharper tuning than that observed in the vibration pattern.

It is evident that as long as a maximum exists in the basilar-membrane vibration pattern, the nerve pathways leading up the auditory cortex can, in principle, isolate it. The sharpening mechanisms proposed by Békésy and Huggins and Licklider both involve some form of differentiation of the motion of the basilar membrane, and this certainly does not seem beyond the capacity of the auditory nervous system. The problem is that the differentiation can be performed in many ways, and the information that could delimit these possibilities is not very well organized.

The fact that some kind of sharpening occurs is clearly evident from the available physiological data, and that it is neural in nature is equally obvious. The pioneer work of Galambos and Davis (1943), and the subsequent work of Galambos (1952), Galambos et al. (1952), Tasaki (1954), and particularly Katsuki (1961), offer important observations on the problem. It is now clear that individual neurons in the eighth (auditory) nerve are very broadly tuned, as we would expect from Békésy's results. The responsiveness of individual nerve fibers becomes sharper and sharper as information passes from the eighth nerve to successively higher stages in the auditory system, i.e., to the cochlear nucleus, inferior colliculus, and medial geniculate body. A typical example of these results is shown in Figure 10. There can be little doubt that the basic features of spatial representation of frequency are preserved through most of the auditory system and that it is sharpened as we move up the auditory system, at least as far as the medial geniculate.

ENVELOPE DETECTION   The several indications of auditory data-processing and sharpening outlined in the preceding section do not raise any fundamental difficulty with place theory. There is obviously a quantitative discrepancy between the frequency resolution indicated by studies of cochlear action and the resolution evident in studies of pitch discrimination. But in all cases, the place mechanism is still assumed to be functioning, and when neural processing occurs, it merely etches the vibratory maximum more sharply than the mechanics of the cochlea permit. Now let us turn to a set of psychophysical observations offering strong evidence for a different kind of pitch.

Fletcher (1929) observed that a tonal complex consisting of components at 400, 600, 800, and 1000 cycles per second is sometimes reported by listeners as having the pitch of a pure tone at 200 cps. He explained the phenomenon as a special case of the "missing fundamental," arguing that the tonal complex is affected by non-linear distortion. The 200-cycle

others seemed much narrower. This suggested that there might be well-defined sharpening mechanisms in the auditory system, and a line of research emerged as an attempt to discover how the sharpening is done. So research has proceeded back and forth, comparing one aspect of the chain with another and filling in the gaps as our ideas have continued to evolve.

The different bandwidths are reminiscent of the different process curves in color vision, and the question of which of them is right is no easier to solve in audition than it was in vision. Each may be right as a description of the transformations imposed by a particular locus along the sensory chain. Huggins and Licklider (1951) note that in sensory systems, theories which seem at first thought to be alternatives may in fact merely supplement one another. The idea is a clear violation of the principle of parsimony. Nevertheless, when nature has constructed a sensory chain in a specific way, our main job is to discover how it works. Criticisms of the form of the mechanism can be left to discussions about the principles of evolution.

Theories of the Threshold

Psychophysics has grown up around the study of thresholds. The color-process curves, masking curves, and pitch-discrimination functions referred to in earlier sections are all based on threshold data. They can be (and will be) considered as large-scale behavioral effects generated by sensory mechanisms and joined together by a constant threshold response (see Graham, 1950). Thresholds, however, are blurred, uncertain regions in which points can be located only in terms of their probability. We now direct our interest to these regions and to the threshold processes themselves. Where do thresholds arise, and what is their relation to the sensory systems in which they are found?

THE CLASSICAL PICTURE OF THE THRESHOLD PROCESS AND SOME MODIFICATIONS   The classical conception of the threshold distribution of sensitivity embodies the normal curve. Fechner (1889) introduced this idea almost from the very beginning of psychophysics, and for many years psychophysical research concentrated on methods for estimating the midpoint of the normal threshold distribution efficiently and without gross error or bias. This particular philosophy is spelled out nicely in the first edition of Guilford's *Psychometric Methods* (pp. 23–214). It was assumed that the uncertainty of the threshold could be attributed to variations in sensitivity either at the periphery or in the noisy passage back to the brain from the periphery, and these variations were assumed to be normally distributed. The assumption was plausible in view of the fact that a large number of variables seem to affect the instantaneous sensitivity of the sense organ, as well as the stages of transmission that are more centrally located. More-over, the *central limit theorem* of statistics establishes that a wide variety of circumstances in which chance variables act in concert must result in the normal distribution. Later work tended to substantiate the normal assumption. Pecher (1939) demonstrated that fluctuations of sensitivity in single nerve fibers are normally distributed. But agreement was not universal; Thurstone (1928), in particular, questioned the normal as-sumption and noted its possible conflict with Weber's Law.

The classical picture was challenged in an unexpected way when Hecht, Schlaer, and Pirenne (1942) showed that the threshold probability distribution for detecting weak light-flashes was comparable with the probability distribution expected of the stimulus itself. These authors measured the absolute threshold for a flash (1 millisecond in duration) of blue-green light (510 millimicrons). They determined that the stimulus at threshold was of the order of 10^{-10} ergs. This is a minute quantity of energy, amounting approximately to 100 quanta of light at this wave-length. Hecht et al. showed, on the basis of measurements of energy losses incurred in the passage through the eye, that roughly 90 per cent of these quanta are dissipated and lost. Perhaps no more than 10 quanta are ab-sorbed by the retina out of the 100 delivered at the surface of the cornea. Moreover, the number of quanta reaching the retina must vary from flash to flash because of the probabilistic emission and absorption of quanta. Physical principles dictate that this number will have a Poisson distribu-tion. Only the average number of quanta (the mean number in the Poisson distribution) is fixed by the intensity of the flash.

Hecht et al. argued that if the subject always reported the stimulus as present when some critical number of quanta reached the retina and never reported it when less than this number was received, the Poisson distribu-tion could be used to trace the probability of quanta in excess of the critical number as a function of stimulus intensity. The resulting cumula-tive distributions for various critical numbers are shown in Figure 11. Notice that they are continuous curves, called "gamma" distributions. The distributions are then compared with empirical data by tabulating the proportion of detections reported by a subject as the intensity of the stimulus is changed in log units. An estimate of the critical number is achieved by comparing the shape of the empirical curve with the various possibilities in Figure 11.

It is important to emphasize that in one important way the formulation by Hecht, Schlaer, and Pirenne cannot be wrong unless existing physical theory about energy emission is wrong. The uncertainty in delivering quanta is exactly linked to the mean number delivered and offers a com-plete specification of the performance of an ideal light detector. It is a lower bound for the psychometric function. The only question in apply-

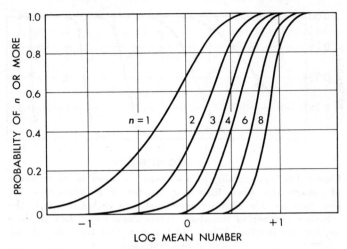

PROBABILITY OF n OR MORE

LOG MEAN NUMBER

Figure 11. **Probability of n or more events in the sampling of a Poisson distribution as a function of the logarithm of the expected number in the sample.** (Adapted from Hecht, Schlaer, and Pirenne, 1942.)

ing this lower bound is the uncertainty in making corrections for quantum losses in transmission through the eye. We do not know exactly how to set the critical number, because we do not yet know the average number of quanta absorbed by the retina when a sharp-eyed subject is at his absolute threshold.

If the critical number is large, say 20 or more, the psychophysical function predicted from variations in the stimulus is very nearly an instantaneous transition. Consequently, it is possible to have all of the circumstances that Hecht et al. envisioned at the retina without attributing to them any appreciable weight in determining the shape of the psychophysical function in behavior. There is evidence to suggest that responses in the optic nerve *are* associated with quantum absorption in the retina. Figure 12 shows the probability distribution of n or more nerve impulses (where n varies from 1–5) recorded from a single fiber of the optic nerve of the horseshoe crab *Limulus* in circumstances similar to those described by the theory. An increase in n, the critical number of impulses, produces a corresponding change in the average intensity required to exceed the critical value and a related change in the slope of the frequency distribution. These changes are remarkably similar to the changes predicted from the gamma distribution.

An interesting feature of the visual quantum theory is its treatment of the threshold. This can be seen by a simple computation based on the Hecht, Schlaer, and Pirenne measurements. Histological studies indicate

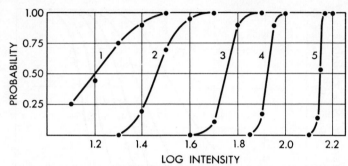

Figure 12. **Probability of *n* or more impulses in the response of a single optic-nerve fiber as a function of the intensity of the test stimulus. The number associated with each curve is *n*, the criterion number of impulses.** (From unpublished data of Mueller. See also Hartline, Milne, and Wagman, 1947, for earlier discussion of this problem.)

that the retinal area they used contained about 500 sense cells. If only 5–10 quanta are absorbed and they are randomly distributed in these 500 cells, the likelihood that one cell captures more than one quantum is small. The suggestion is that a rod cell can be activated by a single quantum and therefore, physically, has no threshold. The threshold imposed by the critical number is dependent on an integrating mechanism. With this model we encounter an idea which has been accorded increasing acceptance in modern psychophysics, namely that events in the receptor may be elaborated by a *decision* mechanism. The Hecht formulation for the visual threshold offers the possibility that other variables, e.g., instruction variables, can be conceived of as manipulating the critical number, and it ought to be possible to account for such variables by manipulating this single parameter. In this respect the work of Hecht et al. portended something of what was to follow later in the theory of signal detection.

Another early threshold model that suggested a secondary decision process transforming sensory information into psychophysical data was the neural quantum model of Stevens, Morgan, and Volkmann (1941). Basing their argument on some earlier work by Békésy (1930), Stevens et al. assumed that neural activity in a sensory system varies in steplike fashion. They argued that on-going stimulation excites some particular number of neural units plus a small random surplus insufficient to stimulate the next higher unit (called a quantum, but unrelated to light quanta). A small increase in intensity might, or might not, excite the next higher unit, depending on the amount of the surplus, which is assumed equally likely to be any fraction of the partly-filled quantum. According to the theory, a given incremental intensity always adds the same number of quanta. (The number does not have to be an integer.) Stevens et al. adopted what they called a "two-quantum" hypothesis. The subject *never* reports an increment if it (plus the surplus) adds less than two quanta to the existing total and *always* reports an increment if it excites two or more additional quanta. Accordingly there will be a range of stimulus increments that the subject will never report as detectably different from a starting intensity, and a range in which the proportion of detections will rise linearly from a value of 0.00 to 1.00, and these two ranges will be identical. Experimental conditions are chosen in such a way as to try to make the assumptions plausible. These conditions define the so-called "quantal method" and provide the circumstances in which the model is tested.

The model has stimulated considerable effort to choose between the sigmoid and linear alternatives for the shape of the psychometric function (Corso, 1956), but it has proved very difficult to tell the two curve shapes apart. The more testable feature of the neural quantum model is the fact that the range of stimulus increments producing no detections and the range in which detections rise from 0.00 to 1.00 are equal, and this seems to hold approximately for rather large ranges of relevant variables.

THE SUBJECT'S CRITERION These two threshold models point up a weakness in the classical theory of the threshold. The classical theory did not offer a quantitative treatment of one of the important parameters of the psychophysical experiment, the subject's "criterion." Anyone who has ever attempted a threshold study has had to develop some way of coming to grips with this problem in order to assure the reliability of his data. In work on absolute thresholds, the experimenter may insert "blank" trials at various points in the experiment, each one carefully contrived to catch the subject off guard. If more than just a few blanks are "detected," the data may be discarded or the subject may be instructed to be more careful. Some experimenters do their work exclusively with good subjects, who are so labeled because they are rarely or never caught by the blank trials.

As soon as it is recognized that a restriction must be imposed on the subject's criterion it is evident that the latter must enter into any adequate theory of the threshold. Later work has shown (as in the case of the two models just considered) that the criterion can be incorporated into the theory by assuming some kind of decision mechanism lying behind (or above) the initial sensory process.

SIGNAL DETECTION THEORY Signal detection theory made its appearance in the psychological literature with the work of Smith and Wilson (1953) and then independently in a paper by Tanner and Swets (1954). The theory was, as we have suggested, a model that attempted to incorporate the subject's criterion.

The idea had its origins in *statistical decision theory*. The latter was worked out by Neyman and Pearson (1928, 1933). These papers and a subsequent book by von Neumann and Morgenstern (1944) have come to occupy a central position in modern statistics.[1] The apparatus of the theory is abstract and rather complicated. However, the underlying notions are simple, and since these notions make direct contact with signal detection and threshold psychophysics, we shall attempt to outline them briefly.

Suppose it is known that an observation comes from one of two populations, N and S, where both populations are distributed along the same dimension. Suppose, in addition, that population S lies mostly above population N, and that the two populations overlap each other. This situation is depicted in Figure 13. Statistical decision theory attempts to

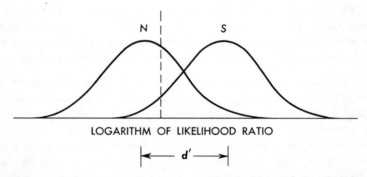

LOGARITHM OF LIKELIHOOD RATIO

Figure 13.   Theoretical decision mechanism. An observation is drawn from one of two populations, S and N. The decision criterion is the dashed vertical line between the distributions. If the observation lies to the right of this line, it is assigned to population S. The distance d' represents the center-to-center separation of the two distributions. So-called "pay-offs" affect the placement of the criterion but not the distributions.

provide a rational guide to choice when a sample is known to come from one of the two populations, but it is not known which one. All of the general features of Figure 13 are assumed known, and in fact this information is crucial for providing a reasonable basis for the decision. Clearly, if the observation is large, it probably comes from population S, whereas if it is small, it probably comes from population N. The real problem is to make an unequivocal choice in the region where the populations overlap. There

[1] There are many expositions of the basic ideas of decision theory. See, for example, Blackwell and Gershick (1954), Luce and Raiffa (1957), and an excellent elementary text by Chernoff and Moses (1959). In addition, Luce (1962) has produced an essay on psychophysics with many of the ideas developed in this section. It should be consulted in detail, and individual citations are omitted.

are four possibilities, corresponding to the two populations and the two decisions. These four possibilities can be arranged in a fourfold table:

DECISION

		N	S
POPULATION	N	Correct	Type I error
SAMPLED	S	Type II error	Correct

We want to partition the possible values of the abscissa in Figure 13 so that if the observation falls in a certain region, we decide in favor of S; if the observation falls outside the region, we decide for N. Evidently, the region associated with one of the decisions determines the region associated with the other, essentially by what is left out, but the region chosen first can be picked in an infinity of different ways. The problem posed by decision theory is to pick the best one.

The term "best" requires specification. We might fix the probability of what is called a Type I error and determine the decision region that minimizes the probability of a Type II error, or we might assign costs or rewards to errors and correct responses respectively and then determine a decision region that will bring the largest expected return. Both of these schemes are best in some sense. Fortunately, both lead to a solution similar to the dashed vertical line in Figure 13. If the observation lies to the right of this line, it is assigned to population S; if it lies to the left of the cut-off, the observation is assigned to population N. The optimal location for the decision criterion will be determined by the a priori probability of sampling from N and S and by the pattern of gains and losses associated with the cells of the fourfold table. For example, if N and S are equally likely, and Type I errors are costly while Type II errors are inexpensive, the decision criterion will be set far to the right in Figure 13; if the costs of the errors are reversed, the decision criterion will be set far to the left. The problem is a bit more complicated when the populations S and N are multidimensional, but Neyman and Pearson showed that the decision problem can be solved by computing a single quantity, the *likelihood ratio* (see Mood, 1950, p. 257) from the multidimensional observation. The likelihood ratio has a certain distribution when the sample is chosen from N and a different distribution when the sample is chosen from S. Thus, the illustration in Figure 13 applies here as well, provided the abscissa represents possible values of the likelihood ratio.

This general conception can now be applied to the problem of determining responses in psychophysics. Signal detection theory assumes that a decision is made on the basis of an evaluation of the effects induced by the stimulus. According to the theory, whatever these effects are, there are also certain effects when no stimulus is presented. This "noise" level is represented by the distribution of N in Figure 13. The distribution might be thought of as reflecting the number of nerve impulses counted during a fixed observation time, although nothing in signal detection theory forces the latter interpretation. It is made merely as a suggestion of what might lead to different values of the likelihood ratio. Myriad possibilities exist, and there need be no reference to physiological mechanisms.

When a stimulus of fixed intensity is presented, the distribution switches to that of S in Figure 13. If the stimulus is weak, there will be considerable overlap of the distributions, and the task of the decision mechanism is to determine a cut-off value for deciding between noise plus signal (S), and noise alone (N). We then have a form of the fourfold table that is specific to the signal-detection problem:

DETECTION

		No	Yes
	Noise	Correct	False Report
STIMULUS PRESENTED	*Signal + Noise*	Missed Signal	Correct

The term *signal detection* suggests that the model did not originate in psychophysics. As a matter of fact, it was borrowed more or less intact from the field of communication theory, where it was used as a guide for constructing efficient radar receivers. A remarkable book on this topic was written by Lawson and Uhlenback in 1950, based on work done at the Radiation Laboratory at MIT during the Second World War. Fully developed treatments of the theory of detectability of a variety of signals in gaussian (i.e., normal curve) noise were presented by Peterson, Birdsall, and Fox (1954) and by Van Meter and Middleton (1954).

One of the principal claims of the psychophysical version of the theory is that the distance between the centers of the distributions S and N (indicated by d' in Figure 13) depends on the intensity of the stimulus. Consequently, d' is a standard distance along a latent continuum that corresponds to the effect of changing the intensity of the stimulus. This conception is almost literally the one proposed by Thurstone (1927). There is a very close relation between a distance on a Thurstone scale, and the distance d' in the signal-detection model. In the latter, the distribution of S moves away from the distribution of N as stimulus intensity is increased. If the criterion remains fixed, the probability of a correct detection (i.e., an observation to the right of the cut-off line when the stimulus is presented) increases systematically with stimulus intensity. Note that this conception yields a psychometric function that is quite similar to the one constructed in classical psychophysics, but the function obtained from detection theory has an additional implication. The probability of a detection can be influenced by shifting the subject's criterion, even though the stimulus intensity remains unchanged. Accordingly, there are infinitely many psychometric functions, all generated by the same changes in d'. These different psychometric functions are produced by different placements of the subject's criterion.

It follows that one of the basic psychophysical problems as seen from the vantage point of the signal-detection model is to determine the relation between d' and stimulus intensity and to show that this relation is 1) independent of the way in which d' is determined and 2) invariant with changes in the subject's criterion.

The second problem can be studied by performing a series of observations in which the stimulus intensity is fixed, but various weights are attached to missed signals and false reports. A plot of a typical empirical relation between the proportion of detections and the proportion of false reports in a visual threshold experiment is shown in Figure 14. The data are taken from Swets, Tanner, and Birdsall (1961), who converted half the stimulus presentations to catch trials and charged subjects for making errors.

The curve in Figure 14 is called an *operating characteristic*.[2] The same general relation can be obtained somewhat more easily by requiring the subject to rate his impression of the stimulus on each trial. For example, the ratings might be as follows:

1. I am sure I saw it.
2. I think I saw it.
3. Don't know whether I saw it or not.
4. I think I did not see it.
5. I am sure I did not see it.

Pollack and Decker (1958) and Egan et al. (1959) showed that these ratings yield data such as might be expected with four different criteria. It is a simple matter to compute the proportion of times the subject makes false reports for each criterion value and the proportion of times he detects the stimulus at each criterion, and then to use this information to plot an operating characteristic. This is a new and powerful interpretation of confidence ratings, which, for a long time, have been known to be

[2] Sometimes it is called an *R.O.C. curve*. These initials stand for *receiver operating characteristic*, a description borrowed directly from electronic signal detection.

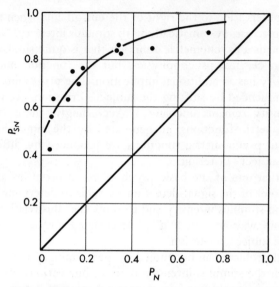

Figure 14. Empirical relation between proportion of detections (P_{SN}) and false reports (P_N) determined on a single observer in a visual-detection experiment. The stimulus was a brief flash of light 0.78 foot-lamberts above the background luminance. However, the stimulus was presented on only half the trials (chosen at random), and subjects' criterion was manipulated by changing the costs of false reports and missed signals. Each point represents a separate criterion setting based on 400 trials and 200 signals. (Adapted from Swets, Tanner, and Birdsall, 1961.)

related to detection probabilities. Signal detection theory offers a suggestion of the nature of the relation and attempts to formulate it in precise terms.

The problem of determining d' is not overly difficult if simple assumptions can be made about the distributions of S and N. For example, if both distributions are normal and have the same variance, the operating characteristic will be a straight line with unit slope on double probability paper. Moreover, each operating characteristic corresponds to some value of d'.

One way of checking the stability of d' with changes in psychophysical method is the following. First obtain a set of ratings (as described above), where half the "stimulus presentations" are catch trials and where many trials are run at a given stimulus intensity. Then study the same intensity, using the method of forced choice. The latter scheme (in the simplest case) provides two observation intervals on each trial. One of these intervals is a blank, and the other contains a stimulus. The subject does not know which is which and must arrive at a decision by comparing his impressions of the two intervals.

A computation of d' is constructed out of forced-choice judgments in the following way. The subject has one sample from S and another from N. Suppose he simply subtracts them and says that S was in the interval containing the larger sample. If both distributions are normal with equal variance and are displaced by d', we can then write down the probability that the observation from S is greater than the one from N. This is identical to the probability that the subject decides correctly. Thus,

$$P\,(S > N) = P\,(S - N > 0)$$
$$= \int_{0}^{\infty}\,n(d';\sqrt{2})$$
$$= \int_{-\frac{d'}{\sqrt{2}}}^{\infty}\,n(0;\,1)$$

where $N(0;\,1)$ is a unit-normal distribution with mean $= 0$ and standard deviation $= 1$. It follows that d' can be determined from a table of the normal curve, if the proportion of correct forced-choice judgments is known.[3] Estimates of d' derived from forced choices can then be compared with estimates of d' derived from stimulus ratings as described above. To the extent that the two estimates are mutually consistent, the outcome is interpreted as an achievement for signal detection theory. Swets (1961) has summarized a number of experiments in which estimates of d' from forced choices, stimulus ratings, and simple yes-no decisions appear to be consistent. This success, together with those already noted for handling changes in motivating conditions and for interpreting confidence ratings, represents a substantial accomplishment and accounts for the widespread recent interest in signal-detection theory.

OPTIMUM DETECTION   One application of signal-detection theory not covered in the above outline involves an attempt to construct an *optimum* model of human detection. If a listener is presented, for example, with a 1000-cycle sinusoid embedded in gaussian "white" noise, the theoretical psychometric function of an optimum detector can be computed, provided that information is supplied about the properties of the noise and about the signal frequency, amplitude, duration, starting time, and phase.

---

[3] This procedure is identical to Thurstone's method for finding scale distances using Case V of the law of comparative judgment (See Torgerson, 1958, Chapter 9). Criterion effects are also possible in forced choice. For example, the subject may decide for S only when the two observations differ by b or more, and flip a coin otherwise. In that event b might be varied by instructions. Such decision making is non-optimum and is usually not treated by signal-detection theory.

Of course, a suitable definition of optimum performance must also be specified.

Peterson, Birdsall, and Fox (1954) and Marill (1956) have shown that a certain physical device for detecting a sine wave in gaussian noise generates a simple detection curve, derived from a normal ogive, when the properties of the signal are known exactly. The median of this detection function is rigidly fixed at a specific signal-to-noise ratio and offers a precise lower bound for the psychometric function. The lower bound cannot be improved if a certain definition of the available information is chosen. The device operates by processing the noisy waveform without losing any of this information. Psychometric functions resulting from threshold studies with humans are almost always found to require higher intensities than such physically defined optima. Psychophysical decision making is nonetheless assumed to be an optimum process because the information available to a decision mechanism in the brain is thought to be a degraded version of the information impinging on the sense organ.

If one adopts these assumptions, it can be argued that studies of the conditions under which psychophysical judgments most nearly approach the physical optimum will yield clues to the major information leaks in the sensory system and in the decision process. For example, Marill (1956) demonstrated that a listener detecting a sinusoid in white noise generates a psychometric function similar to the one produced by a detector that knows the stimulus frequency but not its phase. Even so, the listener is 13 decibels worse than the performance of the physical detector. Green (1960) has reported closer psychophysical approaches to ideal detection (within 6 db) and seems to have shown that these approaches occur when the listener does not have to rely heavily on his memory for the details of the signal. The claim for optimum performance is buttressed chiefly by matching the shape of the psychometric function and not by an actual approach to ideal performance.

It is difficult to know what to say about optimum detection in psychophysics. The real contribution of signal-detection theory is its attempt to formalize the subject's criterion, and this attempt does not stand or fall on the question of the subject's capacity for optimum decision making. The latter appears to introduce a note of premature rationalism. There has been considerable recent discussion of what the performance of an ideal physical detector actually is (Slepian, 1958; Mathews, 1960). Slepian has shown that with certain plausible interpretations of the amount of information available in the noise, there is no lower limit whatever on the detectability of the signal. Hence theoretical limits on detectability reduce to questions of what kind of information is available to the detector. It is evident that if psychophysical detection is evaluated in relation to a physical optimum and if the applicable physical optimum is settled by reference to psychophysical results, the net progress is zero. On the other hand, the behavior of a particular physical detector can be chosen as a standard against which to compare various psychophysical procedures, and an effort can be made in these comparisons to deduce how the information coming back from the sense organ is degraded. This appears to be the approach followed in current research on optima in psychophysics.

SENSORY THEORY AND SIGNAL DETECTION   Despite unquestioned success in handling threshold data, signal detection theory stands in an uncertain relation to sensory psychology. The so-called decision axis, and the criterion that partitions it, the populations S and N, and the distance measure d' are abstractions. No empirical connection with events whose existence is known independently of the signal-detection model has been established. For example, it is not clear at all what kind of information is represented on the sensory version of the decision axis (i.e., the likelihood ratio dimension of Figure 13).

A second ground for uncertainty is the generality of the theory. It is found to work in some rather unexpected circumstances. Egan (1958) has reported an experiment in which the basic model of signal detection is used to analyze recognition memory. Egan gave his subjects a stack of cards with a word written on each card. The subject went through the stack card by card until he had seen every one. Then the experimenter took another stack equal in size to the first, containing new words. These were shuffled in with the orginal set and the subject now had to rate his confidence that he had (or had not) seen each word earlier. The rating technique was similar to the one described above for generating an operating characteristic in the psychophysical case, and Egan was able to produce an operating characteristic for recognition memory. It was possible to assign the stacks of cards to two overlapping distributions on a metric dimension (presumably measuring memory strength) and to compute a value of d' corresponding to the separation of the two distributions.

This finding leads us to re-examine the question of what has been demonstrated in signal-detection experiments in psychophysics. It is certainly worth recalling here that the procedures for determining d' in psychophysical experiments are formally indistinguishable from the methods for determining distances on a Thurstone scale. In fact, Torgerson's (1958) treatment of Thurstone's laws of comparative judgment and categorical judgment (Chaps. 9–10) provides a striking parallel for the forced-choice and stimulus-rating methods in signal detection. The essential point in bringing up these references to Thurstone's procedures is that the latter are built into a very broad scaling technique. Thurstone (1948) pointed out that the law of comparative judgment is easily applied to the stimuli of classical psychophysics, but "the more generally interesting applications are those which involve social, moral, and esthetic values, opinion polls, and consumer preferences."

Thus, the form of the threshold process remains elusive. Despite this uncertainty, threshold data are still important and still usable. The uncertainty is almost always superimposed on a large main effect. In color matching, tone masking, and other data considered in earlier sections of this chapter, the main effect has an unmistakable origin in a sensory process. This is true of much of the psychophysical data cited in describing the operation of sensory systems. If the subject's criterion, now sharply etched by signal-detection theory, is kept stable, the main effect can offer a picture of the operation of a sensory process for comparison with mechanisms emerging from physiological analysis. As we come to understand the local properties of the thresholds themselves, the picture will achieve even sharper definition.

Conclusions

The data of sensory psychology present us with two problems. The first is the problem of accounting for gross changes in sensitivity produced by changes in stimulus conditions. These are the main effects we associate with such phenomena as dark adaptation, intensity discrimination, pitch discrimination, and similar data. The data are acquired with an arbitrary and, at present, incompletely understood definition of the threshold. The second problem is the nature of near-threshold responding. Here the interest is in accounting for the quantitative properties of the threshold, the differences in psychophysical methods, and similar problems.

We have attempted to show that there is little advantage in operating in the area of the first kind of problem without utilizing the available physiological data on mechanism. One of the features of the sensory area is the extent to which one can bring empirical observations to bear on the "as if" model-building encountered in all areas of psychology. In the second class of problems, attempts have been made to develop a framework that will incorporate the subject's criterion and will lead to invariant measures despite the variety of ways in which thresholds can be measured. Exactly how sensory processes and thresholds can be constrained into a single framework is not yet clear. The uncertainty resides mainly in whether the d' distance of signal-detection theory is to be viewed as some kind of sensory magnitude or whether it belongs in the language of the subject's "assurance" that a sensory event took place. In this connection it is instructive to re-read the treatment of signal-detection theory in electronics offered by Lawson and Uhlenbeck (1950) and to compare it with the applications to psychology. Developments dealing with the nature of the noise distribution and the operation of the detector are explicit in electronics; they are vague in the psychological applications. The uncertainty we refer to will persist until the gap is filled.

Despite this uncertainty, there is no ground for hesitation in trying to link the psychophysical data with the knowledge we have of physiological mechanisms when the main effects are large. A theoretical account of dark-adaptation curves that represent changes in sensitivity of a factor of 100,000 or more does not have to wait on an adequate account of problems of changes in threshold involving a factor of five or, at most, a factor of ten. The problem becomes more acute when we are dealing with small main effects, for example, the comparison of monocular and binocular thresholds or sensory interaction effects, where the changes may be of the same order as those involved in our discussions of the theory of the threshold.

References

von Békésy, Georg. Über das Fechnersche Gesetz und seine Bedeutung für die Theorie der akustische Beobachtungsfehler und die Theorie des Horens. *Ann. Physik.*, 1930 7, 329–359. (English translation: Fechner's law and its significance. Reprinted in von Békésy, *Experiments in hearing.* New York: McGraw-Hill, 1960.)

———. Über die Resonanzkurve und die Abklingzeit der verschiedenen Stellen der Schneckentrennwand, *Akust. Zelts.*, 1943, *8*, 66–76. (English translation: On the resonance curve and the decay period at various points on the cochlear partition, *J. Acoust Soc. Amer.*, 1949, *21*, 245–254. This paper is also reprinted in von Békésy, *Experiments in hearing.* New York: McGraw-Hill, 1960).

———. Neural volleys and the similarity between sensations produced by tones and by skin vibrations. *J. Acoust. Soc. Amer.*, 29, 1957, 1059–1069. (Reprinted in von Békésy, *Experiments in hearing.* New York: McGraw-Hill, 1960.)

Blackwell, D., and Girshick, M. A. *Theory of games and statistical decisions.* New York: Wiley, 1954.

de Boer, E. *On the "residue" in hearing.* Doctoral dissertation, University of Amsterdam, 1956. (Complete reference given by Licklider [1959]).

Chernoff, H., and Moses, L. E. *Elementary decision theory.* New York: Wiley, 1959.

Corso, J. F. The neural quantum theory of sensory discrimination, *Psychol. Bull.*, 1956, *53*, 371–393.

De Valois, R. Color vision mechanisms in the monkey, *J. Gen. Physiol.*, 1960, *43*, 115–128.

Doughty, J. M., and Garner, W. R. Pitch characteristics of short tones. I. Two kinds of pitch threshold. *J. Exp. Psychol.*, 1947, *37*, 351–365.

Egan, J. Recognition memory and the operating characteristic. Tech. Note. AFCRC-TN-58-51, ASTIA Document No. AD-152650. Hearing and Communication Laboratory, Indiana University, 1958.

Egan, J. P., Schulman, A., and Greenberg, G. Operating characteristics deter-mined by binary decisions and by ratings, *J. Acoust. Soc. Amer.*, 1959, *31*, 768–773.

Fechner, G. S. *Elemente der Psychophysik*. Leipzig: Breitkopf, 1889.

Fletcher, H. *Speech and hearing*. New York: Van Nostrand, 1929.

———. Auditory patterns. *Rev. Mod. Phys.*, 1940, *12*, 47–65.

Galambos, R. Microelectrode studies on medial geniculate body of cat. III. Response to pure tones. *J. Neurophysiol.*, 1952, *15*, 381–400.

Galambos, R., and Davis, H. The response of single auditory nerve fibers to acoustic stimulation, *J. Neurophysiol.*, 1943, *6*, 39–58.

Galambos, R., Rose, J. E., Bromiley, R. B., and Hughes, J. H. Microelectrode studies on medial geniculate body of cat. II. Response to clicks. *J. Neuro-physiol.*, 1952, *15*, 359–380.

Graham, C. H. Behavior, perception, and the psychophysical methods. *Psy-chol. Rev.*, 1950, *57*, 108–120.

———. Color theory. In S. Koch (ed.), *Psychology: a study of a science*, Vol. 1. New York: McGraw-Hill, 1959, pp. 145–287.

Graham, C. H., and Yun Hsia. Color defect and color theory. *Science*, 1958, *127*, 675–682.

Granit, R. *Sensory mechanisms of the retina*. New York: Oxford, 1947.

Green, D. M. Psychoacoustics and detection theory. *J. Acoust. Soc. Amer.*, 1960, *32*, 1189–1203.

Guilford, J. P. *Psychometric methods* (1st ed.). New York: McGraw-Hill, 1936.

Hartline, H. K., Milne, L. J., and Wagman, I. H. Fluctuation of response of single visual sense cells. *Fed. Proc.*, 1947, *6*, 124.

Hartline, H. K., Wagner, H. G., and Ratliff, F. Inhibition in the eye of *Lim-ulus*. *J. Gen. Physiol.*, 1956, *39*, 651–673.

Hawkins, J., and Stevens, S. S. The masking of pure tones and of speech by white noise, *J. Acoust. Soc. Amer.*, 1950, *22*, 6–13.

Hecht, S., Schlaer, S., and Pirenne, M. H. Energy, quanta, and vision, *J. Gen. Physiol.*, 1942, *25*, 819–840.

von Helmholtz, H. L. *Die Lehre von den Tonempfindungen als physiologische Grundlage für die Theorie der Musik* (1st ed.). Brunswick (Germany): Vieweg-Verlag, 1863. (English title: *On the sensations of tone*. New York: Dover, 1954.)

———. *Handbuch der physiologischen Optik* (2nd ed.). Hamburg and Leip-zig: Voss Verlag, 1896. (See also Graham, 1959, pp. 232–244.)

Hering, E., Zur Erklärung der Farbenblindheit aus der Theorie der Gegen-farben. *Lotos, Jb. f. Naturwiss.*, 1880, *1*, 76–107.

Huggins, W. H., and Licklider, J. C. R. Place mechanisms in auditory fre-quency analysis. *J. Acoust. Soc. Amer.*, 1951, *23*, 290–299.

Hurvich, L., and Jameson, D. An opponent process theory. *Psychol. Rev.*, 1957, *64*, 384–390, 397–404.

Katsuki, Y. Neural mechanism of auditory sensation in cats. In W. A. Rosen-blith (ed.), *Sensory communication*. Cambridge, Mass.: M.I.T. Press (John Wiley), 1961, pp. 561–583.

Lawson, J. L., and Uhlenbeck, G. *Threshold signals*. New York: McGraw-Hill, 1950.

Licklider, J. C. R. Basic correlates of the auditory stimulus. In S. S. Stevens (ed.), *Handbook of experimental psychology*. New York: Wiley, 1951.

———. "Periodicity" pitch and "place" pitch. *J. Acoust. Soc. Amer.*, 1954, 26, 945 (Abstract).

———. Three auditory theories. In S. Koch (ed.), *Psychology: a study of a science*, Vol. I. New York: McGraw-Hill, 1959, pp. 41–144.

Luce, R. D. Detection and recognition. In R. D. Luce, R. R. Bush, and E. Galanter (eds.), *Handbook of mathematical psychology*, Vol. I. New York: Wiley, 1963.

Luce, R. D., and Raiffa, H. *Games and decisions.* New York: Wiley, 1957.

Marill, T. Detection theory and psychophysics. Tech. Report No. 319. Cambridge, Mass.: Massachusetts Institute of Technology, Research Laboratory of Electronics, 1956, 73 pp.

Mathews, M. Mathematical detectability limits and signal perception. *J. Acoust. Soc. Amer.*, 1960, 32, 931 (Abstract).

Miller, G. A., and Taylor, W. G. The perception of repeated bursts of noise. *J. Acoust. Soc. Amer.*, 1948, 20, 171–182.

Mood, A. M. *Introduction to the theory of statistics.* New York: McGraw-Hill, 1950.

von Neumann, J., and Morganstern, O. *Theory of games and economic behavior* (1st ed.). Princeton, N.J.: Princeton University Press, 1944.

Neyman, J., and Pearson, E. S. On the use and interpretation of certain test criteria for purposes of statistical inference. *Biometrika*, 1928, 20A, 175–240, 262–294.

———. On the problems of the most efficient tests of statistical hypotheses. *Philos. Trans. of the Royal Soc. Lond.*, 1933, 231A, 289–337.

Pecher, C. R. La fluctuation d'excitabilité de la fibre nerveuse. *Arch. Int. Physiol.*, 1939, 49, 129–152.

Peterson, W. W., Birdsall, T. G., and Fox, W. C. The theory of signal detectability. *Trans. of the I.R.E. Professional Group on Information Theory.* PGIT-4, 1954, 171–212.

Pollack, I., and Decker, L. Confidence ratings, message reception and the receiver operating characteristic, *J. Acoust. Soc. Amer.*, 1958, 30, 286–292.

Rose, J. E., and Galambos, R. Microelectrode studies on medial geniculate body of cat. I. Thalamic region activated by click stimuli, *J. Neurophysiol.*, 1952, 15, 343–357.

Schaefer, T. H., Gales, R. S., Shewmaker, C. A., and Thompson, P. O. The frequency selectivity of the ear as determined by masking experiments. *J. Acoust. Soc. Amer.*, 1950, 22, 490–496.

Schouten, J. F. The perception of pitch. *Philips. Tech. Rev.*, 1940, 5, 286–294.

Shower, E., and Biddulph, R. Differential pitch sensitivity of the ear. *J. Acoust. Soc. Amer.*, 1931, 3, 275–287.

Slepian, D. Some comments on the detection of gaussian signals in gaussian noise. *I.R.E. Trans. on Information Theory*, 1958, Vol. IT-4, 65–68.

Smith, M. H., and Wilson, E. A model of the auditory threshold and its application to the problem of the multiple observer. *Psychol. Monogr.*, 1953, 67, No. 359 (entire).

Stevens, S. S., Morgan, C. T., and Volksmann, J. Theory of the neural quantum in the discrimination of loudness and pitch, *Amer. J. Psychol.*, 1941, 54, 315–335.

Stiles, W. S. The basic data of colour-matching. *Physical Society Yearbook.* London: Phys. Soc., 1955, pp. 44–65.

————. Color vision: the approach through increment-threshold sensitivity. *Proc. Nat. Acad. Sci.*, 1959, *45*, 100–114.

Svaetichin, G., and MacNichol, E. F. Retinal mechanisms for chromatic and achromatic vision. *Ann. N.Y. Acad. Sci.*, 1958, *74*, 385.

Swets, J. A. Is there a sensory threshold? *Science*, 1961, *134*, No. 3473, 168–177.

Swets, J. A., Tanner, W. P., and Birdsall, T. G. Decision processes in perception. *Psychol. Rev.*, 1961, *68*, 301–340.

Tanner, W. P., and Swets, J. A. A decision-making theory of visual detection. *Psychol. Rev.*, 1954, *61*, 401–409.

Tasaki, I. Nerve impulses in individual auditory nerve fibers of the guinea pig. *J. Neurophysiol.*, 1954, *17*, 97–122.

Thurstone, L. L. Psychophysical analysis. *Amer. J. Psychol.*, 1927, *38*, 368–389.

————. The phi-gamma hypothesis. *J. Exp. Psychol.*, 1928, *11*, 293–305.

————. Psychophysical methods. In T. G. Andrews (ed.), *Methods of Psychology*. New York: Wiley, 1948, pp. 124–157.

Torgerson, W. S. *Theory and methods of scaling.* New York: Wiley, 1958.

Troland, L. T. *Psychophysiology.* Vol. II: *Sensation.* New York: Van Nostrand, 1930.

Van Meter, D., and Middleton, D. Modern approaches to reception in communication theory. *Trans. of the I.R.E. Professional Group on Information Theory, PGIT-4*, 1954, 119–145.

Wagner, H. G., MacNichol, E. F., Jr., and Wohlbarsh, M. L. The response properties of simple ganglion cells in the goldfish retina, *J. Gen. Physiol.*, 1960, *43* (Part 2), 45–62.

Wegel, R. L., and Lane, C. E. The auditory masking of one pure tone by another and its possible relation to the dynamics of the inner ear. *Physical Review*, 1924, *23*, 266–285.

Young, T. On the theory of light and colors. In *Lectures in Natural Philosophy*. London: Printed for Joseph Johnson, St. Paul's Churchyard, by William Savage, 1807, pp. 613–632. (Parts reprinted in R. C. Teevan and R. C. Birney (eds.), *Color vision.* New York: Van Nostrand, 1961.)

Zwicker, E., Flottorp, G., and Stevens, S. S. Critical bandwidth in loudness summation, *J. Acoust. Soc. Amer.*, 1957, *29*, 548–557.

Index of Names

Italic type indicates Bibliographic reference.

Aborn, M., 464, *474*
Ackoff, R. L., 127, *128*
Adler, A., 404–405, 410, *411*
Adorno, T., 386, *387*
Allee, W. C., 287
Allport, F. H., 372–373, *387*
Allport, G. W., 85, *87*, 257–271, 370–378, 387–389, 394–396, 408, *411*, auth. sel. 18: 258–271
Amatruda, C. S., 450, *453*
Amsel, A., 80, *87*
Anderson, C., 423
Anderson, J., 346–358, *367*
Angier, R. P., 443, *453*
Anokhin, P. K., 515, *521*
Ansbacher, H. L., *411*
Ansbacher, Rowena, 405, *411*
Antonitis, J. J., 542, *550*
Aquinas, T., 336
Aristotle, 97, 105, 336
Arnoff, E. L., 127, *128*
Aronson, E., 383–384, *387*, *388* ·
Asch, S. E., 85, *88*, 304, *311*, 372–375, 385n, *387*
Ashby, W. R., 91n, 100
Atkinson, R. C., 131, 495, 537, 553–562, *564*, auth. sel. 33: 551–564
Attneave, F., 567, *574*
Austin, G. A., 476, *491*
Ausubel, D., 343–350, 358–359, *367*
Ayer, A. J., 68–71, *74*

Bacon, F., 290
Baer, D., 354, *368*
Baernstein, H. D., 119n–120, *128*
Bagby, E., 407, *411*
Bakan, D. A., 537, *547*
Baldwin, A., 358, *368*
Bandura, A., 407, *411*
Bard, P., 450, *453*
Barker, A. N., 541, *549*
Barker, R. G., *45*
Barnes, J. M., 462, *472*
Baron, M., *521*

Barron, F., 417, *432*, *519*
Bas ian, J., 469, *472*
Battig, W. F., 537, *547*
Bayley, Nancy, 346
Beach, F. A., 305, *311*
Beer, S., 107, *128*
Békésey, G., 587–600, *611*
Bell, E. T., 54, 65, 74
Bellak, L., 431–*433*
Benjamin, A. C., 27, 44, *45*, 48, *74*, 421–428
Benjamin, J., *433*
Bentley, A. F., 51, 57, 61, *74*, 255
Bergmann, G., 9, 25–26, 34, 44–*45*, 152–162n, 170n–178, 245, *255*, 274, *285*, 500, 508, *521*
Berko, J., 463, *472*
Berkowitz, L., 341, 376–378, 385–386, *387*, auth. sel. 25: 369–388
Berlyne, D. E., 116, *128*, 362–367, *368*, 514–517, *521*
Bersh, P. J., 542, *550*
Bertalanffy, L. von, 246, 254, *255*
Bertocci, P. A., 264n, *271*
Bethe, H. A., 167
Bicknell, Elizabeth A., 542, *548*
Biddulph, R., 593, *613*
Bills, A. G., 51–57, *74*
Bindra, D., 450, *453*
Binet, A., 475, *491*
Birch, H. G., 208–210, 516, *521*
Birdsall, T. G., 604–608, 613, *614*
Bitterman, M. E., 208–210, 516, *521*
Blackwell, D., 602n, *611*
Blodgett, H. C., 534–535, *547*
Blumberg, A. E., 61–63, 69, *75*
Boas, G., *75*
Bohr, N., 83, 326, *338*
Boneau, C. A., 520–*521*
Boring, E. G., 6, 11, 15, 23, *45*, 52, 70, *75*, 102n, 112n, *128*, 158, 259, 262n, *271*, 274, *285*
Borko, H., 489, *491*
Boslov, G. L., 520, *522*

Bousfield, W. A., 467, 471, *472*
Bower, G. H., 463n, *472*, 545, *547*
Braithwaite, R. B., 44, 83–*88*
Brazier, M. A. B., 519, *521*
Brehm, J., 382, *387*
Breland, K., 538, *547*
Breland, Marian, 538, *547*
Brentano, F., 235, 264
Bridgman, P. W., 4, 12, *45*, 49–59, 69, 75, 204, 210, 274, *285*, 532, *547*
Briggs, G. E., 517, *526*
Broadbent, D. E., 114–116, 121, *128*, 521
Brodbeck, May, 43
Bromiley, R. B., *612*
Brown, J. S., 501, *521*, 542
Brown, R. W., 355–356, *368*, 463, *472*
Brown, Ursula, *550*
Bruner, J. S., 378, *387*, 464, *473*–476, 481–485, *491*, 567, *574*
Brunswik, E., 18, 75, 138, 145, 225–226, 249–254, *255*, 277, *285*, auth. sel. 14: 226–237
Brush, Elinor S., 30, *46*, 501, *525*
Bugelski, B. R., 539, *547*
Bühler, K., 236
Bull, Nina, *453*
Bullock, D. H., 538, *547*
Bunch, M. E., 17
Bures, C. E., 75
Burke, C. J., 131, 137, 145, 159, 531, *547*–*548*, auth. sel. 7: 147–159
Burlingham, D., 426, *433*
Busenius, C. E., 145
Bush, R. R., 93, 137, 139n, 145, 543, 547, 557, *563*–*564*
Butler, R. A., 365
Bykov, K. M., *521*

Calvin, A., 396, *411*, 542
Calvin, J. S., *548*
Campbell, D. T., *255*, 532, *548*
Campbell, N. R., 75, *88*, 159, 250–251
Cannon, W. B., 33, 262n, 264, 450, *453*
Cantril, H., 379
Carhart, P. W., 108, *129*
Carlsmith, J. M., 382
Carlson, A. J., 105, *128*, 262n
Carnap, R., 59n–70, 75, 83, *88*, 164, 178, 274, *285*, 527, 532, *548*
Carr, H. A., 17, 442, *453*
Carterette, E. C., 551n
Carterette, T., 138, 146
Cartwright, D., 386, *387*
Cassirer, E., 268, *271*
Cattell, R. B., 398, *411*
Chaisson, A. F., 145
Champion, R. A., 502, 511, *521*

Chance, J., 341n
Chapanis, A., 104–112, 124–127n, *128*, auth. sel. 5: 105–129
Chapman, D. E., 375n, *387*
Charcot, J. M., 391
Chaucer, G., 390
Chernoff, H., 602n, *611*
Child, I., 341n, 366
Chinetti, P., 569, 574
Chomsky, N., 463, 471, *472*
Churchman, C. W., 127, *128*
Claparede, E., 446, *453*
Cochran, S. W., 520, *526*
Cofer, C. N., 467, *472*
Coghill, G., 350, *368*
Cohen, M. R., 190, 201
Comrey, A. L., 159
Conant, J. B., 21, *45*
Connor, J. P., 519, *521*
Conover, D., 107
Conrad, R., 116, *128*
Coppock, W. J., 520–*521*
Corso, J. F., 601, *611*
Cortez, S., 300
Cotton, J. W., 16, *45*, 495, 536–541, *548*–*549*, auth. sel. 32: 526–551
Coyer, R. A., *547*
Cozzens, J. G., 295
Cronbach, L. J., 414, *433*, 466, *472*
Crothers, E. J., 544–545, *548*
Culler, E. A., 539, *548*
Curtis, J. F., 116, 129

D' Abro, A., *88*
Danto, 43
Darwin, C. R., 26, 264, 290–292, 392, 427, 437–438, *453*
Dashiell, J. F., 372, *387*
Davidson, D., 159
Davis, H., 594, *612*
de Boer, E., 596, *611*
de Broglie, L., 85
Decker, L., 605, *613*
Deese, J., 467, *472*
Dembo, Tamara, *45*
Dement, W. C., 425, *433*
Descartes, R., 105
Deutsch, K. W., 118, *128*
Dewey, J., 65n, 372, 443, *453*
De Valois, R., 586, *611*
Diamond, A. L., *574*
Diamond, S., 408, *411*, 569
Dickson, W. J., 127n, *129*
Dingle, H., 75
Dinsmoor, J. A., 542, *548*
Doehring, D. G., 497, *521*
Dollard, J., 291, 365, 373, *388*, 407, *411*

Dostoevski, F. M., 390
Doughty, J. M., 590, *611*
Duffy, E., 450, *453*
Dufort, R. H., *520–521*
Duhem, P., 83, 86, *88*
Duncker, K., 475, *491*
Dunlap, K., 442, *453*
Dunn, B., 570, *574*
Durkheim, E., 309n, *311*
Dykman, R. A., 521, *522*

Ebbinghaus, H., 142–145, 332, 456–457
Edwards, W., 476, *491*, 536, *548*
Egan, J., 605, 609, *611–612*
Einstein, A., 75, 85, 284
Elkind, D., 546, *550*
English, Ava C., 8–9, *45*
English, H. B., 8–9, *45*
Erikson, E. H., 346, 415–416, 429
Escalona, S. K., 420, *433*
Estes, W. K., 5, 44–*45*, 46, 81–82, *88*, 93, 131–146, 376, 463n, *472*, 495–497, *522*, 526–531, 536–553, *564*, auth. sel. 6: 132–146
Eysenck, H. J., 398, *411*, 446, *453*
Ezriel, H., *433*

Falk, J. L., 34, *45*
Farber, I. E., 320, *322*
Farrell, B. A., 431, *433*
Fechner, G. S., *612*
Fechner, G. T., 229, 290, 554, 597
Feigenbaum, E., 488, *491*
Feigl, H., 43, 61–69, 75, 195, 201–210, 248, 255, 274, *285*, *368*, 402, *411*, 414, *433*
Feldman, J., 488, *491*
Felsinger, J. M., 219–221, 372, 382, *535–536*, *548*
Ferster, C. B., 18, *45*, 327, *338*, 543, *548*
Festinger, L., 17, *45*, 96n, 341, 379–386, *387*
Fisher, C., 425, *433*
Fisher, R., 100
Fitch, F. B., 178, *473*, *549*
Fitzgerald, J., *369*
Flagle, W. H., *129*
Flavell, J., 481, *491*
Fletcher, H., *612*
Fletcher, R., 438, 448, *453*, 591, 594
Flottorp, G., 593, *614*
Foley, J. P., 467, *472*
Fox, W. C., 604, 608, *613*
Frank, P., 6, *45*, 59n
Franks, C. M., 520, *522*
Frankmann, J. P., 140, 146
Frege, G., 60n
Frenkel-Brunswik, E., *387*, 413–415, 423, 431–432, *433*

Freud, Anna, 405, 410–*412*, 426, *433*
Freud, S., 207, 263–264, 291, 312, 346–350, 362–364, 377, 391–392, 404–405, *412*, 421–428, 443–445, *453*
Frick, F. C., 464, *472*
Fromm, E., 405, *412*
Fuller, J., 354, *368*
Fulton, J. F., 287

Gagné, R. M., 476, *491*, 529, *548*
Galambos, R., 519, *522*, 594, *612–613*
Galanter, E. H., *46*, 159, 489, *492*, 564
Gales, R. S., *613*
Galileo, G., 163, 292
Gantt, W. H., 510, 521, *522*
Gardner, R. A., 536, *548*
Garner, W. R., 590, *611*
Gauss, K. F., 54
Gehman, R. S., *526*
Gelernter, H. L., 488, *492*
George, F. H., 161, 225, auth. sel. 15: 237–239
Gerall, A., 520, *522*
Gershik, M. A., 602n
Gesell, A., 350, 360–363, 450, *453*
Gewirtz, J., 354, 366, *368*
Gibbs, J. W., 89
Gibson, E. J., 354, *368*, 462n, *472*
Gill, M. M., 410–418, *433–434*
Ginsberg, A., 86, *88*, 545
Ginsberg, Rose, *551*
Girshick, M. A., *611*
Gladstone, A. I., 219–221, 535, *548*
Gleason, H. A., 463, *472*
Goldstein, B., 23, *45–46*
Goldstein, H., *525*
Goldstein, K., 268n, *271*, 519
Goodenough, F. L., *453*
Goodnow, Jacqueline J., 476, *491*
Goodson, F. E., 320, *322*
Gormezano, I., 520
Gough, P. H., 455, auth. sel. 29: 456–474
Graham, C. H., 148, 529, *548*, 566–569, 574, 579–582, 597, *612*
Granit, R., 587, *612*
Grant, D. A., 81, *88*, 510, 520, *522*, *524–525*
Green, B. F., 489, *492*
Green, D. M., *612*
Greenberg, G., *612*
Grice, G. R., 173, 178
Grings, W. W., 495, 515–522, auth. sel. 31: 495–526
Guetzkow, H., 96n
Guilford, J. P., 394–398, *412*, 476–480, 490, *492*, 597, *612*
Gulliksen, H., 159

Guthrie, E. R., 6, *45*, 93, 206, 376, 407, *412*, 500, 508, 515, *522*, 526–536, 543, *549*

Haggard, D. F., 507, 519, *525*
Hahn, H., 59n
Haire, M., 106n, *128*
Haldane, J. B. S., 246
Hall, M., 178, *473*, *549*
Halsey, R. A., 112, *128*
Hammond, W. A., 105, *128*
Hansche, W. J., 520, *522*
Harary, F., 384–387
Harlow, H. F., 17, *45*, 85, *88*, 219, 312, *322*, 363, 365, *368*, 397, *412*, 427, *433*
Harmon, H. H., 477, *492*
Harms, E., 479
Harris, D., 343, *368–389*
Hartley, E., *387*
Hartline, H. K., 569–570, 574, 593, 600, *612*
Hartman, T. F., 520, *522*
Hartmann, H., 312, *322*, 416, 422, *433*
Harvey, O. J., *412*
Harvey, W., 289, 406
Hawkins, J., 592, *612*
Heard, W. G., 521, *525*
Hebb, D. O., 140, 146, *255*, 286, 302, 567, 574
Hecht, S., 567, 574, 598–600, *612*
Heider, F., 277, *285*, 304, *311*, 384, *387*
Heimer, W., 544, *550*
Held, R., 572, 574
Helmholtz, H. L. von, 230, 290, 581, 587, *612*
Hempel, C. G., 64, 75, 248, 251n, *255*, 414, *433*
Henderson, L. J., 299, 546
Henderson, R. L., *550*
Henle, Mary, 17, *45*
Hering, E., 236, 569, 574, 582, 587, *612*
Heron, W., 450, *453*
Hess, E. H., 450, *453*
Heuss, T., 303
Hickson, R. H., 138, 146
Hilgard, E. R., 17, *45*, 142, 146, 197, 202, 261, *271*, 395, 425, *433*, 456, *473*, 496, *523*, *534*, *548*
Hillix, W. A., 11, 17, *46*
Hippocrates, 288, 295
Hobhouse, L. T., 393
Hochbaum, G., 381
Holst, E., von, 574
Holt, E. B., 261, 427, 572, 574
Holt, R. R., *433*
Holton, G., *45*
Homans, G. C., 93, 96n, 386, *387*

Homme, L. E., 140, 146
Hopkins, B. L., 133, 544–545, *548*
Horney, Karen, 404–405, 410–411, *412*
Horton, G. P., 469, 534, *549*
Horwitz, L., 389, auth. sel. 27: 413–434
Hoslett, S. D., *271*
Hovland, C. I., 178, 191n, 202, 378–379, *388*, *473*, 488, *492*, *549*
Howes, D. H., 80, *88*
Hsia, Y., 579, *612*
Huggins, W. H., 129, 593–597, *612*
Hughes, J. H., *612*
Hughes, J. W., 373, *388*
Hugo, V., 390
Hull, C. L., 8, 15–16, 24, 44–*45*, 46, *88*, 120, *128*, 140–146, 156–179n, 188–196, 202–221, 233, 265, *271*, 278–*285*, 291, 364–365, 407–412, 457–467, *473*, 499–508, 526–546, 548–549
Hume, D., 60, 75, 297
Humphrey, G., 475, *492*
Hunt, D. E., *412*
Hunt, E. B., *492*
Hunt, J., 359–361, *368*, 406
Hunt, J. McV., *322*, 488
Hunt, W. A., 34, *45*, 313, 320, *322*, 362
Hunter, W. S., 568, 573, 574
Hurvich, L., 582–587, *612*
Hutten, E. H., 82, *88*
Huttenlocker, J., 520, *525*
Huxley, Julian, 263, *271*
Hyman, R., 116, *128*

Inhelder, Bärbel, 343, *368*, 481–484, *492*
Irion, A. L., 456, *473*
Irwin, J. McQ., 459–461, *473*
Israel, H. E., 23, *46*

Jacobson, C., 287
Jacobson, H., 120–121, *128*
Jagoda, H., 78n
James, W., 23, 47, *75*, 183n, 337, 440, 442, *453*
Jameson, D., 582–587, *612*
Jasper, H. H., 519, *523*
Jeans, J., *88*
Jefferson, T., 374
Jeffress, L. A., 101n
Jenkins, J. J., 455, 468, *473*, 538, auth. sel. 29: 456–474
Jenkins, W. O., *549*
Jensen, G. D., 540, *548*
Jessor, R., 225, 245n, 250, *255*, auth. sel. 17: 245–256
John, E. R., 519, *523*
Johnson, H. M., 19, *46*, 105

Johnson, V., *128*
Jones, J. E., *412, 521, 523, 549*
Jones, M. R., *46, 88*, 404, 502, 511, 520, 545

Kagan, J., *368*
Kant, I., 60, 97, 264
Kantor, J. R., 52, 56, *75*, 148, 161, 180n, 184n, 185n, 249, *255*, auth. sel. 9: 179–186
Karlin, J. E., 464, *473*
Karush, A., 417, *433*
Katsuki, Y., 594–595, *612*
Katz, B., 52, *76*
Keats, J., 300
Kelley, H. H., 386, *388*
Kelly, G., 406, 410, *412*
Kelman, H., 382, *388*
Kendler, H. H., 78n, *80, 81*, 85, *88*, 161, 354, 366, *368*, 516, *523, 549*, auth. sel. 11: 203–210
Kendler, T., 354, *368*, 540
Kepler, J., 162, 293
Keppel, G., 544, *551*
Kessen, W., 44, 245, *255*, 341n, 358–366, *368–369*, 490, *492*
Keynes, J. M., 288
Kimble, G. A., 245, *255*, 496, 501, 511, 518–*521, 523*, 542, *549*
Kimmel, H. D., 510, 520, *523*
Kinchla, R. A., 551n, 553, 558, 561, *564*
Kitt, A. S., 376n, *388*
Kjeldergaard, P. M., 499
Koch, S., 16, 44–*46*, 80, *88*, 168n, 178, 216–221, 358, *368*, 376, *388, 522*, 536, *549*
Koffka, K., 167–168n, 178, 228
Kogan, N., 385, *388*
Kohlberg, L., 341n, 354, 362, *368*
Köhler, W., 166–169, 178, 193, 202, 408
Konorski, J., *523*
Korzybski, A., 72
Kounin, J. S., *45*, 346
Knott, T. A., 108, *129*
Krech, D., 161, 187–193, 200–202, 225, *255–256*, 267, *574*, auth. selections 12 and 16: 211–213, 240–245
Kreuger, R. G., *128*, 199n
Kris, E., *312*, 322, 423–428, 431, *433*
Kris, M., *433*
Kroeber, A. L., 245–247n, 253, *256*
Kubie, L. S., 421–425, *433*
Kuhlman, Clementina, *368–369*, 492
Külpe, O., 475

Lachman, R., auth. sel. 3: 78–89
La Mettrie, J. O., 105
Lane, C. E., 591, *614*
Lashley, K. S., 70, 332, 408

Lauer, D. W., 138
Lawson, J. L., 604, 610, *612*
Lazarsfeld, P. F., *388*
Le Bon, G., 372
Lecky, P., 266, *271*, 408, *412*
Leeper, R. W., 392, 408, *412*, 446, *453*, auth. sel. 26: 389–413
Leeuwenhoek, A., 423
Leibnitz, G. W., 65–66
Leibowitz, H., 565–570, *574*, auth. sel. 34: 565–575
Leighton, A. H., 270, *271*
Lenin, N., 374
Lenneberg, E. H., 463, *472*
Lenzen, V. F., 65n
Lerner, A., 93
Levine, M., *129*
Levine, S., 80–81, *88*, 111, 450, *453*, 540, *549*
Levinson, D., *387*
Levy, N., 538–541, *550*
Lewin, K., 12, *45, 75*, 83, 88, 163–172n, 178, 234–236, 284–*285*, 346, 360, *368*, 374
Lewis, D. J., 540–541, *548–549*
Licklider, J. C. R., 589–597, *612*
Lindley, R. H., 520, *523*
Lindsay, R. B., 57, *75*
Lindsley, D. B., 450, *453*
Lindsley, O. R., 327, *338*, 450, 538, *549*
Lindzey, G., 96n, *387–388*
Littman, R. A., 253, *256*, 258, auth. sel. 21: 303–311
Livingston, J. R., 541, *549*
Loeb, J., 167
Logan, F. A., *523*, 538, *549*
Lorenz, K. Z., 408
Lorge, I., 373–374, *388*
Lotka, A. J., 95
Lowell, E. L., 521–522
Luce, R. D., 563–*564*, 602n, *613*
Lukasiewicz, J., 60n
Lundberg, G. A., 52, *75*, 566
Lundin, R., 395
Luneberg, R., *574*

McAllister, D. E., 520, *523*
McAllister, R., 520, *523*
McConnell, D. G., 140, 146
McCurdy, H. G., 408, *412*
McDougall, W., 265n, *271*, 370–371, *388*, 438–439, *454*
McGeoch, J. A., 17, 52, *75*, 132, 146, 458–461, *473*
McGill, W. J., 495, 565–566, auth. sel. 35: 575–614
McGregor, D., *76*

McGuigan, F. J., 19, *46*, 396
McNemar, Olga W., 476, *493*
Maccoby, E., *387*
MacCorquodale, K., 24, 26, 44, *46*, 161, 187–202, 209n, 210, 213, 219, 221, 240n, 321, *322*, 458, 473, 522, 540, *549*
MacCurdy, J. T., *454*
Mach, E., 86
Machiavelli, N., 289
Mackworth, J. F., 116, *129*
Mackworth, N. H., *129*
MacLeod, R. B., 213
MacNichol, E. F., 585–586, *614*
Maddi, S. R., 81, *88*
Madison, P., 404–408, *412*
Maier, N. R. F., 320, *322*, 408, 475, *492*
Malisoff, W. M., 51, *75*
Mandler, G., 44
Marill, T., *613*
Margenau, H., 57, *75*
Marquis, D. G., 261, *271*, 496, *523*
Martin, W., 355, 362, *368*
Marton, T., *454*
Marx, M. H., 11, 17, *46*, 161, 190, 198n–202, 217, 221, 258, 313–*322*, 418, 476, 546, *550*, auth. selections, 1, 10, 13, 22: 4–46, 187–202, 213–221, 311–323
Maslow, A. H., 191, 202
Masserman, J. H., 320, *322*
Mathews, M., 608, *613*
Mathiev, 87
Mausner, B., 375, *388*
Maxwell, J. C., 283–284
Mead, G. H., 372–373, *388*
Meehl, P. E., 24–26, 44–*46*, 161, 187–193, 196–202, 209n–213, 219–221, 240n, 252–*256*, 321–322, 414, *433*, 466, *472–473*, 522, 540, *549*
Meissner, W. W., 24, *46*
Melton, A. W., 17, 459–461, *473*
Melzack, R., 409, *412*, 450, *454*
Mendel, G., 26, 318
Menger, K., *76*
Merlin, V. S., 518, 520, *523*
Merton, R. K., 376n, *388*
Middleton, D., 604, *614*
Miles, R. C., 542, *549*
Miller, G. A., *46*, 320, *473*, 489, *492*, 531, 596, *613*
Miller, J. G., 19, *46*, 98n, 100
Miller, N. E., 291, *322–323*, 365, 373–377, 381, *388*, 407, *411*, 464, *549*
Mills, J., 383, *387–388*
Milne, L. J., 600, *612*
Mink, W. D., 468
Mittelstaedt, H., 571–572, *574*

Moede, W., 372
Moltz, H., 80–81, *88*, 538–541, *550*
Montgomery, K. C., 365
Mood, A. M., *613*
Moore, J. W., 520, *523*
Morgan, C. T., *522–523*, *613*
Morgan, L., 393, 519, 600
Morganbesser, S., 43
Morgenstern, O., 602, *613*
Morison, R. S., 258, auth. sel. 20: 286–303
Morris, C. W., 60n, 67–72, *76*, 268–*271*
Mosbaek, E. J., *129*
Moses, L. E., 602n, *611*
Mosteller, F., 93, 137–139n, 145, 543, *547*, *557*, 563
Mowrer, O. H., 197–202, 283–*285*, 320–*323*, 365, 496, 501–504, 515, *523*
Moyer, K. E., 520, *523*
Mueller, C. G., Jr., 44, 495, *522*, 534, *550*, 565–566, 600, auth. sel. 35: 575–614
Mullahy, P., 405, *412*
Müller, J., 229
Munitz, M. K., 78n, 81, 85, *88*
Munroe, Ruth L., 405, *412*
Mussen, P., *368*
Murphy, G., *129*, 408, *412*, *434*, 525
Myers, N. A., 520, *524*, 569, *574*

Naddor, E., 111, *129*
Nagel, E., 49, *76*, 190, 201–204, 210
Needham, J., 246
Neilson, W. A., 108, *129*
Neiman, L. J., 373, *388*
Neimark, E. D., 78n
Neumann, J. von, 101n, 602, *613*
Neurath, O., 59n–60n, 64–65, *76*
Newcomb, T. M., 384–*388*
Newell, A., 101n, 309, *311*, 455, 485–488, *492*, auth. sel. 4: 89–104
Newton, I., 105, 162, 289
Neyman, J., 602, 603, *613*
Norris, E. B., 520, *522*
Nowlis, Helen H., 366
Nowlis, V., 366

Odbert, H. S., 389, *411*
Olds, J., 451, *454*
O'Neill, W. M., 390, 468, *473*
Osgood, C. E., 365, 375, 384, *388*, 457, 463–472, *473*
Ost, J. W. P., 521, *523*
Ostwald, W., 86

Parducci, A., 138, 146
Passey, G. E., 510, *523*

Pasteur, L., 289
Pavlik, W. B., 546, *550*
Pavlov, I. P., 93, 166, 178, 229, 286n–289, 325, 407–408, 498–499, 508–517n, 520, *523*
Peabody, D., 303n
Pearson, E. S., 233, 602–603, *613*
Pecher, C. R., 598, *613*
Pennington, L. A., 57, 76
Pennock, L., 542, *550*
Perkins, D. T., 178, *473*, *549*
Peters, G. A., 124–125, *129*
Peters, H. N., 389, 452, *454*, auth. sel. 28: 435–454
Peterson, E., *454*, 604, 608
Peterson, W. W., *613*
Phillips, L. W., 520, *524*
Piaget, J., 346, 350, 360–369, 421, *434*, 455, 475–490, *492*
Pierce, J. R., 464, *473*
Piéron, H., 445, *454*
Pierre, Janet, 391
Pirenne, M. H., 598–599, *612*
Pitts, W., 103n
Platanov, K., 517, *524*
Plato, 148
Plutarch, 288
Poincaré, H., 62, 76
Pollack, I., 605, *613*
Polt, J., 138, 146
Polya, G., 487, *492*
Popper, K., 44
Postman, L., 378, 457–464, *473*, 545, *550*
Potter, S., 287
Poulton, E. G., 115–116, *129*
Pratt, C. C., 10, 12, 44, *46*, 190, 202, 274, *285*, 499, *524*
Pribram, K. H., *46*, 489, *492*
Prince, M., 391, *454*
Progoff, I., 404, *412*
Prokasy, W. F., Jr., *524*

Quine, W., 74, 76

Raiffa, H., 602n, *613*
Raimy, V. C., 311, *323*
Ramond, C. K., 146
Rand, B., 105, *129*
Rappaport, D., 361, *368*, 415–417, 425–430, *434*
Rashevsky, N., 76, 100
Ratliff, F., 570, *574*, 593, *612*
Razran, G. H. S., 495, 500–519, *524*
Rehula, R., 544, *551*
Reichenbach, H., 12, *46*, 48, 60n, 70, 76
Restle, F., 563–564
Reymert, M. L., *454*

Reynolds, B., 546, *550*
Reynolds, W. F., 546, *550*
Richardson, L. F., 95, 100
Richfield, J., 430, *434*
Riecken, H. W., 96n
Robbins, L. L., 417–419, 430, *434*
Robertson, T. B., 133–134, 146
Robinson, H., *388*
Roby, T. B., 534, *550*
Rochester, N., 488, *492*
Rock, I., 544, *550*
Roethlisberger, F. J., 127n, *129*
Rogers, C., 406, 410, *412*
Rogers, W. A., *547*
Roget, P. M., 90, 92
Romanes, G. J., 336
Roosevelt, F. D., 260, 266–267
Rose, J. E., *612–613*
Rosen, E., 253, *256*, 303n
Rosenblatt, T., 567, *574*
Rosenblueth, A., 117, *129*, 194–195, 202
Rosenzweig, S., 55, 76
Ross, E. A., 370, *388*, 507, 519–520
Ross, L. E., 522, *524–525*
Ross, R. T., 178, *473*, *549*
Rouse, R. O., 541, *549*
Roy, R. H., *129*
Rozeboom, W. W., 245–248, *256*
Rubenstein, H., 464, *474*
Ruckmick, C. A., 443, *454*
Ruger, H. A., 145
Runquist, W. N., 457, *474*, 507, 519, 524, *525*
Rushford, G. N., 521–522
Russell, W. A., 60, 65n, 468, *473*, *474*, 488
Ryan, J. J., 469, *474*

Sampson, P. B., 520, *522*
Sanford, R., *387*
Santayana, G., 298
Sargent, H. D., 419, 431, *434*
Schachtel, E., 364, *368*
Schaefer, T. H., 592, *613*
Scharlock, D. P., 539, *550*
Scheerer, M., 364, *368*
Schlaer, S., 598–599, *612*
Schlank, M., 572, *574*
Schlick, M., 59n, 76
Schlosberg, H., 320, *322*, 515, *525*
Schneider, D. E., 510, *522*
Schoenfeld, W. N., 44, *522*, 534, 542, *550*
Schopenhauer, A., 264
Schouten, J. F., 595, *613*
Schroder, H. M., 406, *412*
Schulman, A., *612*

Schulz, R. W., 457, *474*
Schweitzer, A., 331
Scriven, M., 355–356, *368*, 414, 427, *434*
Sears, R. R., 304, *311*, 366, *434*
Seashore, R. H., 52, 76
Sebeok, T. A., 463, 467, *473*
Selfridge, J. A., 464, *473*
Sellars, W., 43, 252, *256*
Semmelweiss, I. P., 400
Senders, Virginia L., 151, 159
Seward, J. P., 16, *46*, 515, 538–542, *524*, 546, *550*
Shaffer, L. F., 406, *412*
Shakespeare, W., 390
Shakow, D., 423–424, *434*
Shaw, J. C., 485–488, *492*
Shannon, C. E., 93, 102n
Shea, R. A., 546, *550*
Sheffield, F. D., 365, 534, *550*
Shepard, J. F., 170
Sherif, M., 375n, 378–379, *388*
Sherrington, C. S., 569, *574*
Shewmaker, C. A., *613*
Shmeley, V., 520, *522*
Shmirnov, G. D., 519
Shoben, E. J., 407, *412*
Shower, E., 593, *613*
Shuttleworth, F., 359, *369*
Sidis, B., 391
Sidman, M., 18, 45–*46*, 537, *550*
Siegel, S., 151–152, 159
Sigler, M., 568, 573–*574*
Silverman, R. E., 520, *524*
Simon, C. W., *129*, 309, *550*
Simon, H. A., 108, *111*, 455, 485–488, *492*, 542, auth. sel. 4: 89–104
Skinner, B. F., 18, 44–*46*, 86–*88*, 148, 191n, 196, 202, 217–221, 258, *285*, 325–*338*, 357, 364–365, 401–402, *412*–*413*, 464–*474*, 497, 508, *524*, 526–543, *548*, *550*, auth. sel. 23: 323–338
Slepian, D., 608, *613*
Sloane, E. H., 320, *323*
Smedslund, J., 250–251, *256*, 354, *369*
Smirnov, G. D., *523*
Smith, M. B., 431, *433*, 601
Smith, M. H., *613*
Snygg, D., 169–170, 178
Sokolov, E. N., 514, 517, *524*
Solarz, A. K., 467, *474*
Solley, C. M., 515, *525*
Solomon, R. L., 30, *46*, 80, *88*, 501, *524*, *525*, 543, *550*
Somerville, J., 76
Sophocles, 390
Spearman, C., 171n, 178, 233, 475, *492*
Spence, K. W., 29, *46*, 80–*88*, 144–162, 171–173n, 178, 188, 196–205, 257, *285*, 320–*323*, *421*, 495–510, 519–520, *524*–*525*, 533, 540–546, 550, auth. selections 8 and 19: 162–178, 272–286
Spencer, H., 96
Sperling, D. S., 542, *548*
Spieth, W., 116, 129
Spitz, R. A., 426, *434*
Staats, A. W., 83, *89*, 467–469, *474*, 521, *525*
Staats, C. K., 83, *89*, 467–469, *474*, 521, *525*
Stagner, R., 395, 407, *413*
Stanley, J. C., Jr., 538, *549*
Stein, K. B., 426, *434*, 476
Stein, M. I., *492*
Stellar, E., 519, *523*
Stevens, S. S., 4, 52, 56, 63, 69n, 73, 76, *88*, 111, 126–129, 148–151, 159, 202, 274, *285*, 592, 593, 600, *612*, *613*, *614*, auth. sel. 2: 49–76
Stevenson, H., 354, 361–366, *368*–*369*
Stiles, W. S., 580–582, 586, *613*–*614*
Stone, C. P., *88*
Storms, L. H., *474*
Straughan, J. H., *88*, 531, *548*
Struik, D. J., 76
Suci, G. J., 464–465, *473*
Sullivan, H. S., 304, *311*, 405, 410
Sullivan, S. N., *526*
Suppes, P., 159, 545, *550*, 553–562, *564*
Suttie, I. D., *271*
Svaetichia, G., 585, *614*
Swets, J. A., 601–606, *614*

Tagiuri, R., 385, *388*
Tannenbaum, P. H., 375, 384, *388*, 464–465, *473*
Tanner, W. P., 601–606, *614*
Tarde, G., 370–375, *388*
Tarski, A., 60n
Tasaki, I., 594, *614*
Tatsvoka, M., 78n
Taylor, D. W., 38, *46*, 455, 476, 493, 507, 596, auth. sel. 30: 475–493
Taylor, Janet, 28, *46*, 476, *525*
Taylor, W. G., *613*
Teuber, H. L., 572, *575*
Thales, 65
Thibaut, J. W., 386, *388*
Thompson, P. E., 116, 129, *613*
Thompson, W., 354, *368*, 450, *454*
Thorndike, E. L., 268, 271, 332, 408
Thouless, R. H., 12, *46*
Thune, L. E., 460, *474*
Thurstone, L. L., 133–136, 146, 171n, 178, 233, 320–*323*, 478, *493*, 598, 604–609, *614*

Tinbergen, N., 408, 448
Titchener, E. B., 235
Tolman, E. C., 24, *46*, 51–56, 69, 76, 148,
    163,   171–172,   176n–192,   195n–206,
    213, 221, 232, 249, *256*, 261–263, *271–*
    279, 281–*286*, 408, 500, 508, 513–515,
    525–536, 539–543, *551*
Tolman, Ruth S., 423, *434*
Tolstoi, L., 390
Torgerson, W. S., 609, 607n, *614*
Toulmin, S., 80, 84, *89*
Trapold, M. A., 519, *525*
Triplett, N., 372
Troland, L. T., *614*
Turing, A. M., 486, *493*
Turner, W. S., 19, 20, 26, *46*
Tustin, A., 94n

Uexküll, J. J., 237
Uhlenbeck, G., 604, 610, *612*
Underwood, B. J., 17, 78, *89*, 109, 129,
    214, 221, 457–462, *472*, *474*, 531, 544,
    545, *551*

Valentine, W. L., 11, *46*
Van Meter, D., 604, *614*
Van Spanckeren, W. J., 199, 202, 320,
    322
Vernon, J., 450, *454*
Verplanck, W. S., 44, *522*
Viek, P., 197–202
Voeks, Virginia W., *525*, 537, 543–544,
    551
Volksmann, J., 375n, *387*, 600, *613*
Volterra, V., 95
von Holst, E., 451, *454*, 570–572
Von Lackum, W. J., 460, *473*
Vygotsky, L. S., 475, *493*

Wagman, I. H., 600, *612*
Wagner, H. G., 586, 593, *612*, *614*
Waismann, F., 60n
Walker, E. G., 520, *525*
Wallach, H., 202
Wallach, M. A., 481, 490, *493*
Wallerstein, R. S., 417–419, 430, *434*
Walter, G., 93
Wapner, S., 567, *575*
Warden, C. J., 532, *551*
Warren, A. B., 520, *525*
Washburn, M. F., 443, *454*
Waters, R. H., 57, 76
Watson, J. B., 148, 229, 261, 272–275,
    286, 289–291, 332, 365, 442, *454*, 465,
    474, 499, *525*
Watt, R., 105
Weaver, W., 298

Weber, E. H., 290
Webster, J. C., 116, *129*
Webel, R. L., 591, *614*
Wegner, Norma, *526*
Weinberg, J. R., 76
Weingarten, Linda, 78n
Weinstock, S. W., 139, 146
Weir, M., 354, *369*
Weiss, R. F., 546, *551*
Wells, H., 475n
Wenger, M. A., *454*
Werner, H., 343–354, 361–363, *369*, 421,
    434, 567, 574
Wertheimer, M., 264, 475, *493*
Westcott, M. R., 520, *525*
Weyant, R. G., 519, *525*
Whaley, F. L., 520, *524*
White, C. T., *525*
White, L. D., 89n, 246–247n
White, R. W., 245, 253, *256*, 365, *369*,
    405, 413, *434*, 515
Whitehead, A. N., 488
Whitehorn, J. C., 521–522
Whiting, J. W. M., 366
Whittaker, E. T., 87, *89*
Wickens, D. D., 11, *46*, 517, 520, *525–526*,
    542, *549–550*
Wiener, W., 117, *129*, 194–195, 202
Wilson, E., 601, *613*
Windle, W., 350, *369*
Wishner, J., 400, *413*
Wittgenstein, L., 60, 76, 84, *89*
Wohlbarsh, M. L., 586, *614*
Wolff, P., 354, 361–363, *369*
Wollen, K. A., 545, *551*
Wolpe, J., *413*
Woodger, J. H., 76, 246–253, *256*
Woodrow, H., 164–165, 174–178
Woodward, J. K., 520, *522*
Woodworth, R. S., 475, *493*, 495, 500–
    503, 513–515, *526*, 568, 572, *575*
Wright, H. F., *45*
Wright, J., *368*
Wundt, W., 235, 290, 437, *454*, 566
Wynne, L. C., 543, *550*

Yamaguchi, H. G., 220–221, 535–536,
    548
Yerkes, R. M., 268, *271*, 332
Young, F. A., *526*
Young, P. T., 446, *454*, 520, 582
Young, T., 614
Yule, G. U., 100

Zajonc, R. B., 383, *388*
Zeaman, D., *526*
Zigler, E., 455, auth. sel. 24: 341–369
Zwicker, E., 593, *614*

Index of Subjects

The following convention is used: *n* for footnote.

Affect, 435–452
Analogy, 93–94, 106, 109
  and models, 85–86
  and science, 103–104
  as theory, 96–98
Analysis, 219
  gross functions, 213–220
Animal psychology, 34–35, 320
Animistic conceptions, 166
Association, verbal, 467–469
Attention, model, 114–116

Behaviorism, 56, 67, 73–74, 179, 182, 228, 257, 272–286
  and physiology, 334
Berlin Circle, 60*n*
Brain functions and classical conditioning, 498

Classical conditioning, 81, 495–521
  contemporary theories, 502–521
  definition of, 495–497
  origins of theory, 497–502
  Russian orientation, 516–519
Clinical theory,
  attitudes, 311–322
  psychoanalysis, 413–432
Clinician, role, 311–312
Cognitive dissonance, 379–384
Color vision theories, 578–587
Computer, 93–94, 477
  and brain, 101, 112, 122
  digital, 101–103
  and thinking, 101–103, 485–489
Concept, 23, 58, 336
  definition of, 9–10, 41
  of personality, 403–410
  reification of, 437
Conceptual focus, 226–237
Conditioning, 93
  classical, 81, 495–521
  instrumental, 496, 504

Confirmation, 13, 37
Conflict and emotion, 443–445
Constancy research, 230–233
Construct, 12, 13, 23, 31, 35, 39
  analysis of, 213–220
  definition of, 9–10, 41
  empirical, 86
  and events, 179–186
  formation, 21–31
  hypothetical, 24–31, 40, 188–196, 240–245
  intervening, 24–29, 40, 181–184, 188–189, 195–201, 213–220, 279–282, 504, 528
  meaning of, 203–210
  modular, 86
  response-inferred, 167–170
  significance, 28
  types, 24–31, 162–177
Constructive explanation, 31–32
Construct validity, 414–415, 432, 466*n*
Control, 39
  events, definition of, 41
  in observation, 11–12, 313–317
  variables, 357, 426
    definition of, 41
Corollary, definition of, 41
Creativity, 13, 37
Curve fitting, 175

Darwinism, 96
Data, 7, 14, 16, 19–20, 23, 40, 127
  definition of, 41
Data language, definition of, 41
Deduction, 15, 19–20, 40
  definition of, 41
Developmental psychology:
  definition of, 343–347
  goals, 347–357
  learning theory, 364–367
  metatheoretical issues, 341–367
  methods, 347–357
Discovery, 13, 29
Discrimination, 53, 58

Drives:
  in conditioning theory, 505
  and emotion, 448–449
  and incentive motivation, 545–546
Dynamic system, 240–245

Emotion, 435–452
  and bodily changes, 439–443
  and classical conditioning, 505
  and conflict, 443–445
  as disruption of behavior, 446
  and drives, 448–449
  as energy, 445–446
  felt, 451–452
  and motives, 448–451
  and perception, 439–443, 447, 449
  theoretical conceptions, 438–446
Empiricism, 9
  definition of, 41
  scientific, 4, 13, 49, 67
  and social psychology, 371–374
Energy and emotion, 445–446
Estes Park seminar, 38–39
Experiment, types, 351–354
Explanation, 40
  constructive, definition of, 41
  definition of, 41
  levels, 33–36
  reductive, definition of, 43
  types, 31–32

Fact, definition of, 41
Factor analysis, 398–401
  and thinking, 477–480, 489–491
Field theory, 33–34, 83, 167–170, 242, 284
Forgetting, interference theory, 458–463
Functionalism, 16–17
  and verbal learning, 456–458

Generalization, 58
  semantic, 469
General systems theory, 98–101, 254
Gestalt psychology, 228–230, 233, 236, 277, 283, 374, 457, 566
Gradualness, principle of, 286–303

Hypothesis, 9–10, 19–21, 31, 39, 54, 314
  definition of, 7, 42
  and observation, 13
  testability, 12–13
Hypothetical construct, 24–31, 40, 188–196, 240–245
  definition of, 42
Hypothetico-deductive theory, 16, 217, 418

Idiographic, definition of, 42
Incentive motivation and drive, 545–546
Incremental learning versus one-trial learning, 543–545
Induction, 20, 40
  definition of, 42
  and theory, 17–19, 375
Inference and models, 80–82
Information processing system, 485–491
Information theory, 464
Instinct and emotion, 438–439
Instrumental conditioning, 496, 504
Instrumental learning,
  theory construction, 526–547
Intention, 264–266
Interaction of laws, 34
Interference theory, 458–463
Intervening constructs, 279–282
Intervening variable, 24–29, 40, 188–189, 195–201, 213–220, 504, 528
  E/C, 29, 197, 200
  physiological properties, 209n
Interview, psychoanalytic, 421–424
Introspectionism, 228, 235–236, 566
Intuition, 316

Laboratory, flight from, 323–338
Language and science, 62–63, 66–72, 90
Latent extinction, 538–540
Latent learning, 238
Law:
  definition of, 7, 42
  of effect, 366
  nomothetic-idiographic, 34
  S-R, 534–538
  types, 279–282
Learning:
  and mathematical models, 551–564
  and perception, 551–564
Learning theory, 333, 335
  developmental psychology, 364–367
Lloyd Morgan's canon, 20
Logic, 122–124
Logical positivism, 4, 49, 59–74, 179

Mathematical model, 81, 132–145, 331–333
  advantages of, 552, 559–560, 563–564
  and perception, 551–564
Mathematics, 62
  theory, 92, 94–96, 219–220
Measurement scales and statistical models, 147–158
Mediating response, 517

Metaphysics, 60, 66, 74
Metatheory, 14
  definition of, 42
Miniature system, 9
  definition of, 42
Model, 39, 78–87, 105–127, 187, 332
  and analogy, 85, 109
  animal, 261–263
  criteria for evaluation, 84–85
  dangers of, 121–127
  definition of, 14, 42, 108
  distinguished from theory, 79–80
  and experiments, 116–119, 127
  functions, 79–85, 113–121
  infant, 263–266
  inference, 80–82
  intuitive, 204–207
  learning, 132–145
  machine, 259–260
  mathematical, 81, 132–145, 331–333, 551–564
  and measurement scales, 147–158
  and overgeneralization, 122
  statistical, 147–158
  and theory, 89, 111–113
  types, 109–111
  uses and limitations, 89–104
Molar:
  and molecular, 237–239
  problems, 258–271
Molecular and molar, 237–239
Motivation:
  classical conditioning, 504–505
  and emotion, 448–451

Neural inhibition, 568–571
Neurology, 211–213
Neurophysiology, 252, 280
  and behavior, 240–245
  theory, 166
Nomological nets, 402, 466
Nomothetic, definition of, 42
Nomothetic-idiographic issue, 312–313

Observation, 10
  and control, 11–12, 313–317
  definition of, 42
  and hypothesis, 13
  and theory, 4–5, 20, 39
One-trial learning versus incremental learning, 543–545
Operationism, 4, 12, 21–59, 179, 187–201, 205, 242, 432
  definition of, 42
Operations research, 106–108
Orienting response and classical conditioning, 516–517

Parsimony, 20–22, 29, 40
  definition of, 42
Perception:
  and emotion, 439–443, 447, 449
  and learning, 551–564
  and mathematical models, 551–564
  and sensation, 566–567, 573–574
Perceptual theory, current trends, 565–574
Personality:
  factor analysis, 398–401
  in literature, 390
  theoretical methodology, 389–411
  theory:
    perceptual, 408–410
    positivistic, 401–403
    S-R, 406–408
Phenomenology, 209, 236, 264
  and social psychology, 374–375
Philosophy, 179–180
  of science, 47–49, 59–63, 179
Physicalism, 49, 63–67, 259
Physiology and behaviorism, 334
Pitch discrimination theories, 587–597
Positivism, 26, 30, 40, 55, 174–177
  definition of, 42
  logical, 4, 49, 59–74, 179
  and theory, 5, 9, 17–19
Postulate, definition of, 8, 42
Pragmatics, 68, 71–72, 179
Prediction in psychoanalysis, 427–431
Probability, 138–139
Psychoanalysis, 195, 234, 300, 324–325, 333, 363–364, 404–406, 444
  interview as research method, 421–424
  theory:
    construction and validation, 413–432
    experimental approaches, 424–427
    learning, 429
    and prediction, 427–431
Psycholinguistics, 456, 463–472
Psychology,
  animal, 34–35
  developmental, 341–367
  gestalt, 228–230, 233, 236
  and psychoanalytic propositions, 427
  S-R, 33
  social, 234, 369–386
  social indifference of, 303–310
  and topology, 12, 236–237
Psychophysics, 228–229, 551–564, 597–610

r_g, 81–82, 84, 86–87, 540
Re-afference principle, 571–572
Reality status of constructs, 24–25
Reciprocity law, 567–568

Reductionism, 34, 85, 245–255
  definition of, 42
Reductive explanation, 31–32
  definition of, 43
Reification of concepts, 437
Representational mediation process, 468
Research training and theory, 36–39

S-R laws of instrumental learning, 534–538
S-R method, 214–220
S-R psychology, 33
S-R theory, 165, 171–177, 260n, 208, 242–245, 279–282, 364, 366, 376, 406–408, 464–467
Sampling, stimulus, 140–145
Science:
  as analogy, 103–104
  definition of, 43
  of science, 49, 56, 67–74
  unity of, 64–67
Scientific attitude, 37
Scientific empiricism, 4, 13, 49, 67
Secondary reinforcement, 541–543
Second signal system, 517
Semantic differential, 466
Semantics, 13, 18, 22, 26, 30, 68–70, 190–192, 198, 335–337
  emotion, 436–437
  in psychology, 9–10, 12
Semiotic, 67–72
Sensation:
  and perception, 566–567, 573–574
  and physiology, 575–577
  theories, 575–611
Sensory deprivation, 450
Sign, 268–269
Signal detection:
  mathematical model for, 553–564
  theory, 601–610
Significance, 277
  of constructs, 28
Social indifference of psychology, 303–310
Social psychology, 234
  cognitive functioning, 377–379
  and empiricism, 371–374
  history, 369–375
  and phenomenalism, 374–375
  theory, 369–386
Statistical learning theory, 81–82, 134, 136
Statistical models and measurement scales, 147–158
Stimulus sampling, 140–145
Structuralism, 235–236

Surplus meaning, 24–25, 30, 40, 532
  definition of, 42
Symbol, 268–269
Syntactics, 68
Synthesis, 219
Systems, 22, 79, 98, 113–114, 244, 350–351
  classical, 9
  conceptual focus, 226–237
  definition of, 43
  dynamic, 240–245
  miniature, 9

Theorem, 16
  definition of, 43
Theoretical concepts defined for learning theory, 527–534
Theory:
  and analogy, 96–98
  axiomatic-model, 86
  clinical, 311–322
  deductive, 15
  definition of, 8, 43
  elegance of, 299–302
  field, 33–34, 83, 167–170, 242, 284
  functional, 16–17
  general systems, 98–101, 254
  geometrical, 93
  as goal, 5–6, 29
  hypothetico-deductive, 16, 217, 418
  inductive, 17–19
  information, 464
  mathematical, 92, 94–96, 219–220
  and model, 86, 89, 111–113
  modes, 39
  neurophysiological, 166
  objection to formalization, 16
  objection to inductive types, 18
  and observation, 4–5, 20, 39
  personality, 401–403, 406–410
  and practice, 293–296
  premature, 292–293
  and research training, 36–39
  role of, 5–6
  S-R, 165, 171–177, 206n, 208, 242–245, 279–282, 364, 366, 376, 406–408, 464–467
  tests of, 19–21
  as tools, 5–6, 15, 16, 39
  types of, 43, 92–93
  verbal, 92, 94–96
Theory construction:
  basic elements, 10–14
  definition of, 43
  general nature of, 4–41
  levels of, 317–321
  model in, 78–87
  modes of, 14–19

Thing-constancy research, 228
Thinking, 475–491
  development of, 481–485, 489–491
  as information processing system, 485–491
  Piaget stages, 481–485, 489–491
Thought, computer analogy, 101–103
Threshold theories, 597–610
Topology and psychology, 12, 236–237
Turing machine, 99, 101

Variable, 7, 32, 124–126, 163, 168, 181–184
  chaining of, 219
  control, 11, 357, 426
    definition of, 41
  definition of, 43
  dependent, 11
    definition of, 41

Variable (*Cont.*)
  hypothetical state, 280
  independent, 11
    definition of, 41–42
  intervening, 24–29, 40, 181–184, 188–189, 195–201, 213–220, 504, 528
    definition of, 42
Verbal association, 467–469
Verbal behavior, Skinner account, 470–472
Verbal learning, 456–463, 544–545
Verbal theories, 92–94–96
Verification of theory, 19–20
Vienna Circle, 4, 59n, 65

Warsaw Circle, 60n
Weber's Law, 598

Yerkes-Dodson Law, 446